Harvard Studies in Business History XXXVII

Edited by Alfred D. Chandler, Jr.
Isidor Straus Professor of Business History
Graduate School of Business Administration
George F. Baker Foundation
Harvard University

Citibank
1812–1970

Harold van B. Cleveland
Thomas F. Huertas

with
Rachel Strauber
Joan L. Silverman
Mary Mongibelli
Mary S. Turner
Clarence L. Wasson, Jr.

Harvard University Press
Cambridge, Massachusetts
London, England

Library of Congress Cataloging in Publication Data

Cleveland, Harold van B.
    Citibank, 1812–1970.

    (Harvard studies in business history; 37)
    Bibliography: p.
    Includes index.
    1. Citibank (New York, N.Y.)—History.   2. Banks
and banking—United States—History.   3. Financial
institutions—United States—History.   I. Huertas,
Thomas F.   II. Title.   III. Series.
HG2613.N54F65812   1985   332.1′223′097471   85–5574
ISBN 0-674-13175-4 (alk. paper)

Editor's Introduction

This history of Citibank is a landmark in the writing of business history. Its story spans more than a century and a half, during which the mercantile bank established in 1812 became by the outbreak of World War I one of the nation's most influential commercial and investment banking houses and then in the 1920s diversified into still other financial activities. After surviving the trauma of the Depression and meeting the challenge of World War II, the bank again became an innovator in banking procedures and strategies. This study is the first to review in depth several of the most significant post-war developments in American banking.

Because Citibank has been at or close to the center of the nation's banking system for many decades, its story is more than a history of an individual enterprise. It provides invaluable insights into the evolution of American banking and indeed of American business in general. The authors have skillfully placed the critical decisions made by senior executives about strategy, policy, and operations within a broader economic and institutional context. The reader has an unparalleled opportunity to observe and analyze the changing activities and functions of investment and commercial banking within the United States; to appreciate the nature of competition between banks for the business resulting from these functions; and to follow the close and constantly changing relationships of the bank with state and federal agencies, which from the beginning defined and enforced regulations that set limits on the activities and operations of American banks.

In addition this book describes and analyzes in precise and dramatic ways the transformation of the bank from a personally run to a professionally managed enterprise. Few other business or economic histories explain so well this transformation, which was central to the evolution of modern managerial capitalism. The adjustments required at all levels by this essential transformation are carefully described. Particularly revealing, for example, is the description of the frustrated hopes of Frank A. Vanderlip, the bank's first modern salaried executive, to reap entrepreneurial rewards comparable to those of his predecessor and mentor, James Stillman.

The authors are successful in illuminating these fundamental changes in American financial and business institutions because they perform so well the tasks of the business historian: they describe and evaluate the decisions that shape the destiny of the enterprise in terms of the situation—the issues, problems, and alternatives—facing the senior decision makers at the time when action was taken. The reader sees how the personalities, biases, and talents of these executives affected the bank's responses to the constantly changing external environment. Nothing was foreordained. With different actors the story would have been different.

The book is a landmark for still another reason. It is a scholarly study written from within the corporation itself. The authors and their staff work for the bank. Both authors are experienced bank executives, and Thomas Huertas is also a trained economic historian. Together with their staff they share a knowledge of banking, business, and economics. As insiders they know the business as few outsiders can. Each step of their work and each page of the manuscript was reviewed by a committee of outside specialists—Professors Vincent Carosso of New York University and Richard Sylla of North Carolina State University in banking history, Anna Schwartz of the National Bureau of Economic Research in monetary history, Stanley Engerman of the University of Rochester in economic history, and myself in business history. The close relationship between the authors and the members of the committee provided a significant learning experience for all involved, and one that certainly strengthened the final product. Such an approach to the writing of a company history permits its executives to understand better their present situation. Thus Citibank itself will reap rich rewards from its enlightened attitute toward its own past. At the same time this history provides information and insights otherwise not available to scholars or the general public about major developments in American business and financial history.

In its comprehensive scope and its skill in illuminating the nature of choice and change in a large bank, *Citibank, 1812–1970*, sets a standard for all future works on this vital industry.

Alfred D. Chandler, Jr.

Foreword

History is the story of people, the organizations they create, and how those institutions cope with the constantly changing challenges of society. All of America's institutions were newly minted in the aftermath of its revolution against the most powerful nation in the world. The founding fathers broke with the current economic dogma and turned away from the mercantilist system that was so pervasive in Europe, opting instead for a market-oriented economy. Such an open economy requires financial institutions that can grow and adapt to the requirements of a dynamic country.

Citibank became one of those financial institutions. Indeed, Citibank is one of the few private institutions that have survived since 1812, through wars and panics, through good times and bad, while steadily building and maintaining a position of leadership at home and abroad. Located in what has turned out to be the financial center of our country, Citibank has been involved in one way or another, in one degree or another, with almost all of the major events in our country's history. And, in a larger sense, it is accurate to say that very few significant events occurring in the world do not have an impact on some of the bank's customers and therefore on its business. Like all institutions that flourish over time, the bank was and is driven by its customers' needs. These requirements are never static. New technologies, ranging from the steam engine to the microchip, produce new businesses and destroy others. As industries rise and fall, many new companies arise, prosper, and then decline as their products become obsolete or they fail to adapt to changing markets and value systems. Of the hundred largest companies in 1900, many that were leaders in that year no longer exist today. In the financial services business, of the original fifty-two banks that founded the New York Clearing House Association in 1853, twenty-two had disappeared entirely by 1910.

Not only are Citibank's customers changing, but so are the needs of each generation of customers. Governments at home and abroad continually alter the ways in which they finance their nations' development. Many countries, our own included, have changed from international debtors to international creditors and back again. That cycle will be repeated in the future. Old colonial empires have disintegrated, and new countries have appeared at such an astonishing rate that there are now almost two hundred nations in various stages of development; each has its own culture and its own financial requirements. New and varying methods of capital finance appear almost daily as old instruments are found to be no longer equal to the task. As economic development proceeds, consumers constitute a growing and more demanding sector of many economies around the world.

The revolution caused by the convergence of computers with telecommunications has moved the global marketplace from yesterday's rhetoric to today's reality. The effect of this revolution on the world of trade and finance is profound, and its consequences are still unfolding. We know that it will continue to call forth new responses to opportunities that are still hidden in the future.

Walter B. Wriston

Acknowledgments

No book is ever solely the product of its authors, and this book is no exception. From the start we have benefited from the assistance, encouragement, advice, and support of numerous individuals and institutions, both inside and outside of Citibank. Without them the book could not have been completed.

Our deepest debt is to Walter B. Wriston, who commissioned the project, and to Leif H. Olsen, who provided continuous encouragement and support. John W. Heilshorn, P. Henry Mueller, and Carl Desch took special interest in the book. Without these sponsors within the corporation, our efforts would have ended up in the same place as the previous attempts to write the bank's history—in a file drawer.

The book began as a brief review of Citibank's history, as background for the preparation of a strategic plan for the corporation by George J. Vojta. It was then decided to transform this review into a history of the corporation. To ensure that it would be a scholarly and objective history, the bank formed a panel of academic advisers to review the work. The panel consisted of Alfred D. Chandler, Jr. (chairman), Vincent P. Carosso, Stanley Engerman, Anna J. Schwartz, and Richard Sylla. At each stage of the project they commented on our work and suggested ways to improve the manuscript. We benefited immensely from their knowledge and expertise. Others who reviewed the manuscript in whole or in part include George Benston and George Smith. Their insights helped strengthen our analysis and sharpen our presentation.

After we submitted an initial draft to Harvard University Press, an anonymous referee, later identified as Mira Wilkins, provided an extensive critique of the entire manuscript. Her comments enabled us to improve significantly the analysis, presentation, and consistency of the manuscript. We were indeed fortunate to have had her review and are most grateful for her careful consideration of our work.

A number of people at Citibank assisted us during the project. These include Thomas Brady, Clemens Canonico, Altheia Courtenay, Sylvia Floyd, Joanna Frodin, Donna Galvani, Daniel Hodas, Chris Jorquera, Charles Klensch, Kenneth McLaughlin, Jack Odette, Conchita Pineda, Anthony Sankitts, Elizabeth Selvaggio, Patrick Walsh, and Jonathan Wiles. Special thanks go to Ann Carolan of the Citibank Library, who tirelessly pursued and successfully procured many obscure yet important references for us. We are also especially grateful to Richard Schultz, Jacqueline Ritter, and Frank Curreri for their skillful preparation of the charts.

We wish to thank the large number of Citibank employees, past and present, who generously granted us interviews concerning their careers at the bank. We are particularly grateful to James Stillman Rockefeller, George S. Moore, Richard Perkins, Walter B. Wriston, William I. Spencer, G. A. Costanzo, and Edward L. Palmer for their comments. All of them spent a good deal of time explaining to us what was second nature to them. Without their personal insights we could not have constructed the story of Citibank's activities in the postwar era.

We owe a special debt to J. Howard Laeri. He not only gave us an extended interview on his own career at Citibank but also made available an extensive collection of interviews and memoirs that he had compiled.

Many people provided thoughtful recollections of people in Citibank's history. We are especially grateful to Frank A. Vanderlip, Jr., who told us much about his father's career in an interview and a memoir. For their thoughts on the career of Charles E. Mitchell, we are indebted to his daughter Rita Cushman, the late Leonard Moore, and A. Hobson Dean.

In addition to Citibank's own library we relied on a number of other collections, especially those of Columbia University, the holder of the Stillman and Vanderlip papers and a depository for the Harrison papers. In addition, the staffs of the New York Public Library, the New-York Historical Society, the Library of Congress, and the National Archives assisted us in consulting their collections, for which we are grateful. We are particularly indebted to the Comptroller of the Currency for permitting us to consult records pertaining to Citibank's activities.

Special thanks are due to Jane Rovensky Grace of Palm Beach, Florida, who graciously permitted us to consult a large collection of private papers belonging to her late father, John E. Rovensky. From these papers we learned a great deal concerning the bank's lending activities during the 1930s and 1940s.

We are indebted to a great many individuals and institutions for permission to cite and quote material taken from various manuscript collections. We would like first to thank Kenneth A. Lohf, Librarian for Rare Books and Manuscripts at Columbia University, for permission to cite and quote material from the papers of George L. Harrison, Herbert H. Lehman,

James Stillman, and Frank A. Vanderlip. Permission to cite and quote from other material in the Harrison papers was kindly given by the Federal Reserve Bank of New York. Calvin W. Stillman and Frank A. Vanderlip, Jr., graciously allowed us to cite and quote extensively from the papers of James Stillman and Frank A. Vanderlip. The Honorable Vincent L. Broderick allowed us to cite and quote a memorandum to Herbert H. Lehman from his father, Joseph A. Broderick. We are also grateful to the Oral History Project at Columbia University for permission to cite and quote from Jackson Reynolds' oral history.

To James H. Hutson, Chief of the Manuscript Division of the Library of Congress, go our thanks for permission to cite and quote from the Charles H. Hamlin diary. We owe a special debt to William M. Kearns, Managing Director of Shearson, Lehman Brothers, Incorporated, for permission to quote and cite from the Kuhn Loeb Syndicate Books for the years 1891 to 1920. Estelle Rebec, Head of the Manuscript Division, University of California, Berkeley, permitted us to cite and quote from material in the papers of John Neylan. Jay Hargis, Associate Archivist, Bank of America, permitted us to quote from the papers of A. P. Giannini. We are grateful to Richard S. Perkins for allowing us to quote and cite from the letters of his father, James Perkins, to John Neylan and A. P. Giannini. We would also like to thank Thomas Dunnings, Curator of Manuscripts at the New-York Historical Society, for permission to cite and quote a memorandum written by Samuel Osgood. The New York Clearing House was very gracious to us, and we would like to thank them for allowing us to cite and quote from their correspondence and record books.

For permission to reprint a cartoon drawn by Daniel Fitzpatrick for the *St. Louis Post-Dispatch*, we are grateful to William Woo, editor of the editorial page of that newspaper. We would also like to thank Prentice-Hall for permission to reprint a portion of "The Regulation of Financial Institutions: A Historical Perspective on Current Issues," by Thomas F. Huertas, from *Financial Services: The Changing Institutions and Government Policy*, edited by George Benston (© 1983 The American Assembly, Columbia University).

Above all, we would like to acknowledge the contribution of Rosalie Quigley, our secretary. The customary accolade for cheerfulness and accuracy through innumerable drafts is not sufficient to express our thanks for her dedication.

On a personal note, we wish to thank our wives for their patience and encouragement. Without their support the book would never have been finished.

Harold van B. Cleveland
Thomas F. Huertas

Contents

Illustrations

A group of Citibank photographs follows page 310. All are from company files except the portrait of Moses Taylor from the New York Clearing House, which is reproduced here with the permission of the New York Clearing House Association.

Tables

Figures

Citibank

1812—1970

Note on the Bank's Name

The original name at the time of the 1812 incorporation was the City Bank of New York. It became The National City Bank of New York when the bank joined the national banking system in 1865. *First* was added to the name in 1955, as a result of the merger agreement whereby the bank took over The First National Bank of the City of New York. In 1962 the name was changed to First National City Bank, the words *The* and *of New York* being dropped. In 1968 the bank became a subsidiary of the newly formed one-bank holding company First National City Corporation, and in 1974 the holding company's name was changed to Citicorp. Two years later the bank's name was changed to Citibank, N.A. In the following pages we have generally referred to the institution by the name in use at the time.

Introduction

This book is a case study of a consistently successful business enterprise, Citibank. Founded in 1812, it emerged in the 1890s as the largest bank in the United States. It has remained at or near the top of the financial services industry ever since.

Lasting success in business is rare. A firm rises to prominence by exploiting an attractive opportunity. But success provokes competition and induces new firms to enter the industry, eroding the initial advantage. In addition, the firm's market may stop growing, or the political climate may deteriorate. Activities once tolerated or applauded may later be perceived as improper or antisocial, provoking regulation that limits the firm's profitability and growth. Each of these factors tends to push the firm back toward the industry norm.

To succeed in the face of such eventualities, the firm must have a strategy that keeps old markets profitable and points the way to new ones. It must carry out the strategy in a manner that maintains the firm's legitimacy in the eyes of its principal constituencies—owners, employees, customers, regulatory authorities, and the general public. The firm's profits must be seen by each of the constituencies as a just reward for its effort.

The qualities that enable a firm to thrive decade after decade may be called entrepreneurship. Yet a modern business enterprise with its complex internal division of labor and its hierarchical structure, with ownership separated from management, can easily become rigid, bureaucratic, complacent. Incentives may weaken, or managers may direct them to their personal ends. To remain successful, the firm must learn how to induce managers to behave as entrepreneurs, not for their own account, but for the firm's. In short, it must institutionalize entrepreneurship. As Citibank's former chairman, Walter B. Wriston, put it, "there is no reason why you can't have an innovative bureaucracy if you put out the word that fame and fortune come from rocking the boat."[1]

1

Choosing and executing winning strategies over a long period of time both form and reflect an institution's character, that is, its values, its traditions, its established ways of seeing problems and opportunities and of responding to them. That character comes from the firm's leaders, particularly the leaders in its formative years. Their values become its values, their policies its traditions. The corporation cannot escape the consequences of this inherited culture, with its particular combination of strengths and weaknesses. Knowledge of the firm's history is therefore of practical value to the executive. To know the history is to understand the kind of things the firm is likely to be able to do well and what it might best avoid trying to do or be.

Knowledge of the firm's history in its environment is also valuable to the executive because history is vicarious experience. Major business problems are hardy perennials; they recur in patterns and sequences that are recognizable to the imagination trained by the study of relevant history. Business history is also a story of encounters with the unexpected. Political turning points, wars, revolutions, nationalizations, and shifts in public sentiment about business have happened often before and will happen again. So, too, will periods of unusual good feeling, prosperity, expansion. Knowledge of the firm's history teaches the executive to be wary of the assumption that tomorrow will be like today. It opens his mind to the probability of the unexpected. "History must be our deliverer," Lord Acton wrote, "not only from the undue influence of other times, but from the undue influence of our own, from the tyranny of the environment and from the pressure of the air we breathe."[2] Business history, then, is a resource for strategic planning. Executives who know history will be better able to make it.

For society at large, business history serves a wider purpose. It deepens understanding of the modern corporation, the dominant form of nongovernmental organization in our society. It explains how the political and economic environment influences the firm and how the firm influences society. In these respects, a case history of Citibank is of considerable interest. Banking has always played a central role in the economy, and Citibank has played a leading role in banking. Size has been only one measure of its leadership; all through its history the bank has been a pioneer. It has been first, or close to it, in adopting the innovations that have shaped modern banking. It has figured prominently in the political process determining the regulation of the financial system.

The elements of banking have not changed since Citibank opened its doors in 1812. Banking was then, as it is now, primarily the business of managing risk. Banks are intermediaries; they bring together savers and investors. They buy assets suited to the preference of investors and sell liabilities suited to the preferences of savers. In doing so, banks make economic life more calculable and predictable both for savers and for investors. For rendering this service they earn a profit.

Banking takes three main forms, which differ in the legal liability and attendant financial risk the bank assumes. In investment banking, the bank is a wholesaler or retailer of financial claims. It acquires securities from the investor for resale to the saver. The bank bears the financial risk, until the securities are sold; thereafter, the saver bears the risk of loss and reaps the reward. In trust banking the bank agrees to administer and invest the saver's funds, assuming a trustee's special legal responsibility in return for a management fee, which may vary with the performance of the client's portfolio. In deposit or commercial banking, the bank acquires claims on investors for its own account and issues its own liabilities or deposits to savers. In important respects such as liquidity, yield, risk, and maturity, the liabilities issued differ from the claims or assets acquired. Thus, a commercial bank does not merely trade in financial claims or manage them for a client. It transforms them, assuming for its own account the risk involved.

To do any of these kinds of banking profitably, a bank needs detailed information about the preferences and financial condition of its clients as well as a knowledge of general financial conditions. Once acquired, this information can be used repeatedly, thereby spreading the cost of acquiring it over many services and allowing them to be sold more cheaply. There is, accordingly, a tendency to combine the three kinds of banking into a single institution. A bank that does so will also be able to serve customers in ways more specialized banks cannot. Because a fully integrated banking firm offers a wider range of services, it can take a more disinterested view of the relative merits of each service from the customer's standpoint and can offer him sound financial advice along with the means of following it.

Commercial banks also differ from other banks and financial institutions in that they issue liabilities—demand deposits and, until 1935, bank notes—which are used as means of payment. The service of providing a means of payment involves the commercial bank in a business distinct from and subordinate to the business of managing risk. We may call it the transactions business: the business of executing payments from one party to another. The bank is compensated for this service by explicit fees or through deposits for which it pays a lower than market rate of interest. In providing this service the bank generates information about a customer's financial condition, information that is useful in assessing his creditworthiness and in selling him other financial services. The bank's cost of producing transactions is accordingly a joint cost, and the bank realizes economies by combining its two kinds of business—risk management and transactions—in a single organization.

Because they are in the transactions business commercial banks are subject to a special regulatory regime; bank notes and demand deposits are money, and governments have always regulated the creation of money. In fact, regulation affects nearly every aspect of a commercial bank's activity. Historically in the United States, regulations have determined where a bank could operate, what services it could offer, to whom it could offer them, and at what price. Further, regulation has not been static. It has changed over time, especially in response to the major financial crises of 1837, 1907, and 1929–33. The resulting rules have reflected a compromise among the banks and their constituencies, each seeking to promote its own self-interest.[3]

Regulation therefore looms large in the determination of a bank's strategy. It sets limits on the choices open to the firm and its competitors, limits that an aggressive bank inevitably seeks to test and to remove. Thus, a certain amount of political activity has always been part and parcel of the business of banking. Like firms in other industries, particularly other regulated industries, banks have fought for competitive advantages in the political as well as the economic marketplace.

Within the changing limits of its franchise, Citibank has evolved from a small mercantile bank to one of the world's leading financial institutions. This is in large part a reflection of the bank's emerging internal culture. At the core of that culture is the institution's view of itself and of the proper scope of its business. First defined by the bank's early leaders, this self-perception was succinctly expressed by George S. Moore, the bank's president from 1959 to 1967 and its chairman from 1967 to 1970: "If it's financial, we do it."[4] From this central idea there flowed a strategy of providing comprehensive financial service, a decentralized structure to carry it out, and an aggressive, innovative style.

1.

The Mercantile Bank
1812—1837

At first, there was little to suggest that City Bank was destined to be a giant. It seemed more likely during its first quarter century to earn a place in history by being one of the first banks in New York to fail. City Bank's unimpressive early record was no accident. During these years the bank lacked a coherent strategy and firm leadership. The merchants who directed the bank subordinated its welfare to their own, using it to finance their own firms. This endangered the bank, ultimately pushing it to the brink of failure in the Panic of 1837.

Despite a shaky start, City Bank benefited from its New York location. Growing out of the political battles over the First and Second Banks of the United States, a regulatory tradition was established in this early period against federal banks and nationwide branch banking and in favor of state-regulated banks without branches. A bank's location, therefore, determined the market in which it could compete. Founded in the city that would become the financial center of the country and then of the world, City Bank had from the beginning the opportunity to become a great bank.

Founding the Bank

When the largest firm serving a large and expanding market suddenly dissolves, an opportunity arises for new firms to take its place. This was the case in the market for banking services in New York City in 1811. Of the six banks in the city the largest, a branch of the Bank of the United States, was about to lose its charter.[1] This prompted proposals for new banks. Among them was a petition to the New York State legislature in February 1811, "praying to be incorporated as a banking company." The new firm was to be known as City Bank.[2]

The petitioners were merchants in a city where "every thought, word, look and action . . . seemed to be absorbed by commerce."[3] In 1811 New York was well on its way to becoming the nation's leading port, being situated better for transatlantic, coastal, and inland trade than its rivals, Philadelphia, Boston, and Baltimore.[4] The city's boosters were already calling it the London of the New World.[5] This natural advantage helped New York's merchants capture a growing share of the nation's commerce. But commerce depended on credit, and here New York was at a disadvantage. As the would-be founders of City Bank noted in their petition to the legislature, Philadelphia and Baltimore had more banking capital, which gave these cities "greater facility in transacting their mercantile business than what is experienced in New York."[6] Thus, the outlook for a new New York City bank was favorable.

The impending demise of the Bank of the United States made the prospects for a new bank even brighter. Congress had established this federal bank in 1791 at the request of Alexander Hamilton, the first secretary of the treasury, to aid the government in the management of its finances and to promote the development of commerce and industry. Compared to other banks, the Bank of the United States had important advantages. The only bank with a federal charter, it received the bulk of the federal government's deposits, and its notes were circulated as legal tender throughout the country. It had, by 1805, branches in New York, Baltimore, Boston, Charleston, New Orleans, Norfolk, and Washington, D.C., in addition to its head office in Philadelphia.[7] In contrast, state-chartered banks received few or no government deposits. They were unit banks without branches, and their circulation was not legal tender. Moreover, the Bank of the United States exercised some control over the amount of notes that its state-chartered rivals could keep in circulation by refusing to accept their notes unless they were convertible into specie. Although this practice promoted the stability of the country's currency, it also restricted the ability of state-chartered banks to expand their loans.[8] With these advantages, it is not surprising that the branches of the Bank of the United States were among the leading commercial banks in each of the cities where they were located.

The power and success of the Bank of the United States were its undoing. When its charter came up for renewal in Congress in 1810, intense opposition developed, fueled by two factors: Much of the bank's stock was held abroad and the country was on the verge of war with England.[9] Those favoring renewal pointed to the bank's role in facilitating the federal government's finances and in promoting a sound currency. Arrayed against the bank's supporters was a heterogeneous coalition. There were four groups: Jeffersonian Democrats, who opposed banks in general and this one in particular as the incarnation of the "money power"; state-chartered banks and would-be organizers of banks; rural communities that favored easier credit; and states' rights advocates, who held that Congress could not constitutionally charter a federal bank. The ensuing struggle brought out most of the ideology and group interest that have dominated the perennial debate on bank regulation ever since.

The vote in the Senate on renewal resulted in a tie, and on February 21, 1811, Vice President Clinton cast the deciding vote against renewal, thereby opposing President Madison, his longstanding political enemy. Clinton had narrowly lost the presidential election of 1808 to Madison, and his nephew, DeWitt Clinton, was working to defeat Madison in the upcoming election of 1812. The Senate vote set a durable precedent in favor of state regulation of banking and against nationwide branch banking.

To City Bank's organizers, the liquidation of the Bank of the United States was more than welcome. It eliminated a major competitor in the expanding New York market for bank credit and removed a potential restraint on the new bank's ability to issue bank notes. This made the chartering of a new bank all the more attractive. Without the Bank of the United States there were only five banks in New York City. Collectively, they enjoyed a local monopoly over note issue. By issuing notes each bank could borrow from the public at low cost—a saving that could be passed on to its merchant-owners in the form of credit on favorable terms. Not surprisingly, the directors of each bank extended loans in a way that promoted their own broader business interests. Merchants not connected with a bank found it difficult to obtain credit. Consequently, "each borrowing interest wanted a bank of its own."[10]

To found a bank, organizers had to obtain a charter from the New York State legislature, for after 1804 the privilege of issuing notes could be granted only in a special act of incorporation.[11] The question of who would be granted a bank charter, therefore, became a hot political issue and a source of no little corruption. Indeed, by 1811 the chartering of banks had become one of the most divisive issues in New York politics.[12]

The Clinton-Madison rivalry threatened the City Bank petition. The would-be organizers were supporters of President Madison and their petition to the Republican-controlled legislature was opposed by the Clinton faction, the dominant force in Republican state politics.[13] On March 22, 1811, the City Bank petition was defeated in the state legislature.[14] There matters stood until January 1812, when the legislature reconvened. In addition to the City Bank petition, there were requests for bank charters from merchants allied with Clinton and from Federalists who had been associated with the former Bank of the United States. The Federalist group proposed to form the Bank of America, which would take over the business of the Bank of the United States in New York. It was opposed by both Republican factions, who saw in it the potential of a banking monopoly and a vehicle of Federalist political influence.[15]

To head off a charter for the Bank of America, Samuel Osgood, a senior statesman of the Republican party, proposed to unite the warring factions of his party behind the City Bank petition. By virtue of his long career in politics, Osgood had close ties to both the Madison and Clinton groups. Born in Massachusetts in 1748, Osgood rose to the rank of colonel in the revolutionary army. After the Revolution he served as commissioner of the United States Treasury (1785–1789) and as the nation's first postmaster general (1789–1791). In 1800 he had been speaker of the Assembly of the State of New York and since 1803 had been the naval officer of the port of New York, one of the highest-paid jobs in the federal government. Although primarily a politician, Osgood had some banking experience. Early in his career he had been a director of the Bank of North America (1781) and cashier of the Massachusetts Bank (1784). In 1799 Osgood had helped Aaron Burr, one of the founders of the Republican party in New York, establish the Bank of the Manhattan Company. Osgood then served as a director until 1803.[16]

Osgood saw the bank charter issue as an opportunity to unite his divided party. "If a republican bank be incorporated," he wrote in February 1812, "surely it ought to be done on principles that will tend to harmonize the republicans of the City of New York."[17] To this end he met with the Madison men who supported the City Bank petition and proposed a coalition with the Clinton group. Each faction would name six men to be directors of City Bank, and Osgood would serve as president. The new bank would have an authorized capital of $2 million, only one-third of that proposed for the Bank of America, but equal to that of the Bank of the Manhattan Company and the Mechanics Bank, the two largest New York City banks in existence prior to 1812.[18] The plan was accepted, and the Clinton men withdrew their own proposal to form a bank. With unified Republican backing, the City Bank charter sailed through the legislature. City Bank's corporate existence began on June 16, 1812, in the building that had housed the New York branch of the Bank of the United States.

A Bank of and for Merchants

The new bank, like nearly all banks of the day, was intended to be a kind of credit union for its merchant-owners. In addition to Osgood, the directors included several merchant-politicians allied with Tammany Hall, the center of opposition to Clinton and support for Madison.[19] Most prominent among them was John Swartwout, a merchant in paint and dyewoods, who served terms as secretary and grand sachem of Tammany. He had been a close associate of Aaron Burr and had been a member of the New York State Assembly. In the latter capacity he helped Burr secure a charter for the Bank of the Manhattan Company. He then served as a director of that bank until 1803, when the Clinton faction succeeded in removing him from office.[20] Three of City Bank's directors were affiliated in a like capacity with insurance companies, and one, William Cutting, was the principal shareholder of a steamboat company; in addition all four conducted mercantile business.[21]

To these men City Bank was to be "a common fund, for the purpose of making loans on commercial paper for the benefit of all, by a division of profits, and for the accommodation of each as funds may be required."[22] The fund consisted of the bank's paid-in capital, its note circulation, and its deposits.[23] Since both notes and deposits were payable on demand, the bank had to manage its asset portfolio carefully in order to remain liquid. During part of the year, each shareholder was permitted to borrow a multiple of the average amount he kept on deposit during the year. During one season the merchant would borrow from the bank to finance his purchases of goods, generally for ninety days. When the loan came due, he would repay the bank from the proceeds of the sale of the goods. For the rest of the year, he would be out of debt to the bank and have a net balance on deposit. This balance, along with the bank's capital and its note circulation, provided resources that the bank could lend to other merchants who needed credit during the first merchant's off-season.

The merchant-owners paid themselves no interest on the funds they deposited with the bank. Compensation came in the form of liquidity and access to credit and services, such as the collection and payment of their checks. Moreover, it was thought that "stockholders themselves constitute the great proportion of the depositors and, consequently, receive back in dividends, the fair proportion of profits arising from such deposits."[24] Thus, through his relationship with City Bank, the merchant-owner could facilitate his transactions, keep his funds in safe and liquid form, gain access to credit at a preferred rate, and participate in the bank's earnings.

In practice things did not work out so smoothly. On June 18, 1812, two days after City Bank's directors had met for the first time, the United States declared war on Great Britain. Soon thereafter British warships blockaded the coast, and British troops threatened to invade New York, as they would Washington. Although some merchants, such as Samuel Tooker, a City Bank director, organized privateers to run the blockade, maritime commerce practically came to a halt.[25] The business of banking became financing war, not trade.

City Bank responded vigorously to the federal government's need for funds. In March and again in September 1813 it subscribed to government bond issues, and in May 1814 it lent Jacob Barker $500,000 to enable him to help underwrite a large bond issue for the government.[26] At the end of that same year City Bank lent the government $200,000 to enable it to meet the interest and amortization payments due on the federal debt.[27] In return, City Bank was designated a government depository, receiving one-third of the federal government's balances held in New York.[28]

When the war ended in January 1815, new problems appeared. In 1816 Congress chartered a new national bank, the Second Bank of the United States. Shortly thereafter, the federal government sharply reduced its deposits at City Bank and other state-chartered banks.[29] In addition, the convertibility of notes into specie, suspended since 1813, was resumed on February 20, 1817. This necessitated more careful reserve management.[30] Finally, credit problems arose. After the war the British dumped textiles and other manufactures onto the New York market, undercutting the local factories that had flourished during the war behind the blockade. Compounding this difficulty was a general decline in prices and economic activity that resulted from the contraction in the money supply.[31]

The sudden shift to a peacetime economy hit City Bank hard, for the bank had failed to live according to the conservative letter of its own charter. The directors did not diversify the bank's loans; instead the bulk of the bank's discounts went to relatively few people. The directors did not collect loans when due; instead they renewed the loans at maturity time after time, overlooking the borrower's inability to repay.

The directors had only themselves to blame. They were among the largest borrowers and among the worst credit risks. They made the credit decisions and, in the bylaws, had given themselves a favored position: "One negative [vote] shall exclude a note from discount, unless the note be offered by a director or the cashier, when a majority of the directors present shall be necessary to reject it."[32] By February 1814, twelve of the bank's 750 customers had over one-fourth of the total amount of discounts outstanding.[33] Moreover, some of the twelve were pressing to have their discounts increased. One was the director William Irving (the brother of the author Washington Irving), whose firm had $50,000 of credit outstanding.[34]

Those directors without large credit lines naturally objected to the concentration of the bank's portfolio in loans to a few persons. Not only did this practice deny others the use of the bank's resources, but it threatened the safety of the bank's capital and its ability to raise resources by issuing notes and attracting deposits. A majority of the directors understood that a loan of "say $50,000 in the hands of one person cannot be so safe as if equal proportions were placed in the hands of four or five persons of equal credit." The majority therefore decided that no borrower "ought to have" any more than $20,000 in discounts outstanding at any one time.[35]

Despite these good intentions, enforcement of the new rule seems to have been lax, particularly in the case of the directors themselves. Some directors and other borrowers were not only indebted to the bank in amounts exceeding $20,000 but remained so throughout the year, although the bank usually extended loans for only ninety days. By September 1816, this "accommodation paper," or loans that were not self-liquidating, amounted to $500,000. Such long-term credits, when added to loans to directors secured by the bank's own stock, amounted to about one-half of the bank's total loans and about one-third of its total capital.[36]

Inevitably, some loans to directors went bad, for the directors were better politicians than businessmen. In several cases, the bank negotiated for years with a director and finally agreed to reduce his debt. John Swartwout, a director, was engaged in an ambitious scheme to drain the Hackensack swamp, and the bank sustained a $50,000 loss when he died insolvent in 1822.[37] Other directors from whom the bank had difficulty collecting debts included Jasper Ward and William van Ness.[38]

Such difficulties led, in 1825, to a change in the ownership and management of the bank. During the early 1820s the bank's earnings had declined, and the stock fell below par. In an effort to boost profitability and the stock's price, the bank reduced its capital from $1.9 million to $1.5 million by buying back 20 percent of its shares in the open market. In 1824 the depressed price of the stock and the reduced number of shares outstanding made it possible for a merchant, Charles Lawton, to acquire a majority of the shares, and in July 1825 Lawton elected a new board of directors, to whom he sold his controlling interest.[39]

Most prominent among the new directors was Isaac Wright, a leading importer of British textiles and the founder of the Black Ball Shipping Line, the first regular packet line service between New York and Liverpool. Wright served as director from 1825 to 1827 and as president of the bank from 1827 to 1832.[40] He brought to the bank's board several prosperous Quaker merchants, including Benjamin Marshall, his partner in the Black Ball Shipping Line, and William W. Fox, secretary and later president of the New York Gas Light Company, New York City's first lighting utility.[41]

An Expanding Market

The new directors had new opportunities not available to their predecessors. During the 1820s and 1830s New York was emerging as the country's leading economic center.[42] The opening of the Erie Canal in 1825 reinforced New York's position as the country's premier port. The canal brought the produce of the western states to New York for export to Europe or reshipment along the Atlantic Coast. New York's position as the country's leading port for European imports had been established in 1815, when New York-based auctions of British manufactures began, and was strengthened in 1819 by the introduction of Wright's packet line service.[43]

The advent of the railroad in the 1830s would consolidate New York's position as the nation's economic center. Transportation attracted manufacturing; by locating in or near New York, manufacturers could reduce their raw materials costs and minimize the cost of distributing their products over a large area. By 1830, the New York metropolitan region ranked with the Boston and Philadelphia regions as a center of industry.

Finance followed commerce and industry. During the 1820s and 1830s New York became a center for insurance, securities trading, and banking. In 1827 the New York Stock Exchange Board traded the shares of nineteen marine and fire insurance companies and twelve banks. In the same year the stock exchange marked the tenth anniversary of its first formal constitution by moving out of the coffeehouse into more permanent quarters at the Merchants' Exchange. In 1830 the stock exchange listed its first railroad security, the Mohawk and Hudson Railroad, opening the way to further growth.[44]

Despite its growth, New York was not yet the country's financial center. Philadelphia was, for that city was the headquarters of the Second Bank of the United States.[45] Chartered by Congress in 1816, the Second Bank had the same advantages as the First had had before the expiration of its charter in 1811. The Second Bank was the only bank with a federal charter and the only one with branches in more than two states. It was the government's fiscal agent, holding its deposits, making payments, and transferring money from one part of the country to another. The Second Bank also exercised control over state banks through its power to limit their note issue, as the First Bank had. Under Nicholas Biddle, its president from 1823 to 1836, it became something like a modern central bank.

But once again, the federal bank was too successful. Its power earned it enemies, most formidable among them the president of the United States. To Andrew Jackson, "Biddle's Bank" was "The Monster"—a symbol of corporate power, of monopoly and privilege, and of political corruption and social inequality.[46] For a Democratic president, the Second Bank was also a useful political issue. With the 1832 election approaching, Jackson vetoed the bill extending the Second Bank's charter, scheduled to expire in 1836, thereby establishing himself as the champion of the people against the money power. After his second inauguration, in March 1833, Jackson declared open war on the Second Bank, drawing down the government's deposits and placing new revenues in state-chartered banks (popularly known as Jackson's pet banks), and thereby undermining the Second

Bank's profitability and weakening its control of state banks' note circulation. The result was a rapid expansion of bank credit across the country; this was complemented by an inflow of specie from abroad, and the two factors led to a powerful boom.[47]

Heading for Trouble

City Bank was unable to take full advantage of these favorable circumstances. Its troubles in collecting loans from its own directors had stunted the bank's growth and reduced its capital. New banks, such as Chemical Bank (chartered 1824), had entered the market, providing competition for loans and deposits. Compared to the total for all New York City banks, City Bank's assets had probably declined. At the end of 1836 its assets amounted to only $2.4 million, or 3.1 percent of the combined assets of the twenty-three banks in New York City.[48]

Moreover, City Bank's expansion was limited by a provision of the New York Safety Fund Act that restricted a bank's loans and discounts to two and a half times its paid-in capital, a limit the bank had nearly reached.[49] As a result, City Bank had to refuse the invitation of a member of Jackson's Kitchen Cabinet to become a federal government depository. Other banks with more capital and unused lending capacity became the "pet banks" of New York.[50] Foremost among them was the Bank of America, which had received its charter in June 1812, at the same time as City Bank.[51]

The directors of City Bank reacted to the constraint on lending with a change in funding. They substituted an increase in both note issue and correspondent balances for balances the bank's merchant-owners had supplied previously. This enhanced the bank's profitability to its owners without an increase in loans but with a significant increase in funding or liquidity risk.

Bank notes were a profitable source of funds if they could be kept in circulation. That was difficult as long as the Second Bank of the United States held a tight rein on state banks' note circulation.[52] In 1833, that obstacle was removed and in the next three years City Bank increased its circulation by 47 percent. To keep its notes circulating, the bank emphasized relationships with correspondent banks, for circulation depended on the notes being acceptable (redeemable) at par in as many banks as possible across the country.[53] Correspondent balances maintained by City Bank at "country" banks, and reciprocal balances held by the country banks at City Bank, helped to assure that the banks would accept each other's notes at par.

As time went on, such correspondent relations became increasingly one-sided. New York was becoming the country's leading commercial and manufacturing center, and an increasing part of the nation's financial transactions took place there. Country banks found that balances with a New York bank served functions other than assuring the acceptance of notes at par. Such balances could be sold to customers wishing to make remittances to New York or used by the banks themselves to purchase securities or commercial paper. Thus deposits with a New York bank constituted a liquid reserve that yielded a considerable return in the form of services and interest. New York City banks came, in this way, to hold a major part of the reserves of the country's banking system. Among them, City Bank was one of the more successful in attracting such balances. By the end of 1836, its net bankers' balances were $250,000, the fifth largest among New York City banks.[54]

Though attractive for many reasons, note circulation and bankers' balances were volatile sources of funds. In the mid-1830s City Bank depended on them for a higher proportion of its total liabilities than did other New York City banks. The directors seem to have made little attempt to reduce this risk by following a more conservative policy on the asset side of the balance sheet. In fact, the bank's assets were probably riskier on the average than those of other New York City banks. At the end of 1836, the bank had a lower reserve ratio and higher loan-to-asset ratio than its New York competitors, and its loans to directors were larger in relation to capital (Table 1.1).

Table 1.1. Banking in New York City before and during the Panic of 1837

	Levels at end of 1836			Changes from end of 1836 to end of 1837	
Financial ratios	City Bank (%)	All other N.Y.C. banks (%)	Selected accounts	City Bank (%)	All other N.Y.C. banks (%)
Reserve[a]	7.5	10.2	Loans	−29.1	−26.4
Loans: assets	63.4	59.8	Circulation	−71.3	−62.8
Directors' loans: capital[b]	25.7	20.4[c]	Bankers' balances	−52.4	−20.8
			Other deposits[d]	−26.3	−15.9

Source: New York State Legislature, Assembly, 60th sess. (1837), Document 78, pp. 26–29; 61st sess. (1838), Document 71, pp. 18–21, 52–53, 60–61.

a. Ratio of specie to circulation plus net deposits. Net deposits are defined as deposits minus the sum of checks and cash items in the process of collection.

b. Directors' loans include loans made or guaranteed by directors. Capital includes capital, profits, and unpaid dividends.

c. Average of ratio at only the thirteen largest New York City banks.

d. Excludes U.S. government deposits.

While in this vulnerable position, City Bank confronted one of the worst panics of U.S. economic history. In the summer of 1836 the Bank of England, alarmed at losses of gold, raised its discount rate sharply. The result was a recession in Britain and a near depression in the United States.[55] The Bank of England's move drained specie from the United States, reducing banks' reserves and forcing them to contract loans. At the same time, British demand for American cotton collapsed, leaving cotton merchants in the United States with unsalable inventories and their banks with uncollectable loans. A move by the outgoing Jackson administration, the Specie Circular of July 1836, worsened the squeeze by requiring that all purchases of land from the federal government be made in specie rather than in bank notes, thereby raising the public's demand for specie and making it more difficult for banks to keep their notes in circulation.

By March 1837, the money crunch had begun to take its toll. Firms were failing and threatening to take their banks down with them. Depositors and note holders rushed to their banks to convert their funds into specie. Panic broke out in New York City at the beginning of May, forcing the banks to suspend specie payments on May 10, 1837.

City Bank fared worse than its New York competitors in the panic. Its note circulation and deposits declined more than theirs. In all probability, the bank stood on the brink of failure. That it did not fail was the result of the suspension of specie payments and, it appears, the support of John Jacob Astor, the richest man in the country, whose representative, Moses Taylor, became a director of City Bank on June 6, 1837.[56]

2.

One Merchant's Bank
1837—1891

Moses Taylor transformed City Bank. From a bank of and for a group of merchants it became one merchant's bank—Moses Taylor's. As such, City Bank had no identity of its own; it was only part of a larger whole, with a limited, but definite role to play. It functioned as a treasury for the many firms that constituted Taylor's personal business empire. Nevertheless, from this experience City Bank acquired two traits of lasting consequence: a comprehensive approach to finance and a strategy of "ready money."

Merchant, Industrialist, Financier

Moses Taylor personified the vast changes in the American economy that took place during the mid-nineteenth century. His career is a textbook case of the merchant turned industrialist and financier. He participated in the transport and industrial revolutions and helped by his investments to open the American frontier, to reconstruct the South after the Civil War, and to build New York into one of the world's largest cities. During more than fifty years of active business life, Taylor assembled a personal empire of industrial, transportation, and business enterprises, many of which were themselves participants in another economic revolution—the rise of big business. From his desk at City Bank, Taylor ran these enterprises by a combination of "personal control, silence, and ready money."[1]

Moses Taylor, said Henry Clews, the noted diarist of Wall Street, "had no social aspirations and no interest in anything but business. It was his idol. Few men have been harder workers from their early life up to their last days."[2] Taylor's life was hardly a story of rags to riches. His father had been business manager for John Jacob Astor, the fabulously rich fur merchant and investor in Manhattan real estate.[3] According to J. A. Scoville, a contemporary chronicler of the New York merchant class, Astor "always backed up Moses Taylor when he needed aid."[4] As already suggested, Taylor entered City Bank as Astor's representative.

Like other nineteenth-century merchants, Taylor began his business career as an apprentice. He started at the age of fifteen in the firm of G. G. and S. S. Howland, the leading merchant house in the Latin American trade. In 1832, at the age of twenty-six, he went into business for himself, opening a firm specializing in importing Cuban sugar. The firm was successful from the outset. Although the great fire of 1835 destroyed Taylor's warehouse, the firm quickly recovered. It began trading in other commodities and invested in ships to carry goods to and from Havana and other Latin American ports. By the time of the 1837 panic and his appointment as a director of City Bank, Taylor was one of New York's leading merchants. By 1855, his firm was reported to be paying more customs duties than any other firm in the United States except A. T. Stewart and Company, the famed dry goods merchants.[5]

Soon after joining the City Bank board, Taylor began to branch out from commodity trading and shipping into other fields. At first invited by his fellow directors to invest in their companies, he later invested in a number of companies on his own initiative and asked his associates in these ventures to become directors of the bank. Gradually, Taylor assembled under his leadership a group of capitalists similar to the Forbes group in Boston.[6] The loose confederation of entrepreneurs was suited to the times. Investment in each other's companies permitted entrepreneurs to diversify their total portfolio as well as to control the executive in charge of each enterprise—an important consideration in an era when little information concerning companies was publicly available.

In all Taylor's ventures, Percy R. Pyne was his closest associate, his indispensable, right-hand man. Pyne had joined Taylor's trading company, Moses Taylor and Company, as a clerk soon after his arrival in New York as an immigrant from England. In 1849 Pyne became a partner in the firm and six years later married Taylor's daughter, Albertina. He became a director of the bank in 1869 and president in 1882, after Taylor's death. Until a stroke forced him to retire in 1891, Pyne managed not only the bank but also Taylor's entire business empire.

Other Taylor associates included John J. Phelps, a prominent New York merchant, and his son William, a business lawyer, railroad investor, and diplomat.[7] William E. Dodge, a partner in the metals trading and fabrication firm of Phelps Dodge and Company, invested with Taylor in a number of enterprises, as did John I. Blair, who was probably the largest railroad construction contractor in the United States.[8] John J. Cisco, investment banker and treasurer of the Union Pacific (1864–1869), was also associated with Taylor, as were Joseph, George, and Seldon Scranton, entrepreneurs in iron and coal.[9]

Taylor and his associates built up an industrial and financial empire (Table 2.1). The process began in 1841 when Taylor became a director of the Manhattan Gas Light Company. Like most directors at the time, Taylor actively involved himself in the management of the company, supervising its accounting, purchasing, and employment contracts and the construction of a new plant.[10] This enabled the company to exploit its franchise: the provision of gas lighting to streets and homes in Manhattan above Canal Street—one of the most rapidly growing urban areas in the world. As a result the Manhattan Gas Light Company had become by 1848 the largest gas company in the United States.[11]

Over time Taylor became the principal shareholder of the Manhattan Gas Light Company, and as such he was concerned about possible competition from new entrants or from the New York Gas Company, which had been established in 1823 to serve the southern tip of Manhattan from the Battery to Grand Street.[12] Taylor countered this challenge by reaching market-sharing agreements and by investing in his rivals. For example, in 1863 the Manhattan reached an agreement with the newly formed Metropolitan Gas Light Company to divide the territory above Canal Street in Manhattan between them; in return the Manhattan Gas Light Company received a sizable equity interest in the Metropolitan.[13] In addition, Taylor made further investments for his personal account in Metropolitan's stocks and bonds.

Taylor had also acquired equity in the New York Gas Light Company. His investments had begun in the early 1850s, probably at the invitation of William W. Fox, its president, who was also a director of City Bank from 1827 to 1861. In 1865 Taylor became a director of the New York Gas Light Company. This brought the entire gas lighting business of New York City under Taylor's influence and direction, and ushered in an era of reduced competition and high profits.[14]

In the 1870s new competitors with more efficient methods threatened Taylor's dominant position. In 1872 the Mutual Gas Light Company was formed, and in 1878 the Municipal Gas Light Company, which utilized a new water gas process, was founded. The older established companies soon found themselves embroiled in an intense price war. The entry of the Equitable Gas Company in 1882, with a more efficient manufacturing process and the financial backing of William Rockefeller and John Archbold of the Standard Oil group, was further threatening Manhattan Gas Light's position when Taylor died in 1882.

The response of Taylor's heir, Percy R. Pyne, was to unify the gas companies of New York into a single entity. This was Consolidated Gas, formed in November 1884. Through this merger Pyne combined Taylor's New York City gas interests into a single firm able to withstand immediate competition from Equitable and the more distant threat from electricity.

Table 2.1. The enterprises of Moses Taylor, circa 1875

Commerce	Railroads	Finance		Insurance	Utilities	Metals and mining	Communications
		Trust companies	Banks				
Moses Taylor and Co.	Delaware, Lackawanna, and Western	Farmers' Loan and Trust Co.	National City Bank	Manhattan Metropolitan	Manhattan Gas Light Co.	Lackawanna Iron and Coal Co.	Western Union Telegraph Co.
	Michigan Central				New York Gas Light Co.	New Jersey Zinc and Iron Co.	
	Chicago and Northwestern						
	Central Railroad of Georgia						
	International and Great Northern (New York and Texas Land Co.)						

With nearly 50 percent of the shares of the merged enterprise, the Taylor family remained firmly in control of what would become New York City's premiere utility.[15]

In the early 1850s Taylor began to invest in the railroads that brought coal to New York City and in the fields where the coal was mined. In 1854, he was named director of the Delaware, Lackawanna, and Western Railroad (DL & W), a road running through the anthracite region of Pennsylvania. The DL & W went bankrupt in the 1857 financial panic and the price of its shares collapsed. Taylor began to buy the stock and during the next few years acquired a controlling interest. In 1867 he installed Samuel Sloan as president of the road; Sloan was a merchant who had been a director and then president of the Hudson River Railroad before Commodore Vanderbilt acquired it. Sloan, who had improved the management techniques of the Hudson road, applied them to the DL & W, helping to make it into one of the most efficient and profitable railroads in the country.[16]

Under Taylor and Sloan the DL & W pursued a two-pronged strategy of route expansion and backward integration into coal mining. In 1856, shortly after Taylor became a director, the DL & W secured a route from Scranton, in the heart of the coal district, to tidewater through the lease of the Central Railroad of New Jersey. In 1868 the DL & W obtained an independent and direct route to Hoboken, New Jersey, across the Hudson from New York City, by leasing the Morris and Essex Railroad. The lease of the Oswego and Syracuse line in 1869 provided the DL & W with access to the Great Lakes at Oswego. In 1882 a spur line was completed to Buffalo, giving the DL & W fuller access to east-west traffic, but also bringing it into competition with the New York Central and other trunk line railroads.

Coal was the main cargo carried by the DL & W, and much of the coal was its own. The DL & W mined coal on its own lands as early as 1851 and during the course of the next twenty years it progressively built up its coal-mining capacity. In 1870 the DL & W acquired the Nanticoke Coal and Iron Company, which was itself the product of several prior mergers. This brought the DL & W's total coal holdings to seventeen thousand acres, giving the road a strong and reliable source of freight shipments. Overall, the DL & W carried about 15 percent of the total anthracite shipped from Pennsylvania during the 1870s and 1880s. By 1890 its net earnings amounted to $8 million per year.[17]

Investment in iron manufacturing was a natural extension of Taylor's interests in coal and railroads. In 1853, Taylor began to acquire stock in the Lackawanna Iron and Coal Company, a leading producer of rails, and ultimately acquired a major interest in the company. Taylor became a director of the company in 1858, and vice president in 1872, after the death of Joseph H. Scranton, who had founded the firm with his cousins, George and Seldon Scranton. As he did in his other companies, Taylor took an active role in managing Lackawanna Iron, especially its finances and sales. In 1861 he negotiated Lackawanna's acquisition of the Mount Hope Iron Company, securing for Lackawanna a stable source of iron ore. This placed Lackawanna in an excellent position to fill a huge increase in orders during the Civil War, and made Lackawanna into one of the largest iron firms in the country. In the 1870s Taylor initiated Lackawanna's conversion to the Bessemer process of steel production, enabling it to remain one of the largest firms in the steel industry after Carnegie's company.[18]

The sales policies of Lackawanna Iron paved the way for further railroad investments by Taylor and his associates. In payment for rails, Lackawanna Iron often accepted the securities of its railroad customers in the Midwest and South, subsequently selling some of the securities to its shareholders, Taylor foremost among them. In this way, Taylor began to acquire holdings in railroads in the South and West, notably the Central Railroad of Georgia and the International and Great Northern Railroad of Texas. When the latter road went bankrupt in 1878, Taylor's holdings of its bonds were converted into shares in the New York and Texas Land Company, which took over the railroad's land grants. Other roads in which Taylor acquired an interest included the Michigan Central, the Chicago and Northwestern, and the Chicago, Burlington, and Quincy.[19]

Still another of Taylor's industrial interests was the telegraph. As a merchant and financier, Taylor appreciated the value of rapid communications. Hence, he responded favorably to Cyrus W. Field's proposal in 1854 to form a company that would link the United States with Great Britain via telegraph. As a first step, Field founded the New York, Newfoundland, and London Electric Telegraph Company to construct a telegraph line from Saint John's, Newfoundland, to Nova Scotia, where it would connect with existing telegraph lines to the United States. This alone cut forty-eight hours off the time needed to send messages to and from Europe. Taylor served as treasurer and director of the new company.[20]

The company soon completed the Canadian line, but experienced difficulty in laying a cable across the Atlantic that would work. By 1858 one cable had been successfully laid, but it soon proved defective. Before the company could replace it with a more reliable model, the Civil War broke out. After the conclusion of the war, three attempts to lay a new cable failed. A fourth attempt proved successful. The Atlantic cable began operation in August 1866, bringing New York into practically instantaneous communication with London.

To exploit more fully the benefits of faster communications with Europe, Field and his associates had formed the American Telegraph Company in 1855. Through the lease and acquisition of other lines, this firm soon became the largest telegraph company in the eastern United States. By 1860 its lines stretched from Maine to Louisiana. Its only major rival within the United States was the Western Union Telegraph Company, whose operations centered on the Mississippi Valley.

Then came the Civil War. The American Telegraph Company had to split itself in two; Western Union did not, and it expanded, building a line to the West Coast and improving its lines in the North. After the war Western Union expanded into American Telegraph's territory by buying the United States Telegraph Company, a new entrant to the business. This put American Telegraph on the defensive. When Western Union proposed a merger in June 1866, American Telegraph accepted. This gave Western Union a monopoly of the telegraph business in the United States, and control over the American side of the transatlantic cable that would be completed two months later. Soon after the merger, Moses Taylor became a director of Western Union, and remained so until his death. As such, he helped guide the policy of the largest firm in the country.[21]

Between the 1840s and the early 1870s, Taylor built a personal business empire, with interests in commerce, public utilities, transportation, iron, coal, and telecommunications. Finance was Taylor's means of controlling this empire. From his Wall Street office at City Bank, Taylor monitored his companies' performance, reviewed their capital expenditure programs, and decided how to finance them. He used a group of financial institutions, all of them more or less under his personal control, to carry out his decisions. Together, Taylor's trust companies, insurance companies, and banks provided his industrial, transportation, and commercial enterprises with comprehensive financial service.

Taylor's trust companies provided the widest range of services, including deposits, short-term loans, and long-term capital, in addition to trust services. Foremost among them was the Farmers' Loan and Trust Company. Founded in 1822 as the Farmers' Fire Insurance and Loan Company, it was the oldest incorporated trust company in the United States. Its original charter from the state of New York empowered the company to offer practically any financial service except the issuance of bank notes. The company initially made broad use of these powers. It offered deposits, made loans, acted as a trustee, and underwrote both fire and life insurance. But after the fire of 1835 in New York City, Farmers' dropped fire insurance as a line of activity, and changed its name to Farmers' Loan and Trust Company. Shortly thereafter it also ceased writing fire insurance.

Taylor became a stockholder in Farmers' Loan and Trust in 1838, and a director in 1843. At first, Taylor probably represented the interests of the Astor estate, which Farmers' Loan and Trust administered. But over time Taylor acquired a controlling interest in the institution and he also became chairman of its executive committee. This enabled Taylor to utilize the trust company to support his broader business interests. Farmers' Loan and Trust not only invested in bonds issued by Consolidated Gas and other Taylor-Pyne enterprises but also acted as a trustee for the bonds issued by these companies. This significantly broadened the market for such bonds, for Farmers' Loan and Trust supervised the companies' adherence to the indenture agreement of the bond. Farmers' also acted as paying agent for the interest and principal due to the bondholders, drawing on funds deposited by the borrower in advance of the payment date. Thus, as the volume of corporate trusteeships grew, so did Farmers' total deposits and assets. The company's practice of paying interest on deposits further spurred growth. From $6.9 million in 1876, total assets rose to $32 million in 1891, or at a compound rate of growth of 10 percent per annum. At the later date Farmers' Loan and Trust was the fourth largest trust company in New York City, and about 50 percent larger than City Bank.[22]

Insurance for Taylor's firms, his ships, and his cargoes apparently was provided by insurance companies in which Taylor was interested. He served as a director of the Manhattan, the Metropolitan, the Union Mutual, and several other insurance companies. Taylor seems to have advised these insurance companies on their investments. In all likelihood, the insurance companies also invested in securities issued by Taylor's companies.[23]

City Bank

Taylor became president of City Bank in 1856, and thereafter acquired a controlling equity interest. Under Taylor, the City Bank became a vehicle for monitoring and controlling the financial performance of the companies that constituted Taylor's business empire. He required his companies to keep their principal deposit account at City Bank, and used the bank to extend short-term credit to his companies as needed. In sum, the bank acted largely as a treasury for Taylor's companies, taking deposits from firms with temporary cash surpluses and lending to those with a deficiency.

Regulation reinforced City Bank's role as a treasury, for it limited the bank's opportunity for growth independent of Taylor and his enterprises. As a chartered bank, City Bank remained exempt until the expiration of its charter in 1852 from the provisions of the New York State Banking Act of 1838. This exemption permitted City Bank to use bank notes as a means of funding any type of asset, including loans. However, the exemption also restricted City Bank's growth. According to the terms of its charter City Bank could make loans amounting to only two and a half times its capital of $720,000 (Table 2.2). In 1852 City Bank's charter expired, and it became subject to the Banking Act of 1838. This restricted the bank's ability to fund its assets through the issue of bank notes; henceforth, the pro-

Table 2.2. City Bank's three regulatory regimes, 1838–1891

Regulation	As a chartered bank, 1838–1852[a]	Under "Free Banking," 1852–1865	Under National Bank Act, 1865–1891
Entry into banking	Charter (1812) as renewed (1831)	Free	Free
Minimum capital	$720,000	$100,000	$200,000
Branching	Prohibited	Prohibited	Prohibited
Circulation	Unsecured	Secured by bonds	Secured by federal government bonds
Lending limit	Total loans cannot exceed 2.5 times paid-in capital	None	Loan to a single borrower cannot exceed 10% of capital and surplus
Minimum reserve requirements	None	None	25%
Deposit rate ceilings	None	None	2% on bankers' balances[b]

a. Items in this column refer to City Bank only. Other New York banks were subject to their own charters or to the Free Banking Act of 1838.

b. Regulation of the New York Clearing House.

ceeds from issuing bank notes could only be invested in assets approved by the state, such as New York State bonds. Although the conversion to a free banking association removed the ceiling on the bank's loan/capital ratio, it did not open the way to untrammeled growth. The Banking Act of 1838 made entry into banking free, subject only to the prospective bank's meeting a minimum capital requirement of $100,000. Along with the continuing prohibition against branch banking, free entry into banking meant that new banks, rather than existing banks, would satisfy much of the increase in demand for banking services that resulted from New York's growth.[24]

This remained so after the introduction of the national banking system in 1863. The new system did not replace the old; it existed alongside it. New York State continued to charter new banks and trust companies. The National Bank Act was modeled on the New York State Banking Act of 1838 and preserved the principle of free entry into banking subject to a minimum capital requirement. It continued to prohibit branching and maintained the rule that banks had to secure their note issue by posting collateral. But the National Bank Act made both the capital and bond requirements more stringent, raising the minimum capital for New York

City banks to $200,000, and restricting bonds admissible as collateral for note issues to securities of the federal government. In addition, the National Bank Act imposed a minimum reserve requirement of 25 percent on all deposits. It limited loans to any single borrower to 10 percent of the bank's capital and surplus. National banks could not extend mortgages; nor could they exercise trust powers. Finally, the National Bank Act created a supervisory authority, the comptroller of the currency, to supervise the national banking system and to ensure the adherence of each national bank to the law through on-site examinations.

Counterbalancing these restrictions were various benefits. National banks could become depositories for the federal government; heretofore the government had acted as its own banker under the Independent Treasury System established in 1846. National banks in New York City could also accept as deposits the required reserves of national banks in other cities. This placed national banks in the city in a unique position, fostering their potential to become bankers' banks. Finally, designation as a national bank carried a certain amount of prestige, for it conveyed to the public that the bank was meeting the higher standards of solvency and liquidity set by the federal government.[25]

It was this final aspect that seems to have swayed Taylor in July 1865 to convert City Bank from a state charter to a national one, and to change the name of the bank to National City Bank. If anything, Taylor's standards of liquidity and solvency were even higher than the federal government's. The national charter was a costless way of affirming this to the financial community.

Ready Money

Taylor was an extremely wealthy man, and this heavily influenced the way he ran City Bank. His personal fortune at his death in 1882 exceeded $33 million.[26] This was more than three times the assets of City Bank. Thus, Taylor did not look to the bank as a primary source of income; his other enterprises provided this in abundance. Instead, he looked to the bank to provide liquidity at all times for himself and his firms. In the language of the day, this was a policy of ready money.

The expression *ready money* meant more than a large cash reserve, though that was its essence; the policy shaped the bank's entire portfolio. On the asset side, the bank stressed liquidity, maintaining high cash reserves and investing heavily in call loans as a secondary reserve. It also limited its investment in long-term government bonds to the minimum required by law, thus limiting interest-rate risk. On the liability side, the bank avoided volatile sources of funds, such as bank notes and bankers' balances. Its funding base was narrow but reliable. Taylor, his business associates, and the firms they controlled supplied most of the bank's deposits.[27]

Taylor ran City Bank "on the formula, not of the ordinary commercial bank, but of the richest and most conservative old time merchant, with a great holding of surplus cash."[28] Taylor's conservative bent as a banker made itself felt soon after his appointment to the bank's board. Before the 1837 panic, the bank's reserve ratio had been lower than that of other New York City banks; from 1838 on, it was consistently higher, often a great deal so. For example, from 1878 to 1891 the bank's average reserve ratio amounted to 42 percent of its net deposits. At times its reserve ratio exceeded 50 percent. In contrast, other New York City banks maintained reserve ratios much closer to the 25 percent minimum required by law.[29]

At City Bank, call loans were increasingly used to buttress the bank's policy of ready money. These were loans made on the collateral of securities and repayable at the demand of the lender. Because of their liquidity, call loans were a second line of defense—after cash reserves—against unexpected deposit withdrawals; they enabled the bank to preserve liquidity and safety without entirely sacrificing yield. They were the nearest thing available in the marketplace at that time to an interest-bearing, risk-free asset.[30] Short-term Treasury securities, the premier money market instruments, were not issued until 1929.

Call loans were a product of New York's rapidly developing securities market. In the period of industrial expansion that followed the Civil War, many merchants made a transition from trading in commodities to trading in securities, and they financed this new line of business as they had the old by borrowing from banks, using their inventory as collateral.[31] Bonds and stocks, however, were generally more liquid than cotton, sugar, or other commodities. They could normally be sold quickly and easily on the stock exchange with little loss of principal. Hence, securities could be offered as collateral for loans repayable at the demand of the lender. This usually meant lower borrowing costs for the merchant-broker than in the case of time loans secured by commodities.

During the years 1878–1891 the bank kept at least one-sixth of its net deposits in call loans. During the last years of Taylor's administration (1878–1881) the bank's liquid assets, including call loans and cash reserves, amounted to nearly 100 percent of its net deposits. This liquidity ratio declined under Pyne's administration (1882–1891), but the reserve ratio remained well above the average maintained by other New York national banks.[32] Thus, National City was one of the most liquid banks in New York.

On the liability side of the balance sheet Taylor was equally conservative. Under his administration, City Bank avoided volatile sources of funds that could suddenly evaporate, squeezing the bank's liquidity. This had happened in the Panic of 1837, and had pushed the bank to the brink of failure (see chapter 1).

Taylor was particularly averse to issuing bank notes. Prior to 1837, bank notes had formed a significant part of the bank's overall funding. In the years 1834 to 1836 they funded nearly 15 percent of the bank's total assets. After 1837, this proportion sank steadily. By 1849 notes funded only 6 percent of the bank's total assets. After 1851 the bank ceased to issue notes. City Bank's original charter expired that year, and City Bank was required to convert itself into a free banking association under New York State's 1838 Banking Act, the so-called Free Banking Act. Under the new regulatory regime, funds raised by issuing notes could no longer be used to fund general assets but had to be invested in long-term government bonds, thus exposing a bank to more interest-rate risk. Notes were in any event costly to keep in circulation and no cheaper than deposits as a source of funds. City Bank responded to these disincentives to note issue by redeeming its outstanding notes shortly after converting to a free banking association. By 1855 the bank, alone among New York City banks, had no notes in circulation.[33] After converting the banks to a national charter in 1865, Taylor's dislike of bank notes remained as strong as ever. The bank issued no national bank notes, preferring to sell its quota to a small bank in Missouri.[34]

Taylor also sharply reduced City Bank's reliance on bankers' balances as a means of funding. In the years 1834 to 1836 bankers' balances had accounted for over half of the bank's total deposits, and funded about one-fourth of its total assets. After 1837 these proportions dropped significantly. By 1849 bankers' balances were less than one-third of total deposits, and by 1864, on the eve of City Bank's conversion to a national charter, bankers' balances were only 5 percent of total deposits. They remained at this relatively low level throughout the Taylor-Pyne years. As late as 1890, the bank had only seventy-nine correspondents, and their balances amounted to only $1.3 million, less than 8 percent of the bank's total deposits.[35]

In contrast, "bankers' banks"—such as the First National Bank of New York, which specialized in correspondent banking—had hundreds of correspondents across the country and got more than half their total deposits from other banks. For these banks the National Bank Act was a big plus. It increased the supply of bankers' balances because it allowed national banks in other parts of the country to count their deposits at national banks in New York toward their required reserves. This helped cement New York's position as the country's financial center.[36]

In sum, the policy of ready money made City Bank's portfolio more liquid and less risky than it had been before 1837, when Taylor became a director. This conservative portfolio policy permitted City Bank to increase its leverage substantially. In the early years of the bank's history, share-holders' capital had funded most of the bank's assets. In 1828 capital amounted to 68 percent of total assets, and as late as 1841, the capital-to-asset ratio exceeded 50 percent. Thereafter, it steadily declined, falling below 35 percent in 1849 and below 20 percent in 1862, where it basically remained until 1891. From 1878 to 1891 the capital-to-asset ratio averaged over 16 percent, slightly less than the average capital-to-asset ratio at other national banks in New York City. Thus, City Bank was about as highly leveraged as its New York City competitors, but it was significantly more liquid.[37] This made it one of the strongest banks, and very possibly *the* strongest bank, in New York City during the second half of the nineteenth century.

The Test of City Bank Policy

The benefits of City Bank's ready money strategy became apparent during the panics that periodically disrupted the nineteenth-century U.S. economy. Unlike Britain and France, the United States had no central bank, no institution with the power to create or destroy reserves, that could stabilize the money market and act as a lender of last resort in a crisis.[38] In a panic, even sound firms could fail if they could not readily obtain bank credit to refinance maturing liabilities, but most banks lost deposits in a panic and could not maintain let alone expand their loans. City Bank, by virtue of its conservative policy, was consistently able to fund its customers (Taylor's companies), thereby shielding them from insolvency, and protecting itself from failure.

Three major panics swept the U.S. banking system during the Taylor and Pyne administrations—one each in 1857, 1873, and 1884.[39] With each, City Bank's reputation for safety grew. Knowledgeable depositors could compare the bank's portfolio with those of other banks. Its relative strength was obvious. John Moody and George Turner, the chroniclers of big business, noted that "whenever there was a panic the [City] bank grew. A panic is a time when everybody puts his money in the safest place he knows. It is the day of reckoning, the time of the survival of the fittest, in the world of business. Moses Taylor's bank was safe and strong; with every panic it grew stronger."[40]

In each panic, pressure focused on New York City banks. Because banks across the country held a large part of their reserves in New York in the form of bankers' balances, the New York banks' own reserves served collectively as the central reserve of the country's entire banking system. But no bank had the power to add to or reduce the reserves of the system in the aggregate, except by importing or exporting gold. Thus, the stability of the system and of the U.S. economy was vulnerable to any shock that caused the reserves of New York banks to decline suddenly. An example familiar to Moses Taylor was the Bank of England's move in 1836 to pull gold from New York. This move helped set off the 1837 panic (chapter 1).

The New York banks found a partial answer to the problems of a panic by cooperating under the aegis of the New York Clearing House Association.[41] Modeled on the London Clearing House, the New York Clearing House was organized in 1853 to eliminate the expense of bilateral clearing and the risk of weekly settlements among the growing number of New York City banks. Soon after its establishment it began to assume other functions. The most important was crisis management. In each of the post-1857 banking panics, the Clearing House formed a loan committee that made loans secured by sound but temporarily illiquid assets to member banks. The borrowing bank received loan certificates, which other member banks pledged to accept in their daily settlements in lieu of currency. Thus, the loan certificate was a form of emergency currency restricted to use among banks. In effect, it enlarged Clearing House members' total reserves. This helped the weaker banks meet depositors' withdrawals and offset the inflexibility of the minimum reserve requirement imposed by the National Bank Act.[42]

If the issuing of Clearing House certificates did not stem the panic, the Clearing House had one final resort: the suspension of the convertibility of deposits into currency at par. This placed currency at a premium relative to deposits, imposing a small, immediate and certain loss on those wishing to convert their deposits into cash. This was preferable to the prospect of a total loss of one's deposits in the absence of suspension, and it was sufficient, in every case in which it was tried, to bring the panic to a halt.

In each of the panics during the Taylor-Pyne years City Bank gained deposits, while the other banks in New York City, on average, lost them (Table 2.3). When a bank's safety became the depositors' paramount concern, depositors rushed to the safest bank around. In New York that was City Bank. Yet the bank made no particular effort to retain such foul weather deposits once the crisis had passed. Taylor and Pyne's view of the bank as a treasury for their other enterprises precluded such competition for deposits. In the panic year 1884, for example, City Bank's deposits increased from $11.2 million to $19.0 million in five months; by mid-1886 they had fallen back to $13.7 million.[43]

Over the longer run City Bank's growth was rapid. As Taylor's business empire grew, so did City Bank. Total assets rose from $1.7 million in 1837, the year in which Taylor became a director, to $22.2 million in 1891, the year in which his son-in-law, Percy R. Pyne, resigned as president. The average rate of growth of assets, corrected for inflation, amounted to 5.6

Table 2.3. Banking in New York City before and during three panics: 1857, 1873, and 1884

Date	Reserve ratio[a] (%)		Date	Change in deposits (%)	
	City Bank	All other N.Y.C. banks[b]		City Bank	All other N.Y.C. banks[b]
10/3/1857	24.1	15.3	10/3–12/4/1857	42.2	18.2
9/20/1873	30.3	23.6	9/20–11/22/1873	32.1[c]	−17.1
4/24/1884	34.4	24.6	4/24–9/30/1884	69.9	−14.6

Source: Bankers' Magazine, 12 (1858): 566–567; Comptroller of the Currency, *Annual Report, 1873* (Washington, D.C.: GPO, 1874), p. 84, and *Annual Report, 1884* (Washington, D.C.: GPO, 1885), p. 214; National City Bank, Call Report, April 24, 1884, September 30, 1884; *Commercial and Financial Chronicle,* September 27, 1873, p. 412, and December 13, 1873, p. 800.

a. Definition of reserve ratio and reserve requirement: 1857—ratio of specie to deposits and outstanding note circulation. No minimum reserve requirement; 1873—ratio of specie and legal tender to net deposits and outstanding note circulation. Reserve requirement of 25% for national banks; 1884—same as 1873 except notes are excluded from ratio.

b. Definition of all other N.Y.C. banks: 1857—state-chartered banks; 1873—N.Y.C. Clearing House banks that are national banks; 1884—national banks.

c. Change in deposits from average for week ending at the commencement of business on September 20, 1873, to average for week ending at the commencement of business on December 6, 1873.

percent per year. Relative to its New York City competitors, City Bank kept pace. At the end of 1836, City Bank was the tenth largest commercial bank in New York. By September 1891, at the end of Pyne's administration, it had slipped to twelfth. Yet relative to the largest bank in New York City, City Bank had improved its standing. In 1836 its assets had been only one-fourth of those of the Bank of America, then New York's largest commercial bank. But by 1891 City Bank's assets had risen to two-thirds of those of Chemical Bank, then the city's largest commercial bank.[44]

The bank's conservatism did not compromise profitability. Its specialized role kept expenses down. Staff requirements were minimal. The president and the cashier were the only officers, and neither Taylor nor Pyne drew a salary. By neither issuing notes nor paying interest on deposits, the bank kept other expenses low. The portfolio of highly liquid, low-risk assets meant a low rate of return on assets, but it also allowed leverage to be increased without compromising safety. Profitability was therefore satisfactory. Net profits as a proportion of stockholders' equity in the years 1879 to 1891 averaged over 7 percent *per annum,* a rate of return only slightly lower than that of other national banks in New York City.[45]

When a stroke forced Percy Pyne to resign as president of the bank in November 1891, National City was far from being New York's most important financial institution. Nevertheless, it had in place the policies and traditions that would in time make it the largest bank in the world: "ready money" and a comprehensive approach to finance.

3.

Stillman Builds the Bank
1891-1908

On November 17, 1891, the board of directors named James Stillman as president of National City Bank to succeed Percy Pyne. Moody and Turner would later write that there were two reasons why the forty-one-year-old merchant was chosen: "First, there was no one else in sight; and second, he was a man of ability, sure to represent, to some extent, the traditions of the institution. He had been familiar, in both a personal and a business way, with the bank since his youth. But no one realized, what was actually the case, that the choice of Stillman meant the choice of a banking genius."[1]

In fact, Stillman would personify National City, becoming "the mind and soul of it."[2] The bank had only two officers, the president and the cashier, and a handful of employees when Stillman took over. It was a small but sound institution. Stillman would make it the largest and strongest in the country.

Much as Taylor had, Stillman used the bank to support his personal business empire, regarding it as a source of ready money for his associates and their business ventures. But there the similarities ceased. Taylor was as much an industrialist as a financier; Stillman was a financier through and through. Taylor dominated his tightly knit group of entrepreneurs, but his firms were regional and so was his bank. Stillman was more of an equal to his associates, and actually inferior to them in personal wealth, but their firms were national, even international in scope. And, Stillman reasoned, the bank should be so as well. "Mr. Stillman," wrote Edwin Lefevre, the financial journalist, "dreams of a great national bank, and thinks he can make one of the City Bank. It is what he is trying to do, what occupies his mind, and animates his actions. He is running his bank, not toward dividends, but toward an ideal . . . To make it great in domestic and in international finance: that is the dream of James Stillman."[3]

Through investment banking, Stillman would make his dream come true. Prior to becoming president of National City, Stillman had underwritten for his own account railroad and industrial issues, selling them to his associates, the country's leading industrial magnates. With the bank under his control, Stillman could and did underwrite on a much larger scale. He continued to take the underwriting risk personally, and used the bank to support these efforts. In doing so he built the bank, expanding its product line and customer base. To the Taylor companies Stillman added leading firms in American industry, Wall Street brokers, correspondent banks across the country and around the world, and the government of the United States. By 1907 National City would become the prototype of modern banking, a big business bank.

Entering Investment Banking

In the 1890s the underwriting and distribution of securities was one of the most profitable and rapidly growing areas of finance.[4] Many of the country's largest firms failed in the wake of the 1893 panic, and hundreds of railroads required recapitalization. After McKinley's election in 1896, there followed nearly twenty years of rapid economic growth. Business investment surged, and larger corporations turned to the securities markets to finance it. A new merger movement, one of the largest and most significant in American history, got under way. Combining to favor the giant corporation were advances in technology favoring mass production, the high tariff, and the Supreme Court's ruling that the Sherman Anti-Trust Act did not prohibit mergers in the form of holding companies. These large firms had the credit standing to make their securities attractive to banks, insurance companies, and wealthy individuals.[5]

Stillman and National City arrived on the investment banking scene a little late. By the 1890s, the top investment houses had a tight grip on the railroad and industrial corporations that were doing most of the borrowing. Relying on their close connections with European investors, both J. P. Morgan and Company and Kuhn, Loeb had built up during the 1870s and 1880s an extensive underwriting business, taking the lead in investment banking away from the Boston houses of Kidder, Peabody and Lee, Higginson. George F. Baker's First National Bank took a different route to the top. It was "less an originator of issues than a most powerful ally," selling securities originated by others, primarily Morgan, to its network of correspondent banks.[6]

Neither Stillman nor the bank could hope to wrest clients quickly from these competitors, nor did Stillman consider it politic to try. But investment banking depended on more than the ability to originate an issue. Of almost equal importance were placing power (relationships with prospective institutional and individual investors) and banking power (the resources to provide short-term credit to syndicate members and brokers to enable them to finance their positions in an issue while it was being sold to the ultimate investors). In placing power, Stillman was strong; he maintained close relationships with America's leading industrialists—an important new source of investment capital. In banking power, the bank, with its tradition of ready money, was strong.

Along with his grasp of finance, Stillman had an extraordinary talent for forming alliances with the rich and powerful of his day. This talent would be the foundation of his success in investment banking. He began his career at the age of sixteen as an apprentice in his father's successful cotton brokerage house on South Street. In 1872, at twenty-two, he was a full partner in the firm, then reorganized as Woodward and Stillman. For many years it was reported to have conducted the largest cotton trade in the country, selling cotton directly to the spinning mills. The senior partner, William Woodward, concentrated on trading cotton, leaving the firm's finances to Stillman. The division of labor suited Stillman well, for he "did not care for routine business. His reticence, which amounts almost to an idiosyncrasy, made the bargaining of buying and selling highly distasteful to him . . . He was a great deal at his place in Newport, and on his yacht—a rich man, and a rich man's son, who didn't have to apply himself to business detail; always silent, yet always with a gift for being with men of power and financial knowledge."[7]

The most important of these men was William Rockefeller, the brother of John D. and the president of Standard Oil of New York. Rockefeller and Stillman became close friends, exchanging invitations and turning to each other for advice. Two of Stillman's daughters would marry Rockefeller's sons. Standard Oil dominated the rapidly expanding business of oil refining and distribution, and William Rockefeller dominated its financial policy. His close relationship with Stillman led him to make National City his own and Standard Oil's main bank. In William Rockefeller and his partners at Standard Oil, Stillman had a ready market for new securities. These men were looking for ways to reinvest their oil profits and to diversify their portfolios, in order to be less dependent on oil. Securities offered that opportunity, and for help they turned to their house banker.[8]

Another valuable and lasting relationship was with James Woodward, the brother of Stillman's partner in the cotton business and president of the Hanover National Bank.[9] Stillman had become a director of the Hanover in 1885 and remained one after his election as president of National City. Instead of competing with the Hanover, which had one of the largest networks of correspondent banks of any New York City bank, Stillman sought to establish an alliance. He retained his large holding of Hanover stock and arranged Woodward's purchase of an interest in National City.[10] When a Texas banker offered to switch his New York account from

Hanover to National City, Stillman refused because the account was "currently held by a friendly bank."[11]

In addition to his relationships with Rockefeller and Woodward, Stillman maintained looser ties with a large number of industrial, financial, and political figures, at home and abroad. They bought securities from him or purchased shares in an investment company he managed, the Union Investment Company. Among the industrialists were Theodore Havemeyer, an executive of the American Sugar Refining Company, and George W. Pullman, of the railroad car company bearing his name.[12] Financiers included John A. McCall, the president of the New York Life Insurance Company, one of the largest institutional investors of the day.[13] Political figures included Grover Cleveland, the former president of the United States, who would be elected to a second term in 1892; Charles S. Fairchild, a former secretary of the treasury; and Daniel S. Lamont, a future secretary of war.[14] As his personal and the bank's corporate counsel, Stillman employed John Sterling, one of the foremost lawyers in the country.[15] Finally Stillman also maintained extensive contacts with European investors. He managed a portfolio of U.S. securities for the United States Trust Company of London, a British investment firm, and advised others, including Lord Revelstoke of Baring Brothers, on conditions in the American securities markets.[16]

Stillman's oldest and most important relationship was with the Taylor-Pyne family. Charles Stillman, James's father, had long been a customer of the bank, and after 1870 Charles's partner, Benjamin Dunning, served as a director of the bank. Before his death in 1882 Moses Taylor asked the young Stillman to participate in several business ventures, notably the reorganization of the Houston and Texas Central Railroad.[17] Thereafter, Pyne continued to cultivate the young merchant. As Pyne's health began to falter in the late 1880s, he invited Stillman to participate in the management of the two key institutions in the Taylor-Pyne network. In 1889 Stillman became a director of Farmers' Loan and Trust Company and in March 1890 he replaced Dunning on the board of National City Bank after the latter's death. A little more than a year later he was elected president, while Pyne remained on the board of directors.

In effect, Stillman became a partner with Pyne in the bank and in many of his other enterprises as well. At the time of his election, Stillman was the junior partner, but it was anticipated that he would gradually increase his ownership in the bank, either through the purchase of Pyne's share or the infusion of additional capital. Thus, over time Stillman would acquire a controlling interest in the bank as well as manage it. Pyne would gradually withdraw from the bank. Such an extended transfer of ownership was a common form of succession among merchants; it enabled the retiring

Table 3.1. Reorganization of the Union Pacific

Date	Issue	Amount (millions of dollars)	Participations (millions of dollars)				
			Kuhn, Loeb[a]	E. H. Harriman	James Stillman	National City Bank	
October 17, 1895	U.P. Reorganization Syndicate	10.50	1.00	0.25	0.20	0.00
November 15, 1895	U.P. 1st Mortgage Bonds	3.50	0.42	0.00	0.00	0.25
January 26, 1897	U.P. Purchase Money	44.00	3.15	1.75	1.51	1.39
June 22, 1897	U.P. Stock Assessment	9.10	0.60	0.23	0.16	0.15
October 28, 1897	U.P. Additional Purchase Money	8.00	0.00	0.00	0.85	0.00
February 2, 1898	U.P. 1st Money Mortgage Bonds	8.20	0.00	0.50	0.50	0.00
February 11, 1898	U.P. Denver and Rio Grande	6.38	1.02	0.00	0.10	0.00
March 9, 1898	U.P. RR Auxiliary Lines	10.00	0.35	0.40	1.25	0.00
August 25, 1898	U.P. 1st Mortgage Bonds	5.00	0.00	0.50	1.25	0.00
Total		104.68	6.54	3.63	5.82	1.79

Source: Kuhn, Loeb, Syndicate Books, 1895–1898.

Note: Table does not include $8.4 million issue of U.P. Collateral Trust Notes and the purchase of securities of the U.P. Denver Gulf Ry., for which no information was available in source.

a. Represents Kuhn, Loeb's participation in selling syndicate. Kuhn, Loeb was the sole originator of each of these issues and bore the entire risk at that stage of the transaction.

owner to realize the firm's good will and the aspiring owner to acquire a going concern. During the transition period the new entrepreneur had to preserve the interests of the retiring one and integrate his own interests with those of the firm. This is precisely what Stillman did during his first years as president of the bank. He continued to operate the bank as the treasury for the Taylor-Pyne group of enterprises, preserving the policy of ready money.[18] At the same time he began to use the bank to support his own business activities.

Shortly after Pyne's death in 1895 Stillman broke into the big league of investment banking, joining forces with Jacob H. Schiff of Kuhn, Loeb to reorganize the Union Pacific. The two were natural allies. Unlike Morgan, Kuhn, Loeb did not complement its investment banking with a large commercial banking business. It had originating and placing power but lacked the banking power to support large issues. For that it preferred to rely on others. Founded in 1867 as a private bank, Kuhn, Loeb had risen to prominence after Jacob H. Schiff became a partner in 1875. Its forte was railroad finance. In 1880 it had become investment banker for the Pennsylvania Railroad, the nation's largest, and in the following years Schiff had formed close relationships with other major roads, including the Illinois Central and the Baltimore and Ohio. To place securities, the firm relied on a large number of houses in the United States and Europe. Thus, Stillman and Kuhn, Loeb each had what the other lacked: Stillman and National City had the banking resources; Kuhn, Loeb had the ability to originate. Both had the ability to place securities. In combination they would be able to underwrite issues of enormous size.[19]

That would prove essential in reorganizing the Union Pacific, which had entered into receivership in October 1893.[20] J. P. Morgan then attempted to recapitalize the road, but he abandoned the effort when the U.S. Congress could not decide on how to settle the government's claims. With Morgan's blessing, Jacob Schiff then took on the task. Recapitalization of the Union Pacific was a major opportunity for Kuhn, Loeb, for Morgan had dominated railroad reorganizations up to that time. But Schiff needed banking support, and he turned to Stillman and National City to get it.

With this backing Schiff organized a committee to represent the bondholders and shareholders in reorganization. Two years elapsed before it could be made final. In the interim Stillman and National City advanced some of the funds needed to keep the road in operation. Stillman participated in an initial syndicate formed to defray the expenses of reorganization. A month later the bank participated for its own account in a $3.5 million syndicate formed to meet the coupon payments of the Union Pacific's first mortgage bonds (Table 3.1). To settle the claims of the U.S. government on the road, three more syndicates were organized in 1897 to

Table 3.2. The enterprises of James Stillman, circa 1905

Railroads	Commerce	Finance			Communications	Industry
		Trust companies	Banks	Insurance		
Union Pacific (f)	Woodward & Stillman (a)	Farmers' Loan & Trust	National City Bank (p)	New York Life Insurance Co. (t)	Western Union Telegraph	UTILITIES Consolidated Gas
Southern Pacific		U.S. Trust	Second National Bank (p)			
Northern Securities Company		New York Trust	Fidelity Bank (v)	British & Mercantile Insurance of London & Edinburgh		METALS AND MINING Amalgamated Copper
Northern Pacific		Lawyers' Title Insurance & Trust	Columbia Bank			Lackawanna Coal
Baltimore & Ohio		Newport Trust Co. (Newport, R.I.)	Citizens Central National Bank	Queen Insurance		
Chicago & Alton			Bank of the Metropolis			
Chicago, Burlington, & Quincy		Industrial Trust (Providence, R.I.)	Lincoln National Bank			CHEMICALS New York Carbide & Acetyline

CONSTRUCTION/
REAL ESTATE

U.S. Realty &
Improvement

Alliance Realty

Century Realty

National Butchers'
& Drovers Bank

National Citizens
Bank

U.S. Trust Co.
(London)

Riggs National
Bank
(Washington,
D.C.)

Delaware,
Lackawanna,
& Western

Hanover National
Bank

Michigan
Central

New York
Central

Bowery Savings
Bank

Source: Directory of Directors in the City of New York (New York: Audit Company of New York, 1905).
Note: Unless otherwise specified, Stillman was a director of the company. a = partner; f = director and member, finance committee; p = president and director; t = trustee; v = vice president and director.

raise the necessary funds. Stillman participated in each. National City bank participated in the first two, and the bank acted as agent to transfer the funds to the U.S. government.

In the course of this complex and lengthy reorganization, Stillman succeeded in cementing his alliance with Kuhn, Loeb and in creating a valuable new relationship with Edward H. Harriman, who would manage the Union Pacific.[21] In the various reorganization syndicates Stillman had personally risked far more than Harriman and nearly as much as Kuhn, Loeb (Table 3.1). In 1899 Stillman became a member of the reorganized road's executive committee, along with Harriman and Otto Kahn of Kuhn, Loeb. In the same year Schiff became a director of National City, followed in 1900 by Harriman. William Rockefeller, already a director of National City, became a Union Pacific director in 1902 along with another Standard Oil man, Henry H. Rogers. This group of five men continued to back the Union Pacific and would eventually provide banking and managerial services for other railroads they came to control.

After the turn of the century Stillman continued to participate prominently in a series of Union Pacific underwritings while Harriman sought to build a vast transcontinental system. James J. Hill, who controlled the Northern Pacific and Great Northern railroads, had the same ambitious plan, and in the ensuing battle Stillman played a prominent part, helping Harriman and the Union Pacific finance an attempt to buy control of the Northern Pacific on the open market. The struggle of the two railroad titans ended in May 1901 in a deal, by which both Harriman and Hill put their Northern Pacific shares into a holding company known as the Northern Securities Company. Stillman was a trustee of this transportation giant, which created a community of interest among the four main roads to the West Coast.[22]

In 1904, the United States Supreme Court, in a landmark decision, found the arrangement to be in violation of the Sherman Anti-Trust Act.[23] The holding company was dissolved, and the Union Pacific received back its Northern Pacific stock. In 1906 the Union Pacific sold these shares and bought shares in other railroads whose routes, if consolidated with its own lines to the West Coast, would have formed a nationwide rail network. The roads included the Illinois Central, Chicago and Northwestern, Chicago, Milwaukee, and St. Paul, the Baltimore and Ohio, and the Pennsylvania—all roads that had long looked to Harriman, Schiff, or Stillman for finance.[24]

These roads formed the core of Stillman's and the bank's business activity. He participated prominently in syndicates to underwrite their bonds, and in many cases he served as a director of the road, offering financial advice and representing his own stock interests and those of his close associates (Table 3.2). But unlike Taylor, Stillman does not seem to have taken an active role in the management of these companies. That he left to others, notably Harriman, who were far more expert at these matters. Stillman specialized in finance.[25]

A Big Business Bank

Stillman's success as an underwriter both depended on and transformed the bank, for he used it to support every stage of the underwriting process. This in turn built the bank, broadening its customer base from the Taylor-Pyne enterprises to include the nation's largest corporations. To these corporations the bank provided an increasingly broad range of financial services, strengthening Stillman's relationships with the industrial magnates who bought securities from him and with the firms that issued them.

In return, the magnates and their corporations boosted their balances at the bank, making it a big business bank. By 1905 total corporate deposits were $142 million, more than eight times what they had been in 1895. Fourteen firms, ten of them railroads, accounted for 56 percent of the bank's total corporate deposits.[26] Overall, the bank's assets rose at an annual rate of 22 percent per annum from 1895 to 1905, a rate more than three times that for all national banks. At the latter date National City's total assets amounted to $308 million, a figure 27 percent higher than the nation's second largest bank, the National Bank of Commerce.[27]

Stillman's success in building the bank is evident from the membership of the board of directors. Throughout his years as president Stillman expanded the board, placing leading figures in American industry alongside the representatives of the Taylor-Pyne enterprises. By 1904 the board included men such as Henry O. Havemeyer (American Sugar Refining), Cyrus H. McCormick (International Harvester), James H. Post (National Sugar), and P. A. Valentine (Armour and Company), in addition to William Rockefeller of Standard Oil and the Union Pacific's E. H. Harriman.

The bank's relations with the Union Pacific illustrate well how Stillman built the bank by using it to support his underwriting efforts. First of all, the bank provided a temporary market for some of the bonds Stillman had committed himself to place. For example, in the Union Pacific Auxiliary Lines Syndicate of March 1898, Stillman took a $1.25 million participation—25 percent of the entire issue. Two months later the bank held nearly half of these bonds in its own portfolio. There they remained for several more months until they were sold.[28] This pattern repeated itself in practically every issue underwritten by Stillman in conjunction with Kuhn, Loeb (Table 3.3).

In addition to purchasing a corporation's bonds, the bank made loans to the corporation and to the executive who controlled it. For example, in the midst of the Union Pacific's attempt to gain control of the Northern Pa-

Table 3.3. National City Bank investments in securities purchased by James
Stillman as participant in Kuhn, Loeb syndicates, 1897–1905 (millions of dollars)

		Participations	
Year	Securities held by National City Bank[a]	Stillman	National City Bank
1897	0.1	9.5	1.4
1898	0.3	5.0	3.2
1899	2.3	10.1	0.4
1900	5.3	4.3	0
1901	4.4	13.2	0.4
1902	3.7	9.3	0
1903	6.2	8.4	0
1904	7.4	15.2	0
1905	8.7	24.5	0[b]

Source: National City, Call Reports, 1897–1905, and Kuhn, Loeb, Syndicate Books, 1897–
1905.
   a. Averages of each year's call dates.
   b. Excludes £2.6 million and 2.0 million yen in foreign securities.

cific, National City lent Harriman's road significant sums, later refunded by
a bond issue.[29] Subsequently, the bank extended credit to Harriman himself for a lengthy period.[30]

Financing Foreign Trade

The bank also provided payment and collection services around the world
and foreign trade financing facilities to corporations with overseas operations. To handle these transactions, the bank opened a foreign exchange
department in 1897. U.S. foreign trade in the nineteenth century was generally financed through the U.S. offices of foreign banks. Nevertheless,
internationally oriented, private U.S. banks, such as Morgan, had long
conducted a foreign exchange business; this was an important part of the
banking service provided to corporate clients. The first U.S. commercial
bank to enter the foreign exchange business was the First National Bank of
Chicago. It began such operations in 1873, in response to the influx into
Chicago of Canadian banks eager to share in financing the growing exports of U.S. wheat. Twenty years later, the Bank of New York became
the first New York bank to set up a foreign exchange department.[31] National City followed four years later in order to serve its largest corporate
customers, such as Standard Oil and American Sugar Refining, which had
extensive operations overseas.[32] By 1902 National City was reportedly
able to pay out "any sum of money . . . in any city in the world within 24
hours."[33]

Through its foreign exchange department, National City not only transferred funds to and from points around the globe but also financed America's rapidly growing foreign trade. To finance imports National City typically authorized the foreign exporter to draw a sterling draft on its London correspondent under a commercial letter of credit, which could be discounted, accepted, and then sold in the London bill market. By the time the bill matured, National City would have collected dollar funds from the importer, converted them to sterling, and transferred them to London for payment to the holder of the bill. In financing exports, the process was reversed. The foreign importer authorized its U.S. supplier to draw a draft on its London correspondent. The U.S. exporter then discounted this bill with National City, which converted the proceeds to dollars and gave the exporter immediate use of the funds. National City could have secured immediate discount of the bill in London. Alternatively, National City could have had the bill accepted by the London bank on which it was drawn and then held it until maturity or sold it at any time.[34] An acceptance created by a London bank was a prime liquid asset easily disposed of. The acceptance in effect substituted the credit of the accepting bank for that of the importer and the importer's bank.

At this time a London or a European connection filled an important gap in the ability of U.S. banks to supply international financial services. National banks were legally prevented from creating acceptances for customers. Nor could they establish overseas branches upon which customers could draw drafts in foreign currencies. Banks in large numbers from other countries set up branches in London for just that purpose. Although there were no legal prohibitions against acceptances or foreign branches for private banks and state-chartered banks, only a handful made these facilities available to customers. But these banks offered no particular advantage. Since sterling was the major currency of international trade, the London discount market was the most liquid in the world. Not surprisingly it was also generally cheaper to finance in London than elsewhere.[35]

The correspondent system, though cumbersome, was nevertheless efficient. Working with its foreign correspondents, National City financed a large volume of foreign trade, especially cotton exports, since Stillman's brokerage business gave him close connections to the major shippers. In the aftermath of the 1907 panic, National City estimated that it alone financed over one-third of the country's cotton exports.[36]

Building a large global network of foreign correspondents was vital to National City's effort to provide its corporate customers with foreign exchange and trade finance services. Fortunately, it was also easy. All National City had to do was open an account with foreign banks in major trading centers, and to maintain balances sufficient to pay for the services it received from the foreign banks. As the largest bank in the United

States, National City had no difficulty in securing the relationships it sought. Correspondents included the London City and Midland Bank, one of Great Britain's largest banks, the Deutsche Bank, Germany's largest, and the Hong Kong and Shanghai Bank, the British overseas bank with branches in the Far East.[37] By 1912 National City maintained accounts with 132 banks in all parts of the world. Total balances on deposit with foreign correspondents amounted to $6 million.[38]

Correspondent Banking

To provide the payment and collection services demanded by large corporations in the United States, National City also required a domestic network of correspondent banks. But in this instance, National City wanted primarily to sell rather than purchase services from its correspondents. The balances bankers would hold as a result would boost National City's resources, enabling it to fund call loans to its syndicate members. In addition, correspondent relationships would bolster Stillman's power to place securities, for banks across the country were purchasing bonds as secondary reserves.[39] For these reasons Stillman dropped National City's longstanding aversion to correspondent banking.

Under Taylor, National City had largely ignored the correspondent banking business, while other New York City banks, such as the First National Bank and the Hanover National Bank, specialized in it, becoming practically "bankers' banks" (see chapter 2). Thus, Stillman first had difficulty building correspondent relationships, even though he abandoned the practice of not paying interest on interbank deposits. As mentioned above, Stillman was reluctant to compete with Woodward's Hanover National for correspondent accounts. In 1893 National City had only 116 correspondents and its interbank balances were only $2 million.[40]

In May 1897 Stillman seized an opportunity to break into the front ranks of correspondent banking. A New York "bankers' bank," the Third National, unexpectedly failed. John Sterling, Stillman's personal lawyer and National City's counsel, was one of its principal owners. Sterling undoubtedly knew of National City's need for correspondents, and a merger agreement between the two banks was quickly concluded. To supervise the details of the takeover, the Third National's former president, A. B. Hepburn, resigned his position as comptroller of the currency to become a vice president of National City Bank.[41]

At the same time Stillman began to acquire stock in a number of banks and trust companies in New York City (Table 3.2). As a director and in some cases officer of these banks, Stillman was in a position to integrate their operations with those of National City. The smaller banks and trust companies used National City as a clearing agent, and kept extensive balances with it. They also participated in National City's loans and used National City to trade securities, including those underwritten by Stillman. By October 1900 the balances of these banks, together with those of the Third National's correspondents, made National City the leading holder of bankers' balances in New York.[42]

Hepburn did not remain long at National City. He resigned in 1899 to become president of the Chase National Bank, and subsequently built it into one of New York's leading banks. But Hepburn's departure would prove to be a stroke of good fortune for National City.[43] To replace Hepburn, Stillman hired a man who would eventually influence the institution's development almost as much as Stillman himself. Frank A. Vanderlip combined experience in government with a flair for publicity. Formerly a journalist who specialized in business and financial news, Vanderlip became the right-hand man of Lyman J. Gage, the secretary of the treasury, and it was Gage who recommended him to Stillman. At the Treasury, where he was an assistant secretary, Vanderlip had managed the public sale of bonds to finance the Spanish-American War and acquired considerable knowledge of finance. Stillman made him a vice president of the bank.[44]

Vanderlip arrived at National City in 1901 afer making a European tour to meet financial and political leaders. From the start Stillman singled him out for special treatment by inviting him to attend meetings of the board of directors. A journalist later described Vanderlip's first day in his new job.

> A desk was given to him in a very good location in the parlors of the bank and possessing a pleasant outlook on Wall Street. But no duties were assigned. Here he was, a high-salaried officer, a part of one of the smoothest-running machines in existence, but with no apparent obligation to make this machine go. Mr. Vanderlip let the *role* of critic alone. There was danger of treading on other people's toes; infinite tact, good nature, and diplomacy were required. What he realized most forcibly was that he had been given a chance to find himself, and that the highest premium paid by the business world into which he had been transplanted was for ideas. Therefore, he looked around to see where he could broaden the scope of the bank.[45]

He began with correspondent banking. At the Treasury, Vanderlip had come to know bankers from across the country and soon after arriving at National City he began to solicit their accounts. He also advertised, something the bank had never done, stressing National City's record of safety and its broad range of services. Bond trading was particularly stressed by Vanderlip. It made bonds more liquid, enhancing correspondents' ability to use them as secondary reserves and thus supporting Stillman's underwriting efforts. To facilitate its trading, National City set up a private wire network to receive orders from correspondents. It offered to buy or sell "bonds of the United States and other Governments, high grade railway securities, and the bonds of larger municipalities."[46] To keep correspondents informed about the bond market and the bank's current offerings, Vanderlip began in 1904 to publish a monthly circular entitled *Economic Conditions, Governmental Finance, United States Securities*. He advised correspondents that "detailed information regarding any issue of bonds in which a correspondent bank may be interested will be furnished."[47]

Although National City traded all types of bonds, it particularly stressed government securities. National bank correspondents required U.S. government securities as collateral for government deposits and national bank notes. National City assured its correspondents that it was "in the market continuously as a purchaser and seller of all the issues of government securities without regard to the amounts offered."[48] In addition, National City set up a special Washington service to facilitate the issuance and retirement of national bank notes by its correspondents. To this end Stillman acquired a controlling interest in the Riggs National Bank in Washington, D.C., directly across the street from the Treasury Department.[49]

Finally, National City offered its foreign exchange and payments service to its domestic correspondents whose customers wished to deal directly with their foreign trading partners rather than conduct business through commission merchants.[50] By 1908 domestic correspondents could draw directly on National City's foreign correspondents, using National City as a silent partner to facilitate the transaction.[51]

These services helped National City keep its lead in correspondent banking in New York. Under Vanderlip, the number of National City's bank accounts grew steadily. The number of U.S. correspondents rose from 606 in 1902 to 1,230 in 1905.[52] Although other New York banks such as Hanover and Chase had more correspondents, none had interbank deposits approaching National City's. By 1905 the bank's interbank accounts were over $44 million and the share of interbank deposits in National City's total deposit base was almost 20 percent, more than double what it had been in the Taylor-Pyne years.[53]

Financing Syndicates

Together, corporate and correspondent balances provided Stillman with the banking power he needed to become a major figure in investment banking. Selling a new issue at the turn of the century was a time-consuming business.[54] To participate in a syndicate, smaller brokers and private banking houses whose own funds were limited had to borrow to carry the securities while they were being sold. Syndicate agreements often included a commitment to pay the issuing corporation in installments regardless of the volume of securities sold. Syndicate agreements also required that securities be sold at or above the syndicate price. To finance installments and ride out downswings in the market, syndicate members looked to the originators of new securities, and National City enabled Stillman to meet these demands.

The success of a new issue depended crucially on such financing, which enabled syndicate members to hold an inventory of the securities or to finance their own customers' purchases. Securities could therefore be sold gradually at the syndicate price rather than dumped on the market all at the same time. Financing took two forms, the syndicate loan and the call loan. In the former, participants pledged the unsold securities of the issue itself as collateral for the loan. In the latter participants pledged older securities in order to purchase new ones. These securities traded in an active secondary market and could be liquidated quickly if the loan were called.

In addition to financing underwriting syndicates, call loans continued to serve as a secondary reserve. Their dual utility induced Stillman to place a growing amount of National City's resources in call loans. In the early 1890s call loans had accounted for about one-third of National City's total loans; after the turn of the century this proportion was more than two-thirds. In absolute terms, call loans rose from $9 million in October 1895 to $142 million ten years later, making National City the largest lender in the call money market.[55]

A Special Relationship

Closely linked to Stillman's underwriting efforts and to his plans to transform the bank into a national institution was his attempt to make National City the federal government's premier bank. The U.S. Treasury was by far the largest participant in the money market and its actions had a pronounced effect on interest rates. Theoretically, the government acted as its own banker under the Independent Treasury System established in 1846, but under the terms of the National Bank Act it was allowed to deposit certain funds in nationally chartered banks. Although not very profitable in itself, a government deposit account revealed important information concerning its finances, permitting its bank to judge the timing and magnitude of changes in its cash position. The bank could thus forecast more accurately changes in the money market. For this reason as well as National City's status as a firm regulated by the Treasury, Stillman thought it "wise and necessary" for the bank "to be on as cooperative relations as possible with the Government."[56]

When Stillman took over the bank in 1891, it had a long history of supporting the government in crises (see chapters 1 and 2) but no current relationship with the government. Its contacts with the government were practically limited to the comptroller of the currency's periodic examinations. Stillman soon changed this. After the panic of 1893 Stillman and the bank actively supported President Cleveland's efforts to maintain the gold standard. Stillman served as a financial adviser to the president and helped persuade other Wall Street financiers to underwrite the two bond issues of 1894.[57] That same year National City became a government depository. In 1897 it became the largest depository, holding for a time the sums due to the government from the Union Pacific after its reorganization. At the outbreak of the Spanish-American War, National City, along with J. P. Morgan and Company, agreed to underwrite any portion of the $200 million bond issue not taken up by the public. This guaranteed the success of the issue.[58]

National City's status as the government's leading bank took on new importance after 1899 when Secretary of the Treasury Lyman J. Gage began to use deposits at National City as a means of preventing crises in the money market. Following the precedents established by previous secretaries, Gage purchased government bonds on the open market, prepaid the interest on the government debt, and allowed the internal revenue receipts to accumulate outside the Treasury in the form of deposits at national banks. National City Bank was appointed to receive the tax revenues and distribute them to other depositories. According to Gage, "no Treasury office is adapted to such a purpose. It was necessary, therefore, to select a bank strong enough and with a volume of securities pledged for such deposits adequate to cover the transactions from day to day. The National City Bank of New York was the only bank which met this requirement, and it was therefore accordingly directed to assume the task."[59]

Gage's successor, Leslie M. Shaw, took such policies to the extreme. Under Shaw the Treasury sought not merely to alleviate crises in the money market but to eliminate them entirely by stabilizing interest rates. To this end Shaw used the Treasury's surplus revenues to build up a large fund, which he could move into and out of the money market at his discretion. To heighten this fund's impact Shaw removed reserve requirements and adjusted collateral requirements on government deposits. Finally, Shaw offered banks temporary inducements to import gold from abroad. This policy helped bring on the Panic of 1907 (see below).[60]

As the largest bank in the country, National City played a key role in Shaw's plans. More than any other bank, National City had the resources necessary to react quickly to changes in Treasury policy. It could rapidly muster the bonds needed as collateral for an increase in government deposits or change their composition as directed. It could meet large withdrawals on demand without difficulty. Finally, National City's foreign correspondent banks and Stillman's personal connections abroad made it possible for the bank to import gold on a large scale. During the years 1902 to 1906 National City served the Treasury in each of these capacities.[61] Consequently, it remained the largest government depository. In September 1906 it held 11 percent of the government's total balances at national banks.[62]

A Strong Base

Stillman's use of the bank to support his underwriting efforts significantly altered the bank's tradition of ready money. Bonds and call loans came to dominate the bank's portfolio; excess reserves declined sharply (Figure 3.1). Alone, these changes would have substantially raised the bank's risk; to offset them Stillman lowered the bank's leverage, increasing its stockholders' equity from $3.4 million in 1891 to $49.3 million in 1907. This enabled the bank to make the major credit commitments required by Stillman's underwriting activities and thus laid the foundation for the bank's future growth.

Most of the increase in stockholders' equity resulted from two issues of new stock in 1900 and 1902. In November 1899, Lyman Gage, the secretary of the treasury, had advised Stillman to raise National City's capital, if he wanted to maintain the large business that the bank had developed.[63] Stillman took Gage's advice and raised the bank's capital from $1 million to $10 million, by selling new stock. In July 1902 he raised the bank's capital again, to $25 million. Following these increases total stockholders' equity amounted to over $40 million, the largest capital of any bank in the United States.

Stillman put in much of the additional capital himself. In March 1898 he had owned one thousand shares of National City stock, or 10 percent of the total. By February 1904 his holdings had risen to fifty-four thousand shares or nearly 22 percent of the higher total.[64] In a letter to the shareholders requesting approval of the second capital increase, Stillman explained the importance to the bank of a strong capital base.

> In the opinion of the Board, the business of the Bank can be further developed and extended by increasing its capital and surplus . . . as the capital of the Bank is still small compared with the volume of its business, especially so compared with that of financial institutions in foreign countries, where a much broader basis of capitalization is customary and is deemed essential to a safe and conservative banking business. With a capital of $25,000,000, a shareholders' liability for the same amount and a

surplus of $15,000,000, this Bank will command a higher degree of confidence, with results which it is believed will be a cause of substantial satisfaction to the shareholders.[65]

Stillman had not overstated the case. The results would indeed be satisfying. Assets spurted ahead, reaching a peak of $334 million in 1908, more than ten times their level in 1891 when Stillman had become president of the bank. Profits mounted steadily, cresting at $5.2 million in 1907.[66]

Figure 3.1

National City Bank portfolio policy, 1891–1908

Leverage and reserve ratios
Yearly average of call dates
percent

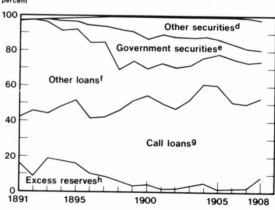

Allocation of net assets[c]
Yearly average of call dates
percent

More important, Stillman's conservative portfolio policy enabled National City to meet the severest test of a bank's strength: a panic. Indeed, the banking panics of 1893 and 1907 made National City a stronger bank relative to its competitors. The 1893 crisis set the stage for National City's subsequent growth. The 1907 crisis confirmed its position as the country's leading bank and enhanced its standing as an investment banker.

The 1893 panic stemmed from uncertainty over the federal government's willingness and ability to maintain the gold standard.[67] Stillman had seen trouble coming, and following Taylor's precept of ready money, he had prepared the bank for it. By October 1894 the combination of ready money and the solicitation of new customers had made National City Bank the largest bank in the United States, giving Stillman the banking power needed to enter investment banking on a large scale.

The Panic of 1907, as mentioned above, stemmed largely from the attempt of Treasury Secretary Shaw to stabilize interest rates. Initially, this policy was successful, for Shaw had the resources to intervene in the market and the skill to invent new ways of increasing the Treasury's influence over the money market. But Shaw's very success induced banks, including

---

Notes to Figure 3.1.

Source: National City Bank, Call Reports, 1891–1908.

Leverage and reserve ratios:

  a. Ratio of excess reserves to deposits is the average reserve for the 30 days preceding the call date minus a constant 25% required reserve ratio.

  b. Ratio of capital to assets is total stockholders' equity (capital, surplus fund, undivided profits, and dividends unpaid) divided by total assets.

Allocation of net assets:

  c. Net assets is computed as total assets minus float and required reserves. Float is the sum due from other national banks, state and private banks and bankers' exchanges for clearing house, and checks and drafts on banks in this city.

  d. "Other securities" is stocks, securities, including premiums on same.

  e. "Government securities" is the sum of U.S. bonds to secure circulation, U.S. bonds to secure deposits, U.S. bonds on hand, and premium on other U.S. bonds.

  f. "Other loans" is total loans, inclusive of overdrafts, minus call loans.

  g. "Call loans" is loans and discounts on demand, secured by stocks and other personal securities.

  h. "Excess reserves" is the difference between legal reserves (lawful money plus the redemption fund) and required reserves (25% of net deposits). Net deposits is the sum due to other national banks, state and private banks and bankers, deposits of trust companies, individual deposits, and U.S. government deposits minus float.

National City, to reduce their excess reserves. This made the entire banking system more susceptible to external shocks.[68]

In 1906 the Bank of England supplied the shock by raising its discount rate in response to the flow of gold to the United States stimulated by Shaw's subsidization of gold imports. Prior to its decision the Bank of England had called on Stillman, as president of the largest bank in the United States and the largest participant in the Treasury's gold importation program, to appeal to the Treasury to halt the program.[69] Stillman did so, but the Treasury refused. In September and October 1906, the Bank of England retaliated by raising its discount rate and asking British banks not to renew American finance bills. These actions reversed the flow of gold and brought on a money crunch in the United States and a slowdown in business activity.[70]

Panic came a year later. When the Knickerbocker Trust Company failed in October 1907, touching off a run on the city's other trust companies, the Treasury could not avert a panic. Under Morgan's leadership, Stillman and other financiers formed a pool to support the call money market and to save the Trust Company of America, the city's second largest.[71] But to stop the panic, the issue of Clearing House loan certificates and the restriction of cash payments to depositors became necessary.

National City again emerged from the panic a larger and stronger institution. At the start National City had higher reserve and capital ratios than its competitors, and during the panic it gained in deposits and loans relative to its competitors (Table 3.4). Stillman had anticipated and planned for this result. In response to Vanderlip's complaint in early 1907 that National City's low leverage and high reserve ratio was depressing profitability, Stillman replied: "I have felt for sometime that the next panic and low interest rates following would straighten out a good many things that have of late years crept into banking. What impresses me as most important is to go into next Autumn [usually a time of financial stringency] ridiculously strong and liquid, and now is the time to begin and shape for it . . . If by able and judicious management we have money to help our dealers when trust companies have suspended, we will have all the business we want for many years.[72]

The bank's performance during the panic capped a remarkable overall achievement. Since 1891 Stillman had built National City from a small treasury unit in the Taylor empire into the country's foremost commercial bank. Stillman had made National City a bank for big business, for Wall Street, and for banks across the country. National City offered them all ready money and comprehensive financial service. No one-man bank could expect to do more.

Table 3.4. Banking in New York City before and during two panics: 1893 and 1907

Date	Reserve ratio (%)		Date	Change in deposits (%)		Change in loans and discounts (%)	
	National City Bank	All other N.Y.C. banks[a]		National City Bank	All other N.Y.C. banks[a]	National City Bank	All other N.Y.C. banks[a]
4/14/1893	42.6	25.2	5/4–10/3/1893	12.4	−14.5	14.7	−9.1
10/26/1907[b]	26.9	24.9	10/26/1907–2/8/1908	23.5	9.2	10.2	3.7

Source: National City Bank, Call Reports, May 4, 1893, and October 3, 1893; Comptroller of the Currency, *Annual Report, 1893*, vol. I (Washington, D.C., 1894), pp. 282–283; New York Clearing House, Statement of the Associated Banks of the City of New York for the weeks ending October 26, 1907, and February 8, 1908 (New York: New York Clearing House, 1907 and 1908).

a. Definition of all other N.Y.C. banks: 1893—national banks; 1907—N.Y.C. Clearing House member banks.

b. Although there is little difference in the reserve ratios between National City and other Clearing House member banks at this date, National City was much more heavily capitalized. Its ratio of capital to net deposits stood at 35.2%; that of other New York banks at 27.5%. This provided National City depositors with an added measure of safety.

4.

Vanderlip and Banking Reform
1909–1913

By moving out of its owner's shadow, National City would be able to do more, much more. Symbolic of the transformation into a modern corporation was the move on December 19, 1908, from the bank's original home at 52 Wall Street to a new building across the street at number 55. The old building was small, but adequate for the bank's role as a cog in its owner's personal business empire. The new building was grand, a banking palace rich in tradition, yet as modern and up-to-date as any commercial office in the nation.[1] Originally built as the Merchants' Exchange in 1843, converted into the U.S. Customs House in 1863, and purchased by National City in 1899, this building, more than any other, signified the rise of New York as the nation's business center. Stillman ordered that its distinctive Ionic colonnade be preserved and that the interior be remodeled after the Pantheon in Rome. The result was a structure suited to the bank's position as the largest and strongest bank in the United States.

Stillman intended National City to retain this position even after his death, and to ensure this he filled the new building with people who shared his own vision and entrepreneurial spirit, people who would build an organization. He would step aside himself and let them run the bank. Stillman had long had this object in view. As he wrote to his mother in December 1908:

> I have been preparing for the past two years to assume an advisory position at the Bank and decline re-election as its official head. I know this is wise and it not only relieves me of the responsibility of details, but gives my associates an opportunity to make names for themselves. They will have all the benefits of my advice and experience, for my pride and interest in the Bank will never be any less and probably greater than in the past. This makes them very appreciative and loyal to me and the Bank and that is of great value to it. The completion of the new building is

> a fitting time for this step and I feel we have erected a superb
> monument and laid the foundation for limitless possibilities,
> greater even for the future than what has been accomplished in
> the past.[2]

Frank Vanderlip would be responsible for finding and exploiting those
opportunities. The directors had elected him president of the bank on January 12, 1909. Stillman moved up to the newly created post of chairman
of the board of directors. Stillman did not attend the meeting but orches-
trated it from his home in Paris, where he planned to spend most of each
year. Indeed, his subsequent visits to New York would be few and far between. He did, in fact as well as in name, delegate considerable executive
authority to Vanderlip, although he expected to be kept informed through
frequent cables and weekly letters regarding events at the bank. Stillman
also retained the right to veto major policy decisions, for he continued to
be the bank's principal shareholder. In sum, the division of executive labor
was this: Vanderlip proposed and Stillman disposed.

New Directions

Even in 1909 the limits of Stillman's strategy were becoming apparent.
The personal element in finance was on the wane; the institutional, on the
rise. The magnates whom Stillman had served would soon depart from
the business scene. Harriman died in 1909, and William Rockefeller would
retire as a director of Standard Oil in 1911. Increasingly, managers rather
than owners would make financing decisions for corporations. As investors, the industrial magnates to whom Stillman had sold securities were
also fading in importance relative to individuals of more modest means
and institutions, such as correspondent banks. The result of these developments was a broader and deeper investment market. New issues rose in
number and size, straining the personal system Stillman had created.[3]

Both Stillman and Vanderlip realized that National City had to institutionalize its relationships with borrowers and investors. This involved
transforming Stillman's personal alliance with Kuhn, Loeb into an institutional arrangement, strengthening National City's ties with other houses,
and developing its own customer base.

National City's banking power paved the way. In 1907, the bond market had collapsed and new issues could only be marketed at high yields or
not at all. Firms seeking to refund maturing issues turned to their bankers
for short-term credit to tide them over until bonds could be sold on a more
reasonable basis. Kuhn, Loeb could not meet these demands; National
City could and did, lending substantial sums to their mutual customers.

This experience would put National City and Kuhn, Loeb on a nearly equal footing. The change came in 1909 when J. Ogden Armour approached Vanderlip and asked National City to underwrite a $50 million bond issue to finance his company's expansion of meatpacking facilities in the United States and Argentina.[4] Armour had been a steady customer of the bank since 1897. Vanderlip was eager to accommodate him, but felt that an issue of $50 million was too big for National City to handle alone. Vanderlip turned to Kuhn, Loeb for help despite his fears of "being eaten alive" there.[5] But he was not. As he wrote to Stillman, no "piece of business in connection with the bank . . . has given me so much pleasure, . . . for the results certainly mark a most distinct progress in the bank's position. I have succeeded in getting absolutely everything that I thought the bank was entitled to, in fairness, and have gotten it with absolute good nature and friendliness throughout all the discussions. I have even gotten the trusteeship for the Farmers Loan, although that was one of the particularly difficult things to do."[6] For the first time National City had succeeded in getting "a definite standing on all fours with K[uhn,] L[oeb] & Co. . . . as joint bankers."[7] The Armour financing established a precedent that governed the division of profits and fees in future National City and Kuhn, Loeb underwritings.

While strengthening its position with Kuhn, Loeb, National City also began to deepen its relationship with other investment-banking houses. The key alliance was with Morgan, the leader in investment banking. Its foundation had been laid in the early 1890s when Stillman participated in a Morgan-led syndicate to reorganize the Northern Pacific. In 1896 a Morgan partner, Robert Bacon, joined National City's board of directors and served until 1903. Another Morgan partner, George W. Perkins, served as a National City director beginning in 1900. After the 1907 panic, the bank became a regular member of the originating group in Morgan-led syndicates. It thereby obtained securities on the same terms as Morgan and earned a larger spread than formerly, when it had been restricted to membership in the selling syndicate. The bank also received a portion of the sale as deposits, pending their use by the borrower. But Morgan clearly remained the senior partner. It retained its close relationships with leading borrowers and probably did not share the "up-front" origination fees on the many new issues it developed. By 1908 National City, Morgan, and the latter's close ally, the First National Bank, regularly shared in one another's underwritings. The three banks agreed that the house originating an issue would offer each of the other two 25 percent, retaining 50 percent for itself.[8]

Alliances with Morgan and Kuhn, Loeb did not prevent National City from venturing into new territory. The bank also participated in syndicates with a number of smaller and newer investment houses. These

houses floated issues for electric and gas utilities, industries largely neglected by Morgan and Kuhn, Loeb. Utilities in the years 1900–1913 were
in much the same stage of development as the railroads were in the 1860s
and 1870s, with many small local companies and frequent price wars.
Technology in the generation of electricity was changing so rapidly that
investments were constantly in danger of becoming obsolete. Utility securities were consequently unpopular with investors and not readily
marketable.[9]

But National City knew the utility field, and the bank was optimistic
about its future. Consolidated Gas had been one of the bank's oldest and
most important accounts. Stillman had been a director of that company
since 1894, and William Rockefeller since 1890. The bank's loans had
helped the company achieve by 1901 a commanding position in the provision of gas and electricity to New York City.[10]

During the years 1900–1914, National City helped underwrite securities
for a number of utilities, extending to smaller investment-banking houses
the banking support they required. The most important of these underwritings was for Pacific Gas and Electric (PG & E), which Stillman helped
N. Wetmore Halsey organize in 1906. This assistance would lead to further underwritings for PG & E and ultimately to National City's acquisition of Halsey's investment-banking firm in 1916 (see chapter 5).[11]

This strategy of strengthening and expanding alliances required considerable diplomacy and tact. As National City moved closer to Morgan, its
alliance with Kuhn, Loeb was threatened. Vanderlip wrote about this to
Stillman in 1909: "It takes some acrobatic ability to be on extremely
friendly and co-operative relations with two sets of people that are dis-
tinctly antagonistic, and the job of keeping on the most co-operative basis
with Morgan, with Kuhn, Loeb, and with Speyer, has its difficulties."[12]
The balancing act was a success. In 1914 Vanderlip wrote to Stillman: "We
are at peace with everybody, we do business with everybody. There is not
a financial house that is not glad to work with us."[13]

Along with developing National City's alliances with other investment
bankers Vanderlip broadened its customer base, increasing its placing
power and laying the foundation for originating securities on its own.
Correspondent banks were a prime target, for in addition to keeping large
deposit balances in New York they continued to buy securities as secondary reserves and were beginning to resell them to their own customers.
As a result of Vanderlip's new business campaigns, the number of National
City's out-of-town correspondents rose from 1,230 in 1905 to 1,889 in
1912.[14]

At the same time National City began to approach investors directly. At
William Rockefeller's suggestion Vanderlip began to develop a network
for the retail distribution of securities. Initial results were favorable. At

the beginning of 1912 Vanderlip reported to Stillman: "Our bond sales are most satisfactory. We have never had anything like such an active demand or wide distribution of orders. The largely increased [sales] force is beginning to show very satisfactory results and our placing power is increasing quite as rapidly as we could possibly hope for."[15]

Vanderlip also established relationships with potential issuers of securities. During the years 1905 to 1913, the bank offered deposit and credit facilities to a large number of corporations, putting it in a position to underwrite their securities when they decided to fund themselves in the bond market. To this end Vanderlip organized calling programs in various sections of the country, most notably Texas, where Stillman had extensive business interests.[16] The result was a greatly expanded and more diversified corporate customer base. To the nucleus of railroad, petroleum, and utility accounts inherited from Stillman and Taylor, Vanderlip added relationships with the leading firms in American industry (see Appendix D).

Thus, by 1913 National City had secured a leading position in both investment and commercial banking. Overall, it remained the largest bank in the country. By forming ties to both Morgan and Kuhn, Loeb, National City gained access to two distinct groups of customers, and in the years 1908 to 1912 National City probably participated in a larger volume of new issues than either of its allies.[17] In commercial lending National City became a leader as well. After the Panic of 1907 the bank substantially increased corporate loans, both to satisfy the demands of its new industrial customers for credit and to reduce its reliance on call loans. By 1912 it was the largest lender to business among all New York City banks.[18] These initiatives were clearly reflected on the bottom line. After the Panic of 1907 the bank's earnings rose sharply, reaching a peak of $7 million in the year ending October 31, 1911. Bond underwriting and trading (including interest earned on the bonds while held in the bank's portfolio) amounted to nearly one-half of the bank's gross income in that year.

Despite the bank's excellent performance, Vanderlip viewed the future with increasing apprehension. Its earnings were highly dependent on bond trading and underwriting; if the volume of new issues fell off, as they did in 1912 and 1913, the bank's overall earnings could sag sharply. As Vanderlip explained to Stillman, "had there been no Bond Department profits, the Bank would only have [earned] about around its dividend this year. Difficult as it is to make money out of this strictly banking side, we are having to compete with trust companies that are offering broadcast to make free collections for commercial accounts and pay three per cent interest on balances."[19]

As a nationally chartered bank, National City stood at a distinct disadvantage compared to less heavily taxed and stringently regulated state-chartered banks and trust companies. Specifically, state-chartered banks and trust companies had a required reserve ratio of 15 percent, as opposed to 25 percent for national banks. Lower reserve requirements allowed these institutions to provide their depositors more services or a higher rate of interest than National City. In addition, state-chartered banks and trust companies had the power to branch, while National City could not. National banks were restricted to a single office, while state-chartered banks could operate branches throughout New York City. Trust companies could open branches overseas, which gave them a considerable advantage in financing foreign trade. Finally, the trust companies had, as their name implied, the power to offer institutions and individuals a full range of trust services. National banks had no trust powers at all. As a result, trust companies had grown far more rapidly than national banks in New York City.[20] Vanderlip's strategy was to launch a counterattack. As he wrote to Stillman, "something radical is going to be necessary in order to meet the banking competition that we are facing."[21]

Banking Reform

At first, Vanderlip worked to change the banking laws. The 1907 panic had focused the attention of the public and its representatives in Congress on banking reform.[22] Vanderlip welcomed the public's concern about an issue crucial to National City's future. For decades National City had acted along with the other leading members of the New York Clearing House as a "one-armed central bank."[23] As holders of the reserves of other banks, these banks had been responsible for the stability of the banking system, even though they had neither the means nor the public support required for the job. Shifting this task to a real central bank would free National City from this responsibility. It would also undermine the rationale for narrow limits on the powers of national banks. A central bank, coupled with broader powers for nationally chartered banks, would enable National City to modify or abandon its ready money strategy and go after more profitable business. As Vanderlip later remarked, "If we have a central bank, at which we can rediscount commercial paper, making commercial paper a liquid asset, then we will have no necessity for devoting a large amount of our funds to call loans on stock exchange collateral, and can divert the funds now used for that purpose to commercial loans."[24]

Vanderlip participated from the start in developing the reform plans then taking shape on Wall Street and in Washington. He was well qualified for the task. He combined practical experience in banking with a knowledge of economics. As a former Treasury official, he knew the Washington political scene and the leading figures in it. As a former journalist, he knew the value of publicity and how to get it. Finally, there was his new position as the president of the largest bank in the country. In his note of congratulations, Andrew Carnegie had reminded Vanderlip, "Now you are in the front just at the right time. We shall have to establish a better currency system and your voice will be powerful."[25]

Vanderlip agreed. Like certain economists, journalists, public officials, and other bankers, he thought the major defect in the country's banking and monetary system was its lack of an "elastic" currency. That term had two very different meanings. The first concerned banks' ability to convert their deposits into currency on demand and at par at all times. The second concerned banks' provision of money adequate to meet the needs of trade. Making the currency elastic in the first sense would help halt a panic. Making it elastic in the second sense would, it was commonly believed, prevent panics altogether and thus ensure continued economic prosperity.[26]

In the wake of the panic, reform proposals concentrated on providing an elastic currency in the first sense. The most pressing problem during the panic had appeared to be a shortage of currency. Banks had to restrict cash payments because they were illiquid. Although banks had large reserves, these could not be used. They were frozen by the comptroller's minimum reserve requirements. Nor could banks readily turn their secondary reserves into cash. Call loans could not be repaid, and securities could not be sold. Investments safe for each individual bank in normal times endangered all banks in a crisis. Faced with the prospect that they and their customers would fail, the New York banks had done two things: They effectively suspended reserve requirements through the issue of Clearing House loan certificates and they restricted the convertibility of deposits into currency at par. These measures succeeded in bringing the panic to an end, although they were accompanied by severe disruptions in commerce and industry.

The disruptions from the 1907 panic convinced congressional leaders that it was time to act. In May 1908, Congress passed the Aldrich-Vreeland Act. As amended in 1913, it provided for the issue of emergency currency. Thus banks could maintain cash payments to depositors even if a crisis forced the issue of Clearing House loan certificates. (This in fact happened in 1914. The outbreak of war in Europe set off a financial crisis and a near panic, which was contained by the issue of Clearing House certificates and emergency currency.)[27]

The Aldrich-Vreeland Act was designed to help halt a panic, not to prevent one. With the latter purpose in mind, Congress established the National Monetary Commission, with Senator Nelson Aldrich of Rhode Island as chairman, to develop a banking and monetary system that would eliminate panics. It was an ambitious task and a problematic one. Imperfect though it was, the national banking system had not prevented nearly five decades of the most rapid economic growth on record. Panics had interrupted, not halted, progress. The traditional Clearing House method—

loan certificates and restricting cash payments—had been effective in halting panics and softening their effects. Supplemented by an issue of emergency currency, these measures could limit the impact of a panic on economic activity, as the 1914 experience would show.

Aldrich knew little about banking, but he was willing to learn. He turned for advice to the leading bankers on Wall Street, Vanderlip among them. Others included Paul M. Warburg of Kuhn, Loeb, Henry P. Davison of J. P. Morgan and Company, and Benjamin Strong of the Bankers' Trust Company.[28] These men turned Aldrich's mind toward the creation of a central bank, to be modeled on the Bank of England or the German Reichsbank. At the beginning of the twentieth century, European central banks were privately owned but publicly sanctioned institutions. Through their operation European countries had been spared panics on the American scale.[29]

At the beginning of 1911 Aldrich was scheduled to report to Congress on the commission's findings and to recommend a plan of banking reform. The commission had assembled much useful and valuable information, but as late as November 1910 Aldrich "had made no progress at all in the direction of crystalizing his ideas further than that he was certain that some sort of a central organization, which should hold reserves for the whole country, was the necessary foundation."[30]

Once again Aldrich turned to Wall Street for help. He invited Vanderlip, Davison, Warburg, and Strong to a secret meeting on Jekyll Island, off the coast of Georgia, to participate in the drafting of a plan for banking reform. After a week of intensive discussion, they produced a document outlining the functions, management, and scope of a centralized banking organization.[31] The plan as presented by Aldrich to Congress on January 16, 1911, envisioned the creation of a national reserve association that would hold the reserves of the nation's commercial banks, rediscount their commercial paper, and issue bank notes. This would assure the liquidity of the banking system. It also granted nationally chartered banks significantly broader powers including the ability to branch in their home city and overseas, to conduct a trust business, and to accept commercial paper.[32] If it had been adopted, it would have given Vanderbilt everything he hoped to achieve for National City Bank.

The Aldrich Plan stood little chance of adoption. Although Warburg and other Wall Street bankers launched a publicity drive to gather support for the plan, its prospects of enactment were slim.[33] Indeed, their support probably did the plan more harm than good, for it awakened fears that the large New York banks would dominate the national reserve association.[34] Bankers also disagreed among themselves about the specifics of the plan, and with the return of economic prosperity, the public had lost interest in banking reform. Finally, there was Senator Aldrich himself. By

1911 he had fallen from the dominant position he had held in the Senate since 1882. He was isolated from his Republican colleagues and distrusted by the Democrats. Presidential hopeful Governor Woodrow Wilson of New Jersey told an interviewer that even though he had not studied the plan, he disliked anything bearing Aldrich's name.[35] Having won control of the House of Representatives in the 1910 elections, the Democrats could prevent the passage of any bill not to their liking.[36] Thus the Aldrich Plan seemed likely to gather dust, as had the reports of other currency commissions before it.

Vanderlip had anticipated this development. After the Jekyll Island meeting he had not been "optimistic about the immediate fate of this plan."[37] During 1911 he grew more pessimistic, finally coming to the conclusion that "there is no prospect whatever for any banking legislation at the present time . . . The plan is so indelibly stamped the 'Aldrich Plan' that the name itself is going to defeat its fair consideration, for the present, at least."[38]

The National City Company

When the prospects for regulatory relief dimmed, Vanderlip began to consider a more direct approach to National City's problem: the formation of an affiliate not subject to the National Bank Act, which would allow National City to enter new areas, offer new services, and win new customers.

For years National City's owners had invested in state-chartered trust companies or banks in order to engage in activities prohibited for the bank itself. For example, Taylor owned and managed the Farmers' Loan and Trust Company, and Stillman had invested in a large number of banks and trust companies in New York City and elsewhere. But such arrangements were personal and depended on the situation and interests of the bank's dominant shareholder. Vanderlip decided to institutionalize the relationship between National City Bank and its owners' other investments. By establishing a corporate affiliate, Vanderlip hoped to employ some of the bank's capital more profitably and to broaden his own managerial responsibility.

In Washington, the Treasury Department had long been concerned with the inability of national banks, which were under its jurisdiction, to compete on an equal footing with the less heavily regulated state-chartered banks and trust companies, and had accordingly looked with favor on the formation of such bank affiliates. In his annual report to the Congress on December 5, 1910, Treasury Secretary MacVeagh stated:

> We have in the national banking system a great institution and one whose usefulness is susceptible of great development. It car-

ries, however, the marks of its imperfect inauguration. It is, in some respects unnecessarily, tied hand and foot. It can not, as I have pointed out, do international banking; and it is restricted closely as to the kind of domestic banking it can do. It can not do the business the trust companies do, though the trust companies can turn from their trust business to become competitors of the national banks in their own restricted field of commercial banking. But why a national bank should not do all kinds of legitimate banking it is hard to say.[39]

The Treasury had in fact recommended legislation to expand the powers of national banks, but Congress had not acted. Pending such legislation, the Treasury had approved affiliates, such as the one Vanderlip had in mind, established by other national banks, as a way of keeping a large part of the banking system within its jurisdiction.

On June 28, 1911, Vanderlip wrote to the National City shareholders: "The officers and directors of the National City Bank of New York are of the opinion that it will be of material advantage to the shareholders of the Bank to unite in establishing a corporation so organized that it may make investments and transact other business, which though often very profitable, may not be within the express corporate powers of a National Bank."[40]

Vanderlip took as his model the First Security Company formed by George F. Baker of the First National Bank in 1908. The shareholders of the First Security Company agreed to vest their ownership rights in three trustees, who would be officers or directors of the First National Bank. The trustees elected the board of directors of the affiliate and agreed to distribute through the bank any dividends paid by the affiliate. Through this arrangement the shareholders of the First National Bank created a corporation whose capital and operations would be distinct from those of the bank but whose ownership and management would be the same. The First Security Corporation had acquired from the First National Bank and its shareholders a controlling interest in the Chase National Bank as well as shares in other New York City banks and the First National Bank of Minneapolis. These transactions received the tacit approval of the comptroller of the currency and passed practically unnoticed by the public. So did the formation of similar affiliates by other national banks such as the First National Bank of Chicago.[41]

Vanderlip's proposal to form an affiliate of this kind was quickly approved by the shareholders. In July 1911 a new company, the National City Company, was incorporated under the laws of the state of New York along the lines of the First Security Company. The first trustees were James Stillman, Frank Vanderlip, and Stephen Palmer, a director of the bank. The shareholders agreed to endow the National City Company with a capital of $10 million, an amount equal to the special dividend that the bank had declared on its stock.[42]

Two factors set the National City Company apart from similar bank affiliates. The first was size. National City was the largest bank in the country, and it formed the largest bank affiliate. The bank's action inevitably attracted attention. The second factor was the way the new corporation was used. Within days of its formation, the National City Company had become a nationwide bank holding company. It acquired from James Stillman and other stockholders some of their shares in other banks and trust companies. These included a controlling interest in several smaller banks in New York City, as well as a minority interest in large banks in New York, Philadelphia, Boston, Washington, Indianapolis, and Kansas City (Table 4.1).

Table 4.1. National City Company stockholdings in banks and trust companies, July 1911

Bank	Number of shares	Percentage of total shares outstanding
New York City banks		
National Bank of Commerce	9,800	3.9
Lincoln National Bank	4,324	43.2
Bank of the Metropolis	3,340	—
National Butchers' & Drovers' Bank	3,000	100.0
Farmers' Loan & Trust Co.	950	—
Columbia Bank	882	—
Second National Bank	10	0.1
Other U.S. banks		
Riggs National Bank (Washington, D.C.)	2,240	22.4
National Shawmut Bank (Boston)	1,000	2.9
Fourth Street National Bank (Philadelphia)	500	1.7
Hibernia Bank & Trust Co. (New Orleans)	423	—
Fidelity Trust Co. (Kansas City)	500	—
Title Saving & Trust Co. (Kansas City)	125	—
American National Bank (Indianapolis)	250	—
Fletcher American National Bank (Indianapolis)	167	0.8
Foreign banks		
Banco de Habana (Cuba)	1,667	—

Source: Frank A. Vanderlip to H. A. Wise (United States Attorney, New York City), July 26, 1911, Taft MSS, Library of Congress, Washington, D.C., and U.S. Congress, Senate Banking and Currency Committee, *Stock Exchange Practices: Hearings on S. Res. 84,* 72nd Cong., 1st sess., 1932, p. 2040.

The acquisition of the smaller New York City banks formalized a long-standing situation. For many years Stillman had held a controlling interest in these banks, and had operated them as if they were branches of National City (see chapter 3). National City granted them loan participations, administered the collection of their out-of-town checks, and extended them overdraft facilities. In effect, Stillman had built up a chain of banks. Although not as efficient as a branch bank, the arrangement enabled him to compete with state-chartered banks, which since 1898 had been able to establish branches in New York City. The City Company brought these smaller banks into a single holding company with unified management.

Through its minority interests in banks outside New York City the National City Company created the possibility of the same type of arrangement across state lines. Coordination of policy was already far advanced with the Riggs National Bank, which administered a representative service in Washington, D.C. offered by National City Bank to its domestic correspondents. Stillman had obtained a controlling interest in the Riggs at the turn of the century and this interest was sold to the National City Company. Holdings in American Fletcher, Fourth Street National, and other out-of-state banks were as yet toeholds, but they could be supplemented by additional purchases. Thus, within days of its creation the National City Company had put together the nucleus of a nationwide chain of banks. The National City organization had leapt over the regulatory barriers that had long confined the bank to a single office at the tip of Manhattan Island.

One of the City Company's investments stood out. That was a block of ninety-eight hundred shares in the National Bank of Commerce, the second largest bank in New York City. Stillman had acquired these shares in March 1911 from the Mutual Life Insurance Company, which was required to divest them under the insurance law passed by the New York State legislature in the wake of the Armstrong investigation of 1905–1906. J. P. Morgan and George F. Baker had acquired the Equitable's holdings of the National Bank of Commerce stock at the same time as Stillman. Thus the three men together held a controlling interest in the Commerce. Rather than fight one another for control, they had agreed to run the Commerce through a finance committee composed of their representatives. Along with the First National's control of Chase and Stillman's influence in the Hanover National Bank, the Commerce arrangement brought five of the six largest holders of correspondent bank balances under the control of Stillman, Morgan, Baker, and their close associates.[43] It was the nucleus of a private central bank.

In this way the National City Company seemed to offer a solution not only to National City Bank's regulatory problems but also to the nation's need for a central reserve bank. Moreover, the City Company with its interests in banks across the country was also the nucleus of a nationwide banking chain. In combination, these two aspects—a central reserve bank and nationwide chain banking—resembled the banking structure of the United Kingdom and Germany, countries where banking panics had practically vanished.

The Money Trust Investigation

In forming the National City Company, Vanderlip had unwittingly touched a raw political nerve, the antitrust issue, and mixed it up with banking reform. The organization of the National City Company inspired Congressman Charles A. Lindbergh, Sr., of Minnesota to call for an investigation of the "money trust," which he likened to the industrial combines controlling the steel, sugar, tobacco, oil, and meatpacking industries. He labeled the Aldrich Plan a "wonderfully devised plan specifically fitted for Wall Street securing control of the world."[44]

Shortly before Lindbergh's statement, Attorney General Wickersham announced that he would conduct an investigation into the National City Company.[45] Evidently he did so on his own initiative, without a request from Treasury Secretary MacVeagh, who was responsible for the supervision of nationally chartered banks. By August 3, 1911, Wickersham was ready to deliver an opinion that the National City Company's ownership of stock in other national banks violated the spirit of the national banking laws. The following day Secretary MacVeagh was reported ready to take the position that the National City Company complied with the letter of the law. Rather than let either of them do so, President Taft requested that the papers on the case be sent to him, so that he could make the decision himself.[46]

For Taft, legal considerations were secondary to politics. He faced a difficult reelection campaign. The Democrats had captured the House of Representatives in 1910 and were sure to mount a strong challenge against him in 1912. Within Taft's own party, former President Roosevelt was increasingly inclined to make another bid for the presidency. The issue of the day was the trust problem.[47] To his opponents Taft had not gone far enough in breaking up the trusts; to his supporters in business he had gone too far. The *New York Times* summed up Taft's predicament: "If he decides [bank] holding companies are unlawful and proceeds to put them out of business he will strike a heavy blow at a great number of important business concerns closely connected with the financial stability of the country. If he decides they are lawful he will at once be accused of giving consent to the establishment of a money trust."[48]

Taft also had to consider the problem of banking reform and whether he wished to see it solved through legislation or by market forces. Congress had adjourned without settling the question of banking reform. Although less than lukewarm toward the Aldrich Plan, Congress still had not rejected it. The formation of the National City Company and its use as a bank holding company aroused suspicion that the "National City Bank interest would in some way dominate the directorate of the National Reserve Association."[49] The *New York Times* remarked in August 1911 that "if any definite attitude toward the extension of the influence of National banks into trust companies and securities companies were announced at this time, the whole question of financial legislation might be entangled when it comes up at the next session of Congress with the Monetary Commission's report."[50] Thus, the wisest political course for Taft to follow was to avoid a decision, which he did.

Nevertheless, Vanderlip decided that the National City Company should get rid of its domestic bank stocks. On November 3, 1911, it began to sell its holdings in state and nationally chartered banks in the United States. On November 14 it completed the process by selling its holdings in the Bank of the Metropolis to the Bank of the Manhattan Company. The National City Company itself was not dissolved, for the affiliate had other uses in international and investment banking. It therefore retained its interests in foreign banks and nonfinancial corporations.[51]

Although National City had yielded Wickersham's main point, Congressman Lindbergh nevertheless introduced, on December 4, 1911, a resolution calling for a congressional investigation of the money trust. In his speech Lindbergh sounded a theme that the Democratic nominee, Woodrow Wilson, would echo in the presidential campaign the following fall: "Wall Street brought on the 1907 panic, got the people to demand currency reform, brought the Aldrich-Vreeland currency bill forward and, if it dares, will produce another panic to pass the Aldrich central bank plan. We need reform, but not at the hands of Wall Street."[52]

After considering and rejecting the Aldrich bill, the House Committee on Banking and Currency set up a subcommittee on April 25, 1912, to "investigate the concentration of money and credit." As Vanderlip had anticipated, the hearings brought to light the existence of interlocking directorates among banks and industrial corporations. National City was portrayed as part of an inner ring—with J. P. Morgan and Company and the First National Bank—that controlled industrial, railroad, public utility, and financial corporations through underwriting their securities and service as directors.[53] The interlocking directorships were viewed as proof of the money trust's existence and its awesome power. By June 1912, when the Pujo committee recessed for the electoral campaign, it had again made

the topic of banking reform a serious one, and one that the new administration would have to address.[54]

The Federal Reserve Act

Thanks to the split between Roosevelt and Taft, the new administration
was headed by a Democrat, Woodrow Wilson. His statements during the
campaign and the Democratic party's platform had been vague, indicating
only opposition to "the so-called Aldrich bill or the creation of a central
bank" and promising to free the country "from panics and consequent unemployment and business depression by such a systematic revision of our
banking laws as will render temporary relief in localities where such relief
is needed, with protection from control or dominion by what is known as
the money trust."[55]

That task of drafting banking legislation fell to Carter Glass, a Democratic congressman from Virginia and the chairman of a subcommittee
of the House Committee on Banking and Currency.[56] At the end of December 1912, he presented the President-elect Wilson with a draft of a bill
prepared by his assistant, H. Parker Willis, professor of economics at
Columbia University. The bill aimed to eliminate the concentration of
bank reserves in New York by providing for a decentralized, privately
controlled reserve system with twenty or more independent reserve
banks, presided over by the comptroller of the currency. Wilson proposed
a "capstone to be placed on the structure," a central board to control
and coordinate the individual reserve banks. The president-elect, Willis
later wrote, "recognized the fact that [a central bank] was politically impossible even if economically desirable, and what was to be sought was
the provision of those central banking powers which were unmistakably
desirable."[57]

The Glass bill was similar to the Aldrich bill in the functions it assigned
to the reserve banks. They were to rediscount commercial paper for member banks, hold a portion of member banks' reserves, and issue bank
notes partially backed by gold. But the Glass bill differed sharply from the
Aldrich Plan in its provisions for the structure and management of the
system. The Glass bill envisioned twelve or more independent regional
banks rather than one central bank with branches throughout the United
States. Although the regional banks were to be owned and managed by
bankers, their operation was to be supervised by the Federal Reserve
Board, a political body dominated by presidential appointees and cabinet
members, ex officio, as Wilson had proposed.

Vanderlip objected strongly to the regional decentralization and political control of the proposed system. He felt "no legislation at all" would be
preferable to the Glass bill.[58] According to Vanderlip:

> The greatest defect of our present system is that there are as
> many unrelated and distinct reserve centers as there are banks.
> The most important thing that legislation can accomplish is to
> relate all these reserves to one another by placing the reserves in
> a common reservoir. The proposed measure fails to accomplish
> this effective mobilization because it creates a considerable num-
> ber of reserve centers which would compete one against another
> in just the same manner as the twenty thousand individual banks
> now compete, but the competition might become even more
> fierce and dangerous for the power of these several regional re-
> serve institutions would be immeasurably greater in a sectional
> struggle for reserves because their strength would be greater
> than is the strength of the existing numerous units.[59]

Vanderlip acknowledged that, in principle, Glass's proposal overcame
this defect, but in practice he thought the board would prove ill suited to
the task. As he said, a "board having on it only one man of technical banking experience, and subject to all the vicissitudes of political pressure and
party trading in its make-up, will fail to assume successfully" the responsibilities of a central bank. To Vanderlip the fundamental flaw in the Glass
bill was its separation of "the control of the credit system of this country . . . from the active responsibility of bank management."[60]

To National City, the organization and management of the reserve system held the key to the bank's future. A single central bank controlled by
bankers seemed far more likely to assume the ready money function than
a government-managed system of regional reserve banks. Thus Vanderlip
continued to campaign for a reserve system owned and managed by its
member banks, even after the Glass bill had passed the House. It was a
losing battle. His campaign probably did his cause more harm than good,
for as he would later remark, he represented "an institution that in the minds
of some people seems to be the very fangs and claws of the 'Money Trust.' "[61]

On October 23, 1913, Vanderlip appeared suddenly to change his position regarding government control of the reserve system. At the request of
several members of the Senate Banking and Currency Committee, he had
drawn up a plan that would combine their desire for government control
and his wish for a single central bank.[62] According to this plan, the president of the United States would appoint all seven members of the Federal
Reserve Board, which in turn would appoint all other Federal Reserve officials. The Federal Reserve would be a single bank with branches
throughout the country rather than a system of twelve or more independent banks. Banks would not own the Federal Reserve Bank; nonvoting
common stock would be sold to the public.

Vanderlip's plan seemed to win the support of the committee. The *New
York Times* commented that the principle of government control "should

appeal to Democrats of the Bryan type."[63] Republicans favored the idea of
a single central bank. In combination the two ideas posed a workable alternative to the Glass bill, one that would eventually be followed in 1935
with the support of Glass himself. But Glass thought that Vanderlip had
proposed the plan to block any banking legislation, and he was vehemently
opposed to any bill but his own.

Wilson stood with Glass. After testifying in the Senate, Vanderlip attempted to discuss his plan with Wilson. The president rebuffed Vanderlip's request for a meeting. He indicated his satisfaction with the Glass-
Owen bill and commented that Vanderlip's plan was "so far from being
along the lines of my thought in this matter that it would be quite useless
for me to discuss it with you."[64]

Undeterred, Vanderlip continued to work for a single bank. On November 10, 1913, he debated the merits of the bill with Glass and Owen
before the Economic Club of New York. To Vanderlip, only blind preju-
dice against Wall Street prevented the adoption of his plan for a single central bank. He therefore prefaced his criticism of the regional bank scheme
embodied in the Federal Reserve Act with a defense of himself and his
right to help shape the currency legislation:

> I stand charged with the offense of being the President of the
> largest bank in the United States. Who are the officers of that
> bank? Let me tell you that with a single exception they are men
> whose boyhood started in poverty. I myself wore the blue over-
> alls of a farm hand and a machine shop apprentice . . .
>
> In such a technical and intricate matter as banking and currency
> legislation do you want the advice of men who have started in
> most humble surroundings and remained there, or men who, in
> spite of every handicap, have surmounted the barriers and have
> made a success of life?[65]

In his reply, Glass chose to ignore Vanderlip's presumption. He treated
Vanderlip's outburst as the last gasp of a frustrated and defeated oppo-
nent. Glass did not refer to Vanderlip by name; he merely refuted Vanderlip's charges that Congress had neglected bankers' advice in framing the
bill. Indeed, Congress had consulted bankers all through the legislative
process. But, Glass contended, at no time did all bankers adopt a common
position for any length of time (a reference to Vanderlip's own apparent
about-face). Glass concluded, "There are many things I can learn, but
what I have been unable to learn is what the American bankers really
want." He added, "This is really admirable currency legislation and you
[bankers] are going to have it."[66]

They did. After debate in the Senate, President Wilson signed the Federal Reserve Act into law on December 23, 1913. In the final version twelve regional reserve banks were placed under the supervision and control of a seven-member Federal Reserve Board, consisting of five presidential appointees and two ex officio members, the secretary of the treasury and the comptroller of the currency.

This structure sharply reduced the public policy role that National City had perforce played as the leading bank in a nation without a central bank. It injected a new organization between the federal government and the banks. Although the Federal Reserve System was to be a collection of bankers' banks, it of necessity reduced the influence of any one bank, however large, on economic policy. Henceforth, the government would seek advice more often from the Federal Reserve than from the leaders of the country's largest banks. All this was in line with Vanderlip's intentions, for it freed National City to pursue new opportunities at home and abroad.

What ran counter to Vanderlip's intentions and boded ill for the future was the direct and strong involvement of the federal government in the supervision of the Federal Reserve System. This made the Federal Reserve banks not only banks for bankers but also regulators of bankers. Thus from the outset there existed a tension within the Federal Reserve System between the dual responsibilities of serving its member banks and serving what it construed to be the public interest. Ultimately the division of control over the Federal Reserve between government and the banking community would prove to be as troublesome to National City and to the nation as Vanderlip had feared.

5.

A New Strategy
1914-1916

The Federal Reserve Act, wrote Vanderlip to Stillman at the end of 1913, "is going to recast the methods of the banking business."[1] At National City it certainly did. The new law gave Vanderlip the freedom to develop more fully his earlier initiatives in commercial and investment banking and to create new ones in international banking. The outbreak of war in Europe, coupled with U.S. neutrality, further heightened these opportunities. The result was a new and more aggressive strategy that transformed National City from a specialized wholesale bank into an all-purpose intermediary providing a wide array of financial services to a variety of customers at home and abroad.

A New Environment

Although not everything Vanderlip had hoped and lobbied for, the Federal Reserve Act did considerably expand National City's private business opportunities and did significantly reduce its public policy role. The Federal Reserve System took direct responsibility for ensuring the stability of the nation's banking system. Instead of a one-armed central bank, National City could become a two-fisted competitor in a wide range of financial services at home and abroad.

The Federal Reserve was created in order to prevent panics, and to this end it was granted powers that no national bank had enjoyed. These were the ability to issue notes based on commercial paper as well as government bonds, to require member banks to keep their required reserves on deposit with it, and to act as the federal government's fiscal agent. These powers enabled it to take over primary responsibility for issuing the nation's currency, to centralize the reserves of the nation's banking system, and, most importantly, to act as a lender of last resort by discounting paper presented to it by member banks. Together these measures enabled the

Federal Reserve System to keep the nation's banks liquid at all times—the key, so it was thought, to preventing a panic.[2]

The introduction of the Federal Reserve banks radically altered the way in which commercial banks, especially central-reserve-city national banks such as National City, could conduct business. The provisions of the Federal Reserve Act significantly reduced the attractiveness of domestic correspondent banking while creating greater opportunities in commercial lending and in international banking. Of equal significance for National City, the Federal Reserve Act also left unaltered the rules concerning call loans and the conduct of investment-banking activities through security affiliates.

Correspondent banking for other U.S. banks was the area most affected by the Federal Reserve Act. The new Federal Reserve banks took over many of the functions formerly performed by National City and other national banks in New York City. First, the Reserve banks became depositories for the reserves that national banks across the country were legally required to maintain. Formerly, under the National Bank Act, national banks outside New York City could include their deposits at national banks in New York City as part of their required reserves (see chapter 2). After the introduction of the Federal Reserve System they could no longer do so, although a three-year transition to the new system was permitted. Second, the Federal Reserve System provided clearing and collection services to its member banks and par clearance to their depositors, eliminating the fees formerly paid to New York City correspondents by out-of-town banks. As a result of these two changes, national banks in New York City were expected to lose a significant portion of their correspondent bank balances.

Compensating for the prospective loss of correspondent balances was the banks' ability to discount commercial paper with the Federal Reserve. This reduced the need for each bank to maintain its own liquidity, and permitted banks to make more commercial loans. Further stimulus to business lending came from the reduction in reserve requirements. For central-reserve-city banks, such as National City, requirements on demand deposits were reduced from 25 percent to 18 percent. In addition, a new category of deposits, time deposits with a maturity of more than thirty days, was created with a reserve requirement of only 5 percent. Taken together, these measures enabled national banks to compete aggressively for corporate business on a national scale.

In addition, the Federal Reserve Act enabled national banks to compete on a global scale, if they chose to do so. In order to promote U.S. foreign trade, the act permitted national banks with more than one million dollars in capital to open branches abroad. This broke the longstanding prohibition against branches of any sort for national banks, and put them more on a par with state-chartered banks, which were permitted by New York State to branch both abroad and throughout New York City. Thus, allowing national banks to open foreign branches not only opened new business opportunities abroad but also dispelled the notion that national banks had to be unit banks. This would open the door to further relaxation of the branching restrictions on national banks.

Linked to the power to open branches overseas was the power to create acceptances based on the importation or exportation of goods, which the Federal Reserve Act granted to member banks. Such trade acceptances were also eligible for discount at the Federal Reserve. This too was intended to promote U.S. foreign trade. By allowing national banks to open foreign branches and to create and discount acceptances, the framers of the Federal Reserve Act hoped to duplicate in America the London discount market, whose smooth operation promoted British trade.

With regard to investment banking the Federal Reserve Act's significance lay in what it did not do. Although the Pujo committee decried the practice of investment banking by commercial banks, Congress sanctioned it, refusing to prohibit it in either the Federal Reserve Act or the Clayton Anti-Trust Act (1914). Indeed, the Federal Reserve Board went a step further, allowing state-chartered banks and trust companies to become members without giving up their investment-banking powers. National banks interpreted this as a sign that they too could engage in investment-banking activities, either directly or through affiliates.[3] This confirmed the legitimacy of National City's investment-banking activities, and promoted their further development.

Shortly after the passage of the Federal Reserve Act war broke out in Europe, fundamentally altering the position of the United States in the world economy and of New York in world finance. European governments requisitioned and liquidated their citizens' dollar securities to help pay for U.S. goods. They also borrowed heavily in this country, transforming the United States from a debtor to a creditor nation. Between July 1914 and April 1917, when the United States entered the war, the New York market was the only major source of credit to the European belligerents.[4]

New York also replaced London as the principal source of trade financing, since access to sterling credit was cut off by British exchange control. The dollar largely replaced sterling as the means of payment not only for U.S. exports and imports but also for most of Europe's trade with Latin America and the Orient. With the pound's convertibility into gold suspended and exchange controls in place, the link of the British overseas banks to the London discount market was broken. This opened the door to U.S. banks to capture a larger share of trade finance. At home the war first touched off a financial crisis and aggravated the mild recession then under way, but by 1915 an inflationary boom began.[5] As orders poured in from Europe, the demand at home for credit surged.

Thus, the outbreak of the war tended to reinforce the changes wrought by the Federal Reserve Act. The war stimulated the demand for bank credit by corporations just when the introduction of discounting made a greater investment in this type of asset more feasible for banks. It enhanced the attractiveness of international banking just when national banks were permitted to establish branches abroad and to create acceptances. Finally, it transformed the scale of investment banking just when commercial banks' ability to engage in that activity had been confirmed.

Nationwide Corporate Banking

Vanderlip saw, beyond the loss of correspondent balances that the advent of the Federal Reserve was expected to entail, the profits to be made from developing corporate business. During the hearings on the Federal Reserve Act, he had remarked:

> We are restrained from coming in competition with the country banks now, for two reasons: We do not want to interfere with our correspondent, our client who keeps his money with us, and we do not want to go into his field and take business away from him. Furthermore, we can not offer quite equal terms to the borrower, because we have to charge for the collection of all of his checks. Under the new arrangement, having no relations with our correspondent bank, his deposit having been withdrawn and placed in his own vault or the Federal Reserve bank, we would have no compunctions, certainly, against invading his field and going after commercial business. Further than that, we can offer to the country commercial borrower the same terms for collecting his checks as his local bank could offer. So I think we will become competitors for business in a much wider circle.[6]

The target market was the smaller corporation. Although National City had established relationships during the years 1909 to 1913 with most of the largest firms in the country (see chapter 4), Vanderlip realized that these accounts could not fuel the bank's growth. Not only were these corporations likely to turn to the bond market for financing, but their primary banking relationships were generally with either Morgan or Kuhn, Loeb. National City was at best their second bank. Smaller firms thus offered more attractive growth prospects. As Vanderlip pointed out, "After all the aggregate of the smaller accounts may be far greater than the aggregate of the great accounts. I welcome the growth in the number of accounts. I know it means more work, more officers, more need of judgment. It is not nearly so easy as handling the big accounts, but in the end it is safer for a bank to have this foundation of a great number of medium-sized growing accounts."[7]

After the passage of the Federal Reserve Act, Vanderlip intensified National City's new business campaigns. Officers crisscrossed the country soliciting accounts from smaller corporations. Aside from questions of credit-worthiness, the only limit on such accounts was that the firms have net invested capital of at least $100,000, and even that limit might be waived if a firm outside New York had sufficient foreign business to justify a New York balance.[8] The campaigns were a huge success. From September 1912 to July 1916 the total number of corporate accounts rose from 2,250 to 4,300, an increase of nearly 100 percent.[9]

National City was thus well positioned to take advantage of the surge in loan demand that followed the outbreak of war in Europe in 1914. During the first two years of the war, firms sought to build up their inventories quickly to secure themselves against rapidly rising prices of raw materials and the vicissitudes of wartime ocean transport. From the end of 1914 to the end of 1916 the assets of large U.S. manufacturing companies increased at a 13 percent annual rate, while inventories grew at a rate of 24 percent.[10] This produced a surge in the demand for credit, especially bank credit, since the assets being accumulated were largely short-term, and since the closure of the stock exchange at the outbreak of the war had limited bond finance.

This combination of rising demand and aggressive marketing swelled National City's commercial loan portfolio. From June 1914 to June 1917 the institution's commercial loans more than tripled, rising from $66 million to $213 million. At the latter date they accounted for 29 percent of total assets, the largest single component of the portfolio.[11] Such success had not been generally expected. As Vanderlip remarked to Stillman, the Federal Reserve Act "was designed to curb the great New York banks in their growth. Instead of that, it has given them the broadest opportunities for development . . . It has made the City Bank far more a national bank than ever before."[12]

International Branch Banking

In its growth during the early war years National City did not differ from other leading New York banks, as Vanderlip was well aware. He saw that if National City was to outdistance its competitors, it would have to provide corporate customers with a reason for preferring National City. Vanderlip soon saw that to attract new accounts in larger numbers and to increase rapidly balances from existing customers, National City would have to offer services that "our strong, well managed neighbors" could not match.[13] As he wrote to Stillman in June 1914, "We have got to find some other reason to influence business. That reason must be found, it seems obvious to me, in some sort of superior service."[14] What he had in mind was a system of foreign branches—now permitted to national banks by the Federal Reserve Act—that would provide corporate customers with banking services abroad.

Vanderlip had good reason to believe that international branch banking would be a success. A number of the bank's largest corporate customers had indicated an interest in having National City open branches in countries where they had manufacturing or distribution facilities. The most persuasive request came from James A. Farrell, president of U.S. Steel, who had developed a large export business for his company. Knowing that his company's lead bank, the First National Bank of New York, was not interested in international banking, Farrell turned to National City, which had been active in foreign exchange trading since the late 1890s (see chapter 3).[15] Farrell proposed that the bank expand its international service to include foreign branches. In return, Farrell promised that U.S. Steel would give the bank access to its credit files on foreign customers and make a substantial deposit.[16]

Other corporate customers with large investments in production and distribution facilities in South America offered Vanderlip similar encouragement. They wanted the bank to finance their foreign inventories and receivables and to provide the money transfer and disbursement services they had been getting from British overseas banks or from local banks abroad. Du Pont, for example, which had recently opened a nitrate factory in Chile, wrote to National City in 1914, asking whether or when National City might open branches in South America.[17]

Several National City directors were connected with firms in the forefront of American direct foreign investment. These firms stood to benefit from National City branches in South America, particularly now that British overseas banks had difficulty in providing sterling financing. W. R. Grace and Company, for example, had extensive shipping, textile, sugar, and other business interests in countries along the western coast of South America.[18] International Harvester had a number of sales outlets and agencies in South America that could use the services of the bank's branches to provide credit to local customers.[19] Armour and Company had bought a meatpacking plant in Argentina that exported beef to Europe.[20] Last and by no means least, Standard Oil of New York, with which the bank's director, William Rockefeller, was associated, had investments in refining and distribution facilities around the world.[21]

Vanderlip had long been intrigued by the idea of international branching. In 1909, before it was legally possible for a national bank to have branches, he had sent an assistant to South America to look into the question of whether local branches would be profitable. Although the assistant turned in a negative report, Vanderlip was convinced that South America's ample resources and growing trade with the United States would eventually provide the basis for profitable branch banking there.

James Stillman had also been interested in foreign banking. In 1905 he had invested for his personal account in the Banco de Habana, a Cuban bank established by a group of American financiers. The Farmers' Loan and Trust Company, a state-chartered institution in which Stillman had a large stake, had established branches in London and Paris in the early 1900s. Perhaps as a result of this experience, Stillman understood how difficult foreign banking could be and how important it was to have experienced management to make branches profitable. He had, accordingly, resisted Vanderlip's suggestion that National City might establish branches abroad. Nevertheless, Vanderlip's interest continued, and from time to time he lobbied actively for a change in the National Bank Act to allow national banks to have overseas branches.[22]

In 1913 the efforts of Vanderlip and others to change the law bore fruit. The Wilson administration, like the Taft administration before it, wanted to promote U.S. foreign trade and saw foreign branches of American banks as a means to that end. Moreover, the authors of the Federal Reserve Act thought foreign branches would help create a trade acceptance market in the United States, similar to the London discount market. They hoped such a market would displace the call loan market, which they distrusted, as a source of liquid investments for banks. Hence the Federal Reserve Act included a provision allowing national banks to have branches outside the United States.[23]

The next year, Vanderlip thought he could risk "a modest trial of South American banking."[24] As Farrell had reminded Vanderlip, opportunity was knocking; if National City hesitated, its customers would go elsewhere. This argument tipped the balance. Vanderlip wrote Stillman, "there is the greatest advantage in being the first in the field . . . If we do not take this step at once, some other bank will, and they will tie up these interests so that we will be much handicapped if we came to the conclusion later to enter the field."[25] National City accordingly applied to the Federal Reserve board and to the Argentine banking authorities for permission to open a branch in Buenos Aires, and on November 10, 1914, the office opened, the first foreign branch of any nationally chartered U.S. bank.[26]

In taking this fateful step for the bank's future development, the immediate aim was modest: to cement the bank's relations with corporate customers. Vanderlip confided to a friend, "I do not expect much profit out of it. Indeed, I shall not be surprised if there is something less than any profit, but I hope to get very considerable return by offering facilities that other banks cannot offer to exporters, and thus attract their accounts to the City Bank."[27]

Despite these expectations, the Buenos Aires branch began to earn a profit almost immediately. By forming good relations with the Banco de la Nación, the largest local bank, the branch quickly integrated itself into the local banking scene. The subsidiaries of U.S. companies opened accounts as they had promised to do, and local firms soon followed suit. A large volume of exchange trading and a rapid increase in Argentina's foreign trade provided the branch with a growing stream of profitable business, for the war had virtually eliminated competition from German and British banks. By 1917 National City's Buenos Aires branch had become the ninth largest bank in Argentina, with 1.8 percent of the banking system's total deposits, a ratio approximately equal to the bank's share of total deposits in the United States.[28]

Stillman and Vanderlip soon came to appreciate that these favorable competitive circumstances would last for some time, because the war would be long. "Nothing but exhaustion will terminate it," wrote Stillman from Paris in October 1914, after the containment of the German offensive in the Battle of the Marne.[29] And Vanderlip noted, "as we are to have the [Latin American] field pretty much to ourselves there will be a large business . . . for us."[30]

Vanderlip opened the bank's second branch in Rio de Janeiro in April 1915, with a subbranch in Santos, the center of Brazil's coffee trade, and followed these a few months later with a branch in São Paulo. In August the same year a branch was opened in Montevideo, Uruguay, where the country's trade in hides was centered, and still another in Havana, which took over the Banco de Habana, in which Stillman had an interest. More branches followed in rapid succession in 1916: in Bahia, Brazil, the center of that country's sugar trade; in Santiago, Cuba; and in Valparaiso, Chile, that country's principal port and the center of its trade in nitrates and copper, two articles in heavy demand during the war. In two short years, National City had put in place the basic elements of a comprehensive Latin American branch network.

Recruiting International Managers

With the branches' potential business as good as it was, the only limit to expansion was a lack of experienced personnel. "Our foreign-branches . . . developed faster than we could find trained men to run them," Vanderlip recalled in his autobiography.[31] Few Americans had experience in international banking, but the distance from New York and slow communications made it necessary to give branch managers considerable operating and credit authority. It was hard to find "men of initiative and vision who at the same time had absolutely conservative credit ideas and a proved ability for credit analysis, and who, in addition to those difficult requisites, could speak Spanish or Portuguese."[32] The staffing problem worried Stillman, too. He counseled his president to proceed cautiously with foreign expansion, reminding him that "the ablest banker is the one who knows how not to do business, meaning . . . what kind not to do, and when to do as little as possible."[33]

After many attempts to hire capable employees from other banks had failed, Vanderlip concluded, "We evidently have got to grow men, rather than hire them."[34] He accordingly developed in 1915 a program with several U.S. universities that combined general studies and practical training in international banking, with the tacit understanding that the successful participants in the program would enter the bank's service after graduation. The same year, Vanderlip commissioned a bank officer, F. C. Schwedtman, to set up the College Training Program, which took a select group of college graduates through a one-year course, working in various departments of the bank, studying foreign languages, and attending lectures by bank officers.[35] A number of the graduates of the early College Training Program eventually reached leading positions in the institution, among them Howard C. Sheperd of the 1916 class, who was to become president and chairman of the bank after World War II.

The International Banking Corporation

The war and its effect on British and European overseas banking opened opportunities for American banks in the Orient as it had in Latin America. Here, too, Vanderlip's vision and aggressiveness enabled him to steal a march on his competitors that would have lasting consequences. But instead of establishing new branches as the bank had in Latin America, Vanderlip gained a foothold in the Orient by acquiring a banking firm that had been in business there almost since the turn of the century.

In 1901 Marcellus Hartley, a Connecticut industrialist and developer of the Remington Arms Company, together with General Thomas H. Hubbard, a lawyer and businessman, and several other prominent men interested in promoting trade with the Far East, organized the International Banking Corporation (IBC) under a special charter from the Connecticut legislature.[36] After the U.S. victory in the Spanish-American War and the acquisition of the Philippines, there was much interest in business and financial circles and in Washington in developing trade with the Orient. The IBC was one manifestation of that interest. Hubbard was named chairman of the new corporation and Hartley president. The latter died soon thereafter and somewhat later Hubbard became president as well as chairman.

Hubbard was the driving force in the expansion of IBC. After opening its first branch in London in April 1902, he started a Far East network with a branch in Shanghai (May 1902) followed by branches in Manila and Singapore (July 1902). He copied the structure and raided the personnel of the British overseas banks, the IBC's main competitors in the Far East. By 1914 IBC had a home office at 60 Wall Street in New York, branches in London, Panama, and San Francisco, and a network of sixteen branches in China, Japan, and other Far Eastern countries, staffed for the most part by Englishmen and Scots. IBC was not the only American-owned bank with branches overseas before World War I, but it was certainly the largest and most successful.[37]

As early as February 1909 Vanderlip had written to Stillman in Paris about the possibility of acquiring control of IBC, with a view to extending its operations to South America, but it was not until 1915, after Hubbard's death, that National City was able to acquire a majority interest.[38] Vanderlip wrote enthusiastically to his boss, "I think the acquisition of the International Bank has been an extremely fortunate stroke. We have got it at a time when it has really gotten pretty well on its feet. It has a serviceable and well tried out staff, although not a brilliant one, and it has a machine that we will be able to develop and make great use of."[39]

With IBC in hand, Vanderlip's vision of City Bank's international role seems to have expanded. Now he foresaw a time when "City Bank will have a well ordered branch in every important center in the world outside the United States."[40] In 1916, he accordingly turned his attention to Europe, particularly to Italy and Russia, countries where National City could hope to take the place of German banks that had been active before the war. The bank opened branches in Genoa and Petrograd; branches in London, Paris, and Madrid were under consideration when U.S. entry into the war postponed for the time being further branch expansion in Europe.

By 1917, then, National City had established a worldwide branch network in embryo. Among American banks, this was a unique asset. Other large banks such as Guaranty Trust, Equitable Trust, the Farmers' Loan and Trust Company, and the First National Bank of Boston had a few branches or banking subsidiaries in Latin America, Europe, and the Far East. There were also a few foreign branches established by so-called American foreign banking corporations, corporate partnerships formed by smaller American banks during the war in order to conduct a banking business outside the United States.[41] But in 1917 and for many years thereafter, no American bank came close to matching National City's system of thirty-five foreign branches, including twenty-two IBC branches.

Foreign Trade Finance

In conjunction with opening branches overseas National City stepped up its efforts to finance U.S. firms' foreign trade. In New York Vanderlip set up a Foreign Trade Department to supply information to American businessmen concerning foreign markets and foreign firms. This new unit collected data from National City's branches concerning the demand for American products and the credit-worthiness of the American firm's prospective trade partners. To areas where it had no branches National City sent representatives. The aim was to promote America's foreign trade and to finance it.[42] The result was a considerable improvement over the indirect methods of finance that National City had employed before 1913 (see chapter 3). The ability to branch overseas and to create acceptances at home gave National City the ability to offer complete financing service to firms engaged in foreign commerce.

Thus when war broke out in 1914, National City was positioned to finance the surge in American trade that would result.[43] Since the declaration of war fell at the start of the cotton harvest, National City immediately set out to ensure that cotton exports would be adequately financed, despite the disruption of financial markets in London and New York.[44] After the crisis subsided, National City turned to financing a broad range of exports, especially to Europe. To do so National City made extensive use of its new acceptance powers. Total acceptances outstanding grew to $20 million by June 1917.[45]

Despite this growth, in financing wartime trade National City remained far behind J. P. Morgan and Company, which acted as the British and French government's purchasing agent for war supplies in the United States. This gave the Morgan firm and affiliated institutions, such as the Guaranty Trust Company, first crack at financing the resulting trade. Moreover, Guaranty had greater experience in the foreign field. It had opened branches overseas and accepted foreign bills long before the Federal Reserve Act empowered national banks to do so. National City, therefore, acquired only a small share of the total acceptance market, amounting to 6.5 percent at the end of 1916.[46]

Banking for Foreign Correspondents

The outbreak of the war and the closing of the London market temporarily made New York the center of world finance. To pay for war materiel from the United States, the European belligerents needed dollar balances. As the dollar replaced sterling as the currency of payment in international trade, many other countries accumulated dollar balances, which they held in New York. Thus New York took over at least for the duration of the war the City of London's traditional role as the center of the international payments mechanism. Inevitably this meant a rapid expansion of dollar balances at New York banks.

National City was well positioned to get a large share of this influx of foreign money. As a result of its foreign exchange activities (see chapter 3), National City had relationships with leading banks around the world. By 1912 over four hundred foreign banks maintained their New York accounts with National City.[47] After the outbreak of the war these banks naturally used their accounts with National City as the depository for the sharply increased volume of dollars that they then wished to hold. Foreign bankers' balances rose from $22.7 million in June 1914 to $175.1 million in June 1917. The increase of $152.4 million amounted to 47 percent of the increase in National City's total domestic deposits. By June 1917 foreign bankers' balances amounted to nearly 30 percent of National City's total domestic deposit base.[48]

In addition to receiving deposits from foreign banks National City also extended them credit. The financing mainly took the form of loans and acceptances drawn by British and French agencies and banks. The most important of these credits was a dollar loan to the Bank of England in February 1915 made in conjunction with Morgan and the First National Bank at a time when the U.S. bond market was closed to foreign issuers (see below). The loan, which was secured by a special deposit of gold in Ottawa, was used to support the sterling-dollar exchange rate.[49] Even after the bond market was opened to foreign issuers, National City continued to lend to correspondents in Britain and France. These credits included a $50 million advance to the London clearing banks, which were borrowing on behalf and on the instructions of the British Treasury, and the purchase of $20 million in London bankers' acceptances.[50]

Two "Banks"

Overall, Vanderlip wrought an immense change in National City Bank in the three years following the passage of the Federal Reserve Act. Under his direction National City built an international "bank" that integrated branch banking abroad, trade finance for domestic corporations, banking for foreign correspondents, and foreign exchange trading. This new "bank" not only provided geographic diversification but also strengthened National City's core business, the domestic wholesale bank built by Stillman to conduct commercial banking for domestic corporations and correspondent banks.

At the same time Vanderlip shifted the focus of the domestic wholesale bank toward corporate banking on a national scale. After the introduction of the Federal Reserve, National City became less a bankers' bank and more of a business bank, less a bank for Wall Street and more a bank for the nation. Although the balances of domestic correspondents and the volume of call loans did grow after 1914, their importance was overshadowed by the deposits and loans of domestic corporations from across the country.[51]

Overall, National City assets and profits grew dramatically in the years 1914 to 1917. Total assets rose from $352.4 million in June 1914 to $970 million by the end of 1917, an annual rate of increase of 34 percent. Profits rose by 65 percent from 5.1 million in 1914, to $8.4 million in 1917.[52]

Much of the increases in these totals came from the newly created international "bank." In the exceptional conditions of wartime, the branches' assets and remitted profits, protected as they were from foreign competition, had become a significant part of the bank's totals. As early as 1916 the bank's own branches remitted nearly $500,000 in profits to Head Office, while IBC's earnings brought the total profit from foreign branch banking to approximately $2 million, or 20 percent of National City Bank's earnings. By the end of 1917, assets booked overseas had grown to $177 million, nearly one-fifth of the bank's total assets.[53] These results, which exceeded all expectations, encouraged Vanderlip to enlarge his conception of the branches' strategic role. No longer did he see them simply as a means of attracting domestic corporate customers. Now they were to become a "foundation upon which is going to be reared the structure of the greatest all-world bank that has yet been seen."[54]

Investment Banking

As in corporate lending and international branch banking, opportunities created by war transformed the conception and execution of another of National City's traditional roles: investment banking. From institutions and the magnates who owned them, National City broadened its customer base to include, for the first time, individuals of more modest means. Once again the change resulted in no small measure from Vanderlip's energy and imagination.

During the first decade of the twentieth century National City Bank had joined the established leaders of investment banking (see chapters 3 and 4). Under Vanderlip's supervision the Bond Department, which did the underwriting, had become one of the bank's most profitable areas. Vanderlip had long appreciated the critical role that distribution played in National City's entry into investment banking. Indeed, National City's prewar success in this field had been based primarily on its ability to distribute bonds rather than to originate them. This was the comparative advantage on which Vanderlip wished to build. As he had written to Stillman just before the war, "distributing facilities are what we must have to occupy the great position we are going to take in the investment field."[55]

By the eve of World War I, the U.S. bond market was growing rapidly, in breadth and depth. Investors were no longer confined to New England, the "cradle of capital," nor were they any longer exclusively institutions and millionaires. Now families of more modest means were a growing factor in the securities market. Vanderlip had seen these trends. For some time before he had started to build National City's own distribution system (see chapter 4), Vanderlip had observed the development of retail-oriented securities firms such as N. W. Harris and N. W. Halsey. They were bringing new buyers to the market and forming relationships with borrowers such as municipalities and public utilities, issuers the established houses tended to overlook. These firms were building the broader securities market of the future. In 1913 Vanderlip had expressed a desire to acquire N. W. Harris and Company, which he considered "the best distributors in the United States."[56] Although the acquisition did not materialize, he continued to look for a way of increasing National City's distribution capacity.[57]

Indeed, Vanderlip thought the task so important that he briefly considered taking it on himself. At the beginning of 1914 he suggested to Stillman that he, Vanderlip, should take over the National City Company, which would be disaffiliated from the bank, and transform it into a major underwriter of bonds.[58] Stillman did not approve the separation, which would have weakened both the bank and the City Company. But he did accept Vanderlip's main point that the City Company should step up its underwriting activity. To that end, two of the bank's vice presidents, Samuel McRoberts and Charles V. Rich, took over management of the City Company as chairman and president, respectively.

The outbreak of the war further heightened the attractiveness of investment banking and the need to build a broader distribution system. Only a handful of foreign issues had been floated in New York before the war, but now the European allies' enormous demand for credit would add a major international dimension to U.S. investment banking. At first, though, the Wilson administration's policy of "financial neutrality" stood in the way. In August 1914, shortly after the war's outbreak, J. P. Morgan had requested the State Department's opinion on a proposed issue of French government bonds. Secretary of State Bryan's reply took the form of a public statement on August 15, 1914, that "loans by American bankers to any foreign national are inconsistent with the true spirit of neutrality."[59]

There the matter rested until October 5, 1914, when the French ambassador to the United States visited Vanderlip in New York with a proposal to borrow $10 million. Vanderlip replied by letter accepting the proposal at 6 percent (call money at the time was about 3 percent) and indicating that National City would place part of the loan with other banks. Then he added that first he had to check with the Department of State.[60] Vanderlip then asked Samuel McRoberts "to lay the matter before Bryan," and on October 23, McRoberts delivered to Counselor Lansing of the State Department a letter stating that the bank would "grant short-term banking credits to European governments, both belligerent and neutral . . . This business was deemed necessary to the general good," and that the bank would "proceed along the lines indicated unless it is objectionable from the government standpoint." Lansing saw Wilson the same day and reported in a memo he showed McRoberts that the president went along with a distinction recommended by Lansing between bank "credits" and "loans." The former were deemed not to violate neutrality on the ground that they were simply to finance trade. The distinction between a "credit" and a "loan" was that the latter was "sold to the public."[61]

Secretary Bryan resigned in June 1915, opening the way for the Allies to float bonds on the New York market. The first issue, in October 1915, was a blockbuster—$500 million of five-year, 5 percent bonds issued jointly by the British and French governments through a syndicate managed by the Morgan bank. It was the largest single issue floated in the New York market up to that time. A nationwide syndicate was formed to place the bonds, and despite intense opposition from pro-German groups, the issue was quickly sold. Other issues followed. Prior to U.S. entry into the war, when the Treasury assumed responsibility for financing the Allies, foreign governments issued over $2.5 billion in new bonds to American investors.[62] It was a sea change in the scale of U.S. investment banking, and it put a new premium on placing power.

Experience in floating the Anglo-French bond issue confirmed Vanderlip's belief that broader distribution held the key to National City's continued success as an underwriter. He therefore kept searching for ways to enhance National City's placing power. Finally, in the summer of 1916 the Halsey firm became available. After Harris, it was the most successful of the retail-oriented houses, with offices in New York, Chicago, San Francisco, and other cities across the United States. It was, in fact, one of the few investment firms with a truly national distribution network.[63]

Stillman and Vanderlip were well aware of what the Halsey firm could contribute to their aim of transforming the National City Company into the "foremost financing house in America."[64] The two firms' underwriting relationships complemented each other, and they had worked together in the past (see chapter 4). As relative latecomers to the field, each had had to develop relationships with borrowers who did not have a regular investment banker. In Halsey's case, these were municipalities and public utilities, but National City's special forte was issues for foreign governments that were now tapping the New York market for the first time. At the time of the acquisition, which was consummated in August 1916, the City Company was already earning almost $4 million a year, or about 28 percent of the total earnings of the National City organization, although this largely reflected the earnings of the bank's Bond Department, which was transferred to the City Company at the time of the Halsey merger.[65]

In one respect, the deal was less than Vanderlip had hoped. He did not get the services of the firm's most capable executive, Harold Stuart, who preferred to set up his own firm.[66] Vanderlip had obtained his nationwide bond house but he still needed someone to run it, a dynamic, aggressive sales executive with broad knowledge of and experience in the bond market. He soon found the man for the job, "a man named Mitchell. He is about 38 years old and has had valuable business and banking experience. He is a very well set-up, intelligent man with a good eye and keen mind. He is undoubtedly going to prove of real strength to the whole situation.[67]

Charles E. Mitchell had started his business career with Western Electric as a salesman of electrical equipment. Just before the Panic of 1907 he became assistant to the president of the Trust Company of America, the institution that Morgan and Stillman decided to rescue in order to stop the panic. Shortly thereafter, Mitchell set up his own investment-banking firm, C. E. Mitchell and Company. Mitchell brought to the City Company a broad background in finance. Most importantly, he brought what Vanderlip would later call "an astonishing capacity to create energy."[68]

Vanderlip's Vision

With the Halsey acquisition, Frank Vanderlip put in place the final panel of the picture he had been creating since the passage of the Federal Reserve Act and the outbreak of the European war. In less than three years, the institution had been transformed. Beginning with a bank whose primary functions were to hold and invest the reserves of domestic correspondents and to serve a select group of domestic corporations, Vanderlip not only preserved and strengthened these traditional core activities but added a series of new functions: a worldwide branch system unique among American banks; a major role as an international correspondent bank; and an investment-banking affiliate with a promising retail distribution system. In doing so he had acquired not only new customers but also new categories of customers: smaller U.S. firms, foreign governments, local firms in foreign countries, and middle-class purchasers of securities at retail.

Together these initiatives formed a new strategy, one that responded to the competitive environment facing National City at the time and that set the pattern for the bank's future development. In 1914 Morgan and Kuhn, Loeb held a tight grip on the major names in the wholesale banking market. National City did not challenge their supremacy; indeed, the core of its business remained secondary banking relationships with Morgan and Kuhn, Loeb customers. This was a profitable and steady business, one to which George F. Baker chose to restrict the First National Bank.[69] But Vanderlip and Stillman had grander ambitions for National City. Their strategy was to exploit the periphery, to put National City into areas that Morgan or Kuhn, Loeb would not enter. Beginning with a strong base, National City diversified, bringing its existing products to new customers, offering new products to its existing customers, and expanding its geographical scope.

The transformation came about gradually, with each new activity growing out of existing functions, but Vanderlip's strategic thinking was critical. Encouraged by success as the institution evolved, Vanderlip held to his vision of the bank, letting this vision determine the decision as each opportunity to enter a new field or develop an old one presented itself. Stillman in his declining years was the balance wheel, the force of continuity with the bank's traditions of high liquidity and cautious management of risk, at times acting to check his protégé's enthusiasm. Vanderlip supplied the drive, the imagination, the vision of what National City could be: an all-purpose, worldwide financial intermediary. "We are really becoming," he wrote Stillman on December 31, 1915, "a world bank in a very broad sense, and I am perfectly confident that the way is open to us to become the most powerful, the most serviceable, the most far-reaching world financial institution that there has ever been. The one limitation that I can see, lies in the quality of management."[70]

6.

Owners and Managers
1917–1921

As 1914 opened, National City Bank was still the unitary institution it
had been during the first century of its existence. Eight vice presidents, ten
junior officers, and fewer than five hundred other employees conducted
the bank's business at a single location on Wall Street. There was little formal organization. Three years later, as Vanderlip's ambitious strategy unfolded, there were more than twenty-two hundred employees, including
nearly six hundred overseas, plus the employees of two affiliates, the National City Company and the International Banking Corporation.[1]

Quite suddenly, it seemed, Vanderlip was faced with the task of managing a large, diversified, and geographically dispersed institution. Two
problems arose, both related to Vanderlip's role in the National City organization. The first concerned the separation of policy making from responsibility for day-to-day operations. The second concerned who would
make policy—Stillman or Vanderlip.

The two issues arose together in early 1915, when overwork and a bout
with paratyphoid fever forced Vanderlip to take a rest of several months,
just at the time when National City was launching its overseas branches.
On this forced vacation Vanderlip came to understand, "There is a defect
in our organization, which results in too many problems being referred to
me."[2] The institution had continued to function in his absence without his
constant attention. He realized that his involvement in day-to-day administration had led to a neglect of larger issues just at a time when great new
opportunities were opening up at home and abroad. Accordingly, on his
return to work early in 1915, he considered creating a committee of four
vice presidents to assume part of his administrative load, develop plans
for expanding into new areas, and take on "larger aspects of the Bank's
management," a task for which no one had previously found sufficient
time.[3] But Stillman was reluctant to approve such a change. Vanderlip
therefore substituted "an hour's conference each morning to which I ask to

be present James A. [Stillman, the elder Stillman's son], Simonson, McRoberts and Perkins."[4]

Meanwhile, a more serious problem was boiling up—the question of Vanderlip's role in relation to that of his mentor, James Stillman, who was also, by virtue of a controlling interest in the bank, his boss. Over the years Stillman had increasingly delegated operating responsibility to his protégé while retaining ultimate authority and the right to be consulted on all major questions. Vanderlip gradually became more Stillman's partner than his employee, but without a partner's share in profits and ultimate control. For many years, Vanderlip had been satisfied with this arrangement. Then in 1915 Stillman, aged sixty-five, fell seriously ill. Vanderlip, who was fourteen years younger than his mentor, became concerned about his own future should Stillman die. Stillman's son and heir, James A., was forty-two years old, a vice president of the bank and a logical candidate to succeed his father as chief executive. As Vanderlip recalled in his autobiography, "In 1915, certain developments, one of which was the frailty of Mr. Stillman's health, made me conclude it was high time I took some steps to secure my own fortune. I was well-to-do, yes; but I wanted to be fixed to maintain myself in the job I had."[5]

Now carrying successfully the main responsibility for the country's largest bank, Vanderlip dreamed of becoming a leading financier in his own right on the model of J. P. Morgan and Stillman himself. To accomplish this end, as well as to consolidate his position at National City, Vanderlip felt that he needed a major stock interest in the bank. But National City stock was closely held and infrequently traded. The six largest shareholders held a majority of the stock.[6] Stillman held nearly 20 percent and various members of the Taylor family together held another 20 percent. If Vanderlip was to acquire a block large enough to control the bank, or nearly so, he would have to get it from one or more of these major shareholders.

In July 1915 Vanderlip wrote to Stillman in Paris asking for two things: an option on a major portion of Stillman's own stock and a multimillion dollar personal loan from Stillman, which would allow Vanderlip to acquire seventy-five hundred National City shares that J. P. Morgan, Jr., had offered him. Together, the Morgan shares and the option would make Vanderlip one of the largest shareholders. He suggested that Stillman set the option price, for price was a secondary consideration; what Vanderlip wanted was to own a large piece of the bank. He wrote to Stillman,

> I believe it would be for the interest of the stockholders to have
> me succeed in doing that. One is apt to be prejudiced in consider-
> ing one's own abilities, and it is possible that I am over-rating
> what I might reasonably expect to look forward to. If my own
> estimate of what I have done, and what I am likely to do, is not

borne out by your sound judgment, I think it is only fair that I
should definitely know that . . .

I have a very deep desire to feel some firm earth under me in
regard to the future, and while I do not expect to have it any
firmer than may be the prospect of my being able to continue
successfully to contribute to the good management of the Bank,
I should like to feel that I know definitely what my relation is to
be to the future success of the institution, if it is to be as successful as I believe it is.[7]

It was, as Vanderlip acknowledged, far from a modest request, and it
proved to be one that Stillman could not grant. He responded by offering
far less than Vanderlip had asked and needed for his purpose, an option
on twenty-five hundred shares of bank stock, which was about 5 percent
of Stillman's holdings and 1 percent of the bank's outstanding shares, with
the promise of an additional twenty-five hundred if Vanderlip could not
acquire them elsewhere. Nor, wrote Stillman, was he able to lend Vanderlip the money to acquire the Morgan shares.[8]

Stillman had a high regard and an almost parental affection for his protégé, but what Vanderlip was asking was to take Stillman's place not only
at National City but also in the financial world. It was too much to con-
cede. No doubt the elder man, sick and lonely as he was, envied the younger
his health, his happy family life, his activity at the head of the bank. Years
later, in his autobiography, Vanderlip was able to see the incident through
Stillman's eyes: "I quite understand him, I think, in the attitude he took toward my request for an option on some of his City Bank stock. Of course
he did not want to surrender any of it! It was a piece of himself that I was
asking for."[9]

At the time, Vanderlip took Stillman's response less philosophically. He
was deeply disappointed. The tone of the refusal was kind, but the "no"
was final.[10] In his reply, Stillman had chosen to ignore Vanderlip's concern
about his future position at the bank as well as his larger ambitions. "Rather
grimly," Vanderlip took up the stock Morgan had offered him—with the
aid of a loan from Morgan himself.[11] Although he thereby became the second largest shareholder, his holdings were barely one-fourth of Stillman's,
far short of what he had wanted and, perhaps, expected. It was a turning
point in Vanderlip's career and would have fateful consequences for the
fortunes of National City.

The American International Corporation

Vanderlip realized that if he were to satisfy his ambition, he would have to
do it without Stillman's help and, to an extent at least, outside the bank. In
the fall of 1915, after Stillman's refusal, Vanderlip hit upon the idea of set-

ting up a firm, to be known as the American International Corporation, that would complement the bank's trade finance activities around the world through the purchase of debt and equity positions in promising local enterprises. Once again, Vanderlip saw in the European war an opportunity for American finance. The new corporation, he hoped, would purchase from European investors "well-tried and profitable undertakings . . . which, owing to the present unhappy position of the European investment markets, are likely in some cases to be for sale at prices that will warrant new investors becoming interested."[12]

Vanderlip proposed to Stillman that the American International Corporation be organized as an affiliate of the bank, similar to the National City Company, but Stillman rejected this out of hand as an inappropriate extension of the bank's business.[13] Stillman did feel, nevertheless, that "the opportunities for investing by such a company . . . after it had secured an able management, would doubtless be many and profitable," and he therefore asked Vanderlip to allot him a large block of stock in the new corporation.[14]

Actually, Stillman was far from enthusiastic about the project. He saw that to Vanderlip the scheme was mainly an attempt to achieve outside the bank the recognition and reward that Stillman's refusal of a large option had denied him, and he feared the consequences for the bank. In a letter to Vanderlip in mid-November 1915, Stillman therefore offered to increase the number of National City shares on which he had offered Vanderlip an option, though the offer still fell short of the latter's hopes. At the same time, he hinted that he found Vanderlip's restlessness and concern for the future unseemly: "For while I expect to recover my health, life is uncertain and when one is seriously ill persons are apt to be a little sensitive in regard to provisions being made which contemplate one's death." He continued, "I do not think, however, that I am very sensitive on that score as Sterling and I have always tried to provide for such contingencies as far as I am concerned. Still I am as you know a very sensitive person."[15] In the same letter Stillman remarked that Vanderlip would profit greatly from his options on the bank's stock, "provided its future management is as wise and able, as it is now and has been in the past."[16] He confessed that his doubts about the American International proposal were prompted to a large extent by the "great fear . . . that it might produce a divided interest and effort on your part as far as the Bank was concerned."[17]

Moreover, Stillman was concerned that in an attempt both to run the bank and to launch the new company, Vanderlip would ruin his health. In closing, Stillman advised Vanderlip to give up the project: "Your health to the bank and to me, and especially to your family, is what you should consider more than anything else put together, otherwise it will be most unfortunate, and to none more so than yourself. So my dear friend, do take heed in time and realize that I am speaking, not only from the depth of my heart, but from the experience from the condition in which I am in."[18] Yet Stillman also told Vanderlip, "You must in spite of my absence consider me in the game." And he asked Vanderlip to include him in any other financial ventures in which he might engage.[19]

The letter surprised Vanderlip and angered him. In a hastily written draft of a reply, Vanderlip poured out his frustration and disappointment.

> I had supposed financial relations between us were pretty much over when you declined to carry City Bank stock for me. I will say frankly that that was the worst financial disappointment I ever had in my life. I was ready at that time to give every bit of my life to City Bank affairs. If you had gone forward with the proposition as I made it in regard to the stock option and carrying Morgan's stock, you could have commanded every bit of financial ability I had . . . I had a very sharp awakening and realized as I never had before that if I was ever going to make any money it was up to me to get busy and make it for myself. No one else was at all likely to do it for me. The results thus far have been quite satisfactory. Now, nothing will please me more than a real cooperative arrangement with you for future business . . . Had you taken a different view of the letter I wrote you last summer, none of these questions would probably ever have risen, for I would have been so bound to the City Bank and to you financially that I would hardly have raised my eyes from my desk to go into these other things, but it is going to be better for the City Bank and for me, I can see now, to have things go as they have gone. The things that I am doing are resulting greatly to the advantage of the Bank. I might say, as you so often have about things you used to do, that they are being done solely for the benefit of the Bank, but that would be disingenuous. They are not being done solely for the Bank, but they are accruing tremendously to its advantage just the same.[20]

On rereading this draft, Vanderlip realized that he had "got some things off my mind by writing it, and I think it is a good deal better not to send it."[21] Instead, he went ahead and set up the new company, despite Stillman's objections. Although it was not organized as an affiliate of the bank, the bank's shareholders made liberal use of their right to subscribe to the common stock of the new corporation. In addition, the board of directors of the new company overlapped considerably with that of the bank. Through his holdings of managers' shares, a special class of securities reserved to the executives of the new company, Vanderlip stood to become a very wealthy man if the American International Corporation were successful.[22] As chairman, Vanderlip was in the position to make it so.

Vanderlip was not alone in his high hopes for the company. Among its directors were some of the biggest names in American manufacturing and finance.[23]

The new venture was launched with fanfare in January 1916. The real significance of the American International Corporation, said the *Wall Street Journal,* lay "in its broad charter and unusually wide scope . . . [It] may be likened to such organizations as the East India Company and the Hudson Bay Trading Company, to which England owes much of her present supremacy in world finance."[24] According to its charter the new corporation could go anywhere and do almost anything, and it soon had investments in South America, China, Europe, and Russia. Not surprisingly, the activities of the American International Corporation followed closely the expanding branch network of National City Bank.[25]

Restructuring Top Management

Guided by the ambitious strategy Vanderlip had created and developed in the expansive wartime environment, National City was now developing a powerful marketing thrust into retail distribution of securities and into international branch banking. Plainly, the organization needed firm and dedicated top management if it were to avoid big mistakes. But as Stillman had feared, Vanderlip's loyalty and attention were now divided between the American International Corporation, the vehicle of his personal ambition, and National City.

Aware of the problem, Vanderlip sought to solve it by restructuring his job so as to have time to make his new venture succeed while continuing to oversee the National City organization. In January 1916 he wrote to Stillman that "the time has come for me to retire from the presidency of the City Bank."[26] He proposed that he become vice chairman of the bank and chairman of the International Banking Corporation and the National City Company, while retaining the position of chairman of the American International Corporation. No doubt he saw in this scheme a way of reducing his administrative load at National City and at the same time enhancing his own status in the financial world.

Stillman was skeptical. As he saw it, Vanderlip's proposal had an internal weakness. With Vanderlip as vice chairman, the job of president would be hard to fill with a man of the highest quality. The position would presumably report to Vanderlip and therefore would lack much of the authority that Vanderlip himself exercised as president. Rather than being chief operating officer, the new president would be at most a deputy to Vanderlip. With Vanderlip's attention divided, the proposed arrangement therefore threatened to cast the bank adrift without the top management needed to steer it through what promised to be a difficult period, especially in the international arena. Stillman had never fully shared Vanderlip's enthusiasm for foreign expansion. He seems to have seen more clearly than his protégé that the end of the war would bring renewed overseas competition from British and German banks, and that National City's foreign branch system had serious weaknesses of personnel and home office supervision.[27]

All this may be read between the lines of Stillman's tactfully worded reply. He wrote,

> It was not a surprise to me that you wished to be relieved of the requirements and details incumbent upon a bank president. How can it be done conscientiously and all interests safeguarded for all concerned? It took me two years to accomplish this in a satisfactory manner.
>
> It should not take you long and I don't expect you to be as equally successful in the choice and the necessity does not exist as even with your divided interest, I know your loyalty and attachment to the bank is greater than ever, that with you as with me it's part of ourselves . . . The bank has been our mother and we owe it all the allegiance of sons. You have inaugurated such developments that your responsibility is very great until they prove sound and are being successfully managed. So it makes but little difference what your title is. What you propose seems to be on the right lines of strengthening the organization, and I have great confidence in your judgment, but as you write who to have for the presidency is not clear and a most difficult proposition.[28]

Stillman's decision was to temporize. "I have," he wrote, "come to the conclusion that the matter will have to be held in abeyance until we meet and are able to discuss the matter fully. This and all other matters I am convinced we should discuss and settle measured by the yardstick of friendship which I am sure is the wisest and safest way in the long run to prevent mistakes and misunderstandings, not only in business but all other affairs."[29] That meeting would have to wait several months; Stillman and his doctors thought him too ill to travel.

By the summer of 1916 Stillman had recovered sufficiently to be able to return to New York. In the months after his return, he and Vanderlip seem to have come to an understanding regarding Vanderlip's proposal and their respective roles in the National City organization. Stillman would remain chairman and retain the final say on policy. Vanderlip could move up to vice chairman as soon as a suitable successor could be found. But the search was unsuccessful. As Stillman had foreseen and Vanderlip later recalled, "It was not easy to get a man sufficiently young to make a change desirable, and yet capable enough to be master of our friendly monster."[30] For under the proposed setup, the position of president would have been devoid of real authority.

Vanderlip and Stillman therefore fell back on the former's old idea of a board of executive managers who would take on many of Vanderlip's administrative duties and also act as a policy committee. Vanderlip had been running the bank with the aid of an informal committee of vice presidents, the system he established in 1915. Together they monitored the bank's liquidity and its major loan commitments, particularly those to belligerents, and supervised the expansion of the foreign branch network. In December 1916 Vanderlip formally designated the members of this group the executive managers of the bank, with the position of general executive manager to rotate among them on a yearly basis, an arrangement borrowed from British banks. William A. Simonson, who had nearly thirty years of experience in the bank, was named the first general executive manager. The other executive managers were Samuel McRoberts, James H. Perkins, Charles V. Rich, and James A. Stillman.

In principle, the system was workable; a similar setup had worked satisfactorily for many years in large British and German banks.[31] But in the National City context it had the same structural weakness as the Vanderlip proposal it replaced. As long as Vanderlip was president, the authority of the executive managers was too limited. Vanderlip did not give them overall operating responsibility for the bank, as was done under the British system. That authority he kept for himself. More fundamentally, the new structure did nothing to cure the defect of Vanderlip's motivation, his divided interest. Although he held onto the power and authority of the presidency, he lacked the incentive to exercise it fully—to control the burgeoning growth of the "friendly monster" he had unleashed. Thus Stillman's fear that the bank would go adrift was realized, though Stillman himself returned to New York and tried, so far as his failing strength allowed, to help steer the ship himself.

An Organization for Marketing

A second organizational change compounded the problem created by Vanderlip's divided interest. In the summer of 1917 Vanderlip restructured National City below the level of the executive managers to give it more marketing thrust (Figure 6.1). Within the bank, divisions were along geographical lines. In the United States, corporate and correspondent banking was set up on a regional basis, with district boundaries corresponding to those of the Federal Reserve System. The vice presidents in charge of the districts reported to the executive managers as a group, an arrangement that no doubt enchanced the vice presidents' freedom though it

Figure 6.1

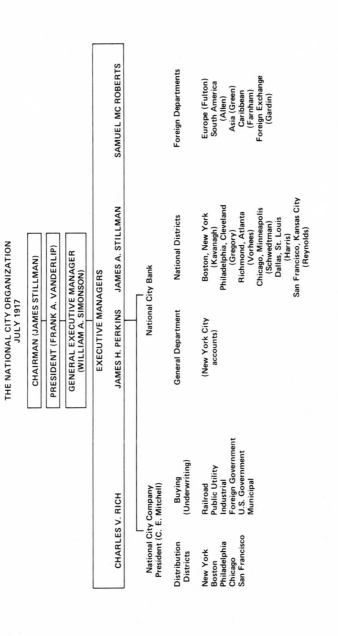

THE NATIONAL CITY ORGANIZATION
JULY 1917

CHAIRMAN (JAMES STILLMAN)

PRESIDENT (FRANK A. VANDERLIP)

GENERAL EXECUTIVE MANAGER
(WILLIAM A. SIMONSON)

EXECUTIVE MANAGERS

CHARLES V. RICH	JAMES H. PERKINS	JAMES A. STILLMAN	SAMUEL MC ROBERTS

National City Company
President (C. E. Mitchell)

National City Bank

Distribution Districts	Buying (Underwriting)	General Department	National Districts	Foreign Departments
New York	Railroad	(New York City accounts)	Boston, New York (Kavanagh)	Europe (Fulton)
Boston	Public Utility		Philadelphia, Cleveland (Gregory)	South America (Allen)
Philadelphia	Industrial		Richmond, Atlanta (Vorhees)	Asia (Green)
Chicago	Foreign Government		Chicago, Minneapolis (Schwedtman)	Caribbean (Farnham)
San Francisco	U.S. Government		Dallas, St. Louis (Harris)	Foreign Exchange (Gardin)
	Municipal		San Francisco, Kansas City (Reynolds)	

Source: Vanderlip to Stillman (Letter), July 6, 1917, Vanderlip MSS.
C. E. Mitchell, "Lectures to Banking III Class," March 18, 1919, p. 144.

weakened central control. A similar looseness seems to have characterized Head Office relations with the branches in South America and Europe, though this was not true of the Far Eastern branches, since they were
lodged in the International Banking Corporation and supervised by its
president, H. T. S. Green.

In contrast, the National City Company was organized along functional lines. A central "buying" or underwriting department, organized on
industry lines, negotiated the terms and amount of National City participations in new bond issues. A sales department, organized on regional
lines, then distributed the securities to institutional and individual investors. Sales offices across the country were supervised from headquarters
in New York and from district offices in Boston, Chicago, Philadelphia,
and San Francisco.

The new organization suited National City's expansive strategy. It decentralized responsibility for day-to-day operations, promoting initiative
down the line. But by improving the institution's marketing capability, the
1917 reorganization also increased the burden on top management to
manage the overall level of institutional risk. Only at the top could decisions be made about the degree and combination of credit risk, and ex-
change- and interest-rate risk National City should bear. Only at the top
could decisions be made about entry into new markets or exit from unpromising ones. Vanderlip had created, with Stillman's approval, a powerful engine for growth. He had chosen to remain chiefly responsible for
steering the vehicle and, if necessary, braking it. But the new organization
diluted accountability and weakened control. National City was now too
big and too dynamic to be run as a one-man show. Moreover, the driver's
mind was not on the road.

Vanderlip was well aware in the early months of 1917 that his zest for
his work at the bank had ebbed. The routine of the presidency weighed
heavily on him as the realization grew that he would never achieve independence from his mentor and full control over the National City organization. When the Federal Reserve Bank of New York asked him to organize the publicity for the Liberty Loan campaign of May 1917, Vanderlip
therefore accepted gladly. He took up the task with all of his old energy,
stumping the state to raise the public's support of the war effort. As he recalled in his autobiography, "During the Liberty Loan campaign of May
and June 1917, I found, somehow, new sources of energy. I suppose I
could find enthusiasm for that work that I could not produce just then for
the heavy routine of the City Bank."[32]

The campaign was exhilarating. Vanderlip was in the limelight day
after day, back in public service and public relations, the activities he had
left behind in 1901 when he came to New York and the National City
Bank. He was playing an independent role and a prominent one that re-

minded him of the career he might have followed if Stillman had not asked him to join National City. Thus, when the secretary of the treasury invited him to become chairman of the War Savings Committee in September 1917, he accepted with alacrity. Now he would do on a national scale what he had done in New York State. So Vanderlip left Wall Street for the banks of the Potomac as a dollar-a-year man, taking an unpaid leave of absence from the bank. Although he stayed in touch by telephone and tried to spend one day a week in New York, the burden of managing the institution fell on William Simonson, the general executive manager, and on Stillman, back from France and again occupying his office at 55 Wall Street.

The Russian Fiasco

At first, Stillman was content to remain in the background and leave the management of the bank to Simonson. But a crisis soon blew up that demanded Stillman's full attention: the nationalization of the bank's Russian branches in the wake of the Bolshevik Revolution.

Vanderlip had long considered Russia a fertile field for development and in 1916 he had welcomed the opportunity to open a branch there. As early as 1902 he had written glowingly of the opportunities for American capital in the development of Russia's natural resources and its agriculture.[33] Some of the bank's major customers, International Harvester and Standard Oil, for example, had seen Russia's potential and invested in production and distribution facilities there in the early 1900s.[34] The bank itself developed close relations with the czarist government, first as underwriter of its bonds and then, after the war began, as a depository for funds used to buy war materiel in the United States.

When the European war began, Vanderlip thought that National City could, by establishing a string of branches across the Russian empire, serve its multinational customers and steal a march on its German banking competitors, as it was doing in South America. After the war, the bank would be in an excellent position to finance the country's trade and development. Russia had been one of the world's leading grain exporters before the war, and in 1916 there was good reason to expect the country to recover that position when peace came. In the early 1900s the Russian economy had entered a phase of rapid industrialization, so that its overall economic growth before the war had been one of the highest in the world. Plainly, the country would offer attractive opportunities for finance, once the war was over.

The Wilson administration encouraged the bank's Russian activities. As early as November 1914, Secretary of Commerce William Redfield had suggested that City Bank open a branch in Russia.[35] The new U.S. ambassador to Russia, David R. Francis, in a letter to President Wilson found the government's interests identical with those of City Bank: the promotion of direct commercial relations between the United States and Russia "without the intervention of any other country or influence."[36] Francis, like Vanderlip, saw in Russia "a better field for the investment of American capital and for the exercise of American ingenuity and enterprise than any country on the globe."[37]

In June 1916 Vanderlip sent Charles V. Rich and Samuel McRoberts, two vice presidents whom he would soon appoint executive managers, to Russia with instructions to investigate at first hand the possibilities of opening branches and to conclude negotiations with the czarist government for a $50 million bond issue. Rich fully reflected Vanderlip's enthusiasm for branches in Russia and wrote his chief from Petrograd in June 1916: "You surely were wise when you decided to send someone to Russia . . . The country, as you know, is one of great opportunity, and I think there will be rapid development. The people themselves are waking up to their opportunities, and will probably be lenient towards foreign capital. The strange part about it all to me is that foreigners who come in here fail to devise any new schemes.[38] Before departing for the United States the following month, Rich began preparations for opening a branch in Petrograd. Vanderlip had applied to the Federal Reserve Board for permission to open eleven branches throughout the Russian Empire from Warsaw to Vladivostok.

Despite Russia's reverses in the war, Vanderlip remained enthusiastic about the country's economic prospects. In November 1916 in a speech to the members of an American underwriting syndicate for a Russian bond issue, Vanderlip commented, "I feel today that of all the foreign countries, there is none that offers a more promising outlook than Russia."[39] Two months later, in January 1917, National City opened its first Russian branch, in Petrograd. Even after the revolution of March 1917, which brought the Kerensky regime to power, Vanderlip remained optimistic about Russia's future. In May 1917 Vanderlip wrote Prince Andre Poniatowski: "The Russian situation, of course, continues to be one of great possibilities. It presents what seems to me to be one of the greatest opportunities in history for great leadership if the right leader or leaders can be found.[40] Vanderlip's high opinion of Russia's prospects was shared by the *New York Times*, numerous banking and trade publications, and the U.S. government at the highest levels. It was widely expected that the Kerensky regime would have "growing pains" but that it would remain in power.[41]

Thus Vanderlip saw no reason to curtail the bank's operations in Russia. He continued to receive optimistic reports from H. Fessenden Meserve, the bank's representative in Petrograd. On September 15, 1917, shortly before Vanderlip began his leave of absence in Washington, Meserve had reported that the Petrograd branch was following "in these unsettled times the most conservative policy possible," namely, the investment of its assets in "liquid, shortest term, lowest rate Russian government securities."[42] Meserve was so confident about the future that he started to prepare for the opening of a second branch, in Moscow.

All during these months the American government was providing credit to the Russian government in order to keep it in the war against Germany. This aid appeared to lend some measure of safety to the bank's holdings of Russian government bonds and to the activities of its branch in Petrograd. As Vanderlip assured Benjamin Strong, the governor of the Federal Reserve Bank of New York, National City stood in a good position, for it would be unthinkable for a Russian government to repudiate its debts.[43]

Less than a month later, on November 6, 1917, the Bolsheviks seized power in Petrograd, and on December 14 the new government declared banking a state monopoly. Now the bank was in a bad position. It held over $5 million of Russian government obligations and had advanced its Russian branches another $2 million. These assets were now presumably worthless. Moreover, the bank's liability to depositors at its Russian branches amounted to $26 million at the official rate of exchange. This was the bank's first experience with nationalization and the legal status of these liabilities was unclear: Did nationalization cancel the depositors' claims, or was the bank liable to pay them in dollars in New York? Among the depositors were subsidiaries of American corporations whose parent concerns might bring suit in the United States to recover their funds. Together, the Russian assets and the branch deposits came to $33 million, or over 40 percent of the bank's total capital. Although the bank's total loss would ultimately be less than $10 million, for many years it appeared that the bank might lose a much larger amount.[44] It was a rude introduction to the problem of sovereign risk.

Exit Stillman . . . and Vanderlip

The disastrous denouement of National City's Russian venture precipitated a break between Stillman and Vanderlip. On November 6, 1917, when the news came that the Bolsheviks had seized power in Petrograd, Stillman canceled all his appointments and assumed direct control of the bank. The same day it was announced that Samuel McRoberts, the executive manager responsible for international banking, had resigned. Three months later, in February 1918, Stillman called Vanderlip, who was still on leave in Washington, to New York. Just what transpired at their meeting is not known, but apparently there was a serious disagreement. It involved in all probability the question of responsibility for the Russian fiasco. As re-

called by Howard Sheperd, later president (1948–1952) and chairman of
the bank (1952–1959), and then a young trainee, "Stillman and Vanderlip
didn't see eye to eye . . . and I saw Mr. Vanderlip walk out of the Bank,
just as if an office boy walked out."[45] Clarence W. Barron said it more succinctly: "Kerensky fell, and so did Vanderlip."[46] How deep the disagreement was, whether it would have led to Vanderlip's resignation, shall never
be known. For immediately after the meeting, Stillman fell desperately ill,
and less than a month later, on March 15, 1918, at his house on East
Seventy-second Street, he died.

The bank's directors met and immediately elected Stillman's son, James
A. Stillman, chairman. The choice was the natural one. Under his father's
will, the younger Stillman owned in his own right and administered as
trustee under family trusts a controlling interest in the National City organization. Vanderlip, still on leave of absence in Washington, continued as
president—for the time being.

Vanderlip's position was now as precarious as he had feared it might become when, in 1915, he had sought to acquire a controlling interest in the
bank. William Rockefeller, a director with a large stock interest, was not
well disposed toward him. Rockefeller and several other directors had
also been openly critical of Vanderlip's long leave of absence and of his
predilection to involve himself and the bank in public affairs.[47]

Such disapproval did nothing to deter Vanderlip from continuing to
participate prominently in the public debate concerning America's proper
role in the postwar world. In the spring of 1919 Vanderlip made a tour of
war-torn Europe, and on his return to New York he addressed the Economic Club of New York on the European situation and what America
should do about it. Before the leaders of the financial community Vanderlip asserted that reconstruction rather than reparations should be the first
priority of the postwar world. And to bring that reconstruction about,
Vanderlip recommended that America lend heavily abroad.[48] The bank's
monthly economic newsletter echoed these sentiments.[49] Although this
won warm applause from the audience and echoes of support from Benjamin Strong, the head of the Federal Reserve Bank of New York, and other
financiers, Vanderlip's proposal fell on deaf ears at the Versailles conference and among the American public. In Paris the Allies had already decided to impose a harsh peace on Germany; at home, people were more
interested in seeing the Allies repay their debts than in lending them additional money.[50]

At this juncture Rockefeller and the junior Stillman decided to push
Vanderlip out. As Vanderlip later told the story, on his return from a trip
to Europe just after the November 1918 armistice, he was met by a colleague who told him about

a kind of movement—"plot" was what my loyal friend called it—to get my resignation from the presidency of the City Bank. He had learned that Jimmy Stillman had said that he now proposed to become president; moreover, that William Rockefeller was behind Jimmy. I felt chagrin the moment Rockefeller's name was mentioned. I wanted to get out. I did not want to be put out.

Well I came on back to Wall Street and saw Jimmy. It was quite true. He did want to be president. We exchanged only a few words, and thereafter I let it be known that I would get out gladly . . .

I could have made a fight; but I cannot say too strongly that I welcomed the chance to get out.[51]

So ended the long and fruitful rule of James Stillman and Frank Vanderlip. Together the two men had made National City into the most powerful, profitable, and dynamic private financial institution in the country. Yet they were unable to provide for an orderly transition to a new top management able and willing to safeguard what they had built.

In retrospect, the reasons for that failure are clear and not untouched by tragedy. In principle, the problem was solvable. The continuity of first-rate management might have been maintained if Vanderlip had been willing to accept permanently the role of top professional manager and if Stillman had been willing to retire from active involvement in management and to sweeten the pot for Vanderlip by granting him a substantially larger option and a large share in the profits—for example, in the form of a bonus plan such as that which Vanderlip had inserted into the charter of his American International Corporation.

But Vanderlip's model of success was that of his heroes, J. P. Morgan and Stillman himself. His ambition drove him to emulate and finally to seek to replace his mentor as owner-manager of National City. This Stillman could not bring himself to allow, despite his affection for his protégé. He was the father who, though his own powers are failing, cannot allow his favorite son to take his place. And so the son must strike out on his own. This Vanderlip did and, in doing so, neglected his responsibility to City Bank and undermined his position with key directors. The National City organization had outgrown the traditional model of the owner-managed firm. The value of the capital it assembled and the complexity of its business were too great to entrust to a top management chosen on any basis other than demonstrated competence. The truth of this proposition was about to be proved.

Vanderlip resigned on June 3, 1919, and James A. Stillman was elected president with full control of the bank. The younger Stillman was a good banker, but he had neither the talent nor the self-confidence to fill his father's shoes. So little did James A. Stillman esteem his ability to take his father's place that he would not occupy his father's private office, preferring to retain his own desk on the platform.[52] The father's shoes would have been hard for anyone to fill. The elder Stillman had been an extraordinary banker with few equals before or since and, according to a biographer, he had once warned his son never to aspire to run the bank.[53]

Lacking strong leadership and with a loose-jointed, marketing-oriented structure, the bank was swept along on a flood of credit demand in the postwar boom. The rule of "ready money"—high liquidity—observed since Moses Taylor's time was forgotten and loans grew rapidly without sufficient regard for credit risk and portfolio balance. The sharp, worldwide depression that began in 1920 therefore caught National City along with many of its competitors in an exposed position both at home and abroad.

Boom and Crash

Early in 1919 an intense boom got under way, reflecting a wave of business spending in an effort to convert from war to peacetime production. The boom was marked by rapid accumulation of inventories and commodity speculation. Commodity prices rose steeply both at home and abroad, stimulating buying for inventory. Credit to fuel the boom was provided mainly by banks, for the bond market was still glutted with Treasury issues.[54] The Federal Reserve underpinned the rapid expansion of bank credit by keeping its discount rates substantially below market interest rates, thereby encouraging member banks to borrow at the discount window. The Federal Reserve's discount rate policy was motivated by "an alleged necessity for facilitating Treasury funding of the floating debt plus unwillingness to see a decline in the prices of government bonds."[55]

In this heady environment, National City along with banks across the country responded readily to business customers' strong demand for credit. From a low in June 1919, the bank's business loans rose nearly 30 percent by the end of 1919. To fund the loans, National City relied increasingly on the Federal Reserve Bank of New York, whose discount rate, at 4.75 percent, was far below the rate the bank could earn. Corporate customers were bidding aggressively for loans, and by the end of the year, the average return on City Bank's loan portfolio was up to 5.6 percent, and new loans were being made at even higher rates.[56] Plainly it was profitable to go on borrowing, and the executive managers did not hesitate to do so. By the end of 1919, borrowings from the Federal Reserve were equal to the bank's required reserves.

Meanwhile, the authorities were growing alarmed about inflation. A controversy developed about how to check the rise in bank credit, since it was generally agreed in Washington and within the Federal Reserve System, that this was causing the inflation. One group, headed by Benjamin Strong, president of the New York Reserve Bank, favored a sharp rise in the discount rate to discourage borrowing. Another group, led by Secretary of the Treasury Carter Glass and including leading members of the Federal Reserve Board, opposed raising the discount rate mainly for fear of the impact on the prices of government bonds. Glass thought the Reserve banks should deny credit to member banks that were using the funds to make "speculative" loans.[57] (The same difference in points of view on how to control a boom was to erupt again and again in the Federal Reserve's history.) The two sides reached a compromise in January 1920. The New York Reserve Bank raised its discount rate to 6 percent, but to ease the impact on government bond prices it kept a preferential (lower) rate for member bank borrowings secured by government securities.

Six percent was still too low. Bank lending rates adjusted for compensating balances were now above 6 percent, and National City and other member banks continued to borrow and expand their business loans. Even an increase in the New York Federal Reserve Bank's discount rate to 7 percent in June 1920 did not keep the executive managers away from the discount window; the preferential rate for borrowings secured by government securities was a loophole that allowed some profitable borrowing to continue.[58]

Nevertheless, the rising discount rate along with a large outflow of gold did succeed in slowing the growth of the money supply. In the summer of 1920 the boom peaked and commodity prices plunged. At home and abroad a severe recession set in. Deposits at the National City declined and the bank's ability to accommodate its corporate customers, some of whom were now experiencing severe cash-flow problems, was reduced. In an effort to meet their needs, the executive managers ran down liquid assets (brokers' loans and securities) and further increased borrowings from the Federal Reserve.

By early 1921, the bank was in trouble. On February 21, the date of the comptroller's call, National City's debt to the Federal Reserve stood at $144 million, nearly three times its required reserves, and many domestic loans were under water or threatened. In a conference called by the comptroller's office the next day in Washington, the examiners reviewed in excruciating detail hundreds of the bank's loans whose soundness was suspect. The examiners also intimated that borrowings from the Federal Reserve should be reduced.[59]

Although the comptroller's examiners found much in the domestic loan portfolio to criticize, it was the situation of National City's Cuban branches that gave them cause for real alarm. For months the Cuban economy had been reeling under the impact of an unprecedented decline in the price of raw sugar, the island's principal export and the basis of its economic life. From a high of 22 cents per pound in May 1920, the price of sugar had tumbled to 3.75 cents in mid-December and to 1.3 cents in early 1921. Mill owners, planters, and merchants had gone bankrupt, leaving the bank's branches with approximately $63 million in nonperforming loans.[60]

In 1919, sugar had seemed a sure thing. During the war, the price of sugar in Cuba had risen steadily, and at the close of hostilities it stood at four cents a pound. After the war, political conditions halted exports of beet sugar from Russia and held down production elsewhere in Europe. In the course of 1919, the price of Cuban sugar rose 60 percent, to eight cents per pound, and in early 1920, as strong speculative buying developed, it soared to twenty-two cents. In the heady days of the postwar boom it appeared that sugar prices could go only one way: up.

The surge in the price of sugar unleashed a capital-spending boom in Cuban sugar production. Mills were constructed and railroads were laid to haul the cane to the mills. Cane land was cleared and new *colonos*, the small farmers who cultivated the cane, entered the industry. Because of its seasonal nature, the industry depended heavily on bank credit, as did local merchants who extended trade credit to *colonos* and mill owners.

In 1918-1919, National City plunged deeply into Cuba. It spread offices across the island, opening twenty-two new branches in 1919 and one more in 1920. Under the administration of Porfirio Franca, whom Vanderlip had recruited from the Banco Nacional of Cuba, the branches booked sugar loans rapidly. National City made loans to finance the working capital requirements of existing mills and to finance local merchants and suppliers to the sugar industry. By mid-1920 the bank's branches had become a major factor in the Cuban banking scene. By June 30, 1920, National City had nearly 20 percent of the total of loans outstanding in the Cuban banking system.[61]

Franca appears to have operated with little Head Office supervision but strong Head Office encouragement; when local funds proved insufficient, the Cuban organization was allowed to tap Head Office for large advances. Head Office also made loans to domestic corporations to finance investments in Cuba and to build up sugar inventories. By the end of 1921 these loans amounted to $37 million. Together with the loans of the Cuban branches the institution's total exposure to sugar was $79 million, or 80 percent of the bank's total capital. Management's bet on this single commodity had been imprudent to the point of folly, though National City was by no means alone in this. Both of its chief U.S. competitors in overseas banking, Chase National and Guaranty Trust, were also deeply involved in Cuban sugar.[62]

When the sugar bubble burst, sugar firms failed, forcing the local Cuban banks to close. National City and other foreign banks on the island were able to keep their branches open and meet depositors' withdrawals by tapping their head offices for funds. But the bank's entire Cuban loan portfolio was frozen under a debt moratorium declared by the Cuban government and it remained so well into 1921.

All this became too much for James A. Stillman. Distracted for many months by a highly publicized suit for divorce, he had had the misfortune to preside over the worst setback in National City's long history. On May 3, 1921, he resigned as president, though he retained his place on the board of directors. To succeed him, the directors elected Charles Edwin Mitchell, the dynamic executive who in four years had built the National City Company into the largest distributor of securities in the United States. At the same time the directors named Eric P. Swenson, a Texas landowner and industrialist, chairman of the board. It was clear from the start that Mitchell, not Swenson, was to be number one.

Mitchell Takes Command

At the age of forty-three, Charles Mitchell took up a challenge that would have daunted many a more experienced banker. The largest bank in the country was tottering. Could he, a successful investment banker and securities salesman, with only limited experience in commercial banking, set National City back on its feet? Could he deal with the scope and complexity of a worldwide commercial bank as well as with the business of underwriting and selling securities?

Three problems confronted him on taking office: the quality of the bank's portfolio, the organization of the bank, and compensation of its key personnel. The first was the most urgent. Practically his first act in office was to request a list of nonperforming loans. Then he set about putting the portfolio in order. During the final months of 1921, the bank's liquidity was substantially increased and by the end of the year its borrowings from the Federal Reserve had been repaid. Much of the institution's reduced operating earnings in 1921 were used to write off bad loans. The extra dividend the bank had been paying on its capital stock was terminated. Overseas, marginal branches were closed and stricter Head Office financial controls were imposed on the branches, based on a new accounting and procedures manual. By the end of 1922, the situation was in hand and a quick, strong economic recovery from the 1921 slump was strengthening the corporate portfolio. At the annual meeting of the bank's shareholders in January 1923, Mitchell was able to report that "at the outset of the year, the items in our loans, discounts and investments, the nature of which was not entirely satisfactory, were subjected to a most careful analysis and treatment, and in the course of the year more than 70 percent of the aggregate amount has been paid in cash or cleared from the balance sheet. This operation resulted . . . in strengthening our position by replacement of such assets with loans, discounts and investments representing the highest credits."[63]

To provide against future losses Mitchell increased the rate at which earnings were allocated to the reserve for bad debts and set up a special contingency reserve of $10 million, although a committee of the New York Clearing House that examined the bank's condition had recommended a figure of $25 million.[64] To keep a closer rein on future credits, Mitchell appointed G. Edwin Gregory as the bank's comptroller with the mandate to improve the quality and increase the frequency of the bank's internal audits. Gregory also received overall responsibility for recoveries and working out bad debts.

One problem remained, and it was a big one—the Cuban sugar loans. Should they be written off or worked out? If the loans were written off, the bank's capital would be severely reduced. The decline in capital would lower the legal lending limit and stunt the institution's future growth by limiting its ability to attract deposits and hold major customers.

But the alternative was fraught with risk. It involved a big bet on the future price of sugar and a continuation of National City's disproportionate exposure to this one commodity, until such time as growth in other areas of the portfolio had reduced the relative importance of the sugar loans. The bank's new president did not underestimate the importance of the decision. Of the Cuban situation he said later that unless "it was handled with extreme care, it would have meant pretty nearly the destruction of our institution."[65]

Apart from the depressed price of sugar, the big problem in managing the sugar loans was that $25 million in loans depended on sugar properties (plantations and mills) that had not been ready to produce when sugar prices collapsed in 1921, forcing their owners into default. Unlike the other Cuban loans, which could be recovered at least in part if and when the price of sugar turned up, these project loans were worthless unless further investment to complete the projects was made. In their uncompleted state, the market value of the mills and plantations, which the bank had acquired through foreclosure, was practically nil. With additional investment and a rise in the price of sugar, the bank might eventually recover both the additional investment and its original loans.

This was the situation as Mitchell saw it in the spring and summer of 1921. To help him make a final decision, he asked Gordon S. Rentschler, the manager of a heavy machinery company in Ohio and a customer of the bank, to survey the bank's sugar properties. As a manufacturer of sugar mill machinery, Rentschler had debts of his own from Cuban planters he was trying to collect. Mitchell had known Rentschler since 1918 when they had worked together on a bond issue for a Miami, Ohio, flood-control program. Rentschler left for Cuba in July 1921 accompanied by Colonel E. A. Deeds, who had been an executive of the National Cash Register Company and who was to return to the company and become its chairman some years later. In their report at the end of 1921, the two industrialists estimated that, with some additional investment, the properties could be made profitable and that, with efficient management, they would generate the revenues needed to repay the bank's loans and to yield a reasonable return on the additional funds. Implicitly at least, Rentschler and Deeds assumed that sugar would rebound from its depressed lows to a more normal level.

In January 1922 Mitchell went to Cuba accompanied by several of the bank's directors. With Rentschler and Deeds at their sides, they decided to follow the conclusions of the report and make the additional investment. The decision was that the bank should go into the sugar business in a big way and bet on the recovery of sugar to a higher price. To oversee the operation, the directors hired Rentschler and Deeds, who formed a firm called the General Sugar Corporation to manage the properties. George Houston, an executive with experience in reviving bankrupt companies, was hired as local manager. Houston and his two bosses apparently did their work well. Within a year, the unfinished plantations, mills, and railroads were producing sugar. When the price of sugar recovered to five cents a pound in 1923, the Rentschler-Deeds report was confirmed. The bank's sugar business began to run in the black, and General Sugar became one of the largest producers of sugar in Cuba.[66] In October 1923 Rentschler joined the bank's board of directors with responsibility for overseeing the bank's sugar interests. Deeds remained with General Sugar and became president in 1927 and a member of the bank's board of directors in 1928.

The Cuban sugar decision in 1922 was fateful in several respects. Ultimately, the bank would pay dearly for its continued exposure to sugar. Because of the recovery of beet sugar output in Europe and the expansion behind a high-tariff wall of beet and cane sugar in the United States and its island possessions, the price of Cuban sugar never made a lasting comeback. The price fell in 1925 and did not exceed four cents a pound again until World War II.

Rentschler's and Deeds' recommendation had been technically but not economically sound, for they had not correctly anticipated developments in the world sugar market. After 1926 even General Sugar's modernized mills operated in the red. At this point Mitchell called a halt to any further infusion of the bank's funds into the mills, aside from seasonal crop loans.

With part of the proceeds of a 1927 stock issue the National City Company acquired the ownership of the General Sugar properties from the bank and repaid most of the sugar loans to the bank. This strengthened the position of the bank's depositors, but left the position of the shareholders unchanged; they still held title to the properties. Further losses were incurred in the Depression. The mills were finally sold in 1945.[67]

At the same time, keeping the Cuban credits on the books at their full face value preserved the bank's capital in a visible, accounting sense. It thereby enabled Mitchell to take advantage of the era of growth and prosperity that lay just ahead. Had he followed a more conservative course, writing off the $25 million in loans on uncompleted projects immediately, the cutback in the bank's capital funds would have forced him to set more modest goals for expansion. The Cuban decision allowed him to adopt a forward-looking strategy not only at home but abroad. In the course of the 1920s the expansion of the bank's capital and portfolio was so rapid that the sugar loans gradually receded from view. Forgotten but not gone, they would come back to haunt Charles Mitchell at the end of his National City career.

The other problems Mitchell faced on taking over the bank were more easily solved. Soon after he became president, Mitchell scrapped the system of executive managers that Vanderlip had set up and substituted straight lines of authority running from the president's office directly to the units that dealt with customers. Within months all but one of the executive managers had resigned. The exception was William A. Simonson, who stayed on as chief credit officer with the title of senior vice president.

The international organization also had a thorough overhaul. During his first months in office Mitchell got rid of almost all the men responsible for the Cuban fiasco. The executive manager in charge of the foreign branches resigned under pressure, and the vice president who headed the Latin American district also left. Joseph H. Durrell, who had had fifteen years of experience in Cuban banking when he joined National City in 1919, was put in charge of the Cuban branches, reporting directly to Mitchell.

There remained the question of motivation: What incentives would drive the organization forward? In this respect, the accession to top leadership of a man who had little equity in the bank posed a problem—the same problem in a different guise that the elder Stillman and Vanderlip had failed to solve in the last years of their regime. This time, fortunately, no incompatibility of personal aims stood in the way of a rational solution.

Although the bank was still closely held in 1921, the major shareholders had no desire to run it. The Stillman and Taylor family trusts together owned a controlling interest in the bank, but no member of either family wanted to play an active role.[68] The bank's management was left to Mitchell. But the separation of ownership and management still raised the possibility of a conflict of interest, just as it had in the case of Vanderlip and his mentor.

Both Charles Mitchell and the directors representing the major shareholders recognized the problem; it was clearly in their mutual interest to solve it rapidly. Accordingly in February 1923 they devised a bonus plan, known as the management fund, to link the pay of key officers to the actual earnings of the bank. A similar plan had existed for City Company executives for some time and some large manufacturing corporations had had such plans since before 1914.[69] In an address to the shareholders, Mitchell stated that the management fund would be "set up from and proportionate to the current earnings of the Bank, to be periodically distributed to those officers who have contributed most effectively to the Bank's development and profitable progress and in recognition of significant achievement. It is believed that this action will promote economical administration, concentrate the attention of the officers upon service to the institution as against any outside personal interest, and will result in the higher efficiency of the institution and in larger returns to the shareholders."[70]

The terms of the plan offered generous remuneration to bank officers at the level of vice president or above, as long as profits were good. It assured them the sort of compensation they could have earned had they been important shareholders in their own institution or partners in an investment bank. It also subjected them to the risk of wide variations in their income from year to year, since the major portion of their total compensation was linked to actual profit performance.[71]

The management fund was a contract between the owners and the executives of the bank concerning the division of risk and reward. Each side guaranteed the other a minimum return in the form of salary or dividend. After these amounts had been paid, remaining profits went to owners and executives in a four-to-one ratio, the same division as in the City Company plan. The executives then divided the total pool among themselves according to their estimates of each individual's contribution. Executives were not explicitly forbidden to receive outside compensation, but the plan was clearly a strong inducement to spend all their working time in the bank. As Mitchell put it, the plan was intended to spur executives to greater efforts and the bank to greater profits.

Within less than two years Mitchell had accomplished a managerial tour de force. The bank was back on its feet and moving forward on several new fronts. The change had been accomplished largely with the help of the men who had been on the scene in 1921. Aside from Rentschler and Deeds, Mitchell hired few new officers. Instead he pruned vigorously, especially at the top of the organization. He gave younger, capable men enough authority to solve problems or take the bank into new fields. The new bonus plan created the incentives needed to make the organization go.

Above all, Mitchell took charge. He made his presence felt throughout the organization. People in the bank began to refer to their new boss as The Chief. The days of the president who concentrated on his own affairs or put his interests ahead of the bank's were past. In a speech to the employees in 1922 Mitchell said, "We are on our way to bigger things. The National City Bank's future is brighter, I believe, than it has ever been. We have been going through a period of readjustment and a time of rebuilding. We are getting ready now to go ahead full speed."[72]

7.

The Financial Department Store (I)
1921–1929

Under Mitchell's leadership, Vanderlip's vision of an all-purpose financial intermediary became a reality. James Stillman had built a wholesale commercial and investment bank serving large domestic corporations and correspondent banks. Vanderlip had added an international bank. Mitchell completed the structure by adding households and smaller firms to National City's list of customers for banking services and for securities.

Both strategy and structure were right for the times. The years 1921 to 1929 were a golden age of economic well-being, eight years of prosperity broken by only two recessions that were almost too mild to be noticed. Contemporaries called it the New Era. The phrase captured people's growing confidence in lasting prosperity, both at home and abroad. There were good, objective reasons for confidence. Inflation was a thing of the past. After falling steeply in 1920–1921, the general price level in the United States was stable or slightly declining during the rest of the decade. Economic growth was strong. After a quick rebound from the 1920–1921 recession, real output rose rapidly through the end of the decade.

In the New Era, economic prosperity was an export commodity as well. The United States came out of the war the world's largest, most dynamic industrial nation. From its shores price stability and economic growth spread to the rest of the world through trade, investment, and credit. With the dollar firmly tied to gold, other countries had only to peg their currencies to the dollar to stabilize their own economies. As they did so, inflation subsided and the investment opportunities created by wartime destruction and undermaintenance of capital became apparent. Aided by a flow of capital from the United States, the European economies boomed. So did world trade.[1]

This environment was good for financial markets at home and abroad. The prospect of rapid economic growth stimulated investment and the demand for credit. After the United States entered the war, the government had dominated the credit markets, lending to domestic firms and foreign governments. After 1919 the Treasury withdrew from the credit business, leaving the field to private lenders.[2] Real interest rates were high, reflecting high returns to investment and strong credit demand, though nominal rates declined during the decade as inflation was forgotten. With prices stable, the yield curve flattened and exchange rates stabilized. Interest and exchange risks were accordingly low, and financial intermediation became primarily the analysis and management of credit risk. This was the banker's long suit, whether applied to loans or bonds.

Three features of the New Era proved to be particularly advantageous to National City. One was the dominant role of the United States in the world economy. This led to a growing role for the dollar as an international currency.[3] The second was the emergence of New York City as the world's leading securities market, the one place in the world where borrowers could raise capital in large amounts on short notice.[4] The third was the emergence of a large, well-to-do middle class in the United States. Vanderlip had seen these trends in the making and had based his strategy on them. Mitchell's contribution was to implement the strategy more fully, with particular emphasis on bringing financial services to the individual.

The market for individual accounts was a mass market. To reach it required changes in National City's traditional business methods and in the low public profile James Stillman had favored. Vanderlip had initiated and Mitchell then perfected the sales methods and public style needed to sell bonds and banking services to a mass market. What General Motors was doing for the automobile and Procter and Gamble for household products, National City now did for financial services.[5] In effect, National City became a financial department store.

The Local Bank

Nowhere was the market for banking services to individuals and smaller firms more attractive than in National City's home town. New York's population included a larger proportion than other cities of well-to-do corporate executives, securities brokers, lawyers and other professionals, and proprietors of successful smaller firms. New York was also the nation's largest manufacturing center and its leading port. From factory lofts in the city and inner suburbs flowed more than 10 percent of the country's industrial output. The Port of New York handled nearly 30 percent of the nation's foreign trade. Thousands of smaller firms were active in the city's leading industries, clothing and printing.[6] Owner-managed for the most part, such firms could not borrow in the securities markets and therefore depended on banks. National City could be particularly helpful to the small business wishing to import raw materials or to sell its product overseas. Through its worldwide branch system it could arrange trade finance and provide credit information on the firm's foreign customers.

New York was also becoming the headquarters of corporate America. Long the nation's principal financial center, New York was fast becoming the industrial and communications capital as well. Many of the country's largest manufacturing firms were putting their executive offices and corporate staff departments in the city, as were the radio networks and many publishing houses. The companies' headquarters personnel were a natural market for the bank, particularly in the case of companies whose lead bank was National City.

In sum, New York offered National City a rich individual and business market right at its doorstep. But to reach it the bank needed branches, especially in the midtown area, and in 1920 it had none. The small businessman, the corporate executive, or the employee living or working in midtown Manhattan would not travel down to Wall Street to do his banking, especially if there were local banks nearby. Some of the bank's Wall Street neighbors, the big state banks and trust companies, had begun after World War I to set up "elaborate uptown branches when the uptown business developed on a scale to warrant specialized attention."[7] In 1921 the Corn Exchange Bank and Trust Company already had over forty branches in the five boroughs, while Guaranty Trust, National City's closest competitor in the 1920s, had three branches in Manhattan outside the Wall Street area.[8]

As long as the elder Stillman was alive, National City could view these developments with a certain equanimity, because Stillman had an equity position in the Second National Bank and a number of smaller uptown banks (see chapter 3). Through these investments he participated in the early expansion of retail banking in New York, even though National City itself could not, forbidden by the National Bank Act to have domestic branches.[9]

At one time Vanderlip had considered converting National City to a state-chartered bank in order to gain local branching powers (see chapter 5). But Stillman had preferred to wait for a change in the national banking law. In 1918 the change began. The National Bank Act was amended to allow national banks to acquire branches, though by a circuitous route. Under the National Bank Consolidation Act, as the amending law was known, two national banks that merged with each other were permitted to retain any branches they might have had. When combined with a provision of the National Bank Act that allowed a state-chartered bank to retain its branches upon conversion to a national bank, the Consolidation Act opened a small door to branching for national banks. Henceforth, a national bank could acquire the existing branches of a state bank if it could persuade the state bank to convert itself to a national bank and then merge. This device did not, nevertheless, permit a national bank to open *de novo* branches.[10]

Soon after passage of the Consolidation Act, merger negotiations were begun with the Commercial Exchange Bank, a small, state-chartered institution with three branches, all in Manhattan well north of Wall Street.[11] But it was not until early 1921, shortly before Mitchell became president, that the Commercial Exchange converted to a national charter, the merger was completed, and National City acquired its first domestic branches. Late the same year, National City merged with the Second National Bank, in which the Stillman family had a controlling interest. William Simonson had served as president of Second National in addition to his duties at National City, and Second National had long operated, for practical purposes, as if it had been a branch of National City. Now the Second National's operations were consolidated with those of the former Commercial Exchange branch at Broadway and Twenty-sixth Street.[12] Thus by the end of 1921 National City had three offices in New York in addition to its headquarters at 55 Wall Street.

In 1922 the comptroller of the currency, D. R. Crissinger, after Congress had again failed to act on his recommendation that the National Bank Act be amended to allow *de novo* domestic branching, reversed a longstanding policy and allowed national banks to establish offices in areas where state banks were allowed to branch. These offices, known as teller's windows, could accept deposits but could not make loans.[13] National City received permits for five such offices in Manhattan, the first of which was opened in 1923 at Fifty-seventh Street and Seventh Avenue, a fast-growing section of the city. By late 1925 National City had a network consisting of seven offices (three full-service branches and four teller's windows) in Manhattan north of the financial district.[14] The bank entered Brooklyn for the first time in 1926 by acquiring the People's Trust Company, a rapidly growing bank with eleven branches and deposits of approximately $65 million.[15]

The way to branching by national banks was opened wider in February 1927 when Congress passed the McFadden Act. This law allowed national banks to have full-service branches so long as they were in accordance with state law. Henceforth, National City could convert teller's windows to branches and open *de novo* branches within the five boroughs of New York City, the geographical limit under state law for branching by banks with headquarters in the city.[16] National City moved quickly to take advantage of the new law. By the end of 1929, the bank had thirty-seven domestic branches in Manhattan, Brooklyn, Queens, and the Bronx. Among New York banks, it had the fifth largest domestic branch system in number of branches (see Table 7.1). In terms of deposits, the bank's local

Table 7.1. New York City banks' branch systems, year-end 1929

Bank	Number of branches
Corn Exchange Bank	67
Bank of Manhattan Trust Co.	64
Bank of United States	58
Manufacturers' Trust Co.	45
National City Bank	37
Bank of America, N.A.	34
Public National Bank	33

Source: Gaines T. Cartinhour, *Branch, Group, and Chain Banking* (New York: Macmillan, 1931), p. 291, and *Polk's Bankers Encyclopedia, March 1930* (New York: Polk's Bankers Encyclopedia Company, 1930).

branches exceeded the total deposits of the Corn Exchange Bank, which had long specialized in local branch banking.[17]

Mitchell's conception of branch banking was that each branch should be the bank in miniature. "At each of these [branches] a full banking service is rendered to the community served. It is our policy to open additional branches in the city from time to time, as the extension of our business or the growth of this or that district seems to require. Urban conditions of life and business seem to us to call for this continuous development of our branch facilities throughout the city. We find them profitable and easy to manage."[18]

In sum, Mitchell had added a successful local bank to the wholesale bank Stillman had built and the international bank Vanderlip had created. By the end of the decade, deposits at the local branches had reached $305 million, nearly one-fifth of the bank's entire deposit base. These deposits funded the branches' rapidly growing portfolio of loans to small businesses in New York City and also yielded a growing surplus of funds for Head Office use (Table 7.2). During the 1920s, the local bank accounted for more that one-quarter of the increase in total deposits (Table 7.3) and by 1929 it was earning $4 million before taxes, or about 14 percent of the bank's total pretax operating earnings.

The local bank was also a retail bank. With domestic branches in place, National City not only increased the number of places where it offered its services but also reached out to a new class of customer, the consumer, or, as Mitchell described him, the "small but developing capitalist."[19] The bank's first local branch, acquired in the Commercial Exchange merger in 1921, was set up with the customer's convenience in mind. It aimed to

Table 7.2. National City Bank's "local bank," 1921–1929 (millions of dollars)

End of December	Deposits			Loans			Due from Head Office[d]	Earnings[e]
	Compound interest	Other[a]	Total[b]	Personal Credit	Other	Total[c]		
1921	0.0	48.1	48.1	0.0	—	—	—	0.1
1922	3.3	49.1	52.4	0.0	20.8	20.8	30.7	0.3
1923	12.4	51.8	64.2	0.0	27.2	27.2	36.1	0.3
1924	19.4	69.4	88.8	0.0	30.7	30.7	57.0	0.4
1925	26.2	76.5	102.7	0.0	41.7	41.7	60.0	0.3
1926	37.0	135.9	172.9	0.0	69.4	69.4	102.3	1.1
1927	47.7	145.4	193.1	0.0	85.3	85.3	106.9	1.2
1928	59.8	193.7	253.5	8.2	125.1	133.3	125.3	2.2
1929	64.7	239.9	304.6	25.0	172.2	197.2	128.8	4.2

Source: National City Bank, Comptroller's Report, 1921–1929, and Daily Statement Book, year-end 1921–1929.

a. "Other" includes a small amount of time deposits that were not compound interest accounts.

b. Only deposits booked at the domestic branches.

c. Only loans and discounts booked at the domestic branches plus all loans of the Credit Department.

d. Gross funds redeposited by domestic branches with Head Office not adjusted for float.

e. Net operating earnings before income tax and securities gains or losses according to the NCB internal accounting system. Earnings may be overstated to the extent that general overhead and the expenses incurred in opening new branches were allocated to the Head Office.

Table 7.3. Deposits at National City Bank's three "banks," 1921–1929 (millions of dollars)

End of December	Local bank	International bank	Domestic wholesale bank	Total deposits
1921	48.1	206.1	394.8	649.0
1922	52.4	254.5	420.9	727.8
1923	64.2	229.3	435.2	728.7
1924	88.8	325.4	498.8	913.0
1925	102.7	308.1	510.7	921.5
1926	172.9	384.6	525.9	1083.4
1927	193.1	531.3	550.6	1275.0
1928	253.5	473.5	622.2	1349.2
1929	304.6	551.1	793.7	1649.4
Increase (1921–1929)	256.5	345.0	398.9	1000.4
Rate of growth in percent per annum (1921–1929)	27	13	9	12

Sources: Tables 7.2, 7.5, and 7.6.

make banking "as simple as buying a dress, a pair of gloves or a piece of furniture."[20] Located on Forty-second Street, the branch was in "the best uptown neighborhood, adjacent to the hotel, theatre and shopping district, and at a point where transportation arteries converge to a remarkable extent."[21]

To serve this new customer group National City tailored its "products" to customers' tastes and incomes. It reduced the minimum balance required in a checking account. Soon after opening, the Forty-second Street branch began to solicit checking accounts with "a monthly average balance of three figures." But a minimum balance of $500 was required, so that checking accounts were still restricted to the businessman and to fairly successful members of the middle class.[22]

The next step was to meet the needs of small depositors. This was done by offering a new kind of time deposit. Late in 1921, at the suggestion of bank officer Roger Steffan, the bank set up the Compound Interest Department in the basement of the Forty-second Street branch, with Steffan in charge. When the bank said "small," it meant it. "Accounts from $1 and up will be received, on which interest compounded semi-annually will be paid on balances of $5 or more," the bank announced. The new accounts could not be called savings accounts because that name was restricted under New York law to savings banks.[23]

The interest the bank paid on savings deposits in the 1920s was 3 percent, the maximum allowed by New York Clearing House rules. Although below the nearly 4 percent average paid by mutual savings banks, 3 percent was competitive.[24] There was no state or federal deposit insurance at the time. National City's reputation for safety as well as the wider range of services it offered its customers was apparently enough to give it an edge over savings banks in attracting customers within reach of the branches.

In June 1922 the bank had just 6,300 savings depositors with an average balance of less than $300. Total savings deposits amounted to less than $2 million. Seven years later, in mid-1929, the average balance was still less than $300, but the number of depositors had grown nearly fortyfold, to 232,000, and total savings deposits had risen to $62 million. In the last six months of 1929, National City added over 90,000 savings accounts. As the decade ended, one out of every twenty people living in New York City held a National City passbook.[25]

Rapid penetration of the New York market for personal savings provided an important new source of funds. By 1929 the bank's compound interest deposits were half as large as its deposits from domestic correspondent banks, traditionally a significant source of funds. Moreover, savings deposits were subject to lower reserve requirements than demand balances, so that a larger part of the funds was available for investment in earning assets.

The Compound Interest Department led to another successful innovation in banking for the retail customer. Roger Steffan, as a former journalist, had long been interested in the loan shark problem in New York City. The problem was serious in the 1920s because the large demand for personal credit was not being met. Commercial banks did not make small, unsecured loans. The few so-called licensed lenders and industrial banks, which were allowed to charge rates above the New York usury ceiling on unsecured personal loans, could not expand rapidly enough to meet the need, because their capital base was too small and their loan portfolios too undiversified.[26] In his administration of the Compound Interest Department, Steffan had acquired much information about the finances of his customers and their need for small loans. He became convinced that the bank could make small, unsecured personal installment loans safely and profitably, charging 6 percent discounted.[27] In doing so, Steffan argued, the bank would render an important service to the public. He convinced Mitchell. As the latter commented,

> Our contact with this great number of small depositors has brought us to an understanding of their problems, their periodic necessitous financial requirements, and a realization that to give

to them the opportunity of safeguarding their savings by deposit without furnishing on the other hand a means by which they can, under necessity, borrow on reasonable terms, constitutes an unbalanced relationship and points to a lack of comprehensiveness in financial service . . . Our contact with people of this class has given to us a confidence in the integrity and character of the average individual. While it is not our purpose to encourage anyone to borrow except under the stress of circumstances, we have faith that loans so made can and will be paid.[28]

Early in 1928 the New York attorney general made a plea for more lenders to enter the personal lending business to combat loan sharking, and National City responded positively, the only New York commercial bank to do so. The Personal Credit Department was set up in the Forty-second Street branch under Steffan's direction. The step was a public relations sensation (Figure 7.1) and an almost instant business success. Widespread favorable press comment on the bank's move into a field hitherto untouched by major commercial banks brought in a flood of borrowers. In the first seven months, the new department made twenty-eight thousand individual loans for a total of $8.5 million. Steffan funded the loans with 3 percent money from his Compound Interest accounts, so that the 12 percent effective rate of interest (6 percent discounted on a twelve-month installment note) provided an ample spread. Loss experience was good. Two cosigners were required on each loan, and Steffan's knowledge of his customers and a credit-scoring system he devised enabled him to make good credit decisions, while his administrative skill kept expenses under control. The new department was soon operating in the black.[29]

As head of both the Compound Interest and the Personal Credit Departments, Steffan reported directly to Mitchell and imparted a drive and spirit to his departments that largely explain their success. Other New York commercial banks would follow National City into personal lending, but City Bank's head start gave it a lead in this field that lasted many years.

The International Bank

In the wake of the 1920–1921 recession, the directors of National City Bank, dismayed by the reverses in Russia and Cuba, considered closing the bank's entire foreign branch system.[30] Other U.S. banks with branches abroad were closing them and bowing out of the foreign field.[31] But National City chose to stay abroad, and the decision would set it apart from other U.S. banks for many years to come. Mitchell and his directors made this decision because the bank's original reasons for going abroad—to assist American firms operating overseas and to aid in financing U.S. trade—

Figure 7.1

—Clive Weed, New York Evening World
Reprinted National City Bank, Number Eight, April–May 1928, p. 12.

were as valid as ever. Moreoever, the International Banking Corporation (IBC) continued to earn a profit through the recession—proof that a well-managed foreign banking system could contribute to the bottom line. Two of the bank's directors, Joseph P. Grace and Cyrus H. McCormick, headed large multinational enterprises (W. R. Grace and Company and

International Harvester). They had also suffered in the 1920–1921 recession, but they were committed to direct foreign investment as a means of geographical diversification and growth. A number of the bank's other major corporate customers felt the same.[32] As a result, the bank's branches overseas could count on a firm customer base.

Mitchell's emphasis in international branch banking was on improving the existing network rather than on enlarging it. Rather than enter more countries, Mitchell sought to strengthen the existing system with a view to deepening its market penetration. To prevent a repetition of the Cuban disaster, much tighter control was exercised over the foreign branches, especially in the lending area. Teams of inspectors arrived unannounced to audit the branches and ensure their adherence to Head Office policy. To gain greater control, Mitchell also transformed IBC branches into branches of the bank, except where local law prohibited such a change. Upon completion of this process in 1930 Mitchell created the Overseas Division, with management responsibility for all foreign branches, the IBC, all exchange trading, and the dollar accounts that foreign institutions and individuals held at Head Office in New York. This step firmly institutionalized the international bank.

At the beginning of the 1920s National City or its subsidiary, the International Banking Corporation, already had branches in twenty-one countries. Paris was the only major financial market without a National City branch—surprising, perhaps, in view of James Stillman's long residence there. This gap was filled in 1922 when the bank acquired the Paris branch of the Farmers' Loan and Trust Company. National City opened offices in only two other countries during the 1920s, Haiti in 1922 and Mexico in 1929. At the end of the decade it had ninety-eight branches in twenty-three countries—a system many times larger than that of any other American bank with operations abroad in the 1920s.[33]

Despite this growth, during the 1920s the big British banks began to offer National City stiff competition overseas. Prior to the war the large British clearing banks had avoided international banking, leaving the field to the merchant banks, overseas banks, imperial banks, discount houses, and foreign banks, each of whom performed a specialized function or served a particular region.[34] The clearing banks concentrated on building domestic branch systems throughout the United Kingdom, largely by merger, as English law encouraged them to do.[35] In this way the big five clearing banks came to rank among the largest banking institutions in the world.

By the 1920s the domestic amalgamation movement in the United Kingdom was practically complete, and the big clearing banks began to look upon overseas banking as the route to further growth. They opened branches on the European continent and acquired existing overseas and imperial banks, and started to offer customers integrated international banking services.[36]

The relaxation of British exchange controls first imposed during the war and the revival of the pound as an international currency further intensified the competition that the British banks gave National City overseas. The pound's stabilization and Britain's return to gold in 1925 made sterling once again the principal currency of invoice for Europe's trade with Latin America and the Far East. This restored the position of the London discount or acceptance market in the financing of these major trade flows.

Nevertheless, demand for trade financing in dollars did not disappear. In fact, it increased relative to the prewar period. America's own imports and exports were now mainly invoiced and financed in dollars, and the U.S. share of world trade was much larger than before the war. National City's branches thus had plenty to do. Indeed, the branches' main activity was trade finance. In Latin America and the Far East, the business centered on financing each country's major export. Business was brisk, for the boom in Europe and North America meant strong demand for primary materials and food. In Chile, the bank financed the copper exported to the United States for wiring and plumbing in the great building boom of the 1920s. The Singapore branch extended credit to producers of rubber used by tire manufacturers in the United States and Europe. In other countries the story was the same: coffee in Brazil, silk in Japan, hides in Uruguay, beef in Argentina (Table 7.4), all financed in dollars.

The dollar's continuing role in trade finance also supported modest growth of the market for acceptances at home. The Federal Reserve provided further impetus to this market through a ruling that ultimately encouraged banks to increase acceptances based on transactions involving the foreign storage and shipment of goods.[37] National City participated in this market directly and indirectly. On its own it became the leading issuer of dollar acceptances; by 1928 the bank had $100 million in acceptances outstanding (Table 7.5), 8 percent of the total market.[38] Through the Discount Corporation, which it had helped establish in 1918 and which it partially owned, National City was also involved as a leading dealer in bankers' acceptances.[39]

Along with trade finance went foreign exchange. The bank was active in the exchange markets in the branches as well as in New York, trading for the accounts of its customers and for its own account. In the China branches, Shanghai in particular, such trading was particularly profitable. The exchange market there was entirely unregulated and the branches not only conducted the exchange business of their regular customers (mainly U.S. firms) but also traded actively for the bank's account in a variety of Chinese and foreign currencies and in gold and silver. Ex-

Table 7.4. Foreign branches, National City Bank, June 1929 (millions of dollars)

| Country | Selected accounts[a] | |
	Loans	Deposits
Argentina	26.0	31.8
Brazil	26.2	25.9
Chile	19.0	11.9
Colombia	1.3	0.3
Cuba	45.8	54.1
Dominican Republic	3.3	4.5
Panama	3.8	12.0
Peru	7.2	2.7
Puerto Rico	10.5	5.2
Uruguay	4.9	4.4
Venezuela	3.3	7.6
LATIN AMERICA	151.4	160.4
Belgium	8.9	8.7
Italy	7.7	7.9
United Kingdom	35.0	51.9
EUROPE	51.6	68.6
China	36.8	53.1
India	14.1	9.6
Japan	28.9	8.0
Java	1.3	1.5
Singapore	6.1	3.6
FAR EAST	87.1	75.8
Total	290.1	304.8

Source: Comptroller of the Currency, Annual Report, 1929 (Washington, D.C.: GPO, 1930), pp. 340–345.

a. Does not include affiliates in France, Haiti, and Spain. The Mexico City branch had just started operation and hence is not in this table. Note that figures are not comparable to those in Table 7.5 because of differences in date.

change transactions were, in fact, the principal source of branch earnings in the 1920s not only in China but in the bank's overseas system as a whole.[40]

In New York the chief exchange trader in the 1920s was Bernhart Duis, a German who had served with the International Banking Corporation. Duis was a brilliant trader, as Head Office exchange profits during his tenure attest. He was, for example, on the right side of the market during the stabilization of the pound and the French franc in 1925 and 1926, earning large profits in these years (Table 7.5). He ran his little empire virtually without supervision and reportedly accumulated a large reserve off the bank's regular books to cover trading losses. The story is told that in 1921,

Table 7.5. National City Bank's "international bank," 1921–1929 (millions of dollars)

End of December	Selected accounts							Earnings	
	Deposits			Loans			Acceptances outstanding New York[e]	New York (foreign exchange trading)[f]	Foreign branches[g]
	New York[a]	Foreign branches[b]	Total	New York[c]	Foreign branches[d]	Total			
1921	105.1	101.0	206.1	—	—	—	25.8	0.9	0.4
1922	143.3	111.2	254.5	9.4	—	—	29.3	1.2	0.4
1923	111.4	117.9	229.3	13.0	—	—	34.6	1.2	1.6
1924	186.2	139.2	325.4	20.1	—	—	44.2	1.8	2.7
1925	140.6	167.5	308.1	21.0	198.9	219.9	57.5	4.2	3.0
1926	150.4	234.2	384.6	15.9	246.8	262.7	49.4	2.9	3.9
1927	256.5	274.8	531.3	30.9	263.3	294.2	89.8	1.2	4.4
1928	172.0	301.5	473.5	40.1	319.9	360.0	98.8	0.6	5.0
1929	213.8	337.3	551.1	24.1	330.4	354.5	139.8	0.8	6.5

Source: National City Bank, Comptroller's Report, 1921–1929, Daily Statement Book, year-end 1921–1929, and Call Reports for year-end 1921–1929.
a. Foreign deposits in New York are those funds at Head Office due to foreign banks and bankers and to individuals plus time deposits due to foreigners.
b. Deposits in foreign branches are limited to deposits booked at the branch.
c. Foreign loans in New York are foreign bills discounted, foreign currency bills bought, and foreign overdrafts booked at Head Office.
d. Loans at foreign branches are limited to loans and discounts booked at the branch.
e. Acceptances outstanding issued by National City Bank to finance trade and to furnish dollar exchange.
f. Gross profits from foreign exchange trading at Head Office before deductions for expenses and taxes.
g. Net operating earnings remitted to New York less foreign branch expenses at Head Office. These earnings are generally after the payment of foreign income tax but before the payment of U.S. tax. These figures do not include earnings or foreign branches' deposits with Head Office.

after the bank had suffered a $5 million exchange loss in Brazil because of the dishonesty of a trader there, Duis at Mitchell's request found enough in his unofficial reserve to cover the entire loss.[41]

Where possible, National City sought to extend its foreign branches' business beyond trade finance and exchange to include local currency deposits and loans to local firms and individuals. In places where confidence in local banks was low—China and Cuba, for instance—this effort was particularly successful. In Cuba the bank was already a large factor in the local banking scene. The closing of local banks in the 1921 sugar crisis, while National City's branches remained open, increased the branches' appeal to local depositors.[42] National City Bank did, nevertheless, reduce its loans. By mid-1929 loans at the Cuban branches were down to 16 percent of all loans booked in the bank's foreign branches, compared to a high of 46 percent in 1921.[43] The bank's equity in the General Sugar Corporation was also transferred to the National City Company (see chapter 6).

In 1927 a program was launched to attract passbook savings accounts at the foreign branches—the bank's first try at retail banking abroad. The program was quite successful. By the end of 1928 over 160,000 individuals had savings accounts at National City's overseas branches with aggregate balances of $40 million.[44]

At Head Office in New York, the bank continued to seek foreign deposits, although in the 1920s such deposits remained below the high levels reached during the war. The balances reflected the dollar's growing international role as well as foreign borrowing in New York. Foreign governments, banks, and firms needed dollar balances to pay for U.S. exports. A large part of the balances were the proceeds of bond issues floated in the New York market. For most of the decade, foreign balances in New York accounted for about one-fifth of the bank's domestic deposit base.

All in all, National City's international bank became, in the course of the 1920s, nearly as important as its domestic wholesale business. By 1928 the international bank's deposits at Head Office and the branches approached those of the wholesale bank. Toward the end of the decade, the foreign branches accounted for 20 percent of the bank's total assets and a still higher proportion of total loans. The branches also contributed significantly to total earnings. From 1923 to 1929, profits from the foreign branches and subsidiaries supplied about one-quarter of the bank's pretax operating earnings. Vanderlip's commitment to international branch banking was paying off.

The Wholesale Bank

At the center of the National City organization was the third and largest of its banks, the wholesale bank at Head Office that served the nation's corporations and correspondent banks. This was the core business from which the institution had diversified into other areas of intermediation. The wisdom of this strategy became apparent in the course of the 1920s, for the bank's relationship with major corporations was changing and its business with domestic correspondents was flat.[45] As a result, the whole-sale bank grew more slowly than the local and international banks (Table 7.3).

Indeed it is surprising that National City's domestic wholesale business grew at all. After the recession of 1920–1921, the country's largest corporations altered the role they assigned banks in their financial plans. The recession had taught them that bank loans could be unreliable as a source of "permanent" financing. In the following years corporate treasurers took precautions to ensure that they would not again be strapped for liquidity as they had been in 1920–1921. Large firms came to consider their banks as lenders of last resort. They repaid bank loans and relied for external financing on new issues of securities.[46]

This change in corporate financial policy was a challenge to New York banks, National City among them. At the peak of the 1919–1920 boom, corporate loans had provided a major part of the bank's assets and earnings. Now the bank's best customers were reducing their balances and repaying their loans. If National City was to keep business customers, it had to find a way of adjusting to these changes.

It found two ways. As corporations shifted from bank loans to bond finance, the National City Company took up where the bank left off (see chapter 8). During the 1920s, the bank's securities affiliate originated or participated in issues for many companies that had borrowed from the bank during the postwar boom. In late 1920, for example, the bank had extended a credit of $1.2 million to the Goodyear Tire and Rubber Company. The following year the National City Company participated in a $30 million bond underwriting as part of that company's reorganization.[47]

The bank also found new business customers. They were acquired principally at the branches in New York and overseas, although Head Office also succeeded in establishing new domestic relationships. The bank also continued Vanderlip's policy of reaching out to smaller firms across the country. Such firms did not have access to the bond and equity markets, and they looked to banks to finance their asset growth. These smaller accounts gave a boost to the wholesale bank's lending. In fact, between mid-1924 and mid-1929 wholesale loans doubled (Table 7.6). By 1928 there were over six thousand domestic corporate and correspondent bank accounts at Head Office, about one-fourth more than in 1912, shortly after Vanderlip had begun his thrust into the corporate market.[48]

To protect liquidity, treasurers of large corporations in the 1920s began to use their deposit balances more effectively. Funds were placed with

Table 7.6. National City Bank's "domestic wholesale bank," 1921–1929 (millions of dollars)

End of December	Selected accounts									
	Deposits[a]						Loans			Earnings[d]
	Demand deposits			Other deposits		Total deposits	Brokers' loans[b]	Other[c]	Total	
	Domestic banks	Other	Total	Time	Trust funds and other					
1921	83.8	281.6	365.4	26.0	3.4	394.8	—	—	—	12.1
1922	76.3	297.7	374.0	36.0	10.9	420.9	109.2	296.7	405.9	7.5
1923	92.8	300.2	393.0	38.6	3.6	435.2	113.1	209.9	323.0	8.0
1924	112.4	347.8	460.2	28.9	9.7	498.8	125.1	270.5	395.6	7.4
1925	92.3	391.9	484.2	17.1	9.4	510.7	118.4	253.8	372.2	11.3
1926	97.7	384.3	482.0	32.6	11.3	525.9	150.1	299.7	449.8	11.4
1927	84.2	375.2	459.4	46.3	44.9	550.6	345.4	331.9	677.3	11.9
1928	96.7	457.4	554.1	57.2	10.9	622.2	174.1	334.1	508.2	15.2
1929	126.4	547.6	674.0	42.1	77.6	793.7	149.1	558.2	707.3	19.8

Source: National City Bank, Comptroller's Report, 1921–1929, and Daily Statement Book, year-end 1921–1929.

a. All deposits other than foreign at Head Office.

b. Brokers' loans are demand loans to brokers collateralized by marketable securities.

c. "Other" loans are loans other than brokers' loans booked at Head Office with the exception of loans to foreigners (as recorded in Table 7.5).

d. Net operating earnings of Head Office before tax and securities gains and losses. This includes revenues from foreign loans booked at Head Office as well as general overhead expense for the foreign and domestic branches. For the years 1923, 1928, and 1929, the figures are after the payment of income tax.

banks that would extend a firm credit line on which the customer could draw as needed. This practice gave National City an advantage over its many competitors. The largest bank in the country, National City could extend large lines. Moreover, National City made it clear to corporate customers that their credit lines would be directly proportional to their balances.[49] This explicit commitment to lend up to the amount of the line if called upon gave corporate treasurers the assurance of liquidity they wanted. An example is General Motors, which in 1922 designated National City one of its "preferential" banks, and kept in excess of $2 million on deposit with Head Office, principally because National City gave it a firm line of credit of $6 million.[50]

Another service National City offered to coax balances from reluctant treasurers was a cash management system known as the transcontinental banking service. The bank initiated the service in 1928 in cooperation with correspondent banks across the country. The system allowed corporations to reduce their deposits to the minimum required for transactions purposes, thereby freeing the company's resources for other uses, including investment in higher-yielding liquid assets such as call loans.[51]

Call Money

In the 1920s call loans—demand loans to brokers and securities firms secured by stock and bonds—were the liquid asset that was most widely available apart from cash and bank deposits.[52] In the later 1920s, brokers' demand for credit surged. They were selling a record volume of new securities and providing credit to their customers, enabling them to buy securities on margin. Beginning early in 1928 the Federal Reserve began to follow a restrictive policy to damp the market boom, and call money rates rose steeply. But so high was confidence and so great was the momentum of the bull market that rising interest rates on call money neither halted the growth of brokers' loans nor checked the rise in stock prices.

As call money rates rose, it became profitable for corporations and correspondent banks to shift funds from bank deposits into call loans, for deposit rates were no longer competitive. The New York Clearing House had set a ceiling of 2.5 percent on the rate National City and other member banks could pay on corporate and interbank demand deposits, whereas by April 1928 the call loan rate was above 5 percent and headed higher. Under the circumstances and since they were unwilling to raise the Clearing House ceilings, National City and the other Clearing House banks could only accommodate their customers by placing the funds with brokers for the customer's account rather than the bank's. As call money rates continued to rise, funds poured in from banks and firms across the country and from abroad. At National City, outstanding "loans on the stock exchange for the account of others" totaled over $225 million to-ward the end of 1928. The following year they rose further, reaching a peak of over $500 million in October 1929 (see Table 7.7).

The growing volume of call loans for the account of others created a formidable problem of liquidity management for National City and the other big New York banks. The banks were well aware that the bull market might break. If that occurred, they had to be prepared to take over customers' loans to brokers if the customers wanted to take their funds out of the stock market. If Clearing House banks failed to act in this way, panic in the money market would be the predictable consequence.[53]

But to do so, National City and the other banks needed funds of their own. They might get them by persuading customers to convert call loans to deposits. Alternatively, the banks would have to sell liquid assets. To prepare for this second eventuality, National City and other Clearing House members built up their holdings of liquid assets such as bankers' acceptances and government securities. These holdings increased rapidly in the late 1920s as call loans for the account of others rose. New York banks also cut back their own lending to brokers and may have held down commercial lending as well, in order to acquire liquid assets.

Clearing House members were naturally uneasy about this state of affairs, which made them responsible for the liquidity of a money market that might break at any time. Mitchell called the practice of booking brokers' loans for the account of others a "dangerous trend" that "not only

Table 7.7. Brokers' loans, National City Bank, 1920–1929

Date	For account of others (millions of $)	For own account (millions of $)	Rate on call loans (%)	Clearing House ceiling (%)
2/13/20	48.3	18.2	9.75	3.0
6/15/23	30.9	107.7	4.70	2.5
11/23/23	26.9	74.0	4.75	2.5
6/05/25	44.0	135.5	3.90	2.0
11/27/25	94.5	152.0	4.63	2.0
10/21/27	141.4	265.4	3.90	2.0
3/30/28	169.1	225.6	4.65	2.0
10/19/28	227.0	72.4	7.00	2.5
3/09/29	305.8	126.8	8.80	2.5
10/04/29	512.9	106.0	8.20	2.5

Sources: Brokers' loans: Comptroller of the Currency, Examination Reports for National City Bank for dates cited. Call loan rate: average renewal rate on stock exchange call loans for week of examination date. Board of Governors, Federal Reserve System, *Banking and Monetary Statistics, 1914–1940* (Washington, D.C.: GPO, 1943), pp. 452ff. Clearing House ceiling: New York Clearing House.

deprives member banks of legitimate profits as a result of decreases in deposits, but also, owing to a lack of banking understanding of the majority of lenders, throws upon Clearing House members a moral responsibility that is inadequately compensated by the present rate, and in addition, introduces . . . a lending factor which is a menace because it recognizes no responsibility for the maintenance of a sound banking situation and holds for itself a freedom of action that is of itself dangerous."[54]

Federal Reserve officials agreed. They, too, were alarmed about the level of stock prices and the volume of call loans for the account of others. In their view such loans were "speculative": They tended to divert credit from "legitimate needs of commerce" and threatened to depress business activity. The officials disagreed, however, about what to do. The Federal Reserve Bank of New York argued forcefully for an increase in the discount rate. This would raise the rate on brokers' loans and induce investors to sell part of their holdings, thus slowing the rise in stock prices. The board in Washington argued that higher interest rates would raise the cost of credit to "legitimate" business and bring on a business contraction. The board's proposal was that the Reserve banks should ration credit to their member banks, discounting the paper of banks that were not lending at call in the New York market. It was the same difference of view between the same parties that surfaced in 1919–1920.[55]

Circumstances thrust Charles Mitchell into the center of this dispute. Shortly before his death in October 1928, Benjamin Strong, governor of the Federal Reserve Bank of New York, had chosen Mitchell to be a director of that bank.[56] Mitchell assumed his new duties in January 1929, just as the debate concerning Federal Reserve policy was heating up.

Late in March 1929 the emergency occurred. Stock prices wavered and funds were withdrawn from the market. Call money rates shot up to nearly 15 percent. On March 25, stock prices broke sharply and call money went to 20 percent. Suddenly the collateral supporting billions of dollars in brokers' loans looked shaky. It looked as though credit to carry stocks might not be obtainable at any price and that panicky selling of stock would follow. At this point Mitchell decided to act. With the tacit approval of the Federal Reserve Bank of New York and the assurance of its support at the discount window, Mitchell announced that National City would lend up to $25 million in the call loan market, "whatever might be the attitude of the Federal Reserve Board."[57] The market was reassured. In a few days call money was down to 8 percent and still falling.

The crisis was over for the market, but not for Charles Mitchell. The Federal Reserve Board, annoyed not so much at what Mitchell had done but at what he had said, wrote asking him to "clarify" his statement.[58] Politicians in Washington were less restrained. Senator Carter Glass of Virginia, a principal author of the Federal Reserve Act, accused Mitchell of "slapping the Federal Reserve Board squarely in the face," and of treating its policies "with contempt and contumely."[59] He called on the board to demand that Mitchell resign as a director of the Federal Reserve Bank of New York. Other senators supported the suggestion.[60] Later, in the depths of the depression, these charges would be remembered and revived.

In New York, where people had a closer view of the markets, opinion in business and financial circles held that Mitchell's actions had been correct, though his words ill chosen. The *Commercial and Financial Chronicle*, while agreeing that Mitchell's remarks were "unfortunate" and that "he laid himself open" to Senator Glass's attack, concluded that "his declaration was that of a courageous man and one . . . alive to the dire disaster that threatened if there should be complete shutting off of new money supplies. In the circumstances his stand was entirely justified.[61] The *New York Times* editorialized that "Senator Glass seems to have confused a temporary emergency with a permanent policy. The banks did not come forward with funds to promote speculation, but to prevent what threatened to be a serious crisis in the money market." The *Times* concluded, "Mr. Mitchell and his action has saved the day for the financial community. No one can say how great a calamity would have happened had he not stepped into the breach at the right moment."[62]

The Bottom Line

The dispute over Mitchell's intervention soon faded from the headlines and Mitchell turned again to fulfilling his longstanding ambition: to make National City Bank "not only . . . the largest and most powerful, but the most solid institution in the world."[63] On April 2, 1929, he announced that National City would merge with the Farmers' Loan and Trust Company. This strengthened National City's position in the trust field (see chapter 8). It also kept the bank comfortably ahead of its nearest U.S. rival, the Guaranty Trust Company, in terms of assets and deposits, although Guaranty had recently announced a merger of its own with the National Bank of Commerce. National City thus remained the largest bank in the country, with only the Midland Bank ahead of it in world ranking.[64]

In connection with the Farmers' Loan and Trust merger, National City raised its capital again. For it was the bank's policy to maintain "a larger ratio of capital and surplus to deposits than is dictated by general banking practice."[65] Not only did a larger capital base raise the bank's legal lending limit, but it also gave added safety to depositors in an era when bank failures were common. At the time of the merger the bank issued 500,000 new shares, bringing the stockholders' equity in June 1929 to almost $250 million, one-eighth of total resources. Leverage was lower than at any time since 1921 (Table 7.8).

Table 7.8. Summary statistics, National City Bank, 1921–1929

| End of December | Selected accounts (millions of dollars) | | | | Net profits[b] (millions of $) |
	Assets	Loans	Deposits	Stockholders' equity[a]	
1921	821.9	526.8	649.0	101.0	3.8
1922	950.8	543.9	727.8	91.1	0.9
1923	920.1	472.5	728.7	91.9	6.8
1924	1,142.3	584.7	913.0	95.3	3.1
1925	1,215.0	635.0	921.5	115.3	13.2
1926	1,374.4	789.0	1,083.4	116.3	12.8
1927	1,682.8	1,060.1	1,275.0	146.2	17.9
1928	1,847.7	995.6	1,349.2	167.0	19.8
1929	2,206.2	1,245.4	1,649.4	239.7	22.8

Source: National City Bank, Comptroller's Reports, 1921–1929, "Condensed Statement of Condition" (including domestic and foreign branches), Annual Report, 1921–1929 (New York: National City Bank, 1922–1930), Appendix B.

a. Stockholders' equity is composed of capital, surplus, and undivided profits.

b. Figures do not include income of City Bank Farmers' Trust Company but do include income of National City Bank Trust Department.

Profits were excellent. They soared from $900,000 in 1922 to approximately $13 million in 1925 and 1926 as a result of Mitchell's management and the recovery from the 1920–1921 recession. In the years 1927 to 1929, as market interest rates climbed above Clearing House ceilings on deposit rates, the bank's profits surged again, reaching a high of $22.8 million in 1929.

When Mitchell became president in May 1921, the institution was floundering. In 1929 it was breaking records. During his tenure assets, earnings, and capital had grown at double-digit rates (Table 7.8). The bank's strategy had positioned it to make the most of the New Era.

8.

The Financial Department Store (II)

1921-1929

Symbolic of National City's approach to its customers was its building on Madison Avenue and Forty-second Street. The building housed a branch of the bank, an office of the City Company, and a representative of the Trust Department. National City did not simply intend to be the "bank for all," as Mitchell called it in 1922. It also wished to bring to each customer all things financial.

Securities and the Individual Investor

Vanderlip had seen, beyond National City's traditional clientele of institutions and millionaires, the emergence of a "great bond-buying public," people who had not previously been considered investors. They were the managers and technicians who were revolutionizing the corporate world. They were independent businessmen who owned small manufacturing firms. They were lawyers, doctors, and other professionals. These men and women were looking for ways to invest their savings in something more profitable or more liquid than bank deposits, life insurance, or their own homes. Securities offered that opportunity. Bonds and stocks could be combined in a portfolio tailored to their investment objectives. In return for accepting some risk, the saver could obtain a significantly higher return than that available from bank deposits. Yet his investment would be far more liquid than an investment in real estate.

This middle class was large and growing rapidly. In 1922 nearly 600,000 people in the United States had incomes of over $5,000 per year, an amount that allowed the individual to maintain a comfortable standard of living and to save significant sums. By the end of the decade over one million people counted themselves so fortunate.[1] For the most part these people had little previous investment experience. The City Company therefore attempted to teach them the basics. Mitchell's method was to persuade people by advertising and direct selling to see the regular purchase of securities as a normal means of household saving. At the same time he intended through volume to cut the unit cost of distributing securities in order to reach a mass market. He explained,

> We felt that if we could tear from the investment banking profession the veil of mystery and false dignity that surrounded it; if we could get the people to look upon securities as something they were themselves vitally interested in and could readily understand; if we could bring the investment banking house to the people in such a way that they would look upon it as a part and parcel of their everyday life; if, by advertising, we could spread the gospel of thrift and saving and investment; if we could, by developing a very large volume of business, reduce the unit cost—we then, by spreading the expense over this large volume, could afford to render a service to the individual investor and the bank investor such as had theretofore never been rendered. We felt that if we could take from the books of successful merchandisers and distributors, the country over, those pages that had spelled success for them, those that had to do with successful advertising, and those with successful education, within and without their organization, we could then, by adaptation of those pages, lift this investment banking business to a level it had never reached before.[2]

To this end, the City Company opened offices across the country. By 1919 the company had offices in fifty-one cities. Mitchell compared them to chain stores: "Our branch offices throughout the United States are already working to make connections with the great new bond-buying public. Our newer offices are on the ground floor . . . [We] are getting close to the public . . . and are preparing to serve the public on a straightforward basis, just as it is served by the United Cigar Stores or Child's Restaurants."[3]

The company's sales method was educational: to teach customers the basics of bonds as investments. Although the Liberty bond campaigns of World War I had developed "a great understanding among the people as to what thrift and investment mean," much remained to be done.[4] The prospect was first told that through saving he could begin to accumulate a portfolio of bonds that would give him a second income or help him build a substantial estate. To help its salesmen spread this message of thrift, the City Company advertised in magazines such as *World's Work*, *Harper's*, and the *Atlantic Monthly*. The prospect was then taught the investment characteristics of a bond—that bonds were a "promise to pay to those who buy them specified sums on specified dates," that they could be sold before maturity or could be pledged as collateral for a loan if the investor needed cash, and so on.[5] The company's sales brochures pointed out that bonds were not all equally safe and that apart from the bonds of the United States government, they all carried some risk that the borrower would default, and even government bonds fluctuated in market price with interest rates.[6]

The City Company salesmen were told to encourage customers to make a "sharp distinction . . . between good bonds *as a class* and what may prove to be a good bond *for you.*"[7] Bonds have a number of characteristics, such as marketability, call protection, and tax exemption, and "every added feature of yield or security has its own special price tag attached."[8]

The City Company's sales effort was aimed at the "person of limited resources, all of whose capital and income are necessary to insure life's future comforts."[9] To them it recommended both bonds as the "ideal investment medium" and diversification as the first principle to observe in any bond portfolio. Bonds should be chosen in a way that avoids undue concentration in any one industry, geographical location, or maturity; and some portion of the portfolio should be readily marketable in case the investor faces an unanticipated need for cash.[10]

Investment, then, was a complex matter, but the City Company's sales literature assured prospective customers that if they saved, it would advise them how to invest (Figure 8.1). It encouraged them to set financial goals and then talk to a National City representative about how to reach them. Finally, the City Company reminded the investor that "to get the fullest benefit of its judgment and vigilance, [he] must be as frank and open in discussing his investment problems as he is in discussing legal problems with his lawyer or his health with a doctor."[11]

Over the long run the success of this approach depended on putting the customer's interests first. The company's policy was not to market an issue unless it considered the security to be attractive as an investment, one whose price fairly reflected the company's judgment of its risk. To that end, the company, with the aid of a headquarters research staff, examined new issues before deciding to present them to the public with the National City "seal of approval." It also refused until 1927 to underwrite common stocks. Then "because of the past prosperity enjoyed by many corporations and the favorable outlook for the future, plus improved capital position," the City Company classified some common stock issues as "investments."[12]

All this was a wide departure from previous investment-banking practice. But the City Company was confident of its ability to advise the small investor capably. It employed the most advanced methods of investment analysis available. It recommended securities on the basis of their "intrinsic value" and encouraged the small investor to accumulate a well-diversi-

"I shouldn't decide it alone"

A MAN with a few thousand dollars to invest has a perplexing range
of possibilities before him. Values must be appraised, past records
studied and future trends estimated. But the investor should not
try to decide alone. He can get the considered opinion of a worldwide investment organization—it is his for the asking. National City
judgment as to which bonds are best for you is based on both strict
investigation of the security and analysis of your own requirements.

The National City Company
The National City Bank Building, New York

OFFICES IN 50 AMERICAN CITIES : INTERCONNECTED BY 11,000 MILES OF PRIVATE WIRES
INTERNATIONAL BRANCHES AND CONNECTIONS

Figure 8.1

fied bond portfolio.[13] In the expanding world economy of the 1920s the safety of this conservative course seemed assured; after all, bonds had first claim on the rapidly expanding revenues of governments and corporations.

Mitchell was well aware of the high profile the City Company had acquired and the responsibility this entailed:

> The time will never come, certainly so long as I am connected with The National City Company, when, pressed with the need for securities for our great selling organization, we will let down in our exacting requirements. We have gained the confidence of the investor and we are building our institution upon that confidence. We want the public to feel safe with us. We are going to make more exacting our yard-stick, because the small investor who buys from us today a thousand or a five hundred dollar bond is not in a position to know whether that security is good or not and must rely on us. I often think that, in nine cases out of ten, we might just as well be selling this small investor a gold brick, so far as the extent of this knowledge is concerned. But we recognize that as between ourselves and this small investor, the law of *caveat emptor* cannot apply, and that if we are to fulfill our trust, we must supply that which means safety and a reasonable return to him.[14]

Underwriting

In the 1920s the added placing power provided by the retail distribution system cemented National City's position as one of the top underwriters and enabled it to become a leading originator of securities as well. Overall the City Company participated in or originated over one-fifth of all bonds issued in the United States during the 1920s (Table 8.1), putting it in the front rank of all underwriters.[15]

Under Mitchell the City Company followed the tack taken by Stillman and Vanderlip, working closely with Morgan and Kuhn, Loeb in floating issues for their clients and working hard to develop new alliances and new relationships of its own. This strategy of cementing and expanding alliances dictated the pattern of National City's underwriting activity. In floating issues for seasoned borrowers, participations were the rule; in this area Morgan and Kuhn, Loeb had firmly established relationships with the major issuers. Participations in their syndicates provided the City Company with a steady stream of income and a base on which to build. With issuers new to the securities market National City had more opportunity to develop relationships of its own. Its success with foreign governments and corporations made it a major originator of new securities.

Table 8.1. Role of National City Company in new bond issues in the United States, 1921–1929 (millions of dollars)

Type of bond	Total issued	National City Company issues		
		Total	Originations	Participations
Railroad	6,195	1,854	100	1,754
Utility	11,065	1,529	395	1,134
Industrial	9,210	1,581	511	1,070
Total domestic corporate	26,470	4,964	1,006	3,958
Domestic state and municipal	11,892	1,422	1,016	406
Federal agencies	1,643	564	2	562
Total domestic	40,005	6,950	2,024	4,926
Foreign	10,267	3,783	1,195	2,588
Total	50,272	10,733	3,219	7,514

Sources: Col. 2, Domestic corporate bonds: W. Braddock Hickman, *The Volume of Corporate Bond Financing since 1900* (Princeton: Princeton University Press, 1953), pp. 253–255. Col. 2, Domestic state and municipal bonds and federal agency securities: Board of Governors, Federal Reserve System, *Banking and Monetary Statistics, 1914–1941* (Washington, D.C.: GPO, 1943), p. 487. Col. 2, Foreign bonds: U.S. Department of Commerce, Bureau of Foreign and Domestic Commerce, *Trade Promotion Series*, no. 104, 1930. Data are adjusted to include total amount of issues, not just amount purchased in the United States, to exclude issues for companies incorporated in the United States where proceeds are used abroad and to exclude entities in Alaska and Hawaii. They are further adjusted to include private placements. Cols. 3–5, Domestic corporate bonds: *The Cumulative Daily Digest of Corporation News* (1921–1924) (New York: Poor's Publishing Co., 1921–1924), and *American Underwriting Houses and Their Issues* (1925–1929), ed. O. P. Schwarzchild (New York: National Statistical Service, 1925–1929). Cols. 3–5, Domestic state and municipal bonds and federal agency securities: *The Cumulative Daily Digest of Corporation News* (1921–1923); *Poor's Feature Volume: Government, State, and Municipal Securities* (1924) (New York: Poor's Publishing Co., 1925); *Poor's Government and Municipal Supplement* (1925) (New York: Poor's Publishing Co., 1926); *Poor's Descriptive Tabulation of Government, State, and Municipal Bonds* (1926–1928) (New York: Poor's Publishing Co., 1927–1929); *Poor's Bank, Government, and Municipal Volume* (1929) (New York: Poor's Publishing Co., 1930). Cols. 3–5, Foreign bonds: U.S. Congress, Senate Committee on Finance, *Sale of Foreign Bonds or Securities in the United States: Hearings Pursuant to S. Res. 19*, pt. 1, 72nd Cong., 1st sess., 1931, after p. 162.

Financing Domestic Corporations

During the 1920s two factors produced a surge in new security issues by domestic corporations. The first was a rise in new investment. The second was the change in corporate financial practice that followed the 1920–1921 recession (see chapter 6). In reaction to this downturn, large corporations turned away from bank loans and toward means of finance that would match more closely the expected life of the additions to plant and equipment the companies were making. When these capital investments outran companies' earnings, they turned to the securities market for funds. At first, that meant bonds, but as the decade progressed, it increasingly involved equities. From 1921 to 1929 corporations issued new bonds totaling over $26 billion (Table 8.1).

Nearly one-fifth of these bonds were originated by or underwritten with the participation of the National City Company (Table 8.1). From 1921 to 1929 the City Company had a hand in issuing nearly $5 billion in bonds for domestic corporations, plus a small amount of common and preferred stock. Corporate bonds were the core of National City's underwriting business, and participations in Morgan and Kuhn, Loeb syndicates the rule. During the 1920s the City Company continued to benefit from the working relationships established by Stillman and Vanderlip with J. P. Morgan and Company and Kuhn, Loeb (see chapters 3 and 4). Morgan led nearly half the syndicates in which the City Company participated. Kuhn, Loeb led another 10 percent (Table 8.2). National City's placing power remained the chief attraction. These wholesale firms had no retail distribution of their own, while National City had the country's best.

The pattern of National City's underwriting activity demonstrates its basic strategy of innovation and diversification from an established and secure base. In railroad finance, which accounted for 37 percent of its total underwritings, National City continued to follow in the wake of Morgan and Kuhn, Loeb. These firms continued to maintain strong relationships with the major railroads. Although the railroads had little demand

Table 8.2. Domestic corporate securities originated by others and issued with National City Company participation, 1921–1929 (millions of dollars)

Lead house	Total	Railroads	Utilities	Industrial
J. P. Morgan	1,963	1,160	739	64
Kuhn, Loeb	493	483	0	10
Dillon, Read	248	0	0	248
Guaranty Co.	301	0	0	301
Lee, Higginson	177	0	0	177
Bankers Trust	85	0	0	85
Others	691	111	395	185
Total	3,958	1,754	1,134	1,070

Source: As in Table 8.1, cols. 3–5, Domestic corporate bonds.

for new capital, they refunded a large volume of maturing issues. Thus National City had little opportunity to originate securities; participations accounted for 95 percent of its railroad underwritings, the vast majority of it in association with Morgan and Kuhn, Loeb.

In financing public utilities the City Company played a more prominent role, but here too its performance rested on longstanding relationships. City Company originated nearly $400 million in new bonds, largely for Consolidated Edison, the New York City utility that Taylor had helped build, and Pacific Gas and Electric, the California firm that Stillman had helped establish in 1906 (see chapters 3 and 4).

The rest of the City Company's underwriting for public utilities took the form of participations. Once again Morgan led the majority of syndicates in which National City participated. The primary client was American Telephone and Telegraph (AT & T) and National City's increasing role in AT & T syndicates provides a good example of its development as an investment banker. In 1906 AT & T abandoned its practice of soliciting competitive bids for new security issues in order to work with investment bankers. Morgan formed an originating group consisting of itself, Kuhn, Loeb, Baring Brothers, and Kidder, Peabody. Starting in 1908 Morgan allocated National City a share in its share of issues for various AT & T subsidiaries. In 1913 National City Company was admitted to the originating group along with the First National Bank. Each was given a 10 percent share, a percentage that was formalized in a 1920 agreement. In subsequent years AT & T's capital requirements continued to grow rapidly, providing a steady source of underwriting income. Between 1921 and 1929 the City Company purchased $62.2 million of securities on original terms from AT & T and grossed close to $600,000 on sales to the selling syndicate. It earned additional profits in distributing these securities to the public.[16]

Financing industrial firms represented a major opportunity for the National City Company. Until World War I relatively few manufacturing and mining firms had reached the stage where a trip to the bond market was either feasible or necessary. Perhaps as a result Morgan and Kuhn, Loeb had largely neglected industrial securities. Thus, when industrial companies began to borrow heavily in the 1920s, the newer investment-banking houses competed vigorously for this business.

National City Company was fairly successful. It participated in 11 percent and originated 6 percent of the bond issues floated for industrial corporations in 1921–1929. To do so the City Company developed relationships with other investment-banking houses and the issuers themselves. During the 1920s it participated in issues managed by Dillon Read, the Guaranty Company, Lee, Higginson, and other wholesale houses (Table 8.2). It teamed up with retail-oriented houses such as Halsey, Stuart and

Harris, Forbes. Smaller, regional firms also found National City attractive as a participant in their syndicates. As local corporations extended their activities, their financing needs outpaced the capacity of local securities firms. To keep the corporation as an investment-banking client, the local underwriter had to expand his syndicate. National City's nationwide distribution system made it a natural choice.

Participations were profitable, but the best part of investment banking was origination. The lead underwriter not only earned higher fees but also was able to build with the borrower a broader banking relationship that might include deposits, bank loans, and trust services. The City Company was lead underwriter for only a handful of major industrial companies in the 1920s, in the oil, copper, and sugar industries. Foremost among them was Sinclair Crude Oil Purchasing, a joint venture of Harry Sinclair and Standard Oil of Indiana, for which the City Company originated $92 million in new securities.

During the 1920s the City Company also took on as clients small but rapidly growing firms in the textile, chemical, paper, and cement industries, as well as a number of public utilities. In many cases the company, as the sole underwriter, took the risk of selling the entire issue. These smaller underwritings probably contributed little to the City Company's profits, but they were a base for growth. Successful investment banking usually required the underwriter to establish a relationship with the borrowing firm early in its history. That was the path Morgan had taken and the one City Company now wished to follow.

Financing Domestic Municipalities

In underwriting municipal bonds the National City organization had long followed the strategy of establishing close relationships with major borrowers. During the 1920s this led to numerous underwriting assignments as municipalities turned to the bond market to finance needed additions to the social infrastructure, such as roads, schools, sewers, and waterworks. From 1921 to 1929 National City Company originated or participated in municipal securities totaling $1.4 billion (Table 8.1), predominantly for the governments of major U.S. cities (Table 8.3).

During the 1920s New York City was far and away the largest issuer of municipal securities and National City Company was its principal investment banker. From 1921 to 1929 the National City Company originated $463 million in securities for the nation's largest city. This amounted to nearly half of its total originations of municipal securities and to one-seventh of its originations of all securities, domestic and foreign.

National City's close relationship with New York City dated from the turn of the century, when the city chose the bank to be its chief bank of de-

Table 8.3. Municipal bonds underwritten by National City Company, 1921–1929 (millions of dollars)

Issuer	Originations	Participations	Total
Cities			
New York City	463	55	518
Philadelphia	63	30	93
Detroit	5	83	88
San Francisco	48	24	72
Los Angeles	49	0	49
Chicago	32	14	46
Other cities and local governments	189	71	262
Total cities	849	277	1126
States			
North Carolina	27	36	63
Pennsylvania	30	8	38
Michigan	0	31	31
Other states	47	54	101
Total states	104	129	233
Other entities			
Port of New York Authority	63	0	63
Total	1016	406	1422

Source: As in Table 8.1, cols. 3–5, Domestic state and municipal bonds.
Note: Figures are par value of bonds.

posit. The bank also provided the city with short-term loans and began to underwrite its notes and bonds. Most notable was the assistance rendered New York City by National City and other Clearing House banks together with J. P. Morgan and Company and Kuhn, Loeb during the crisis following the outbreak of World War I in 1914. In return for a loan of $100 million that permitted New York City to repay bonds maturing in Europe, the city agreed that after 1918 it would fund non-revenue-producing improvements, such as schools, from general taxes, rather than through bonds, as it had done previously. Thereafter, the city agreed to finance only revenue-producing improvements, such as rapid transit or docks, through the issuance of new bonds. This so-called pay-as-you-go policy brought the unbridled growth of New York City's debt under some control, although not before its total net debt had reached $942 million—an amount nearly equal to the interest-bearing debt of the federal government.[17]

Under the pay-as-you-go policy New York City continued to borrow in the 1920s, although at a less rapid pace than in the years prior to its agreement with the bankers in 1914. As promised, new financings were used to refund maturing issues and to finance capital improvements, such as the IND subway, that would generate revenues. During the years 1921 to 1929 New York City issued $715 million in new securities. Nearly two-thirds of these issues were originated by the National City Company.

In addition to New York City, other major cities giving underwriting mandates to the National City Company included Philadelphia, Detroit, San Francisco, Los Angeles, and Chicago. State governments for which National City underwrote securities included North Carolina, Pennsylvania, and Michigan. All in all, the City Company floated 309 issues for governments in 37 different states during the 1920s.

Financing Foreign Firms and Governments

The strategy of building relationships and expanding alliances was even more successful in the area of foreign bonds. In fact, during the 1920s the underwriting of foreign bonds propelled much of the National City Company's growth.

The City Company was well positioned to take advantage of the surge in foreign borrowing that occurred in the 1920s. James Stillman had cultivated relationships with a number of foreign governments at the turn of the century, when they first became interested in floating bonds on the New York capital market. During World War I, National City had strengthened and expanded these relationships, aided by its foreign branches.

As was the case in corporate finance, the Morgan relationship benefited the City Company in its efforts to underwrite foreign bonds. It provided National City with a steady stream of high-quality foreign issues for resale to the public. In fact, Morgan led over half of the foreign bond syndicates in which the City Company participated. Morgan had firm relationships with major European borrowers such as Great Britain, France, and Italy and with governments in other areas of the world such as Australia and Argentina. These were a product of its close links to the Morgan partnerships in London and Paris, its prominence in financing the Allies during World War I, and the State Department's confidence in Morgan's ability to float difficult issues. Morgan looked to others to distribute the securities it originated, and it relied heavily on the National City Company to do so.

Overall, the City Company originated or participated in over 150 foreign bond issues for borrowers from 26 different countries from 1921 to 1929. In these years the City Company originated or participated in issues amounting to $3.8 billion, 37 percent of the foreign bonds floated in New York in that period (Table 8.1). Of this total, the company underwrote 30 percent for its own account and sold $673 million to the public, earning over $20 million in doing so (Table 8.4). Aside from Canada and Germany, no country's bonds amounted to more than 10 percent of the total underwritten by the company. With the possible exception of the house of Morgan, no other firm played so prominent a role in the sale of foreign bonds on the New York market.

The rise in foreign borrowing in the 1920s was primarily a result of the war. During the war much of Europe's capital stock had been destroyed or allowed to deteriorate. The effective stock of capital was low, and the return on investment high. The same was true in Latin America, but for a different reason. There, capital was scarce compared to natural resources. In the United States, in contrast to Europe and Latin America, the supply of savings was large compared to investment opportunities.[18]

These imbalances in the demand and supply of capital called for international financial intermediation on a large scale. It fell to City Company and other American investment houses to provide it. Neither Britain nor France, the leading international lenders before 1914, was prepared to resume its former role. Neither permitted free access to their capital markets in the 1920s. The Bank of England restricted foreign borrowing in the Lon-

Table 8.4. Role of National City Company in new foreign bond issues in the United States, 1921–1929 (millions of dollars)

Lead house	Total volume of issues	National City Company's role	
		Underwriting group[a]	Selling group[b]
National City Company	1,195[c]	624	393
J. P. Morgan	1,406	355	141
Kuhn, Loeb	215	30	39
Dillon, Read	346	55	32
J and W Seligman	105	31	18
Others	516	68	50
Total	3,783[d]	1,163	673

Source: As in Table 8.1, cols. 3–5, Foreign bonds.
Note: Data referred to in columns 3 and 4 are not available for domestic corporate issues.
a. Refers to National City Company's own financial responsibility or underwriting share.
b. Refers to National City Company's share in selling syndicate, that is, to the securities it actually sold.
c. Conforms to Table 8.1, row 8, col. 4.
d. Conforms to Table 8.1, row 8, col. 3.

don capital market in order to support British government securities and the pound sterling.[19] The French government was itself borrowing abroad early in the decade and later preferred accumulating gold to permitting the export of capital.[20] Thus the task of international lending fell primarily on the United States.

However, the U.S. government wanted no direct role in foreign lending. Although it wanted the loans to be made, it did not want to make them itself. "It is not the policy of our Government," said Secretary of State Charles Evans Hughes, "to make loans to other governments, and the needed capital, if it is to be supplied at all, must be supplied by private organizations."[21] In fact, the U.S. government not only refused to extend aid to Europe but insisted that Allied governments repay the loans extended to them during the war.[22]

But behind the scenes the Harding, Coolidge, and Hoover administrations encouraged Wall Street bankers to float foreign bonds. The three administrations sought to restore a balance of power in Europe and the Far East and to maintain U.S. influence in Latin America. Economic recovery and development were considered necessary means to these political ends, and foreign lending was the essential instrument. The government realized this and sought to direct foreign lending into channels it thought politically desirable.[23]

In 1921 the State Department began to review foreign bond issues prior to their flotation, so that it would "have the opportunity of saying to the underwriters concerned, should it appear advisable to do so, that there is or is not objection to any particular issue."[24] As John Foster Dulles remarked in 1926, "While thus nominally a request, the source from which it emanated was such that the request became in fact a command."[25] The "command" to consult the State Department gave the U.S. government de facto veto power over foreign bond issues in the United States.[26]

Europe. European firms and governments were far and away the largest borrowers underwritten by National City (Table 8.5), even though in the immediate aftermath of war most European countries were hardly attractive to private lenders. The risks were too high. European economies had been battered by war and in some cases dismembered in the peace. Inflation was rampant and output stagnant. Political conditions were unsettled. Without economic stabilization, political disorder seemed likely to persist and the risk of lending to remain prohibitively high. A successful German stabilization was the key to a general European recovery, but France's position on reparations, hardened by U.S. insistence on the payment of war debts, stood in the way. In 1923 French and Belgian troops moved into the Rhineland to collect German reparations by force. The German government tottered and inflation skyrocketed.[27] After a trip to

Table 8.5. Foreign bonds underwritten by National City Company, 1921–1929 (millions of dollars)

Country	Government or government- guaranteed	Private	Total
Europe			
Germany	326	144	470
France	235	40	275
Belgium	220	0	220
Italy	130	26	156
Netherlands	136	10	146
Norway	65	20	85
Sweden	30	50	80
Finland	57	10	67
Austria	55	0	55
Switzerland	50	0	50
Czechoslovakia	48	0	48
Denmark	45	0	45
Greece	17	0	17
Ireland	15	0	15
Total Europe	1,429	300	1,729
Far East			
Japan	252	99	351
Australia	195	0	195
Total Far East	447	99	546
Latin America			
Chile	204	0	204
Argentina	160	0	160
Brazil	142	0	142
Peru	105	0	105
Cuba	59	2	61
Haiti	18	0	18
Dominican Republic	13	0	13
Panama	12	0	12
Uruguay	8	0	8
Total Latin America	721	2	723
Canada	280	505	785
Total all countries	2,877	906	3,783

Source: Same as Table 8.1, cols. 3–5, Foreign bonds.
Note: Figures are par value of bonds.

Europe late in 1922, Charles Mitchell had returned convinced that "international debts, reparations, currency inflations and the absence of equilibrium in budgets are all questions which comprise footballs of politics in every country in Europe; but they are all so interrelated that I would look to see a settlement of one question, and especially that of reparations, have a potent settling influence on all others and quickly bring an unravelling of the snarls."[28] The settlement came not long thereafter, in 1924, in the form of the Dawes Plan for Germany. The plan reduced German reparations and included a $200 million loan from Britain, France, and the United States to the German government. The loan would enable the Reichsbank, the German central bank, to acquire the gold and foreign exchange needed to put the reichsmark back on gold.[29]

The United States government was unwilling to put up the U.S. share of the Dawes loan itself. Instead, it asked J. P. Morgan and Company to assemble a syndicate, which included the National City Company, to underwrite the loan.[30] The success of the issue was far from certain. Germany had just come through ruinous hyperinflation. French troops still occupied the Rhineland, and the Weimar government's ability to command the loyalty and resources of its citizens was in doubt. As National City commented, if underwriting houses "are to act as agents in placing the loan with the American public, they must consider the terms and conditions upon which they will be willing to recommend it as a sound investment to buyers accustomed to look to them for advice."[31]

Indeed, the conditions imposed on the German government by the Dawes loan were strict. The German government consented to the appointment of an agent general for reparations payments, who was given far-reaching supervisory powers over German economic policy. The German government was required to balance its budget, reparations included. The Reichsbank was forbidden to advance funds to the German government and had to keep a minimum reserve of gold and foreign exchange equal to 40 percent of its note issue. The bondholders had a first lien on the revenues of the German State Railway, and interest and amortization on the loan took precedence over the government's other external obligations, including reparations.[32] For the remaining risk, bondholders were compensated with an attractive rate of return—nearly 7.3 percent, about 2 percent higher than the rate of return on bonds of the United Kingdom. With these conditions, the issue was a success. The City Company took a participation of 15 percent, or $16.5 million of the U.S. issue. The company sold bonds totaling $8 million directly to the public.[33]

National City then became particularly active in floating German issues. With the reichsmark back on gold, reparations scaled down, and inflation at an end, the German economy took off. Attractive investment opportunities abounded, and German firms and municipalities turned to the U.S. capital market to finance them. As the German boom gathered momentum, U.S. investors' confidence in Germany rose and there was a ready market for German bonds. In the years 1921–1929 the City Com-

pany managed issues totaling nearly $500 million for eight German bor-
rowers. These borrowers included leading German companies such as
Allgemeine Elektrizitaets Gesellschaft, Rhine Westphalia Electric Power,
Iselder Steel, and the U.S. subsidiary of I. G. Farben. The City Company
was the sole underwriter of most of the bonds these companies issued in
New York and distributed on average 40 percent of the bonds sold. During
the years 1925 to 1929 German bonds were a third of the company's foreign business and contributed 43 percent of its net profits from the underwriting and sale of foreign bonds.[34]

China and Japan. In the Far East, National City faced a situation different
from that in Europe. In the case of China the borrowers were politically
acceptable, but economically weak. In the case of Japan the borrowers
were economically strong, but politically questionable, at least in the eyes
of the U.S. State Department. As the leading United States financial institution in the Far East, the bank and its securities affiliate inevitably became deeply involved in the 1920s in financing the economic development
of the region. In doing so, the bank had to weigh the relative political stability of the area's two major countries, China and Japan. Naturally this
question also concerned the makers of U.S. foreign policy, who wished
United States bankers to adopt policies that would enhance the official
policy of the United States—the maintenance of an independent China.[35]

After World War I the Wilson administration sought to promote Chinese development by sponsoring an international consortium of banks,
including National City, that would raise funds for the Chinese government. But no use was ever made of this consortium, for the Chinese government defaulted on its existing obligations in 1921.[36] Thereafter, U.S.
policy shifted to restricting Japan's use of foreign credit to further its interests in China.

Shortly after the failure of the Chinese consortium the National City
Company turned to financing Japan. In 1921 it entered into negotiations
with the Oriental Development Company for a public bond issue to be
floated in the United States with the guarantee of the Imperial Japanese
government. The Japanese government itself maintained a significant equity interest in the firm, which had been established in 1908 to promote
the colonization of Korea. After initial success in this area the Oriental
Development Company had expanded its activities to Manchuria, Mon-
golia, and other areas of East Asia. The State Department viewed this expansion with alarm; further Japanese encroachment in Manchuria would
jeopardize the Open Door policy. Indeed, Japan might extend its sphere of
influence in China directly through the quasi-governmental Oriental Development Company. Therefore, when the City Company inquired about

the State Department's views concerning the proposed loan, the Department of State replied that the United States did indeed have an objection to the loan. National City dropped the proposed issue.[37]

In December 1922 the City Company again proposed to float a loan for the Oriental Development Company in the United States. Japan had recently bound itself to respect the Open Door in China in the Nine-Power Treaty (February 1922). At the same time it had ceded Shantung to China in a separate treaty. With these assurances, the State Department dropped its initial objection to the loan for the Oriental Development Company, once the Japanese had pledged to use the proceeds of the loan in Japan. In 1923 the City Company therefore syndicated a $19.9 million bond issue (forty million yen) for the Oriental Development Company.[38]

The City Company had less success with another proposal. The City Company had to drop its plans to issue bonds for the South Manchuria Railway, a quasi-governmental Japanese enterprise that was the focal point of Japanese investment in Manchuria, even though the contract contained provisions for partial use of the loan proceeds in the United States. The State Department objected that such a loan would harm American business interests in Manchuria. The objection stood; the City Company did not issue the loan.[39]

In sum, National City's experience in underwriting bonds for various Japanese quasi-governmental agencies illustrates the blend of political and business considerations determining when, for whom, and on what conditions a U.S. house could underwrite bonds for foreign borrowers. Overall, the National City Company originated or participated in eleven issues totaling $350 million for Japanese borrowers in the years 1921 to 1929, a figure larger than that for any other country except Canada and Germany (Table 8.5). Most of the issues aroused no controversy; they were clearly for domestic purposes by domestic borrowers, such as the city of Tokyo and the city of Yokohama. Only when Japanese borrowers intended to use the proceeds to finance colonial expansion did the U.S. State Department raise an objection, and in some cases these were overcome.

Latin America. In contrast to Europe and the Far East, politics played a relatively minor role in determining National City's underwriting activities in Latin America. The U.S. government neither promoted underwriting, as it had for Germany, nor attempted to hinder underwriting, as it had for certain Japanese agencies. Instead, the U.S. government played a passive but nevertheless powerful role. The State Department's review process held a broad umbrella over all foreign bonds. The Monroe Doctrine provided additional protection. Under it, the U.S. government had previously intervened in several Latin American countries to safeguard the bondholdings of U.S. investors. This created the expectation that the United States would act similarly in the future.[40]

Nevertheless, actual underwriting decisions were generally left to the issuers and to the investment-banking houses themselves. That made underwriting largely an economic proposition. Bonds were to be sold based on the underwriter's assessment of the country's ability to repay, a calculation that reflected not only the country's potential for development but also the prospects for the world economy to which the country would sell its exports.

About Latin America's economic potential there was no doubt. The region was rich in natural resources and unharmed by the war in Europe. Indeed, during the war many Latin American countries had amassed significant trade surpluses, strengthening their foreign exchange reserves and positioning themselves for further development. Foreign borrowing was a way to accelerate that process.

Nevertheless, National City Company approached underwriting for Latin American issuers cautiously. From 1921 to 1929 the City Company originated or participated in $723 million in bonds for Latin American issuers, less than 20 percent of its total foreign issues. All but $2 million was government-issued or government-guaranteed. Chile, Argentina, Brazil, and Peru, four of the region's largest economies, were the leading borrowers. The City Company issued relatively few bonds for Cuba ($61 million), even though it had an extensive branch system there.

Canada. In contrast to other foreign bonds underwritten by the National City Company, its Canadian issues were mostly for private corporations. In 1923 the City Company had bought control of the United Financial Corporation of Montreal, one of Canada's largest investment houses, and this acquisition became the vehicle for selling American issues in Canada and of underwriting Canadian issues in New York.[41] From 1921 to 1929 the City Company originated or participated in $785 million in bonds for Canadian issuers. Overall, Canadian issues accounted for 55 percent of the private foreign bonds and about 20 percent of all foreign bonds underwritten by the National City Company in the years 1921–1929 (Table 8.5).

Growth and Profits

The National City Company at the end of the 1920s was reputed to be "the largest agency in the world for the distribution of securities to the public."[42] Its network spread across the country and around the world. In the United States it had offices in over fifty cities. Overseas the company had representatives in the bank's branches, as well as offices of its own in London, Amsterdam, Geneva, Tokyo, Shanghai, and throughout Canada. Linking the U.S. offices was an elaborate private communications system. Over its lines the City Company sent a steady stream of "flashes" to its salesmen in the field, outlining the merits of securities to be sold. Through this system the company conducted a secondary market in bonds, which made the bonds it distributed more liquid and enhanced the company's ability to market an issue. The salesmen, the offices, and the private wire system together spelled placing power.

To support the company's growth, Mitchell and his directors increased its assets and capital. Total assets more than doubled from year-end 1920 to September 1929, rising from $85.4 million to $209.4 million (Table 8.6). Total capital rose even more rapidly, from $15.7 million to $129.5 million. Thus Mitchell significantly reduced the City Company's leverage, in line with his belief that "investment banking earnings are never stable."[43] Although this was certainly true at the City Company, the dominant trend in profits was up. During the years 1926 to 1929 the City Company's profits were on average probably 35 percent as large as the bank's.[44]

Trust Administration

As the market for securities broadened in the 1920s the demand for the services of institutional trustees grew also.[45] Earlier, National City Bank had had close ties of common ownership with the Farmers' Loan and Trust Company, the oldest trust company in the country, and during Moses

Table 8.6. Summary statistics, National City Company, 1920-1929 (millions of dollars)

Date	Assets	Stockholders' equity[a]	Leverage[b]
December 31, 1920	85.4	15.7	5.44
June 30, 1923	75.9	21.8	3.48
November 30, 1925	60.4	33.2	1.82
April 30, 1926	94.4	32.9	2.87
September 30, 1928	139.9	106.1	1.32
September 30, 1929	209.4	129.5	1.62

Source: Comptroller of the Currency, Examination Reports, National City Bank, for dates cited.

a. Capital, surplus, undivided profits, and reserves.

b. Column 2 divided by column 3.

Taylor's regime the two institutions had been run as parts of a single enterprise. James Stillman had continued this arrangement, but after his death in 1918 ownership of both institutions became dispersed, and they went their separate ways. The Farmers' Trust Company began to develop a commercial banking business and, in 1919 after the trust powers of national banks had been clarified by legislation, National City opened its Trust Department.[46]

The bank entered the trust business at an initial disadvantage. In trust administration, much depended on close relationships of long standing with wealthy families and large corporations—the sort of relationships Farmers' Loan and Trust and other established trust companies had built over a long period. The bank accordingly bypassed these traditional markets and directed its efforts in the trust field toward the middle class, a market segment largely neglected by the trust companies. In the 1920s many business executives and professional people were building estates in excess of $50,000, the practical minimum for commercial trust administration.[47] In New York alone, estates valued at $800 million were being filed for probate every year.[48] Increasingly, this wealth was in the form of securities. Professional administration was required in order to preserve the value of an estate during the lengthy process of settlement and later to enhance it for the benefit of the survivors.

National City's Trust Department adopted much the same sales philosophy as the rest of the bank and the City Company in their retail markets. Trust officers tailored their products to suit the customer's needs and then approached him by a combination of advertising and personal solicitation.[49] The department devoted most of its sales efforts to securing appointments as executor and trustee. Its advertisements sought to convince potential customers that they should have a will, in order to protect their heirs from the delays, expense, and extra taxes that would result if the estate was settled by a court-appointed administrator. Prospects were offered an "estate survey" by which they could calculate what their heirs would receive, what taxes would be paid, and the amount of ready cash the executor would need to settle the estate.[50] Advertisements in legal journals offered to help attorneys prepare the "preliminary drafts of any will in which this bank is named executor or trustee," and assured them that "whenever legal services are required in connection with the administration of an estate, it is the policy of the National City Bank of New York to employ the attorney who drew the client's will, and is therefore familiar with his personal affairs."[51] The Trust Department's ads also appealed to life insurance underwriters, promoting the use of life insurance payable to the estate to provide ready cash so that the executor would not have to liquidate estate assets on short notice to pay taxes and expenses.[52]

By virtue of such imaginative marketing, National City's trust business grew rapidly. Assets under trust management increased from $20.9 million in June 1923 to $41 million in April 1926 (Table 8.7). By May 1929, with a boost from the merger with the People's Trust Company, trust assets had grown to $158 million, or about 3 percent of the trust assets of all national banks.[53] The business generated sizable profits. In 1928 the Trust Department earned about 10 percent of the bank's net operating revenue.[54]

Despite this growth, National City still ranked far behind the older, state-chartered trust companies. Merger was the only way to get into the big leagues, and the logical partner was the Farmers' Loan and Trust Company. Like National City, Farmers' Loan and Trust had begun to broaden its customer base and line of services in the 1920s. In 1927 it had introduced a uniform trust. With a minimum investment of $5,000, this trust operated much like a mutual fund. Acknowledged to be the invention of James H. Perkins, the president of Farmers' Loan and Trust, the new instrument certainly fitted into National City's strategy of providing individuals with comprehensive financial service.[55]

From the standpoint of Farmers' Loan and Trust, a merger with National City was attractive, too. Farmers' had been trying to build its commercial banking business but had found it difficult to persuade customers to do their banking with a firm they had always thought of as a trust company.

Table 8.7. Summary statistics, National City Bank Trust Department, 1923–1929 (millions of dollars)

Date	Assets held in trust[a]	Annual earnings
1923	20.9	—
1924	23.2	0.3
1925	23.3	0.3
1926	41.0	0.6
1927	75.0	0.7
1928	81.9	2.4
1929	158.2	1.7[b]

Source: Col. 2: Comptroller of the Currency, Examination Reports, National City Bank, 1923–1929, on various dates in March, April, or June. Col. 3: National City Bank, Report of Earnings and Dividends to the Comptroller of the Currency, 1923–1929.

a. As of examination by comptroller of the currency on various dates in March, April, or June.

b. Six months ending June 30, 1929.

A merger would allow each institution to do what it did best and at the same time gain the benefits of greater size: scale economies, a larger capital base, and more prestige in the marketplace. The merger was announced on April 1, 1929.[56]

To reap the potential benefits of merger, a restructuring of both institutions was necessary. On the one hand, the two firms' trust and commercial banking operations had to be integrated. On the other hand, the combined trust operations needed more autonomy and status within the merged institution than they would have as a department of National City Bank. These considerations underlay Mitchell's decision to make Farmers' Loan and Trust a third corporate affiliate on the same level as the bank and the City Company within the merged institution. Renamed City Bank Farmers Trust Company, the affiliate remained a state-chartered institution and was affiliated with the bank and City Company through the same device of common stock ownership that had been used in 1911 to affiliate the City Company and the bank. Commenting on the arrangement Mitchell said, "Our experience convinced us . . . that the trust business was far too important to be looked upon and operated as a side line of a commercial banking institution and that it could better be administrated by a separate corporate entity devoted exclusively to that field and operated by men of long trust experience."[57]

The merger was accomplished by an exchange of certificates representing shares in all three affiliates for shares in the Farmers' Loan and Trust Company. The bank's trust accounts were transferred to the new affiliate, and Farmers' Loan and Trust's commercial banking accounts were assigned to National City's domestic banking groups. Like the earlier acquisitions of Halsey and the International Banking Corporation, the merger with Farmers' Loan and Trust established National City's position in a rapidly growing field.

The Vision Realized

With the addition of City Bank Farmers Trust to the National City organization, Vanderlip's vision of a global, all-purpose financial intermediary became reality. From offices around the world the institution now provided corporations, households, and governments with commercial banking, investment banking, and trust services. Its annual earnings approximated $30 million. It was without question the world's leading financial intermediary.

Completing this institution was Mitchell's achievement. The organizational structure he created at the time of the merger with Farmers' Loan and Trust tells much about his role (Table 8.8). At each of the affiliates, a capable executive was in charge of day-to-day operations. Gordon S.

Table 8.8. The National City Organization, June 1929

Office	National City Bank	National City Company	City Bank Farmers Trust Company
Chairman	C. E. Mitchell	C. E. Mitchell	C. E. Mitchell
President	G. S. Rentschler	H. B. Baker	J. H. Perkins

Rentschler was president of the bank. Rentschler had become a director of the bank in 1923 after his reorganization of the bank's Cuban sugar properties, and since 1925 he had been groomed for the presidency while serving as Mitchell's assistant. The president of the City Company was Hugh B. Baker, who had directed its sales of new securities since 1919. James H. Perkins became president of the City Bank Farmers Trust Company. He had been president of Farmers' Loan and Trust at the time of the merger. From 1916 to 1919 he had served as an executive manager of National City Bank. Ultimate authority rested with Mitchell, and in the 1929 reorganization he became chairman of each of the three affiliates. Thus the new organization reflected his belief in "the typical U.S. system . . . the concentration of responsibility in the hands of one accountable individual."[58]

Mitchell's task was a large one. Each of National City's affiliates occupied a leading position in its field. In June 1929 National City was the largest bank in the country, with over $2 billion in aggregate resources, and was challenging Britain's Midland Bank for the position of largest bank in the world.[59] The National City Company was the largest distributor of securities in the world and a leading underwriter as well. City Bank Farmers was not the largest, but it was the oldest and one of the most prestigious of the trust companies. The three affiliates were in the business of assuming, and being compensated for taking, three different kinds of financial risk. The bank guaranteed depositors a fixed rate of return on their funds and invested their balances and its own capital in loans and investments. The bank and its shareholders assumed the credit, interest-rate and exchange-rate risks inherent in this transformation. The City Company took underwriting risks; like a retailer, it purchased securities with the expectation of reselling them at a higher price. The Trust Company assumed a fiduciary's risk. It did not own the securities and other investments it administered, but it assumed a trustee's legal responsibility to manage them competently and prudently. Together, the affiliates offered a range of financial services no other institution could match.

Common to the three affiliates was a knowledge of the customer's financial requirements. National City knew the borrower's credit-worthiness and the saver's investment preferences. Doing business separately, each affiliate would have had to acquire this information independently. Grouped in a single enterprise, they could share this basic information, lowering the organization's cost per transaction and enabling it to tailor financial packages to the customer's requirements. That was the rationale underpinning National City's comprehensive strategy. As Mitchell summed it up:

> I think the trend is always toward giving to a clientele a complete banking and investment and trust service. I think that the public are indicating that that is what they want. Now, if those businesses can be done by a single organization it is very much better . . . Unless it is done that way we are constantly going to get the wrong answer for the client on some problem that he brings to us. There is always the time when a commercial banking client has problems that should be solved through application of investment banking practice and principle, and there are times when individuals, and with the corporate customer as well, when their need for fiduciary service is very definite. Those are all functions which the average client likes to conduct under one roof, so to speak, and the profits from which are legitimate to the single institution as an institution.[60]

9.

Into the Abyss
1930-1933

Within four years of the merger with Farmers' Loan and Trust, National City's comprehensive strategy was gone. So were the profits. Both fell victim to the Great Depression. With economic recovery, profits would return. The strategy would not, at least not fully, for government regulation would limit the strategic options available to the bank.

In the years from 1930 to 1933 the well-ordered financial system achieved in the late 1920s fell apart. In the United States an abrupt, massive, and unexpected decline in the money supply induced firms and individuals accustomed to monetary and price stability to slash their spending. From October 1929 to March 1933 the stock of money fell 33 percent, producing disastrous declines in output, prices, and employment. At the trough, the U.S. real gross national product was little more than two-thirds of the peak reached in 1929. By 1933 prices had fallen 25 percent and unemployment had risen to one-fourth of the labor force. Over one-third of the nation's banks failed.[1]

Conditions abroad matched those at home. Monetary contraction and business depression were transmitted from the United States to the rest of the world via the gold standard. International trade shrank, and the gold standard crumbled. Protectionism spread. Debtor countries' export revenues sagged, and the weight of their debt service in real terms increased. Many countries preferred default to the economic sacrifice that would have been required to pay foreign creditors. Exchange controls proliferated.

On National City, the depression had a devastating effect. By the end of 1932 the bank had already written off $86 million in loans, with additional write-offs to come. From year-end 1929 to year-end 1932, its total resources fell from $2.2 billion to $1.6 billion, a decline of 27 percent. In the same period deposits dropped 21 percent, and loans, 50 percent. On the bottom line the ink turned from black to red, from a profit of $22.8 million in 1929 to a loss of $12.6 million in 1932 after write-offs and recoveries. In addition, there was a sharp rise in nonaccrual assets, or bonds and loans that were not performing as stipulated when first issued. Such assets soared from $5.1 million at the end of 1929 to $89.4 million at the end of 1932, a figure equal to 37 percent of the bank's capital (Table 9.1).

The City Company fared worse. Corporations' profits virtually disappeared, and new investment almost ceased.[2] New issues of securities dried up.[3] The business of underwriting and distributing securities practically came to a halt. So did the City Company's underwriting activities. Securities originated by or underwritten with the participation of the City Company plunged from $1.4 billion in 1930 to $350 million in 1932. On its investments in General Sugar and in marketable securities, the company suffered major capital losses. By the end of 1932, its capital had shrunk to $20.8 million from $129.5 million in September 1929 (Table 9.2). Total losses incurred by the company probably exceeded $100 million.[4]

Worst of all fared National City's reputation, and that of commercial banks in general. As the *New Yorker* quipped in 1933, "We regret to announce the loss of a handsome set of iridescent halos. Finder will kindly return to the officers of National City Bank."[5] As the depression deepened, the press increasingly pictured banks as villains rather than victims. Bankers, Charles E. Mitchell foremost among them, were reviled as "banksters." Gradually, Congress also adopted this assessment, laying the foundation for a punitive system of banking regulation enacted in 1933 (see chapter 10).

Table 9.1. Summary statistics, National City Bank, 1929–1932 (millions of dollars)

Year	Assets	Loans	Deposits	Stock-holders' equity[a]	Net profits[b]	Non-accrual assets[c]
1929	2,206.2	1,245.4	1,649.6	264.4	22.8	5.1
1930	1,944.2	1,015.4	1,460.0	247.2	0.5	12.7
1931	1,858.0	913.2	1,418.7	272.6	−7.3	66.8
1932	1,615.3	619.8	1,299.4	242.3	−12.6	89.4

Source: National City Bank, Comptroller's Reports, 1929–1932.

Note: All figures are on a consolidated basis and include the foreign branches. All figures are as of year-end, except for net profits, which are for the calendar year.

a. Capital, surplus, undivided profits, and reserves for dividends, taxes and contingencies.

b. Net operating income minus write-offs plus recoveries.

c. Assets either not accruing interest or not being amortized at originally contracted rates.

Table 9.2. Summary statistics, National City Company, 1929–1932 (millions of dollars)

Year	Assets[a]	Stockholders' equity[a,b]	Securities underwritten[c]
1929	209.4	129.5	1,305
1930	—	—	1,469
1931	33.5	22.0	888
1932	29.9	20.8	351

Source: Comptroller of the Currency, Examination Report, National City Bank, September 30, 1929; *Poor's Bank, Government, and Municipal Volume* (1929–1932) (New York: Poor's Publishing Co., 1930–1933); *American Underwriting Houses and Their Issues* (1929–1932), ed. O. P. Schwarzchild (New York: National Statistical Service, 1930–1933); U.S. Congress, Senate Committee on Finance, *Sale of Foreign Bonds or Securities in the United States: Hearings Pursuant to S. Res. 19*, pt. 1, 72nd Cong., 1st sess., 1931, after p. 162.

a. Figures are for September 30, 1929, and for year-end 1931 and 1932.

b. Capital, surplus, undivided profits, and reserves for dividends, taxes and contingencies.

c. Figures represent the par value of domestic corporate, state and municipal, federal agency and foreign debt securities, as well as the market value of common and preferred stock of domestic and foreign corporations originated by or underwritten with the participation of the National City Company during the calendar year.

Four Crises

In retrospect, the depression looks like one continuous slide, starting in late 1929 and continuing through early 1933. Actually, it developed in stages, with each downward thrust marked by a liquidity crisis that weakened public confidence in the financial system and business confidence in the economy. Each of the crises was severe in itself. Except for the first, each crisis was marked by a banking panic. The cumulative effect was catastrophic, for the economy and for banks. Yet National City survived, in no small measure because of its continuing adherence to the precepts of ready money. In fact, it was even able to take actions and participate in programs designed to alleviate the crises. Tragically, these programs were far less effective in stopping crises than had been the actions of the Clearing House in earlier panics.

The first crisis was the stock market crash of October 1929. Quick action by National City and other New York City banks to supply funds to the call money market with the help of the New York Federal Reserve Bank brought the market slide under control, though not until stocks on the Big Board had lost more than a third of their market value. The second crisis was marked by runs on banks and bank failures all over the country and culminated in the failure of a large New York bank in December 1930. The third crisis was triggered by the fall of sterling from gold in September

1931 and the Federal Reserve's response in raising the discount rate. Another wave of runs and bank failures followed. The fourth and final crisis was also the worst—the 1933 banking panic that ended in the Bank Holiday of March 1933.

These successive crises and the Federal Reserve's failure to counteract them by raising sufficiently the supply of high-powered money (currency in circulation and bank reserves) turned what otherwise would have been a serious recession into the Great Depression. The bank panics progressively undermined confidence in banks, causing people to increase the proportion of money that they sought to hold in the form of currency.[6] Banks lost deposits, and in response they contracted loans and scurried to obtain the liquidity needed for survival. As a result, expenditures for consumption fell and those for investment sagged sharply from the levels achieved in the late 1920s. Unemployment soared, and output and prices plummeted.

There had been bank panics before, but the establishment of the Federal Reserve System was supposed to have made them obsolete (see chapter 4). The Reserve banks had the power to discount eligible paper for member banks or purchase government securities in the open market. This would aid solvent, but temporarily illiquid banks and prevent a fall in the money supply, nipping possible panics in the bud. In 1928 Andrew W. Mellon, treasury secretary and an ex officio member of the Federal Reserve Board, had remarked that thanks to the Federal Reserve, there was no longer "any fear on the part of the banks or the business community that some sudden and temporary business crisis may develop and precipitate a financial panic such as visited the country in former years . . . We are no longer the victims of the vagaries of business cycles. The Federal Reserve System is the antidote for money contraction and credit shortage."[7]

Mellon was mistaken. In the following years the opposite would be closer to the truth.

The First Crisis

In October 1929 the stock market collapsed, and the sudden slide in securities prices threatened to disrupt the money market. At noon on Thursday, October 24, with panic gathering momentum, Mitchell joined a small number of New York's leading bankers at the offices of J. P. Morgan, across the street from the stock exchange. The bankers formed a pool to buttress stock prices and dispatched Richard Whitney, the Morgan broker, to the floor of the exchange to buy large blocks of key issues, such as U.S. Steel. When Black Thursday ended, more than thirteen million shares had changed hands, but the panic seemed to be over.[8]

It was not. The market rallied on October 25, but on Monday, October 28, it opened lower and kept on drifting down. At 4:30 that afternoon the bankers met again. It was clear they could not halt the market slide. The best they could do was keep panic from spreading to the money market by taking over brokers' loans they had placed for the account of customers who were now calling their loans. This would enable brokers to hold securities. If not forced to dump their holdings, brokers could remain solvent. So would their banks. This program required the support of the Federal Reserve Bank of New York. If the banks were to take over the loans placed for their customers, they needed assurance that the Federal Reserve would discount freely or provide reserves to the banks through open market operations. As he had in March 1929, Governor George L. Harrison of the New York Reserve Bank let it be known that he would do so.[9]

It was a remarkably effective exercise in crisis management. Together the New York banks and the Federal Reserve had prevented a bad situation from getting much worse. Although the banks and the Federal Reserve could not prevent the steep fall of stock prices, they did enable brokers to hold securities for a time rather than dump them on the market all at once. If the latter had been allowed to happen, it would have accelerated the downward spiral in securities prices, bankrupted brokers wholesale, forced some banks to close their doors, and in all probability brought on a run on banks generally.[10]

National City suffered significant losses in the market collapse, the most important of which was the failure of an intended merger with the Corn Exchange Bank and Trust Company. The Corn Exchange was an attractive merger partner because of its large local branch system. On September 19, 1929, when the intended merger was announced, Corn Exchange had sixty-seven branches. They largely complemented National City's. The Corn Exchange had an extensive network in Queens and the Bronx, two boroughs where National City had just started to branch. Together the two systems would have led by a large margin in local banking.[11]

Another aspect of the merger appealed to Mitchell as well. As the *New York Times* noted in a September 21, 1929, editorial,

> The merger of the National City and Corn Exchange banks undoubtedly interests most people chiefly as giving America, for the first time, the largest bank in the world. In a way, it had been a matter of mortification that, with the post-war United States outstripping Great Britain in the field not only of industry but of home and international finance, London should still possess the premier institution, measured by total banking resources. With this new merger at New York, $2,386,000,000 resources pass un-

der a single management, as compared with $2,303,000,000 shown in its last report by the Midland Bank of London.[12]

To the Corn Exchange, the merger was also attractive. During the 1920s its growth had been sluggish; from 1922 to 1928, deposits had grown only 4 percent a year.[13] By merging, the Corn Exchange would have the benefit of National City's larger capital base and lending limit, its worldwide branch network, and its rapidly growing Personal Credit Department.

Under the agreement of merger, Corn Exchange shareholders were to receive either 0.8 shares of National City stock or $360 in cash for each of their Corn Exchange shares, so that as long as National City stock sold at more than $450 per share, the merger would be effected by an exchange of shares.[14] At less than $450 Corn Exchange shareholders would have found it profitable to take the cash option. When the agreement was signed, National City stock was quoted at $492.[15] As the stock price fell, Mitchell acted "to keep the market from collapsing where it would be destructive to the interests of our shareholders."[16] In an effort to save the merger, Mitchell borrowed $12 million from J. P. Morgan on the security of his own holdings of National City stock, in order to support the price. But no man could stand against the market. On November 7, 1929, as the stockholders of the two institutions met to vote on the merger, the bank's stock stood at $295. Naturally enough, the Corn Exchange shareholders voted overwhelmingly for the merger, which promised them an immediate payment of $360 for Corn Exchange stock, then selling in the market at less than $200. But the National City shareholders, at Mitchell's recommendation, rejected the merger.[17]

In the supercharged atmosphere that followed the stock market crash, the failure of the merger gave rise to worries about the condition of National City Bank. The governor of the Bank of England, Montagu Norman, cabled Harrison at the New York Reserve Bank to ask if the failure of the merger had caused uneasiness and distrust that might precipitate a run on banks.[18] The Federal Reserve Board shared Norman's concern and ordered a special examination of National City Bank.[19] Governor R. A. Young of the board thought that "Mitchell had his back up against the wall, the most discredited man in New York," but the examination showed the bank to be "in first class condition."[20]

Indeed it was. Despite the failure of the Corn Exchange merger, National City ended 1929 as the largest bank in the world.[21] Its aggregate resources of $2.2 billion exceeded those of London's Midland Bank, and its capital position was stronger than at any other time since Mitchell had taken over. Liquidity was high, too. During 1929 the bank's holdings of cash, government securities, and other liquid assets in New York had averaged 63 percent of its net domestic deposits.[22] Despite the crash, profits were running at a record pace.

The Second Crisis

As 1930 opened, Mitchell thought the worst was over. He commented to the shareholders in January 1930, "A general feeling of confidence exists throughout the country . . . [It] does not appear probable that business will remain below the normal stage of activity for any protracted period."[23] History seemed to be on Mitchell's side. Since the turn of the century, business contractions had been short. Even the deep recessions of 1907 and 1920–1921 had been quickly followed by strong recoveries.

In the first months of 1930 confidence seemed justified. The City Company's business picked up once again as corporations and foreign governments raised funds to finance new investment or to refund maturing issues. The Trust Company began to market its uniform trust, a commingled investment account that approximated a mutual fund and appealed to smaller investors (see chapter 8). At the bank, plans were laid to expand overseas and to open additional local branches in place of those the bank had hoped to acquire by merger. Mitchell could accept calmly Chase's merger with the Equitable Trust Company in March 1930, which made Chase the largest bank in the world.[24]

But the recovery aborted. Instead of "forcing funds" on the banks through open market purchases, the Federal Reserve waited for banks to come to the discount window to borrow. They were reluctant to do so, since the market rate of interest was significantly below the discount rate. Moreover, the Federal Reserve did little to publicize that it had reversed the policy of "direct pressure" in effect since 1928. As a result of this passive policy the stock of high-powered money fell, and the rate of growth of the money supply declined.[25] The combined effect of a declining money stock and the blow to confidence administered by the crash caused spending, incomes, and prices to fall. Industrial production, which had seemed to stabilize in the first few months of 1930, fell in June and continued to fall steeply for the rest of the year.

At home and abroad, National City's loan losses mounted. In Cuba alone the bank lost $9 million in 1930 as the price of sugar fell. The bank's management concentrated on liquidity. In 1929 the ratio of liquid assets to net deposits had averaged 63 percent and never fell below 59 percent in any month. In 1930 these ratios rose to 67 percent and 63 percent, respectively.[26] "In such times as these," said Mitchell in January 1931, "a high degree of liquidity has been considered of far more importance than large earnings."[27]

In December 1930, another blow fell. For several months, the Bank of United States, a large, poorly managed New York bank with 440,000 depositors, had been in trouble—in fact, insolvent.[28] National City executives had been working with other Clearing House banks and the Federal Reserve on a plan to rescue the bank by merging it with three other banks. National City and other Clearing House banks stood ready to subscribe to $30 million of capital in the new institution to facilitate the rescue. But the prospective partners could not agree on the terms of the merger.[29] The question was then whether the bank should be allowed to fail. No Clearing House bank was willing to take it over. The Bank of United States was a member of the Federal Reserve System, but the Federal Reserve's discount window was not open to an insolvent bank.[30]

On December 11, 1930, the bank closed its doors for the last time. Clearing House members created a fund so that depositors could immediately withdraw 50 percent of their funds.[31] National City Bank was appointed liquidator, and depositors eventually got over 80 percent of their money back.[32] But the damage had been done. Allowing the Bank of United States to fail was, as Joseph Broderick, New York superintendent of banks, had predicted before the failure, "the most colossal mistake in the banking history of New York."[33] Because of the bank's apparently official name, its large size, and its Federal Reserve membership, the failure had a devastating effect on the public's confidence in banks.[34] For the first time since the onset of the depression, the public began to shift significant sums from deposits into currency. This added to the decline in the money supply and deepened the slide in income and employment.[35]

The contrast with 1907 was marked. Then, the large Wall Street banks had stopped the panic by issuing Clearing House certificates and suspending the convertibility of deposits into currency at par. This increased the effective supply of bank reserves and reduced the public's demand for currency, bringing the panic to a halt (see chapter 3). In 1930 this solution was out of the question. The existence of the Federal Reserve made it impossible for the New York banks to resort to these traditional and effective measures of panic control without appearing to challenge the central bank's authority.[36] Yet the spectacle of a major bank being allowed to fail would not soon be forgotten. In the public's view, Wall Street banks and the Federal Reserve had had the opportunity to save the institution's depositors, but had chosen not to do so.

Even worse in the public's mind were the practices that had been allowed to take place at the Bank of United States. As the *New York World Telegram* noted editorially, "The bank officers, taking the name of the nation for the institution, obtaining the right to do so through political influence and buying up bank after bank as they would so many drug stores until they owned fifty-nine branches, seemingly looked upon the undertaking as a private speculative venture, as a sort of racket."[37] For Wall Street, it would be all downhill from here.

The Third Crisis

In May 1931 the third crisis began. Austria's largest bank, the Credit-Anstalt für Handel und Gewerbe, failed. So did the attempts of major central banks to confine the crisis to Austria. Panic spread from Austria to Germany, to the United Kingdom, and then to the United States. By September 1931 the international gold standard, so laboriously restored during the 1920s, lay in shambles. So did the world economy.

For this sorry turn of events three factors were responsible: deflationary policies in the United States and France, the determination of central bankers despite deflation to maintain the gold standard, and their unwillingness or inability to commit sufficient resources to achieve the purpose. The passage of the highly protectionist Smoot-Hawley Tariff Act by the United States Congress in June 1930 aggravated the situation, for it provoked retaliatory tariff hikes by other nations, further disrupting the international economy. The expedient adopted to defuse the May 1931 crisis, the standstill agreement, actually made matters worse, for it froze creditors' assets, transferring the liquidity crisis from the borrower to the lender.[38]

The Austrian crisis began on May 11, 1931, when the Credit-Anstalt announced that it had incurred heavy losses. Although the Austrian National Bank came to the Credit-Anstalt's aid, it soon became apparent that only a large infusion of foreign credit from London, New York, or Paris could keep the Austrian schilling on the gold standard. If the schilling fell, the reichsmark and possibly the pound would be in serious trouble. The Bank of England extended a credit to the Austrian National Bank, and National City and other leading U.S. and European banks agreed to "stand still," that is, to roll over their Austrian credits at maturity. It was not enough.[39]

The crisis spread to Germany.[40] Foreigners, fearing that the reichsmark would go off gold or that German banks would fail, withdrew funds from Germany. The Reichsbank's reserves of gold and foreign exchange dwindled; by mid-June 1931 they had fallen below the legal minimum of 40 percent of the note issue. As the crisis intensified, the United States intervened. On June 20, President Herbert Hoover proposed a one-year postponement of both interest and principal payments on intergovernmental obligations, including both war debts and reparations. Although a step in the right direction, the Hoover moratorium could not solve the fundamental problem facing Germany: a lack of foreign exchange reserves. Massive foreign assistance would be required to keep the reichsmark on gold. It was not forthcoming.

The efforts that were undertaken were too little and too late. On June 25, under the auspices of the newly created Bank for International Settlements (BIS), the central banks of France and England, together with the Federal Reserve Bank of New York, lent $100 million to the German Reichsbank for a period of three weeks.[41] Although this loan was renewed, it was not increased. At the beginning of July, in another rescue effort, the Federal Reserve Bank of New York set up a committee to persuade leading U.S. commercial banks to renew their short-term credits to Germany. Mitchell joined the committee, for he recognized the danger to the world financial system and to the National City organization posed by the German crisis.

The committee succeeded in its immediate aim. Leading U.S. banks, including National City, agreed to renew their short-term credits to Germany as they matured.[42] This was later formalized into a standstill agreement. In the case of acceptances, the principal form of short-term credit to Germany, National City, along with other leading banks, agreed to pay the holder of the acceptance at maturity without demanding payment from the German borrower, who would in effect receive an unsecured loan from National City or another U.S. bank for the amount due. But it was not enough; the Reichsbank continued to lose reserves. On July 13, 1931, the Darmstädter und Nationalbank failed, and Germany abandoned the gold standard de facto. All commercial banks in Germany were subsequently ordered closed for two days, and the first of a long series of exchange controls was put in place.

Consequently, $57 million of National City Bank's assets—mostly short-term credits but some bonds as well—were frozen, immobilized by German exchange controls.[43] Although German borrowers were solvent and able to pay in reichsmarks, they could not obtain foreign exchange to pay the bank. The German financial crisis had other repercussions for National City. At the end of July 1931, Chile defaulted on its foreign debt; a precipitating cause was Germany's imposition of a 120 percent duty on nitrates, one of Chile's principal exports. National City Bank was left with $20 million of practically worthless Chilean assets, an amount equal to nearly 10 percent of its capital.[44]

Germany's departure from the gold standard led to heavy speculative pressure on sterling, and in September 1931 the pound also went off gold. Market pressure then shifted to the dollar. Within a few months the Federal Reserve lost 10 percent of its stock of gold. To stem the pressure on the dollar, the Federal Reserve Board raised discount rates sharply. Bond prices sagged, further weakening the position of the nation's banks. Banks suspected of being weak lost deposits rapidly. Another U.S. banking panic soon developed.[45]

Merger with the Bank of America. One of the weak banks was the Bank of America, an old New York bank that had received its charter in May 1812, just a few weeks before City Bank. In 1928 the Bank of America had been acquired by the Transamerica Corporation, the bank holding company founded by A. P. Giannini as a vehicle for nationwide branch banking. Giannini had merged his other banking interests in New York with the Bank of America, giving it a network of thirty-two branches in New York City.[46]

For some time, the New York-based Bank of America had been a troubled bank. It had suffered losses in Cuba and South America during the 1920–1921 recession, from which it never fully recovered. To these were added the problems of the depression. Between June 1930 and September 1931, the bank had lost 50 percent of its deposits, compared to an 8 percent decline at National City and a 12 percent decline on average at all Federal Reserve member banks.[47]

Again, a large Federal Reserve member bank in New York with a seemingly official name was on the brink of failure. But this time National City Bank stepped into the breach. A hastily concluded merger agreement with the Bank of America was announced on October 1, 1931. The announcement "was greeted by Wall Street as one of the first major constructive steps in months of cautious dealings and depressing developments."[48]

The addition of the Bank of America's local branches made National City's network the largest in New York. The merger also made Transamerica the largest single shareholder in the National City organization, with 8.7 percent of the outstanding shares. But the merger agreement provided that Transamerica would reduce its holdings in National City "in a constructive and gradual manner" and that it would not "seek to influence the policies and management of National City Bank."[49] Later, Giannini would have second thoughts. He would demand and receive representation on National City's board of directors.

The National Credit Corporation. The Bank of America was by no means the only bank in trouble in 1931. The crisis had pushed weak banks further toward insolvency. To meet depositors' withdrawals they had sold their high-grade securities and were holding illiquid loans and lower-grade securities that were ineligible for rediscount at the Federal Reserve. Bank examiners made matters worse by adopting rules for valuing securities that helped relatively healthy banks but forced the weakest banks to reveal to the public just how weak they were.[50]

In contrast, National City and other large banks had strengthened their liquidity as the depression deepened. They had large holdings of cash and assets eligible for rediscount at the Federal Reserve. To some officials this seemed overly cautious. Owen D. Young, chairman of the board of General Electric and a director of the Federal Reserve Bank of New York, commented that "if the rest of the country looks to New York [banks] for leadership in recovery . . . we shall not get anywhere, and banks will become no more than safe deposit boxes."[51]

President Hoover agreed with this view. So did Eugene Meyer, the head of the Federal Reserve Board. Both believed that a lack of credit was the cause of the continuing depression. They contended that business would increase output if it could obtain credit. But those who would lend lacked the reserves to do so. Depositors' withdrawals had depleted their reserves. To Hoover and Meyer, it appeared that if some way could be found to transfer reserves from strong to weak banks, the public's confidence in the banking system would be restored, business could once again obtain credit, and production would expand.[52]

On October 4, 1931, President Hoover outlined a proposal along those lines to Mitchell and other leading New York bankers at the home of Treasury Secretary Andrew Mellon. Hoover suggested forming the National Credit Corporation that would make loans to banks throughout the country secured by whatever assets they might have, whether or not they were eligible for rediscount at the Federal Reserve. The corporation would be entirely private, without government funds or control. Commercial banks would subscribe to its capital in proportion to their net deposits.

Like other New York bankers, Mitchell was skeptical that the proposal would do much good, but ultimately he supported it. In particular, he did not accept the view that banks were holding back the recovery through an excess of caution in lending. To his way of thinking, "the banks, individually, were trying to maintain liquidity and . . . they would not lend nor invest freely, either at home or abroad, even though the Federal Reserve promised to bail them out if the necessity arose."[53] Instead, Mitchell thought that "fear is the dominant difficulty and the essential thing is to find something which will destroy fear." He doubted that the National Credit Corporation was the tool for the job, for it lacked government participation.[54] Indeed, he thought the proposal might actually "increase nervousness by bringing the public to the realization that the banking situation is such as to call for unusual action."[55] Nor could he see the benefit of strong banks sacrificing their liquidity with no assurance of a successful result.

Nevertheless, after the meeting with Hoover, Mitchell delegated Rentschler to participate in organizing the new corporation, and in early November National City subscribed to $20 million of the capital notes of the new National Credit Corporation.[56] The plan met with a poor reception in the rest of the country, and was replaced in January 1932 by the government-owned Reconstruction Finance Corporation (RFC).[57]

Although Mitchell hoped that the RFC would succeed where the National Credit Corporation had failed, prudence dictated that National City rebuild its own liquidity. By the end of 1931, the depression had taken a heavy toll on National City and participation in various rescue efforts had contributed to it. In 1930 and 1931 it had written off $51 million in losses net of recoveries. The crisis of 1931 had reduced the bank's liquidity. By the end of September 1931, the proportion of net domestic deposits invested in cash and paper eligible for rediscount at the Federal Reserve had dropped below 40 percent, in contrast with the 50 percent average in 1930. The loan portfolio, too, was less liquid. Many short-term credits had been transformed involuntarily into long-term loans—the German credits, for example. There was also $80 million of "bridge" financing extended to certain City Company customers in late 1930 and early 1931. At the time, the bond market was expected to revive, so that borrowers could repay the bank from the proceeds of bonds to be issued through the City Company. But the bond market did not revive and the loans remained on the bank's books.[58]

With the economy showing no sign of improvement and the Bank of America to be absorbed, rebuilding the bank's liquidity had to be given priority. Everything else was secondary to this requirement. Expansion plans were shelved. All through the year 1932, management used every means to build liquidity. Abroad the branches restricted operations to short-term self-liquidating loans and accumulated cash reserves. By the end of 1932 cash reserves amounted to one-third of the foreign branches' deposits. In New York the bank was on a parallel course. By the end of 1932 the proportion of net domestic deposits invested in cash and paper eligible for rediscount at the Federal Reserve had risen above 60 percent, a ratio that prompted *Time* to call National City's balance sheet "the envy of every bank in the United States."[59] Liquidity again seemed adequate, particularly since Mitchell felt that thanks to the actions of the Federal Reserve and the RFC, "the panic has been overcome."[60]

The Fourth Crisis

He was mistaken. In the coming weeks National City would need every bit of liquidity it could command. Even as Mitchell spoke, the RFC's ability to help banks was being undermined and another banking panic was in the making. In July 1932, John N. Garner, Speaker of the House and the Democratic nominee for vice president, had ordered the clerk of the House to make public the reports of the RFC regarding its subsequent loans to banks. Since depositors regarded a loan from the RFC as a sign of a bank's weakness, this action made banks that needed help reluctant to go to the RFC lest they spark a run by their depositors. On January 6,

1933, in the interval between the 1932 election and Roosevelt's inauguration in March 1933, the House passed a resolution at Garner's insistence
requiring the RFC to publish the names of banks to which it had extended
credit prior to July 1932.[61] Garner's action baffled his contemporaries, for
he had ignored protests from banking organizations and supervisory authorities that publishing the banks' names would undermine confidence.[62]
Arthur A. Ballantine, under secretary of the treasury in the Hoover administration and in the first few months of Roosevelt's, feared publication
would lead to increased pressure on the banks.[63] Raymond Moley, a member of Roosevelt's original brain trust, termed Garner's forcing publication
an act of "irresponsible demagoguery."[64]

When the names were published, runs followed, as predicted. They
spread rapidly from state to state. Rather than let their banks fail, the governors of Iowa, Louisiana, and Michigan declared banking holidays,
which made it impossible to convert deposits into currency. This aggravated the panic in other states as depositors rushed to convert their balances into currency before a holiday could be declared. Pressure on National City increased as correspondent banks pulled out their balances to
meet their depositors' withdrawals. In the first three weeks of February
1933, such balances fell by $68 million, or 33 percent. National City's total
domestic deposits declined in the same period by 12.5 percent, and its liquidity ratio (cash and paper eligible for rediscount at the Federal Reserve
relative to net domestic deposits) was slashed back to 50 percent.[65] The
nation's banking system was collapsing, and National City was struggling
to avoid being dragged down with it.

Wall Street on Trial

As crisis followed crisis and the depression deepened, the public mood
darkened. Shock and dismay gave way to anger and bitterness and a need
to assign blame. Wall Street bankers became the object of the public's
mounting wrath.

The conventional wisdom of the day, which bankers shared, espoused a
credit theory of the business cycle. National City summarized it in April
1929.

> As finance is but the handmaiden of industry, it follows that the
> test of normalcy in the rate of credit expansion is the relationship
> which it bears to the rate of growth of industry and trade. If the
> rate of credit increase falls below the rate of business growth, we
> have a condition wherein business is starved, progress is retarded,
> and production and distribution fall into a decline. Conversely,
> if the rate of credit increase rises above the rate of business

growth, we have a condition of inflation which manifests itself in rising prices in some departments of the business structure, over-confidence, excessive speculation, and an eventual crash.[66]

The doctrine made banks seem the autonomous engines of the credit cycle. As the editors of the *Saturday Evening Post* had written in a laudatory article published in December 1928, bankers are the "stewards of the whole intricate credit system."[67] Such were the economic theory and morality in whose terms Wall Street was now to be tried in Congress and in the court of public opinion.

Establishment of the RFC early in 1932 helped bring these ideas into focus. Business appeared to be languishing for lack of credit. Bankers' request for a new government body to help out the banks and the bond market was seen as an admission that they had failed to discharge their own responsibility. Big city bankers were too timid to lend and were trying to get the federal government to do their job. Along with the criticism of banks' failure to lend went another charge that cut deeper: Banks had lent too much in the 1920s, and this overextension of credit and the resulting speculation were the root cause of the Great Depression.

In this damaging charge there was more than an echo of the venerable real bills doctrine on which bankers had been nurtured and which underlay the Federal Reserve Act. According to this doctrine, economic stability depended on banks' restricting their investments to short-term self-liquidating loans. Banks had violated this rule in the 1920s by investing heavily in loans on securities. Such "speculation" had led to the stock market crash. Moreover, large banks had promoted speculation by selling securities through their securities affiliates and by placing call money in the stock market for the account of their customers. Speculation, then, caused the depression, and bankers had been responsible for speculation. So read the indictment as it unfolded in 1931 and 1932 in the course of a series of congressional investigations. That the doctrine underlying the indictment was false, and had been shown to be false as early as 1803, mattered not one whit.[68] That the Federal Reserve, in adhering to the real bills doctrine, had inadvertently caused the depression (see above) occurred to practically no one.

As congressional committees probed the activities of banks, Mitchell, as the head of the country's second largest bank and largest security affiliate, traveled frequently to Washington to testify. At first he appeared as an expert witness; congressmen sought his opinion on the depression and possible remedies. As the public mood soured, Mitchell found himself increasingly in the role of defendant. It did not help his case that his explanation of the depression and that of his Wall Street colleagues had much in common with that of his accusers.

In December 1931 Mitchell appeared before the Senate Committee on Manufactures to testify on a bill to establish a national economic council. In response to Chairman Robert La Follette's questions, he outlined his theory of the depression and the role played by the nation's banks.

> *The Chairman.* Will you outline for the committee what you consider to be the major factors that caused the present depression?
>
> *Mr. Mitchell.* Essentially, one factor—the war. The situation as it exists today is a backwash of the war and all that it brought about in the way of inflation—inflation both in the volume of production and in the price level. It caused a great flow of gold to this country which became the basis of a great overexpansion in real estate and the stock market. The ultimate collapse of this inflation and the progress of deflation are primarily responsible for the condition of world-wide economic disorder which exists today.
>
> *The Chairman.* Do you think that any of the factors which caused or aggravated this situation in the period following the war could have been subjected to any sort of control which would have mitigated or lessened the severity of the depression?
>
> *Mr. Mitchell.* As we look back upon it now, I should say yes; but the afterlook is so much better than the forward look that it is really unfair to criticize too severely. All the activities of production and distribution, banking, investment banking, consumer buying, went on without perhaps as heavy curbs as might have been put upon them. A reaction could not have been averted, in my mind, but its severity could have been lessened.
>
> *The Chairman.* As we look back on the situation, was the credit policy of the American banking system too liberal during the period from 1923, say, to 1928 and 1929?
>
> *Mr. Mitchell.* When you speak of the banking system, have you in mind the central banking system or banks as a whole throughout the United States?
>
> *The Chairman.* I should like your opinion concerning the banks as a whole.
>
> *Mr. Mitchell.* Again looking backward, their policy was undoubtedly too liberal. They were too ready to loan, too ready to meet the competition of neighbors, too willing to cut down their margins to a point of encouraging excessive borrowing. They were at fault with others; yes.[69]

Mitchell pointed out that bankers had been aware of speculation at the time but that "they were foiled in their attempts to stop it."[70] In particular, he deplored the practice of brokers' loans for the account of others, repeating the statements he made in the late 1920s that individuals and corporations "ran around the banks."[71] National City was forced by competitive pressures to join this trend or face the loss of its business.

Regarding the role of investment banking, Mitchell was equally forthright.

> *The Chairman.* Do you think the policy of investment banking institutions had any bearing on the encouragement of, or in producing, the condition of excessive speculation prior to the depression?
>
> *Mr. Mitchell.* Unquestionably; yes. It was part of the machine that developed inflation. It came about in part by reason of the demands of corporations seeing the possibility of changing their capital structure to their advantage. It came about in part by reason of the public's interest in and fever and fervor for investments and speculation, if you will. It came about as a result of the demands of foreign countries for funds, and an obvious appetite on the part of the American public for investments therein. The investment banking community became one of the tools by which the demands on each side operated to satisfy their requirements.[72]

Foreign Bond Investigation

As part of the investigation into the causes of the depression, the Senate Finance Committee had been looking into the sale of foreign bonds by the National City Company and other investment banks during the 1920s. Many of these bonds were now in default. In March 1932, in a speech summarizing the results of the investigation, Senator Hiram Johnson added a new, damaging count to the indictment: Bankers had not only been guilty of speculation and poor judgment but also of conscious wrongdoing. The committee's conclusion was that the default of foreign governments on bonds sold to the American public had worsened the depression and that the bonds had been sold by men who knew they were unlikely to be repaid.

The charge leveled against Mitchell and other bankers was fraud on a massive scale. According to Congress the bankers knew, or should have known, at the time of the original underwriting that these securities were unsound, that is, certain to default. As Senator Hiram Johnson put it, the investment bankers had abused the public's "childlike confidence" in selling them foreign securities.[73]

Specifically, Congress pointed to the National City Company's participation in two bond issues for the Peruvian government originated by J. and W. Seligman and Company in 1927 and 1928. Although these bonds amounted to only 2 percent of the total underwriting commitments for foreign bonds made by the National City Company in the years 1921–1929, and although these bonds had the worst price record of any foreign bond underwritten by the City Company, Congress and later historians viewed the company's involvement in the underwriting and distribution of these Peruvian bonds as characteristic of the City Company's investment-banking activities. They ignored those foreign bonds that appreciated in price or were redeemed at or above par during the depression. The critics cited the Peruvian case as proof that the National City Company hoodwinked investors into buying worthless securities. They alleged that the National City Company either knew or should have known that Peru would default and that investors therefore bought the bonds at prices far in excess of their intrinsic worth.[74] Yet it was impossible for the City Company, or anyone else, to have known with certainty in 1927 and 1928 that Peru would default. Nor could the City Company have known with certainty in 1927 and 1928 that Peru would not default. All that anyone in 1927 or 1928 could have was an opinion.

In fact, there existed a wide range of opinions in 1927 and 1928 concerning the credit-worthiness of Peru and the riskiness of its bonds. In making their allegations of wrongdoing against the National City Company, the investigators of the Senate Finance and Banking committees alluded to statements by various officials, including some in the employ of National City Bank or the City Company itself, that Peru was too poor a credit risk to justify putting the National City Company "seal of approval" on its bonds. But when Congress conducted its investigation, it knew which bonds had gone into default and which had not. With the benefit of hindsight, Congress found pessimistic opinions on Peru to be more authoritative than they actually were at the time that they were written.

Moreover, the Senate completely ignored more favorable assessments of Peru's condition. For example, it ignored the fact that in 1927 Moody's, an independent rating service, graded Peru's bonds A, "still good, but further down the investment scale" from Aaa and Aa bonds.[75] In November 1929 Moody's downgraded the bonds one notch to Baa, the lowest 'investment' grade, with the comment, "granted strict budgetary control and an efficient Comptroller's department, the debt of the Republic should be adequately protected."[76] This too the Senate ignored. Similarly, the Senate passed over a statement by E. L. Kemmerer, a Princeton University economist who undertook a special mission to Peru in 1930; Kemmerer held that Peru could still service its debt if policy adjustments were made.[77]

This diversity of opinion is characteristic of any well-functioning financial market. Some investors think the bond is overpriced, that it offers too low a return to compensate them for the risk that the borrower will default. These investors will therefore not hold the bond. Other investors think the bond is underpriced, that it offers a rate of return that more than compensates them for the risk that the borrower will default. They will tend to hold the bond. In the market the price of the bond will rise or fall until the total issue is distributed among investors who feel that the bond is either underpriced or correctly priced relative to the risk that the borrower will default. Thus the price of the bond or the prospective return offered to investors will reflect the range of opinion regarding the creditworthiness of the borrower.

In underwriting a new issue the investment house must take the market into account and exercise its own judgment on the quality of the securities that it recommends to its clients. As an intermediary between the borrower and the investor, the underwriter prices a new issue at a level that will produce an acceptably low cost of funds for the borrower and an appropriately high prospective rate of return to the investor, that is, at a price that will compensate him for the risk that the borrower may default.

For a firm like the National City Company, an established firm with a reputation to protect, there was little or no incentive to sell deliberately overpriced securities. The inevitable decline in the market price of such securities would damage the underwriter's credibility with investors, making it more difficult for the underwriter to sell securities in the future. Thus the underwriter intending to build business would carefully consider the risk of the securities it offered the public to ensure that its offerings were fairly priced.[78]

During the 1920s the National City Company exercised precisely this care in selecting issues for sale to the public. It zealously guarded its reputation (see chapter 8) and openly stated in its advertisements that it "buys and offers to investors only such securities as it can recommend after thorough investigation."[79] Practically all securities underwritten by the company received an investment-grade rating. Foreign bonds were no exception. Moreover, except for Canadian issues, the vast majority of the foreign bonds underwritten by the National City Company were either government obligations or government-guaranteed (see Table 8.5). This was done to limit risk, for the City Company thought that "a borrowing country must at all costs keep good its foreign credit, on which its commercial life depends."[80]

In the case of Peru, National City Company exercised particular care. Although President Leguia of Peru had offered the National City Company the opportunity to become the nation's investment banker and financial adviser after the opening of the Lima branch of National City Bank in 1919, the City Company passed up several opportunities in the early 1920s to float bond issues for Peru in the United States, since it was not confident that the bonds would be repaid. But during the mid-1920s the Peruvian economy improved. Exports increased, as did investment by

U.S. and British companies to develop the country's copper and petroleum resources. The government brought its current budget nearly into balance and was borrowing primarily to finance capital expenditures. The central bank had curtailed its note issue and, with the encouragement of the Federal Reserve, was trying to stabilize the exchange rate and to build its foreign exchange reserves preparatory to a return of the gold exchange standard. The political atmosphere was also favorable. The Coolidge administration considered Peru a good friend of the United States, as did President-elect Hoover, who praised Leguia for his pro-American policies during a visit to Peru in 1928.[81]

As Peru's economy improved, the City Company's representative in Lima, C. W. Calvin, began to revise his pessimistic assessments of the country's future. In December 1925 Calvin commented, "The general situation of the Peruvian government has improved during the past two years to the extent that I feel renewed consideration should be given to the advisability of the National City organization interesting itself in Peruvian financing." Calvin concluded that "a Peruvian Government bond would offer no greater, if as much, risk as that involved in other issues which have been floated by the National City Co."[82]

In 1927 the City Company adopted Calvin's view, agreeing to participate in a bond issue for the Peruvian government originated by J. and W. Seligman and Company. According to later testimony by Victor Schoepperle, a City Company vice president, the City Company based its decision on President Leguia's progress in stabilizing the economy and on his desire to restructure the country's external debt. Almost two-thirds of the 1928 bond issue was used to retire existing debt. As a result, the country's debt service was considerably reduced as a proportion of outstanding debt. In the loan agreement, the Peruvian government consented to a reduction in its public works program. To oversee this agreement the fiscal agents of the issuers (Seligman and National City Bank) named a representative to serve as a director of Peru's central bank and of the Caja, a corporation that administered the government's receipts. According to the loan agreement the Caja would first pay interest and amortization on the foreign loans before turning over the remainder to the government for other expenditures.

Despite these safeguards, there remained some probability that Peru would default. The country was still developing. It was dependent on the export of only four commodities (copper, petroleum, sugar, and cotton) for about 85 percent of its foreign exchange earnings and a significant portion of its tax revenues. Its program of public works contained some uneconomic projects, such as road building in sparsely populated regions. It also had a significant amount of external debt already outstanding, and its service of its foreign debt had been spotty up to January 1924, when it had regularized its payments to foreign creditors.[83]

The underwriters priced Peru's bonds to reflect the country's problems and prospects. In 1927 its bonds yielded 6.6 percent to maturity, approximately equal to the average for bonds similarly rated A by Moody's.[84] They offered a prospective return commensurate with the risk of default as perceived at the time of the original underwriting. Thus the Peruvian bonds appear to have been priced fairly to investors, contrary to the Senate's later assertion that they were inherently unsound securities.

Price movements of Peruvian bonds subsequent to their initial distribution to investors bear out this conclusion. For example, the 7 percent bond maturing in September 1959 was originally underwritten in March 1927 and issued to investors at 96½. Two years later its price was 102½ (Figure 9.1). It sold above its original issue price as late as May 31, 1930, or more

Figure 9.1

Price of Peruvian bonds, January 1928 to March 1933

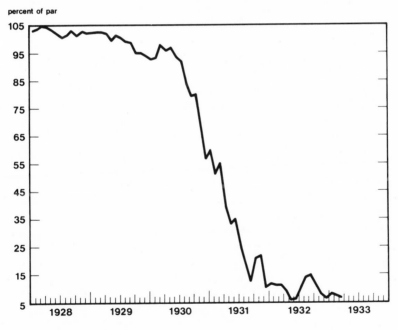

Source: New York Times.

Note: Prices are highest end-of-month prices bid for Peruvian National Loan maturing in September 1959 with 7% coupon.

than three years after the initial underwriting. Only then did the bond plummet in price as a result of the depression's impact on the Peruvian economy. As output in the industrial countries fell in 1930 and 1931 so did the demand for Peru's principal exports. Copper, petroleum, sugar, and cotton all dropped sharply in price on world markets. The total value of Peru's exports declined precipitously, from $134 million in 1929 to $55 million in 1931.[85] This limited Peru's ability to service its foreign debt. Moreover, the collapse in foreign trade made a shambles of its domestic economy. This led in August 1930 to a revolution that deposed President Leguia. The new government promptly undertook a massive devaluation, but this could not, in the face of a deepening world depression, reverse the erosion of Peru's balance of payments. For practical purposes, Peru's commercial life, which had led National City Company to deem the government creditworthy, had ceased to exist.

Consequently, Peru was forced to default on its foreign debt payments. In March 1931 it abrogated its loan agreement and ordered the Caja to pay to the Treasury the funds needed to service the national loan of 1927. In May 1931 the Peruvian revolutionary junta declared a temporary moratorium on debt repayments, which was extended indefinitely in January 1932. As William H. Wynne concluded in a 1951 study, "political unsettlement intensified the effects of the world-trade depression and the total default on the foreign debt was the result."[86]

All this was reflected in the prices of Peru's bonds. From 97 in May 1931, the 7 percent issue fell to 80 shortly after the revolution, to 55 shortly before the first default, and to 33 when the moratorium was first announced. By March 1932, at the conclusion of the Senate's foreign bond investigation, the Peruvian bonds had fallen to 11, or 89 percent below their original issue price.

Other foreign bonds were also adversely affected by the depression, although not as severely as Peru's. Throughout the 1920s foreign bonds had appreciated in price, and even after the stock market crash in October 1929 their prices held fairly firm. But when the gold standard collapsed in 1931, yields soared and prices tumbled (Figure 9.2). Naturally, the price decline was steepest for bonds of countries that defaulted, such as Peru, Chile, and Brazil. Still, not all foreign bonds defaulted, and not all foreign bonds declined as steeply in price. In fact, most foreign bonds recovered. For example, Aa-rated bonds rose in price during the first nine months of 1932 to the point where their yield was again below that of August 1931. Bonds of the gold bloc countries (France, Belgium, Switzerland) even rose significantly above par after Roosevelt's election in November 1932, when it became obvious that they would redeem their obligations in gold, whereas the United States might not.

Figure 9.2

Yields on foreign dollar bonds by rating, September 1928 to March 1933

percent (inverted scale)

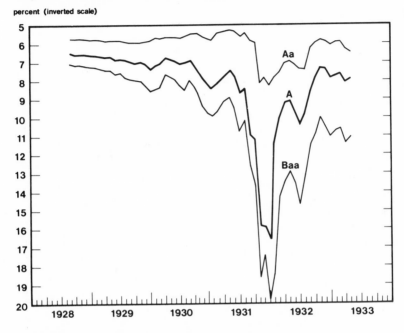

Source: <u>Moody's Investment Survey</u> (New York: Moody's Investors Service, 1928–1933).

Note: An increase in yield is equivalent to a decline in the price of the bond.

Domestic bonds behaved similarly to foreign bonds in response to the depression (Figure 9.3). During the 1920s bonds generally declined in yield and rose in price. In the years 1930 to 1932 the reverse was true. As the depression deepened bond yields climbed and prices plunged. The change—up in the 1920s and down in the 1930s—was greater for lower-rated and presumably riskier bonds. But all bonds, even U.S. government bonds, declined in price and rose in yield during the depression.

This evidence strongly suggests that the depression caused the defaults, and that underwriters had not deliberately issued unsound securities. Bonds were issued and subsequently traded at prices that reflected inves-tors' perception of risk among different borrowers and global economic conditions. Lower-rated bonds, with presumably higher risk, traded at lower prices and offered higher yields than higher-rated bonds with lower

Figure 9.3

Yields to maturity on domestic corporate bonds, by rating, January 1928 to March 1933

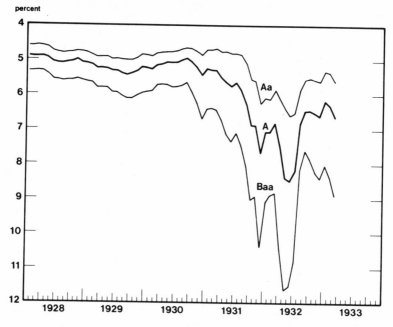

Source: Board of Governors, Federal Reserve System, <u>Banking and Monetary Statistics, 1914–1940</u>
(Washington, D.C.: GPO, 1943), pp. 469–470.

risk. As economic conditions improved in the 1920s risk premiums declined and bond prices climbed, reflecting borrowers' greater ability to repay. After the onset of the depression, this trend was reversed. Risk premiums rose, and bond prices plunged. Thus the evidence strongly
suggests that the market for foreign bonds was efficient, that is, that bond
prices at the time of issuance and thereafter fully reflected the relative
probabilities of default by various issuers.[87]

Had the depression not been as deep, or had the depression not occurred at all, investors in bonds would have done better. As Henry C.
Wallich pointed out in 1943 in reference to Latin American dollar bonds,
"If the depression in the 1930s had been mild, and if the steady expansion
of world trade and capital exports had continued thereafter, defaults
would probably have been settled without much difficulty."[88] But the depression was an extraordinary event, unforeseen and unforeseeable.
Bankers and investors had only foresight, and this was and is imperfect.

Stock Exchange Practices

In June 1932, in an investigation of the New York Stock Exchange, the Senate Banking Committee applied Senator Johnson's thesis of conscious wrongdoing to the domestic scene. The committee added a new note of conspiracy to the accepted theory that the stock market boom of the late 1920s had led to the depression. Bankers and brokers, the committee alleged, had worked together to push stocks up before October 1929 and afterward to push them down. Through pools and the use of inside information, they allegedly took profits both on the way up and on the way down, all at the expense of the public.

In the course of the hearings, the members of the committee looked into the dealings of the National City Company in Anaconda Copper stock. In the summer and fall of 1929, the National City Company had accumulated a block of Anaconda common, some of which it resold to the public. National City recommended the stock to its customers as a sound investment after research into the copper company's prospects. At the time of the offering in 1929, the stock sold for over $100 a share. In June 1932 it was selling at $4. To the committee, the decline in the price and the existence of a pool in Anaconda stock were enough to establish a *prima facie* case that National City had helped manipulate the price of the stock for its own profit at the expense of the public.

In Senator Glass's view, the Anaconda pool and similar pools active across the whole Big Board had driven the entire market down and devastated the economy. Mitchell in the witness chair could only react with incredulity to such an assertion: "You do not hold us responsible for that?"[89] Even the fact that the City Company took its own advice and lost heavily on the Anaconda shares it retained made no impression on Glass and his colleagues, who only insinuated in their questioning that the loss must have been the result of incompetence. That the depression itself was responsible for the decline in share prices and that Glass's own creation, the Federal Reserve System, had been chiefly responsible for the depression (see above) never occurred to the Senate committee.

Choosing the Scapegoat

The congressional hearings were grist for the media mill. The *Saturday Evening Post*, once effusive in its admiration of the nation's billion dollar banks and the men who ran them, now thought that depressions were made, "not by real bankers, but by men who during booms get into banks and banking firms."[90] In the *American Mercury* Clifford Reeves commented, "The title of banker, formerly regarded as a mark of esteem in the United States, is now almost a term of opprobrium. There seems some danger, in fact, that in forthcoming editions of the dictionary it may be necessary to define the word as a peculiar American colloquialism, synonymous with rascal . . . and we may even see the day when to be called a son-of-a-banker will be regarded as justifiable ground for the commission of assault and mayhem."[91]

On February 21, 1933, in the midst of the worst banking panic in the nation's history, Charles E. Mitchell made his second appearance before the Senate Banking Committee in its continuing investigation of the New York Stock Exchange. Wall Street banks and bankers were already indicted in the public mind and in the eyes of the committee's majority on the charge of having brought on the depression by promoting speculation. The committee's new chief counsel, Ferdinand Pecora, saw it as his job to turn the indictment into a conviction by nailing down the evidence that prominent bankers had fostered speculation and engaged personally in it.

Pecora picked Mitchell as his lead witness because, as Pecora later wrote, "National City was one of the very largest banks in the world, and had but recently been surpassed in this country only by the Chase National. The prestige and reputation of these institutions were enormous. They stood, in the mind of the financially unsophisticated public, for safety, strength, prudence, and high-mindedness, and they were supposed to be captained by men of unimpeachable integrity, possessing almost mythical business genius and foresight."[92] If Mitchell could be convicted, all bankers would stand guilty.

For Pecora's purpose Mitchell was an ideal witness. By January 1933 he had become to the editors of *Time* "a rampant bull . . . the popular scapegoat of the Crash."[93] Forthright, self-confident, convinced of his own integrity, and anything but a political animal, Mitchell had always stated his views clearly and without equivocation. He shared the common belief that credit had fueled speculation and helped cause the depression, but he believed that National City had attempted to combat these tendencies and had always adhered to sound banking and investment principles. That its judgment in several instances had been wrong, he admitted. That the bank or he personally might have been guilty of conscious wrongdoing never crossed his mind.

Pecora began his questioning by probing into Mitchell's personal finances. He quickly established that Mitchell had earned well over $1 million in salary and management-fund bonus in 1929 but had not paid any income tax that year because of a capital loss incurred in the sale of National City stock to his wife. Pecora seems to have had two purposes in mind in bringing out this evidence. One was to discredit Mitchell personally. Given the temper of the times, he succeeded. Senator Burton K. Wheeler's reaction was extreme but not atypical: "The best way to restore confidence is to take these crooked presidents out of banks and treat them the same way as they treated Al Capone when Capone avoided payment of his tax."[94] The second purpose was to suggest that large salaries and bonuses had been an incentive to sell bad securities and depart from sound banking principles. "These unreasonable salaries and these bonuses lead to unsound banking and unsound sales of securities," remarked Senator James Couzens, a member of the committee, during Mitchell's first day in the witness chair.[95] With depositors storming banks across the country, such an assertion seemed to require no proof.

Indeed, as the following excerpts from the record of the hearing suggest, the committee was satisfied to bring out a few actions taken by National City and to leave it to the Congress and the press to fill in the implied but unexplained connection to bank failures and the depression.

Regarding the call loan controversy of March 1929 (see chapter 7):

Senator Brookhart. If you had let it [the call money market] collapse in March, that would have saved hundreds of thousands of dollars to people who invested later on, prevented them from buying, and the collapse would not have suffered such purchases to mean a loss; is not that a fact?

Mr. Mitchell. I do not believe that any man who has it within his power to stop a money panic is going to take the responsibility of seeing the money panic develop.

Senator Brookhart. That is what is wrong with our financial system; nobody is going to stop this speculation.

Mr. Mitchell. I may be an inferior banker, but so long as I am in the banking business and can find a way to stop a money or a credit panic every bit of the weight I can put into the situation is going to be put in.

Senator Brookhart. You helped to inflate matters later and on up to the 25th of October, and you could not stop it then.

Mr. Mitchell. No; I beg pardon, Senator Brookhart. We stepped in in a critical moment, and we stopped the development of a panic at a critical moment.[96]

Regarding the transfer of the General Sugar Corporation from National City Bank to the City Company in February 1927, an action that actually strengthened the position of the bank's depositors (see chapter 6):

Mr. Pecora. . . . this $25,000,000 bailing out.

Mr. Mitchell. This was a transfer. You speak of it as a "bailing out" and I am afraid again that that creates in the public mind an incorrect impression. That was the passage from the part of the institution where it is vital that liquidity prevail, of certain loans that were bound to be slow under the condition of the industry, and in the stockholders' interest it seemed far better to carry those in the form of a permanent stock investment in the National City Co.[97]

There was no controversy about the facts in these episodes and a few others brought out in Mitchell's testimony. Only the significance of the facts presented was at issue. As Mitchell remarked to Senator Brookhart, "You are viewing it through different eyes than I would view it."[98] Mitchell and other National City executives testified that they had acted according to their judgment of the situation at the time, acknowledging that "just as long as men are human and judgment has the element of error in it, just so long there will be mistakes made by the National City Co[mpany] or any investment house that puts out securities."[99]

To the members of the Senate Banking Committee and their counsel, National City and bankers generally had been swept into a speculative fever during the 1920s. Bankers had not been faulty in their judgment; they had failed to use it, and their failings had caused the panics and the depression. As Pecora later wrote, the testimony of National City officials was "an amazing recital of practices, to which the catastrophic collapse of the entire banking structure of the country seemed but the natural climax."[100]

The press agreed (Figure 9.4). Mitchell's testimony, coming in the midst of the banking panic, put people in an "ugly mood."[101] Pressure mounted on Mitchell to resign. The *New York Times* commented, "No banking institution, not even the next to largest in the world, could afford even to appear to approve or condone the transactions of which he was a guiding spirit and one of the beneficiaries."[102] The *New York World Telegram* called for "resignations as well as reforms."[103] Eugene Meyer, governor of the Federal Reserve Board, found Mitchell's testimony embarrassing to the board and urged his removal.[104] President-elect Roosevelt reportedly urged him to step down.[105] The bank's directors, who had earlier defended him consistently, now reconsidered and requested his resignation.

On February 26, 1933, Mitchell resigned. In his letter to the board he stated:

My first loyalty is to The National City Bank of New York to which I have given the best years of my life, and I am not willing that the criticism which has been directed at me as a result of the public misunderstanding of testimony given in ex parte hearings before the Senate Committee on Banking and Currency during the past week shall react upon the institution on my account . . . As the chief executive officer of The National City Company as well as of the Bank, I personally have been brought under a

Figure 9.4

No Wonder the Country Went Haywire
—Fitzpatrick in the St. Louis "Post-Dispatch."
Reprinted in the Literary Digest, March 11, 1933.

cloud of criticism from which I conceive that the institution should not be permitted to suffer by my continuance in office.

[The bank's] financial strength is such that it needs no restatement by me, but it will always be my deepest source of pride.[106]

The directors met to accept Mitchell's resignation and to elect James H. Perkins, president of City Bank Farmers Trust Company, to succeed Mitchell as chairman of the National City organization. In *Time's* report of this event, the caption under Mitchell's photograph read, "The U.S. Senators got their man" and under Perkins's, "National City got an old-time banker."[107]

10.

Rehabilitation and Recovery
1933-1939

With Mitchell's resignation, National City touched the low point of its corporate existence. "Nobody could possibly envy James H. Perkins, the new head of National City Bank," said *The Nation.* "There has been dumped upon him a mess which was once a great banking institution."[1]

But Perkins was equal to the task. As the *New York Herald Tribune* would later comment, "In appearance and manner, as well as in conduct, he was calculated to inspire confidence at a time when that was the most desperately needed commodity in the financial world." In contrast to Mitchell, Perkins was "quiet, scholarly," and had about him "a certain homespun, friendly quality that stamped him . . . as 'a country banker in Wall Street.'"[2] A member of a socially prominent family and a wealthy man, Perkins counted President-elect Franklin Roosevelt among his friends.[3] Perkins was respected within the National City organization as well. During World War I, he had been a member of Vanderlip's top management. During the depression he had kept the Trust Company free of the public criticism that surrounded the bank and City Company. Moreover, he knew what had to be done. He wrote to A. P. Giannini,

> I have been "drafted" into this position to do what I can to reestablish confidence in the Bank and to convince people of the soundness of its operation. I shall need all the support possible . . .
>
> My inclination will be to conduct things in the most conservative way possible; and if I have time and the confidence of my friends I feel no doubt of our ability to produce the desired results . . .
>
> I ask you to believe that everything I do will be done with all sincerity of purpose, and although I shall undoubtedly make mistakes, I shall try to see that they are made on the side of sound banking.[4]

The Bank Holiday

For National City, Perkins's appointment came none too soon. With each day's testimony at the Pecora hearings, the banking panic had worsened. State after state declared a banking holiday. Where banks remained open, runs continued. At National City, withdrawals by correspondent banks and other depositors accelerated. To help cope with the outflow, the bank, for the first time during the panic, turned to the Federal Reserve's discount window.

On March 2 and 3, the bank felt the full fury of the panic. By the close of business on March 3, its domestic deposits were down to $810 million, 11 percent below their level two days before and 29 percent less than on February 1.[5] No program of liquidity management could cope with such an environment. To meet the withdrawals National City could only rely on the Federal Reserve. At the close of business on March 3, 1933, the bank owed the Federal Reserve $117 million, a sum in excess of its required reserves.[6] But even the Federal Reserve's ability to help was threatened. Speculation that the incoming administration would devalue the dollar or abandon the gold standard made gold appear to be the only safe money. A surge of demand for gold caused the Federal Reserve's gold stock to decline toward the legal minimum required to back its notes, threatening to limit the central bank's ability to help banks in trouble.[7]

Evidently, immediate action was needed to stem the outflow of deposits. On the evening of March 3, Governor Harrison of the Federal Reserve Bank of New York joined Perkins and the heads of the other Clearing House banks at a meeting to urge Governor Herbert H. Lehman to declare a banking holiday in New York.[8] Earlier the bankers had hoped Hoover would declare a nationwide holiday as his term of office ended, but Hoover refused to act without Roosevelt's approval, and Roosevelt was unwilling to commit himself before his inauguration. When word came in the early hours of March 4 that the federal government would take no immediate action, the bankers were sitting with Governor Lehman in his New York apartment, negotiating the terms of a state holiday. Only hours remained before the banks were to reopen, and depositors were lining up to take their money out. At 3:30 A.M. on March 4, the banks reached agreement with Governor Lehman, and a state banking holiday was declared, effective immediately. The statement issued that morning by the Clearing House read in part as follows:

> The request of the Clearing House Committee to the Governor is based on the continued and increasing withdrawals of currency and gold from the banks of the country.

The unthinking attempt of the public to convert over $40,000,000,000 of deposits into currency at one time is on its face impossible.

While the condition of the Clearing House banks in New York is such that they could, through the facilities of the Federal Reserve Bank, pay on demand every dollar of their deposits, the above limitation and such tremendous withdrawals through the country as a whole, and upon a rapidly increasing scale, render imperative a halt to enable the proper authorities to consider and adopt remedies to meet this situation, not only for New York primarily, but for the nation as a whole.[9]

Hours later, Franklin D. Roosevelt took the oath of office as president of the United States. As his inaugural address began, banks across the country were closed and business was practically at a standstill. For this unprecedented economic disaster Roosevelt chose to blame the country's leading bankers, "the rulers of the exchange of mankind's goods," the "unscrupulous money changers" who, "through their own stubbornness and their own incompetence, have admitted their failure, and have abdicated." Having thus driven the money-changers "from their high seats in the temple of our civilization," Roosevelt promised to request Congress to grant him "broad Executive power to wage a war against the emergency, as great as the power that would be given to me if we were in fact invaded by a foreign foe."[10] Two days later, on March 6, 1933, without waiting for Congress, the president issued an executive order closing every bank in the United States and prohibiting the export of gold.[11]

Perkins called on Roosevelt at the White House the same day to discuss the banking situation and the condition of National City Bank.[12] As Roosevelt knew, the public's loss of confidence in banks had aggravated the depression. Recovery would come only when the public came again to believe that its money was safer in a bank than under a mattress. Rehabilitation of the nation's second largest and now most notorious bank would help restore that confidence.

On March 9 Roosevelt extended the Bank Holiday under authority of the hastily enacted Emergency Banking Act.[13] The act empowered the president to license banks to reopen when they were found to be in "satisfactory condition." The purpose of the licensing procedure was, as Treasury Secretary William Woodin announced, to "insure . . . that banks, when reopened, [are] capable of remaining open."[14] National City received a license to reopen on March 13, the earliest day permitted by the legislation.[15] Open again for business, National City faced two tasks: to assess the damage done by the depression and to rehabilitate its image. Each would lay the foundation for a return to National City's comprehensive strategy.

Drawing a Line under the Depression

The first step was to assess the damage done during 1929 to 1933. Perkins had begun to evaluate the bank's portfolio immediately after his appointment as chairman. With the aid of a special committee of the board of directors, he and his staff examined the assets of the bank, paying special attention to items criticized by the national bank examiners. Reserves were created on the bank's books, "against items the collection of which may be delayed or doubtful."[16] During 1933, $50 million was added to the bank's contingency reserve, a part of which was used to write off $21 million in bad loans and bonds at the end of the year.[17]

Two weeks later, on January 13, 1934, additional assets were written off, in conjunction with the sale of $50 million in preferred stock to the Reconstruction Finance Corporation (RFC). The RFC had been authorized by the Emergency Banking Act of 1933 to buy preferred stock from banks. Perkins had consented to the sale of stock to the RFC to "support the President of the United States in his program of strengthening the capital structure of the banks of the country and in his campaign to bring about business and industrial recovery," even though National City itself did not need additional capital.[18]

In effect, Perkins took the opportunity afforded by the sale of stock to draw a line under the depression on the bank's books. Losses amounting to $60 million were written off, bringing the total losses incurred by the bank since the end of 1929 to $167 million net of recoveries, or 68 percent of its stockholders' equity at the end of 1929. Assets remaining on the bank's books were written down to their most conservative values. After the recapitalization, the common stockholders' equity amounted to $113 million, or 8.5 percent of the bank's total assets. In addition, the bank had $40 million in unallocated reserves.[19] Regarding these moves, Perkins commented to the shareholders, "The drastic writing down of assets and accounts beyond what may appear at the moment to be necessary and the provision of unallocated reserves . . . [are] the part of prudence and conservatism by a bank which must keep its demand deposits in mind, and over the course of the years should increase the value of the shareholders' investment.[20]

Restoring Legitimacy

Money was not the most important loss National City had incurred during the depression. Far more damaging was the loss of its legitimacy as a result of the Pecora hearings. Perkins hoped to put the Mitchell era behind him as rapidly as possible, but a stockholders' suit against National City directors stood in the way. In February 1933, Celia Gallin and a few other stockholders brought a stockholders' derivative action against National City's directors in the New York State Supreme Court, alleging negligence or wrongdoing damaging to shareholders. The main charges involved matters that had just been brought out in the Pecora hearings, including the handling of Cuban sugar loans and the management fund. If the plaintiffs had been successful in making all or most of their charges stick, the damages, for which the directors would have been personally liable, would in all probability have bankrupted them as well as further damaged National City's reputation.

The court exonerated the directors on all but one count. In approving periodic allotments of bonuses to officers from the management fund, the directors had accepted management figures on earnings and failed to look into the underlying accounting. The court found the accounting to be faulty in several respects. Total damages assessed to the directors were $1.8 million, to which was added a large allowance for the plaintiffs' legal expenses.[21] Many of the directors were reportedly "relieved at the modesty of the judgment."[22] There was no appeal.

Perkins also took steps to disassociate the institution from Mitchell. Bank officers and directors were apparently advised to have no contacts with Mitchell.[23] Mitchell's indictment, on March 24, 1933, and subsequent trial for federal income tax fraud may have helped the bank to shed his image. Mitchell was acquitted, and the publicity surrounding the case, in which Roosevelt took a more-than-usual interest, directed the public's attention toward Mitchell and away from the National City institution.[24]

Perkins realized that if National City were to regain public acceptance, its officers had to recover their own self-esteem. Indirectly, they had been maligned in the Senate investigations; though the policies had been Mitchell's, the execution had been theirs. Many key bank employees were also deeply in debt as a result of commitments to buy National City stock at pre-crash prices. Perkins did not want financial worries to keep officers from putting their full energies into rebuilding National City. He therefore established a loan fund for bank officers. At a meeting held shortly after his appointment, Perkins told employees that "they should not try to defend the past, nor should they stay home in shame. They should get out, face the music; and should speak of the future NCB, the new policies, and do their banking business effectively and capably, as they well knew how to do."[25]

A Revolution in Regulation

In the aftermath of the banking holiday, the public clamored for legislation to reform the banking system. In June 1933 Congress passed a comprehensive banking bill, the Banking Act of 1933 (Table 10.1). This act and subsequent banking measures radically altered the environment facing National City, severely circumscribing its comprehensive strategy.

The New Deal banking legislation reflected the general conviction that the banking practices of the 1920s, identified as speculative, had caused the panics and the depression.[26] According to Congress, stability depended on a safe banking system, and this required that each bank be safe. That in turn implied that each bank should be consistently profitable. The solution was to limit the risk to which a bank could expose itself and to restrict the competition to which a bank could be exposed. In practical terms this meant two things: first, segmenting banking from other forms of finance and, second, creating a cartel among the banks that had survived the Great Depression.

Segmentation of commercial and investment banking was the first priority. In the vocabulary of 1933, *speculation* meant primarily the activity of banks and their affiliates as investors, underwriters, and distributors of securities. It followed logically that if banks had been forbidden to invest in securities, to finance such investments by others, or otherwise to participate in the securities markets—if, in other words, they had been confined to commercial banking, and bank assets had been limited to short-term commercial loans and government bonds, as the real bills doctrine demanded—there would have been no depression. Thus the main thrust of the 1933 legislation was to separate commercial and investment banking. Department store finance was to end. Firms were to choose which they wanted to be—commercial banks or investment banks. Each type of firm would be regulated separately.[27]

Commercial banks became subject to extensive and detailed regulation. The nation's banking laws were to have only one purpose: to prevent banks from competing too much either against each other or against other financial intermediaries. Banks were to be protected against the judgment of the bankers who ran them: They were to restrict their activities to a set of "safe," low-risk activities. Entry into banking was restricted. According to the Banking Act of 1935, applications for new banking charters became subject to a "needs" test, and other laws prohibited nonbanks, such as thrift institutions, from offering demand deposits and other commercial banking services. Competition among banks was limited by restrictions on branching and on the rates payable on deposits and by deposit insurance.

The Banking Act of 1933 retained the prohibition against interstate branching. Each state determined where the banks within it could branch; but a national bank could branch anywhere that a state bank could. In theory, the restrictions on branching gave each bank a protected local market.[28] Competition within banking markets was limited by restrictions on the interest rates payable on bank deposits. It was commonly but

Table 10.1. New Deal banking legislation

Objects of new or re-regulation	Banking Act of 1933	Banking Act of 1935	Other measures
Investment banking	Partial separation of commercial and investment banking		
Credit collateralized by securities	Banks prohibited from acting as agent for nonbank lenders in placing loans collateralized by securities	Federal Reserve granted power to regulate credit advanced by banks and bankers for purchasing and carrying registered securities	Federal Reserve granted power to impose margin requirements on loans collateralized by securities (Securities Exchange Act of 1934)
Rates paid on deposits	Prohibition of interest on demand deposits Provision for ceilings on interest rates payable on time and savings deposits to be set by Federal Reserve	Federal Reserve's power to set interest-rate ceilings extended to include differential ceilings on rates payable on various classes of time and demand deposits	

Deposit insurance	Imposition of temporary system of deposit insurance for accounts up to $2,500 (later raised to $5,000). Creation of Federal Deposit Insurance Corporation	Permanent plan of deposit insurance
Reserve requirements		Federal Reserve Board granted increased power to change reserve requirements
Branching/entry into banking	Prohibition against interstate banking confirmed. Equalization of branching powers with states for state and national banks	Entry into banking made more difficult through "needs" criterion for new bank charters

incorrectly held that excessive competition by banks for deposits in the 1920s had forced up their costs, propelling them into securities-related activities and from there into receivership. To prevent this from recurring, the legislation of 1933 and 1935 prohibited the payment of interest on demand deposits and empowered the Federal Reserve Board to set ceilings on the interest rates payable on time deposits.[29]

Deposit insurance provided a safety net. It was intended to prevent panics by convincing the small, unsophisticated depositor that the failure of one bank did not mean that all banks were in danger of failing. His own deposits were guaranteed; there was no need to start a run. But deposit insurance restricted competition as well, as the small banks who supported its passage were well aware. It tended to make the deposits of one bank equivalent to the deposits of any other, and made a small bank as safe as a large geographically diversified (branch) bank. Thus deposit insurance prevented banks from competing for funds by offering deposits with lower risk, and blunted the movement toward branch banking.[30]

A strong central bank was to be the final guarantor of economic stability. New Deal legislation broadened the powers of the Federal Reserve and concentrated the authority to use those powers in the hands of the Federal Reserve Board. In line with the theory that the depression was caused by excessive credit creation and extensive credit diversion to the securities markets, the new powers accorded the Federal Reserve were largely aimed at controlling the amount and use of credit.

Broadest in scope was the power granted to the Federal Reserve Board, by the Securities and Exchange Act of 1934, to set margin requirements for loans on the collateral of securities, whether granted by banks or by securities dealers. This extended the Federal Reserve's authority from participants in the securities market (member banks) to the market itself. This would be the precursor of later regulations and legislation empowering the board to regulate consumer credit and the use of credit generally.

Within its traditional banking domain, the Federal Reserve also received broader powers. The Banking Act of 1935 granted the board the authority to vary reserve requirements, a tool thought necessary to control the total volume of bank credit. The Banking Act of 1933 made permanent the power of the Federal Reserve to grant member banks credit on the basis of any asset rather than just government securities or "real bills." Coupled with deposit insurance, this enabled the regulatory authorities to prevent, or at least delay, the failure of any bank.

In sum, segmentation and sedation were the guidelines of the New Deal financial system. In order to preserve stability, it was thought necessary to ensure the safety of not only the banking system but also each individual bank. This demanded a less competitive, and hence less efficient, banking system—in fact, a cartel, similar to those proposed for industries under the National Recovery Administration.[31] The adverse effects of the new regulatory scheme would surface only after World War II, in the buoyant economic conditions of the 1950s and 1960s.

The End of the City Company

For National City the major blow inflicted by the 1933 legislation was the requirement to disaffiliate or liquidate the City Company. The company's underwriting and distribution of securities had been the cornerstone of Stillman's and Vanderlip's diversification program and had provided a large and growing share of National City's profits in the 1920s. Now most of these activities would have to be renounced. The Banking Act of 1933 prohibited the bank from affiliating itself "with any corporation . . . engaged principally in the issue, floatation, underwriting, public sale, or distribution at wholesale or retail or through syndicate participation of stocks, bonds, debentures, notes or other securities." The bank itself was permitted to underwrite certain debt securities, notably federal government securities and general obligation municipal securities.

Perkins had anticipated this outcome. On March 7, 1933, the day after Perkins's talk with Roosevelt about the state of National City and the banking situation, the bank's board of directors voted to work toward a separation of the bank and the City Company. Effective immediately, the bank and the City Company would have no common directors. The City Company would be sold "as soon as it could be done in an orderly manner without sacrifice of the assets of the Company and of the value which exists in its facilities for the purchase and distribution of investment securities of the highest grade."[32] National City would confine itself to the underwriting and distribution of U.S. federal, state, and local government securities.

With the passage of the Banking Act of 1933, the City Company's chief mission became its own sale or liquidation by June 16, 1934, the deadline fixed in the act. Perkins confessed, "The problem of disposing of the City Company is a sticker [sic] to me . . . From the Bank's point of view I want to get rid of the thing, but I want to keep the organization together because it will be necessary for the men to handle a number of bond issues which have gone bad [,] to service those issues and give the best results possible to the owners of the bonds."[33] Various possibilities were explored. A merger with the affiliates of Guaranty Trust or the First National Bank of Boston was rejected, on the ground that the prospective partner's business was competitive rather than complementary. A merger with Banc-America-Blair was considered but ruled out because of that firm's relationship with Transamerica, the largest National City shareholder. Another plan called for a group of City Company executives to take over the business, which would be recapitalized by issuing new stock, with the stipulation that any of the new shares held by a shareholder of the bank would be nonvoting. This plan was also rejected on the ground that the public might think the new company was still connected with the bank.[34]

Finally, a month before the deadline, it was decided to liquidate the City Company, and on June 4, 1934, it went out of business except as liquidator of its assets. As Perkins wrote the shareholders, "Good-will is a nebulous thing. In so far as it is attached to the name of City Company it cannot be realized on, because the continued use of the name would identify the user with the Bank and that cannot be permitted without control by the Bank, which is forbidden by law. In so far as it may be represented by personnel trained in the investment banking business, such personnel consists of free individuals whom the City Company is not in a position to deliver to a prospective purchaser."[35]

The end of the City Company did not spell the end of National City's involvement in investment banking. Its Bond Department continued to underwrite and distribute U.S. government securities and general obligation municipal bonds. Thus National City exploited to the fullest the investment-banking franchise remaining open to it after enactment of the Banking Act of 1933.

The Strategy Reaffirmed

Perkins worked from the beginning of his tenure as chief executive to ensure that National City would retain the structure needed to pursue anew its comprehensive strategy once times improved. In January 1934 he confirmed that National City "is prepared to serve all classes of customers, large or small, at home or abroad, and, as trade becomes more normal throughout the world, to contribute its share to the rehabilitation of industry and commerce, with results that would be satisfactory to the shareholders."[36] Within the constraints imposed by the New Deal legislation and given the uncertainty of the times, this strategy meant preserving the bank's liquidity while keeping intact the wholesale, international, and local banks built by Vanderlip and Mitchell.

Perkins aimed to "keep the Bank strong in resources, ready to meet contingencies, and also prepared to profit by any improvement in conditions."[37] Perkins recognized, nevertheless, that "the immediate course of economic affairs, both national and international was and still is involved in uncertainties."[38] In the United States, doubts centered on how long the recovery from the depression would last. In the long, steep slide of 1929-1933 there had been brief interludes of rising production, most notably in late 1932. In each case, a banking panic had halted the advance, and despite the New Deal legislation there was still the chance that another panic might occur. Adding to uncertainty were changes in industrial organization and labor relations introduced by the New Deal. Thus during the recovery, businessmen continued to fear a relapse into depression. Although real output advanced at the extraordinarily rapid rate of 9.5 percent per annum from 1933 to 1937, investment remained sluggish and demand for credit, weak. Interest rates fell to extraordinarily low levels. Then in 1937 the public's fears seemed to be confirmed. Recovery was interrupted by a sharp recession.[39]

Overseas, the outlook was worse. Except for Germany and Japan, where rearmament spending spurred growth, industrialized countries recovered more slowly from the depression than did the United States. Recovery was particularly slow in the gold bloc countries, such as France, that attempted through continued deflation to keep their currencies on gold.[40] As the decade drew to a close, the probability of war increased. In the Far East Japan invaded Manchuria (1931) and then attacked other parts of China (1937). In Europe Spain erupted into civil war, and Germany annexed Austria and the Sudetenland. The world moved inexorably toward war.

Back to "Ready Money"

In essence, the problem confronting Perkins in the aftermath of the depression was the same that Taylor and Stillman had faced after the panics of the nineteenth and early twentieth centuries. Although the public's confidence in the nation's banks had started to return after the nationwide Bank Holiday, a sharp and sudden decline in deposits could not be ruled out. Until economic conditions improved, profitability at the bank had to take a back seat to liquidity. Writing in December 1933, Perkins recognized that "in these times the obligation of a commercial bank to its depositors, customers and shareholders is to pursue a conservative policy, maintain an adequate degree of liquidity, reduce expenses, and increase reserves."[41] But for one interlude in 1936-1937, that policy would prevail for the next seven years not only at National City but at banks generally.[42] After the Bank Holiday, fear that the depression would return prompted National City Bank to build liquidity. A high margin of liquidity would not only attract deposits but also protect the bank if deposits should take flight again, as they had during 1929-1933. Thus National City would be prepared for either prosperity or depression.

From early 1934 to the end of 1935 National City raised its ratio of government securities and excess reserves to deposits from 40 percent to nearly 60 percent (Figure 10.1). In 1936 the bank began to reduce its liquidity. At first, it did so voluntarily, in response to the confidence and loan demand generated by the ongoing recovery. But after August 1936 much of

Figure 10.1

National City Bank, excess reserve[a] and liquidity[b] ratios, July 1933 to December 1938

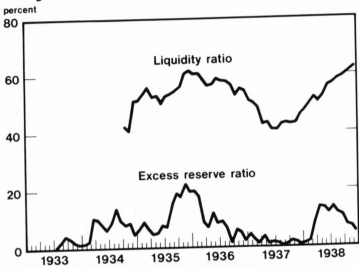

Source: National City Bank, Daily Statement Book, 1933–1938.

a. Ratio of excess reserves to revised deposits (total deposits minus float minus required reserves).

b. Ratio of excess reserves and U.S. government bonds (including bonds directly guaranteed by U.S. government) to revised deposits.

the decline in liquidity was forced upon the bank by the Federal Reserve's doubling of reserve requirements. This step by the central bank contributed heavily to the severity of the 1937-1938 recession, and to National City's subsequent rebuilding of liquidity. From a low of 40 percent in mid-1937, National City raised its liquidity ratio to over 60 percent by the end of 1938.

Although fear that the depression would return prompted the bank to build liquidity in 1934-1935 and 1938, concern that the recovery would last induced it to hold that increased liquidity in the form of excess reserves. This enabled the bank to limit interest-rate risk. Perkins believed that interest rates normally rose during a recovery. Hence he was reluctant in 1935 and again in 1938 to invest in longer-term government securities, whose price would decline if interest rates rose. Perkins preferred to keep the bank's liquidity in the form of cash and short-term Treasury bills.[43]

By mid-1935 interest rates had fallen to what Perkins considered to be unrealistically low levels. The yield of long-term bonds had dropped continuously since the Bank Holiday and their price had risen sharply. Perkins doubted that the rally could last.[44] Accordingly, when National City's deposit growth accelerated in the second half of 1935, Perkins put practically all of the resulting increase in investable funds into short-term assets. This meant excess reserves, since the yield on short-term Treasury bills had fallen to little more than one-tenth of one percent, a rate so low that the yield probably did not cover the cost of administering the portfolio. From July 3 to December 4, 1935, National City's excess reserve ratio soared from 3.4 percent to 25.1 percent—a surge so rapid that it alone accounted for approximately one-third of the total increase in excess reserves at all Federal Reserve member banks.[45]

Similar reasoning led National City to increase its excess reserves after the 1937-1938 recession. Once again, the recession induced National City to increase its liquidity; once again, Perkins shied away from the interest-rate risk inherent in long-term government bonds. In February 1938 he wrote to John Neylan, one of the bank's directors, that because of the extraordinarily low level of interest rates (short-term Treasury bills were yielding less than 0.1 percent), "I can't see how we can make any money at all for the Bank this year, and I am troubled by it. Of course, if we wanted to buy long time governments, we could make a fine showing; but I am not willing to risk the drop [in price] that might come."[46] As a result National City once again accumulated excess reserves. From 1.2 percent at the end of 1937, the bank's excess reserve ratio rose to 11.0 percent in June 1938 (Figure 10.1).

There Perkins called a stop to the accumulation of cash. The deepening recession caused him to change his mind about the future course of interest rates. In June 1938 he wrote to Giannini that he had "made a mistake in not going into long-term governments two or three years ago and staying with them."[47] With three-year to five-year tax-exempt Treasury notes yielding nearly thirty times the taxable rate on Treasury bills, lengthening the maturity of the portfolio promised an immediate increase in income at what Perkins now felt to be an acceptable increase in risk. In mid-1938, the bank began to shift from excess reserves to long-term government securities while continuing to build liquidity. By the end of 1938 its excess reserve ratio had fallen back to less than 5 percent, while its total liquidity ratio again topped 60 percent.

The Wholesale Bank

Like National City, corporations sought to increase their liquidity after the depression. This common objective dominated the activity of the wholesale bank, which maintained relationships with approximately six thousand institutional customers across the United States. Growth was intensive, rather than extensive, and centered on increasing deposit balances rather than loan volumes. In fact, the number of institutional accounts actually fell by 9 percent from 1933 to 1939, while the average balance per account more than doubled.[48] In contrast, loan volumes remained roughly constant.

This pattern of growth, common to most major banks, was highly controversial. Both contemporary and later commentators contended that banks' penchant for liquidity and reluctance to lend slowed the recovery from the depression and contributed to the 1937-1938 recession. Pilloried in 1932 and 1933 for lending too much in the 1920s, bankers were taken to task in 1934 and 1935 by the administration for lending too little. Seen in the light of the credit theory of the business cycle, banks' policy of holding down loans and building excess reserves was doubly dangerous. Officials charged that business was starved for credit and that the slow expansion of credit from 1933 to 1935 hindered the recovery.[49] In contrast, officials at the Federal Reserve were concerned about what might happen when banks did begin to lend. Excess reserves could finance a too-rapid expansion in loans to business. As officials in Washington saw it, excess reserves had the potential for an explosion in bank credit that could, according to the credit view, induce a speculative bubble, whose inevitable bursting would plunge the economy into a new depression.[50]

But this view is too one-sided. Although banks were reluctant to lend, corporations were also leery of borrowing. Like banks, corporations sought to strengthen their balance sheets after the depression as a precaution against a new economic downturn. They too rebuilt liquidity, accumulating cash and marketable securities and paying down their existing debt, especially short-term bank debt. The one exception to this pattern came in 1936-1937, when the accelerating recovery and the imposition of a tax on undistributed profits temporarily boosted corporations' demand for credit.[51]

Thus deposits were the banking service of primary interest to the large corporate customer in the years after the Bank Holiday. In competing for these deposits National City had several advantages over other banks: its large capital base, highly liquid portfolio, and comparatively good earnings record. In an era when deposit insurance was still untried, National City's deposits therefore appeared to carry a lower risk than those of other less well capitalized or less liquid banks. Moreover, the uncertain economic environment and the prohibition of interest payments on demand deposits heightened the attractiveness of such low-risk deposits. As a result average corporate balances at the wholesale bank rose 58 percent from 1933 to 1935 (see Table 10.2).[52]

Table 10.2. National City Bank's "domestic wholesale bank," 1929–1939 (millions of dollars)

| | Deposits | | | | | Loans | | | |
| | Demand | | | | | | | | |
Year	Correspondent banks	Other	Total	Time	Total deposits[a]	Loans to brokers	Other	Total	Earnings[b]
1929	92.3	383.9	476.2	48.2	576.7	118.9	384.8	503.7	19.0
1930	98.2	337.9	436.1	44.7	551.9	166.9	334.8	501.7	10.2
1931	99.8	338.8	438.6	46.2	545.2	90.7	350.6	441.3	8.5
1932	118.6	323.5	442.1	30.2	519.6	15.9	310.8	326.7	10.6
1933	113.3	309.4	422.7	27.3	485.0	25.8	229.9	255.7	7.8
1934	147.4	363.9	511.3	28.3	564.5	26.6	216.2	242.8	7.1
1935	205.7	489.4	695.1	34.3	759.8	29.5	250.9	280.4	2.0
1936	251.8	532.3	784.1	30.8	862.2	54.8	233.2	288.0	3.8
1937	211.6	495.0	706.6	28.7	819.5	68.9	273.1	342.0	4.9
1938	241.2	534.4	775.6	25.8	835.5	45.6	232.2	277.8	4.3
1939	316.1	610.7	926.8	22.0	974.0	59.0	208.9	267.9	4.0

Source: National City Bank, Comptroller's Reports, 1929–1939.

Note: Data are yearly averages.

a. The difference between total deposits and the sum of total demand and time deposits represents other deposits, including the deposits of National City affiliates.

b. Operating earnings after tax.

In contrast, loan volumes remained fairly constant over the entire 1933 to 1939 period, and were significantly below the volume extended during the depression. Large, profitable firms had little or no demand for credit, and these were the core of National City's corporate customer base. Less prosperous firms wished to obtain credit, but in the uncertain economic environment of the time they generally seemed to lack enough earning capacity or capital to make them credit-worthy.

What National City sought was firms midway between these two extremes—companies that had excellent business prospects but only limited access to the securities markets. To such firms National City could safely and profitably extend increasing amounts of credit. For example, in 1933 it began a relationship with United Parcel Service (UPS), even though the company had lost money in 1930, 1931, and 1932. In the years after 1933 National City periodically lent UPS significant sums to increase its fleet of delivery trucks and to expand into new areas.[53]

Firms like United Parcel seemed few and far between to National City executives in the early stages of the recovery from the depression. In March 1934 Perkins lamented, "It is almost impossible to lend money to anybody from whom you have a reasonable chance of getting it back."[54] On average, the wholesale bank's loan volume actually fell from 1933 to 1934. Even during the later stages of the recovery, loans expanded only modestly, reaching a peak of $273 million in 1937 (Table 10.2).

The recession of that year prompted banks and corporations alike to rebuild liquidity. Once again, the wholesale bank was faced with a situation in which those to whom it wished to lend would not borrow. More precisely, corporations were reluctant to borrow short-term funds, the traditional form of bank finance, lest they be unable to renew these credits upon maturity.

The solution to this dilemma was the term loan, which was equivalent to a nonmarketable bond with a sinking fund and a maturity of one to ten years. Various regulatory rulings opened the way to this new form of bank financing for corporate customers. In 1934 a joint conference of bank examiners recommended that loans reasonably certain of repayment should not be criticized on the basis of their maturity alone.[55] The Securities and Exchange Commission also ruled that a term loan was not a security. Hence it was exempt from registration requirements. That gave term loans a considerable advantage over bonds of equivalent maturity, for with interest rates low, the cost of registration loomed large.[56]

National City was quick to take advantage of the new rulings. By accepting the interest-rate risk of the longer-term, fixed-rate loan, National City could acquire assets whose credit risk was low. One of the bank's early term loans was to a major oil company at a rate of 1.66 percent, only marginally higher than the 1.5 percent prime rate. This loan reportedly "touched off a stampede on the part of virtually all of the major oil companies who came in and wanted, and received, the same deal."[57] From a total of $35 million at the end of 1937, the bank's term loans rose to $106 million two years later, accounting at the later date for nearly 25 percent of the domestic loan portfolio.[58]

Nevertheless, National City remained skeptical of the term loan. It saw the innovation as a temporary phenomenon, doomed to die as the securities markets revived and regulations changed.[59] Instead, it relied on the advice of analysts in the Bond Department, who subjected term loan proposals to the same cash-flow analysis that investment bankers would have undertaken prior to a new issue of securities.[60] Finally, the principle of safety first dictated that the term loan play a limited role. As Perkins commented in 1939, "the amount of such loans should be limited in relation to our total assets."[61]

The International Bank

After investment banking, international branch banking had been the first of Vanderlip's diversification efforts. From the outset, the international bank's performance had been uneven. Losses in Russia and then in Cuba in 1917–1921 were followed by years of rising profits during the 1920s. Then came the Great Depression. Losses again mounted, especially in Cuba. Nonetheless, Perkins resolved to keep the branch system intact. As he noted to the shareholders in January 1934:

> Under anything like normal conditions the foreign branches make handsome earnings and contribute largely through their services to the building up of domestic deposits.
>
> In building up this foreign organization a great deal of money has been spent, for which values over and above those appearing in the Statement have been created. These values consist of our experience in the foreign field and our facilities for foreign commercial business which would take any other bank many years and great expense to duplicate.[62]

Against this long-term commitment to international banking, National City balanced current considerations of cost and risk. Maintaining branches abroad was expensive. It required large outlays for salaries and other operating expenses, though some economies were possible. After the depression the bank reviewed the situation branch by branch and closed thirty unprofitable or marginal branches, including twelve in Cuba. It also refrained from adding branches. In 1933, for example, it passed up an opportunity to open a branch in Geneva, Switzerland.[63] The refusal to enter Switzerland, an island of economic and political stability and one of the world's financial centers, indicates how wary National City was; until conditions improved, it wished to keep its international organization in place, but to limit its risk.

After the Bank Holiday, National City quickly reduced the volume of problem credits inherited from the depression, writing off $33 million in foreign branch assets in January 1934. This brought total foreign branch write-offs net of recoveries since the end of 1929 to $77 million, or nearly half of the total net write-offs taken by the bank during this period. The one remaining problem of major importance was the bank's German credits frozen under the terms of the standstill agreement (see chapter 9). By December 9, 1933, these credits had been reduced to $43 million, approximately half of the amount outstanding on July 31, 1931, when the agreement became effective; so far the bank had suffered no losses on these credits, but Hitler's rise to power made it unlikely that this record could be maintained.[64] Thus the bank faced a choice: the possibility of full payment on the restoration of exchange convertibility or the certainty of an immediate, but partial payment.

In 1934 Perkins traveled to Germany for a firsthand look. He concluded that "the more money we could get out quickly—even at a discount—the better off we would be."[65] Under the standstill agreement, a creditor had the option of accepting payments in "travel marks," a special form of currency available only for certain purposes, including travel in Germany. The marks could be sold for dollars for what they would bring. At this time travel marks were selling at a discount of 30 to 40 percent below the official exchange rate. Under this option, the bank's German credits were reduced to less than $25 million by the end of 1935. Liquidation continued until the eve of World War II in 1939, when the bank called home its special representative in Berlin, Sterling Bunnell. The remaining credits were then written off, bringing the total exchange and credit loss on these loans to $18.5 million.[66]

Caution guided the Overseas Division in its current operations as well. To enhance liquidity and limit credit risk, new lending was largely restricted to trade finance secured by goods in transit. In addition, the branches were instructed to lend only to the subsidiaries of American companies and to local customers of long standing.[67] This policy brought the branches back into the black. Profits in 1935 were $1.9 million and rose to over $4 million at the end of the decade (Table 10.3).

For this turnaround there was one reason: a recovery in world trade. During the depression world trade had fallen nearly 60 percent in value, but after 1932 it made a strong comeback. Recovery spurred increases in both the volume of trade and the price of goods traded. By 1937 the volume of world exports had again surpassed the level achieved in 1928, and the prices of principal commodities had reached double their depression

Table 10.3. National City Bank's "international bank," 1929–1939 (millions of dollars)

Year	Deposits			Loans			Earnings	
	Head Office[a]	Foreign branches	Total	Head Office[b]	Foreign branches[c]	Total	Head Office (exchange)	Foreign branches[d]
1929	161.0	331.5	492.5	27.0	317.2	344.2	0.8	4.0
1930	179.1	339.1	518.2	15.5	287.1	302.6	0.9	−8.0
1931	140.2	285.5	425.7	19.1	247.1	266.2	3.0	−1.9
1932	71.6	233.8	305.4	32.0	163.8	195.8	2.5	−11.8
1933	49.8	203.6	253.4	25.0	145.9	170.9	−0.9	−6.1
1934	50.9	208.3	259.2	14.4	137.9	152.3	2.1	−37.3
1935	62.5	207.1	269.6	8.1	127.8	135.9	0.4	1.9
1936	90.6	236.9	327.5	9.2	111.4	120.6	2.6	0.2
1937	121.1	265.8	386.9	11.8	142.4	154.2	0.6	2.7
1938	101.6	273.4	375.0	10.6	109.7	120.3	1.0	4.4
1939	196.8	270.5	467.3	7.8	106.0	113.8	1.6	4.3

Source: National City Bank, Comptroller's Reports, 1929–1939. Figures for 1929 do not match those of Table 7.5 because of difference in dating.

Note: Except as noted, all data are yearly averages.

a. Demand and time deposits due foreign individuals, corporations, and banks by Head Office plus deposits denominated in foreign currency.

b. Foreign overdrafts, foreign bills discounted, and special foreign credits at Head Office.

c. End of June.

d. Net remitted income after allowance for losses, recoveries, branch expenses at Head Office, and branch capital adjustments. Excludes income from and dividends paid by the International Banking Corporation and other overseas subsidiaries.

lows.[68] This provided National City's overseas branches with opportunities to finance exports and imports and to trade foreign exchange. Even in adverse political circumstances, such activities, if conservatively managed, could produce profits.

The China branches were proof of this. Originally established as branches of the International Banking Corporation in the first decade of the twentieth century, they had by 1930 obtained a broad customer base consisting of local Chinese businesses and the subsidiaries of American and other foreign firms. In dealing with Chinese businesses, the branches employed a comprador, a local Chinese factor who guaranteed loans made to Chinese customers in return for a commission. Most of the branches' activity involved international trade. For example, the Manchurian branches (Harbin, Mukden, Dairen) financed exports of furs, bristles, and soybeans. So did the Tientsin branch. Hankow financed tung oil exports. Shanghai also financed trade, but its chief activity was trading silver and foreign exchange.

After the Japanese invasion of Manchuria in 1931, National City's branches there were forced to curtail their activity. Much the same happened in the remaining Chinese branches (Tientsin, Hankow, Peking, and Canton) after 1937, when the Japanese attacked the rest of China. Only the branches in Hong Kong and Shanghai operated freely. They continued to trade silver and foreign exchange, and thanks to a foreign exchange trader named Red Reed, they made substantial profits. Overall the Chinese branches earned over $7 million in the years 1934 to 1939, or nearly 40 percent of the total gross remitted branch earnings for those years. Foreign exchange probably accounted for most of these gains.[69]

In New York, foreign exchange trading also yielded substantial profits. To earn them, the bank took large positions on what amounted to one-way bets. For example, after the dollar's devaluation in 1934, it became evident that France and the other gold bloc countries would be forced sooner or later to devalue. The bank accordingly kept a short position in the French franc and other gold bloc currencies. When the franc was finally devalued in September 1936, the Overseas Division profited handsomely. According to Joseph H. Durrell, head of the Overseas Division at the time, "sufficient profit resulted from the transaction to cover the major part of the Bank's entire 1936 dividend."[70]

Overall, the performance of the international bank justified Perkins's decision to keep it intact. The foreign branches were consistently profitable from 1934 on, even after allowing for loan losses and adjustments to the branches' capital (Table 10.3). In combination with Head Office foreign exchange profits, the branches' net operating earnings accounted for nearly 40 percent of the bank's net profits in the years 1935-1939.

The Local Bank

During the 1920s Mitchell had built the foundations of a thriving local bank that opened relationships with the consumer and small businessman and helped fund National City's asset growth. Perkins recognized the contribution of the domestic branches to National City's comprehensive strategy and resolved to keep them intact after the depression. This was an easy decision, for as Perkins noted to the shareholders in January 1934, "the domestic branches of the Bank are all situated within New York City and represent an organization that has been created during the past ten years. Even during the past year these branches have rendered a good account of themselves and have turned in a profit, which, under the conditions which have existed, has proved their value and justified their creation and existence."[71]

Like the international bank, the local bank expanded cautiously after 1933. It added few branches; instead it worked to consolidate the branches acquired in the merger with the Bank of America (N.Y.) in 1931. Loans to local businesses expanded only modestly from the trough reached in 1933, although deposits rose steadily (Table 10.4).

Personal credit paced what expansion there was. During the depression National City had continued to extend personal credit on an experimental scale. By 1935 it had developed sufficient expertise and gained sufficient

Table 10.4. National City Bank's "local bank," 1929–1939 (millions of dollars)

		Loans				Net operating earnings
Year	Deposits	Personal credit	Time contracts	Other business	Total	
1929	304.6	12.8	—	144.6[a]	157.4	4.2
1930	308.4	15.7	—	192.1[a]	207.8	2.9
1931	346.5	15.5	—	135.3[a]	150.8	3.4
1932	387.5	14.6	—	99.7[a]	114.3	4.3
1933	338.4	12.6	—	69.9[a]	82.5	2.2
1934	350.8	13.6	—	70.6[a]	84.2	1.8
1935	392.2	20.1	—	71.4	91.5	1.6
1936	460.1	37.3	—	73.2	110.5	1.2
1937	498.8	54.1	6.1	84.5	144.7	0.7
1938	512.4	53.7	16.4	72.9	143.0	0.5
1939	616.3	53.6	21.2	81.4	156.2	2.6

Source: National City Bank, Comptroller's Reports, 1929–1939; Daily Statement Book, 1929–1934.

Note: All data are yearly averages.

a. End of June.

confidence in the economy to increase its personal loan portfolio substantially.[72] Total personal loans rose to $53.6 million in 1939 (Table 10.4), accounting for approximately 13 percent of the volume and 30 percent of the interest income of the bank's domestic loan portfolio.[73]

In addition, the bank began to make personal loans indirectly by buying time installment contracts from retailers. For example, in 1939 it signed an agreement with Sears, Roebuck to buy over 500,000 of the retailer's installment or conditional sales contracts with its customers. Sears gave a guarantee that limited the bank's potential loss.[74] Similar deals to acquire consumer paper from other large retailers were made in 1938 and 1939, at rates averaging 2.6 percent, about 20 percent higher than the average the bank received on other domestic credits.[75] By 1939 such contracts were 40 percent as large as the volume of the bank's direct personal loans.

Profits and Performance

Overall, National City rebounded strongly from the setbacks suffered during the depression. From 1933 to 1939 deposits grew at an annual rate of 10 percent and assets at a rate of 7 percent. By the end of the decade National City's assets topped $2.5 billion, making it the second largest bank in the country after Chase.[76]

This rapid growth, coupled with write-offs and recoveries, enabled National City to reduce substantially the burden of nonaccrual assets. These were assets on which interest was either not being paid at all or being paid at a rate less than the originally contracted rate. At the end of 1933 such assets amounted to nearly $120 million, or 51 percent of the bank's total capital. After the recapitalization in January 1934, this percentage declined steadily. By the end of 1939 nonaccrual assets amounted to only 11 percent of capital, or $16.6 million.[77]

Profits rebounded as well. National City's ready money policy generated a small but safe stream of earnings amounting to approximately $14 million per year (Table 10.5), though this was heavily dependent on earnings from the sale of long-term government securities. The combination of low interest rates and sluggish credit demand severely depressed earnings in selected years, such as 1938.

Although important, current earnings were not Perkins's primary concern. He sought to maintain the bank's ability to earn significant profits as times improved. As he wrote to A. P. Giannini in 1935, "the earnings from our regular commercial business are very small indeed. They will continue to be so, I fear, until there is a greater demand for money." But, he continued, "Things are going smoothly, but slowly, and I am waiting anxiously the time when we can use our money. When that time comes we can make some really respectable profits in the Bank as it is set up at present."[78]

Table 10.5. Summary statistics, National City Bank, 1933–1939 (millions of dollars)

End of December	Assets	Loans	Deposits	Common stockholder's equity	Net profits[a]	Nonaccrual assets
1933	1,448.4	555.1	1,117.2	232.4	−7.3	120.9
1934	1,640.1	482.8	1,394.6	126.4	−58.1	50.9
1935	1,880.7	547.2	1,652.4	134.3	11.1	50.5
1936	1,904.8	588.4	1,713.8	147.3	12.8	39.1
1937	1,899.3	609.4	1,711.6	150.2	6.2	30.0
1938	2,099.2	531.4	1,835.3	149.4	4.1	20.7
1939	2,509.4	539.1	2,331.3	156.9	16.1	16.6

Source: National City Bank, Daily Statement Book, 1929–1939; Comptroller's Reports, 1929–1939.
a. Net profits less write-offs plus recoveries for the calendar year.

Perkins's Legacy

In July 1940, Perkins died, the victim of a heart attack at the age of sixty-two. As his successor the board chose Gordon S. Rentschler, who had been president of the bank since 1929. To fill Rentschler's slot the board selected William Gage Brady, Jr., the head of the Domestic Branch Division. W. Randolph Burgess remained as vice chairman. Perkins had recruited him for that post in 1938 from the Federal Reserve Bank of New York, where he had worked for many years as an economist and close adviser to its governor, George L. Harrison.[79]

To this top management team Perkins left a valuable legacy. Early in his career he had helped Vanderlip initiate the bank's comprehensive strategy; as chairman he kept that strategy intact after the ravages of the depression. When he assumed responsibility for the National City organization in 1933, it was battered financially and politically. Its capital was reduced; its reputation was shattered; its future was uncertain. Regulation curtailed its comprehensive strategy, and the profitability of its remaining commercial banking activities depended on economic recovery that many thought would never occur.

Into this situation Perkins went calmly and purposefully. He viewed National City's course as fundamentally correct, and the economy's course as temporarily aberrant. Recovery, he thought, was bound to come. Perkins therefore instituted no radical changes in National City's strategy and structure beyond the divestiture of the National City Company as mandated by the New Deal banking legislation. Instead, he worked to preserve and strengthen National City's position. He had kept the institution liquid, maintained its branches at home and abroad, restored its profitability, and reestablished its legitimacy in the eyes of the administration and public. In sum, he rescued the bank.

11.

War and Peace
1940–1949

In September 1939, ten months before Gordon Rentschler became chairman of National City Bank, Germany invaded Poland and World War II began. This halted National City's attempt to revive its comprehensive strategy. Most of the bank's branches in Europe and the Far East were closed. In the United States controls limited lending to firms and individuals. For all practical purposes National City became like other banks across the country, an arm of the U.S. Treasury, an engine of war finance.

This experience tested anew National City's commitment to its comprehensive strategy. Many businessmen were inclined to accept the popular theory that traced the depression back to World War I, so that the outbreak of this war filled them with foreboding. "The great depression," wrote National City's management in its annual report to shareholders early in 1940, "was the aftermath of war, and many of the problems with which we have struggled in the United States during the past ten years have descended in a straight line from August 1914." From this new and greater war, management expected another cycle of boom and bust, "with inflationary movements [bringing] only an illusion of prosperity, and [ending] in debts, taxes and depression."[1] This dark prognosis would characterize management's thinking throughout the war and into the postwar period.

Banking for the U.S. Treasury

Wartime banking at National City and other banks was largely a matter of helping the Treasury sell bills and bonds needed to finance the war. The Treasury and the Federal Reserve cooperated to this end. Bank reserves and deposits grew rapidly as the Federal Reserve, responding to the Treasury's needs, supplied reserves in large quantities to the banking system in order to peg the Treasury bill rate close to the low level (three-eighths of one percent) reached in 1939-1940. This kept bank deposit rates low as well and also locked in the steeply sloped positive yield curve for government securities that had prevailed in the late 1930s, creating strong incentives for banks to invest in longer-term Treasury securities.[2] As a further incentive, the Federal Reserve allowed a member bank to pay the Treasury for newly issued securities by crediting a "war loan account," or deposit, in the name of the Treasury. After 1943 such deposits were exempt from reserve requirements, thereby widening a bank's spread on the investment. Required reserves on regular demand deposits for the largest banks were also reduced, in order to free more funds to invest in Treasury issues.[3] To make sure bankers got the message, Allan Sproul, president of the Federal Reserve Bank of New York, sent a letter to member banks in the New York district, instructing them that "banks should now abandon the practice of holding large amounts of excess reserves, with the knowledge that by investing their funds more fully through purchases of Treasury securities, they will be assisting in the war effort without sacrificing their ability to meet any demands for cash which may be made upon them."[4]

Other regulations closed off normal civilian demand for bank credit. The Federal Reserve's Regulation W precluded consumer finance for the duration. War Production Board orders forbade the production of automobiles and most other consumer durables as well as most construction for civilian use. Inventories were strictly controlled and firms producing war materiel received advances from the government to finance production. This reduced the demand not only for business credit but for export credit as well. The Federal Reserve also discouraged loans secured by Treasury issues if the borrowed funds would be used to pay for the securities.

National City responded quickly to these various measures. From June 1941 to June 1945 it raised its holdings of government securities by $1.3 billion. At the later date, the bank owned $2.5 billion in government bonds, an amount equal to two-thirds of its total domestic earning assets. The bank paid for about 70 percent of the increase in its holdings of government bonds by crediting the Treasury's "war loan account," the bonds being pledged as collateral to secure the deposit. In this way Treasury deposits at National City Bank rose from $6 million in June 1941 to $917 million in June 1945, accounting at the later date for 22 percent of the bank's domestic deposits.[5]

From June 1941 to June 1945 the bank's loans for the purchase of securities, mostly Treasury issues, increased from $71 million to $678 million.[6] In the same period, the increase in the bank's bond portfolio together with that in loans to purchase securities accounted for more than the entire increase in the bank's earning assets, as corporate loans and personal and consumer credit declined.

Finally, the bank also acted as a sales agency for the Treasury, selling bonds to the public. National City participated energetically in each of the Treasury's eight war-bond campaigns, selling almost $6 billion in bonds—well in excess of its quota and 3.6 percent of the national total.[7]

The bank's profits during the war years were excellent. Wartime profits were the bank's compensation for helping the Treasury finance the war, rather than returns for assuming credit and interest-rate risks—the normal business of a commercial bank. By stabilizing short- and long-term interest rates, the Federal Reserve assured the bank a good spread while eliminating interest-rate risk on the bank's investments. At the same time, wartime boom conditions together with government guarantees and regulatory obstacles to normal lending virtually eliminated credit risk. The rapid growth in deposits and lowered reserve requirements made possible an 80 percent increase in the bank's funds and earning assets between 1941 and 1945. All these favorable influences on bank earnings more than outweighed a sharp decline in overseas earnings and a hike in the federal corporate tax rate. Profits after taxes and securities gains increased from $18.4 million in 1941 to $23.7 million in 1945—a 29 percent increase—and the rate of return on stockholders' equity (including securities gains) in 1945 was 10 percent.[8]

Wartime Maintenance

With the balance sheet largely determined by government regulations and profitability assured, top management's attention was mainly directed to maintaining a functioning organization despite the loss of personnel to the armed forces; to preserving relations with major corporate customers, who for the time being had little need for bank credit; and to improving the institution's public image.

Perkins had done a great deal to restore the bank's reputation; through their war work Rentschler and Burgess would complete the job. They participated prominently in war bond drives and served on committees to advise the Treasury on war finance. Burgess was active in the American Bankers Association, becoming its president in 1944. By speeches and personal contacts, he sought to marshal support from the banking community for the war effort along the lines desired by the Treasury and the Federal Reserve.[9]

Rentschler concerned himself particularly with corporate customers. During the war, U.S. industry got most of its financing from the government, but after the war it would need a lot of credit to convert to peacetime production and to finance investments deferred during the war. The bank's account officers were instructed to keep in touch with corporate customers and Rentschler traveled across the country to see corporate executives and assure them that the bank would be ready to meet their needs when peace came. John Neylan wrote to Rentschler in February 1944:

> I do not have to tell you what a cordial and warm feeling there is throughout the whole area toward the bank as a result of the top officers getting out here, meeting and knowing the crowd and having an understanding of the situation . . . You could not have spent $500,000 in advertising and have accomplished the good in this area for the bank that flowed from the visits here during the last ten years, the expense of which must have been relatively nominal—and the City Bank apparently is the only one that has sensed the situation. This condition should not be permitted to go stale.[10]

Voluntary enlistment and the draft sharply reduced the bank's staff soon after the war began. Total staff fell from 10,000 at the end of 1941 to 8,650 at the end of 1943. New recruits were needed to maintain services to depositors. Some retired employees were recalled; on them and on older staff members fell the task of training the recruits. The bank, like the rest of American industry, hired many women. By the end of 1945 the bank's staff again exceeded 10,000. Women were less than a quarter of the bank's labor force in December 1940; two years later the proportion was 43 percent, and women were assigned a wider range of duties than before the war.[11] The new recruits and older hands managed to keep the bank functioning, despite the added administrative burdens of Treasury bond sales and the distribution of ration coupons.

More important in the longer run was management's ability to draw back, at the war's end, the many key employees who had left the bank to join the armed forces. A program was established to keep in touch with every employee on military leave and to reassure him that his job was waiting and that the lines of promotion would remain open. As Rentschler explained in a letter to his friend Neylan:

> If the crowd can hold out physically until the boys come back from service it will in itself be a great accomplishment because we will then have a wide open door not only to welcome these fellows back but more than welcome them because we will need them so badly and will have kept their place in line of promotion definitely open for them. We are working out a system of refresher courses for the older fellows and of intensive study for the younger ones, and in our intensive study plan we may send some of these boys back to college to enable them to go ahead on our job faster. It is a challenging problem but we know we can-

not let a lot of these men start in anywhere near the place they left off . . . I think when they come back they will be a great group to train intensively with the idea that they will run this show while some of us are resting under the shade trees watching the Herefords fatten up.[12]

Fitting ex-servicemen back into the organization posed problems. Many had gained valuable experience in management and organization; some had held positions of great responsibility with the armed forces. Rentschler recognized that the veterans had to be given an opportunity to take on added responsibility. Lewis B. Cuyler, the bank's manager of personnel and an Air Force veteran, was given the task of developing a program to reintegrate the veterans.[13] His and the bank's success in this regard is shown by the high proportion of servicemen who returned to National City after the war. By the end of 1945, 673 veterans, 85 percent of the bank's employees released from military service, had come back.[14]

A Cautious Reentry

The veterans returned to an institution on the verge of change. To Rentschler and his colleagues, the world in the first postwar years was an uncertain, even threatening, place. The prospect of prosperity was dimmed by the probability of a depression and the possibility of another war. As Vice Chairman Burgess remarked, the major question facing the country was "whether we can avoid a boom and bust. We are set for it, just as after World War I."[15] Management's apprehension about the short-term outlook at home and abroad dictated that the bank's reentry into its major markets would be cautious.

Financing Peacetime Production and Consumption

Soon after the end of the war, a vigorous inflationary boom got under way in the United States. For the first time since the 1920s, National City faced a rapidly rising demand for bank credit. The bank responded, expanding loans to corporations and individuals and funding them by reducing its holdings of government securities. From June 1945 to June 1948 the bank's commercial and industrial loans more than doubled, rising from $279 million to $661 million.[16] Despite the bank's belief that term lending was a passing fancy, much of this increase took the form of term credits to firms in capital-intensive industries such as public utilities, petroleum, machinery, and chemicals, with whom the bank had remained in close contact during the war.[17] When these customers wished to finance the acquisition of new plant and equipment for peacetime production, the bank readily extended the credit. Personal credit grew even more rapidly.

As the Federal Reserve relaxed wartime regulations, consumers borrowed to finance the purchase of automobiles, refrigerators, and other durables unavailable during the war. In New York City National City captured much of this business, for few of its major bank competitors had entered the personal loan field as yet.[18] As a result, the bank's loans to consumers more than tripled, rising from $47 million in June 1945 to $167 million in June 1948.[19]

Despite this growth, the bank's domestic portfolio was still dominated by U.S. government securities. As late as June 1948 they accounted for 56 percent of the bank's domestic earning assets.[20] The continued emphasis on highly liquid, low-risk assets (the Federal Reserve's peg was still in effect) reflected management's lack of confidence in the economy and its expectation of a postwar depression. As Rentschler remarked to the shareholders at the beginning of 1948, "so far as industrial activity and employment are concerned, the immediate prospect could hardly be more satisfactory. It also seems to be true, however, that uneasiness over the outlook is increasing. The country is riding the boom not confidently and comfortably, but rather with a sense that the position becomes precarious as time goes on."[21]

Rebuilding the Foreign Branch Network

Overseas, the bank was cautious as well. Before the war it had had the most extensive international network of any United States bank. After the war Rentschler intended to rebuild this overseas network, for it was a characteristic that not only gave National City an edge over its domestic competitors but also provided significant earnings and diversification. Although the immediate postwar outlook was bleak, the only questions were how quickly to rebuild the foreign branch network in Europe and the Far East and when to expand the network elsewhere.

In Europe, the bank followed a policy that Leo Shaw, who became head of the Overseas Division in 1946, described as "opening on the best corners first."[22] With the cold war heating up in Europe and revolutions in progress throughout much of the Far East, prudence dictated a policy of opening offices that would be safe from nationalization and of restricting the branches to trade finance and to servicing the foreign affiliates of the bank's corporate customers. Expansion into new areas, such as the Middle East, where the bank had no branches, was postponed.

Under these guidelines the bank reopened offices in Japan and the Philippines, where the branches could share the business and enjoy the protection of the U.S. military. The branches flourished in that sheltered environment.[23] Concerning plans for expansion in other areas, senior management said at the start of 1946, "Reopening of other branches in the Far East will depend, first, on the needs and requests of our armed forces, and, second, on the reestablishment of conditions under which foreign trade can be carried on safely and with profit."[24] At first, senior management thought conditions in China would be favorable. Shortly after V-J Day, the bank reopened the branches in Shanghai, Tientsin, and Hong Kong. At the time it seemed that these branches would be only the first steps toward reestablishing the bank's entire prewar Chinese branch system. It was thought that the bank would soon reopen in Hankow, Peking, and possibly Harbin.[25]

It soon became apparent, however, that the civil war would eventually bring the communists to power. As James MacKay, the head of the Overseas Division's Far Eastern District, recalled, "We had great plans, but then, we realized when we went back out there that there was no hope."[26] The branches in Shanghai and Tientsin began to curtail their operations, shifting as much of their business as possible to the branch in Hong Kong. In the final months of the Nationalist regime, the bank prepared for the storm. Loans were called, deposits repaid, emergency records prepared, the staff cut to a minimum, and families evacuated. In December 1948, the Tientsin branch closed. In May 1949, after the capture of Shanghai by the communists, the Shanghai branch ceased operations and was officially closed in August 1950.[27] Elsewhere in the Far East, management was deterred by chaotic or uncertain political conditions. Half of the bank's prewar Asian branches remained closed, and only two new ones were opened.

In Europe the bank took a more cautious approach right from the beginning. To National City's management after the war, the prospects for banking in postwar Europe appeared dim. Communism was spreading westward. In 1948, democracy in Czechoslovakia succumbed to a Stalinist coup, completing Soviet domination of Eastern Europe. Communist guerrillas aided by Russia and Yugoslavia occupied a large part of Greece. The French Communist party had twice received about a quarter of the nation's votes; it had been put out of the government in 1947, but it remained a serious threat to a struggling Fourth Republic. In Italy, the Communists with their Socialist allies had polled 40 percent of the popular vote in 1947. In both countries, the most important labor unions were controlled by communists.

Economic conditions in Western Europe were discouraging. In France and Italy, production was well below prewar levels and inflation was on the rampage, with French wholesale prices up more than 50 percent in 1946 and in 1947. Conditions in Western Germany were worse. In the first two postwar years, the German economy had virtually reverted to barter as the mark lost all its value.

National City had closed all its branches on the continent of Europe at the beginning of the war, keeping only its London office open. In 1948, it reopened in Paris but chose to do so inconspicuously, under the label of the International Banking Corporation in temporary quarters rather than in the bank's handsome building at No. 60 Champs Elysées. Jean Le Pelley, an officer in the Paris branch, wrote in a 1963 memoir:

> With the hindsight of today, it seems impossible that we wait-
> ed so long to reopen [in Paris]. The motive was the ever present
> fear in those days of seeing Russian tanks rolling across Europe.
> The grapevine has it that up till his trip to Europe in 1949, Mr.
> Brady, our President, was ready to write off Europe as a total
> loss at any moment . . . When at last we reopened in 1948, it
> was under the name of the International Banking Corporation,
> not as NCB. This IBC label was unknown in Paris and the fact
> that we were on the third floor in temporary premises did con-
> siderable harm and gave our organization in this city an inferior-
> ity complex it has taken years to recover from.[28]

Similarly, the bank's decision to close the branches of its Spanish affiliate in 1941 had lasting adverse consequences. In 1946 National City allowed its license in Spain to expire. It was not able to reopen a branch in that country until the 1970s.[29]

The bank also suffered a setback in South America. During the war National City's branches in Argentina and Brazil had flourished as these countries, along with the rest of Latin America, were lifted on a tide of wartime demand for raw materials and foodstuffs. After the war, external economic conditions continued to be favorable, but domestic conditions in the two largest countries, Argentina and Brazil, deteriorated. There followed in both countries a decade of economic mismanagement, inflation, and slow growth. In Argentina, Perón's government imposed in 1946 an onerous form of control over bank credit known as the nationalization of deposits for the account of the Banco de la Nación, the central bank, an arrangement amounting to a 100 percent reserve requirement.[30] In Brazil, exchange controls imposed in 1947 eliminated the free exchange market, where the bank's branches had been making the major part of their earnings.[31]

Despite setbacks in China, Europe, and Latin America, National City retained the most extensive foreign branch system of any U.S. bank. In Latin America, Japan, and the Philippines it was strongly entrenched. In London, the world's leading financial center after New York, it maintained a branch. Although fewer in number than in 1930, its offices sat on the major trade routes of the world.

New Management

Gordon Rentschler died suddenly on March 3, 1948, while on a trip to Cuba. The directors assembled and asked William G. Brady, Jr. to move up from president to chairman. Brady had over thirty years of experience in National City, much of it as the head of the domestic branches. A banker's banker, nicknamed the Iron Duke within the bank, he was also an inside man with expertise in operations and administration. During the war he had been responsible for internal administration, while customer and external relations had fallen to Rentschler and Burgess. With Brady as chairman, the directors wanted a president with a gift for dealing with the outside world, a grasp of the economic and political environment, and skill in developing new business. The choice narrowed down to the three senior lending officers: Arthur Forward, William Lambie, and Howard Sheperd.

The board chose Sheperd, an open, gregarious man with wide banking experience. According to *Finance Magazine*, Sheperd combined a "genial, winning personality with a keen and sound judgment. From the outset, he has had what many describe as a 'natural-born banking talent.' "[32] He had joined National City in 1916 as a member of one of the first college training classes. After a hitch in the army during World War I, he had returned to the bank in 1920, and his subsequent career included the supervision of the European branches in the 1930s and the domestic branches during World War II.

At the time of Sheperd's appointment Burgess became chairman of the executive committee, a newly created post that also ranked second in the bank's hierarchy. From this spot he continued to supervise the bank's bond portfolio, its overall investment policy, and its public relations. Brady retained control over the personnel function and over the administration of the bank. Into Sheperd's lap fell the key tasks of supervising the existing loan portfolio and acquiring new business.

At this juncture Lambie decided to take early retirement. Sheperd thereupon unified the administration of the bank's relationships with its corporate customers and named Forward the head of the Domestic Division. As his successor in the Domestic Branch Division (New York metropolitan area branches) Sheperd named his right-hand man, James Stillman Rockefeller. Leo Shaw was confirmed as head of the Overseas Division. Lenfestey continued as cashier and head of back office operations.

Overall, the succession had been orderly and quiet, in marked contrast to the furor surrounding the resignation of Mitchell or even the mild controversy surrounding Rentschler's appointment as chairman. At last, the echoes of the Great Depression had faded away. Within the bank, the succession marked a new maturity, another stage in its development as an institution, beyond the separation of ownership and management that had been achieved in the 1920s. The bank was now generating its own executives. In contrast to other leading banks, such as the First National Bank, it had actively groomed several contenders for the top spot. Thus the board had the luxury of choosing from among several highly qualified candidates within the institution.

In a way, therefore, the 1948 succession marks the bank's coming of age. One test of an organization's capacity to survive and prosper over long periods of time is its ability to provide in an untraumatic and orderly way for the transfer of legitimate authority from one generation of top management to the next. In a business organization, the legitimacy of management's authority cannot be guaranteed by a constitutional formula, still less by a general election. It depends on more subtle, fragile, intangible factors. The institution must establish a custom of encouraging the rise of new leaders and of testing them in varying assignments so that the ultimate selection is almost self-evident. Top management's choice and the board's formal election then become a ratification of the consensus of the officers. The institutionalization of this process presupposes both a common loyalty to the institution and a sense of fair play in the officers that keep personal rivalries and politics under control and assure that the outcome will be accepted with good grace by disappointed candidates and their supporters. It presupposes, in short, institutional maturity. In 1948 and after, the bank demonstrated its maturity as an institution in this critical sense.

A Big Bank with a Big Return

After his appointment, Sheperd's immediate concern was profits. Maintaining a large, indeed a growing, organization in a poor business environment was not good for the bottom line. The bank's earnings in the first three postwar years were sluggish, the product of a decline in deposits and a low average yield on its assets. At the war's end the Treasury had withdrawn its $900 million of deposits at the bank, sharply reducing the resources available for investment in earning assets. By 1949 total deposits were down 8 percent from their level at the end of the war. In selling government securities to meet this withdrawal, the bank had realized substantial capital gains, but such gains diminished in 1947-1948 as the Federal Reserve gradually relaxed its control of long-term bond prices. Low average yields on domestic assets resulted from the high proportion of government securities in the bank's portfolio. But in the uncertain environment of the late 1940s, management dared not risk a major portfolio shift from the safety and liquidity of government bonds to higher-yielding loans. Overseas, good earnings in the Philippines, Japan, and parts of Latin America were partly offset by diminished profits in Argentina and Brazil and the loss of China branches. Total earnings before taxes were flat in 1946, 1947, and 1948. Adjusted for the high inflation rate of the postwar boom, these results were poor indeed.

They threatened to get worse. Convinced that the rapid expansion of bank credit had contributed to postwar inflation, the Federal Reserve in 1948 reimposed controls on consumer credit and raised reserve requirements. The rate of money growth declined sharply. By the end of 1948 the U.S. economy had slipped into the long-expected postwar recession.[33] At home and abroad, the outlook was dark. Senior management commented to the shareholders at the beginning of 1949, "We face today a period of low visibility with the threat of war and, at home, the threat of an inflationary boom ending in recession."[34]

Sheperd acknowledged that poor earnings appeared to raise a major strategic issue. At a meeting early in 1949 he remarked that "we [had] to make up our minds whether we wanted to be a big bank with a low return . . . or whether we would abandon business and go after profits."[35] The question was mostly rhetorical. The National City tradition and the decisions of Rentschler and Perkins to maintain the organization's potential for future expansion through the depression and the war virtually precluded the first option. National City's destiny was to be both profitable and big. The only question was how.

To help find an answer, Sheperd formed a committee in December 1948 to make recommendations to improve profits. The committee, first known informally as the New Look Committee, was subsequently named the Survey Committee. To head the study, Sheperd chose George S. Moore, a forty-three-year-old vice president in charge of the out-of-town accounts in the Domestic Division, charging him to "take a new look at everything—to see if new methods, procedures or profit-making ideas can be suggested."[36]

The assignment was much to Moore's liking. It was a blank check to dig into any or all of the bank's activities and look at them from the standpoint of senior management. As a training ground and launching pad for an ambitious, energetic, and talented banker who wanted to reach the top, no better assignment could be imagined.[37]

In the unpromising environment of 1948-1949, the emphasis in management's thinking about profitability was on cost cutting; most of the Survey Committee's work was concerned with reducing expenses. Nevertheless, Sheperd made it clear in his initial instructions to the group that management "was properly disposed to spare no reasonable expense to build the bank." The committee's final report noted that the members had taken it for granted at the outset that "the project put before our Committee differed substantially from expense-cutting jobs which previous committees have tackled . . . [and that] any areas of economy which we might develop must stand the critical test that their adoption would not restrict the growth of the bank."[38] As Sheperd said to the committee in 1948, it is "often dangerous to abandon a reputation for bigness."[39] The means to future expansion were not to be sacrificed to a desire to improve profits in the short run.

The Survey Committee's most valuable contribution was the development of a divisional profitability statement—a management tool long used by the bank's industrial customers. The information provided by divisional and subdivisional profit analyses is in many ways the quintessential requirement of effective overall management. It is necessary not only for strategic decision making but also for the key management task of motivating and rewarding officers in a manner that reflects their relative contributions to the institution's overall profits and growth.

Apparently, such information was overdue. At the end of 1948 Moore reported to Sheperd, "National City Bank is a composite of a number of different types of banking businesses. It is probably fair to say that in the development of this business, at least in recent years, more emphasis has been placed on size growth than on the profit factor. We have never really known just where we made our net profits, but have generally proceeded on the assumption that we should encourage the growth of all these businesses to the maximum, on the theory that the more they grew the more money we would make."[40] Moore and his committee set out to remedy this weakness. Sheperd encouraged them and indicated senior management's desire for an annual divisional profit and loss statement that would enable it to compare divisional performance from one year to the next. The Survey Committee put together divisional profit and loss statements for each of the three years from 1948-1950, and its final report recommended that in future such reports be prepared on a regular basis.[41]

A Strong Base

These divisional statements brought out forcefully National City's basic strength—its broad diversification. In 1949 it already occupied a leading position in each of the major markets for banking services in the United States and overseas. Unlike other, more specialized banks, it did not face the prospect of entering entirely new lines of business in order to survive. It had moved back into its traditional lines of business at a pace that reflected senior management's assessment of the economic outlook.

National City's strongest point was the international bank, which combined branch banking abroad with foreign exchange trading and dollar-based banking services for foreign customers in New York. Although it now had far fewer branches overseas than in 1930, National City was the only bank with a worldwide branch system. Both Chase and the Bank of America, its nearest rivals in the United States, had only skeleton networks overseas, and British banks were shackled by exchange controls. In its more than fifty branches in nearly twenty countries National City functioned as a local bank, accepting local currency deposits and making loans to local firms as well as to the subsidiaries of U.S. multinational corporations.

The international branch system also helped National City attract balances in New York. During the war foreigners accumulated dollar balances in New York to conduct international trade and to invest in U.S. securities. National City captured much of this inflow. At the outset of the war in 1939, foreign balances at Head Office doubled, rising to $197 million (see Table 10.3). From there they kept on rising throughout the war and its aftermath. By year-end 1948 they topped $500 million. Since the bank made few loans to foreigners from New York, these deposits, after deductions for float and required reserves, were used to fund a portion of the bank's bond portfolio. The Overseas Division, in turn, received credit for the earnings of the Bond Department funded by its deposits. Together with the earnings of the branches and foreign exchange trading profits, these bond earnings made the international bank the largest earner among National City's three banks in 1948, with 41 percent of the bank's total pretax operating earnings (Table 11.1).

The importance of the Overseas Division was likely to increase. The United States had emerged from the war as the world's dominant economic power. The dollar reigned supreme as the international currency. With the return of stable political and economic conditions in Latin America and the Far East, National City would be well positioned to finance trade and investment for local and American firms. Although other banks might follow, National City would have the advantage of an established customer base, a knowledge of local conditions, and an experienced staff. It was a formidable head start.

In domestic retail banking National City was as well positioned as the law would allow. Within New York City, to which federal and state regulations confined it, National City remained the undisputed leader in personal credit. In 1949 the branches had 270,000 checking accounts and 460,000 savings accounts, both figures a substantial increase over those of 1940. Total deposits amounted to $1.6 billion, enough to fund the branches' own loans and furnish substantial balances to Head Office for investment in bonds (Table 11.1).

Within New York, National City had the third largest branch system, after Manufacturers' Trust and the Corn Exchange. Its sixty-seven branches were spread throughout the city and conveniently located near the subway, the city's major means of transportation. They were well managed. After returning from military service, James Stillman Rockefeller had made a survey of the branches at the request of Brady and Sheperd. He was then given the task of putting his recommendations into effect and had succeeded Sheperd as the head of the Domestic Branch

Table 11.1. National City Bank's three "banks," 1948

"Banks"	Loans[a] (billions of $)	Deposits[b] (billions of $)	Earnings[c] (millions of $)	No. of deposit accounts[d] (thousands)
Domestic wholesale	0.8	1.7	11.2	7
International	0.3	1.3	12.5	12[e]
Local	0.2	1.6	4.8	744[f]
Total	1.3	4.6	30.7	763

Source: National City Bank, Comptroller's Reports, 1948; Survey Committee Reports.

a. End of June.

b. Average for year.

c. Net income before taxes. According to the Survey Committee, "In the preparation of this earnings statement, each division was credited with the income of its own loans, and the deposits not employed directly in the division were credited with the average earned rate of the Bond Department's portfolio (about 1.5 percent in 1948). Certain items of income and expense were prorated on the basis of estimates developed by the Analysis and Interest Department's unit costs [and by] departmental activity and opinions, with adjustments made by the Comptroller's Department." The difference between the three banks and the total is the net income attributed to "Capital." This is the book value of shareholders' equity and other capital accounts, multiplied by the Bond Department's earnings rate.

d. As of November 30, 1948.

e. Foreign accounts at Head Office. The number of accounts in the foreign branches is not available.

f. There were 472,000 savings accounts and 272,000 checking accounts.

Division when Sheperd became president in 1948. Under Rockefeller's administration the domestic branches had contributed 16 percent of the bank's pretax operating income in 1948 (Table 11.1).

Nevertheless, the future of retail banking at National City was problematic. New York City was losing population to the suburbs and to other parts of the country. This benefited banks in faster growing regions, such as the California-based Bank of America, the country's largest. National City would also face increasing competition in the personal credit field from wholesale banks looking for higher yields. Thrift institutions also posed a threat to National City's consumer savings deposit base, for they were willing to grant home mortgages, a field National City was reluctant to enter. Moreover, consumers were beginning to shift their savings away from bank deposits. The income tax code favored investments in one's own home and saving for retirement through institutions, such as company pension plans. As the economy improved, consumers would once again invest in stocks and bonds, either directly or through mutual funds. Because of the New Deal banking legislation, National City would be powerless to follow.

In domestic wholesale banking National City lagged behind its more aggressive New York competitors, particularly Chase. In the 1948-1949 recession National City allowed commercial and industrial loans, particularly term loans, to decline sharply from the heights attained in the immediate postwar boom.[42] Although this policy was certainly prudent, it ran the risk of damaging the corporate relationships that the bank had striven during the war to preserve. So did the bank's attitude toward pension management. It took a dim view of investing pension assets in common stock, a stance that is reported to have cost the City Bank Farmers Trust Company much lucrative business, including managing the pension funds of General Motors and Ford.[43]

These were depression attitudes. Then the accent in the corporate relationship had been on deposits. National City's tradition of ready money had given it an advantage over other banks. Now the accent was on credit. Deposit insurance and banks' wartime accumulation of government bonds had made all banks safe and liquid. If National City wanted to keep its corporate customers, it had to meet their demands for credit. These were likely to be large, if the economy did not slip back into a depression. Plant and equipment had depreciated during the war and the corporate tax code favored financing new investment through debt.

Sheperd realized what was at stake. If the economy remained depressed, National City's prudence would spare it substantial loan losses. If the economy turned around, National City would have to move quickly, or risk losing its corporate customers to the securities markets or other banks.

12.

Back in the Business of Banking
1950-1956

In 1950, the turnaround came. North Korea invaded South Korea and the United States was again at war. The economic prospects for the country changed for the better. Fear of depression evaporated and the economy entered a decade of rapid expansion.

This was the change National City had been waiting for since the 1930s. The large cushion of government securities built up during the war was no longer needed. In the new, expansive environment, the risks of corporate and personal lending declined, while loans yielded substantially higher returns than government securities. National City responded by shifting its portfolio from bonds to loans, raising the average rate of return on assets. The profit squeeze of the late 1940s was over.

In response to the rising demand for business credit, National City strengthened its credit procedures and reorganized its corporate lending departments. The bank merged with a longtime rival and changed its corporate name. It raised new capital. These changes were all made with a view to deepening existing corporate relationships and adding new ones. They succeeded. Corporate banking became more than ever before the core of the bank's business.

From Bonds to Loans

In June 1950, just before the Korean War began, government bonds still accounted for more than half of the bank's domestic earning assets, and commercial and industrial loans accounted for one-sixth (Figure 12.1). Commercial loans were actually $100 million lower than they had been in 1948. During the 1948-1949 recession, firms had paid down their loans and little effort had been made to replace loans with new credits as business recovered in 1949-1950, for credit demand was sluggish and senior management was pessimistic about the recovery.[1]

228

Figure 12.1

First National City Bank, composition of domestic earning assets, June 1950 – 1956

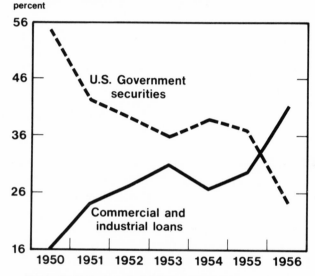

Source: First National City Bank, Call Reports, 1950–1956.

With the outbreak of war, both negative factors disappeared. Expectations of shortages sparked a surge in demand for raw materials, consumer durables, and capital equipment. Industrial output spurted, dissipating fear that the recovery would abort. The war boom altered profoundly the country's views and those of its business leaders about the future. Talk of economic stagnation ceased; henceforth, *growth* would be the term most often used to describe the country's economic prospects. Families and firms began making their spending decisions on the expectation that prosperity would be permanent.

To some extent believing made it so. The economy advanced rapidly, fueled by wartime demand for military equipment and by consumer spending for housing, automobiles, and other durables, such as the television set. Although the administration and the Federal Reserve feared the surge in spending would bring on inflation and took steps to restrain demand, they were wary of a relapse into depression. In 1953, when restrictive monetary policy brought on a crisis in the bond market and a brief recession, policy was promptly relaxed. By the mid-1950s the country was again enjoying peace with prosperity and growth without inflation, with a Republican, Dwight Eisenhower, in the White House.

Not since the 1920s had the business environment been so favorable. As one banker remarked, "Anybody who can't find cause for at least selective optimism is just congenitally morose."[2] Most businessmen became anything but. In the early 1950s they launched a powerful capital-spending drive to prepare for the growth of sales they saw ahead. Plant and equipment expenditure rose at rates that practically equaled those of the short-lived but explosive post–World War II boom.[3]

To finance capital expansion, firms borrowed heavily. Although profits were growing, retained earnings and depreciation allowances were insufficient to finance the additions to plant and equipment planned by major corporations, and firms turned to the securities markets and to banks. An environment of steady growth and high corporate tax rates tilted external funding away from equity toward debt. The demand for credit soared, particularly in capital-intensive industries such as petroleum refining and electric utilities.[4]

National City booked business loans rapidly, with much of the money coming from sales of government securities. Between June 1950 and June 1957, the bank's commercial and industrial loans increased more than four times, from $561 million to $2.4 billion.[5] In the same period, holdings of government securities declined about 40 percent. By June 1957 the bank had restructured its domestic portfolio. Commercial and industrial loans accounted for close to half of the bank's domestic loans and investments, while government securities amounted to less than one-fourth of the total.

Shifting from bonds to loans, along with a higher general level of interest rates, lifted the bank's yield on loans and investments booked in the United States. Between 1950 and 1957, it practically doubled on a taxable equivalent basis, rising from 2.1 percent to 4.0 percent. Interest expense remained low, and the bank's domestic interest spread increased from 1.9 percent in 1950 to 3.5 percent in 1957. With expenses under control and leverage unchanged, the rate of return on stockholders' equity rose. In 1950-1957 it averaged 5.4 percent after adjustment for inflation—well above the rate in the late 1940s.[6] The boom in corporate lending had put the bank back in business.

Term Lending

Much of this improved performance resulted from the bank's shift into term loans. The postwar reservations regarding this financing technique were dropped. Henceforth, it would be the bank's primary means of extending credit to its major corporate customers.

Since the 1930s the term loan had evolved into a sophisticated financial instrument, capable of competing with securities as a means of corporate finance.[7] Term loans could be quickly arranged and tailored to fit the lender's requirements and the customer's needs. This enabled corporations to acquire credit on terms difficult or impossible to obtain in the securities markets. As a bank credit, the term loan was not subject to registration with the Securities and Exchange Commission (SEC). This saved time, costly registration fees, and underwriting commissions. Term loans were thus ideal vehicles for acquisitions, where speed and confidentiality were essential, or for smaller companies whose limited credit needs and unknown reputation made an issue of securities impractical.

Unlike publicly issued and traded debt instruments with standard sets of terms and conditions, term loans could be individually designed. Repayment schedules, collateral, and commitments to lend in the future could all be written into the loan agreement to suit the customer. At times this flexibility permitted the bank to finance a customer it might not have lent to at all. For example, in 1949 the Greek shipowner Aristotle Onassis came to the bank for a loan to finance one of his ships. He was not as well known and certainly not as wealthy as he would later become. Walter Wriston, then a young lending officer, later recalled how Onassis got his loan.

> Ship loans were invented by Onassis, and when he had one Canadian liberty ship, which he bought for $50,000, he used to come in the Bank and stand at the door and wait till what he called "the pope" was free—it was Howard Sheperd. Shep sat in the catbird's seat on the East Platform and Onassis would go over to see him, and Shep would kid him along the way Shep does . . . I eventually got in the act. And he (Onassis) came up with a Texaco bare-boat charter, signed by . . . [the] chairman of Texaco. And he said he'd assign that Texaco charter, *and* his personal guarantee, with great trepidation.
>
> And that was the first ship loan as far as I know. Everybody takes credit for it, but the facts are that to my knowledge Onassis invented the concept and we all were pretty wise after the event. My father-in-law was an admiralty lawyer and spent half his life foreclosing ship mortgages, so I decided to go up to his apartment two or three nights a week and study admiralty law, bare-boat charters, contracts of affreightment, and got a lecture on departing that nobody ever got a good ship loan, that we were going to lose our tail. But that pattern of ship loans that Onassis invented is still our pattern.[8]

Credit Policy Supervision

The shift from bonds to loans and the advent of term lending brought credit risk again to the fore. Term lending required more complex credit analysis than the traditional secured credit or working capital loan. Under a term loan the bank committed funds for a long period. In analyzing a term loan, projections of cash flow and profitability over a number of years are more important than analysis of a current balance sheet or valuation of collateral.[9]

Consequently, the bank's credit review process needed strengthening. Traditionally, the bank's president had personally shaped credit policy. He had done so informally, largely by the decisions he made on large loans. The number of senior lending officers was small, and in periodic meetings the president would review each major credit proposed. Approval was case by case, though occasionally a general memorandum was circulated to inform lending officers what kinds of loans were likely to be approved. Credit policy in a formal written sense did not exist.

Until the late 1940s this procedure was adequate. The number of individual credits to be reviewed was not large, since most credits could be analyzed with the aid of simple rules. Many loans were backed by securities or by goods in transit; to limit the bank's risk, the lending officer only had to make sure that the value of the collateral exceeded the loan by an ample margin. Unsecured credits were mainly for working capital. If the ratio of the borrower's current assets to his current liabilities met a conventional standard, the loan was considered safe.

With two outstanding exceptions, these simple approaches to credit analysis had served the bank well. The exceptions were the Cuban sugar loans and the bridge financing (loans to be repaid from the proceeds of bond sales) undertaken by National City in 1930-1931. In both instances, a large, unexpected deterioration of economic conditions had invalidated the assumption of continuing economic stability implicit in a loan officer's estimate of a borrower's balance sheet ratios or in the valuation of collateral. In the Cuban sugar case, the bank had compounded the error in credit analysis by allowing sugar loans to become too large a proportion of the bank's total portfolio. When sugar prices collapsed in 1921, the bank almost did too (see chapter 6).

The growth of term lending in the 1950s meant the bank would be making more loans, larger loans, and more complex loans. Sheperd could no longer hope to review proposals personally in order to set credit policy, along with all his other duties. He had to delegate the job of setting credit policy.

Sheperd chose D. Arthur Forward for the task. Forward had been in charge of the Domestic Division and was reputed to be one of the best credit men in the country.[10] Like Sheperd, he had joined the bank in 1916 as a member of a College Training Class and had occupied a variety of positions, beginning in the Foreign Department. After the People's Loan and Trust merger, he headed the Brooklyn branches and switched to corporate lending in the 1930s. In 1948 he had been in the running for president (see chapter 11). Now he would take on an important aspect of what was traditionally the president's job.

As Forward conceived it, the function of credit policy supervision was to set formal standards applicable to individual credits and to maintain overall portfolio balance. Much of his work was done in weekly meetings with the bank's senior lending officers. As the bank's directors had done a century earlier, this group—though not yet formalized as a credit policy committee—reviewed major proposed credits and reached a consensus on what loans to make. Forward saw to it that credit judgments followed common standards, so that firms in similar circumstances in different geographical areas and industries would have similar chances of receiving credit approval. As the standards became known in the bank, lending officers could negotiate loans more confidently, knowing what preliminary commitments were likely to be approved. When problems in collecting a loan developed, Forward's staff monitored the accounts closely. If the borrower defaulted, the staff took the account over and tried to work out the loan.

The weekly credit meeting also gave Forward an overview of the loan portfolio and an opportunity to hold back on commitments to industries or regions that were already too heavily represented. Forward or another member of top management also conducted daily "money meetings" with senior officers to review the bank's liquidity and take steps to meet the bank's reserve requirements. With these credit and liquidity controls in place, lending officers could safely be given and were given a stronger marketing thrust. Account officers could focus on deepening existing relationships and developing new ones.

A New Leader

Howard Sheperd's decision in 1951 to move Forward out of his position as head of the Domestic Division seems to have been motivated in part by concern for the coming presidential succession. Brady, the bank's chairman, would retire in 1952; it was clear that Sheperd would succeed him. Sheperd's candidate for president was James Stillman Rockefeller, the head of the New York branches. Moving Forward out of the Domestic Division freed that spot for Rockefeller, giving him an opportunity to deepen his experience in the core business of the bank, corporate lending.

Rockefeller had strong family ties to the bank. His grandfathers, James Stillman and William Rockefeller, had been two of the men most responsible at the turn of the century for building the bank. After a brief stint at Brown Brothers Harriman and Company, James Stillman Rockefeller came to the bank in 1930. He spent his first years at National City handling corporate accounts in New York City. After military service in World War II, Rockefeller returned as Sheperd's deputy in the Domestic Branch Division, succeeding him when Sheperd became president in 1948. When Rockefeller took over the Domestic Division, he did not relinquish his responsibility for the New York branches. Thus for a time he was in charge of the entire domestic business of the bank. He passed this final exam, and when Sheperd became chairman at the end of 1952, Rockefeller moved up to president.

W. Randolph Burgess, chairman of the Executive Committee, was disappointed at this turn of events. He decided to leave the bank and return to public service as under secretary of the treasury in the Eisenhower administration. In his fourteen years as a member of top management, he had served the institution well, in managing the investment portfolio, advising management on economic and money market conditions, and maintaining good relations with the Federal Reserve and the Treasury.

Burgess's departure left the institution without a senior manager of its bond portfolio. To fill the gap, Sheperd asked Richard S. Perkins, president of City Bank Farmers Trust Company, to come over to the bank as vice chairman. Like Rockefeller, Perkins had strong family ties to the bank; James H. Perkins, chairman from 1933 to 1940, was his father. After a career in investment banking that culminated in a partnership in Harris Upham, Richard Perkins joined City Bank Farmers Trust as executive vice president in March 1951. In December the same year, he succeeded Lindsay Bradford as president of the Trust Company. From the start, Perkins had breathed new life into City Bank Farmers Trust. He built up the pension business, carried out a major reorganization of the company, and overhauled its systems, procedures, and investment policy. He brought in young men and aggressively sought new business.

Perkins's move to the bank in late 1952 completed the top management team. He brought the experience in investment management needed to oversee the bond portfolio and to develop the Trust Company. Rockefeller had the administrative skill, the knowledge of banking, and the soundness of judgment needed to run the bank from day to day. Sheperd shaped policy, worked with directors, and helped build the more important customer relationships. Together the three men launched an assault on the corporate market. Their front-line commanders were Howard Laeri and George Moore, who respectively divided between themselves Rockefeller's previous responsibility for both the local (Domestic

Branch Division) and domestic wholesale (Domestic Division) banks. Each man hoped to follow Rockefeller into the presidency. Their rivalry would propel the bank forward.[11]

Geography or Industry?

As the corporate market took off in the early 1950s, the question of how best to organize the corporate lending officers came to the fore. The question was: What form of organization would best allow a lending officer to acquire the knowledge or expertise he needed to market the bank's services and to judge the quality of his customers' credit?

Traditionally, National City had grouped its lending officers into geographical districts and divisions. Frank Vanderlip had adopted this pattern during World War I when the bank first subdivided its lending officers into units (see chapter 5). The assumption underlying such geographical specialization was that a loan officer needed most to know his customer's firm in its local or regional setting. From a marketing standpoint, intimate knowledge of the local scene could be turned into leads to new business. In time, a lending officer could acquire real stature in his district, representing as he did one of the largest banks in the country, a valuable marketing plus. From a credit standpoint, the officer would know his customers' local reputation, what his business acquaintances and competitors thought of his firm, what the local bankers thought of the business. Lending officers brought up in this tradition were generalists. The successful ones among them, in addition to having a gift for salesmanship, knew a great deal about business generally and were able to make credit judgments based as much on their knowledge and judgment of human character as on the numbers.

Until the mid-1950s, the bank's corporate accounts had been subdivided essentially along geographical lines. Although within the Metropolitan (New York City) Group of the Domestic Division some accounts were organized by industry groups, this was because industries within the city were often concentrated geographically (clothing on Seventh Avenue, brokers and insurance companies around Wall Street). The Out-of-Town Group of the Domestic Division was subdivided into regional districts that divided up the country. Some large accounts were domiciled in the Metropolitan Group because the customer's headquarters were in New York City although the firm's main business was elsewhere—the Union Pacific Railroad, for example. The result was that firms in some important borrowing industries such as oil refining were scattered among the various groups and districts.

In the early 1950s, the lack of industry knowledge on the part of lending officers came to be seen as a serious drawback from both a marketing and

Figure 12.2

THE CREATION OF THE SPECIALIZED INDUSTRIES GROUP

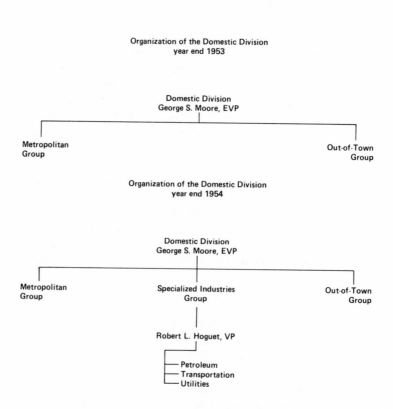

Organization of the Domestic Division
year end 1953

Domestic Division
George S. Moore, EVP

Metropolitan
Group

Out-of-Town
Group

Organization of the Domestic Division
year end 1954

Domestic Division
George S. Moore, EVP

Metropolitan
Group

Specialized Industries
Group

Out-of-Town
Group

Robert L. Hoguet, VP

— Petroleum
— Transportation
— Utilities

a credit standpoint in the case of certain industries, oil and electric utilities
among them. The problem surfaced when these industries began to borrow heavily, mainly in the form of term loans. Marketing and credit analysis for these accounts required a deep understanding of the customer's
business in its regulatory, economic, technological, and competitive aspects, as well as the ability to project these factors well into the future. Frequently, large term loans had to be tailored to a firm's capacity to provide
unconventional forms of collateral, such as an assignment of charter revenues in shipping loans. By itself, the bank's streamlined credit review
process was not adequate for the job. Nor was the small staff of specialists
in the Bond Department. Although they advised account officers on the
techniques of cash-flow analysis and supplemented account officers' knowledge of individual industries, the bond specialists were not organized to

support or promote large increases in the volume of term loans. Unlike Chase and the First National Bank of Chicago, National City had not integrated its industry specialists into the lending divisions or the credit review process.[12]

To compete effectively for corporate business, the account officer had to know the borrower's finances and prospects inside out. Moore had already set up regular in-house briefings to keep his officers informed about industries in their region. He had also put more officers on the road, sending them to visit customers more frequently. But as the bank's business grew, officers found it difficult to keep up to date on many different industries.[13] They were encountering tough competition from industry specialists at other banks, particularly Chase, whose highly successful Petroleum Department had been organized in the 1930s.[14]

In 1954 the bank moved toward industry specialization as well. At Moore's recommendation, the Specialized Industries Group was created within the Domestic Division to handle the bank's relationships with firms in the petroleum, transportation, and public utility industries (Figure 12.2). Each of these industries contained relatively large firms that demanded large amounts of credit for new plants and equipment. These industries operated under special tax codes and regulatory constraints, which made their far-from-ordinary economics still more complex. The accounts of firms in these industries were among the largest in the bank. The 550 accounts transferred to the new group had an average balance more than twice as large as the rest of the accounts in the Domestic Division (Table 12.1). Accounts of this size could support the extra cost of developing lending officers with specialized industry knowledge.

Robert L. Hoguet, Jr., a vice president in charge of the district in the Metropolitan Group that had been responsible for many of the bank's pe-

Table 12.1. Account domicile, Domestic Division, November 1954

Group	No. of accounts	Average balance (thousands of $)
Metropolitan	2,589	185
Out-of-town	3,483	250
Specialized industries	550	492
Petroleum	151	890
Public utility	146	440
Transportation	253	285
Domestic Division	6,622	245

Source: National City Bank, Comptroller's Report, 1954, p. D48.

troleum accounts, was asked to head the new group. He brought together a team of account officers from the Domestic Division and a number of analysts from the Bond Department who had long been advising corporate lending officers on cash-flow projections and other aspects of term lending. Under the new setup, the analysts took a direct part in lending and credit decisions.

At first there were the usual problems accompanying a major reorganization. The head of the new Transportation District was not effective and his second in command, Walter B. Wriston, ran the district. There was resistance to the transfer of some of the bank's largest and most prestigious corporate accounts to the Specialized Industries Group, particularly on the part of those New York City branches where big petroleum accounts had been domiciled. "We had a lot of trouble at the start," Hoguet said in an interview, "because it was fairly easy to take a business away from the geographic district [of the Domestic Division] but the shoe bound badly in New York City. The branches . . . didn't want to give up these big relationships and there was a push and a pull."[15]

These problems soon faded, and the new unit was not long in proving itself. From 1954 to 1957 its loans more than tripled, rising from $257 million to $785 million.[16] By the later date the Specialized Industries Group was extending one-third of the bank's total domestic commercial loans. About half of that increase came from accounts in the petroleum group, at first under the administration of J. Ed Warren, a petroleum engineer, and then under William I. Spencer, an experienced lending officer who had left Chemical Bank to join National City in 1951.

The Petroleum District demonstrated the power of the industry approach to lending. During the mid-1950s drilling for new oil was proceeding at a record pace. Increased expertise in the industry enabled the bank to employ innovative financing techniques. By and large, the independent producers who did much of the drilling were too small to have access to the bond or equity markets; for external finance they depended on their bankers. Their business was risky; only one in five wells drilled found oil or gas in commercial quantities. If a bank had to depend on future gushers to repay its loans, few such loans could be made.

But many drillers had interests in wells that were already producing crude, and this oil could serve to secure a loan that was "bankable." An assignment of revenues by the borrower became collateral for a loan to finance a new well. As the oil from the old well was pumped to the surface, it provided a cash flow that could reasonably be expected to amortize the loan. Thus the bank would be repaid, whether or not the new well struck oil. Invented by the Republic Bank of Dallas, the production-payment loan, as it came to be called, was taken over by Spencer and his colleagues in the Petroleum District and transformed into one of the bank's major financing vehicles.

To translate this concept into practice required specialized knowledge. A petroleum engineer had to determine the amount and quality of the oil in the ground and how quickly it might be drawn out. A petroleum economist had to estimate the future price of crude and the limits the state regulatory authorities might place on oil output in the future. The lending officer had to know enough about his borrower and the quality of his organization to judge whether the borrower could produce the oil on the schedule promised. With this information, the bank could make a loan to the well owner with the expectation that it would be repaid. For the remaining risk the bank was compensated by an attractive spread.[17] Largely on the basis of such production-payment loans, the average credit outstanding in the bank's Petroleum District rose from $62 million in 1954 to $324 million in 1957.[18] Within three years the bank had become one of the leading lenders to the petroleum industry.

Merger with First National

Soon after the Specialized Industries Group got under way, National City made another move to enlarge the bank's share of the corporate market. On March 31, 1955, it merged with the First National Bank. The merged institution was named the First National City Bank of New York.

First National at the time of the merger was much smaller than National City—$700 million in assets compared to $6.5 billion. Founded in 1863, First National was a specialized wholesale bank whose portfolio consisted for practical purposes of a handful of major corporate accounts. But it was an elite bank with a distinguished past. Its corporate accounts included such household names as U.S. Steel and the Ford Motor Company, for which the First was lead bank. First National, in sum, was still the blue ribbon corporate bank George F. Baker had built in the days of J. P. Morgan, Sr., and James Stillman. Nearly all the bank's major accounts dated from Baker's day, and the shadow of the grand old man still lay heavy on the institution he had created, though he had been dead more than twenty years.[19]

At the turn of the century, Baker's bank had closely resembled Stillman's. Both serviced a cross section of the nation's leading corporations. In time the two banks grew increasingly different. Baker set up a securities affiliate for First National in 1908 and confined it to underwriting securities. Stillman's National City Company, set up three years later, broadened its activities to include the retail distribution of securities. In the 1920s Mitchell extended the thrust into retail finance by opening domestic branches and emphasizing retail securities distribution. Baker confined First National to a single office in Wall Street. He spoke contemptuously of branch banking as "chain-store banking." To strengthen ties with large corporations and to attract new customers, National City opened branches abroad as soon as the law permitted it to do so. Baker held that no American banker knew enough about international banking to venture safely abroad. For this reason Baker sold the First National's security affiliate's controlling interest in the Chase National Bank, which had begun to open branches abroad. Nevertheless, in the 1920s both National City and First National were remarkably profitable. In that expansive environment, more than one strategy worked.

The New Deal banking legislation would weaken Baker's bank. No longer able to underwrite its clients' securities, First National also lost its power to attract their deposits. The *New York Times* commented at the time of the merger, "Ironically, the niche that George F. Baker had carved for the First became less important with the end of the Bank Holiday, the early Thirties, and especially the establishment of deposit insurance. When people began to cease worrying about the safety of their deposits the premium declined on a bank that had made a name for itself as the epitome of conservatism."[20] At the end of World War II, 60 percent of the bank's deposits came from just six customers.[21] If the First was to survive, it had to widen its deposit base. Edwin Thorne, a vice president of the First National in the early 1950s, recalled, "We had very substantial balances from a very small number of accounts and this was because in those days money wasn't worth very much and so corporations were keeping very large liquid assets, that is, cash which was left on demand deposit. We realized this wasn't going to continue and people were going to work their cash a lot harder, and therefore to tread water and keep our position balancewise, we had to work very hard to build up new business."[22]

It was a losing battle. The First's small cadre of lending officers was of high quality, and its relatively large capital enabled it to undertake some innovative financing in the postwar period, but the bank steadily lost deposits. In 1945 its total assets had exceeded $1 billion. Nine years later they had declined to $700 million.[23] Flexibility and speed of response to credit inquiries could not offset the regulatory handicaps and the failure to build a branch network to capture deposits.

The First's days were numbered and its management knew it. The erosion of deposits had depressed earnings relative to the bank's large capital base. Although the First paid out approximately 95 percent of its earnings as dividends, it had a capital-to-asset ratio far higher than other New York City banks. But with the premium on safety substantially reduced by deposit insurance and post-Korea prosperity, this large capitalization served no purpose. Rather it reflected the obsolescence of a strategy of exclusive specialization on corporate banking. As Thorne recalled, "We saw that we were not in a position to really compete, to develop deposits rapidly so that we could make proper use of our capital for our stockholders."[24] Merger with a bank that had what the First lacked, deposits, was the obvious next move.

After considering a merger with a predominantly retail branch bank such as the Corn Exchange, or another wholesale bank such as the New York Trust Company, First National opened merger discussions with National City.[25] Alexander Nagle, president of the First, was Howard Sheperd's close friend, and Percy Chubb, one of First National's more active directors, had done much business with National City. These personal relationships undoubtedly influenced Nagle and his directors in the choice of a merger partner and smoothed the transition from two banks to one.

National City's aggressive corporate lending officers were delighted to acquire the First's prestigious accounts. As George Moore remembered, "The First National Bank . . . had lost ground steadily . . . [It] had lost 50 percent of its size in the 10 post-war years while Citibank had doubled! But it had some remarkable business relationships: U.S. Steel, American Can, American Radiator, National Biscuit, the 'Hill' railroads, Burlington, Great Northern, Northern Pacific . . . [The First] people were good but many drifted out . . . but not until we had locked up the valuable business relationships we acquired in the merger. This was a great deal for Citibank, business-wise."[26]

The Trend to Diversification

Beginning in 1954, other major New York banks had entered into a series of mergers, creating diversified wholesale-retail banks like First National City. For big banks, the days of specialized banking were over. A wholesale bank like the Chemical Bank needed a retail bank like the Corn Exchange Bank to help fund its assets and to match its corporate customers' demands for larger credits, and in October 1954 the two banks merged.[27] Bankers Trust, another wholesale bank, merged in February 1955 with the Public National Bank, a retail bank with the fourth largest branch network in the city but without enough corporate business to make full use of its ability to generate deposits.[28] Later, in 1961, Manufacturers Trust, with the largest local branch network, would merge with Central Hanover Bank, a strictly corporate institution.[29]

The largest union came in January 1955, when the Chase National Bank agreed to merge with the Bank of the Manhattan Company, a retail bank, under the latter's original 1799 state charter. Chase had already begun to diversify in the 1920s, opening branches at home and abroad. It grew rapidly through a series of mergers, overtaking National City in total assets and deposits in 1930. By 1948, Chase had again fallen behind National City, but the merger pushed the new Chase Manhattan Bank ahead, making it the largest bank in New York and second in the country, after the California-based Bank of America.[30]

Among New York's major wholesale banks, only Morgan was able to resist moving into retail banking. In 1959 it merged with the Guaranty Trust, significantly boosting its resources. It remained a purely wholesale bank.[31] With this exception, First National City Bank's closest competitors paid its longstanding strategy of diversification the sincerest compliment of imitation.

Despite these positive signs, more funding problems lay just ahead. The explosion of corporate lending depended on rapidly increasing deposits, and in the late 1950s, even for diversified banks with large branch networks, deposits were getting to be harder to find.

13.

The Funding Squeeze
1957-1961

Scarcely a year after its merger with First National, the bank was running out of money to lend. Deposits were not keeping pace with loan demand. As early as 1956 management reported to the shareholders that "lending capacity has not been sufficient for all demands."[1] The recession of 1957-1958 eased the problem temporarily, but as the economy recovered, so did loan demand. In January 1960 management described the situation:

> Our principal problem in 1959 therefore has been to meet greater loan demand in a period when our deposits have shown little gain. To obtain funds for loans we have reduced our holdings of U.S. Governments and other securities substantially, accepting necessary losses on the sales. However, the extent to which banks can liquidate investments for the purpose of adding to loanable funds is limited. In addition to the cash reserves required by law, we must always hold quickly convertible assets sufficient to meet temporary deposit downswings, with a good margin for the unforeseen, and we must have substantial amounts of government securities to pledge against deposits of public bodies as required by law. Except as deposits increase, these requirements impose an approximate ceiling on lending capacity.[2]

The slow growth of deposits reflected changes in banks' relationships with their large corporate customers. Traditionally, corporations had borrowed from banks to finance inventories and goods in process or in transit. Such short-term borrowings were normally seasonal, and loans were fully repaid at least once a year. At times when it had no loan outstanding, the customer maintained balances at the bank, which entitled the firm to credit, as a matter of custom if not of legal right, when its borrowing sea-

son came round again. Since seasonal patterns of inventory buildup, production, and shipment differed among industries and trades, a well-managed bank had sufficient deposits to cover loan demand in all seasons. As
a group, a bank's business customers funded themselves.

In the 1950s major changes in corporate banking altered this familiar
pattern. One was the term loan. Term lending had enabled National City
to respond, in the early 1950s, to its corporate customers' rapidly growing
demand for credit. But term lending to finance investments in plant and
equipment was not seasonal; the corporate customer remained in debt
throughout the year, thereby utilizing fully for its own loans the balances
it had on deposit. The bank's large corporate customers no longer funded
each other as a group. Their loans came to depend on funds from other
sources.

Rising interest rates and the changes they induced in corporate cash
management, were a second factor. In 1951 the Federal Reserve's "accord"
with the Treasury had freed the central bank from its residual wartime obligation to peg interest rates. Since then, rates had been rising, impelled by
rising prices and strong credit demand. As rates rose, it became costly to
corporations to hold idle demand balances. As in the 1920s, corporate
treasurers began to trim bank balances to the minimum required to transact business, and to invest the excess in marketable securities.[3]

These changes showed up in rising loan-to-deposit ratios, particularly
in the case of the Specialized Industries Group, where much of the bank's
term lending was concentrated (Table 13.1). In 1954, when the group was

Table 13.1. Ratio of loans to deposits, First National City Bank,
1954–1961

Year	Specialized industries group	Entire bank
1954[a]	86.0	40.7
1955	117.0	43.8
1956	162.5	56.9
1957	151.0	60.0
1958	171.5	56.8
1959	175.3	59.2
1960	179.7	59.7
1961	164.6	55.9

Source: First National City Bank, Comptroller's Reports, 1955–1961;
Head Office Consolidated Statement of Condition, 1954–1961.

Note: Ratio for the Specialized Industries Group is the average for the calendar year; that for the bank as a whole is for the end of June.

a. 1954 ratios are for National City Bank.

set up, it had loans of $257 million and deposits of $299 million—a loan-to-deposit ratio of 86 percent. Two years later the group's loans had more than doubled, but its deposits had increased less than 30 percent, and its loan-to-deposit ratio was up to 163 percent. Specialized Industries had to draw on other parts of the bank to fund its expanding portfolio of term loans.

But the rest of the bank was providing less funds to the wholesale bank. Both the local bank and the international bank were experiencing the same squeeze. Loans rose rapidly, but deposits increased slowly. Thus these banks had fewer deposits available to fund corporate loans (Table 13.2). The bank therefore had to sell securities.

The amount of bonds the bank could sell without jeopardizing its liquidity was limited. A higher loan-to-deposit ratio therefore made the bank's lending more sensitive to any tightening of credit engineered by the Federal Reserve. Thus when the Federal Reserve tightened in 1956, the bank had to ration credit to corporate borrowers, taking care to give the best customers priority. Management told the shareholders, "In 1956 factors other than the creditworthiness of the borrower have had to be taken into account . . . Close control over lending policy has been necessary to assure our ability to meet our customers' short-term needs, which we regard as our primary function, and to determine what part of their longer term needs we can and should supply. Within that framework we consider that our first obligation is to customers who have had established relationships and have carried good deposit balances with us over the years."[4]

Rationing credit was hardly a solution to the problem of how to serve corporate customers. By the late 1950s, the bank's large corporate custom-

Table 13.2. Net excess deposits, First National City Bank's three "banks," 1954–1960 (millions of dollars)

Year	Wholesale bank	Local bank	International bank	Total
1954	145	858	787	1,790
1955	95	862	762	1,719
1956	−417	741	653	977
1957	−473	734	562	823
1958	−375	893	600	1,118
1959	−534	866	547	879
1960	−642	878	555	791

Source: First National City Bank, Comptroller's Reports, 1954–1960.
Note: Net excess deposits are deposits minus float, required reserves, and loans extended by that "bank." A negative figure denotes that the "bank" borrowed funds from the general pool.

ers had alternatives. If First National City could not offer them credit when they needed it, they could go to the bond market—or to regional banks in the South and West, whose deposits were still growing rapidly. Deposit growth along with lower required reserves enabled regional banks to compete effectively with banks in New York. A regional bank could also help a corporation's local plant managers to open doors locally and could provide convenient banking facilities for the company's plant and its employees. Corporate treasurers accordingly began to spread their firms' banking business among dozens of banks across the country, downgrading the relationship with First National City and other money center banks.[5]

In sum, the funding squeeze threatened First National City in its core business. In 1962 management told the shareholders that during the 1950s, "the Bank's loans more than doubled, while deposits expanded by less than one half. Our ratio of loans to deposits has therefore risen substantially. Since we expect a continuing expansion of demand for loans over the years ahead, it has become increasingly evident that it will be necessary to accelerate the rise in our deposits if we are to meet the future credit needs of our customers and continue to make our full contribution to the growth of the American economy and world trade."[6]

Funding through Branches

The traditional response to a funding squeeze was to expand the deposit base by opening new branches. In the 1920s, the bank had found funds for business lending by building a local bank consisting of branches throughout New York City. In the 1950s this tactic was no longer promising. Economic and demographic trends were unfavorable to New York City after the war. Earlier, migration into the city had more than offset the general westward movement of population. But in 1940 the city's population peaked as a share of the nation's and after the war the middle class began its exodus to the suburbs in pursuit of the American dream, taking with it its rising incomes and bank deposits. Now, better highways and general ownership of automobiles allowed people to commute longer distances to work, and they were moving beyond the city limits to Westchester County, Long Island, Connecticut, and New Jersey. Business, too, was beginning to leave as transportation and communications improved.

In the 1920s, when people had moved from crowded Manhattan to the less crowded boroughs of Brooklyn, Queens, and the Bronx, the bank had followed its customers, opening branches in all the boroughs. In the 1950s this natural response was blocked by law; under New York's Stephens Act of 1934 and the McFadden Act of 1927, the domestic branches of a national bank with headquarters in New York City were confined to the city.[7] The bank's location, once one of its greatest assets, now became something of a liability. Deposits at city banks were hardly rising, and competition for them among commercial banks and a host of savings institutions was intense. First National City could hardly hope to solve its funding problem by taking a larger piece of this limited pie.

The First New York Corporation

For some time, the bank's management had been looking for a way to reach the suburbs, and in 1956 management saw an opportunity to do so. It was presented by a new federal law, the Bank Holding Company Act of 1956. Although the act restricted the formation of multibank holding companies and required prior approval of a new holding company by the Federal Reserve Board, it also seemed to suggest that a merger between National City and a suburban bank might now be possible through a holding company. The bank's attorneys advised that the new holding company law appeared to authorize intrastate bank mergers that took the form of a multibank holding company, even in the absence of a state statute expressly authorizing such mergers.[8]

A suitable merger partner was soon found: the County Trust Company of Westchester County, the largest of the twelve commercial banks in Westchester, with assets in 1956 of $382 million and thirty-nine branches in the county.[9] A state bank formed in 1903, County Trust had grown primarily by serving the local retail market. Its loan portfolio consisted mainly of mortgages and consumer loans. The rapid development of the county after the war had brought County Trust many opportunities for growth, but providing consumer services, in addition to wholesale banking for major firms that were moving their headquarters into Westchester County, strained the bank's resources. The banking needs of a multinational enterprise were beyond the capacity of a local bank. Andrew Wilson, County Trust chairman, hoped to find relief from the bank's growing pains in a holding company merger with National City.[10]

For First National City, affiliation with County Trust offered the bank the opportunity to gain deposits quickly and to establish its presence in a rapidly growing suburban market, much as it had done in Brooklyn in 1926 by merging with People's Loan and Trust. The two banks quickly agreed to merge and a joint application was submitted to the Federal Reserve Board to approve a new holding company, to be called the First New York Corporation, which would control both banks. A joint announcement of the new holding company explained its advantages: "[It] will establish a community of interest and make possible a beneficial exchange of management ideas, methods and experience. The holding company can provide specialized managerial talent, in such matters, for example, as in-

vestment management . . . accounting, tax service and business development at a low unit cost . . . It can facilitate raising necessary capital to
support future growth."[11]

Then the trouble began. Small suburban banks protested the invasion
of their market by a large New York City bank. The press saw it as the
"biggest story in banking since the holiday of 1933," "the little man against
the giants and Main Street versus Wall Street." Politicians sensed an attractive issue. The proposed merger, said the *New York Times,* raised the
"desire of both political parties to be viewed as the champion of the little
man. In New York State, this desire gains urgency because of the gubernatorial election next year."[12]

Running for reelection was Governor Averell W. Harriman, the son of
E. H. Harriman, James Stillman's associate in the Union Pacific reorganization at the turn of the century (chapter 3). When First National City and
County Trust announced that the Federal Reserve Board had been asked
to approve the holding company, Governor Harriman called for a temporary freeze on the formation of bank holding companies in the state. The
state legislature was quick to oblige him. On January 29, 1957, it passed
legislation prohibiting the formation of bank holding companies pending
consideration of comprehensive banking legislation. As the state superintendent of banking acknowledged, it was the First New York Corporation
proposal that had provoked the "freeze law": "The dangers inherent in this
proposal—a breaching of banking district lines and a threat to the survival of
smaller independent banks—were such as to require immediate remedy
by the Legislature."[13]

The Federal Reserve did not take kindly to New York's attempt to pre-
empt its jursidiction, and in February 1957 the board ruled that the New
York freeze law did not preclude an examination of the holding company
proposal on its merits under the Bank Holding Company Act.[14] But for
First National City and County Trust, the win was only procedural. Focusing mainly on the point that the proposed holding company would be
much larger than any other existing bank holding company—because of
the size of First National City—the board on July 10, 1958, denied the application. The board's opinion found that the Westchester community's
banking needs were already satisfied by banks in the county and that the
threat to competitors far outweighed any favorable effect the holding company might have.[15] New York's banking system, said Governor Harriman,
has been "preserved from the threat of monopolistic domination . . . The
chain reaction toward stifling independent banking . . . has now been
prevented."[16]

Two members of the board dissented. They saw no evidence that the
merger would lessen competition, and they rejected the proposition that
big city banks should be kept out of the suburbs simply because they were

big: "To hold otherwise would be tantamount to saying that entry into Westchester County and comparable suburban areas around New York City should be denied forever to any except the smaller New York City banks that might wish to extend the scope of their services through the holding company device. Such [a] position would confer preferred status in this regard upon smaller New York City banks merely because of their lesser size."[17] But the board's majority felt otherwise. To them, size was a four-letter word.

First National City did not seek a review of the Federal Reserve's decision in the courts. It preferred to await an expected change in the New York banking law that might make it possible to reach the suburban market. Harriman had lost the 1958 gubernatorial election to a Republican, Nelson A. Rockefeller, and the new state administration was thought to favor a more liberal state banking law. Even so, it was not until March 1960 that the New York Assembly passed an omnibus banking bill. The new law authorized New York City banks to branch into Nassau and Westchester counties.[18]

Another Attempted Merger

Welcome as it was, the new banking law had limitations from First National City's standpoint. In particular, it prohibited banks with headquarters in New York City from opening a branch in any suburban area that contained the home office of a bank. This "home office protection" clause blocked First National City from opening branches in some of the most attractive suburban markets, such as White Plains. To enter such a market, the bank would have to merge with an existing suburban bank. Once again the search was on for a suitable partner. County Trust was no longer available; it had announced a plan to affiliate with Bankers Trust.[19] On February 9, 1961, First National City announced a plan to merge with the National Bank of Westchester, the second largest of the county's nine commercial banks.[20] The Westchester bank was about half the size of County Trust, with twenty-two branches in the county and a home office in White Plains.

Chances for regulatory approval of the merger looked good. Under the New York Omnibus Banking Act and the federal Bank Merger Act of 1960, First National City and the Westchester bank could affiliate by ordinary merger rather than by means of a multibank holding company. This procedure made Federal Reserve approval unnecessary, although the comptroller of the currency had to approve. The shareholders of both banks voted for the merger on April 18, 1961, in a mood of optimism. The bank's chairman, James S. Rockefeller, commented, "We hope our case is so clear that no one will object."[21]

On May 15, 1961, the two banks submitted a memorandum on the proposed merger to the newly appointed comptroller of the currency, James J. Saxon. Every aspect of the competitive situation that would result from the merger was documented. The memorandum concluded:

> By careful, factual analysis, we have demonstrated that the proposed merger would . . . make readily available to the residents and business firms of Westchester County the full range of services, the better quality of services, and the lower rates and charges of a large-scale, efficient New York City bank. It would not alter the distribution of banking assets in Westchester. It would intensify competition not only among Westchester banks but among nonbank institutions as well. It would bring to the public in this part of the metropolis the benefits of the intense banking competition which exists in the city center. It would supply more healthy competition with the leading bank in the area. It would intensify competition not only in Westchester but throughout the entire New York Banking District. It would help one of the nation's major banks to continue to contribute to the economic progress of the nation.
>
> In view of these facts, which are documented in detail in this application, it is urged that the proposed merger be approved.[22]

Nevertheless, Saxon disapproved. Again, size was the determining factor. Saxon's opinion was a litany of the virtues of competition in banking and stressed the benefits to be expected from the entry of New York City banks into Westchester. But he ruled that these benefits should come gradually, by *de novo* branching, rather than rapidly by merger. The decision protected the local monopoly rights of suburban banks while at the same time prohibiting the sale of those rights to an outsider. Saxon concluded, "The smaller banks in Westchester County, to the extent that they are able properly to service the needs of their respective communities, should be given the opportunity to grow and to prosper."[23]

Other major New York City banks fared no better in their attempts to effect a quick penetration of the suburban banking market through mergers or holding companies. The application of Bankers Trust and County Trust to form a bank holding company was turned down.[24] In 1962 the Federal Reserve said no to Chemical's plan to merge with the Long Island Trust, the third largest Nassau County bank, and Chase Manhattan was refused permission to merge with the Hempstead Bank, another Nassau County bank.[25] In May 1962 Morgan Guaranty's bid to form an intrastate bank holding company, the Morgan New York State Corporation, was turned down.[26] In this way, a legal and regulatory environment developed that penalized the big New York City banks for their size and granted their smaller competitors a preferred status.[27] Subject to "home office protection," First National City could enter the suburbs with its own branches, but not otherwise.

Funding in the Market

With quick entry into the rich suburban deposit market blocked, competing for corporate funds by paying for them was the only recourse remaining for coping with the funding squeeze. But here too there were regulatory obstacles, most obviously the prohibition of interest payments on demand deposits. Devised in the depression to protect banks' solvency by preventing them from paying too much for deposits, the prohibition now limited commercial banks' access to corporate funds in an environment of rising market interest rates.

Bankers compounded the difficulty by their own resistance to paying for deposits. Bankers assumed that corporate treasurers were less sensitive to interest rates than they in fact were and bankers therefore opposed lifting the ban on interest payments. New York banks, said First National City's senior management in a 1959 report to shareholders, are the "natural depositories for corporations."[28] Management thought the bank should and would receive a certain volume of deposits, no matter what rate of interest was paid. Thus paying more for corporate deposits would reduce profits without attracting new funds in significant amounts. Other New York City banks shared this view. A special study prepared by a committee of the New York Clearing House in 1959 concluded:

> This committee would oppose removal of the prohibition of payment of interest on demand deposits. With respect to the payment of interest on time deposits, no legal prohibition exists, although Regulation Q of the Federal Reserve Board imposes a rate ceiling. While the committee recognizes that practices with respect to payment on corporate time deposits are for banks individually to determine, since the dominant factors in such decisions are essentially competitive position, effect on profit and loss account, and similar practical considerations, it doubts the efficacy of such payment in improving the relative position of New York City banks, at least to an extent commensurate with the costs assumed.[29]

But the markets were not listening. First National City and other banks were forced slowly and reluctantly to pay more for funds. On May 1, 1956, the bank raised its rate on passbook savings from 2 percent to 2.5 percent, the Regulation Q ceiling. A year later the passbook ceiling was raised to 3 percent and the bank followed. These and other changes to increase the attraction of savings accounts were relatively successful. The volume of savings at the bank's New York branches more than doubled, rising from $382 million in 1955 to $781 million in 1961, and accounted for nearly half of the increase in the bank's total domestic deposits in that period. But this was plainly insufficient to fuel the bank's long-term growth.

First National City also began to compete more vigorously for funds from correspondent banks, bidding aggressively in the rapidly developing interbank market for overnight balances. An interbank market in reserve balances at the New York Federal Reserve Bank had grown up in New York in the 1920s, when the Federal Reserve Board discouraged rediscounting and New York City banks began to lend and borrow among themselves to adjust their reserve positions instead of borrowing from the Federal Reserve. Banks needing funds to meet reserve requirements on a particular day would borrow overnight the excess reserves of another bank. This market in reserves or "federal funds" disappeared almost completely in the 1930s. Banks generally had large excess reserves and hung on to them, while interest rates were too low to make overnight lending profitable. In the 1940s a funds market was again unnecessary. With Treasury bill rates pegged by the Federal Reserve, bills were the equivalent of cash. Banks, heavily laden with bills, could make necessary reserve adjustments by selling or buying bills.

A federal funds market sprang up again in the 1950s, after the 1951 "accord" freed the price of Treasury bills. In a climate of rising rates, buying and selling bills to make reserve adjustments could impose a capital loss on a bank. The Garvin Bantel Corporation, a firm whose regular business was trading government securities, is credited with having resurrected the federal funds market in 1949 by creating a market in the reserve balances of New York banks.[30]

First National City, like other money center banks, was active in this market. At first, the bank both bought and sold funds, but by the late 1950s it was predominantly a buyer. The market became increasingly divided between money center banks, such as First National City, that borrowed continuously and banks across the country that had more deposits than loans and lent in the funds market day in and day out. By the late 1950s the federal funds market, along with security repurchase agreements with other banks ("repos"), had become an important and growing source of funds for money center banks. In 1961 First National City Bank was borrowing $160 million a day on average from those two sources at an average interest rate of slightly over 2 percent, compared to $26 million at a rate just over 1 percent in 1954.[31] Still, federal funds and repos were no solution to the funding squeeze. They placed the bank second in line for the balances needed to fund corporate loans. Banks in the rest of the country had first claim on their deposits and were using them to attract large corporations away from New York banks.

By the end of the 1950s, then, the bank's "natural depository" thesis had been invalidated. Corporate funds were available but not as interest-free balances. "Attractive interest rates on Treasury bills and other short-term investments," the bank noted in its 1959 annual report, "have . . . diverted corporate funds to those markets. The New York banks . . . are especially affected by this diversion."[32] Providing additional services offered little prospect of attracting more balances. Indeed, as interest rates rose, the bank had to provide more and better services to corporate customers just to keep their balances from declining. The services were costly to provide and difficult to account for. To attract corporate deposits, the bank needed to compete openly for them by paying a market rate of interest.

Eurodollars

In 1959 the bank began to tap a new source of funds, a market for dollar time deposits in banks located outside the United States. The Eurodollar market, as it came to be known, had its origins in the cold war. Communist governments in the mid-1950s needed to hold dollar deposits but wished to avoid making deposits in banks located in the United States, where they might be blocked or sequestered by the United States government. Instead these dollars were deposited in London with British banks or the London affiliates of East European banks. The subsequent development of the market depended far more on foreign exchange controls and on national regulation of commercial banking than on East-West politics. The British supplied the necessary first step when in defense of the pound in 1957 the authorities imposed severe restrictions on sterling credits to foreigners but imposed no regulation of any kind on transactions denominated in dollars or other foreign currency. A series of U.S. capital controls beginning in 1963 interrupted the development of New York as a substitute for London in the finance of international trade. Moreover, the absence of reserve requirements and deposit interest ceilings provided greater returns and lower costs in London than in New York.[33] Consequently, the banking market for time deposits and loans denominated in dollars that emerged in London in the late 1950s grew and expanded rapidly over the course of the next twenty-five years.

In November 1959 money was tight in the United States and the bank, in a new departure, began to use its London office to attract dollar deposits; these would then be advanced to Head Office to help fund the domestic loan portfolio. It was not difficult to attract such funds in London, for the branch was able to accept deposits denominated in dollars as well as in sterling. The dollar shortage was over, and the bank was willing and legally able to pay a rate above the Regulation Q ceiling that applied to domestic time deposits. Further, funds advanced to Head Office by the London branch (they were then called special funds), unlike time deposits booked directly at Head Office, were not subject to reserve requirements.

At the outset, Eurodollar borrowings at First National City were primarily a substitute for the Federal Reserve discount window.[34] Although the market became an important marginal source of funds, in the 1960s it was never intended to be more than that. In those days management was concerned that the market might not continue to be viable. While there was some small degree of sovereign risk, the major problem was a fear that the market might simply and suddenly evaporate.

The Negotiable Certificate of Deposit

Even though the development of the Eurodollar market was important, the bank did not regard it as a solution to the problem of funding domestic assets except for brief periods during the credit crunches of 1966 and 1969. From that perspective, the Eurodollar market merely permitted First National City and other money center banks to gather dollar deposits in additional locations. The solution to the funding problem, pioneered by First National City, lay instead in offering customers a new domestic investment vehicle.[35]

In this effort, the bank had the implicit blessing of the Federal Reserve. The regulators had also become concerned about the erosion of member banks'—particularly money center banks'—deposits. But their concerns differed from those of the banks. Federal Reserve doctrine held that the Reserve's control of credit conditions in the economy depended critically on money center banks. According to this view, ease or tightness imposed by the Federal Reserve was transmitted to the whole credit structure mainly through the money center banks. If their weight in the credit system was reduced because they were unable to attract deposits, the Federal Reserve's control would be weakened. Accordingly, in January 1961 Howard D. Crosse, a vice president of the New York Federal Reserve Bank, made a pointed suggestion: "As I see it, it is no more than wishful daydreaming to hope that holders of temporarily idle excess funds will leave them as non-interest-bearing demand deposits in commercial banks when they can sell them in the market. If banks are to use these funds they will have to pay for them . . . The burden of my remarks is to suggest that commercial banks consider the extent to which they might rebuild their own liquidity through more active participation in this market for short-term, interest-bearing funds; and that if changes in the law or regulations are required, the commercial banks should aggressively make the case for such changes."[36]

One month later, on February 20, 1961, First National City announced a major innovation: "We have now decided to offer negotiable certificates of deposit—'Bankers Certificates'—to selected corporate customers, domestic as well as foreign. These Certificates, evidencing the fact that FNCB will pay to bearer at a stated maturity a stated amount of money plus interest, will be issued in units of not less than $1 million . . . The Discount Corporation of New York has now agreed to undertake to make a market in these Certificates and it is our hope that as they and we gain experience, this new market instrument will come to be accepted as a new short-term medium of investment which will enjoy a ready market."[37]

The certificate of deposit (CD) in the generic sense of an instrument setting forth the terms of a time deposit agreement between a bank and a large depositor was hardly new in 1961. Such certificates had appeared on bank balance sheets before the turn of the century. In 1928 the Federal Reserve published a detailed breakdown of time and savings deposits indicating that one-fourth of all member bank time deposits were accounted for by open account deposits and "time certificates." In form, too, the new CDs, as they would now be known, were little changed. Their language was similar to that recommended by the Federal Reserve Board in 1933 to member banks as an aid in drafting time certificate contracts that would satisfy the requirements of Regulation Q.[38]

What was new was effective negotiability. Traditionally, deposit certificates had been nonnegotiable by their terms or by custom, and in practice they were not marketable; there was no secondary market. A secondary market transforms an illiquid investment into one the investor can quickly convert into cash at a low transaction cost. To succeed, the new CD had to have an efficient secondary market; it would compete for corporate funds with Treasury securities and commercial paper, which traded in well-organized markets. This point was clear to the man at First National City most responsible for introducing the negotiable CD: Walter B. Wriston, head of the Overseas Division.

The Overseas Division had traditionally offered its foreign customers time deposit open accounts. Early in 1960 it concluded that time deposits might be more attractive to foreign customers if they were marketable. In the summer of 1960 "bankers' certificates," described as a marketable instrument, were offered to a few customers. The first certificate, for $1 million, was issued to the Union Bank of Switzerland on August 23, 1960. But this first essay did not get very far. Marketable by their terms, the certificates were not effectively so. "You tell me it's negotiable," said a Union Bank official, "and I can't see any place to sell it. It really isn't negotiable at all."[39]

But Wriston had grasped the CD's potential if it had a secondary market. He persuaded the Discount Corporation of New York, a dealer in government securities, to start a market in CDs. The Discount Corporation was willing, provided the bank supported the venture with an unsecured loan of $10 million. The bank broke its rule of not lending to brokers on an unsecured basis, and the market was made.[40]

The CD, said Wriston in a 1977 interview, "probably changed the world [of banking] as much as anything."[41] It would solve the funding problem, thereby opening the way to faster growth. Instead of matching loan commitments to the supply of bonds that could be sold, banks would now be able to book loans they thought profitable, knowing the funds would be available in the market at a price. Moreover, market funding would solve another traditional banking problem: liquidity. If banks could find funds whenever needed in large, efficient CD and Eurodollar markets, they would be able to shift their asset portfolios away from low-yielding but highly liquid U.S. government securities toward higher-yielding but less liquid assets such as loans and municipal securities. In effect, market funding would come to serve the purpose Frank Vanderlip had once hoped the Federal Reserve's discount window would serve. It would make banks liquid without sacrificing yield on assets.

But such gains would come at a price. With market funding, banking would become more like other businesses—that is, more competitive, with profits more dependent on cost-conscious management, imaginative product development, and aggressive marketing. In traditional commercial banking, a bank enjoyed a privileged relationship with its customers. Deposits were raised in markets partly protected from competition by geographical restrictions on branching, by a prohibition of interest payments on demand deposits, and by banks' exclusive franchise to offer checking accounts. Thus traditional banking consisted of the exchange of a bundle of financial services, particularly ready access to credit and third-party payments, for deposits on which the bank paid a less than fully competitive rate of interest.

With profitability protected by low-cost funds, banks did not have to know in depth the cost of the individual services they provided, or to understand fully the differences in the risks they assumed on different classes of assets and lines of business. Cheap funding made it possible to earn a global profit without having to worry too much about exactly where and why. If assets grew and credits were analyzed conservatively, the bank would earn an adequate return on its capital.

Market funding would change bankers' perception of their business and alter, accordingly, the business of banking itself. Commercial bankers would come to see that their business consists of two distinct but related activities: the management of risk or financial intermediation in a broad sense and the manufacture of financial transactions, particularly the execution of third-party payments. In time, the desirability of partially unbundling and separately costing, pricing, and marketing these and other services would become apparent. But such far-reaching implications of the shift from demand deposits to market funding were hardly visible when the CD was introduced in 1961. They would not emerge into the full light of day until the 1970s.

14.

A New Era
1961–1967

Solving the bank's funding problem was a necessary requirement for growth but not the only one. For growth also depended on the demand for bank credit, and there the outlook was clouded. The bank's bread-and-butter business, corporate lending, which had fueled the institution's expansion in the 1950s, was turning sluggish.[1]

Business loan demand at First National City and other banks peaked in 1957, near the top of the business cycle, and thereafter declined until 1962. In this decline, money center banks fared worse than commercial banks generally, and First National City fared worse than its major money center competitors.[2] The bank's special problem was its particular mix of customers, especially the utilities companies whose borrowing in the mid-1950s had ballooned the assets and earnings of the Specialized Industries Group, and had now tapered off. More significant was the difficulty the bank shared with other money center banks: greater dependence than in the case of regional and local banks on a core of large corporations whose borrowing had become increasingly cyclical. Large firms typically did the bulk of their financing in the securities markets and out of retained earnings. They turned to their banks primarily in the later stages of a business expansion, when other credit was becoming scarcer and more expensive. Thus for large firms, banks like First National City were becoming lenders of last resort.

Between 1955 and 1962, the bank's commercial and industrial loans varied from 40 percent to 50 percent of the domestic portfolio of loans and investments. Such variability, while hardly disastrous for earnings, was not the stuff of which a strong, steady expansion could be made. Moreover, in the 1960s, unlike the 1920s, the institution could not follow its corporate customers into the securities markets to offset a weakness in the demand for bank credit.

Banks' traditional advantage in commercial lending—their accumulated knowledge of their customers' business—was also diminishing in the

1960s. A revolution in business information—advances in the theory and practice of business analysis, a wave of business school graduates trained in the new methods, an explosion of economic, financial, and company data from federal agencies and private information services, and, last but not least, electronic data processing—made it easier and cheaper for all participants in financial markets to make credit judgments, at least with respect to leading domestic corporations. As a result, large and rapidly growing nonbank financial intermediaries such as insurance companies, finance companies, and pension trusts as well as nonfinancial corporations themselves could compete more effectively with money center banks in lending to large firms. Moreover, firms could more easily raise capital in the securities markets.

In sum, lending to large firms was becoming a less dependable source of growth. Charles Mitchell had faced the same strategic problem and responded to it by diversifying into other lines of business. Now James Stillman Rockefeller and George Moore would define and carry out a similar strategy. Together, they would lead the bank into its most successful period since the 1920s.

George Stevens Moore had become president in 1959, when Rockefeller moved up to chairman after Howard Sheperd's retirement. Moore's entrepreneurial style was well suited to the times. A man "hell bent on doing things yesterday," he knew how to impart his own drive to those who worked for him. Throughout his career he had been a builder, first in the Domestic and then in the Overseas Division. Now he would build the bank. Balancing Moore's creativity and enthusiasm was Rockefeller's judgment. Much as James Stillman had done when Frank Vanderlip was president, Chairman Rockefeller allowed his dynamic president to drive the bank forward, braking him rarely and only when something was clearly going wrong. In manner and style, Rockefeller and Moore were a study in contrasts, and their relationship was not without friction. Yet each complemented the other and valued the other's contribution.

Shortly after becoming president, Moore and his close associate in the Overseas Division, Walter B. Wriston, defined their vision of where the bank should be going. As Moore recalled, "Around 1960, we in Citibank took a new position. We would not be merely a bank. We would become a financial service company. We would seek to perform every useful financial service, anywhere in the world, which we were permitted by law to perform and which we believed we could perform at a profit."[3]

Actually, the position was as old as it was new. It was a reaffirmation of the institution's traditional strategy. The aim to be everywhere and do everything harked back to Frank Vanderlip's vision, which Mitchell had carried forward in the 1920s and his successors, to the extent permitted by regulation, had preserved through the long years of depression and war.

"The fundamental aims of the Bank have not changed," said the bank's 1961 annual report. "We remain committed to the concept of the 'all-around' bank."[4]

As in the 1920s, the times were ripe for a strategy of this kind. After the 1960–1961 recession, the world economy entered a period of extraordinary prosperity. In the United States, beginning with the first quarter of 1961, real economic activity advanced for thirty-five consecutive quarters, the longest economic boom on record. Prosperity seemed permanent. *Time* wrote on February 5, 1965, "The amazing U.S. economy could defy even the law of physics: what goes up need not necessarily come down." Abroad, growth was still more rapid than at home. In continental Europe and Japan, the economic miracle of postwar recovery continued. Growth in the industrialized world propelled other economies forward. Brazil, Korea, Mexico, Taiwan, and some other developing countries industrialized rapidly. U.S. firms' direct foreign investment ballooned. World production and trade grew at rates never before seen on a sustained basis. This expansive environment was a consequence of the stabilization of the world political balance, of the lowering of barriers to international trade and investment, of reasonably stable prices and exchange rates, and of the steady, moderate expansion of the world money supply—converging influences all reflecting in one way or another the hegemony and policies of the United States in the world political, monetary, and trading systems.

In such an environment, the concept of an all-around bank could again become reality. First National City diversified its activities, building on its strong position overseas and in the local retail market. It undertook a program of branch expansion at home and abroad and broadened its product line. Geographical expansion and product diversification served a common goal: to deepen relationships with existing customers and to find new ones.

International Banking

International banking had long been the bank's strong suit, and during the 1960s First National City played it to the hilt. Beginning with the largest overseas branch system of any U.S. bank, the bank expanded the network, entering new countries and adding offices in countries where it was already established. At the branches, the bank provided a wider range of financial services, using them to broaden the local customer base and to strengthen connections with its major customers, U.S. multinational corporations. Walter Wriston, who took command of the Overseas Division in 1959, described the program: "The plan in the Overseas Division was first to put a Citibank branch in every commercially important country in the world. The second phase was to begin to tap the local deposit market by putting satellite branches or mini-branches in a country. The third phase was to export retail services and know-how from New York. All of these phases ran concurrently and sometimes overlapped."[5] The groundwork had been laid in 1956, when Chairman Howard Sheperd asked George Moore to have a look at the bank's European and Latin American branches. Moore returned from a survey trip with a series of recommendations for expanding and improving the branches. Soon thereafter, Sheperd asked him to replace Leo Shaw, who was close to retirement, as head of the Overseas Division. As Moore remembered it, "Sheperd said, 'You're in charge of the foreign department effective at 1:00 P.M.' It was a quarter to twelve."[6]

Moore took over an organization badly in need of change. The overseas establishment had been eroded by long years of depression and war, hot and cold. The outbreak of war in Korea in 1950 had brightened the domestic outlook, but abroad it had had the opposite effect. In 1948 the bank had reopened a branch in Paris, but further openings in Europe were deterred, despite Europe's developing recovery, by visions of Soviet tanks rolling across Germany and France. In the Far East, the Overseas Division's postwar stance had been equally unaggressive. The bank's newly reopened China branches had been lost in 1949 when China fell to the communists. Thereafter, apart from the Philippines and Japan, where a U.S. military presence guaranteed security, branch expansion had ceased. The bank had also suffered a setback in South America. After the war, a turn of the political wheel brought populist regimes to power in Argentina and Brazil. In both countries there followed a decade of economic mismanagement, inflation, and exchange control that reduced the bank's branch earnings in these two countries to a trickle (see chapter 11).

At the end of 1955, the bank's foreign branches numbered 61, down from 83 in 1930, and 63 in 1940. There were only 3 branches in Europe, and the Far Eastern network numbered 12 in five countries, compared to 17 in six countries before the war. Still, the network was far larger than those of the bank's nearest U.S. competitors.[7] The overseas staff was competent and possessed a wealth of knowledge about foreign countries, but it was aging and morale was low. Few Americans had been sent overseas. Moreover, those stationed outside the United States tended to remain in a particular region, and had little contact with Head Office or with their counterparts in other regions. In 1947 there were only 165 Americans overseas, out of a total overseas staff of 4,200. Since then, there had been little hiring, promotions had been rare, and management had been more interested in controlling expenses than in building the business. All in all, the value of the foreign branches to the bank had declined sharply. They contributed 16 percent of total earnings before tax in 1955, compared to 30 percent in 1930. The foreign branches' share of the bank's total deposits and loans in 1955 was 11 percent and 14 percent, respectively, down from 25 percent and 29 percent in 1930. Business in the branches was largely confined to trade finance and foreign exchange.

Moore moved promptly to put new life into the Overseas Division. To speed change, he built a new informal structure inside the old one, infusing into this shadow organization his own enthusiasm for growth.[8] He brought officers who were eager to become agents of change from the rest of the bank, particularly from the Domestic Division, and added new recruits—about fifty a year—from the country's leading universities and business schools, whom he posted for training to the bank's branches around the world.

At the supervisory level Moore effected nothing less than a "complete personnel reconstruction."[9] By the end of 1959, two-thirds of the Overseas Division's supervisors abroad had been changed, either retired or called back to New York.[10] It left "a lot of people in shock," but to those who identified with Moore's aim, it was exhilarating.[11] In 1957 Moore began holding annual meetings of senior officers from all branches. Few of the men knew one another at first, and they had little sense of belonging to a worldwide team. By these meetings held at the Westchester Country Club and his own extensive travels, Moore created the feeling of a united organization on the move. Formerly a ticket to nowhere (before his transfer, Moore once called the Overseas Division Siberia), a job there now appeared to be the way to early responsibility and large rewards.[12]

"De facto decentralization," one participant called Moore's management style.[13] Officers in New York and abroad were expected to have a definite strategy, a "game plan," but also to be opportunistic and creative as they sought out and responded to chances to expand the bank's business and its profits. Although the reins were loose, control of credit and personnel ultimately remained in New York, where a small group around Moore administered the division and planned the bank's entry into new countries. Within this group Walter Wriston became Moore's deputy and chief administrator, helping to give concrete, practical form to his boss's sense of political and economic trends and business opportunities. Wriston and Moore formed a cohesive management team from which the bank and the two men's own careers would benefit.

Wriston continued to build the international organization after Moore moved up to president in 1959. Wriston's philosophy of branch expansion was simplicity itself: to be everywhere there was a reasonable chance of turning a profit. He reasoned that many countries open to First National City would not remain so. Sooner or later, the combination of nationalism and resistance by local banks would exclude latecomers. Being "everywhere" also helped diversify the bank's portfolio, and the depth and experience of the international staff enabled the bank to make money in countries where its competitors could not.[14] Accordingly, the first priority was "to establish an institutional presence, particularly through branch banking, with the widest possible dispersal along the trade routes and financial centers of the world."[15]

The process was well under way when Wriston took over in 1959, but gaps remained, particularly in Europe, where the formation of the European Economic Community (EEC) in 1957 and restoration of currency convertibility in 1959 had set off a near stampede of U.S. firms to put manufacturing and distribution facilities inside the EEC's common external tariff. In 1959 the bank had branches only in London and Paris, plus a representative office in Frankfurt. Soon branches were opened in other financial centers, beginning in October 1960 with the conversion of the Frankfurt office to a branch. In 1962 the bank opened in Brussels, the headquarters of the EEC, and reentered Italy with a branch in Milan. By 1965 the bank had a branch in each of the major European countries, and in the next two years it opened additional offices in several of them. By 1967 the bank's branch coverage in Europe was adequate, in marked contrast to what had been in place at the beginning of the decade.

Elsewhere overseas, the branch network was exploding. In 1964 and 1965, branches were opened in the Republic of China (Taiwan) and in Dubai on the Arabian Gulf. During the 1960s, the bank deepened its existing network in India by adding branches in Madras and New Delhi and second offices in Calcutta and Bombay. Additional offices were also opened in Hong Kong and Singapore, where business was particularly brisk because of the absence of exchange controls and restrictive banking regulations. In Latin America, where the bank already had an extensive network, there were opportunities to enter smaller countries. In the first half of the 1960s, offices were opened in Bolivia, Ecuador, El Salvador, Honduras, Jamaica, and Trinidad and Tobago. In Argentina, Brazil, Chile, Colombia, Panama, Paraguay, Peru, and Puerto Rico, the bank opened additional branches, deepening its penetration into these markets.

Even this torrent of branch openings did not exhaust the list of countries First National City would have liked to enter. Profitable opportunities remained, particularly in rapidly growing countries where there was relatively little competition among domestic banks. But entry into these protected markets was difficult, for local banks had successfully appealed to nationalism as a reason to exclude foreign banks. Acquisition of an existing bank was therefore the only way to enter the local banking market.

In Canada this approach seemed at first quite promising. The rapidly growing Canadian economy was served by a closed club of eleven chartered banks, to which the Canadian Banking Act afforded protection against competition from new entrants, domestic and foreign. So oligopolistic a market along with the rapidly growing Canadian economy spelled big profits for any foreign bank that could manage to get in. In 1963 First National City managed to do so, buying control of the Mercantile Bank, the smallest of the Canadian chartered banks.[16] Through this acquisition First National City would be able to reach the entire Canadian market, and other U.S. banks would be unable to follow.

Top management felt with some justification that they had pulled off a coup, but the Canadian government and Canadian bankers retaliated. In May 1967 the new Canadian Banking Act became law.[17] It required the Mercantile Bank to limit its liabilities to twenty times its authorized capital of $10 million (Canadian), unless First National City agreed to reduce its ownership to 25 percent or less. Ultimately, the bank chose the latter course. Thus the bank's first major attempt to break into the rich Canadian banking market ended in something close to defeat.[18]

Canada was not the only country with an attractive banking market where the combined opposition of local banks and nationalist political interests proved to be an insurmountable barrier. Spain and Sweden would let no foreign bank open a branch. Australia took the same position, although First National City did open a representative office in Sydney and acquired a controlling interest in a faltering finance company. In Egypt and Cuba, socialist regimes closed down the bank's operations, though in Egypt the decision was later reversed; the bank departed in 1960 and returned in 1975.[19] Banishment from Cuba has proven more lasting. The bank lost a sizable sum when Castro clamped down exchange controls and nationalized its Cuban branches in 1960, and had to forgo the large stream of earnings the branches had formerly remitted each year.[20]

Despite these reverses, by 1967 First National City had reached its goal of establishing an institutional presence in most of the world's financial markets. Between 1960 and 1967, the bank established a total of 85 foreign branches: 54 in Latin America and the Caribbean, 14 in the Far East, 15 in Europe, and 2 in the Middle East. By the end of 1967, Citibank had 148 direct foreign branches in forty-two countries. In addition, there were 93 offices of bank subsidiaries or affiliates in twenty-one countries. These totals placed it far ahead of Chase Manhattan and the Bank of America, its nearest U.S. competitors.

Local Banking Abroad

Traditionally, the overseas branches had done what George Moore called a "a rivers, ports and harbors kind of facilitation of trade business."[21] The boom in world trade in the 1960s increased such business rapidly, but

Wriston decided to diversify the branches' customer base and their activities. Fully developed, this strategy could give First National City nearly the status of a local bank without compromising the advantages of being a U.S. bank. But this was only possible in countries where the bank had been present for many years and where local competitive and regulatory conditions were favorable to a foreign bank. Argentina and Brazil were the two best examples. There First National City had numerous branches. Well integrated into the local banking scene, they had been doing business with local firms continuously since World War I. Elsewhere, the bank could only work toward this ideal as far as local conditions allowed.

Traditionally, the bank had confined its local business lending to self-liquidating loans to prime names. In the 1960s, the bank began making term loans and soliciting customers whose credit standing was less than prime. To do so without heavy losses, the bank introduced into its Latin American and Far Eastern operations techniques of credit analysis and account management that had worked successfully in the Specialized Industries Group in the United States. Frequently, they required the customer to adapt his own accounting and management to the requirements of modern banking, U.S. style. A successful example was the bank's lending to the cattle industry in Panama, where the bank combined its credit analysis and account management techniques with expert advice to ranchers on breeding and feeding. The result was a substantial boost to the industry and the local economy.[22]

To acquire local currency deposits, the bank began to develop individual banking abroad. Mini-branches ("deposit-catchers") to attract household deposits were opened in several countries. In Argentina and Honduras, the bank acquired local banks, in part for the same purpose. Consumer lending at foreign branches was introduced for the first time in the 1960s in a number of countries, while in Argentina, Australia, Hong Kong, and the United Kingdom the bank acquired consumer finance companies.

Further diversification was provided by acquiring other nonbank financial firms: trust companies in Canada, the Bahamas, and the United Kingdom, industrial development banks in Brazil, Venezuela, the Philippines, Pakistan, and Liberia, and an interest in a merchant bank (Hill and Samuel) in London.[23] Such acquisitions, minor in themselves and some of them unprofitable, were important mainly as an expression of the institution's will to move beyond traditional banking into what Wriston would later call congeneric activities.

Banking for the Multinational Corporation

First National City opened its first foreign branch in Buenos Aires in 1914 at the suggestion of American firms with affiliates there (see chapter 5).

The branching explosion of the 1960s was also in large part a response to the rapid foreign deployment of American multinationals, as they would now be called. Between 1960 and 1970, the book value of American direct foreign investment increased from $21 billion to $55 billion.[24] The largest industrial firms accounted for the bulk of it, and most of them were bank customers of long standing. A Harvard Business School study in the mid-1960s showed that 187 firms accounted for three-quarters of all U.S. foreign direct investment in manufacturing and for one-third of the total sales of all U.S. manufacturing firms.[25] Of these 187 companies, 165 were bank customers and their accounts were among the bank's largest.[26] By serving those firms abroad, the bank could strengthen valuable corporate relationships that conditions in the domestic market were weakening.

As U.S. corporations' international operations grew in importance relative to their domestic business, firms reshaped their organizations. The traditional separation of domestic and international operations gave way to a global, functional structure with supervisory departments at company headquarters responsible for such functions as production, marketing, research, and treasury or finance, worldwide. Assistance to the global treasurer in managing cash and raising capital presented a major opportunity for First National City.

Until the late 1950s, affiliates of multinational firms had managed their cash positions country by country. They had raised funds for working capital locally and called on headquarters for financing of plant expansion, much as individual General Motors plants had done before Sloan introduced a companywide treasury system in the early 1920s.[27] The obvious opportunity costs and inefficiencies of such decentralized financial management were unavoidable as long as foreign currencies were inconvertible and the movement of funds out of foreign currencies was blocked by exchange controls. But once European currencies became convertible and European exchange markets were working freely again, the global treasury function came of age. Now the treasurer could transfer liquid funds from a country where the firm had a surplus to countries where it had a cash deficit, in search of the best return. His firm could make investment decisions independently of the cost of availability of local financing, and the treasurer could raise funds where they were available and least expensive.

With its extensive foreign network and its leading position in the Eurodollar market, First National City was positioned to assist the global treasurer in these tasks. But to do so the bank had to increase its ability to move a customer's funds between, and to operate in, national money markets. Like its customers, the bank focused on Europe, where exchange and local money markets had been liberalized after the restoration of convertibility in 1958. There the bank strengthened its branches' money-trading capability, stressing arbitrage in and among local money markets, exchange markets, and the Eurocurrency market. Beginning in the Frankfurt branch in the early 1960s, exchange trading, operations in local money markets, and Eurocurrency operations were gradually brought together within each of the European branches into a treasury unit. [28] This setup made it possible for the bank to fund a customer's loan in any European currency and to transfer his funds quickly from one country to another without exchange risk for the bank or the customer.

In doing so, First National City and the few other U.S. banks with foreign branches would recreate in the 1960s, for the first time since the 1920s, an integrated international money and capital market. "It is clear," the Federal Reserve Board reported in 1968, "that overseas branches, operating in many diverse deposit and loan markets, tend to shift funds quickly among financial centers in response to changes in supply, demand and rates. They have become the major medium through which changing conditions in individual money markets are transmitted to other money markets—the major channel for the movement of short-term capital among international financial centers." [29] On the credit side of the relationship with multinational customers, First National City supplied funds to overseas affiliates either in dollars or in local currency. Dollar loans to U.S. corporations to finance their foreign operations had traditionally been made at Head Office in New York and had been funded domestically. In the 1960s dollar funding of foreign loans moved offshore to the Eurodollar market, under the impulse of U.S. balance-of-payments controls. The Federal Reserve's decision in 1966 to let Regulation Q ceilings on domestic CD interest rates become effective had, temporarily, a similar effect (see chapter 15). To First National City Bank, with its strong offshore funding base in London and its close relations with multinational firms' affiliates through the bank's branch network, these artificial incentives to fund dollar loans in London rather than in the United States were a godsend. They boosted the bank's value to its corporate customers at the expense of U.S. banks without London branches or with less extensive foreign branch systems. As the bank noted in 1965, its corporate customers "had problems complying with the Government's balance-of-payments program. We were able to assist many of them in finding sources of funds in local currencies or Eurodollars to finance some of their activities abroad." [30]

Two variants of Eurodollar lending helped the bank serve its multinational firms. One was the floating-rate loan, which made credit available at a fixed markup or spread over the cost of Eurodollar funds in London. By eliminating the lender's interest-rate risk, the floating-rate loan allowed the bank to extend substantially larger credits to its customers. Another variant was the syndicated loan. This allowed the bank to play the part of a bond underwriter, negotiating the terms of a credit with the borrower and then arranging for the participation of other banks. For managing such syndicates, the bank would later earn an "up-front" fee in addition to interest on its own share of the loan, thereby enhancing the profitability of its relationship with the borrowing firm.[31]

The floating-rate loan and the syndicated loan began life together in Eurodollar lending to multinational corporations in the early 1960s.[32] The concepts quickly took hold. The bank soon introduced floating-rate loans in the United States. Eurodollar loan syndicates became larger, more banks took part in them, and more borrowers used them. By the early 1970s the floating-rate syndicated loan would be the dominant form of credit in the Eurodollar market and the principal vehicle of international lending to governments as well as to private firms. In the 1970s, it would play the same international role that bond financing had played in the 1920s.[33]

The bank's ability to provide loans in local currencies was even more valuable, for U.S. firms' affiliates overseas sometimes found it difficult to secure credit from local banks, which tended to favor local firms. In countries where the bank's branch system was large and well established— Brazil and Argentina, for example—the bank had ample local currency deposits and a strong position in the local interbank market, and could fund a large volume of local currency loans. Elsewhere the bank's local deposit base was narrow and its position in local money markets less developed, while the needs of its corporate customers were growing rapidly. In Europe, the branches therefore raised local funds by converting dollars raised in the Eurodollar market into local currencies, covering the exchange risk by a forward sale of the local currency for dollars. Less frequently, dollars would be advanced by Head Office to a branch abroad to be exchanged into local currency. In Japan, this method was used to fund a rapidly growing portfolio of yen loans to U.S. and Japanese firms.

Profitable in themselves, services provided to multinationals abroad had the additional attraction of strengthening relationships at home. In return for cash management services or for local currency credits provided by a foreign branch, the corporation was often willing to hold additional balances at the bank's Head Office, in New York. The Federal Reserve Board reported that "on the strength of the services supplied by branches to affiliates of U.S. corporations, the head offices usually request the parent companies to provide appropriate balances. In fact, such commensurate balances are a prerequisite for branch loans in markets where local-currency deposits are scarce and loan facilities at a premium. There are indications that the balances thus held in United States banks in compensation for loans and services provided by the overseas branches are very substantial."[34]

Corporate Banking

International expansion was only one aspect of the bank's response to the competitive threats to its core business. At home, the bank sought to strengthen existing corporate relationships and to add new customers by expanding credit, trust, and merchant-banking services, with the goal of becoming or remaining a customer's "primary banking connection in New York."[35]

Achieving these tasks would not be easy, for competition in domestic lending to business was getting tougher. In New York two new rivals emerged. In 1959 J. P. Morgan and Company had joined with the Guaranty Trust Company, forming Morgan Guaranty. The result was a formidable competitor in corporate lending with a high loan limit. Two years later, Manufacturers Trust merged with the Central Hanover Bank to form Manufacturers Hanover Trust Company. The combination of Manufacturers Trust's large retail deposit base with Hanover's experience in corporate banking created another powerful rival in the wholesale market. Across the country regional banks were growing rapidly. Their competitive power was considerable because they were close to the local firms and had more demand deposits in proportion to their assets than New York City banks. Moreover, until 1962 they had the benefit of lower reserve requirements. They could also offer local firms some services New York banks could not—payroll accounting, for example.[36]

Furthermore, all banks faced increasing competition for corporate business from the securities markets. In the early stages of the recovery from the 1961 recession, firms' cash flow outran their expenditures for inventory accumulation and new plants. They began to repay bank loans and to fund their fixed assets by issuing bonds or stock. Demand for bank credit was therefore sluggish. It was particularly so at First National City, whose customer base was heavily concentrated in such capital-intensive industries as petroleum, utilities, and transportation. The bank's total domestic commercial and industrial loans actually declined in the years 1959–1962, while those of its New York competitors were rising.[37]

To make matters worse, as the recovery of the early 1960s got under way, risk premiums on corporate debt began to fall, and they would continue to fall until late 1964. This development led banks to prefer forms of domestic business lending less subject to competition from the securities market and with higher spreads. Credit risk in such lending would be higher, too, but it could be kept within bounds by good credit analysis, by proper structuring of the loan's terms and collateral, and by the added diversification that such lending implied.

One example was First National City's adaptation of the production-payment loan, developed in the 1950s for petroleum producers (see chapter 12), to mining. Another was lease financing, adopted by the bank in 1963 after the comptroller of the currency had ruled that a national bank could engage in lending of this kind.[38] In leasing, a bank buys equipment from a supplier with its own funds and leases it to the borrower. The lease agreement provides for periodic payments that amortize the cost of the equipment and also yield the bank a return on its funds. The bank has a property interest in the equipment, which normally has a residual market value when the term of the lease has run. Such lending is suited to financing the purchase of aircraft, railroad rolling stock, computers, and other more or less standardized capital goods with a secondary market, where the borrower's uncertain cash flow makes a fully secured, high-yielding loan necessary. By 1967 the value of leases on jet aircraft, railroad cars, computers, and the like extended by First National City Bank had reached $41 million, amounting to about 1 percent of the bank's domestic commercial loan portfolio.[39]

Factoring, the purchase of a firm's accounts receivable at a discount, was another established form of high-yield business credit and was also adopted by First National City in the 1960s. Again, the comptroller of the currency lent a helping hand, ruling in 1963 that a national bank could engage in factoring. Two years later, First National City acquired Hubshman Factors, a firm that had been consistently profitable for fifty years.[40] Hubshman had recently been acquired by a company that made vending machines. George Moore thought that that acquisition made no business sense and inquired whether Hubshman's might be for sale. The reply was, "It's for sale and everything is negotiable except for price, $30 million."[41] The bank decided to go ahead on condition that Henry Hubshman, the head of the firm, stay on, which he agreed to do. The merger was successful. By the end of 1967, the bank had outstanding $31 million in factored accounts receivable, or about 1 percent of the value of its domestic commercial loan portfolio.[42]

Of the high-yield business loan techniques adopted by the bank in the 1960s, mortgages on commercial real estate proved to be quantitatively the most important. Loans secured by real estate had been authorized for national banks since 1914, but considerations of risk and unfamiliarity with such credit kept First National City's involvement in this activity low until 1960. Thereafter, the bank moved in aggressively, helping to finance the 1960s building boom. From $9 million outstanding in June 1961, loans secured by commercial real estate rocketed to nearly $164 million in June 1967, or 2 percent of the bank's entire domestic loan portfolio.[43]

After the 1964 tax cut, the bank's more traditional forms of business lending, especially term loans, picked up dramatically. The lower tax rate on corporate profits reinforced the incentive to capital spending given by the investment tax credit in 1962. Coupled with growing confidence in strong economic growth, these tax incentives spurred a debt-financed capital-spending boom. Thanks to its efforts to deepen and widen its corporate relationships, First National City was in a position to take advantage of it. Overall, the bank's commercial and industrial loans more than doubled from 1961 to 1967.[44]

To strengthen relationships with major corporations, First National City supplemented its credit facilities with an increasingly diverse array of financial services. During the 1960s, the bank offered improved corporate services of traditional kinds, such as corporate trust administration, and added new ones—financial planning, for example—in exchange for balances or fees. The new importance given to corporate trust administration was underlined in 1963 by the merger of City Bank Farmers Trust into the bank.[45] All trust operations were consolidated in the bank's Trust Division and an experienced corporate banker, Robert L. Hoguet, was put in charge of the division. He began to integrate his division's stock transfer, bond trustee, and pension management services more closely with other elements of the corporate relationship.

The Trust Division's main emphasis was on pension management. By 1960 practically every large corporation had a pension plan for its employees, and such plans covered about twenty-six million workers and had assets of $53 billion, up from $5.6 billion in 1955.[46] To tap this rapidly growing market, the Trust Division strengthened its investment research. Improved portfolio performance won the bank new pension accounts.

Finally, in the early 1960s the institution began to offer to business customers services normally associated with investment banking. It could not underwrite corporate securities, but it could compete with investment houses in providing such services as financial planning to corporate customers. Bank officers knowledgeable in corporate finance would review a company's capital structure in light of its business goals and suggest financing plans. Advice was not confined to bank financing; other options were included, such as an issue of securities. Officers might suggest candidates for merger or acquisition and help to arrange and finance the marriage.[47] Beginning in 1967, the bank made direct equity investments in smaller enterprises through a subsidiary, FNCB Capital Corporation, a venture capital firm.[48]

In sum, First National City Bank responded to competitive pressures in the domestic corporate market during the 1960s by offering, at home and abroad, an increasingly diverse array of credit and noncredit services, some of them far removed from traditional corporate banking. Overall, the program was successful. By 1967 First National City had penetrated the large corporate market more deeply than either of its closest competitors, Chase Manhattan and Morgan Guaranty.[49]

Consumer Banking

In the household market, First National City followed the same strategy of branch expansion and product diversification as in the corporate market. It sought to become, as its local advertisements in the 1960s put it, "the only bank your family ever needs."

An ambitious program of branch expansion was launched in New York City and after January 1, 1960, when the New York banking law was amended to allow it, in the suburban counties of Nassau and Westchester. The day the change in law became effective, the bank applied for permission to open five branches in Westchester and two in Nassau. Not all the applications were approved, but the bank became the first New York City bank to have a suburban branch when its Plainview, Long Island, office opened for business in October 1960.[50] Six years later, the bank had thirty-six branches in Nassau and Westchester. Within the city limits, the branch network was enlarged as well. Between 1960 to 1966, the bank added forty-three branches to its local network, mainly in midtown Manhattan and in the boroughs of Queens and Staten Island, where the population was still increasing. By the later date, the bank had 164 domestic branches, putting it in first place for the first time in local branch banking, ahead of Chase Manhattan, Manufacturers' Hanover, and Chemical Corn Exchange. Thomas R. Wilcox, who took command of the New York Branch Division in 1957, was the principal architect of this expansion.

In the 1960s, as earlier, a primary purpose of local branch expansion was to acquire deposits to help fund the corporate portfolio. Consumer demand and savings deposits at the local branches were considered a cheaper and more stable source of funds than CDs, and the branches competed aggressively for deposits, advertising heavily in local media, running deposit contests, and upgrading the branches. By 1965 savings deposits at the New York branches were up to $1.3 billion, about the same level as the bank's outstanding CDs.

On the asset side of the balance sheet, the bank introduced a new consumer product, the residential mortgage, which it and other New York commercial banks had previously left to savings banks, mortgage companies, and life insurers. The home mortgage business grew rapidly in the 1960s housing boom. From mid-1959 to mid-1967, the bank's home mortgage portfolio increased ninefold, accounting at the later date for nearly 9 percent of the entire domestic loan portfolio.

In personal lending the institution had led its competitors since 1928 (see chapter 7), but in the 1960s the bank began to lose ground to other New York City banks as they bid more aggressively for consumer business. Traditional sales finance credits—loans to purchase automobiles and other consumer durables and home improvement loans—actually declined at First National City between 1960 and 1967. Nevertheless, the bank's portfolio of personal credits in the 1960s grew at an annual rate of 7 percent, creditable but below that of its competitors.[51] Helping to fuel this growth were two new forms of consumer credit. One was ready credit, introduced by the bank in 1958, a product that had been invented by the First National Bank of Boston shortly before. This was a line of credit on which an individual customer could draw simply by writing a check. To qualify the arrangement for the higher usury ceiling allowed on installment loans and to reduce credit risk, the credit was repayable in monthly installments. The plan was immediately successful.[52]

The other new consumer product was the credit card, which the institution was not quick to adopt. The credit card combined the two classic services of a commercial bank: credit and a means of making third-party payments. The possessor of a card could buy consumer goods or services on credit, and the card served both to identify him to the merchant and to entitle the merchant to be paid by the bank or credit card company that had issued the card. The bank or credit card company was compensated by fees paid by card holders and by paying the merchant the card holder's charge less a discount.

Potentially, the credit card was a remarkable invention. It would allow a bank to do a nationwide consumer credit business without local branches. It allowed the merchant to insure against credit losses by shifting the credit risk to an institution specialized in managing it. Moreover, it simplified the credit process, enabling a bank to make small loans at low cost and at spreads that, at the time, were attractive relative to the risk involved in lending on an unsecured basis. In the 1970s the credit card would emerge as a leading means of extending credit to individual customers. Finally, the credit card was an alternative to cash and checks as a means of payment. It offered the consumer the opportunity to manage money more efficiently and a bank an opportunity to earn a fee for executing payments that would otherwise have been made in cash.

Though the credit card was promising and simple in concept, it took a long time and heavy losses to learn how to make the new product profitable. The first credit card with the features just described was issued by the Diner's Club in 1949 for use at restaurants. Banks began to issue similar cards in the early 1950s. Indeed, something amounting to a craze developed, and between 1951 and 1955, according to a Federal Reserve study, about a hundred plans were set up by banks. By the end of 1955 only twenty-seven were still in operation. The high start-up costs of launching a card, the high fixed costs of a card operation, the difficulty of getting merchants to sign up in sufficient numbers to cover these costs, and the lack of experience in and systems for making credit judgments in this new kind of lending were responsible for the high failure rate.[53]

Charge cards moved into the big time in 1958 when the American Express Company and the Hilton Hotel chain launched card operations, the latter with the Carte Blanche card. The same year, the Bank of America in California started its BankAmericard program, and the Chase Manhattan Bank launched the Chase Manhattan Charge Plan. These two bank plans offered a new, installment credit feature not then available from American Express or Carte Blanche. The card holder could repay his credit balances in installments with a monthly interest charge on the unpaid balance.

The two banking giants were confident their cards would be profitable, but these second-generation bank card programs still had a hard time breaking even. The Bank of America, with its many branches throughout the state of California, was able to achieve the volume necessary to cover fixed and start-up costs and to acquire the necessary credit experience, and in a few years its card operation was in the black. But Chase Manhattan gave up after a four-year try and sold its card business to Uniserv Corporation.[54]

First National City Bank had watched the credit card's ups and downs from the sidelines. Impressed, perhaps, by Chase's experience, the bank had been content to stick to its profitable and growing business in other forms of consumer credit. But in 1966 George Moore learned that Conrad Hilton was interested in selling Carte Blanche, and a deal was soon arranged. The bank acquired a 50 percent equity and 100 percent control for $12 million.[55] Carte Blanche at this time was third in volume of the nonbank cards but had had only one good year since its establishment in 1958. Nevertheless, management was confident that under the bank's control, with an infusion of experienced personnel and the aid of the bank's foreign branches, the operation could succeed.[56]

It was not to be. Even before the acquisition papers were signed, the Department of Justice made inquiries, indicating that the merger raised antitrust questions. The Justice Department maintained that a large bank should enter the credit card business *de novo*, rather than by means of an acquisition.[57] Thomas Wilcox recalled, "We weren't long into the mission when the Justice Department made inquiry as to what this was all about and would we please respond to the following questions which were about the size of a book. We caucused, and I remember Stillman Rockefeller saying, 'Hell, we'll fight 'em. Don't worry. We'll fight 'em. You go right ahead with . . . the development program.' Well, the Justice Department came on a little stronger. It was obvious that we were going to court, so we eventually folded."[58] The bank's 50 percent equity in Carte Blanche was sold to AVCO Financial Services Corporation, for $16.4 million.[59] In 1967 the bank introduced its own First National City Charge Service. Popularly known as the Everything Card, it was converted in

1969 to Master Charge, becoming part of the Master Charge interbank card system.[60]

First National City's record in the consumer business in the 1960s was clearly mixed. On the plus side, consumers' demand for credit grew rapidly and spreads on consumer loans were attractive compared to the risks assumed. The bank's portfolio of personal loans and residential mortgages grew at about the same rate as its corporate loans, so that the higher spread raised the rate of return on the whole loan portfolio while also contributing to diversification.

On the negative side of the ledger was intense competition from savings banks and other commercial banks in the New York market for individual deposits. Further, the interest and noninterest costs of consumer banking were rising. Like corporate treasurers, individuals were becoming more sophisticated as cash managers and were shifting their demand balances into time deposits. This shift coupled with higher interest rates led to a substantial increase in the bank's interest expense on household funds. The noninterest expenses of local branch operations were also rising rapidly. There were serious delays in automating back office operations (see chapter 15), and rents for office space were rising as older branches' long-term leases expired and new branches were opened. As a result, the profitability of the consumer business appears to have been well below that of the bank's corporate and international activities.[61]

Growth and Transformation

On the whole, the bank's performance in the 1960s was excellent—not surprising perhaps, considering the favorable economic and political environment. In terms of total assets, the institution caught up with its traditional rival, Chase Manhattan, and narrowed the lead of the California-based Bank of America. From 1961 to 1967 assets rose at an annual rate of 11 percent and net operating earnings at 8 percent, growth rates among the highest in the bank's history and the highest since the 1920s.[62]

Overseas expansion in the 1960s altered the balance between the bank's domestic and international operations. The Overseas Division's loans, deposits, and profits grew more rapidly than those in the bank's domestic divisions. From $970 million in 1960, international loans booked in the bank's foreign branches and affiliates and in New York rose to $2.7 billion in 1967, an annual increase of 16 percent, and the Overseas Division's share of the bank's total loan portfolio rose from 22 percent to 30 percent.[63] The institution was finally able to realize the potential of the foreign branch system that Frank Vanderlip had begun and his successors had developed and preserved. When George Moore took over the Overseas Division in 1956, the foreign branches' cumulative contribution to the bank's bottom line since 1914 was written in red ink, mainly reflecting the losses incurred in 1920–1921 and 1929–1934. By 1967, that record would be and could be forgotten, and thereafter the bank's center of gravity would continue to shift toward the international market. By the mid-1970s, more than half of the bank's assets would be foreign.

As significant as this geographical shift were the changes wrought by market funding in the nature of banking. The traditional core of banking was the corporate relationship. Since the Great Depression, that relationship had consisted of an exchange of a bundle of financial services for non-interest-bearing demand deposits. But now demand deposits were declining. In 1961 they still accounted for 77 percent of the bank's domestic deposits; by 1967 the proportion was down to 57 percent, reflecting the shift to market funding.[64]

Although necessary for the bank to go on growing, the change in funding was hard on profitability. Demand balances were cheap compared to "bought money," even considering the rising cost of servicing them; they were raised in a market protected from competition by restrictions on branching, by the prohibition of interest on demand deposits, and by the rule that only a commercial bank could offer a demand deposit. Thus the price of growth in the 1960s was declining profitability. Domestic net interest revenue as a proportion of the bank's domestic earnings assets fell from 3.75 percent in 1961 to 3.17 percent in 1967.[65]

The bank's responses to the profit squeeze would begin to alter the outlines of the business of banking. Some services the bank had traditionally provided as a package to corporate customers in exchange for balances would be "unbundled," marketed aggressively and sold separately for a fee. New services that made use of the Bank's expertise in risk management or in executing financial transactions would be similarly managed. Income from such fee services, many of which required no funding, would help to raise the institution's revenue relative to expenses. In the 1960s these new departures in banking were only in their infancy. The bulk of the bank's activity remained within the traditional framework of relationship banking. Yet basic change was under way. George Moore and Walter Wriston had captured its essence at the beginning of the decade when they began to refer to their institution as a financial service company. As in the 1920s, the business of banking was becoming the business of finance.

15.

The Global Financial Services Corporation
1968-1970

Walter Bigelow Wriston's record in the Overseas Division propelled him into the presidency of the bank when Rockefeller retired in 1967 and Moore was named chairman. The board of directors decided at the same time to change the definition of the president's and chairman's roles, making the president number one, with responsibility "for formulation and execution of policy."[1]

Facing the new management team were familiar challenges cast in new guises. Business was becoming global, and so was finance. As barriers to trade and investment fell, development spread to industrializing countries in Latin America and the Far East. In the process the extraordinary predominance of the United States in the world economy began to wane. This was accelerated by the emergence of domestic inflation and the consequent weakening of the dollar as the world currency. The result was a more pluralistic world economy, more volatile financial markets, and, from First National City's perspective, a wider range of competitors, which henceforth would include not only other leading U.S. banks but also the leading banks of other nations, such as Deutsche Bank and Barclays Bank, that were building worldwide branch networks.

Business was also becoming more oriented toward the consumer. As economies grew, so by and large did the middle class. Consumers were becoming an increasingly important factor in financial markets, especially in the United States. They accounted for a growing share of total saving, borrowing, and spending. Facilitating their fund flows as an intermediary or as a processor of payments appeared to be an increasingly attractive business opportunity not only to First National City but also to other commercial banks and other financial firms, such as Merrill Lynch and American Express.

Finally, business was becoming both faster paced and more analytical. The advent of the computer and advances in telecommunications made financial information more readily and more cheaply available. Although this promised First National City significant cost savings through automation and significant improvements in its own internal management systems, it also offered customers better access to the information needed to make financial decisions. Thus for ordinary, "plain vanilla" finance, firms could and increasingly did turn to the commercial paper or security markets, rather than to commercial banks.

Thus to be at the leading edge of finance, an institution had to be more than a dollar-based, U.S. bank dealing principally with corporations. To take full advantage of the opportunities afforded by the changing environment First National City had to broaden its geographical scope, its customer base, and its product line.

Two obstacles stood in the way. The first was the bank's size, a product of its past success. Growth from an institution of 15,300 employees in 1955 to one of 27,000 in 1967 was a change in kind, one that strained the largely personal process of management that the bank employed. As the bank grew, so did the problems of coordinating activities in diverse markets, measuring performance, providing incentives to managers on the line, and, last but not least, handling the mounting volumes of paper in the back office. Although Moore and Rockefeller had done much to improve the bank's budget, personnel, and management information procedures, much remained to be done, particularly with respect to organization, if the bank was to exploit the opportunities offered by an expanding market.

Regulation posed a second, and more serious, barrier to growth. It limited the bank's ability to adapt to a changing and highly competitive environment. The nation's historic aversion to any concentration of financial power manifested itself in prohibitions against interstate branching and limitations on branching within states. As a result, First National City was prevented from expanding within the United States beyond New York City and its adjacent suburbs of Nassau and Westchester counties. The banking legislation of the 1930s further restricted the bank's ability to attract funds, since it prevented banks from offering depositors fully competitive rates of return on their balances.

Regulation also prevented First National City from providing customers with as broad a range of financial services as they demanded, especially in the United States. The Banking Act of 1933 separated commercial and investment banking and the Bank Holding Company Act of 1956 (see chapter 13) limited a multibank holding company's activities to those that the Federal Reserve Board "determined to be so closely related to the business of banking . . . as to be a proper incident thereto." Despite the introduction of the CD, the Eurodollar, the credit card, the term loan, leasing, and other forms of business credit, the regulations ruling the nation's banks in 1967 remained basically those of the cartel banking system designed in the 1930s.

As a result of this regulatory regime commercial banks lost ground in the larger domestic market for financial services. First National City was not immune to this trend. Although its share of the domestic assets of all U.S. commercial banks held steady at about 3 percent between 1950 and 1965, its share of the domestic assets of all U.S. financial intermediaries fell from 1.6 percent to 1.4 percent.[2]

To reverse this decline and participate in the burgeoning market for financial services First National City therefore had to take two steps: first, exploit its existing franchise and, second, broaden that franchise. Symbolic of what these steps would achieve was a set of overall financial targets, the first the corporation had ever had. The targets were deliberately high: a 15 percent annual increase in earnings per share and a 19 percent return on equity.[3] The bank had approached such numbers in the 1920s, but they were far above anything achieved since World War II, though rising inflation would subsequently bring them within reach. Initially at least, the targets were intended, not as guides to specific action at lower levels of the organization, but as a general call to action. They were a reminder to the institution of its traditional self-confidence and its dedication to profitable growth. They would become a symbol of the new regime.

Reorganizing the Bank

As part of the first task, Wriston asked McKinsey and Company, a leading firm of management consultants, to look at the bank's organization. The new president had major changes in mind. As he recalled, he wanted "to completely reorganize this thing so that we're faced off against the marketplace and get generally in the twentieth century."[4] In the early 1960s Wriston had helped Moore reformulate the bank's traditional mission to go everywhere and do everything financial. Now Wriston would emphasize a third dimension of that mission—to serve everyone. By focusing on the customer, Wriston would position First National City Bank for future growth.

A task force, the Organization Steering Committee headed by Howard Laeri, was set up to work with the McKinsey team. The consultants' task was to help this group to find answers and to make sure that its conclusions got top management's attention. Toward the end of 1967, McKinsey presented a preliminary report that raised two organizational issues. The report asked: "1. Is Citibank organized soundly—and for optimum profits—against the separate markets that it serves? 2. Is Citibank organized to provide sufficient top-management direction to its evolution as a financial conglomerate?"[5] The report's answer to both questions was no.

In 1967 the bank was still set up about the way that Mitchell had structured it in the 1920s (chapter 7). Within the bank, geography was still the dominant organizational criterion. The National Division was basically the domestic wholesale bank created by Stillman and Vanderlip. It handled corporate accounts outside New York City and was structured internally into regional districts. The local bank developed by Mitchell, formerly called the New York Branch Division, was now named the Metropolitan Division. It managed the bank's branches in New York City and the suburbs, serving both corporate and consumer accounts. The Overseas Division represented the international bank created by Vanderlip and continued to manage the bank's foreign branches and the accounts that foreign residents held in New York. Three product or functional divisions completed the organization: the Trust Division and Bond Department, vestiges of the Trust Company and City Company, respectively, and the Operations Division, a unit that supplied back office support to the domestic banking divisions.

The one exception to the rule of geographical specialization in the banking divisions was the Specialized Industries Group, and its success demonstrated the benefits of organizing to focus on the customer. George Moore, who had pioneered the concept in the bank, had wanted to apply it more widely, but had not been able to persuade Rockefeller or to overcome the resistance of officers in the National Division who favored the geographical structure. Yet from the standpoints of marketing, credit analysis, and a lending officer's rapid professional development, structuring business lending along industry lines seemed to work.

In contrast, assigning the local bank responsibility for both corporate and consumer accounts increasingly created problems. Since the 1920s the branches in metropolitan New York had functioned as if each were the bank in microcosm. Until the late 1950s, this pattern had been workable, because large corporate accounts in New York City were domiciled at Head Office rather than in the branches. Most large corporations with headquarters in New York had their offices close to the bank's Wall Street headquarters, and their accounts were handled there. The branches had only the accounts of smaller, local firms, whose needs were not beyond the capacity of a branch whose main business was individual banking.

Then in the 1950s many large corporations moved their New York headquarters uptown, away from the Wall Street area. Some of the bank's Wall Street competitors, Chase, Chemical, and Bankers Trust, had transferred large corporate accounts to midtown branches and were soliciting First National City customers there.[6] Chase in particular had stressed a concept of "department store banking," which meant combining wholesale banking for a large corporate customer with retail services for its officers and employees, all provided through a branch near the customer's midtown headquarters.[7] In 1960 First National City followed its competitors' example and transferred a number of major corporate accounts from Howard Laeri's National Division at 55 Wall Street to branches near the companies' headquarters, under the jurisdiction of Thomas Wilcox's Metropolitan Division. The move was made over strong objections from officers in the National Division.[8]

Personal and personnel considerations played a part in this decision. Laeri had just lost to Moore in the 1959 race for the presidency, whereas Wilcox, several years younger than Laeri, was in the running to succeed Moore as president. Transferring major corporate accounts to Wilcox's division broadened his responsibility and gave him a chance to compete for the presidency on equal terms with Wriston, who was then the head of the Overseas Division.

By 1967 there was a consensus that domiciling major corporate accounts in midtown branches had been a mistake. The bank had moved its headquarters uptown to 399 Park Avenue in 1961, making obsolete the original rationale of the 1960 decision. Moreover, experience had shown that a branch manager could not do justice to his major corporate accounts and to his retail customers. An ambitious manager would neglect the retail customers, since the larger corporate accounts were more profitable and were also a steppingstone to Head Office, where career prospects were brighter. A branch manager was also at a disadvantage in serving a large corporate customer. He had neither the means to supply all the services demanded nor the authority to commit the bank to a major loan. "The branch-manager function we originated in 1921 has grown so complex as to be untenable," Wriston noted in 1968.[9] Nor were the big customers happy to be in the branches, removed from the place where major decisions could be made.[10]

To solve the bank's organizational problems, the task force and the consultants labored for more than a year. Their recommendation was adopted by top management and the board of directors, effective January 1, 1969. The domestic divisions were reorganized according to customer group and industry; geographical specialization was abandoned. Officers were placed opposite different segments of the market for banking services with the intention that each officer would develop the specialized knowledge appropriate to his market segment. The bank as a whole consisted of six groups plus the Bond Department, renamed the Money Market Division (Figure 15.1). Domestic banking was divided among the Personal Banking, Corporate Banking, and Commercial Banking groups. Otherwise the organization remained unchanged. The Operating Division was renamed the Operating Group, and the Overseas Division, the International Banking Group.

Figure 15.1

FIRST NATIONAL CITY BANK ORGANIZATION
JANUARY 1969

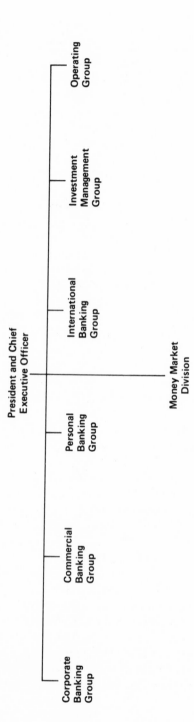

The Personal Banking Group was given responsibility for the consumer or personal banking business of the New York branches. This group would administer a volume business—the checking and savings accounts and personal loans of hundreds of thousands of individual customers at more than 150 metropolitan branches. It would devote itself exclusively to this task, employing the mass-marketing and credit-scoring techniques essential in banking of this kind.

For wealthy individual customers, a more personal approach was needed. High-net-worth individuals, as they were called, demanded a variety of services not sought by the bank's regular individual customers. They included estate and tax planning, investment advice and investment management, and complex forms of credit. These accounts, seven thousand in number, were therefore transferred from the New York branches to the Investment Management Group, formerly the Trust Division. This group also continued to manage investment portfolios for institutional investors and to administer corporate trust activities.

The Corporate Banking Group took over the bank's relationships with larger corporations. Smaller companies, mainly in the New York area, were assigned to the Commerical Banking Group.[11] Internally, the Corporate Banking and Commercial Banking groups were organized on industry lines. Thus industry or market segment specialization became the principle on which the whole domestic bank was organized.

Laeri had recommended extending the principle of specialization by market segment to the bank's overseas markets, assigning large multinational corporations to one banking unit and other overseas customers to another. But G. A. Costanzo, who headed the division, said no and Wriston agreed. Nevertheless, the recommendation reflected a growing problem. Responsibility for the bank's relationships with its major multinational customers was fragmented, divided among the Corporate Banking Group, the International Banking Group, and the branches in countries where the customer firms did business. No unit or officer had responsibility for the relationship as a whole. "It is not unusual," a McKinsey report noted, "to find as many as 20–40 Citibank officers working in different locations and at different times on a single institutional account. Therefore it is critical that the actions of these officers be coordinated and directed in the best interests of Citibank as a whole."[12] The bank accordingly adopted in 1969 a "worldwide account management system" for its largest multinational customers. An officer in the Corporate Banking Group was designated global account manager for each firm, with responsibility for coordinating the whole range of the bank's activities with respect to the firm. It was a first step in the direction Laeri had recommended and would eventually lead to the formation of a separate banking group for multinational customers.[13]

With the reorganization approved, someone had to decide case by case where each corporate account would be domiciled. That delicate political task fell to Howard Laeri. Now an elder statesman, Laeri commanded the respect of the people who would be most affected by his decisions: the officers in what had been the National and Metropolitan divisions. Despite the inherent difficulties in splitting up accounts, "everyone had confidence that Laeri would make it go."[14] A transition team was set up to explain the changes to those affected and smooth the way to the new organization. The "new" First National City Bank, as a press release called the reorganized institution, opened for business on January 2, 1969.

Personnel

The new organization was potentially a powerful engine for growth, but to make it run First National City needed managers, many of them. The need was urgent, too, for the bank had not only to staff its expanding businesses but also to replace retiring executives. Thus along with the reorganization the bank revamped its personnel procedures, accelerating training and development.

First National City was already moving at a fast pace in these areas. Developing the bankers of tomorrow had long been top management's first priority. As James Stillman Rockefeller commented in 1965:

> If we collapse the recent years and put them together, the thing to which we have devoted the greatest attention and will in the future is, without question, personnel. That means starting from the beginning, the recruitment, training, assigning, and development of people in the Bank. That goes for the whole staff no matter what they may be doing but naturally it is directed primarily toward those we hope will assume management responsibilities. It has been going on in this Bank for a long, long time. Our predecessors started training classes back in 1917, if not before. We have seen too many businesses—and that goes for banks—wither and die for lack of adequate management and we just don't want that to happen to the ones who will be here after we move along. We've got a lot of things on the fire and we are dreaming about a lot of things. The days and weeks and months are just not long enough to get them done, and the only way we can get them done it to train more people, let them develop the know-how, give them the responsibility, and then be on with these jobs and look for some more.[15]

The bank had begun at a disadvantage. In the long years of depression and war banks had expanded slowly. With business sluggish, promotions were few and far between. To a young, ambitious person of talent banking seemed an unlikely path to either fame or fortune. If First National City was to attract the men and women it would need to grow, senior management had to convey to them their own enthusiasm for banking. This, in effect, is the lesson First National City learned from its first futile efforts to recruit at the Harvard Business School in the mid–1950s. If the bank wanted the best talent, it would have to compete for it, just as it did for deposits and loans. The bank had to sell itself as an exciting place to work.[16]

George Moore took on the task at Harvard and then at other schools across the country. In his talks to prospective recruits he would outline the bank's plans and how, as employees, they might help the bank achieve its goals. In those who joined the bank, Moore retained a continuing interest, meeting with them as trainees and following their progress in their first assignments. Each was rated on a regular basis. The best were rotated through different areas of the bank, and given successively heavier doses of responsibility. This rounded out their experience, giving them the broad perspective necessary to manage the bank.

Still this was not enough. As late as 1966 the bank had only 235 senior officers, many of whom were close to retirement. Their training had been on the job, a slow, but cumulative process. Experience had made them bankers. Now First National City had to develop quickly new bankers to take their place and to fill the slots its expanding business would create. As the director of personnel commented, "The challenge is clear. We don't have the time to prepare men for responsible positions in the same way as we prepared their predecessors. The velocity of experience must be increased and performance more quickly assessed, for our selections must be made earlier in the men's careers."[17]

To meet this challenge the bank employed "a systems approach to the development of human resources in the form and quantity required by the organization in achieving its business goals."[18] By adapting concepts developed by the armed forces, the bank began to project its personnel needs, to centralize training, and to track people's development more closely.

To this effort the reorganization provided considerable support. Industry specialization would make it easier to train lending officers to the point where they were deemed competent to handle customers and make credit judgments on their own. It takes less time to learn the facts and problems of one industry than of many. With industry specialization, a bright, well-educated recruit could reasonably be expected to assume considerable marketing and credit responsibility within a couple of years. It had traditionally taken much longer, in a geographical district, to develop a recruit into a lending officer. As a McKinsey report put it, "A new calling officer will be able to develop and increase his responsibility faster, be-

cause he can concentrate his efforts within a specific segment of the wholesale market—a segment that permits transferability of experience from
one account to another. Also, he will be able to develop a real degree of
expertise and professionalism at an earlier age and within a shorter time
span than is possible under the present system."[19]

Yet potentially the reorganization created a problem. By stressing specialization it tended to produce specialists, managers who knew their own
area in depth, but lacked the overall view of the corporation and its businesses needed by a senior executive. To develop new executives the bank
would convert some specialists into generalists. Those chosen would land
on the fast track; they were handed large responsibilities and given the resources necessary to carry them out. With senior management following
their progress closely, these managers competed intensely against one another.

Management Information

To ensure that this competition promoted the bank's interest as well as
that of the players involved, decentralization had to be balanced by greater
top management control. Without that balance, delegating authority to
managers in the field could prove disastrous, as the Cuban sugar loans of
the early 1920s amply demonstrated. Accordingly, the reorganization
took steps to establish incentives and controls that would make officers
look on the institution's goals as their own. Improved systems of management information and for the control of risk were, therefore, necessary
complements to decentralization.

Potentially, the computer offered a solution to the problem, since it
could process masses of data quickly and cheaply, presenting management with information about the bank's business that formerly would
have been too costly to collect or process. But the first question was what
data to collect and how to organize and analyze them. The question was
not trivial; the answer would shape top management's view of the bank's
business, form the basis for appraisal of officers' performance, and set implicitly the standards by which they would be rewarded.

The conventional budget and accounting numbers by which the bank
had been managed were insufficient. The principal McKinsey consultant
recalled, "We found, in the first place, that the management . . . didn't
even have a good profile of its markets and its customers. It didn't really
know in summary form what is our position with respect to discrete market segments. And without that sort of information it is pretty difficult to
manage the business . . . There was very little account-profitability information and not even market-segment profitability."[20]

In 1966 the bank had set up a task force to determine the information needed to run the bank. The task force made two valuable contributions. The first was an improved definition of the transfer-pool rate, which would make the concept operationally useful. The pool rate was the rate at which one division could lend to or borrow from another. Traditionally, it had been a retrospective accounting concept rather than a management tool. Divisions with net deposits in excess of loans, such as the New York branches and the Overseas Division, supplied these funds to an investment pool from which they were lent to divisions with loans in excess of net deposits. The remainder was invested in bonds. In the bank's divisional profitability statements, divisions lending to the pool were credited with the average rate of return realized on the bank's investment portfolio, and divisions borrowing from the pool were charged the same rate.

The task force redefined the transfer-pool rate to be the effective cost of newly issued CDs, in other words, the marginal cost of funds to the bank. The new definition, adopted in 1968, changed the pool rate from an accounting concept to a day-to-day decision-making tool. It established within the bank an internal money market linked to the actual money market. It became an unambiguous guide to account officers in loan-pricing decisions, helping to push profit consciousness and accountability down to the level of the account officer. "Our objective," said Edward L. Palmer, the new head of the Corporate Banking Group, "was to develop a mechanism which would describe to our Account Managers the effect of their pricing decisions on the bank's income statement."[21]

The task force's second contribution was a management profitability report (MPR). This reporting system was based on one that had been adopted in the Overseas Division in the early 1960s. It incorporated the new transfer-pool rate into the calculation of net interest revenue of each business segment and divided expenses into controllable and noncontrollable items. It highlighted the segments of the business that could be managed to yield greater profits and became the basis for treating the divisions as profit centers. It would give senior management a more useful overview of the business than that afforded by the traditional divisional accounting reports.[22]

In this early form, the MPR system left a good deal to be desired. For example, a large part of the bank's operating and corporate overhead expenses was not transfer-priced to the banking division but allocated arbitrarily across the divisions. Nor did the system recognize differences in credit risk among business segments. Nevertheless, the system was a significant advance over the previous one. Greater accountability made it possible to give the business segments more autonomy and a correspondingly greater marketing thrust.

Risk Management

The rising cost of funds in an era of market funding underlined the need for better risk management. As demand deposits declined compared to total liabilities, the bank became more of a pure intermediary, earning a greater proportion of its profits from assuming risk—credit risk, interest-rate risk, and exchange-rate risk. In traditional banking, funding with non-interest-bearing demand deposits had cushioned profits against errors in risk management. Even considering the associated operating costs, demand deposits were cheap compared to market funds of comparable maturity, such as federal funds. Thus demand deposit funding yielded an extra margin of profit. With market funding that margin disappeared, making it necessary to manage risk more effectively.

Of the three types of risk financial intermediaries assume, market funding most directly affected the management of interest-rate risk. Until 1960 the bulk of the bank's liabilities were payable on demand; even some deposits technically classified as time deposits, such as passbook savings accounts, were largely payable on demand. Thus the bank borrowed short and lent long, assuming interest-rate risk across its whole asset portfolio, especially in the case of assets of longer maturity: bonds and fixed-rate term loans that might have a maturity of ten years or more. In contrast to demand deposits, CDs and Eurodollars had fixed maturities. Market funding thus allowed the bank for the first time to control the maturity profile of its liabilities and accordingly to manage the interest-rate risk incurred.

Liability management was the name bankers gave to this new dimension of their profession. Liability management is the art of raising the funds necessary to fund a bank's loans and investments while at the same time adjusting the maturity structure of the CD and Eurodollar portfolios in the light of expected interest rates, the shape of the yield curve in the market, and the rates and maturities of the loan portfolio, all with the aim of maximizing potential gains at an acceptable level of interest-rate risk. Until 1970 this complex function had been managed informally by the chairman of the Credit Policy Committee in cooperation with the Bond Department's money desk, which issued the CDs.

In that year, the task was assigned to a new committee, the Asset and Liability Management Policy Committee (ALCO), which included representatives of the banking divisions, the Money Market Division (formerly the Bond Department), the chairman of the Credit Policy Committee, the Economics Department, and top management. The committee met weekly to review the interest-rate outlook, to determine the maturities at which CDs would be issued, and to set the bank's prime lending rate. "ALCO functions as a corporate overseer in our search for an asset and liability mix that will maximize Citibank's earnings," said Edward L. Palmer, AL-CO's first chairman.[23]

The new emphasis on market penetration along with the bank's increased size had implications for credit-risk management. Going after higher-yielding assets and deeper penetration of market segments meant assuming greater credit risk. Making the trade-off work to the bank's advantage required a better flow of information to top management on the bank's credit-risk profile, as well as tighter control of methods and standards of credit analysis down the line. Such improvements were the more necessary because after more than ten years of uninterrupted prosperity, lending officers had grown accustomed to an environment of lower credit risk. Rapid expansion, moreover, had brought into the bank a large number of younger officers whose experience in banking did not include a serious business recession. "We worry," E. Newton Cutler, Jr., a senior lending officer, said in 1966, "that there are so few loan officers today who have experienced a period of frequent credit problems. We do the best we can to pass on the recollections and the written record of past credit failures and successes, but every officer retirement of the past decade has robbed us of some hard-earned credit understanding which we can only duplicate at a miserable price. While we are teaching our young wizards the technical skills of banking practice, we must also give them an understanding that such education and such skills are vulnerable to obsolescence but that the wisdom they should seek is not of a temporal quality."[24]

Designing and supervising credit policy in the bank had traditionally been centralized (chapter 12). As long as the institution was not too large and was growing moderately, such centralization had been natural and efficient. Credit policy supervision, said P. Henry Mueller, "was fairly easy in the 1950s when the Bank was uncomplicated and small enough for key members of management to be close to all credit developments on a daily basis . . . When the Bank was smaller, there was a feeling of tighter controls, and credit issues seemed to be more absorbing. Communication was good. George Moore's credit comments were within earshot of almost every lending officer and were well noted by those who didn't get them first hand. All senior credit officers, including senior management, could fit into the same room every Monday afternoon at four to discuss credit."[25]

The bank's rapid growth during the 1960s, along with decentralization, made delegation of credit authority necessary also. In 1969 the weekly meetings of senior credit officers were terminated "when the number of senior credit officers and their deployment made the meetings unfeasible."[26] The number of credits that required the approval of the Credit Policy Committee chairman or his staff before the loan agreement was signed was also reduced, and credit policy supervision came to consist increasingly of written guidelines and informal consultation between the central staff and lending officers.

Overseas expansion in the 1960s exposed the institution to more exchange-rate risk. The bank's exchange traders had traditionally traded for the account of customers, earning a spread. They also traded for the bank's own account, and in this activity they would take uncovered positions in the hope of gain, thereby incurring a risk of loss. The freeing of European exchange markets after 1959 and the greatly increased volume of activity in those markets multiplied the opportunity for such gains while also exposing the bank to more exchange risk.

Two factors limited total exchange-rate risk. The first was the commitment to fixed exchange rates by the world's central banks. This restricted exchange-rate movements to a narrow band around the official parity; barring a devaluation, the maximum possible loss from carrying an open position was strictly proportional to the size of the position. The second factor was the bank's own policy on open positions. To curb exchange traders' risk-taking propensity, First National City, like many other banks, had rules that limited the size of a trader's uncovered positions during the day and required that all positions be covered at the end of the business day. In addition, First National City took steps to hedge its capital position in the overseas branches, especially in countries whose currency was inconvertible or subject to exchange controls.

Despite the care taken in setting policy, these rules were not sufficient to prevent large exchange losses in the bank's Milan and Brussels branches in 1964 and 1965. In both cases the loss was caused by traders who exploited loopholes in the bank's positioning rules in order to attempt to profit from a projected devaluation. In particular, the traders engaged in a practice known as maturity gapping. The bank's rules required traders to cover their long or short exchange positions at the end of each trading day but did not require that the maturities of the contracts be matched. Gapping was left to the traders' discretion.

In the Brussels case, the branch's trader, anticipating that the pound would recover from a bout of weakness, made substantial forward purchases of sterling at large discounts for periods as long as twelve months and was covering them with sales for shorter periods. He was betting against the market that the pound would not be devalued but would strengthen, and that, as a result, the discount in the forward exchange market would decline. If he guessed right, he stood to make a big gain. The pound remained weak, however, and the discount in the forward exchange market did not decline. In view of the size of the position, the decision was made to liquidate by buying shorter-term and selling longer-term forward contracts. Consequently, the forward discount on sterling rose, creating a loss to the bank of nearly $8 million. Failure to liquidate, however, might have resulted in substantially larger losses. Although the bank was unwinding a position created on the theory that the pound would recover, it did not appear that way; market participants, including European central bankers, believed that the bank had gambled on a devaluation and lost. On balance, the Brussels episode may well have been a blessing, for it led the bank to adopt tighter rules governing exchange trading well in advance of the exchange crises of the late 1960s and early 1970s.[27]

The Back Office

With the reorganization completed and management information and risk control systems in place, there remained only one major internal obstacle to faster growth and higher profits: the growing mountain of paper in the bank's back office. Nearly every financial service provided to a customer gave rise to a bookkeeping operation, such as crediting or debiting an account. Each operation meant a piece of paper to be read and its contents recorded or used to prepare another piece of paper. The paper added up to a major management headache.

The back office problem was common to all large financial institutions in the 1960s. In commercial banks it was compounded by rising interest rates, which caused corporate treasurers and individual customers to work their demand balances harder, multiplying the number of checks and other pieces of paper banks had to process per dollar of deposits. Between 1940 and 1960, the dollar volume of checking accounts at the bank's Head Office and the New York branches had grown by 40 percent, while the number of checks processed had increased by 75 percent. In this twenty-year period, the number of transactions processed per dollar of demand deposits had therefore increased by a little over 1 percent per year. In the 1960s the growth in the number of checks processed at the bank accelerated sharply compared to the volume of demand balances. The number of checks processed by the bank seems to have been rising about 4 or 5 percent a year in the early and mid 1960s, at a time when the volume of domestic demand deposits was flat.[28]

This development raised the direct cost of demand deposit money to the bank, both at Head Office and in the branches. No one yet knew how to automate a bank's back office, and the response to more paper at First National City and other large banks had been to hire more people. This had not been efficient. By the late 1960s, operating costs were rising more rapidly than revenues, costly errors were multiplying, and service to customers was deteriorating. To respond effectively to the interest-differential squeeze, the bank had to find a way to control operating costs.

It was not for want of trying that the problem persisted. For years, management had known in a general way that the key to a solution was automation, and that the electronic computer would eventually make automation possible. George Moore's Survey Committee in 1949 had pointed out the savings to be made by automating operations. Since then, one generation of operations executives after another had been unable to solve the automation problem. It took long years of frustration to learn that applying the computer effectively presupposed major changes in procedures and work flows.

Check processing, the associated demand deposit accounting, and preparation of customers' statements were the functions most in need of automation. Beginning in 1951 the bank invested heavily in a partnership with IT & T in developing a mechanical sorting machine to process checks and prepare customers' statements. While the machine was still in the development state, the banking industry adopted a common check encoding system known as Magnetic Ink Character Recognition (MICR) as an aid to banks in automating check processing. The new system made the IT & T machine obsolete before it was fully operational. The machine, too large to dispose of in any other way, was loaded on a barge and sunk in the Atlantic Ocean. Down with it went several million dollars of the bank's money.[29]

After adopting the MICR system, the bank had installed several general purpose IBM computers in its new headquarters at 399 Park Avenue. Hopes were high that the new machines would solve the bank's demand deposit accounting problems and perform other functions as well. Management commented to the shareholders in 1962: "The large-scale introduction of automation and electronics into financial record-keeping constitutes a major revolution. While the equipment is expensive both to acquire and operate, it is essential in order to keep pace with mounting volume and it will eliminate many monotonous work assignments, thus making possible higher pay scales. It is also highly versatile in its applications and will enable us to improve the quality of our services."[30]

The bank had tried to fit the computers into existing work flows, looking on the machines as "yet another tool to do conventional banking as usual, only faster." The results, said management with considerable understatement, were "somewhat less than our expectation."[31] The head of the Operations Division later expressed his frustration in terms of what he called Schwartz's Law, which decreed "that the application [of the computer] would take twice as long to put in as we had estimated that it would, and that it would do half the work that we estimated that it would, and it would cost twice as much as we estimated it would. And you can see that with . . . Schwartz's Law . . . a great many thousands of dollars were poured down the drain in the transfer of business and bank accounting from mechanical to electronic means."[32]

Against the background of disappointment with the computer, George Moore had decided in 1964 to call in an outside consultant to study, from a different point of view, the problem of rising payroll costs, particularly in the Operations Division and the New York branches. The consultants' method was that of the traditional efficiency expert: to study and measure the way jobs were done, to define them in terms of work units, to set work-unit standards for each task, and then to eliminate people who were judged redundant based on these standards. Relying on previous experience in manufacturing firms, the consultants had told Moore they could reduce personnel in operations at Head Office and the New York branches by 33 percent and still get the same work done, without raising average salaries. To this promise a condition was attached: The consultants' teams were to have authority not only to determine the number of redundant employees but also to have them discharged. In effect, the outside experts had asked for the right to fire bank employees without appeal to their supervisors. Moore had accepted this proposal over the objections of the bank's director of personnel.

The results were bad. Morale in the operating departments and New York branches was severely affected. Turnover rose, service deteriorated, and there was a threat of unionization. Finally, early in 1966 Rockefeller called it off. An officer from the operations area had come to him with the disturbing news that union organizers were active with the employees, and Rockefeller had ordered the consulting arrangement terminated.[33]

In 1968 Wriston decided to launch an assault on the overall problem, and he asked William Spencer to take it on. Spencer was not happy to have been chosen. He had always been a line banker and enjoyed corporate banking as he had known it in the Petrolem District and as the head of the Specialized Industries Group. He had, as he told Wriston, no experience in operations and little taste for it. But Wriston was looking for other qualities: Spencer's calm under fire and his ability to build a team. Spencer finally accepted and on January 1, 1969, was appointed to head the newly renamed Operating Group.

Spencer would succeed where his predecessors had failed because he asked, through a task force headed by John S. Reed, not how to apply computers to traditional operating functions and work flows, but rather a different question—how to redefine the functions and reshape the flows so as to realize the machines' cost-reducing potential. By 1970, when Spencer and Reed became president of the bank and head of the Operating Group, respectively, the operations problem was on its way to a solution, and the bank on its way to taking full advantage of its franchise.[34]

Regulatory Restrictions

Broadening the corporation's franchise was the next step toward more rapid growth and higher profitability. But here First National City ran into the obstacle of obsolete regulation and an antiquated definition of banking. Characteristically, the bank would seek to overcome that obstacle, and in the process it would redefine the business of banking.

Just how confining banking regulation was became apparent when the bank attempted to introduce a promising new product, the Commingled Investment Account, similar to the uniform trust introduced by James Perkins in 1927 (see chapter 8). Set up in the bank's Trust Division, the account pooled the interests of a number of customers in a portfolio of securities, in order to gain the diversification of risk and economies of scale in research and administration that pooled investment makes possible. Investors could choose among several pools invested in different categories of securities. With a minimum investment of $10,000, far less than the $100,000 required to open an individual investment advisory account or investment management trust, an individual investor in the Commingled Account could have the benefit of the bank's expertise in investment management. It was a mutual fund by another name. In 1966 the bank applied for and received the blessing of the comptroller of the currency to operate the account and also registered it with the Securities and Exchange Commission (SEC) as an investment company.

Everything pointed to the success of the new venture. During the 1960s the number of middle-class families in New York and across the nation was rising rapidly. These families were looking for investment opportunities in addition to bank deposits and their own homes. The booming stock market seemed the place to go. A mutual fund offered the small investor a way of participating in the gains the market promised without the risk of putting his money in a few stocks. Mutual funds were accordingly proliferating and enjoying rapid growth.

The similarity of the Commingled Account to a mutual fund or investment company did not escape the National Association of Securities Dealers and the Investment Company Institute. When the plan was announced, the association and the institute brought suit in a federal district court, asking the court to overturn the comptroller's and SEC's ruling on the ground that the rights of the investors in the account were securities, which the bank could not legally issue under the Banking Act of 1933. The district court agreed, holding on September 28, 1967, that the investors' interests were indeed securities within the meaning of the Banking Act of 1933 and the bank could not legally issue them. The bank and the regulatory agencies appealed the case to the court of appeals, which disagreed with the district court, only to be, in turn, overruled by the United States Supreme Court in 1971.[35] Thus First National City's attempt to compete for the saver's dollar on an equal footing with mutual funds was blocked. Management commented to the shareholders, "This problem highlights the fact that not everyone likes innovation, particularly when it begets competition . . . We strongly believe that the public will benefit from free, vigorous competition in these markets which we are willing and able to serve."[36]

The same year that the bank launched its abortive attempt to get into the mutual fund business, it encountered another, more serious regulatory setback, one that threatened to restrict its already narrow franchise still further. The CD, on which money center banks had become dependent for funding the growth of their corporate loan portfolios, depended on the continued willingness of the Federal Reserve to keep Regulation Q ceilings above market interest rates. But what the Fed had given the Fed could take away. Regulation Q, said George Moore in 1964, was a "sword of Damocles."[37] In July 1966 the sword fell. To accommodate the Johnson administration's effort to fight simultaneously a war in Southeast Asia and another against poverty at home, Federal Reserve policy had become inflationary. Market interest rates rose, and in July 1966 the yield on negotiable CDs in the secondary market bumped the Regulation Q ceiling. The Federal Reserve allowed the ceiling to become effective, for the first time since the regulation was issued in 1933.

The ensuing credit crunch was brief, but the experience had disturbing overtones. In explaining the decision to allow Regulation Q ceilings to become effective, officials had invoked traditional Federal Reserve doctrine, which held that excessive expansion of bank credit was the root cause of "speculation" and economic instability. That doctrine, it will be recalled, had led the board in 1928–1929 to resort to "moral suasion"—jawboning at the discount window—to persuade member banks not to lend in the call money market (chapter 7). In 1966 it was business loans rather than loans to brokers that troubled the Federal Reserve, but philosophically the policy was the same, with Regulation Q ceilings likely to become effective whenever conditions appeared to the Federal Reserve to call for monetary restraint.[38]

The new policy was particularly troublesome to New York money center banks. Their business lending, predominantly to major corporations, was cyclical. Business loans at New York banks accordingly rose most when the Federal Reserve least wished to see them rise: at the top of the business cycle. The Federal Reserve therefore aimed its controls at New York banks. In 1966 the board noted that its restrictive policies were aimed at "larger member banks issuing savings certificates and other certificates of deposit (CDs) in substantial volume."[39] Bankers at First National City knew whom the Federal Reserve was talking about.

The Holding Company

Management's response to regulatory restriction was a bold attempt to enlarge the bank's franchise. In June 1967, just before he became president,

Wriston had received an interesting memorandum. It pointed out that the Bank Holding Company Act of 1956 applied only to holding companies that owned "two or more" banks. The same was true of New York State's own holding company law.[40] Therefore, a holding company that owned a single bank—a one-bank holding company—would not be subject to these laws and, not being itself a bank, could enter lines of business that the bank could not. Nor would the geographical restrictions of the New York banking law and the McFadden Act apply to the company's activities. If, therefore, the bank were to organize a one-bank holding company that controlled the bank, the holding company could engage in activities beyond the confines of the bank's own franchise. The move also could be made without the Federal Reserve Board's approval. The memorandum observed, "Under this program, after a series of mechanical transfers, FNCB would become a wholly owned subsidiary of a holding company formed under the laws of any state. FNCB stockholders would end up with the stock of the holding company . . . As long as the holding company held the stock of only one bank it would not be subject to the Federal or State Holding Company Act. Accordingly, it would be free to engage directly or indirectly in most other activities without limitation based on the character of the business involved."[41]

One-bank holding companies were not a new idea in 1967. A number of well-known nonbanking firms such as Goodyear Tire and Rubber Company, Sears, Roebuck, and Montgomery Ward had long owned a bank.[42] In fact, the 1956 act had been drafted to apply only to multibank holding companies in order to exempt cases of this kind, where a manufacturing or commercial firm owned a bank that was incidental to its main business.[43] What was new was the idea that an existing bank could create *de novo* its own holding company for the purpose of enlarging its legal franchise.[44]

On October 31, 1968, the stockholders turned in their stock in First National City Bank in exchange for shares of the First National City Corporation, a newly organized holding company that owned all shares of First National City Bank.[45] The bank had given birth to its own parent. With one stroke, it had pushed back the geographical and functional frontiers that had for so long defined the permissible scope of its business. In a letter to the shareholders requesting approval of the change, Wriston and Moore wrote that through the new entity "Citibank can be more useful to more people." Specifically, the new company would enable the institution to meet increasing competition in the rapidly growing market for financial services by "establishing new services either *de novo* or through acquisition which build upon Citibank's professionalism and expertise in the financial field." Wriston made it plain that the bank had "no intention to diversify into unrelated businesses or to become another conglomerate. Our goal instead is to preserve and strengthen our competitive position in the financial services business, which we are convinced can best be achieved by becoming a financial congeneric corporation, that is, a corporation which brings together allied activities which have a common relationship."[46]

Although subsequent amendments to the Bank Holding Company Act in 1970 restricted the businesses that First National City could enter, the holding company did succeed in liberating the corporation from some of the confines of the New Deal banking legislation.[47] In particular, it permitted subsidiaries of the corporation to engage in some banking activities, such as consumer finance, free from geographical restrictions applicable to bank branches. During the 1970s the corporation would utilize these expanded powers to establish a nationwide presence. More importantly, the holding company broadened the concept of banking from the narrow definition implicit in the New Deal legislation. Henceforth, banks would view themselves, not as something special, but as what they are—part of the highly competitive and rapidly growing financial services industry. Thus the holding company created a framework for further regulatory reform.

For First National City all this was in line with tradition. Since the time of James Stillman, it had viewed its business as finance, not merely banking. Its comprehensive strategy dictated developing new products, opening in new locations, and reaching out to new customer groups. The holding company was another step. It would make First National City what it had always aspired to become—the global financial services corporation.

16.

The Dynamics of Success

Consistent success in business is rare. Few firms achieve it. Citibank has, and its history suggests how companies generate superior performance over time. Although unique in its details, the case of Citibank parallels the development of other major business firms. In response to a changing economic, regulatory, and competitive environment, Citibank made the transition from a small, owner-managed firm serving a local market to a large, manager-controlled enterprise serving a global market. In the process Citibank became a leader in the financial services industry. With the appropriate change in the name of the industry, much the same might be said of Du Pont, General Electric, General Motors, or other leading firms.[1]

The dynamics of success apparent from the case of Citibank are deceptively simple. The environment sets the strategic choices open to the firm. From the range of options open to it a firm selects a strategy intended to secure it a sustainable competitive advantage and then designs a structure to implement that strategy. Together environment, strategy, and structure dictate performance—a firm's profitability and growth relative to its competitors.

So far this is textbook corporate strategy, but it leaves the loop incomplete.[2] History provides the final link, for it demonstrates the role of feedback from past performance in influencing future strategy. How a company performs influences not only its position vis-à-vis competitors but also how the firm will view the strategic choices open to it and how the firm will implement its strategic decisions.

Paths and Barriers to Growth

A firm generally begins business in a certain niche. It has only one market: It sells a single product to a single type of customer from a single location. To grow from this base it can either specialize or diversify.

The specializing firm seeks growth through greater penetration of its market niche. It aims to dominate its chosen market through a combination of cost control and product differentiation. Its strategy will therefore aim at isolating its target market and at overcoming competition within that market. It will seek to create barriers to entry, including regulatory barriers, that will repel firms invading its 'turf.' Overall, therefore, the specializing firm grows at a rate approximately equal to the rate of increase in its market share plus the rate of growth of the target market as a whole.

The structure of the specializing firm tends to be relatively simple. With a single product line, a single location, and a narrow customer base, there is little need for elaborate organization. Management tends to be centralized, and the organization follows functional lines, such as production, purchasing, sales, and finance. Frequently, management also owns a significant share of the company; there is unity between ownership and control.

In contrast, the diversifying firm seeks growth through entry into new markets as well as through greater penetration of existing ones. Its strategy is to cover a broad array of target markets, not a narrow niche, and to do so it may expand from its original market by developing new products, selling to new types of customers, or opening new locations. Accordingly, it will seek to overcome barriers to entry, including regulatory barriers, to any market that fits within its vision of what the firm should be. Overall, the rate of growth of the diversified firm will be a weighted average of the rates of growth in its existing and its new businesses.

The structure of the diversifying firm is generally more complex than that of the specialized firm. It is both more hierarchical and more decentralized. Operating authority is delegated to managers of individual business units. The better are the firm's internal accounting and financial controls, the more authority top management can safely delegate to managers of individual business units. Top management deals with crises, monitors performance, allocates capital for expansion, and, most importantly, sets overall strategy for the corporation.

Rarely is the diversified firm organized along functional lines, for that would weaken the efficiency of the individual business units. Instead, it tends to be organized along product, customer, or geographical lines. That leaves each of the business units free to specialize within its own market, and concentrates responsibility for ensuring integration of the firm's many businesses in the hands of upper-level managers.

Finally, the diversified firm generally separates ownership from management. Although top managers may have the bulk of their personal wealth tied up in the company, they generally do not own a controlling interest in the firm. This allows the firm to attract management talent and capital from their respective marketplaces. Each is needed for growth, and only rarely are they found together. Thus the separation of ownership and control will allow the firm to grow faster, particularly if the firm employs compensation incentives to make its executives entrepreneurs.

In sum, the strategy and structure of a firm depend largely on its choice between specialization and diversification. And that choice depends largely on its executives' vision of what the firm has been and what it could be.

The Case of Citibank

Citibank's history illustrates well these two paths to growth. For the first seventy years of its existence, it was a specialist. It provided commercial banking services—short-term loans and demand deposits—to a small group of New York City merchants from a single office on Wall Street. During these years the bank grew because it dominated its niche and its niche grew.

Under Moses Taylor specialization became extreme (see chapter 2). The bank became a treasury unit for the firms of Taylor and his business associates. Its single task was to provide these customers with ready money— risk-free deposits and short-term loans as needed. Its structure was accordingly simple. Moses Taylor owned the bank and managed it.

That Citibank was a relatively large bank in 1891 was therefore the result of three factors. The first was the rapid growth of Taylor's business empire. The second was the state of business generally. Until relatively late in the nineteenth century firms had only a limited demand for financial services. They were small, local entities whose simple banking needs were within the scope of a small, local bank. The third factor was regulation. Both state and national banking laws prohibited branching, and this prevented banks from growing through geographical diversification. Thus Citibank stood on a par with other leading New York City banks when James Stillman became its president in 1891.

Growth through Diversification

Together with Frank Vanderlip, James Stillman radically changed Citibank's orientation. Instead of specializing, the bank diversified. Stillman and Vanderlip took a broad view of the possibilities open to the bank. They saw within the United States the rise of big business, the emergence of the middle class, and the growth of the securities markets. They recognized that the United States would surpass Great Britain to become the world's dominant economic power and that this would make New York the world's financial center.

James Stillman was the bank's principal owner and chief executive from 1891 to 1918. But for him, Citibank would be today just another New York commercial bank or the forgotten junior partner in a long-ago merger. He saw that big business demanded big banking—in size, in the range of its products, in its view of finance. From Stillman came a concept of banking that has guided Citibank ever since: "I firmly believe . . . that the most successful banks will be the ones that can do something else than the mere receiving and loaning of money. That does not require a very high order of ability, but devising methods of serving people and attracting business without resorting to unconservative or unprofitable methods, that opens limitless fields for study, ability and resourcefulness and few only will be found to do it."[3] To play a major role in the financial world, Stillman transformed the bank from the narrow, parochial firm it had been under Taylor and Pyne. After 1891 Citibank expanded its product line, broadened its customer base, and opened offices in new locations. It instituted a decentralized, multidivisional structure and, after a severe crisis, succeeded in separating ownership and management. As a result, Citibank became a fully modern corporation and a leading firm in the financial services industry.

Diversification came step by step. Continuing Taylor's policy of "ready money," Stillman led Citibank into related areas, offering new products to existing customers or selling existing products to new customers. The key initial thrust was the entry into investment and correspondent banking at the turn of the century. This made Citibank a big business bank (chapter 3).

At this time J. P. Morgan and Kuhn, Loeb held a tight grip on the nation's leading corporations. Unable to compete directly for the business of these firms, Stillman and Vanderlip sought to attract these accounts to Citibank by offering services that complemented those provided by its competitors. Morgan's and Kuhn, Loeb's strength lay in the origination of securities; Citibank therefore stressed the distribution of securities to institutions and to individuals. Morgan and Kuhn, Loeb had affiliations overseas, but only in Europe. Citibank therefore built up a global branch network, with a particular emphasis on Latin America and the Far East, where the largest U.S. corporations were beginning to invest heavily. Finally, Citibank sought to establish relationships with smaller, but rapidly growing firms across the country, positioning itself to be the lead bank for firms that might in time become giants.

In this way Stillman and Vanderlip gradually developed a comprehensive strategy. Citibank's business was to be not merely "receiving and loaning money" but providing any financial service. Its customers were to be not merely Taylor's firms but also institutions and individuals. And it would operate not only from Wall Street but across the United States and around the world.

This strategy both depended on and fostered a change in the perception of a bank's proper role and in the way banks were regulated. Until 1913 banks, especially members of the New York Clearing House Association, such as Citibank, were considered quasi-public institutions, responsible for the stability of the money market and, indirectly, of the economy at large. As a result, Citibank operated under severe regulatory restrictions that limited its ability to branch or to provide a broad range of financial services. Reducing this public role, Stillman and Vanderlip realized, was critical to Citibank's expansion as a private business. Their creation of the National City Company, an affiliate not subject to regulation by the banking authorities, helped prompt the passage of the Federal Reserve Act. This act created a central bank, diminishing but not eliminating the public role ascribed to commercial banks, and opened the door to international and ultimately domestic branch banking and to the exercise of broader powers by national banks and their affiliates (chapter 4).

Citibank was among the first to take advantage of this broader franchise. During the years 1914 to 1916 Vanderlip initiated the development of an international bank with branches around the world. He also transformed the domestic wholesale bank into a truly national institution by initiating relationships with firms across the country. Finally, he expanded National City's investment-banking activities by creating a retail distribution system. This brought individuals of modest means into National City's customer base for the first time. By 1916 Citibank's long-term strategy was set: It would offer a broad range of financial services to institutions and individuals around the world (chapter 5).

During the 1920s a new chief executive, Charles E. Mitchell, filled out the vision of Vanderlip and Stillman by adding new, but related businesses to the structure they had left him. After further revisions in the banking laws, Citibank opened branches in New York City, establishing a local bank to serve small businesses and individuals. This fueled much of the bank's growth during the 1920s, for larger corporations had begun to trim their cash balances and to turn to the securities markets for financing. National City also added trust services to its product line for individuals and corporations, while at the same time developing further the corporation's commercial and investment banking activities around the world (chapters 7 and 8).

By 1929 these initiatives had made National City the world's leading financial institution. Each of its three affiliates occupied a primary position in its field. The bank was the largest in the world. Its investment-banking affiliate was the world's largest distributor of securities and a leading underwriter as well. Its trust affiliate also served institutions and individuals. Though not the largest trust company, it could, through its merger with Farmers' Loan and Trust Company, lay claim to being the oldest and most prestigious. Together the three affiliates provided a range of services from a network of offices that no other financial institution could match.

Then came the Great Depression. The immediate result was a sea of red ink (chapter 9). The lasting effect was a system of regulation that narrowed the bank's franchise. Commercial banks—Citibank and its chairman, Charles E. Mitchell, in particular—were made scapegoats for the worst economic disaster in the nation's history. Regulation became punitive. The efficiency of the financial system was sacrificed in the name of safety. Laws were enacted to prevent banks from competing with other financial institutions and with each other. The new restrictions struck at the heart of Citibank's comprehensive strategy. The Banking Act of 1933 mandated the separation of commercial and investment banking, forcing the bank to liquidate its securities affiliate. Deposit insurance lowered the value of the reputation for safety that the bank had built. Interest-rate ceilings, along with state and federal branching laws, limited the bank's ability to compete for deposits (chapter 10).

Nevertheless, in the years after 1933 James Perkins preserved the organization necessary to implement anew the comprehensive strategy. He kept the branches open at home and abroad and maintained the bank's internal structure, cutting staff sparingly. Gordon Rentschler continued this policy during World War II and its aftermath, even though the bank suffered additional reverses. During World War II enemy troops occupied most of its branches in Europe and the Far East. In the United States, government regulations restricted lending to corporations and individuals. For all practical purposes, the bank was reduced to a repository for U.S. government bonds (chapter 11).

Thus, despite the reverses resulting from depression and war, a second generation of chief executives held fast to the principles established during the corporation's formative years. Both Perkins and Rentschler had personally known either Stillman, Vanderlip, or Mitchell, and had participated in the execution of their comprehensive strategy. The new leaders remembered the success of the old, and believed they could improve on it when times improved.

Perkins's and Rentschler's decisions to keep intact the bank's strategy and structure were vindicated after 1950, when the economy revived. At home, there was a surge in corporate investment and in the demand for credit as well as an expansion of the middle class. Abroad, countries began growth miracles, and the dollar reigned supreme as the world's currency. It was an environment favorable to the diversified, dollar-based bank that Citibank had remained. Unlike other, more specialized institutions, Citibank did not have to enter entirely new markets after the war in order to survive. It had already established a position in many markets; as these grew rapidly, so could the bank.

Leading Citibank's further development were two old hands who had joined the bank while Vanderlip was president. William G. Brady, chairman from 1948 to 1952, began his Citibank career in 1914 and helped Mitchell fill out Vanderlip's vision by administering the local branches in the 1920s. Howard C. Sheperd, chairman from 1952 to 1959, entered the bank fresh from college as a trainee in the year 1916. After hearing Vanderlip's lectures on banking, Sheperd went on to help implement the bank's comprehensive strategy, first in the international bank and then as head of the local bank. During his tenure as chairman, Sheperd continued that strategy, reviving the bank's corporate and international business (chapter 12). With the retirement of Howard Sheperd in 1959, leadership of Citibank passed to James Stillman Rockefeller and George Moore, executives who had had no direct working relationships with either Stillman or Vanderlip. Nonetheless, they saw the environment and the bank's situation to a large extent from the founders' perspective. They were as much a product of the bank's history as they would become makers of it.

Confronting the bank's new leaders at the beginning of the 1960s was a critical, but not entirely unfamiliar problem. Regulation threatened to choke off the bank's growth; a combination of branching restrictions and ceilings on the interest rates payable on deposits limited the bank's ability to fund new loans. Without such funding Citibank's days as a leading bank were numbered. Necessity was the mother of invention. In 1961 the bank introduced the negotiable certificate of deposit, an instrument that would usher in the age of liability management (chapter 13).

Thereafter, banking was simply not the same. With funding available in the marketplace, banks could aggressively bid for new business. Citibank led the way. As the world economy grew, business and finance became global. So did Citibank. As corporations and consumers became more sophisticated, so did the financial services they demanded. Citibank responded, with leasing, factoring, merchant banking, the credit card, and other innovations. In sum, the strategy was to remain an all-around bank (chapter 14).

A Decentralized Structure

The comprehensive strategy developed by Stillman, Vanderlip, and their successors demanded a decentralized structure. Growth made Citibank both a larger and a more complex institution. From 22 employees in 1875, the bank grew to 37,000 in 1970. From a single location on Wall Street, total offices rose by 1970 to over eight hundred in more than eighty countries. Taylor's simple, centralized structure could not support such growth. A managerial hierarchy was needed. Stillman recognized this, as did Vanderlip. In 1915 Stillman wrote, "Organization, organization, with a system, that will give the fullest attention to details and the wisdom of careful and deliberate council in shaping policies, impresses me more and more as of vital importance to avoid making mistakes and insuring permanent and ultimate success."[4] Three principles guided Vanderlip and his successors in creating an organization to implement Citibank's comprehensive strategy. These were decentralization, risk control, and top management leadership. Each factor complemented the other; together they made the bank's growth possible.

Decentralization was key. Citibank's strategy was to enter many different markets. To pursue these opportunities successfully managers on the scene had to have the authority to make business decisions. Vanderlip's solution (chapter 6) was to create market-oriented business units, and to give their managers the responsibility and resources required to penetrate those markets.

The actual organization was along product and geographical lines. Product dominated; the corporation was divided into commercial banking, investment banking, and trust banking units. Within these units, geography was the dominant organizational principle. The commercial bank, for example, was partitioned into domestic and overseas divisions. Within these divisions, further geographical subdivisions were made. Similarly, the sales force of the investment-banking affiliate was organized along geographical lines. Even after the liquidation of the investment-banking affiliate in 1934, this product-geographical organization was maintained, for it created units with a clear marketing thrust.

Balancing decentralization was better risk control. Indeed, early reverses in Russia and Cuba (chapter 6) taught the bank that control, particularly over credit, was a precondition for decentralization. Thus in 1918 the bank instituted a specialized Comptroller's Department responsible for financial accounting and auditing of the bank's diverse operations. This enabled top management to monitor more closely the performance of individual business units. Another control that permitted greater decentralization was the creation of the credit policy function in 1952 (chapter 12). This centralized the bank's credit standards and review procedures and provided a balance to greater marketing emphasis in the line divisions, particularly the Specialized Industries Group.

The third leg of Citibank's structural triangle was greater freedom for top management to focus on its primary task: leading the corporation. Decentralization transferred day-to-day responsibility for running the businesses to line managers. Controls enabled top management to monitor their performance. Top management therefore had more time to do what only it could do: deal with major crises, present the corporation's position to shareholders, regulators, and other "outside" constituencies, and, finally, determine the corporation's overall strategy. As James Stillman Rockefeller put it in 1965, the task of top management was "to avoid the day-to-day details and try to set the broad general policies for the good of the institution."[5]

Performance

Profits demonstrate the success of strategy and structure. Indeed, they are the lifeblood of the firm. Without the prospect of profits, a firm cannot attract capital and employees, nor can it undertake new initiatives. Thus profits are integral to growth. Except for a few years in the depths of the Great Depression, Citibank's strategy of diversification always produced profits. Overall, net profits rose from $314,000 in Stillman's first full year as chief executive (1892) to $141 million in 1970 (see Appendix B), or at an annual rate of 6 percent, corrected for inflation.

Profitability fluctuated with economic conditions (Figure 16.1). During the years 1891–1929, when the economy was expanding and Citibank was unfolding its comprehensive strategy, profitability was high, averaging 6.9 percent in real terms. Particularly high real returns were achieved during Stillman's first years as head of the bank (1891–1900) and during the years 1920–1929, when the real rate of return on equity averaged 9.2 percent and 10.4 percent, respectively.

Then the depression put Citibank deeply into the red. Corrected for the deflation of the period, total losses during the years 1929 to 1934 amounted to 46 percent of stockholders' equity at the end of 1929. Practically the entire loss was recorded in 1934, when the bank wrote off its bad loans and securities in conjunction with the sale of preferred stock to the Reconstruction Finance Corporation. Afterward, recovery was slow, and the rate of return on equity was low, averaging 4.4 percent in real terms from 1934 to 1961. In the 1960s it picked up again as the bank resumed its diversification strategy. From 1961 to 1970 the real rate of return on equity averaged 6.5 percent, about the same rate as that achieved during the years 1891–1929, when the bank first developed and implemented its comprehensive strategy.

Profitability went hand in hand with gains in market share (Figure 16.1). In 1891 Citibank's assets were a mere 0.3 percent of the total for all U.S. banks. By 1929, this percentage had risen nearly ten times, to 2.8 percent. It then remained at roughly that level until 1961, before rising again to 3.7 percent in 1970. Thus diversification enabled Citibank to grow faster than other banks, especially during the years 1891 to 1929 and 1961 to 1970, when it could more freely and more fully implement its comprehensive strategy (Table 16.1).

Table 16.1. Real rate of growth in assets, Citibank and all U.S. banks, 1834–1970 (in percentages)

Years	Citibank	All banks
1834–1891	5.0	4.9
1891–1929	7.7	4.2
1929–1961	2.4	2.4
1961–1970	8.1	5.5
1834–1970	6.7	4.5

Source: Appendix B and U.S. Bureau of the Census, *Historical Statistics of the United States: Colonial Times to 1970* (Washington, D.C.: GPO, 1975), pt. 1, pp. 201, 224, 1019–20.

Figure 16.1

Real rate of return on stockholders' equity and share of assets of all U.S. banks, 1891–1970

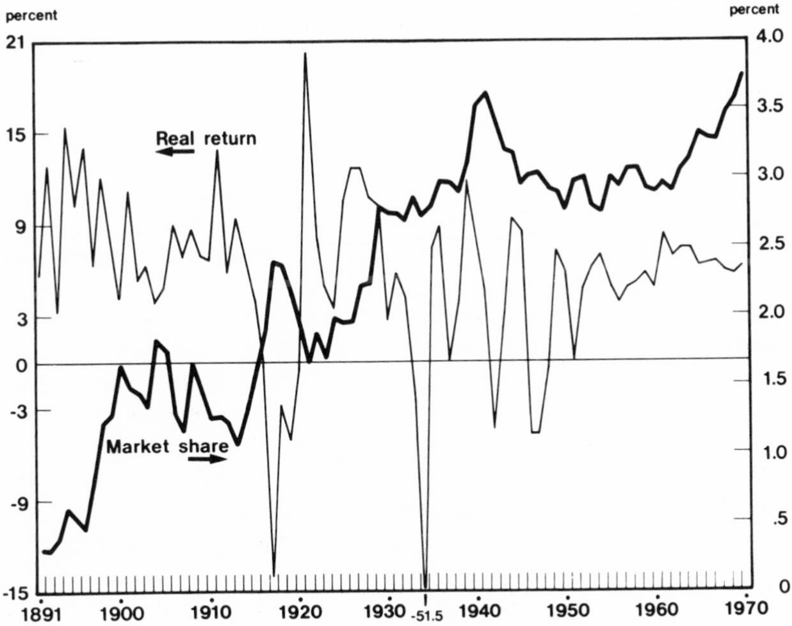

Source: Appendix B; U.S. Bureau of the Census, Historical Statistics of the United States: Colonial Times to 1970 (Washington, D.C.: GPO, 1975), pp. 1019–20 (ser. 580).

Most of Citibank's growth was self-generated. In contrast to Chase Manhattan and the Bank of America, its two leading rivals among U.S. banks, Citibank did not heavily rely on mergers to fuel its growth. Indeed, Citibank's mergers were relatively few and far between. They were generally undertaken in order to establish a position in a new product or market segment after the bank had gained experience in the field. For example, the merger with the Third National Bank in 1897 opened the door to correspondent banking; that with the International Banking Corporation in 1915 gave the bank a branch network in the Far East; that with Farmers' Loan and Trust pushed the bank into the forefront of the market for trust services. Moreover, the acquired firms were generally small relative to the bank in terms of assets, capital, and personnel. Hence, they were fairly easily assimilated into the bank.

As a result, the bank developed a strong, internal culture centered around its comprehensive strategy and decentralized structure. Expansion produced opportunities for younger people to run businesses of significant size. This attracted capable managers, and the practice of promoting from within encouraged successful ones to remain with the bank. Over time, Citibank developed a distinctive character, one in which "self-doubt has a small place . . . and arrogance a large one," according to outsiders.[6] To Citibank executives, however, self-confidence was a virtue, for it enabled them to pursue aggressively and innovatively the corporation's traditional goal: to be a global financial services corporation serving both institutions and individuals.

The Global Financial Services Corporation

This was exactly the task that Walter Wriston set for the corporation when he became its chief executive in 1967. As it had in the past, the corporation continued to seek growth through deeper penetration of its existing markets and through expansion into new, but related markets. Also as in the past, the obstacles to this strategy were twofold: disintermediation and regulation. The bank's best corporate customers were tending to bypass it entirely, by funding themselves in the securities markets and by investing their surplus cash there, as they had done after the turn of the century and in the 1920s.

Regulation prevented the bank from responding effectively to this challenge, at least in the United States. Regulation restricted the bank's ability to compete with other banks and with other financial firms. According to U.S. law, banks were still considered as much quasi-public institutions as private financial intermediaries, even though the federal government and the Federal Reserve in the postwar era had increasingly assumed and were increasingly held to have responsibility for economic growth and stability.

Concretely, regulation hindered the bank from offering new products to existing customers and from soliciting new customers for its existing products. It could not offer investment-banking services to its best corporate customers, at least not in the United States. Nor could the bank easily offer commercial banking services to U.S. customers, particularly individuals, outside New York. Branching restrictions prevented that. Thus an outmoded system of bank regulation denied banks the right to participate fully in the rapidly expanding market for financial services. In essence, Wriston faced a problem similar to the one that had confronted Stillman and Vanderlip after the Panic of 1907.

Wriston's solution was similar as well: to increase the profitability of the bank's existing business and to broaden its franchise. Sharper focus on the customer was the key to achieving the first objective. The 1968 reorganization of the bank's domestic business separated banking for institutions and individuals into two independent units, permitting each to develop specialized marketing and credit techniques. Decentralization reinforced the reorganization; each business unit was given greater responsibility to generate profits and greater authority to deploy resources as it saw fit. To balance decentralization, better risk controls were put in place and better information systems were devised. Finally, the bank tackled the problem in its back office, paving the way toward more efficient operations. The result of this internal restructuring was a more competitive bank, prepared to do battle with its traditional competitors in its traditional markets.

Through the formation of a one-bank holding company the bank secured a broader franchise. This device distinguished between a bank and the corporation that owned it. While the former might have quasi-public functions, the corporation as a whole surely did not and therefore should be free to offer a broad range of financial services. Although the 1970 amendments to the Bank Holding Company Act restricted the permissible range of services to something considerably less than what the corporation had planned to offer, an important point had been confirmed. Bank holding companies were to be regulated differently from the banks they controlled. It was a first step toward further reform. Henceforth, banks were again part of the financial services industry; to become a leader in that broader market Citibank transformed itself into Citicorp, a global financial services corporation.

It was a bold stroke and a characteristic one—a concrete expression of the bank's traditional strategy and a fitting note on which to end our story. The holding company reflects the bank's view that its business is finance in the broadest sense. It exemplifies the decentralized structure appropriate to that strategy. And in creating the holding company, the bank acted with its customary panache, making no secret of its intention to change the face of banking.

Citibank
Photographs

Samuel Osgood, President, 1812–1813.

Moses Taylor, President, 1856–1882. Painting
by Daniel Huntington in the New York
Clearing House.

James Stillman, President, 1891–1909, and
Chairman, 1909–1918.

Frank A. Vanderlip, President, 1909–1919.

Charles E. Mitchell, President, 1921-1929, and Chairman, 1929–1933.

The National City branch at Petrograd, 1917.

James H. Perkins, Chairman, 1933–1940.

Gordon S. Rentschler, President,
1929–1940, and Chairman, 1940–1948.

William Gage Brady, Jr., President,
1940–1948, and Chairman, 1948–1952.

Howard C. Sheperd, President, 1948–
1952, and Chairman, 1952–1959.

55 Wall Street, Headquarters, 1908–1961.

In 1961, Headquarters moved uptown to 399 Park Avenue.

James Stillman Rockefeller, President,
1952–1959, and Chairman, 1959–1967.

George S. Moore, President, 1959–1967,
and Chairman, 1967–1970.

Walter B. Wriston, President, 1967–1970,
and Chairman, 1970–1984.

William I. Spencer, President, 1970–1982.

APPENDIX A

Citibank: Directors, 1812–1970

| Directors | Duration of service | |
	From	To
Chairmen		
James Stillman	January 12, 1909	March 15, 1918
James A. Stillman	April 2, 1918	June 3, 1919
Eric P. Swenson	May 3, 1921	April 2, 1929
Charles E. Mitchell	April 2, 1929	February 27, 1933
James H. Perkins	February 27, 1933	July 12, 1940
Gordon S. Rentschler	July 23, 1940	March 3, 1948
William Gage Brady, Jr.	March 9, 1948	December 30, 1952
Howard C. Sheperd	December 30, 1952	November 1, 1959
James Stillman Rockefeller	November 1, 1959	July 1, 1967
George S. Moore	July 1, 1967	July 1, 1970
Walter B. Wriston	July 1, 1970	September 1, 1984
Presidents		
Samuel Osgood	June 19, 1812	August 12, 1813
William Few	August 17, 1813	July 1, 1817
Peter Stagg	July 3, 1817	July 1, 1825
Thomas L. Smith	July 1, 1825	February 12, 1827
Isaac Wright	February 15, 1827	July 2, 1832
Thomas Bloodgood	July 2, 1832	May 18, 1843
Gorham A. Worth	May 18, 1843	April 3, 1856
Moses Taylor	April 15, 1856	May 23, 1882
Percy R. Pyne	May 31, 1882	November 13, 1891
James Stillman	November 17, 1891	January 12, 1909
Frank A. Vanderlip	January 12, 1909	June 3, 1919
James A. Stillman	June 3, 1919	May 3, 1921
Charles E. Mitchell	May 3, 1921	April 2, 1929

Directors	Duration of service	
	From	To

Presidents

Gordon S. Rentschler	April 2, 1929	July 23, 1940
William Gage Brady, Jr.	July 23, 1940	March 9, 1948
Howard C. Sheperd	March 9, 1948	December 30, 1952
James Stillman Rockefeller	December 30, 1952	November 1, 1959
George S. Moore	November 1, 1959	July 1, 1967
Walter B. Wriston	July 1, 1967	July 1, 1970
William I. Spencer	July 1, 1970	August 1, 1982

Other Directors

Benjamin Bailey	June 16, 1812	July 1, 1825
Abraham Bloodgood	June 16, 1812	May 15, 1820
William Cutting	June 16, 1812	July 1, 1817
Henry Fanning	June 16, 1812	July 1, 1813
William Furman	June 16, 1812	March 20, 1815
William Irving	June 16, 1812	November 9, 1821
John L. Norton	June 16, 1812	July 1, 1813
Isaac Pierson	June 16, 1812	July 1, 1825
Ichabod Prall	June 16, 1812	July 1, 1825
Peter Stagg	June 16, 1812	July 3, 1817
John Swartwout	June 16, 1812	July 1, 1817
Samuel Tooker	June 16, 1812	October 23, 1823
Jasper Ward	June 16, 1812	July 1, 1815
Grove Wright	June 16, 1812	July 1, 1825
Fidele Boisgerard	June 1, 1813	December 1, 1817
William P. van Ness	July 1, 1813	July 1, 1817
John Adams	July 1, 1815	July 1, 1825
John Graham	July 1, 1815	December 19, 1822
Isaac Carow	July 1, 1817	July 1, 1825
George Gallagher	July 1, 1817	July 1, 1825
James Magee	July 1, 1817	July 1, 1825
Edmund Smith	July 1, 1817	July 1, 1825
Benjamin Desobry	January 19, 1818	May 3, 1819
Joseph Bouchaud	July 1, 1819	September 6, 1824
Jacob Drake	July 1, 1820	July 1, 1825
Goold Hoyt	July 1, 1822	July 1, 1825
William Stewart	July 1, 1823	July 1, 1825
Peter I. Nevins	October 30, 1823	April 14, 1825
Cornelius W. Lawrence	September 30, 1824	October 6, 1825
Thomas Sands	April 14, 1825	July 1, 1825
Abraham Bell	July 1, 1825	May 8, 1837

	Duration of service	
Directors	From	To

Other Directors

Thomas Bloodgood	July 1, 1825	July 2, 1832, and
	May 18, 1843	July 1, 1844
William G. Bull	July 1, 1825	July 1, 1827
Job S. Comstock	July 1, 1825	June 6, 1826
Benjamin Corlies	July 1, 1825	July 1, 1838
Nicholas Gouverneur	July 1, 1825	July 1, 1827
William Israel	July 1, 1825	July 1, 1827
Charles Lawton	July 1, 1825	September 15, 1825
William H. Legett	July 1, 1825	July 1, 1825
Jethro Mitchell	July 1, 1825	July 1, 1827
Samuel F. Mott	July 1, 1825	July 1, 1825
Alfred S. Pell	July 1, 1825	December 23, 1825
William F. Pell	July 1, 1825	July 1, 1834
Cornelius R. Suydam	July 1, 1825	July 1, 1840
Jordan Wright	July 1, 1825	July 1, 1838
William Stevens	September 15, 1825	July 1, 1830
Isaac Wright	October 3, 1825	February 15, 1827, and
	July 2, 1832	July 1, 1833
James Barker	October 6, 1825	June 6, 1826, and
	July 1, 1827	July 1, 1829
James Byers	June 6, 1826	July 1, 1831
Joseph Foulke	June 6, 1826	June 5, 1845
William W. Fox	July 1, 1827	March 1, 1861
Fred W. Rhinelander	July 1, 1827	July 1, 1828
Robert I. Walker	July 1, 1827	June 4, 1846
Richard S. Williams	July 1, 1827	July 1, 1828
Benjamin Marshall	July 1, 1828	July 1, 1831
Thomas Tobias	July 1, 1828	July 1, 1834
Herbert Van Wagenen	July 1, 1829	May 18, 1843
James T. Burr	June 1, 1830	July 1, 1831
Charles A. Davis	July 1, 1831	December 9, 1833
Henry Delafield	July 1, 1831	June 28, 1853
John P. Stagg	July 1, 1831	July 1, 1850
Oliver Corwin	July 1, 1833	July 3, 1837
Richard M. Lawrence	July 1, 1834	June 28, 1853
Daniel Parish	July 1, 1834	September 25, 1863
Gabriel Wisner	July 1, 1834	July 1, 1848
Moses Taylor	July 1, 1837	April 15, 1856
Thomas H. Mills	July 1, 1838	July 1, 1839
Ellis Potter	July 1, 1838	June 4, 1846
Richard S. Williams	July 1, 1838	July 1, 1839, and
	July 1, 1840	July 1, 1842

| Directors | Duration of service | |
	From	To
Other Directors		
Lora Nash	July 1, 1839	June 28, 1853
Henry Shelden	July 1, 1839	June 28, 1853
John H. Brower	July 1, 1842	April 16, 1867
Stewart C. Marsh	July 1, 1844	June 30, 1857
Tarrant Putnam	June 3, 1845	July 15, 1870
Abraham Bell	June 4, 1846	June 28, 1853
Thomas E. Walker	June 4, 1846	June 29, 1858
Thomas W. Gale	July 1, 1848	July 1, 1849
Aaron L. Reid	July 1, 1849	June 28, 1853
John J. Cisco	July 1, 1850	March 23, 1884
George Greer	April 15, 1856	July 26, 1870
Lewis A. von Hoffmann	June 30, 1857	April 6, 1875
William G. Read	June 29, 1858	June 28, 1864
John Alstyne	June 25, 1861	August 31, 1869
Henry Parish	September 25, 1863	June 17, 1890
John J. Phelps	June 28, 1864	May 28, 1869
Samuel Sloan	April 16, 1867	September 22, 1907
William W. Phelps	May 28, 1869	June 17, 1894
Percy R. Pyne	August 31, 1869	May 31, 1882, and
	November 13, 1891	February 14, 1895
Benjamin Dunning	July 15, 1870	February 21, 1890
Edwin W. Holbrook	July 26, 1870	July 24, 1883
Jose V. Onativia	April 6, 1875	July 6, 1876
David M. Turnure	January 9, 1877	February 21, 1889
Lawrence Turnure	January 9, 1883	May 2, 1889
Rosewell G. Rolston	July 24, 1883	August 25, 1898
George W. Campbell	January 13, 1885	June 4, 1893
Cleveland H. Dodge	November 1, 1889	June 24, 1926
James Stillman	March 4, 1890	November 17, 1891
Henry A. C. Taylor	December 26, 1890	May 28, 1921
Francis M. Bacon	January 8, 1895	September 21, 1912
George D. Meeker	January 8, 1895	January 14, 1896
William Rockefeller	January 8, 1895	June 24, 1922
H. Walter Webb	January 8, 1895	June 26, 1900
Moses Taylor Pyne	May 14, 1895	October 6, 1908,
	January 12, 1909	October 9, 1916, and
	January 9, 1917	April 22, 1921
William D. Sloane	January 14, 1896	March 19, 1905
Robert Bacon	June 23, 1896	January 13, 1903
John A. McCall	January 11, 1898	February 18, 1906
Charles S. Fairchild	January 25, 1898	August 24, 1909
John S. Sterling	January 25, 1898	July 5, 1918

	Duration of service	
Directors	From	To

Other Directors

James H. Post	October 4, 1898	March 5, 1938
Henry O. Havemeyer	January 10, 1899	December 4, 1907
Stephen S. Palmer	January 10, 1899	January 29, 1913
Jacob H. Schiff	February 7, 1899	July 7, 1914
W. S. Bogert	January 9, 1900	September 10, 1901,
	July 29, 1902	November 18, 1902, and
	January 13, 1903	January 9, 1906
E. H. Harriman	January 9, 1900	September 9, 1909
Moses Taylor	January 9, 1900	October 14, 1916
Archibald G. Loomis	January 9, 1900	January 17, 1905
George W. Perkins	November 8, 1900	January 9, 1912
John D. Rockefeller, Jr.	September 10, 1901	January 12, 1904
Edwin S. Marston	July 29, 1902	October 10, 1916
Cyrus H. McCormick	November 18, 1902	March 25, 1930
W. Ashley de Wolf	January 13, 1903	January 27, 1903,
	January 8, 1907	February 26, 1907, and
	January 14, 1908	October 6, 1908
P. A. Valentine	January 13, 1903	February 15, 1916
Henry C. Frick	January 27, 1903	June 13, 1916
James A. Stillman	January 12, 1904	April 2, 1918, and
	May 3, 1921	January 13, 1944
Gibson S. Whitson	January 9, 1906	November 24, 1907
Frank A. Vanderlip	January 8, 1907	January 12, 1909
Joseph P. Grace	February 26, 1907	January 22, 1946
Samuel Sloan, Jr.	October 22, 1907	October 9, 1916, and
	April 29, 1930	November 26, 1939
J. Ogden Armour	August 24, 1909	August 16, 1921
J. P. Morgan, Jr.	September 14, 1909	June 30, 1914
George H. Church	January 11, 1910	November 6, 1912, and
	January 9, 1917	April 4, 1922
Gerrish H. Milliken	January 11, 1910	June 11, 1947
Eric P. Swenson	January 9, 1912	August 14, 1945
Robert S. Lovett	November 6, 1912	March 12, 1918, and
	January 14, 1919	August 30, 1921
Frank Trumbull	November 6, 1912	May 25, 1920
Beekman Winthrop	September 15, 1914	October 11, 1916, and
	June 28, 1921	December 26, 1933
Edgar Palmer	December 7, 1915	May 16, 1922
William C. Procter	January 11, 1916	July 2, 1929
Philip A. S. Franklin	August 1, 1916	August 14, 1939
Percy A. Rockefeller	August 8, 1916	April 11, 1933
Earl D. Babst	January 9, 1917	July 3, 1923

	Duration of service	
Directors	From	To

Other Directors

Henry A. Lindsay	January 9, 1917	April 15, 1919, and
	January 13, 1920	June 28, 1921
Charles H. Toy	January 9, 1917	June 28, 1921, and
	January 10, 1922	January 9, 1923
John A. Garver	July 30, 1918	December 26, 1933
Guy Cary	January 14, 1919	August 27, 1950
Nathan C. Kingsbury	April 15, 1919	January 24, 1920
Nicholas F. Brady	May 18, 1920	March 27, 1930
Horace S. Wilkinson	October 5, 1920	November 7, 1928
James E. O'Neill	June 7, 1921	August 23, 1927
Percy R. Pyne	June 28, 1921	August 22, 1929
Robert W. Stewart	August 16, 1921	January 13, 1931
Joseph T. Cosby	January 9, 1923	June 29, 1926,
	January 11, 1927	June 14, 1927,
	January 8, 1929	April 2, 1929,
	June 29, 1929	July 23, 1929, and
	November 7, 1929	January 9, 1934
G. Edwin Gregory	January 9, 1923	November 7, 1928
F. C. Schwedtman	January 9, 1923	June 23, 1925
Thomas A. Reynolds	January 9, 1923	January 13, 1925
Gordon S. Rentschler	October 2, 1923	April 2, 1929
William A. Simonson	January 13, 1925	March 5, 1937
Sosthenes Behn	June 23, 1925	December 4, 1956
Cleveland E. Dodge	June 29, 1926	February 29, 1960
John D. Ryan	June 29, 1926	February 11, 1933
H. S. Black	June 14, 1927	July 19, 1930
Fred J. Fisher	November 9, 1927	December 26, 1933
Edward A. Deeds	November 13, 1928	January 22, 1952
Hugh B. Baker	April 2, 1929	February 27, 1933
Allen G. Hoyt	June 29, 1929	December 10, 1929
James A. Jackson	January 14, 1930	January 9, 1934
James H. Perkins	June 29, 1929	July 12, 1940
Charles A. Peabody	July 2, 1929	April 26, 1931
Gerard Swope	July 23, 1929	January 27, 1942, and
	March 10, 1942	December 30, 1952
Percy R. Pyne II	September 3, 1929	January 13, 1931
Floyd L. Carlisle	April 1, 1930	December 26, 1933
Samuel Sloan	April 29, 1930	November 26, 1930
Curtis E. Calder	January 13, 1931	March 8, 1955
Gayer G. Dominick	January 12, 1932	November 14, 1933, and
	May 6, 1947	May 24, 1947
A. P. Giannini	September 12, 1933	June 3, 1949

| | Duration of service | |
Directors	From	To

Other Directors

John F. Neylan	September 12, 1933	February 14, 1939
Reginald B. Taylor	January 9, 1934	March 15, 1966
Amory Houghton	September 7, 1937	April 2, 1957, and
	March 7, 1961	May 28, 1968
W. Randolph Burgess	September 14, 1938	December 30, 1952
Robert Winthrop	November 28, 1939	May 19, 1964
James R. Hobbins	June 30, 1942	November 14, 1949
J. Peter Grace, Jr.	January 22, 1946	—[a]
Roger Milliken	June 24, 1947	—[a]
Frederick B. Rentschler	June 29, 1948	April 25, 1956
Lawrence M. Giannini	June 21, 1949	August 19, 1952
William H. Hoover	December 6, 1949	June 6, 1952
Boykin C. Wright	September 19, 1950	November 16, 1954
Harry C. Hagerty	January 8, 1952	February 18, 1964
Keith S. McHugh	January 8, 1952	April 28, 1959
Stanley C. Allyn	January 29, 1952	June 4, 1963
Roy H. Glover	June 24, 1952	March 31, 1958
R. Gwin Follis	October 28, 1952	April 4, 1967
Richard S. Perkins	December 30, 1952	July 1, 1970
Nathan C. Lenfestey	January 13, 1953	August 8, 1954
DeWitt A. Forward	August 10, 1954	October 1, 1959
Charles C. Parlin	November 16, 1954	June 21, 1966
George A. Guerdan	January 11, 1955	October 30, 1956,
	November 24, 1959	March 7, 1961, and
	December 5, 1961	February 6, 1962
Charles G. Mortimer	January 11, 1955	March 16, 1971
George F. Baker, Jr.	March 30, 1955	October 5, 1965
Percy Chubb II	March 30, 1955	May 19, 1971
Edward S. Moore, Jr.	March 30, 1955	October 23, 1959
Alexander C. Nagle	March 30, 1955	April 16, 1963
William C. Stolk	March 30, 1955	August 1, 1968
H. Mansfield Horner	May 8, 1956	October 15, 1968
Leo D. Welch	October 30, 1956	November 15, 1968
Alan H. Temple	December 4, 1956	October 1, 1961
Joseph A. Grazier	May 28, 1957	February 3, 1970
Charles M. Brinckerhoff	June 3, 1958	January 20, 1970
Clifton W. Phalen	April 28, 1959	October 31, 1967
Carl W. Desch	November 24, 1959	February 15, 1960, and
	March 18, 1969	January 20, 1970
John E. Bierworth	February 16, 1960	April 30, 1967
John R. Kimberly	March 15, 1960	April 20, 1971
William M. Batten	February 6, 1962	June 22, 1976

| | Duration of service | |
Directors	From	To

Other Directors

Directors	From	To
Michael L. Haider	April 16, 1963	March 17, 1970
Robert S. Oelman	June 18, 1963	March 15, 1977
George P. Jenkins	June 2, 1964	February 19, 1980
C. Sterling Bunnell	November 10, 1964	June 21, 1966
Charles H. Sommer	October 19, 1965	May 16, 1967
Joseph C. Wilson	April 5, 1966	May 16, 1971
Albert L. Williams	June 21, 1966	March 20, 1979
Frederick M. Eaton	June 21, 1966	March 19, 1974
Gordon M. Metcalf	June 6, 1967	January 16, 1973
James Stillman Rockefeller	July 1, 1967	April 8, 1970
Gordon Grand	September 3, 1967	January 16, 1972
John D. deButts	November 1, 1967	September 18, 1979
Amory Houghton, Jr.	May 28, 1968	—[a]
Charles B. McCoy	August 2, 1968	December 17, 1974
William P. Gwinn	October 15, 1968	September 30, 1972
Louis K. Eilers	January 20, 1970	March 16, 1976
John G. Hall	January 20, 1970	October 29, 1971
Milo M. Brisco	March 17, 1970	November 21, 1972
Lawrence E. Fouraker	March 17, 1970	—[a]
Edward L. Palmer	July 1, 1970	September 1, 1982
Franklin A. Thomas	December 15, 1970	—[a]

a Member of the Board of Directors as of December 31, 1984.

Citibank: Principal Assets and Liabilities and Net Profits, 1834–1970 (millions of dollars)

Year	Total assets or liabilities[a]	Assets			Liabilities			Net profits[c]
		Total loans	Total investments	Total cash	Total deposits	Bank notes	Capital accounts[b]	
1834	2.3	1.8	0.0	0.5	1.1	0.3	0.9	
1835	2.6	1.8	0.0	0.7	1.3	0.3	0.9	0.1
1836	2.4	1.5	0.0	0.8	1.1	0.4	0.9	0.1
1837	1.7	1.1	0.0	0.6	0.7	0.1	0.9	0.1
1838	1.9	1.4	0.0	0.5	0.8	0.2	0.8	0.1
1839	1.5	1.0	0.0	0.4	0.5	0.1	0.8	0.1
1840	1.9	1.2	0.0	0.6	0.8	0.2	0.8	0.1
1841	1.6	1.0	0.0	0.5	0.6	0.2	0.8	0.0
1842	1.7	1.1	0.1	0.4	0.7	0.2	0.8	0.1
1843	2.2	1.2	0.0	0.9	1.2	0.2	0.8	—
1844	2.1	1.4	0.0	0.6	1.1	0.2	0.8	—
1845	2.2	1.6	0.0	0.6	1.2	0.2	0.8	—
1846	1.9	1.3	0.0	0.5	0.9	0.2	0.8	—
1847	—	—	—	—	—	0.2	—	—
1848	—	—	—	—	—	—	—	—
1849	2.5	1.5	0.0	1.0	1.5	0.2	0.9	—
1850	—	—	—	—	—	—	—	—
1851	—	—	—	—	—	—	—	—
1852	—	—	—	—	—	—	—	—
1853	2.5	1.7	0.0	0.6	1.4	0.2	0.9	—
1854	2.2	1.6	0.0	0.6	1.1	0.0	1.1	—
1855	2.4	1.7	0.0	0.7	1.3	0.0	1.1	—
1856	2.7	1.8	0.0	0.7	1.5	0.0	1.1	—
1857	2.5	1.9	0.0	0.6	1.4	0.0	1.1	—
1858	3.3	2.2	0.0	1.2	2.2	0.0	1.1	—
1859	3.3	2.2	0.0	1.0	2.1	0.0	1.1	—
1860	3.4	2.6	0.0	0.8	2.2	0.0	1.2	—

Year	Total assets or liabilities[a]	Assets			Liabilities			Net profits[c]
		Total loans	Total investments	Total cash	Total deposits	Bank notes	Capital accounts[b]	
1861	3.5	2.1	0.0	1.4	2.3	0.0	1.2	—
1862	6.5	3.4	0.3	3.0	5.4	0.0	1.1	—
1863	7.2	1.5	2.4	3.3	6.0	0.0	1.2	—
1864	8.8	3.1	2.7	3.4	7.3	0.0	1.4	—
1865	8.2	3.3	2.0	2.9	6.4	0.0	1.7	—
1866	9.3	2.9	0.4	5.9	7.7	0.0	1.6	—
1867	7.5	2.7	0.4	4.2	5.6	0.0	1.9	—
1868	9.1	3.6	0.4	4.8	7.0	0.0	2.0	—
1869	9.4	4.3	0.4	4.4	7.3	0.0	2.1	—
1870	9.0	5.1	0.4	3.2	6.8	0.0	2.2	—
1871	9.0	4.9	0.4	3.5	6.8	0.0	2.2	—
1872	8.7	4.4	0.4	3.7	6.4	0.0	2.3	—
1873	8.4	4.8	0.3	3.1	6.0	0.0	2.4	—
1874	11.6	6.2	0.1	5.1	9.0	0.0	2.6	—
1875	10.4	6.0	0.1	4.1	7.8	0.0	2.6	—
1876	13.2	6.2	0.1	6.7	10.7	0.0	2.5	—
1877	11.1	5.9	0.1	4.9	8.5	0.0	2.6	—
1878	13.1	5.5	0.1	7.1	10.5	0.0	2.6	0.0
1879	12.9	6.9	0.1	5.5	10.3	0.0	2.5	0.1
1880	18.9	9.2	0.1	9.4	16.3	0.0	2.6	0.2
1881	16.0	9.1	0.1	6.7	13.2	0.0	2.8	0.3
1882	15.1	6.6	0.1	8.2	12.2	0.0	2.9	0.3
1883	14.4	7.3	0.1	6.7	11.5	0.0	2.9	0.2
1884	21.9	8.4	0.1	13.1	19.0	0.0	2.8	0.1
1885	26.5	9.9	0.1	16.1	23.7	0.0	2.8	0.2
1886	18.2	9.3	0.1	8.6	15.2	0.0	3.0	0.2
1887	18.8	9.3	0.1	9.2	15.6	0.0	3.2	0.3
1888	22.2	10.7	0.1	11.1	18.9	0.0	3.4	0.3
1889	24.6	10.5	0.1	13.7	21.1	0.0	3.5	0.2
1890	20.7	10.5	0.1	9.9	17.2	0.0	3.5	0.2
1891	22.2	10.8	0.1	11.1	18.7	0.0	3.5	0.2
1892	23.5	13.2	0.1	10.0	19.7	0.0	3.7	0.3
1893	29.7	13.3	1.1	15.1	25.0	0.9	3.8	0.2
1894	47.4	23.3	1.5	22.4	42.6	0.8	4.0	0.4
1895	42.9	21.7	1.7	19.3	37.9	0.8	4.2	0.4
1896	37.1	19.8	2.6	14.5	31.8	0.8	4.6	0.5
1897	67.9	40.1	3.2	24.6	62.2	0.8	4.7	0.3
1898	113.8	50.3	31.9	31.3	94.5	0.8	5.3	0.7
1899	138.4	70.9	24.2	43.0	123.8	0.8	5.8	0.6
1900	188.6	88.7	33.5	66.2	159.1	4.3	15.5	1.2
1901	194.5	90.5	33.9	69.9	165.8	4.3	16.5	1.7
1902	202.8	89.1	40.4	73.2	151.4	5.0	40.4	2.7

Year	Total assets or liabilities[a]	Assets			Liabilities			Net profits[c]
		Total loans	Total investments	Total cash	Total deposits	Bank notes	Capital accounts[b]	
1903	197.6	105.7	41.3	50.4	142.7	5.4	41.9	3.2
1904	290.4	150.5	45.5	94.3	231.5	5.5	42.4	2.1
1905	307.9	178.1	42.8	87.0	238.8	10.5	43.0	3.1
1906	242.4	126.0	35.6	80.5	181.9	5.0	45.7	5.1
1907	231.5	119.6	43.3	68.4	165.1	9.0	48.6	5.2
1908	334.1	146.8	47.1	135.8	269.6	8.0	50.6	4.0
1909	317.1	157.7	49.6	104.4	252.6	3.9	54.0	5.6
1910	290.4	127.4	45.8	111.8	224.9	2.8	56.5	5.3
1911	307.0	132.2	51.2	118.2	238.9	2.2	59.7	7.3
1912	313.8	163.5	44.7	100.8	252.4	2.2	53.5	5.3
1913	276.1	132.0	40.9	98.1	211.2	3.4	55.5	4.9
1914	352.4	179.0	39.8	119.0	283.8	3.5	57.9	5.1
1915	441.1	196.4	44.9	180.6	366.0	3.4	61.9	5.4
1916	615.3	330.0	49.4	203.6	530.0	1.8	65.8	8.2
1917	902.1	444.7	176.1	248.6	706.3	1.8	72.0	7.3
1918	977.3	531.6	55.0	361.7	840.9	1.4	76.4	7.4
1919	1,039.4	622.8	53.4	291.9	767.2	1.4	80.8	7.1
1920	1,032.1	650.3	39.7	265.1	698.6	1.4	116.1	12.3
1921	868.0	531.2	51.8	221.0	609.7	1.3	104.5	3.8
1922	849.4	492.7	109.2	201.8	667.0	1.8	89.8	0.9
1923	851.0	468.9	170.7	164.6	662.2	2.1	91.5	6.8
1924	1,027.1	537.0	184.6	248.5	841.6	2.1	94.1	3.1
1925	1,154.7	531.4	241.4	300.2	910.9	0.8	112.3	13.2
1926	1,281.5	716.5	177.3	275.6	963.6	0.1	113.1	12.8
1927	1,537.4	849.7	189.0	347.7	1,200.0	0.1	143.8	17.9
1928	1,623.7	921.8	236.3	298.8	1,168.5	0.1	164.0	19.8
1929	2,062.4	1,249.1	242.6	365.5	1,470.9	0.1	235.3	22.8
1930	2,078.3	1,147.1	263.7	453.0	1,560.3	0.1	243.0	0.5
1931	1,973.1	1,003.8	366.4	343.6	1,460.6	0.0	225.8	− 7.3
1932	1,567.7	696.6	394.8	302.3	1,214.3	0.0	205.4	− 12.6
1933	1,475.9	559.9	439.7	334.2	1,134.8	25.0	179.7	− 7.3
1934	1,466.9	490.4	493.8	358.4	1,226.6	0.0	182.5	− 58.1
1935	1,627.1	542.8	636.7	342.5	1,397.1	0.0	184.7	11.1
1936	1,969.9	551.9	843.1	482.8	1,730.0	0.0	192.6	12.8
1937	2,006.2	710.2	664.3	549.8	1,807.8	0.0	145.5	6.2
1938	1,936.9	525.4	725.1	610.3	1,761.3	0.0	147.4	4.1
1939	2,232.8	496.9	850.9	824.5	2,062.8	0.0	153.5	16.1
1940	2,774.8	506.6	969.1	1,247.1	2,592.0	0.0	170.3	17.5
1941	3,145.9	610.4	1,455.6	1,030.3	2,934.8	0.0	191.8	23.6
1942	3,128.3	600.9	1,547.2	935.7	2,917.1	0.0	212.9	16.7
1943	3,735.6	589.6	2,285.6	806.9	3,512.1	0.0	225.8	24.2
1944	4,410.4	833.4	2,491.1	906.7	4,157.8	0.0	258.7	30.7

Year	Total assets or liabilities[a]	Assets			Liabilities			Net profits[c]
		Total loans	Total investments	Total cash	Total deposits	Bank notes	Capital accounts[b]	
1945	4,776.2	1,139.5	2,713.5	870.2	4,503.1	0.0	275.0	31.0
1946	5,184.5	1,078.0	2,875.8	1,176.8	4,872.6	0.0	294.9	20.4
1947	5,044.2	1,184.8	2,504.9	1,301.2	4,720.5	0.0	302.0	21.3
1948	4,955.7	1,310.8	2,150.5	1,461.5	4,645.5	0.0	301.4	19.4
1949	4,945.4	1,369.9	2,118.9	1,411.3	4,579.5	0.0	312.1	21.2
1950	4,966.2	1,334.4	2,396.0	1,164.4	4,593.5	0.0	315.8	23.1
1951	5,579.9	1,839.4	2,174.6	1,490.2	5,079.0	0.0	368.4	24.1
1952	6,025.7	2,199.3	2,229.0	1,542.0	5,541.6	0.0	379.0	26.9
1953	5,762.7	2,277.0	1,935.3	1,496.7	5,267.5	0.0	404.0	28.6
1954	5,966.6	2,202.4	2,314.1	1,385.7	5,455.4	0.0	427.2	38.3
1955	6,856.0	2,673.9	2,467.4	1,629.9	6,174.8	0.0	571.7	37.3
1956	6,969.6	3,517.0	1,732.4	1,611.3	6,249.7	0.0	574.2	41.7
1957	7,434.1	3,905.3	1,526.0	1,843.9	6,614.2	0.0	591.8	55.1
1958	8,056.4	3,965.5	2,086.5	1,825.6	7,132.7	0.0	731.5	57.3
1959	7,871.1	4,078.2	1,845.8	1,781.9	6,966.1	0.0	749.5	55.7
1960	8,162.6	4,266.9	1,766.5	1,884.6	7,173.3	0.0	780.4	50.3
1961	8,630.3	4,066.6	2,537.7	1,753.8	7,455.9	0.0	828.2	80.6
1962	9,196.1	4,385.1	2,566.3	1,927.7	8,023.0	0.0	861.9	68.2
1963	10,599.4	5,176.2	2,697.2	2,366.4	9,236.3	0.0	920.8	80.3
1964	11,752.3	6,199.8	2,700.3	2,425.0	10,174.8	0.0	957.3	86.0
1965	13,756.0	7,929.3	2,633.0	2,601.6	11,802.8	0.0	1,250.4	88.7
1966	14,744.4	8,737.6	2,668.2	2,684.5	12,588.6	0.0	1,295.2	93.4
1967	15,649.9	9,116.3	2,894.4	2,940.8	13,221.3	0.0	1,337.9	102.6
1968	18,385.1	10,790.7	2,748.7	3,982.1	15,461.3	0.0	1,381.8	109.3
1969	21,205.6	12,459.8	3,020.2	4,563.2	17,390.2	0.0	1,406.7	121.6
1970	23,445.0	13,326.9	2,947.9	5,115.2	19,674.9	0.0	1,393.6	140.6

Source: Cols. 2–8: 1834–1846: New York State Legislature, Assembly (1834), Doc. 102; (1835), Doc. 74; (1836), Doc. 80; (1837), Doc. 78; (1838), Doc. 71; (1839), Doc. 101; (1840), Doc. 44; (1841), Doc. 64; (1842), Doc. 29; (1843), Doc. 34; (1844), Doc. 4; (1845), Doc. 25; (1846), Doc. 25; (1847), Doc. 5. 1853–1865: New York State Superintendent of Banking, *Annual Report* (Albany, N.Y.: n.p., 1853–1866). 1866: *Bankers' Magazine* 21 (1866): 303. 1867–1877: Comptroller of the Currency, *Annual Reports* (Washington, D.C.: GPO, 1868–1878). 1878–1916: National City Bank, Call Reports. 1917–1920: National City Bank, Comptroller's Reports. 1921–1970: (First) National City Bank, Statement of Condition, June 30.

Col. 9: 1835–1842: New York State Legislature, Assembly (1836), Doc. 80; (1837), Doc. 78; (1838), Doc. 71; (1839), Doc. 101; (1840), Doc. 44; (1841), Doc. 64; (1842), Doc. 29; (1843), Doc. 34. 1878–1900: National City Bank, Report of Earnings and Dividends to the Comptroller of the Currency. 1901–1917: National City Bank, Earnings, Organization File, Vanderlip MSS. 1918–1970: Citibank, Comptroller's Report, Annual Report.

a. Principal assets and liabilities are as of June 30, except for the years 1834 to 1842, which are for December 31; 1843 to 1846, which are for November 1; 1878 to 1910, which are for the call date nearest to October 1; and 1917 to 1920, which are for December 31. The figures refer to the consolidated assets and liabilities of the Head Office and the domestic and foreign branches for the bank, except for the years 1915 and 1916, when the assets and liabilities of the foreign branches are excluded.

b. Capital accounts include capital, surplus, undivided profits, unallocated reserve for contingencies, preferred stock (1934–1936), and convertible long-term debt (1965–1968). Figures for 1969 and 1970 represent the capital of the bank alone, and include as part of surplus the obligation for the convertible capital note assumed by the parent holding company.

c. Net profits represent net operating earnings minus net write-offs except for the years 1835 to 1842 and 1901 to 1917, when they are calculated as dividends plus the change in undivided profits (an equivalent measure). Net profits for the years 1878–1899 are for the year ending October 31. Net profits for the years 1835 to 1842 and 1901 to 1970 are for the calendar year. Net profits for the year 1900 are for the 14 months ending December 31, 1900. Net profits for the years 1834 to 1968 are for the bank only. Net profits for the years 1969 and 1970 are for the holding company. All profit figures are after tax.

Citibank: Number of International Branches, 1914–1970

Selected years	Western Hemisphere	Europe	Asia and the Far East	Middle East	Total
1914	1	0	0	0	1
1915	8	1	12	0	21
1916	12	2	13	0	27
1917	17	4	13	0	34
1918	19	4	15	0	38
1919	48	8	18	0	74
1920	55	8	18	0	81
1925	62	9	19	0	90
1930	67	11	19	0	97
1935	44	9	18	0	71
1940	42	6	18	0	66
1941	41	3	5	0	49
1942	41	3	1	0	45
1943	41	3	1	0	45
1944	41	2	2	0	45
1945	41	2	7	0	50
1950	38	3	10	0	51
1955	42	3	11	3	59
1956	46	3	11	3	63
1957	49	3	11	3	66
1958	50	3	11	3	67
1959	57	3	13	3	76
1960	50	4	13	3	70
1961	57	4	13	3	77
1962	59	6	16	2	83
1963	62	7	17	2	88
1964	63	9	18	3	93
1965	70	12	23	3	108

Selected years	Western Hemisphere	Europe	Asia and the Far East	Middle East	Total
1966	80	14	25	4	123
1967	98	19	27	4	148
1968	122	25	33	4	184
1969	145	32	35	4	216
1970	157	32	36	6	231

Source: Paul Rainey, Vice President, Office of the General Counsel, Citibank.

Note: A foreign office is counted as a branch if it accepts deposits, cashes checks, or approves loans. Years were chosen to highlight the speed of the initial buildup, the impact of the Great Depression and World War II, and the revitalization of the branch network after 1955.

National City Bank: Corporate Customers, August 1914

Industry	Rank[a]	
	Within industry	All industrial corporations
Food and like products		
Meatpacking		
Armour & Co.	1	4
Morris & Co.	4	57
Sugar refining		
American Sugar Refining	1	28
Brewing		
Jos. Schlitz	1	228
Tobacco manufacturing		
American Tobacco Co.	1	18
American Cigar Co.	4	111
Textile mill products		
American Woolen Co.	1	36
American Thread Co.	3	195
Fall River Iron Works	7	263
Apparel and related products		
Hart, Schaffner & Marx	2	213
Chemicals		
E. I. Du Pont de Nemours & Co.	1	8
Virginia Carolina Chemical Co.	3	55
New Jersey Zinc	5	73
Petroleum refining		
Standard Oil[b]		

	Rank[a]	
Industry	Within industry	All industrial corporations
Rubber products		
U.S. Rubber Co.	1	9
Firestone Tire and Rubber	4	96
Leather and its products		
Central Leather	1	23
Endicott, Johnson	2	112
Primary metal industries		
Iron and steel		
Lackawanna Steel Co.	6	40
Crucible Steel of America	9	58
U.S. Cast Iron Pipe & Foundry		184
Nonferrous metals		
Phelps Dodge	1	10
American Smelting and Refining	3	13
Fabricated metal products except ordnance, machinery, and transport equipment		
American Brass Co.	4	108
Machinery, except electrical		
International Harvester	1	7
Rumely Co.	12	173
Electrical machinery		
General Electric	1	11
Western Electric Co.	3	38
Transportation equipment		
Automobiles		
Ford Motor Co.	1	16
Detroit Cadillac Motor Car Co.		
Packard Motor Car Co.	9	121
Peerless Motor Car Co.		
Railroad equipment		
Pullman Co.	1	25
Westinghouse Air Brake		118
Shipping		
W. R. Grace		52
Utilities		
Telephone		
American Telephone & Telegraph		
Consolidated Telephone		

	Rank[a]	
Industry	Within industry	All industrial corporations
Electric		
New York Edison		
Gas		
Consolidated Gas		
Railroads		
Pennsylvania	1	
Southern Pacific	2	
New York Central	3	
Union Pacific	4	
Baltimore & Ohio	6	
Chicago, Milwaukee, & St. Paul	13	
Chicago & Northwestern	15	
Illinois Central	16	
Chesapeake & Ohio	20	
Missouri, Kansas, & Texas	23	
Seaboard	26	

Source: Organization File, National City Bank, Accounts, Vanderlip MSS. Classification and rank according to tables in Alfred D. Chandler, Jr., *The Visible Hand: The Managerial Revolution in American Business* (Cambridge, Mass.: Harvard University Press, 1977), pp. 503–513.

a. Rank in 1917.

b. Standard Oil accounts listed as one account. However, Standard Oil was in the process of dissolution in accordance with the Supreme Court's decision.

First National City Corporation: Board of Directors, December 31, 1970

Lord Aldington
William M. Batten
Milo M. Brisco
Frederick M. Eaton
Louis K. Eilers
Lawrence E. Fouraker
J. Peter Grace, Jr.
William P. Gwinn
John G. Hall
Amory G. Houghton, Jr.
John R. Kimberly
J. Howard Laeri, Vice Chairman
Charles B. McCoy
Roger Milliken
Charles G. Mortimer
Robert S. Oelman
Edward L. Palmer, Chairman of the
    Executive Committee
William I. Spencer, President
Franklin A. Thomas
Thomas R. Wilcox, Vice Chairman
Joseph C. Wilson
Walter B. Wriston, Chairman

Notes

Introduction

1. John Brooks, "The Money Machine," *The New Yorker*, January 5, 1981.

2. Lord Acton, *Lectures on Modern History* (London: Macmillan, 1906), p. 33.

3. See Thomas F. Huertas, "The Regulation of Financial Institutions: A Historical Perspective on Current Issues," in *Financial Services: The Changing Institutions and Government Policy*, ed. George J. Benston (Englewood Cliffs, N.J.: Prentice-Hall, 1983), pp. 6–28.

4. Interview, October 3, 1980.

1. The Mercantile Bank, 1812–1837

1. On the First Bank of the United States see Bray Hammond, *Banks and Politics in America from the Revolution to the Civil War* (Princeton: Princeton University Press, 1957), pp. 197–226. U.S. National Monetary Commission, *The First and Second Bank of the United States* (by John T. Holdsworth and Davis R. Dewey, 1910), S. Doc. 581, pp. 9–144; Richard H. Timberlake, Jr., *The Origins of Central Banking in the United States* (Cambridge, Mass.: Harvard University Press, 1978), pp. 6–11. The five other banks in the city in 1811 were the Bank of New York (established 1784), the Bank of the Manhattan Company (1799), Merchants Bank (1803), Mechanics Bank (1810), and Union Bank (1811).

2. New York State Legislature, Assembly, 34th sess. (1811), Journal, pp. 68–69.

3. Bayrd Still, *Mirror for Gotham* (New York: New York University Press, 1956), p. 56. Little is known about the 1811 petitioners aside from the fact that they were led by Thomas Stagg, Jr. He was probably a relative of Abraham Stagg, one of the leading members of Tammany Hall, and of Peter Stagg, one of the original directors of City Bank and its third president (1817–1825). Thomas Stagg, Jr. never became a director of City Bank.

4. Unlike the other cities mentioned, New York possessed both a natural harbor and a natural waterway to the interior, the Hudson River. According to Herman Krooss's essay "Financial Institutions" in *The Growth of Seaport Cities, 1790–1825*, ed. David T. Gilchrist (Charlottesville: University Press of Virginia, 1967),

p. 105, "It was New York's external environment and its entrepreneurs that gave it its preeminent position."

5. Joseph Dorfman, "Economic Thought," in *Seaport Cities*, ed. Gilchrist, p. 157. This notion of an American counterpart of London does not appear in writings concerning other cities.

6. New York State Legislature, Assembly, 34th sess. (1811), Journal, pp. 68–69.

7. Hammond, *Banks and Politics*, p. 127. On the operation of these branches see James O. Wettereau, "The Branches of the First Bank of the United States," *Journal of Economic History*, 2 (1942): Supplement, 66–100. On the New York branch itself, see Edward Hardenbrook, *Financial New York: A History* (New York, 1889), p. 145.

8. Timberlake, *Origins of Central Banking*, pp. 8–12. Fritz Redlich, *The Molding of American Banking, Men, and Ideas*, pt. 1, 1781-1840 (New York: Johnson Reprint, 1968), pp. 96–100.

9. For a discussion of the business and political forces opposed to renewing the charter of the Bank of the United States see Hammond, *Banks and Politics*, pp. 213–225.

10. Hammond, *Banks and Politics*, p. 147. Similarly, Richard Hildreth, *The History of Banks* (Boston, 1837), pp. 133–134, wrote that people who wanted to borrow started banks.

11. Hammond, *Banks and Politics*, p. 159. In the early nineteenth century incorporation was relatively rare and reserved to firms with a distinct public purpose, such as turnpikes and hospitals. Banks were required to incorporate if they wished to issue notes, a close substitute for government coinage as currency. Cf. Oscar Handlin and Mary F. Handlin, "Origins of the American Business Corporation," *Journal of Economic History*, 5 (1945): 1–23.

12. Hammond, *Banks and Politics*, pp. 158–161, relates the struggle in 1804 over the charter of the Merchants Bank between the Federalists, who favored it, and the Republicans, who sought to block it. Bonus payments to the state and to the legislators for their favorable votes persisted until the passage of the Free Banking Act in 1838. See Frank Otto Gatell, "Sober Second Thoughts on Van Buren, the Albany Regency, and the Wall Street Conspiracy," *Journal of American History* 53 (1966): 19–40.

13. On the rivalry of Clinton and Madison in New York see Jabez D. Hammond, *History of Political Parties in the State of New York* (Syracuse, 1852), pp. 230, 264–265. Before 1800 the Federalists had dominated New York State politics and had appropriated to themselves the only banking charter, that of the Bank of New York. Under the leadership of Aaron Burr the Republicans succeeded in obtaining a charter for the Bank of the Manhattan Company in 1799. Soon after that the Republicans divided into two factions, one led by George Clinton and his nephew DeWitt Clinton and the other led by Aaron Burr. After Burr's duel with Hamilton and the end of his political career, his supporters transferred their allegiance to James Madison, the enemy of their enemies, George and DeWitt Clinton.

14. New York State Legislature, Assembly, 34th sess. (1811), Journal, p. 303.

15. Hammond, *Banks and Politics*, pp. 162–163.

16. Dumas Malone, ed., *Dictionary of American Biography*, vol. 14 (New York: Charles Scribner's Sons, 1943), pp. 81–82. Osgood was the stepfather of DeWitt Clinton's wife (cf. Dorothie Bobbe, *DeWitt Clinton*, new ed. [Port Washington, N.Y.: I. J. Friedman, 1962], p. 61). In addition to his career as soldier, legislator, administrator, and banker, Osgood was a theologian as well. He published a number of studies on religion. Concerning Osgood's role as director of the Bank of North America and cashier of the Massachusetts Bank, see Ben Ames Williams, Jr., *Bank of Boston 200: A History of New England's Leading Bank, 1784–1984* (Boston: Houghton Mifflin, 1984), pp. 3–10.

17. Samuel Osgood, Memorandum, February 22, 1812, on the subject of the incorporation of a new bank under Republican managers, Osgood MSS, New-York Historical Society, New York.

18. J. van Fenstermaker, *A Statistical Summary of the Commercial Banks Incorporated in the United States prior to 1819* (Kent, Oh.: Bureau of Economics and Business Research, Kent State University, 1965), pp. 159–160.

19. Gustavus Myers, *The History of Tammany Hall*, 2nd ed. (New York: Boni and Liveright, 1917), pp. 17–36.

20. Joseph A. Scoville (Walter Barnett, *pseud.*), *The Old Merchants of New York City*, 5 vols. (New York, 1885), II, 227; IV, 249–255; V, 222. Another Tammany man was Abraham Bloodgood, a prosperous leather merchant and an alderman for the Fourth Ward (ibid., I, 280–282).

21. Jasper Ward was a director of the Phoenix Insurance Company. Benjamin Bailey served as a director of the Columbian Insurance Company, and Peter Stagg was president of the Commercial Insurance Company (*Elliotts Improved New York Double Directory* [New York, 1812], p. 31). For Cutting's ownership of the Brooklyn Steamboat see Scoville, *Old Merchants*, II, 237.

22. New York State Legislature, Assembly, 51st sess. (1828), Documents, January 2, 1828. Petition Peter Stagg et al. to form the National Bank of the City of New York. Peter Stagg was one of the original directors of the City Bank and its third president (1817–1825). He was ousted from office in 1825 after a change in the bank's ownership. Although the quotation refers to the formation of another bank, we can infer from the charter and bylaws of City Bank that its directors viewed the business of banking in the same way.

The multiple determining a merchant's line of credit relative to his deposits depended not only on his credit standing but also on the size and composition of the bank's liabilities. Larger credit lines could be safely and equitably extended to each shareholder when the bank's paid-in capital was larger. The less variable were the bank's aggregate deposits, the lower was its need to maintain reserves and the higher its credit lines could be without endangering the bank's liquidity. The shorter the maturity of the average loan, the larger the credit multiple could be without compromising the access of other shareholders to credit. Each shareholder would have a more equal access to credit, the more evenly their borrowing demands were distributed over the year.

23. Actual capital was considerably less than authorized capital. At City Bank capital was paid in gradually, reaching a total of $1.4 million by February 1814 (City Bank, Board of Directors, Minutes, February 28, 1814). Shares had a par

value of $50, but shareholders were required to pay only $2.50 per share or 5 percent of the total at the commencement of business (City Bank, Board of Directors, Minutes, June 27, 1812). Further installments of 5 percent and 10 percent were due on September 11, 1812, and November 27, 1812, respectively, for a cumulative total of 20 percent of the par value of the stock (City Bank, Board of Directors, Minutes, August 1, 1812, and October 26, 1812).

Although shareholders were generally required to pay each installment in cash, two exceptions to this rule were made. The first concerned shareholders of the former Bank of the United States. They could purchase up to ten thousand shares of City Bank stock (one-fourth of its total authorized capital) for a cash payment of $2.50 per share and the tender of their shares in the Bank of the United States. About seventy-five hundred City Bank shares (19 percent of the total authorized) were sold in this fashion.

A second exception was made for the directors of City Bank. They did not have to pay cash for their shares. The bank extended them a loan against the collateral of the stock at a rate of 6 percent for an indefinite term (City Bank, Board of Directors, Minutes, July 3, 1812, and October 5, 1812).

24. New York State Legislature, Assembly, 51st sess. (1828), Documents, January 2, 1828. Petition Peter Stagg et al. to form National Bank of the City of New York.

25. Scoville, *Old Merchants*, I, 262.

26. City Bank, Board of Directors, Minutes, March 13, 1813, September 30, 1813, and May 23, 1814.

27. City Bank, Board of Directors, Minutes, December 5, 1814, December 12, 1814, and December 15, 1814.

28. City Bank, Board of Directors, Minutes, May 23, 1814. City Bank received these deposits as a result of the intercession of Jacob Barker. As part of his loan agreement with City Bank, Barker promised to write the Treasury, requesting them to deposit one-third of their New York balances with City Bank.

29. On March 30, 1815, the U.S. government reduced its balances at City Bank from one-third to one-fourth of its total deposits in New York City (City Bank, Board of Directors, Minutes, March 30, 1815). After the chartering of the Second Bank of the United States, the government withdrew its remaining deposits. Cf. Timberlake, *Origins of Central Banking*, pp. 18–22.

30. Specie payments were resumed on February 20, 1817, the day that the Second Bank of the United States began operations. In anticipation of resumption, City Bank took steps to purchase specie to hold as reserves against its note issue and deposits (City Bank, Board of Directors, Minutes, December 20, 1816).

31. Timberlake, *Origins of Central Banking*, p. 22.

32. City Bank, Bylaws, June 19, 1812. In addition, an early resolution of the board allowed directors to subscribe to the stock on favorable terms. These included the provision of a loan of indefinite maturity at 6 percent interest with the stock of the bank as collateral (City Bank, Board of Directors, Minutes, July 3, 1812). The resolution expressly stated that such loans for the purpose of acquiring stock would not diminish the loans to which the directors might otherwise be entitled.

33. City Bank, Board of Directors, Minutes, February 28, 1814.

34. City Bank, Board of Directors, Minutes, December 6, 1813.

35. City Bank, Board of Directors, Minutes, February 28, 1814. In September 1814 this resolution was reinforced by another requiring merchants with discounts above $20,000 to pay interest at 7 percent instead of the customary 6 percent (City Bank, Board of Directors, Minutes, September 19, 1814). The following day the directors resolved that no discounts over $20,000 would be renewed, unless the borrower reduced his indebtedness by 20 percent at the maturity of the note (City Bank, Board of Directors, Minutes, September 20, 1814). The loan limit was raised to $40,000 on June 29, 1815 (City Bank, Board of Directors, Minutes). On October 17, 1817, the board appointed a committee to determine if the bank should ask for additional collateral from large borrowers.

36. City Bank, Board of Directors, Minutes, September 9, 1816.

37. Henry W. Lanier. *A Century of Banking in New York, 1822–1922* (New York: Gilliss, 1922). Swartwout was an associate of Aaron Burr and was involved with DeWitt Clinton in building the Erie Canal. On the bank's negotiations with Swartwout see City Bank, Board of Directors, Minutes, November 2, 1820. Swartwout had ceased as director in 1817.

38. On the bank's difficulty in collecting debts from Jasper Ward see City Bank, Board of Directors, Minutes, February 27, 1816, and May 5, 1816. The bank's difficulties with William van Ness were discussed at the board meeting of November 15, 1819. In addition, the bank had problems with its loans to the Osgood estate (see City Bank, Board of Directors, Minutes, March 13, 1815, and May 1, 1815). Earlier, City Bank had declared Henry Fanning, one of the original directors and the owner of one thousand shares of stock (2.5 percent of the total authorized), to be in default. See City Bank, Board of Directors, Minutes, December 18, 1812, and June 10, 1813. Thereafter Fanning did not stand for reelection to the board.

39. The new directors bought fifteen thousand shares (a majority of the outstanding stock) from Lawton on September 9, 1825, at a 7 percent premium in order to prevent him from selling his controlling interest in the bank to interests "fatal to the character and credit of the institution." As a condition of the sale, Lawton resigned as a director of the bank. City Bank, Board of Directors, Minutes, June 25, 1825, and September 24, 1827.

40. Scoville, *The Old Merchants*, III, 217.

41. Ibid., IV, 217; I, 245–248.

42. Robert G. Albion, *The Rise of New York Port, 1815–1860* (New York: Charles Scribner's Sons, 1939; rpt. Hamden, Conn.: Archon Books, 1961); Charles P. Kindleberger, *The Formation of Financial Centers: A Study in Comparative Economic History*, Princeton Studies in International Finance, no. 36 (Princeton: International Finance Section, Department of Economics, Princeton University, November 1974), pp. 52–53.

43. Albion, *New York Port*, p. 13, writes on the Black Ball Shipping Line that "the regularity of service, as anticipated, attracted shippers almost at once and helped to clinch New York's leadership as the chief receiving port for the offerings of European markets."

44. Edmund Clarence Stedman, *The New York Stock Exchange* (New York: Stock Exchange Historical Company, 1905), pp. 62–87. New York's position as the center of transportation and commerce also helped make it the information center

of the United States, the point at which news about Europe and European markets entered the United States and from which it was distributed to the rest of the country. This too promoted New York's role as a financial center. Cf. Allan R. Pred, *Urban Growth and the Circulation of Information* (Cambridge, Mass.: MIT Press, 1973), pp. 28–32.

45. Hammond, *Banks and Politics*, pp. 351–353. On the Second Bank of the United States see Redlich, *The Molding of American Banking*, pt. 1, pp. 101–161; Timberlake, *Origins of Central Banking*, pp. 26–41.

46. Marvin Meyers, *The Jacksonian Persuasion: Politics and Belief* (Stanford, Calif.: Stanford University Press, 1957), pp. 22–24.

47. For a summary of the Bank War and its effects, see Susan P. Lee and Peter Passell, *A New Economic View of American History* (New York: Norton Books, 1979), pp. 117–122.

48. New York State Legislature, Assembly, 60th sess. (1837), Document 78, pp. 26–29. Comparable asset figures for 1812 are not available. At that time City Bank accounted for 12.7 percent of the authorized capital of New York City's eight commercial banks (Fenstermaker, *Statistical Summary*, pp. 159–160). At the end of 1836 City Bank's actual capital amounted to only 3.8 percent of the total capital of all New York City banks.

49. The occurrence of several bank failures and the difficulty of redeeming notes issued by remote country banks prompted the New York State legislature in 1829 to pass the Safety Fund Act. Each bank chartered by the state paid a tax equal to 0.5 percent of its capital into a fund maintained by the state. The fund was to be used to reimburse the note holders of failed banks.

The law was poorly designed to accomplish its objectives. The establishment of a state-sponsored fund lowered the risk of bank notes relative to specie and thus enhanced their acceptability to the public. This permitted banks to increase their circulation. At the same time, the 1829 act encouraged banks to reduce their capital in order to avoid the tax. Other things equal, this increased the risk of bank failure.

The fundamental flaw of taxing capital rather than the notes themselves was worsened by another deficiency in the plan. The original law provided that the fund would guarantee not just bank notes but all the liabilities of a failed bank with the exception of stockholders' equity. When several banks failed in the early 1840s, the fund was quickly depleted by payments to depositors. Although the legislature amended the law in 1842 to conform with its original intention that only notes be covered, City Bank and other solvent Safety Fund banks were taxed at a penalty rate in order to replenish the fund.

On the Safety Fund see U.S. National Monetary Commission, *The Safety Fund Banking System in New York State, 1829–1866* (by R. E. Chaddock, 1910), S. Doc. 581; Redlich, *The Molding of American Banking*, pt. 1, pp. 88–95; Hammond, *Banks and Politics*, pp. 556–563.

During the 1820s, the bank had reduced its capital several times from the $2 million originally authorized under the charter of 1812. In 1831, on the occasion of the renewal of its charter by the legislature, the bank had set its capital at only $720,000. The reduction reflected the write-off of loans to former directors as well as losses incurred in a robbery in 1831 (City Bank, Board of Directors, Minutes, March 22, and March 24, 1831).

At the end of 1832 City Bank had loans and discounts amounting to 76 percent of its lending limit (New York State Legislature, Assembly, 57th sess. (1834), Document 102, p. 23). In contrast, the Bank of America and the Mechanics Bank, two of the three original pet banks in New York City, had loans amounting to 58 percent and 70 percent, respectively, of their ceilings. At the end of 1835 these pet banks exhausted their aggregate loan limits, a factor that may have been responsible for the passage of the Deposit Act of 1836 and the increase in the number of pet banks.

50. George B. Hotchkiss, "A History of National City Bank" (New York: unpublished, 1912), p. 261. In addition to the limit on aggregate loans, other factors such as the government's demand for collateral against its deposits may also have influenced City Bank not to become a pet bank. It should be noted that the original pets agreed to several restrictions on their operation as a condition of their receiving the government's deposits. According to contracts between the secretary of the treasury and the pets, the latter agreed to pledge collateral for deposits in excess of one-half the bank's paid-in capital. The pet banks also agreed to perform for the government all the services formerly rendered by the Second Bank. They were forbidden to issue small notes and were required to keep one-third of their reserves in specie. In addition, the pet banks agreed among themselves to accept one another's notes and drafts (U.S. National Monetary Commission, *The Independent Treasury of the United States* [by David Kinley, 1910], S. Doc. 587, p. 17). In effect the Treasury sought to produce a decentralized version of the Second Bank, thereby capturing the bank's economic benefits while eliminating Biddle's power. Thus, the conditions imposed on pet banks may have limited the profitability of government deposits relative to the free issue of bank notes.

51. Frank O. Gatell, "Spoils of the Bank War: Political Bias in the Selection of Pet Banks," *American Historical Review*, 80 (1964): 35–47.

52. Peter Stagg, City Bank's president from 1817 to 1825, thought that the circulation of bank notes could not "be depended on as the source of any considerable profit" (New York State Legislature, Assembly, 51st sess. [1828], Documents, January 2, 1828).

53. On the early development of correspondent banking see Margaret G. Myers, *The New York Money Market*, ed. Benjamin H. Beckhart, vol. 1, *Origins and Development* (New York: Columbia University Press, 1931), pp. 103–126.

For example, in 1816 City Bank agreed with the Bank of Lansingburgh that it would continue to redeem their notes although the amount received might occasionally exceed the balance of their account. The Bank of Lansingburgh agreed to pay City Bank 6 percent interest on any funds advanced to it, the same rate commercial borrowers paid. The Bank of Lansingburgh also promised that it would endeavor to keep such advances "as low as possible," clear evidence that City Bank viewed its correspondents primarily as a source of deposits to fund its own commercial loans (City Bank, Board of Directors, Minutes, July 11, 1816).

54. New York State Legislature, Assembly, 60th sess. (1837), Document 78, pp. 26ff.

55. On the causes of the Panic of 1837 see Lee and Passell, *A New Economic View*, pp. 117–122.

56. City Bank, Board of Directors, Minutes, June 6, 1837. Kenneth W. Porter, *John Jacob Astor: Business Man*, 2 vols. (Cambridge, Mass.: Harvard University Press, 1931), p. 1057, notes that Astor was a customer of City Bank. On Taylor's relationship to Astor see chapter 2.

2. One Merchant's Bank, 1837–1891

1. John Moody and George Kibbe Turner, "City Bank: The Federation of the Great Merchants," *McClure's Magazine*, May 1911, p. 78.

2. Henry Clews, *Fifty Years on Wall Street* (1908; rpt. New York: Arno Press, 1973), p. 677. Much of the following section relies on Daniel Hodas, *The Business Career of Moses Taylor: Merchant, Finance Capitalist, and Industrialist* (New York: New York University Press, 1976).

3. Kenneth W. Porter, *John Jacob Astor: Business Man*, 2 vols. (Cambridge Mass.: Harvard University Press, 1931), p. 1048, writes that John B. Taylor was a "sort of chief business man for John Jacob Astor." Astor was a customer of City Bank in the early 1830s (ibid., p. 1057), and the owner of 150 shares in the Farmers' Loan and Trust Company (ibid., p. 973). Thus, Moses Taylor's association with each of these institutions probably arose as a result of his connection with Astor. For a contemporary assessment of Astor, see Sigmund Diamond, *The Reputation of the American Businessman* (1955; rpt. Gloucester, Mass.: Peter Smith, 1970), pp. 23–52.

4. Cited in Porter, *Astor*, p. 1048. Similarly, Moses Y. Beach, *The Wealth and Biography of the Wealthy Citizens of the City of New York* (New York, 1855), p. 28, noted that Moses Taylor's "connection in business with the Astors brought gold to his coffers."

5. Beach, *Wealth and Biography*, p. 28. For a history of Moses Taylor and Company's activities in the Cuban sugar trade see Roland T. Ely, "The Old Cuba Trade: Highlights and Case Studies of Cuban-American Interdependence during the Nineteenth Century," *Business History Review*, 38 (1964): 456–478.

6. The activities of the Forbes group are described in Arthur M. Johnson and Barry E. Supple, *Boston Capitalists and Western Railroads* (Cambridge, Mass.: Harvard University Press, 1967).

7. John J. Phelps (1809–1869) was associated with Taylor in the Manhattan Gas Light Company and the Delaware, Lackawanna, and Western Railroad (Hodas, *Moses Taylor*, pp. 67, 69–70, 89–90, 149–150). Phelps served as a director of National City Bank from 1864 to 1869; at this time he was the second largest shareholder in the bank, with 3 percent of the outstanding shares, second only to Taylor himself, who held 8 percent (ibid., p. 55).

After Phelps's death, his seat on National City's board passed to his son, William Walter Phelps (1839–1894). The younger Phelps was a prominent investor in his own right. For a number of years he controlled the Rock Island Railway. Through his investment in the bonds of the International and Great Northern, Phelps became the largest shareholder in the New York and Texas Land Company. Phelps also had an interest in the Second National Bank of New York and was instrumental in saving this institution from bankruptcy in the Panic of 1884. The Second National merged with National City in 1921. In later life Phelps turned from business to politics, serving as a representative from New Jersey and as ambassador to Germany. Cf. Hugh M. Herrick, *The Life of William Walter Phelps* (New York: Knickerbocker Press, 1904).

8. William E. Dodge (1805–1883) was associated with Taylor in the Delaware, Lackawanna, and Western Railroad, the Lackawanna Iron and Coal Company, and various western railroads, including the International Great Northern and the Houston and Texas Central (Hodas, *Moses Taylor,* pp. 86, 89, 148–150, 235). Dodge's partner and father-in-law, Anson G. Phelps (1781–1853), was a distant relation of John J. Phelps, another City Bank director.

For further details of Dodge's career see *National Cyclopaedia of American Biography* (New York: James T. White, 1893), III, 174–175; Richard Lowitt, *A Merchant Prince of the Nineteenth Century, William E. Dodge* (New York: Columbia University Press, 1954). Dodge never became a director of City Bank, although his son Cleveland H. Dodge did, serving from 1889 to 1926.

John Inslee Blair (1802–1899) was also associated with Taylor in the Delaware, Lackawanna, and Western Railroad, the Lackawanna Iron and Coal Company, and various western railroads, including the International and Great Northern and the Houston and Texas Central (Hodas, *Moses Taylor,* pp. 87, 104, 144, 235, 252). For further details of Blair's career see *National Cyclopaedia of American Biography* (New York: James T. White, 1897), VII, 28.

9. John J. Cisco was a New York merchant and banker, who served as a director of City Bank from 1850 to 1884. He was affiliated with Taylor in the Manhattan Gas Light Company and the Houston and Texas Central Railroad. Cisco's other business interests included the United States Trust Company, which he helped found in 1853. From 1853 to 1865 Cisco also served as assistant secretary of the United States Treasury at New York. Cf. United States Trust Company of New York, *Promise Fulfilled: A Story of the Growth of a Good Idea from 1853 to 1953* (New York: United States Trust Company of New York, 1953), p. 27; James P. Baughman, *Charles Morgan and the Development of Southern Transportation* (Nashville, Tenn.: Vanderbilt University Press, 1968), pp. 201–206.

George W. Scranton (1811–1861) and his brother Seldon started in the iron business in 1839 through the purchase of an iron furnace at Oxford, New Jersey. A year later the two brothers founded the Lackawanna Iron and Coal Company to mine the anthracite deposits of the area around Scranton, Pennsylvania. The firm developed a process to smelt iron with anthracite coal in 1842, and in 1846 it contracted to supply railroad iron to the Buffalo, New York, and Erie Railroad. This was the foundation for the firm's later success. In 1846 the Scranton brothers' first cousin, Joseph H. Scranton (1813–1872), joined Lackawanna Iron and Coal as manager of the iron works. In 1858 Joseph succeeded his cousin George as president of the company. Joseph remained president until his death in 1872. See Dumas Malone, ed., *Dictionary of American Biography* (New York: Charles Scribner's Sons, 1943), XVI, 513–514.

10. Hodas, *Moses Taylor,* pp. 64–65.

11. Louis Bader, "Gas Illumination in New York City, 1823–1863" (Ph.D. diss., New York University, 1970), p. 261.

12. Hodas, *Moses Taylor*, p. 74; Frederick L. Collins, *Consolidated Gas Company of New York: A History* (New York: Consolidated Gas Company, 1934), p. 152.

13. Collins, *Consolidated Gas*, p. 155.

14. Hodas, *Moses Taylor*, p. 74.

15. Collins, *Consolidated Gas*, pp. 184–199; Hodas, *Moses Taylor*, p. 78.

16. On the history of the DL & W see Jules I. Bogen, *The Anthracite Railroads: A Study in American Railroad Enterprise* (New York: Ronald Press, 1927), pp. 80–107; Robert J. Casey and W. A. S. Douglas, *The Lackawanna Story: The First Hundred Years of the Delaware, Lackawanna, and Western Railroad* (New York: McGraw-Hill, 1951).

17. Thomas C. Cochran, *Railroad Leaders, 1845–1890* (New York: Russell and Russell, 1965), pp. 31–32; Eliot Jones, *The Anthracite Coal Combination in the United States* (Cambridge, Mass.: Harvard University Press, 1914), pp. 23–25, 39–41; H. V. Poor and H. W. Poor, *Manual of the Railroad of the United States for 1894* (New York: H. V. and H. W. Poor, 1894), pp. 438–443.

One of the coal-mining concerns ultimately absorbed by the DL & W was Union Iron and Coal Company. Taylor had originally invested in this concern in 1853, a year before he became a director of the DL & W. He did so in conjunction with Lewis von Hoffmann, a New York City broker, who served as a director of City Bank from 1857 to 1875. See Hodas, *Moses Taylor*, p. 89.

18. Hodas, *Moses Taylor*, pp. 102–116, 226–229; J. A. Clark, *The Wyoming Valley, Upper Waters of the Susquehanna, and the Lackawanna Coal Region* (Scranton, Pa.: J. A. Clark, 1875), p. 179. In 1884 Lackawanna Iron and Coal was reincorporated as Lackawanna Iron and Steel. In 1902 this was changed to simply Lackawanna Steel. In 1922 Lackawanna was merged into Bethlehem Steel. At the time of the merger Lackawanna was the fourth largest steel producer in the United States, with approximately 3 percent of the industry's total capacity. Cf. Robert A. Hessen, *Steel Titan: The Life of Charles M. Schwab* (New York: Oxford University Press, 1975), pp. 265–266.

19. Hodas, *Moses Taylor*, pp. 200–264.

20. Henry M. Field, *The Story of the Atlantic Telegraph* (New York: Charles Scribner's Sons, 1893), p. 36.

21. Robert L. Thompson, *Wiring a Continent: The History of the Telegraph Industry in the United States, 1832–1866* (Princeton: Princeton University Press, 1947), pp. 299–333, 424–425, 434–435; James D. Reid, *The Telegraph in America: Its Promoters and Noted Men* (New York: Derby Bros., 1879; rpt. New York: Arno Press, 1974), pp. 399–434; Gerald W. Brock, *The Telecommunications Industry: The Dynamics of Market Structure* (Cambridge, Mass.: Harvard University Press, 1981), pp. 55–88.

22. For the early history of Farmers' Loan and Trust Company see Henry W. Lanier, *A Century of Banking in New York, 1822–1922* (New York: Gilliss, 1922); Edward T. Perine, *The Story of Trust Companies* (New York: G. P. Putnam Sons, 1916), pp. 11–17, 108–110. For a history of the development of corporate trust services during this period see James G. Smith, *The Development of Trust Companies in the United States* (New York: Henry Holt, 1928), pp. 295–309.

Taylor was also an investor in and director of the New York Life Insurance and Trust Company, established in 1830. Two of its officials, Daniel Parish and his son Henry, served as directors of City Bank, from 1834 to 1863 and from 1863 to 1890, respectively. Henry Parish's son-in-law, Cleveland H. Dodge, then served as a director from 1889 to 1926 (see note 8, above). Cf. Hodas, *Moses Taylor*, p. 57. Like Farmers' Loan and Trust, the New York Life Insurance and Trust Company stopped underwriting life insurance soon after its establishment. It had no connection with the New York Life Insurance Company, a mutual insurance company established in 1845.

23. Hodas, *Moses Taylor*, p. 38.

24. On the origins of the Free Banking Act see Bray Hammond, *Banks and Politics in America from the Revolution to the Civil War* (Princeton: Princeton University Press, 1957), pp. 572–600; Fritz Redlich, *The Molding of American Banking, Men, and Ideas*, (New York: Johnson Reprint, 1968), I, 187–204. On the economics of free banking see Hugh Rockoff, "The Free Banking Era: A Reexamination," *Journal of Money, Credit, and Banking*, 5 (1974): 141–167. Rockoff notes that the strict security provisions of the New York law promoted sound banking. In contrast, the laws of Michigan, Minnesota, and other states allowed banks to issue notes in excess of the market value of bonds deposited as collateral and thus promoted wildcat banking.

25. On the origins of the National Bank Act see Redlich, *The Molding of American Banking*, pp. 99–113; U.S. National Monetary Commission, *The Origins of the National Banking System* (by Andrew M. David, 1910–1911), S. Doc. 572. David M. Gische, "New York City Banks and the Development of the National Banking System," *American Journal of Legal History*, 23 (1979): 21–67, argues that the designation of New York as the reserve center for other national banks was the key to the success of the national banking system, for it brought the large New York City banks into the system and enabled them to continue to act as correspondents for banks in other sections of the country that converted to a national charter.

26. Hodas, *Moses Taylor*, p. 279. Hodas estimates that Taylor's fortune may have been as high as $50 million.

27. A 1907 National City Bank memorandum to this effect is cited in John K. Winkler, *The First Billion: The Stillmans and the National City Bank* (New York: Vanguard, 1934), p. 67.

28. Moody and Turner, "City Bank," p. 74.

29. Between 1882 and 1891, national banks in New York City had an average reserve ratio of 29.2 percent. National City buttressed an already high reserve ratio with a large volume of demand loans to brokers. Consequently, the bank's liquidity ratio reached an average of close to 100 percent in the period between 1878 and 1881 and dropped to an average of 78.5 percent between 1882 and 1891. See National City Bank, Call Reports, 1878–1891; Comptroller of the Currency, *Annual Report, 1881* (Washington, D.C.: GPO, 1882), p. 191, and *Annual Report, 1892* (Washington, D.C.: GPO, 1893), p. 175. Data are all averages of call dates for the years indicated. The reserve ratio is calculated as the sum of specie, legal tender, U.S. certificates of deposit, and redemption fund divided by net deposits.

The liquidity ratio is defined as reserve ratio plus the ratio of call loans to net deposits.

30. On the origin and development of the call loan market see Margaret G. Myers, *The New York Money Market*, ed. Benjamin H. Beckhart, vol. 1, *Origins and Development* (New York: Columbia University Press, 1931), pp. 126–148, 265–287.

31. Vincent P. Carosso, *Investment Banking in America: A History* (Cambridge Mass.: Harvard University Press, 1970), p. 13.

32. See note 29, above.

33. *Bankers' Magazine*, 10 (1855): 406–407.

34. National City Bank, Board of Directors, Minutes, May 16, 1867. Under the act of March 3, 1865, the aggregate amount of national bank notes was limited to $300 million. This total was apportioned among the banks according to a complex formula. Banks such as National City, which had joined the national banking system relatively early, received a large quota. These quotas could be sold to recently organized banks in the South and West, which could circulate notes more easily than the New York banks, but had low quotas or none at all. The aggregate limit on national bank notes was raised in 1870 and eliminated in 1875. Cf. John A. James, *Money and Capital Markets in Postbellum America* (Princeton: Princeton University Press, 1978), pp. 76–77.

35. Comptroller of the Currency, Examination Report, National City Bank, January 9, 1890. Most of National City's correspondents were probably located in cities where Taylor's enterprises conducted their principal operations. In some, Taylor himself had an equity interest. For example, Taylor helped set up the First National Bank of Scranton, Pennsylvania, to serve the local banking needs of the Lackawanna Iron and Coal Company and the Delaware, Lackawanna, and Western Railroad. See Hodas, *Moses Taylor*, p. 269.

36. Myers, *The New York Money Market*, p. 230; Charles P. Kindleberger, *The Formation of Financial Centers: A Study in Comparative Economic History* (Princeton: Princeton University Press, 1974), pp. 54–55. On the development of the correspondent banking system see Myers, *The New York Money Market*, pp. 234–264; James, *Money and Capital Markets*, pp. 89–148; and Richard Sylla, "The United States, 1863–1913," in *Banking and Economic Development*, ed. Rondo Cameron (New York: Oxford University Press, 1972), pp. 249–254.

37. National City Bank, Call Reports, 1878–1891; Comptroller of the Currency, *Annual Reports, 1878–1891* (Washington D.C.: GPO, 1879–1892).

38. Although the United States had no central bank, the Treasury did assume central banking functions, intervening on several occasions to stabilize the money market. Up to 1900 these activities were sporadic, and did not form a consistent policy. Cf. Esther R. Taus, *Central Banking Functions of the United States Treasury, 1789–1941* (New York: Columbia University Press, 1943), pp. 49–84. After 1900 the Treasury exercised its central banking powers more consciously and consistently (see chapter 3).

39. On the Panic of 1857 see George W. van Vleck, *The Panic of 1857: An Analytical Study* (New York: Columbia University Press, 1943); Jonathan R. T. Hughes, "The Commercial Crisis of 1857," *Purdue Faculty Papers in Economic History* (Homewood, Ill.: Irwin, 1967), pp. 207–234. On the panics of 1873 and

1884 see O. M. W. Sprague, *History of Crises under the National Banking System* (Washington, D.C.: GPO, 1910), pp. 1–123.

40. Moody and Turner, "City Bank," p. 78.

41. On the origin of the New York Clearing House see Hammond, *Banks and Politics*, pp. 705–707; Redlich, *The Molding of American Banking*, pp. 45–59.

42. The Clearing House loan certificate was invented in 1860 by George S. Coe, the president of the American Exchange Bank, in response to the financial crisis following Lincoln's election. Moses Taylor was a member of the loan committee in this and subsequent crises. See Redlich, *The Molding of American Banking*, pp. 158–174. Although national banks in New York City had to maintain a minimum reserve ratio of 25 percent, they could not draw on these reserves during a crisis. Banks with reserve deficiencies were not permitted to make new loans, and banks that failed to bring their reserves above the minimum ran the risk of losing their charter. Nor could the comptroller suspend or change banks' reserve requirements. Thus, reserve requirements were more of a tax on national banks than a prudential measure.

43. National City Bank, Call Report, April 24, 1884, September 30, 1884, and August 27, 1886.

44. Comptroller of the Currency, *Annual Report, 1891*, (Washington, D.C.: GPO, 1892), II, 255–271; New York State Superintendent of Banking, *Annual Report, 1891* (Albany, N.Y.: Lyon, 1892), pp. 82, 165. This ranking is for commercial banks only. There were also many trust companies and private banks, most of which engaged in commercial banking. The United States Trust Company, the largest of the trust companies, with $50.6 million in assets, was bigger than any of the city's commercial banks (New York State Superintendent of Banking, *Annual Report, 1891*, p. 399). Some savings banks were bigger still. The largest was the Bowery Savings Bank, with $57.5 million in assets (ibid., pp. 274–277). Of all financial institutions in New York City (commerical banks, trust companies, and savings banks) National City ranked twenty-fourth in 1891.

45. National City Bank, Report of Earnings and Dividends, 1879–1891; Comptroller of the Currency, *Annual Report, 1879–1891*.

3. Stillman Builds the Bank, 1891–1908

1. John Moody and George Kibbe Turner, "City Bank: The Federation of the Great Merchants," *McClure's Magazine*, May 1911, pp. 77–78. Stillman's life has been the subject of two books, one sympathetic (Anna Robeson Burr, *The Portrait of a Banker: James Stillman, 1850–1918* [New York: Duffield, 1927]) and one antagonistic (John K. Winkler, *The First Billion: The Stillmans and the National City Bank* [New York: Vanguard, 1934]).

The directors may have first offered the job of president to Lawrence Turnure, a partner in the mercantile house that Moses Taylor had established. Turnure had become a partner in 1851, two years after Taylor's son-in-law Percy Pyne. At Taylor's death in 1882 Turnure was named an executor and trustee of his estate. Shortly thereafter in 1883 Turnure was elected to the board of National City Bank. In 1888 Pyne resigned from the mercantile house, and on January 1, 1889, its name changed from Moses Taylor and Company to Lawrence Turnure and Company. The history of that firm relates that Turnure declined to assume the presidency of

National City Bank, preferring to build up the firm to which he had only recently been able to give his name. Cf. *Lawrence Turnure & Co.: A Short History, 1832–1942* (New York: n.p., 1942).

2. Edwin Lefevre, "James Stillman," *Cosmopolitan*, 35 (July 1903): 334.

3. Ibid.

4. On the development of investment banking during this period see Vincent P. Carosso, *Investment Banking in America: A History* (Cambridge, Mass.: Harvard University Press, 1970), pp. 51–78; Fritz Redlich, *The Molding of American Banking, Men, and Ideas* (New York: Johnson Reprint, 1968), pt. 2, pp. 371–396; and Thomas R. Navin and Marian V. Sears, "The Rise of a Market for Industrial Securities," *Business History Review*, 29 (1955): 105–138.

5. On the rise of the large corporation see Alfred D. Chandler, Jr., *The Visible Hand: The Managerial Revolution in American Business* (Cambridge, Mass.: Harvard University Press, 1977). Chandler analyzes the turn of the century merger boom in chapter 10. See also Ralph L. Nelson, *Merger Movements in American Industry, 1895–1956* (Princeton: Princeton University Press, 1959), pp. 25–38, 71–105. On the Supreme Court's interpretation of the Sherman Act see William Letwin, *Law and Economic Policy in America: The Evolution of the Sherman Anti-Trust Act* (Chicago: University of Chicago Press, 1965), pp. 143–181.

6. Redlich, *The Molding of American Banking*, pt. 2, p. 390. On the activities of the leading investment firms see Carosso, *Investment Banking*, pp. 79–109. Morgan actually started its existence as a British firm. In the 1890s it consisted of two partnerships: J. S. Morgan and Company of London, and the interlocking partnership of Drexel, Morgan in the United States (Philadelphia and New York) and Morgan, Harjes of Paris. On January 1, 1895, the U.S. partnership became J. P. Morgan and Company. Cf. Vincent P. Carosso, "The Morgan Houses: The Seniors, Their Partners, and Their Aides," in *American Industrialization, Economic Expansion, and the Law*, ed. Joseph R. Frese and Jacob Judd (White Plains, N.Y.: Sleepy Hollow Press, 1981). For biographies of Morgan see Jonathan R. T. Hughes, *The Vital Few: American Economic Progress and Its Protagonists* (Boston: Houghton Mifflin, 1965), pp. 399–454; Frederick L. Allen, *The Great Pierpont Morgan* (New York: Harper, 1949); and Herbert L. Satterlee, *Pierpont Morgan: An Intimate Portrait* (New York: Macmillan, 1939). These works focus more on the man than on the firm. The latter is the subject of a forthcoming book by Vincent P. Carosso, which will be based on the Morgan papers.

On the First National Bank see Redlich, *The Molding of American Banking*, pt. 2, pp. 388–391; N. S. B. Gras and Henrietta M. Larson, *Casebook in American Business History* (New York: F. S. Crofts, 1939), pp. 512–517; and Sheridan P. Logan, *George F. Baker and His Bank, 1840–1955: A Double Biography* (St. Joseph, Mo.: George F. Baker Trust, 1981). The First National Bank merged with National City in 1955 (see chapter 12).

On Kidder, Peabody see Redlich, *The Molding of American Banking*, pt. 2, pp. 387–388, and Vincent P. Carosso, *More Than a Century of Investment Banking: The Kidder, Peabody & Co. Story* (New York: McGraw Hill, 1979), pp. 13–42. On Lee, Higginson see Redlich, *The Molding of American Banking*, pt. 2, p. 388. On Kuhn, Loeb see below, note 18.

7. Moody and Turner, "City Bank," p. 77. As Lefevre ("James Stillman," p. 334) commented, Stillman's, "is not an easy psychological portrait to paint."

Stillman's father, Charles, an important businessman in his own right, was a cotton merchant with extensive landholdings near Brownsville, Texas, on both sides of the U.S. border. In 1859 he and several partners established themselves as private bankers in Brownsville. Earlier, Charles Stillman had helped establish the first steamboat company on the Rio Grande. By placing the ships in Mexican registry Charles Stillman was able to continue exporting cotton throughout the Civil War, adding considerably to the family fortune. Cf. *Charles Stillman, 1810–1875* (New York: Printed for Chauncey Devereux Stillman, 1956).

Like Taylor, James Stillman retained an interest in his trading firm throughout his business career. After moving to Europe in 1909, Stillman became a limited partner in the firm, while his son Charles took active control (*The Trow Copartnership and Corporation Directory of the Boroughs of Manhattan and Bronx, City of New York* [New York: Trow Directory Printing and Binding Co., 1911], p. 976). James Stillman also continued to own land and various businesses in and around Brownsville, Texas. These were the bases of his cotton trading, railroad, and banking activities in the state and the basis for National City Bank's business there. Stillman's heirs sold these Texas interests in 1921. Cf. Tom Lea, *The King Ranch* (Kingsville, Tex.: King Ranch, 1957), II, 453n, 781n.

8. Business History Foundation, *History of Standard Oil Company (New Jersey)*, vol. 1, *Pioneering in Big Business, 1882–1911*, by Ralph W. Hidy and Muriel E. Hidy (New York: Harper, 1955), p. 26. William Rockefeller was active in Standard Oil far longer than his brother John D., who retired from active business in 1891. William Rockefeller was responsible for the execution and possibly the design of Standard Oil's policies of self-finance and high liquidity, a key factor in the firm's growth, according to Ralph and Muriel Hidy (ibid., p. 607).

Stillman's association with William Rockefeller dates back to at least 1884, when both men became directors of the Chicago, Milwaukee, and St. Paul Railroad. Thereafter, the two men cooperated closely, often buying securities for a joint account. For an example see James Stillman to William Rockefeller, February 13, 1891, Stillman MSS, Columbia University, New York, hereafter cited as Stillman MSS.

9. Burr, *Portrait of a Banker*, pp. 49–50.

10. Stillman to James T. Woodward, December 7, 1891, Stillman MSS. Although Woodward purchased only 100 shares, this represented 1 percent of the total outstanding, and made him one of the largest shareholders in the bank, after Pyne (753 shares), Stillman (616), W. W. Phelps (350), and Samuel Sloan (250). Comptroller of the Currency, Examination Report, National City Bank, February 25, 1892.

11. Stillman to J. Garrity (president, First National Bank, Corsicana, Texas), December 11, 1891, Stillman MSS.

12. Stillman to Theodore A. Havemeyer, February 24, 1891, Stillman MSS, indicates that Havemeyer was a shareholder in the Union Investment Company. Pullman is listed as one of the persons to whom Stillman resold Northern Pacific securities from his participation in a syndicate managed by J. P. Morgan and Company. Stillman to George W. Pullman, July 21, 1896, Stillman MSS.

13. Stillman to John A. McCall, July 21, 1896, Stillman MSS. McCall also bought Northern Pacific bonds.

14. President Cleveland was a shareholder in the Union Investment Company (Stillman to Cleveland, February 24, 1891, Stillman MSS), as was Fairchild. After leaving the Treasury, Fairchild had become president of the New York Security and Trust Company, and he joined Stillman in a wide range of business ventures, including an investment in one of the Taylor-Pyne enterprises, the Georgia Central Railroad (Stillman to Fairchild, September 14, 1891, Stillman MSS). Stillman served as a director of the New York Security and Trust Company, as did Lamont. See New York State Banking Department, *Annual Report, 1890* (Albany: New York State Banking Department, 1891), p. 258.

15. On Sterling's life and career see John A. Garver, *John William Sterling: A Biographical Sketch* (New Haven, Conn.: Yale University Press, 1929), and *Shearman and Sterling, 1873–1973* (New York: Shearman and Sterling, 1973), pp. 1–191. In 1873 Thomas G. Shearman and John W. Sterling left the law firm of Field and Shearman to set up their own firm. Their former partner, David Dudley Field, had written New York State's Code of Civil Procedure, the model for the laws of many of the southern and western states. Field's brother Stephen was an associate justice of the U.S. Supreme Court and his brother Cyrus had cooperated with Moses Taylor to promote and finance the first submarine telegraph across the Atlantic (see chapter 2). The new firm of Shearman and Sterling became one of the first to specialize in corporation law. Among its clients it numbered Jay Gould and the Consolidated Gas Company, a Taylor concern. Sterling's connection with Stillman dates from the latter's request that Sterling investigate affairs related to his land interests in Texas.

Sterling also had indirect political connections with President Cleveland. He was a friend of William Scott, one of Cleveland's intimate friends, and became executor of Scott's estate in 1891.

16. James Stillman to A. J. Balfour (U.S. Trust Company, London), February 13, 1891, Stillman MSS. Stillman also worked with E. D. Adams, the New York representative of the Deutsche Bank (Berlin), in the reorganization of the Northern Pacific. Cf. James Stillman to E. D. Adams, October 27, 1893, Stillman MSS.

17. *National Cyclopaedia of American Biography* (New York: James T. White, 1916), XV, 28. Henry V. Poor, *Manual of the Railroads of the United States for 1873–74* (New York: H. V. and H. W. Poor, 1873), pp. 641–642, records that Moses Taylor and his close associates, W. W. Phelps and William E. Dodge, were directors of the Houston and Texas Central, whose completion in March 1873 linked the entire existing railroad system of Texas to those of other states.

18. For example, Pyne was one of the largest bondholders of the Mobile Street Railway Company when it went into bankruptcy in 1892. Stillman became chairman of the Bondholders Committee and actively managed the reorganization of the company, including the electrification of the line and the laying of new track. During this process he directed the local manager to purchase rails from Lackawanna Iron and Steel. Following Taylor's precepts, Stillman also insisted that the Mobile Street Railway hold its New York account at National City Bank. Cf. James Stillman to R. Semmes (manager of Mobile Street Railway), April 6, 1893, to February 8, 1897, Stillman MSS.

After his appointment as president of the bank, Stillman consistently increased his stockholdings in the institution. He began with 105 shares (1.1 percent of the total outstanding), but by February 1892 had raised this to 616 shares (6.2 percent), probably by purchasing them from Pyne, who had reduced his holdings from 1,245 to 753 shares. Comptroller of the Currency, Examination Report, National City Bank, February 16, 1891, and February 25, 1892.

19. On the history of Kuhn, Loeb prior to 1914 see Carosso, *Investment Banking*, p. 19, chapters 3–5, and Redlich, *The Molding of American Banking*, pt. 2, pp. 379–381, 385–387. Kuhn, Loeb's extensive European connections included relationships with Ernst Cassel, the London financier, Edward Noetzlin of the Bank de Paris et Pays-Bas, and Robert Fleming of the American-Scottish Investment Company. From the German banking house of M. M. Warburg, Kuhn, Loeb drew two of its younger partners: Felix M. Warburg and his older brother Paul.

Relative to Morgan or National City, Kuhn, Loeb had a small deposit base in the years 1907–1912. At the Pujo hearings in 1912 Schiff indicated that as a matter of general policy Kuhn, Loeb did not become the depository of corporations whose securities it floated. See Redlich, *The Molding of American Banking*, pt. 2, p. 386, and U.S. Congress, House Committee on Banking and Currency, *Money Trust Investigation: Investigation of Financial and Monetary Conditions in the United States*, 4 vols. 62nd Cong., 2nd and 3rd sess., 1913, pp. 1677, 1695. The statement in the text assumes that this was also the situation in the late 1890s.

For a biography of Schiff see Cyrus Adler, *Jacob H. Schiff: His Life and Letters*, 2 vols. (New York: Doubleday Doran, 1929).

20. On the reorganization of the Union Pacific and its subsequent financial history see Stuart Daggett, *Railroad Reorganization* (Cambridge, Mass.: Harvard University Press, 1908), pp. 220–262; Nelson Trottman, *History of the Union Pacific: A Financial and Economic Survey* (New York: Ronald Press, 1923; rpt. New York: Augustus M. Kelley, 1966); and Thomas W. Mitchell, "The Growth of the Union Pacific and Its Financial Operations," *Quarterly Journal of Economics*, 21 (1906–1907): 569–612.

21. For a biography of Harriman see George Kennan, *E. H. Harriman*, 2 vols. (Boston: Houghton, Mifflin, 1922).

22. Trottman, *Union Pacific*, pp. 285–297; Adler, *Jacob H. Schiff*, pp. 82–107. The Harriman-Hill contest started as a struggle for the Chicago, Burlington, and Quincy Railroad, which each sought to use as a link between his transcontinental road and Chicago. In 1901 Hill won control of the Chicago, Burlington, and Quincy, purchasing its stock through the Northern Pacific. Harriman counterattacked by attempting to buy control of the Northern Pacific in the open market.

In all probability National City helped the Union Pacific finance its purchase of the Northern Pacific stock (Adler, *Jacob H. Schiff*, p. 180). More permanent financing came later. Beginning at the end of June 1901 Kuhn, Loeb underwrote for the Union Pacific $60 million in convertible bonds. Stillman's personal participation amounted to $10 million, or one-sixth of the total (Kuhn, Loeb Syndicate Book [1901]).

Harriman's raid on the Northern Pacific made it clear that the same thing could happen to the Union Pacific. To forestall the possibility Kuhn, Loeb organized a pool at the beginning of 1903, to purchase Union Pacific preferred stock.

Harriman, James Stillman, and Kuhn, Loeb each took a one-fifth interest and became managers of this pool, with the discretion to buy and sell as they saw fit. Other participants included Rockefeller and Henry H. Rogers. Kuhn, Loeb also ran two common stock pools. The first was limited to Harriman, Stillman, and Kuhn, Loeb; the second was expanded to include Rogers and Rockefeller. The pools were dissolved in 1905 (Kuhn, Loeb Syndicate Books [1903–1905]).

23. Balthasar H. Meyer, *A History of the Northern Securities Case* (Madison: University of Wisconsin Press, 1906). For a comment on the case's significance in legal history see Letwin, *Law and Economic Policy*, pp. 182–237.

24. Mitchell, "Growth of the Union Pacific," pp. 599–606, and Trottman, *Union Pacific*, p. 315.

25. Stillman would therefore seem to refute the thesis of finance capitalism that maintains that investment bankers, through their position as directors, determined the operating policies of industrial and railroad enterprises. Cf. George Edwards, *The Evolution of Finance Capitalism* (London: Longmans Green, 1938), pp. 161–202.

26. The adjective *corporate* is not strictly correct. It includes individual deposits subject to check, certified checks, cashier's checks, and certificates of deposit. Excluded from the definition are the deposits of banks, trust companies, and the U.S. government. Thus, "corporate" deposits would include deposits from wealthy individuals, such as Stillman, or from state and local governments, such as New York City.

The estimates in the text are based on averages from National City Bank call reports for 1895 and 1905 and Organization File, National City Bank, Accounts, Vanderlip MSS, Columbia University, New York.

27. Comptroller of the Currency, *Annual Report, 1905* (Washington, D.C.: GPO, 1906), and National City Bank, Call Reports, 1895–1905.

28. National City Bank, Call Reports, May 5, 1898, July 14, 1898, and Table 3.3. Such practices raise the possibility of a conflict of interest between Stillman's private underwriting activity and his role as president of the bank. Although there is no information available on the prices at which these transactions took place, two factors limited the possible conflict of interest. First, Stillman was the bank's principal shareholder as well as its president. To some extent, therefore, these transactions merely transferred profits from one area to another. Moreover, the bank's other major shareholders were his business associates, and they were well aware of what Stillman was doing. Second, depositors' funds were well protected, first by the bank's large capital (see below) and second by the double liability clause on national bank stock. If the bank had failed, Stillman and the other shareholders would have been personally liable for any loss incurred by depositors up to the par value of their stockholdings. In Stillman's case this contingent personal liability amounted after 1902 to over $5 million.

The question of conflict of interest between investment bankers and the corporations with which they were associated first came to the public's attention during the New York State Armstrong investigation of the big life insurance companies in 1905–1906. Charles Evans Hughes, the committee counsel, for example, established that Equitable Life owned or had close affiliations with ten banks, trust companies, and title companies, and Mutual Life owned twenty-two banks and trust companies. Jacob Schiff of Kuhn, Loeb, a member of Equitable's board of directors, had sold that company more than $50 million worth of securities. George W. Perkins served simultaneously as vice president of New York Life and vice president and partner of J. P. Morgan and Company. In this dual capacity, he purchased securities for the insurance company and sold them for the House of Morgan. Although neither Schiff nor Perkins saw anything improper in his activities, the press and public had a field day. Legislation requiring insurance companies to divest themselves of their stockholdings in banks and trust companies and imposing strict regulation of insurance companies' investment programs was passed at the conclusion of the Armstrong investigation. See Douglas C. North, "Life Insurance and Investment Banking at the Time of the Armstrong Investigation of 1905–1906." *Journal of Economic History*, 14 (1954): 209–228; and Morton Keller, *Life Insurance Enterprise, 1885–1910: A Study in the Limits of Corporate Power* (Cambridge, Mass.: Harvard University Press, Belknap Press, 1963), pp. 245–264.

29. See above, note 22.

30. National City Bank, Call Reports May 14, 1908, and April 28, 1909.

31. Paul P. Abrahams, *The Foreign Expansion of American Finance and Its Relationship to the Foreign Economic Policies of the United States, 1907–1921* (New York: Arno Press, 1976), p. 2. On the early history of the New York foreign exchange market see Margaret G. Myers, *The New York Money Market*, ed. Benjamin H. Beckhart, vol. 1, *Origins and Development* (New York: Columbia University Press, 1931), pp. 338–350, and Arthur H. Cole, "Evolution of the Foreign Exchange Market of the United States," *Journal of Business and Economic History*, 1 (1929): 384–421.

32. Mira Wilkins, *The Emergence of Multinational Enterprise: American Business Abroad from the Colonial Era to 1914* (Cambridge, Mass.: Harvard University Press, 1970), pp. 70–110.

33. Cited in Abrahams, *Foreign Expansion*, p. 2.

34. Fred I. Kent, "Financing Our Foreign Trade," *Annals of the American Academy of Political and Social Science*, 36 (November 1910): 492–501.

35. Clyde William Phelps, *The Foreign Expansion of American Banks: American Branch Banking Abroad* (New York: Ronald Press, 1927), p. 94.

36. National City Bank, *Currency Association Law* (New York: National City Bank, 1908), p. 16.

37. John E. Gardin (manager, Foreign Department, National City Bank) to Vanderlip, January 22, 1909, Vanderlip MSS.

38. Gardin to Vanderlip (Memorandum), September 9, 1912, Vanderlip MSS. Just as National City required balances at foreign banks, so did foreign banks keep balances at National City despite the international insignificance of the dollar. As early as 1905, these balances amounted to nearly $6 million. A small amount of trade was financed in dollars and the customers of foreign banks as well as the banks themselves had sizable investments in U.S. securities and other assets in the United States. Comptroller of the Currency, Examination Reports, National City Bank, January 19, 1905, and June 20, 1906.

39. Jacob H. Hollander, "The Security Holdings of National Banks," *American Economic Review*, 3 (1913): 793–814.

40. Comptroller of the Currency, Examination Reports, National City Bank, March 7, 1893, and February 16, 1891. In March 1893 National City paid up to 2 percent on correspondent bank balances, the maximum allowed under New York Clearing House regulations. The deposit totals do not include trust companies. Farmers' Loan and Trust, the bank's largest correspondent, maintained a balance in excess of $3 million at the bank. In lieu of interest it received a lump sum of $12,000 per year plus payment and collection of its checks free of charge.

Stillman's extensive business interests helped attract some of the new correspondents. Along with his replies to proxy requests and his acknowledgments of dividends received from banks around the country, Stillman sent back brief notes requesting the bank to place its New York account with National City. For example, to the president of the Temple (Texas) National Bank Stillman wrote: "Being a stockholder in some fifteen Texas banks and the Treasurer of an investment company that is interested in some thirty others, I am thoroughly familiar with the requirements of banks in your state, and from my long experience in the cotton business, with the requirements of the cotton factors also." To W. Goodrich Jones, December 10, 1891, Stillman MSS.

41. National City Bank, Board of Directors, Minutes, May 20, 1897. The Third National had failed because of the overcertification of a check by one of its officers. The bank had been founded in 1863 shortly after the passage of the National Bank Act. From the first it had specialized in correspondent banking, receiving well over half of its total deposits from other banks. In October bankers' balances amounted to 77 percent of the Third's total deposits, a ratio somewhat above that at the First National Bank (70 percent) and more than five times that at National City (15 percent). Cf. Comptroller of the Currency, *Annual Report, 1896* (Washington, D.C.: GPO, 1897). Until 1880 the Third National was among the leading holders of bankers' balances in New York; thereafter, its business began to decline. See Myers, *The New York Money Market*, pp. 245–246. On Sterling's role in the merger see Garver, *John William Sterling*, p. 90.

42. Myers, *The New York Money Market*, p. 246. On Stillman's use of other banks see *Commercial and Financial Chronicle*, April 29, 1899, p. 804.

43. On Hepburn's career see B. C. Forbes, *Men Who Are Making America* (New York: B. C. Forbes, 1917), pp. 197–203.

44. Frank A. Vanderlip with Boyden Sparkes, *From Farm Boy to Financier* (New York: D. Appleton Century, 1935), pp. 90–96.

45. Charles S. Speare, "Three Men of Mark," *Review of Reviews*, quoted in *Literary Digest*, March 28, 1908, pp. 452, 454.

46. National City Bank, *Interest Tables* (New York: National City Bank, 1905), p. 43.

47. Ibid.

48. Ibid., p. 51.

49. Ibid., pp. 45–47. A former assistant secretary of the treasury, Milton E. Ailes, supervised this service. Ailes was a vice president of the Riggs National Bank, and National City Bank also employed him as its special Washington representative. On Stillman's ownership of a controlling interest in the Riggs banks see Table 4.1.

50. National City Bank, *National Bank Organization, 1812–1904* (New York: National City Bank, 1904), pp. 125–127.

51. National City Bank, *Currency Association Law*, p. 15.

52. Vanderlip to Stillman, April 17, 1906, Vanderlip MSS.

53. Interbank balances consisted of $37.8 million in deposits from other national banks and $6.7 million in deposits from state banks, for a total of $44.5 million. In addition, National City received $39.6 million in deposits from trust companies, bringing total deposits from financial institutions to $84.1 million, or about 36 percent of total deposits. These figures are averages of call dates for the year 1905 and are derived from National City Bank call reports for that year.

54. Carosso, *Investment Banking*, pp. 53–76.

55. National City Bank, Call Reports, 1895–1905, and Figure 3.1. The increasing proportion of call loans also reflects the shift in corporate finance from loans to bonds. Cf. Vanderlip to Stillman, February 9, 1906, Vanderlip MSS. On the distinction between syndicate and call loans see Bartow Griffiss, *The New York Call Money Market* (New York: Ronald Press, 1925), p. 7.

56. Stillman to Vanderlip, January 10, 1914, Vanderlip MSS.

57. Redlich, *The Molding of American Banking*, pt. 1, pp. 369–370. For a summary of National City's relationship with the government in the years 1894–1900, see U.S. Treasury, *Transactions with Certain National Banks* (U.S. Senate, 56th Cong. 1st sess., 1900), S. Doc. 71, pp. 7–16.

58. U.S. Treasury, *Transactions*, pp. 3–4.

59. Ibid., pp. 13–14.

60. Myers, *The New York Money Market*, pp. 381–390; Milton Friedman and Anna J. Schwartz, *A Monetary History of the United States, 1867–1960* (Princeton: Princeton University Press, 1963), pp. 149–156; Phillip Cagan, *Determinants and Effects of Changes in the Stock of Money, 1875–1960* (New York: Columbia University Press, 1965), pp. 213–219; and Richard H. Timberlake, Jr., *The Origins of Central Banking in the United States* (Cambridge, Mass.: Harvard University Press, 1978), pp. 171–185. For Secretary Shaw's description of his own policies see U.S. Treasury, *Annual Report, 1906* (Washington, D.C.: GPO, 1907), pp. 36–50.

61. National City Bank, Call Reports, 1906–1907, shows that the bank utilized other securities as collateral for its government deposits. U.S. Treasury, *Annual Report, 1906*, pp. 116–121, documents National City's leading role in the Treasury's gold import program.

62. U.S. Treasury, *Annual Report, 1906*, pp. 201, 211.

63. November 10, 1899, Gage MSS, Library of Congress, Washington, D.C.

64. Comptroller of the Currency, National City Bank, Examination Reports, March 22, 1898, and October 27, 1902. On the use of the capital increases to tie the interests of the directors (especially Stillman) to those of the bank see *Commercial and Financial Chronicle*, December 9, 1899, p. 1175.

65. April 30, 1902, Citibank Library, New York.

66. Organization File, National City Bank, Earnings, Earnings of the National City Bank of New York from 1901 to 1917 Inclusive, Vanderlip MSS.

67. Friedman and Schwartz, *Monetary History*, pp. 104–113.

68. Shaw believed that the Treasury had the duty as well as the ability to prevent panics by stabilizing interest rates in the New York money market. In the U.S. Treasury's *Annual Report* for 1906 he stated, "Believing it the duty of the Government . . . to protect the people against financial panics, which, in this country, have caused more mental and more physical suffering than all the plagues known to man, and recognizing that under our system no possible cooperation can be secured among banks, each independent of the other, and finding these institutions in the interior sending their money to be loaned on call in the cities, and the reserve of the country, even in the idle season, very low, the Secretary of the Treasury undertook the task of making some slight provision for the inevitable" (p. 41).

Shaw's apparent success led him to proclaim, "No central or Government bank in the world can so readily influence financial conditions throughout the world as can the Secretary of the Treasury under the authority with which he is now clothed" (ibid., p. 49).

Shaw recognized that the banks had reduced their own reserve ratios, but he did not feel that this resulted from his own policies. Instead, he argued that banks' reserve behavior demonstrated the need for even greater powers for the Treasury to intervene in the money market.

In March 1907 Shaw stepped down as secretary of the treasury and was succeeded by his subordinate, George Cortelyou. The new secretary pledged to follow his former chief's policies, but his actions were radically different. Specifically, Cortelyou failed to contract the volume of government deposits in the national banks during the summer of 1907. Thus, as the fall approached, he had already committed the vast proportion of the resources at his disposal. He had little in reserve to stabilize the market in case a stringent market should develop. Nevertheless, Cortelyou started to deplete his remaining resources. Beginning on August 23, 1907, he added government deposits at national banks at the rate of $5 million per week, assuring the financial markets that this would be sufficient to prevent a panic that fall. It was not.

Contemporaries recognized that Shaw's policies promoted the panic he professed wishing to avoid. Cf. A. Piatt Andrew, "The Treasury and the Banks under Secretary Shaw," *Quarterly Journal of Economics*, 21 (1906–1907): 519–568, and "The Partial Responsibility of Secretaries Gage and Shaw for the Crisis of 1907," *Bankers' Magazine*, 76 (1908): 493–499.

69. Stillman to Vanderlip (Cable), April 24, 1906, Vanderlip MSS.

70. Friedman and Schwartz, *Monetary History*, p. 156.

71. On Stillman's actions during the panic see Saul Engelbourg, "Behind the Throne: A Non-Morgan View of the Panic of 1907," *Revue International d'Histoire de la Banque*, 4 (1971): 141–157. After the failure of the Knickerbocker Trust Company Stillman immediately joined forces with Baker and Morgan to try to keep the financial disturbance from spreading to the stock market and to other banks. They started by rescuing the Trust Company of America. After a cursory examination confirming the institution's solvency, Stillman, Baker, and Morgan agreed to lend it the cash needed to stop the run. National City, the First National, and the Hanover National banks supplied the funds required.

Treasury Secretary Cortelyou agreed to bolster the banks by increasing the government's deposits. On October 23, he placed an additional $10 million in the New York banks, $4 million in National City alone. U.S. Congress, *Money Trust Investigation*, p. 487.

This action saved the trust companies but failed to halt the spread of the panic to the stock market. To gain cash, trust companies refused on October 24 to renew their call loans. This sudden demand for cash by some of the largest lenders in the call market sent call money rates soaring and stock prices plunging. If brokers were forced to liquidate their securities at such prices, most members of the stock exchange would fail. To prevent this the president of the New York Stock Exchange appealed to Stillman, who referred him to Morgan (ibid., p. 457). Morgan then organized a $25 million money pool among the city's leading banks. Stillman was the first banker to pledge his institution's participation. National City committed itself to lend $8 million and actually advanced $6.3 million to brokers on October 24, 1907. Again, the Treasury bolstered the banks, depositing $15.7 million in the New York banks, $4 million in National City alone (ibid., p. 487).

Although this pool stabilized the stock market, it failed to prevent the spread of the panic from New York to other sections of the country. News of the financial disturbance in New York induced banks across the country to withdraw their balances from New York. This pushed the reserves of the New York banks below the legal minimum.

This was precisely the situation Cortelyou had claimed the Treasury could and would prevent. Yet he had already exhausted the resources at his command. The banks therefore had to step in. On October 26 the New York Clearing House Association restricted cash payments and issued Clearing House loan certificates. As in previous episodes, these steps proved effective in curbing the panic. By December 1907 deposits were back to par against currency and in March 1908 the last of the Clearing House loans certificates was retired. By June 1908 the yearlong slide of the economy had been halted.

72. Stillman to Vanderlip, February 12, 1907, Vanderlip MSS.

4. Vanderlip and Banking Reform, 1909–1913

1. For a description of the 55 Wall Street building and its history see Citibank, *55 Wall Street: A Working Landmark* (New York: Citibank, 1979), and *Number Eight*, January 1909. The bank's acquisition of the building sparked a controversy. The government sold the building at auction to National City in 1899 and then leased it back from National City while the new customs house was being erected at Bowling Green. The terms of the lease were criticized during congressional hearings on the policies of Treasury Secretary Gage. Cf. U.S. Treasury, *Transactions with Certain National Banks* (U.S. Senate, 56th Cong., 1st sess., 1900), S. Doc. 71, pp. 15–21.

2. Quoted by Anna Robeson Burr, *Portrait of a Banker: James Stillman, 1850–1918* (New York: Duffield, 1927), p. 249.

3. On the development of the securities market in the years 1907–1914 see Vincent P. Carosso, *Investment Banking in America: A History* (Cambridge, Mass.: Harvard University Press, 1970), pp. 79–109.

4. In all likelihood, the Armour account grew out of Stillman's presence on the board of directors of the Chicago, Milwaukee, and St. Paul Railroad. When Philip D. Armour joined the board a year after Stillman in 1885, he was the leading stockholder. Armour, like Stillman, was a conservative, cautious businessman who placed a heavy emphasis on a large supply of ready cash. Armour, like other meatpackers, borrowed short-term to meet seasonal requirements and avoided the bond markets. J. Ogden Armour was bolder than his father. When he succeeded to the leadership of the company after the death of his father in 1901, he embarked on a major expansion program. To fund the accumulated floating debt and to finance new plants in the United States and Argentina, Armour decided to tap the securities market. He contemplated a $25 million issue and offered the business to Vanderlip. The amount, which was later raised to $50 million, was more than National City could comfortably handle on its own. For a history of Armour and Company see Alfred D. Chandler, Jr., *The Visible Hand: The Managerial Revolution in American Business* (Cambridge, Mass.: Harvard University Press, 1977), pp. 391–402. On Armour's expansion into Argentina see Mira Wilkins, *The Emergence of Multinational Enterprise: American Business Abroad from the Colonial Era to 1914* (Cambridge, Mass.: Harvard University Press, 1970), p. 190.

5. Frank A. Vanderlip to James Stillman, April 22, 1909, Vanderlip MSS.

6. May 21, 1909, Vanderlip MSS. Kuhn, Loeb, however, did drive a hard bargain on this transaction, finally agreeing to a sixty-forty split in their favor of the total business and attendant profits from origination and syndication.

7. Vanderlip to Stillman, April 22, 1909, Vanderlip MSS.

8. Fritz Redlich, *The Molding of American Banking, Men, and Ideas* (New York: Johnson Reprint, 1968), pt. 2, p. 391. See also U.S. Congress, Temporary National Economic Committee, *Investigation of Concentration of Economic Power: Hearings on Pub. Res. 113* (75th Cong., 1938–1940), XXIII, 11853–4.

9. Frank A. Vanderlip, "Electrical Securities," Address to the 32nd Convention of the National Electric Light Association at Atlantic City, New Jersey, June 2, 1909.

10. The Consolidated Gas relationship dated back to at least 1827, when William Fox, a director of one of its predecessor companies (New York Gas), joined City Bank's board of directors (see chapter 1). In 1914 the Consolidated Gas account (including the balances of its subsidiaries) was the twelfth largest nonbank account in the bank. See Organization File, National City Bank, Accounts, August 17, 1914, Vanderlip MSS. For a history of the company see Frederick L. Collins, *Consolidated Gas Company of New York: A History* (New York: Consolidated Gas Company, 1934), pp. 316–323.

11. The creation of the Pacific Gas and Electric Company was an early example of the consolidations that were to mark the light and power utilities in the 1920s. California Gas and Electric, a major component of the new company, grew through the steady absorption of a number of small local companies in central California. The company lacked a major metropolitan market and relied exclusively upon water power to generate electricity, problems that made it difficult to attract funds from investors. Merger with an appropriate partner was the remedy. The Halsey firm, which had issued securities for other California utilities, was se-

lected to assist in the birth of the new company, and N. W. Halsey became the first chairman of the board. Cf. Charles M. Coleman, *P. G. and E. of California: The Centennial Story of the Pacific Gas and Electric Company, 1852–1952* (New York: McGraw-Hill, 1952), pp. 162–233.

Halsey cooperated closely with Stillman throughout the project, keeping Vanderlip well informed throughout the months of planning before the company was officially launched in early 1906. Vanderlip to Stillman, February 22, 1905, and February 24, 1905, Vanderlip MSS.

Stillman's interest in the project probably stemmed from his relationship with Prince Andre Poniatowski, whom he had met in the early 1890s. Poniatowski had come to the United States to gather information on business conditions for a group of European bankers. He then settled in San Francisco, where he became involved in a project to supply electric power to the city. His company was later absorbed into a predecessor of PG & E.

12. May 21, 1909, Vanderlip MSS.

13. January 4, 1914, Vanderlip MSS.

14. U.S. Congress, House Committee on Banking and Currency, *Money Trust Investigation: Investigation of Financial and Monetary Conditions in the United States*, 4 vols., 62nd Cong., 2nd and 3rd sess., 1913, p. 1208. Vanderlip to Stillman, April 17, 1906, Vanderlip MSS.

15. January 5, 1912, Vanderlip MSS. Rockefeller's suggestion is reported in a letter of July 8, 1911, from Vanderlip to Stillman, Vanderlip MSS.

16. Vanderlip to Stillman, November 29, 1912, Vanderlip MSS. After a trip to the Southwest Vanderlip hired Herbert Eldredge as a vice president of National City with the responsibility for building up the bank's business in the Southwest. Eldredge had been a vice president of the First National Bank of Houston and president of the Texas Bankers Association.

17. The statement in the text is necessarily conjectural. It is based on incomplete information for the years 1908–1912. These data come from the committee report that summarized and analyzed the testimony and exhibits presented in the course of the Pujo hearings. See U.S. Congress, *Money Trust Investigation*, pp. 1737–62, 2111–20, 2127–40; U.S. Congress, House, *Report of the Committee Appointed Pursuant to House Resolutions 429 and 504 to Investigate the Concentration and Control of Money and Credit*, 62nd Cong. 3rd sess., 1913, pp. 92–100.

The report of the committee contains a compilation of the securities issues of ten major banking houses, showing the amount of each issue and the role of the banking houses involved. The compilation is based on lists of transactions submitted by the ten banking houses and therefore suffers from the shortcomings of these lists. There are many. For example, National City's list omitted some transactions because they were neither joint account nor syndicate deals. In addition, the bank's list used a dating scheme for issues that differed from those of other houses, making comparisons difficult. The Morgan and Kuhn, Loeb lists were limited to issues for interstate corporations. The Morgan list was further limited to issues that were publicly advertised. The compilation published in the report also omitted issues for states and municipalities and for foreign governments. For National City such issues amounted to roughly $250 million between 1908 and 1912. Poor as the data are, they are all that are available on any sort of comparable basis for the period, and they do provide a rough indication of the activity of the major houses and how National City compared with them.

According to this compilation, for the years 1908–1912, National City participated in nearly $1.9 billion of securities issues, over half of which were with Morgan and more than 25 percent of which were with Kuhn, Loeb. (This comparison is somewhat misleading because National City's share of Kuhn, Loeb issues was larger than its share of Morgan-led issues. Thus, the Kuhn, Loeb connection could have been as profitable as the Morgan relationship, especially since Kuhn, Loeb and National City split origination fees, while Morgan probably retained these for itself.) On the basis of the compilation of the report, Morgan either originated or participated in issues totaling about $1.2 billion and Kuhn, Loeb either originated or participated in issues totaling about $1.0 billion.

18. The statement in the text is based upon a comparison of total loans as reported on the condition statements of leading New York banks and their total loans secured by stock exchange collateral as reported to the congressional committee. Subtracting the former from the latter, for dates as close as possible, provides a rough estimate of loans to business for this period for individual banks. See New York Clearing House Association, "Condition of National Banks in the City of New York on Wednesday, June 23rd, 1909, as Shown by Their Official Statements to the Comptroller of the Currency," and same for Friday, June 14, 1912; "Condition of State Banks of the City of New York on Friday, June 14, 1912, as Shown by Their Official Statements to the Superintendent of Banks," and "Condition of the Trust Companies in the City of New York at the Close of Business Monday, September 9, 1912, as Shown by Their Official Statements to the Superintendent of Banks." See also, U.S. Congress, *Money Trust Investigation*, pp. 1192–1211.

19. January 5, 1912, Vanderlip MSS.

20. U.S. National Monetary Commission, *Digest of State Banking Statutes* (compiled by Samuel A. Welldon, 1910), S. Doc. 353, pp. 457–486. U.S. National Monetary Commission, *Clearing Houses* (by James G. Cannon, 1910), S. Doc. 399, p. 177, observed that because they had no specific reserve requirements, trust companies had an "immense advantage" over Clearing House members and hence were able to make "considerable inroads" into their business.

21. February 1, 1907, Vanderlip MSS. There was increasing competition from the financial markets as well. In 1907 Vanderlip had noted with dismay the tendency of the bank's best customers to bypass it and place money directly in the call money market. As he wrote Stillman, "we must not lose sight of the fact that there are coming into the banking situation radically new methods and the day has passed when we can expect the largest deposits without interest or at 2% interest" (ibid.).

22. "Lessons of the Panic," *Literary Digest*, November 9, 1907, pp. 674–675, and "Demand for a Central Bank," *Literary Digest*, December 21, 1907, pp. 943–944.

23. Vanderlip used this phrase in testimony concerning the Federal Reserve Act. U.S. Congress, Senate Committee on Banking and Currency, *Hearings on H. R. 7837 (S. 2639): A Bill to Provide for the Establishment of Federal Reserve Banks*, 63rd Cong., 1st sess., 1913, p. 1939. The governor of the Bank of England was

quoted at the annual meeting of the Clearing House in 1910: "It seems to me that the American currency laws are barbarous. They seem to us extremely inequitable; you have no central bank; there is no government provision for concentrating banking resources to meet the situation in time of need; but there is one thing we can understand—there is one institution we recognize—that is the New York Clearing House. When it makes a declaration declaring what the situation is, we feel that we know it is true, and we can base our acts and calculations on it." Archives, New York Clearing House Association, New York.

24. U.S. Congress, *Hearings on H. R. 7837, Federal Reserve Banks*, p. 1941.

25. January 1, 1909 (in the possession of Frank A. Vanderlip, Jr.).

26. Milton Friedman and Anna J. Schwartz, *A Monetary History of the United States, 1867–1960* (Princeton: Princeton University Press, 1963), pp. 168–169.

27. Ibid., pp. 192, 196.

28. Frank A. Vanderlip with Boyden Sparkes, *From Farm Boy to Financier* (New York: D. Appleton Century, 1935), pp. 213–216.

29. See for example Paul M. Warburg, "Essays on Banking Reform in the United States," *Proceedings of the Academy of Political Science*, 4 (July 1914): 7–22, 62, 117.

30. Vanderlip to Stillman, November 29, 1910, Vanderlip MSS.

31. Vanderlip, *Farm Boy*, pp. 213–219. Also present at the meeting was A. Piatt Andrew, a Harvard University economist associated with the National Monetary Commission. Preliminary studies for the plan were based on interviews in Europe with leading economists and central bankers. The plan was designed to meet the objections to a central bank and "conquer historical and geographical prejudices" while avoiding political controversy. See Frank A. Vanderlip, "The Aldrich Plan for Banking Legislation," Address to the Commercial Club of Chicago, February 25, 1911.

32. In addition, the reserve association would receive the deposits of the federal government and issue currency based upon gold and commercial paper that would be the liability of the reserve association and not of the government. For the text of the original Aldrich Plan see U.S. National Monetary Commission, *Suggested Plan for Monetary Legislation* (submitted by Nelson W. Aldrich, 1911), S. Doc. 784, pt. 2. Warburg, "Banking Reform," pp. 173–203, compares the Aldrich bill with the Federal Reserve Act (Glass bill).

33. The New York backers of the Aldrich Plan organized the National Citizens League for the Promotion of a Sound Banking System under the leadership of University of Chicago banking authority J. Laurence Laughlin. But certain Chicago bankers and Laughlin refused to commit themselves wholeheartedly to the Aldrich Plan. In July 1911 Laughlin told Warburg that Aldrich's name on the bill would kill it politically. See Gabriel Kolko, *The Triumph of Conservatism* (New York: Free Press, 1963), pp. 186–189. For a summary of the National Citizens League's position see J. Laurence Laughlin, ed., *Banking Reform* (Chicago: National Citizens League for the Promotion of a Sound Banking System, 1912).

34. Vanderlip, "The Aldrich Plan," p. 13, attempted to disarm fears that large Wall Street banks would control the national reserve association. He claimed that "the plan is so designed that there never could by any possibility be a successful effort to secure control of a large amount of stock by any single interest."

35. Wilson's interview with Henry Beach Needham originally appeared in *Outlook*, August 26, 1911, and is reprinted in Arthur S. Link, ed., *Papers of Woodrow Wilson*, 47 vols. (Princeton: Princeton University Press, 1966–1984), XXIII, 292–300.

36. Followers of William Jennings Bryan, three-time Democratic candidate for president, shared with him his "almost Jacksonian" fear of banks. See Paul W. Glad, *The Trumpet Soundeth* (Lincoln: University of Nebraska Press, 1960), p. 92.

37. Vanderlip to Stillman, November 29, 1910, Vanderlip MSS.

38. Vanderlip to Stillman, September 29, 1911, Vanderlip MSS.

39. U.S. Treasury, *Annual Report, 1910* (Washington, D.C.: GPO, 1910), pp. 6–7.

40. Citibank Library, New York.

41. The First National Bank of Chicago formed the first securities affiliate in the United States in 1903. By the time the National City Company was organized in 1911 there were more than two hundred bank affiliates in existence (*New York Times*, November 4, 1911). See W. Nelson Peach, *The Security Affiliates of National Banks* (Baltimore, Md.: Johns Hopkins University Press, 1941), pp. 59–61, on George F. Baker's First Security Company.

42. F. A. Vanderlip (president) to the shareholders, June 28, 1911, Citibank Library, New York. For a discussion of the various models used to set up securities affiliates see Peach, *Security Affiliates*, pp. 66–67.

43. Carosso, *Investment Banking*, pp. 125–126. The National Bank of Commerce was the second largest bank in the country and the second largest holder of bankers' balances, trailing only National City. Together the Equitable and Mutual Insurance companies held a controlling interest in the Commerce, which they had to sell under the terms of the New York insurance law passed after the Armstrong investigation of 1905–1906.

Originally Stillman had considered merging National City with the National Bank of Commerce and continuing operation under the latter's special charter, which exempted its shareholders from the double liability clause applicable to national bank stock. (For details of this charter see David M. Gische, "New York City Banks and the Development of the National Banking System," *American Journal of Legal History*, 23 [1979]: 50.) Stillman's motives in seeking a merger were partly defensive. In June 1905 he wrote to Vanderlip regarding the offer of a large block of stock in the Commerce by a European broker: "In my judgement the serious aspect for us to consider is how it would affect us to have some other banking interests obtain control and what likelihood there is of it" June 24, 1905, Vanderlip MSS.

From the start, the merger encountered problems. First, after the Armstrong investigation the Equitable Insurance Company underwent a change of ownership and a sweeping overhaul of its policies and procedures. The task of disposing of its shares in the Commerce was postponed. Second, the Panic of 1907 turned public opinion against large corporations. Stillman was reluctant to flaunt it by merging the two largest banks in the country. Stillman to Vanderlip, March 31, 1908, Vanderlip MSS. Third, rival bidders for the Commerce appeared, including E. H. Harriman, and J. P. Morgan. Harriman intended to use the Commerce to finance his ambitious scheme of creating a worldwide transportation network. But Harriman died in 1909 before either of these plans could be realized.

That left Morgan and Stillman. During the course of 1910 and 1911 the two men worked out a compormise in which each would own a portion of the Commerce stock. Thus, Commerce became an expression of the community of interest among New York's leading financiers. Its executive committee consisted of representatives from Morgan, National City, and the First National Bank.

This brought the five leading correspondent banks under the control of the trio (Stillman, Morgan, Baker) that had formed the money pool in the 1907 panic and had concluded an underwriting agreement among themselves. Stillman controlled National City and had considerable influence at the Hanover National. Baker controlled the First National, which owned a controlling interest in the Chase National. And, together with Morgan, Baker and Stillman controlled the Commerce. In 1910 these five banks held 63 percent of the bankers' balances on deposit in New York. See Margaret G. Myers, *The New York Money Market*, ed. Benjamin H. Beckhart, vol. 1, *Origins and Development* (New York: Columbia University Press, 1931), pp. 241, 246.

44. *New York Times*, July 24, 1911.

45. Ibid., July 15, 1911.

46. Ibid., August 24 and 25, 1911.

47. To shore up his faltering political fortunes, Taft and his attorney general, George W. Wickersham, intensified their attacks on the trusts. Mark Sullivan saw this as an act "men in desperation sometimes do when they find the strength of the tide running against them too strong for their mental footing" (*Our Times*, [New York: Charles Scribner's Sons, 1930–1932], IV, 406). See also Matthew Josephson, *The President Makers: The Culture of Politics and Leadership in an Age of Enlightenment, 1896–1919* (New York: Harcourt, Brace, 1940), pp. 368, 426–428. Josephson regards the renewal of legal warfare against the trusts as a "diversionary political movement."

48. *New York Times*, August 25, 1911.

49. Ibid.

50. Ibid., August 24, 1911.

51. It was "specifically encouraged" by the State Department to retain its holdings in banks in Latin America as a means of cementing closer relations with Latin America. *New York Times*, November 4 and 15, 1911.

52. Cited in Sullivan, *Our Times*, IV, 580.

53. Hearings by the subcommittee of the House Committee on Banking and Currency adjourned at the end of June for the duration of the presidential campaign, resumed December 9, 1912, and concluded February 27, 1913. Arsene Pujo of Louisiana served as chairman of the subcommittee, and Samuel Untermyer, a prominent New York lawyer, as its counsel. For an aspiring politician the assignment was a godsend, the type that had made Charles Evans Hughes governor of New York after his conduct of the Armstrong investigation into the insurance industry in 1905. Not knowing that such an opportunity would come his way, Untermyer had stated in November 1910, "The fact is that monopolies and substantial domination of industries created in that form could be counted on the fingers of your hands," and he attacked "political partisans who seek to make personal

and Party capital out of a demagogic appeals to the unthinking" (cited in Kolko, *Triumph of Conservatism*, p. 220). A year later, Untermyer reversed himself, observing in a letter to the *New York Times* (December 22, 1911) that the money trust was the greatest peril facing the country and its power was "sadly underestimated." The committee's report also concluded on this note, stating that "there is a well-defined community of interest between [sic] a few leaders of finance, which has resulted in a great and rapidly growing concentration of the control of money and credit in the hands of these few men."

54. Kolko, *Triumph of Conservatism*, p. 220. The Pujo committee concluded that five firms—J. P. Morgan and Company, First National Bank, National City Bank, Guaranty Trust Company, and Bankers' Trust Company—had 118 directorships in 34 banks and trust companies, 30 directorships in 10 insurance companies, 105 directorships in 32 transportation systems, 63 directorships in 24 producing and trading corporations, and 25 directorships in 12 public utility corporations, having aggregate resources or capitalization of $22 billion. Within two days of Wilson's election, November 7, 1912, Carter Glass wrote to the president-elect, requesting an interview to discuss revising the currency system and formulating a substitute for the Aldrich bill. Link, ed., *Papers of Woodrow Wilson*, XXV, 531.

55. Quotation is from the 1912 Democratic party platform. During his campaign, Wilson ambiguously announced he was "for big business and against trusts." Prior to the nominating convention, Wilson attacked the money trust as the "most dangerous of all monopolies." The *New York Times*, for June 16, 1911, asked if he were making a deliberate bid for the support of Bryan and his agrarian followers. The *New York World* for July 31, 1911, asked if Wilson were playing to the gallery to promote his presidential candidacy.

56. Colonel E. M. House, presidential adviser, reported to Wilson after an hour spent with Carter Glass: "He candidly confessed that he knew nothing about banking or the framing of a monetary measure. I congratulated him upon this for I told him that it was much better to know nothing than to know something wrong." Link, ed., *Papers of Woodrow Wilson*, XXV, 564.

57. H. P. Willis to Carter Glass (Letter), December 31, 1912, cited in Arthur S. Link, *The New Freedom* (Princeton: Princeton University Press, 1956), pp. 203–204. See also Carter Glass, *An Adventure in Constructive Finance* (Garden City, N.Y.: Doubleday, Page, 1927); H. Parker Willis, *The Federal Reserve System* (New York: Ronald Press, 1923); Robert C. West, *Banking Reform and the Federal Reserve, 1863–1923* (Ithaca, N.Y.: Cornell University Press, 1974), pp. 89–172; Richard H. Timberlake, Jr., *The Origins of Central Banking in the United States* (Cambridge, Mass.: Harvard University Press, 1978), pp. 186–206.

58. National City Bank, *Pending Banking Legislation* (New York: National City Bank, 1913), p. 10.

59. Ibid., pp. 7–8.

60. Ibid., pp. 8–9.

61. *New York Times*, November 11, 1913.

62. U.S. Congress, *Hearings on H. R. 7837, Federal Reserve Banks*, p. 2891. Vanderlip prepared this plan solely at the insistence of four members of the Senate

Banking and Currency Committee: James A. O'Gorman (D, N.Y.), Gilbert M. Hitchcock (D, Nebr.), James A. Reed (D, Mo.), and Joseph L. Bristow (R, Kans.).
  63. *New York Times*, October 24, 1913.
  64. Link, ed., *Papers of Woodrow Wilson*, XXVIII, 428–430. See also Link, *The New Freedom*, p. 231.
  65. *New York Times*, November 11, 1913.
  66. Ibid. Cf. also Glass, *An Adventure*, pp. 166–174.

5. A New Strategy, 1914–1916
  1. September 27, 1913, Vanderlip MSS. Vanderlip briefly considered keeping National City out of the Federal Reserve System. Vanderlip to Stillman, December 29, 1913, Vanderlip MSS. This would have involved converting National City into a state-chartered bank, possibly through a merger with the Corn Exchange Bank, a bank with a rapidly growing local branch system. Vanderlip to Stillman, January 4, 1914, Vanderlip MSS. These plans were soon dropped. As Charles V. Rich, a National City vice president, reminded Vanderlip, National City would be accused of trying to sabotage the Federal Reserve if it did not join the system. Rich to Vanderlip (Memorandum), January 13, 1914, Vanderlip MSS.
  2. For a discussion of the impact of the Federal Reserve Act on the commercial banking system see Thomas Conway, Jr., and Ernest M. Patterson, *The Operation of the New Bank Act* (Philadelphia: J. B. Lippincott, 1914); Milton Friedman and Anna J. Schwartz, *A Monetary History of the United States, 1867–1960* (Princeton: Princeton University Press, 1963), pp. 189–196.
  3. Edwin J. Perkins, "The Divorce of Commercial and Investment Banking: A History," *Banking Law Journal*, 88 (1971): 491.
  4. On the impact of World War I on the U.S. economy see Friedman and Schwartz, *Monetary History*, pp. 196–216.
  5. On the crisis of 1914 see National City Bank, *Monthly Economic Letter*, September 1914, p. 1, October 1914, p. 3; E. V. Morgan, *Studies in British Financial Policy, 1914–1925* (London: Macmillan, 1952), p. 3. Frank A. Vanderlip's actions during the 1914 financial crisis are discussed in his 1936 munitions investigation testimony. See U.S. Congress, Senate Special Committee on Investigation of the Munitions Industry, *Munitions Industry: Supplemental Report on the Adequacy of Existing Legislation*, 73rd and 74th Cong., 1936, p. 17.
  6. U.S. Congress, Senate Committee on Banking and Currency, *Hearings on H. R. 7837 (S. 2639): A Bill to Provide for the Establishment of Federal Reserve Banks*, 63rd Cong., 1st sess., 1913, p. 1939. Vanderlip's optimism contrasted with the widespread expectation that the new Reserve banks would limit the growth of the securities market and diminish the power of the New York banks. Typical of the expectations regarding the Federal Reserve Act were the remarks of two professors of finance at the University of Pennsylvania: "Every one will be interested to know whether it [the Federal Reserve Act] will destroy or impair the efficacy of the so-called 'Money Trust', which is founded primarily on the control of a comparatively small number of banking institutions that hold these bankers' deposits from the other sections of the country." Conway and Patterson, *Bank Act*, p. 364.

The framers of the Federal Reserve Act certainly intended to reduce the correspondent bank business of the New York banks, since their competition for bankers' balances was held to have led to the pyramiding of reserves in New York and to have promoted the instability of the entire banking system. It was widely anticipated that the Reserve banks would take over many, if not all, of the functions that the New York banks had formerly performed for their correspondents. Vanderlip subscribed to this analysis and expected National City to lose most of its correspondent bank balances. Vanderlip to Stillman, December 29, 1913, Vanderlip MSS.

7. National City Bank, "Lectures to Banking III Class," First Lecture by Frank A. Vanderlip, n.d., p. 8.

8. National City Bank, "Lectures to Banking III Class," Fifth Lecture by Frank A. Vanderlip, December 3, 1918, pp. 39–40.

9. Most of the new accounts were small (less than $5,000 in balances), but National City also succeeded in adding seven new large accounts (balances in excess of $1 million). These large accounts continued to account for over 40 percent of the bank's total deposits from corporations and individuals, so there was little change in the mix of the customer base. See Organization File, National City Bank, Accounts, July 1916, Vanderlip MSS.

10. Estimates are based on a sample of eighty-four large manufacturing companies prepared by the National Bureau of Economic Research, Financial Research Program, and refer to nominal values. *Corporate Financial Data for Studies in Business Finance,* Section A (Large Corporations), Confidential and Preliminary Draft, May 1945.

On corporate financial policy during the war see Ralph A. Young and Charles Schmidt, *The Effect of War on Business Financing: Manufacturing and Trade, World War I* (New York: National Bureau of Economic Research, 1943), pp. 25–26, 39.

11. National City Bank, Call Reports, June 30, 1914, and June 20, 1917.

12. Vanderlip to Stillman, July 2, 1915, Vanderlip MSS.

13. Vanderlip to Stillman, June 5, 1914, Vanderlip MSS.

14. Ibid.

15. N. S. B. Gras and Henrietta M. Larson, *Casebook in American Business History* (New York: F. S. Crofts, 1939), p. 525. George F. Baker, president of the First National Bank, thought that no American banker had the training necessary to enter the foreign field.

16. Vanderlip to Stillman, June 5, 1914, Vanderlip MSS.

17. John E. Gardin (vice president, National City Bank) to Vanderlip (Memorandum), February 15, 1914, Vanderlip MSS. Regarding Du Pont's stake in Chile see Mira Wilkins, *The Emergence of Multinational Enterprise: American Business Abroad from the Colonial Era to 1914* (Cambridge, Mass.: Harvard University Press, 1970), p. 183.

18. Wilkins, *Emergence,* pp. 176, 189, 193–194. Joseph P. Grace was a director of the bank.

19. Ibid., p. 211. W. C. Downs, "The Commission House in Latin American Trade," *Quarterly Journal of Economics,* 26 (1911): 129. Cyrus McCormick, the president of International Harvester, was a director of the bank.

20. Wilkins, *Emergence*, p. 190. On National City's relationship with Armour see chapter 4.

21. Ibid., pp. 209–210. Other National City customers with extensive international operations included American Tobacco, British American Tobacco, Virginia Carolina Chemical, U.S. Rubber, Ford, General Electric, International Steam Pump, Western Electric, and Westinghouse Air Brake. Cf. Wilkins, *Emergence*, and Appendix D.

22. Robert Mayer, "The Origins of the American Banking Empire in Latin America: Frank A. Vanderlip and the National City Bank," *Journal of Interamerican Studies and World Affairs*, 15 (1973): 63–64.

23. Paul P. Abrahams, *The Foreign Expansion of American Finance and Its Relationship to the Foreign Economic Policies of the United States, 1907–1921* (New York: Arno Press, 1976), pp. 12–13.

24. Vanderlip to Stillman, June 5, 1914, Vanderlip MSS.

25. Ibid.

26. It was not the first foreign branch of any United States bank. State-chartered banks and trust companies had established foreign branches beginning in 1895. Cf. Abrahams, *Foreign Expansion*, p. 8; Clyde William Phelps, *The Foreign Expansion of American Banks: American Branch Banking Abroad* (New York: Ronald Press, 1927), pp. 85–86.

27. Vanderlip to Henry S. Pritchett (a personal friend), July 17, 1914, Vanderlip MSS.

28. *Federal Reserve Bulletin*, 6 (1920): 599.

29. October 30, 1914, Vanderlip MSS.

30. October 9, 1914, Vanderlip MSS.

31. Frank A. Vanderlip with Boyden Sparkes, *From Farm Boy to Financier* (New York: D. Appleton Century, 1935), p. 260. It was particularly difficult to find an executive capable of directing the entire foreign branch system. Originally, Vanderlip had hoped that Herbert Eldredge, the former president of a Houston bank who had been responsible for building up National City's business in Texas, would be able to supervise the bank's international business. But Eldredge died just as the expansion into South America was beginning. Consequently, the branches lacked overall supervision. As a provisional measure the manager of the Buenos Aires branch, John Allen, was given overall responsibility for the South American branches while the search for a senior executive continued. Vanderlip to Stillman, November 27, 1915, and April 29, 1916, Vanderlip MSS.

32. Vanderlip to Stillman, June 5, 1914, Vanderlip MSS.

33. January 15, 1915, Vanderlip MSS.

34. Vanderlip to Stillman, May 14, 1916, Vanderlip MSS.

35. "W. S. Kies on National City Bank's Efforts to Develop Foreign Trade," *Commercial and Financial Chronicle*, February 19, 1916, p. 667. Kies was a vice president of National City Bank.

36. State of Connecticut, General Assembly, January sess. (1901), Senate Joint Resolution No. 231, Section 2, incorporating the International Company. The charter was amended by the Connecticut legislature on December 19, 1901, to change the corporate name to International Banking Corporation (IBC).

The founder of the IBC, Marcellus Hartley, became associated with Moses Taylor as early as 1866, when Hartley participated in the financing of the Atlantic cable. Closer contact with the Taylor-Pyne circle of entrepreneurs arose through the marriage of two of his daughters to Norman White Dodge and James Stokes, two of Taylor's business associates, in the early 1880s. For most of his career Marcellus Hartley had specialized in the manufacture and distribution of guns and ammunition. Toward the end of his life he founded the Remington Arms Company, which became a customer of the bank. He also became the chief investment officer of the Equitable Life Assurance Society. In addition, Hartley occupied the post of vice president of the Westinghouse Electric Company, into which he had merged his own firm, the United States Electric Lighting Company. Cf. *Marcellus Hartley: A Brief Memoir* (New York: privately printed, 1903).

Hartley appointed General Thomas Hubbard to manage the IBC. Hubbard was the financial officer of the Southern Pacific Railroad and a partner in the law firm Stillman and Hubbard. Hubbard's law partner may have been related to James Stillman.

37. Set up expressly to aid American business abroad, IBC differed from the private banking houses that established foreign offices. They did so in order to attract funds to the United States. Foremost among these was J. P. Morgan and Company, with a banking house of its own in London, founded in 1864, and an interest in one in France dating back to 1871. Four trust companies also had branches: Equitable Trust, Guaranty Trust, Farmers' Loan and Trust, and Empire Trust. See Phelps, *Foreign Expansion*, pp. 7–8, 147–148, 211.

38. February 12, 1909, Vanderlip MSS.

39. October 29, 1915, Vanderlip MSS.

40. Ibid. The Middle East was the major exception to Vanderlip's plan for a worldwide branch system, for it was closed to U.S. investment, and conducted little trade with the United States. The region therefore offered little opportunity for branch banking by U.S. banks. It was not until 1928, and not without the help of the U.S. State Department, that U.S. oil companies gained access to Iraq. See Mira Wilkins, *The Maturing of Multinational Enterprise: American Business Abroad from 1914 to 1970* (Cambridge, Mass.: Harvard University Press, 1974), pp. 117–120.

41. Phelps, *Foreign Expansion*, p. 163.

42. "W. S. Kies on National City Bank's Efforts to Develop Foreign Trade."

43. From 1914 to 1917 the total nominal value of U.S. foreign trade more than doubled, with exports rising 186 percent and imports 66 percent. U.S. Bureau of the Census, *Historical Statistics of the United States: Colonial Times to 1970*, Bicentennial ed., pt. 1 (Washington, D.C.: GPO, 1975), p. 864.

44. Vanderlip to Stillman, October 9, 1914, October 21, 1914, and October 30, 1914, Vanderlip MSS.

45. National City Bank, Call Report, June 1917.

46. National City Bank, Call Report, December 1916; Benjamin H. Beckhart, *The New York Money Market*, ed. Benjamin H. Beckhart, vol. 3, *Uses of Funds* (New York: Columbia University Press, 1932), p. 311.

47. Gardin to Vanderlip, September 9, 1912, Vanderlip MSS.

48. National City Bank, Daily Statement Book, June 1914, June 1917.

49. R. S. Sayers, *The Bank of England, 1891–1944* (Cambridge: Cambridge University Press, 1976), pp. 86–93.

50. Vanderlip to Stillman, May 26, 1916, Vanderlip MSS.

51. As indicated in the text, the increase in the balances of foreign banks made National City more rather than less of a bankers' bank during the first years of the Federal Reserve System. Bankers' balances, both foreign and domestic, rose as a proportion of total domestic deposits from 42 percent in 1914 to over 50 percent in 1917. Contrary to initial expectations after the passage of the Federal Reserve Act, domestic correspondent balances also rose, although by only modest amounts. National City Bank, Daily Statement Book, June 1914, June 1917.

All types of domestic banks increased their deposits, even national banks, the institutions most affected by the Federal Reserve Act. Under the new law, national banks were allowed, during a three-year transition period, to count balances at New York banks toward their required reserves. Out-of-town banks found it profitable to retain balances with National City to pay for such services as foreign exchange transactions and collections of foreign checks that the Federal Reserve could not provide. State-chartered banks and trust companies also increased their balances at National City. Those that were not members of the Federal Reserve (and most state-chartered institutions were not) could generally continue to count their deposits at National City toward their legally required reserves.

52. National City Bank, Call Reports, June 1914, June 1917; Organization File, National City Bank, Earnings, Earnings of the National City Bank of New York from 1901 to 1917 Inclusive, Vanderlip MSS. The figure for 1917 includes $1.1 million in profits from the IBC in addition to $7.3 million in profits from the bank, listed in Appendix B.

53. National City Bank, Comptroller's Report, 1917; International Banking Corporation, Statement of Condition, June 30, 1917; Organization File, National City Bank, Foreign Trade Department, Vanderlip MSS.

54. Vanderlip to Stillman, April 14, 1916, Vanderlip MSS.

55. November 1, 1913, Vanderlip MSS.

56. Ibid.

57. Vanderlip to Stillman, July 2, 1915, Vanderlip MSS.

58. Vanderlip to Stillman, January 4, 1914, Vanderlip MSS.

59. William Jennings Bryan to J. P. Morgan and Company (Letter), August 15, 1914, cited in George Edwards, *The Evolution of Finance Capitalism* (London: Longmans Green, 1938), p. 205. In September, Russian Minister of Finance Bark approached the head of National City's London branch with a request for a loan of 300 million rubles in order to purchase war supplies in the United States. In compliance with Bryan's declaration, National City replied that the loan was "out of the question." But National City added that it would be willing to grant a three-month credit of $5 million in the form of an overdraft on the New York bank account of the Russian minister of finance to be used for purchasing war supplies in this country. Thus, the bank adhered to the letter of the neutrality policy by substituting a commercial transaction for an outright loan.

60. U.S. Congress, *Munitions Investigation: Supplemental Report*, p. 17.

61. Charles C. Tansill, *America Goes to War* (Boston: Little, Brown, 1938), p. 75.

62. Vincent P. Carosso, *Investment Banking in America: A History* (Cambridge, Mass.: Harvard University Press, 1970), p. 212. National City was made a depository for the proceeds of the issue and helped sell the bonds through correspondent banks across the United States. Cf. Vanderlip to Stillman (Letters), October 22 and 29, 1915, Vanderlip MSS.

63. Carosso, *Investment Banking*, pp. 101–102. Prior to the merger Stillman seems to have had a personal financial interest in Halsey and Company. In June 1907 Stillman agreed to lend Halsey up to $800,000 for use in his bond business. In addition to interest, Stillman received access to Halsey's records and limited veto power over Halsey's activities. Organization File, Halsey and Company, Vanderlip MSS. The exact terms of the 1916 merger are not known.

64. Vanderlip to Stillman, January 4, 1914, Vanderlip MSS.

65. Organization File, National City Bank, Earnings, Vanderlip MSS.

66. Carosso, *Investment Banking*, pp. 259, 274. Vanderlip to Stillman (Letter), December 31, 1914, Vanderlip MSS.

67. Vanderlip, *Farm Boy*, p. 287.

68. Ibid.

69. A 1916 conversation between Baker and Vanderlip pointed up the difference between the First National and National City. According to Vanderlip, who reported the conversation to Stillman in a letter, Baker "spoke in terms of high appreciation of the enterprise of the City Bank, but said that he had no ambition at all to broaden the field of the First National. He didn't want to take on any more work, and was much better satisfied to run along as he was doing, and thought that was the wise course for most other banks to follow, because he doubted that other banks could get together such an organization as we have." January 22, 1916, Vanderlip MSS.

70. Vanderlip MSS.

6. Owners and Managers, 1917–1921

1. Frank A. Vanderlip, "Remarks," at Dinner given by Mr. Vanderlip to the Officers of the National City Bank, the National City Company, the International Banking Corporation, and the American International Corporation, November 21, 1918 (New York 1918), pp. 8–9. These figures do not include either the National City Company or the International Banking Corporation.

2. Frank A. Vanderlip to James Stillman, July 23, 1915, Vanderlip MSS.

3. Vanderlip to Stillman, July 2, 1915, Vanderlip MSS.

4. Vanderlip to Stillman, July 23, 1915, Vanderlip MSS. William A. Simonson, Samuel McRoberts, and James H. Perkins were vice presidents of the bank, as was James A. Stillman.

5. Frank A. Vanderlip with Boyden Sparkes, *From Farm Boy to Financier* (New York: D. Appleton Century, 1935), p. 262. The last sentence probably refers to the possibility that Stillman's son, James A., might take over the bank after his father's death.

6. Comptroller of the Currency, Examination Report, National City Bank, December 29, 1916.

7. July 7, 1915, Vanderlip MSS.

8. July 31, 1915, Vanderlip MSS. Stillman wrote: "I am distressed that you got an impression last summer when the purchase of the Morgan stock was alluded to that I could carry it, for I know I was scrupulously careful to avoid giving any such impression, having made commitments which would sometime use practically all the cash I had accumulated and possibly oblige me to borrow. So I cannot imagine how you got any such impression and regret it extremely as it would be manifestly unwise for me in my state of health and situation to become a borrower for any very considerable amount."

9. Vanderlip, *Farm Boy*, pp. 279–280.

10. July 31, 1915, Vanderlip MSS. From his vantage point Stillman could not understand Vanderlip's concerns, especially about money, and assured his younger colleague, "Certainly with your large salary and opportunities for investments you will make all the money you and your family require."

11. Vanderlip, *Farm Boy*, p. 265.

12. *Number Eight*, January 1916, p. 7.

13. October 26, 1915, Vanderlip MSS. Stillman reasoned, "I doubt extremely the advisability of offering the stock of such a company for subscription to the shareholders of the bank, and do not believe any considerable amount will be taken by them, nor do I think it would create confidence to have such a company too closely affiliated with the bank as it will be more or less speculative, nor do I see how the officers of the bank and such a company can be identical without creating criticism and possibly being illegal."

14. December 2, 1915, Vanderlip MSS.

15. November 18, 1915, Vanderlip MSS.

16. Ibid.

17. Ibid.

18. Ibid.

19. November 10, 1915, November 18, 1915, Vanderlip MSS.

20. Draft of letter not sent, November 13, 1915, Vanderlip MSS.

21. Vanderlip to Stillman, November 19, 1915, Vanderlip MSS.

22. Frank A. Vanderlip (Letter on the organization of the American International Corporation), November 27, 1915, Citibank Library, New York. The charter called for $50 million in capital and, as the letter noted, "It provides for $49,000,000 of common stock and $1,000,000 of preferred stock or Managers' Shares. The purpose of these shares is to enable the Corporation to secure men of exceptional talent and experience for the difficult work of managing this enterprise. It is obvious that its success will hinge almost entirely upon the quality of its management; and as its field will be world-wide and its problems of the most varied character, there will be needed a group of men of as wide vision and as sound judgment as can be brought together in America. These shares will be paid for at par, as will the common stock; and they have no advantage over the common stock in any respect until earnings sufficient to warrant the payment of more than seven percent dividends on both stocks have been made. When dividends to the extent of seven percent per annum on both classes of stock have been declared, any surplus earnings then remaining are to be divided, to the extent that dividends of such earnings are declared, in the

proportion of one-fifth to the Managers' Shares and four-fifths to the common stock."

23. In addition to Vanderlip, the American International Corporation's board of directors included J. Ogden Armour (Armour and Company), Charles A. Coffin (General Electric), Joseph P. Grace (W. R. Grace and Company), James J. Hill (Great Northern Railway), Robert S. Lovett (Union Pacific), John D. Ryan (Anaconda Copper), William L. Saunders (Ingersoll Rand), and Theodore N. Vail (American Telephone and Telegraph).

Charles A. Stone, head of the Boston engineering concern of Stone and Webster, served as president of the American International Corporation. Other officers included Willard Straight, a one-time Morgan associate and former consular official in China, who became vice president. R. P. Tinsley, formerly treasurer of the Standard Oil Company of New York, became secretary and treasurer of the new company.

24. Cited in *Number Eight*, January 1916, p. 9.

25. Ibid., p. 10. After the 1921 recession, the American International Corporation restricted its activities to portfolio investments in domestic securities. The Stone and Webster Company remained affiliated with AIC, but the other directors resigned. In 1969 the AIC was merged into the Adams Express Company, a closed-end investment company.

26. January 7, 1916, Vanderlip MSS.

27. Stillman to Vanderlip, January 5, 1916, Vanderlip MSS.

28. February 3, 1916, Vanderlip MSS.

29. Ibid.

30. Vanderlip, *Farm Boy*, p. 286.

31. *Number Eight*, January 1917, p. 27.

32. Vanderlip, *Farm Boy*, p. 290.

33. "The American 'Commercial Invasion' of Europe," *Scribner's Magazine*, January 1902, pp. 3–22. Vanderlip wrote, "Russia's need for capital is like the Sahara's thirst for water."

34. The first American companies to do business in Russia were the New York Life Insurance Company starting in 1885 and International Harvester in 1898. Vacuum Oil also became interested in Russia prior to 1900. See Mira Wilkins, *The Emergence of Multinational Enterprise: American Business Abroad from the Colonial Era to 1914* (Cambridge, Mass.: Harvard University Press, 1970), pp. 62–64, 82–85.

35. Vanderlip to Stillman, October 19, 1915, Vanderlip MSS.

36. April 8, 1916. Francis reported that J. P. Morgan and Company would have preferred to have Russian financing arranged through London. U.S. Congress, Senate Special Committee on Investigation of the Munitions Industry, *Hearings on S. Res. 206*, pt. 28, 74th Cong., 2nd sess., 1936, pp. 8706–07. The committee counsel suggested that during the war Russia had been in City Bank's "sphere of influence" (ibid., pt. 25, pp. 7553–54) and that Morgan had designated England and France as its own special preserve. Vanderlip denied the existence of special spheres: "It so happened that we had branches in Russia and because of that, we did do Russian business."

37. Ibid., pt. 25, p. 8707.

38. June 19, 1916, Vanderlip MSS.

39. Frank A. Vanderlip, Address delivered at the Hotel Biltmore to the Representatives of the Underwriters of the Imperial Russian Government External Loan, November 16, 1916. At that same meeting, National City Bank vice president Samuel McRoberts praised the abilities of the Russian government and the country's economic potential, comparing Russia to the United States after the Civil War. Ironically, he also pointed out that "the Russian people . . . have recognized that they cannot go on in old channels politically and industrially."

Vanderlip was not alone in his enthusiasm for Russia. Businessmen coveted the country's vast resources and this led them to overlook the very real problems that the czarist regime confronted. The *Annalist* announced April 16, 1917, that "businessmen share with bankers the hope and expectation that rejuvenated Russia will, with the end of the war, become a far greater factor in the American market than ever before." In October 1917 the same periodical declared "broken and economically helpless as she appears, the new Democracy stands forth as the only possible rebuilder of war-battered Europe, her timber lands exceeding those of any other European nation by millions of acres." *Iron Age* predicted that Russia would be the most promising postwar market for American products, especially cotton goods and agricultural and road-building equipment. *Electrical World*, in turn, foresaw a great market for electrical equipment (January 4, 1917, February 10, 1917, and September 9, 1917).

Like many others, Vanderlip saw World War I as an interlude in Russia's progress toward a liberal state. Thus, entry into Russia during the war appeared to present a splendid opportunity for an American bank to supplant the German banks as a conduit for direct investment in Russian industry. "Russia," Summary of article regarding views of a leading Russian economist and banker, Ivan Ozeroff, which apeared in the *New York World*, December 13, 1914, Vanderlip MSS. Concerning the realism of Vanderlip's hopes for Russian liberalism see Theodore H. von Laue, "The Prospects of Liberal Democracy in Russia," in *Essays on Russian Liberalism*, ed. C. E. Timberlake (Columbia: University of Missouri Press, 1972), pp. 164–165.

40. May 17, 1917, Vanderlip MSS.

41. In retrospect, the *New York Times* did not provide its readers with an accurate analysis of the ongoing Russian political situation. In 1920, three years after the Bolshevik takeover, Walter Lippmann and Charles Merz concluded that the coverage by the *Times* was "almost always misleading." During the period from the overthrow of the czar to the failure of the Galician offensive in July 1917, Lippmann and Merz found the newspaper's captions and emphasis "so optimistic as to be misleading." The *Times* persisted in its sanguine tone until the Bolshevik Revolution: "It may fairly be said that the growth of the Bolshevik power from July to November must have been seriously underestimated." See Walter Lippmann and Charles Merz, "Test of the News: An Examination of the *New York Times* Reports on the Russian Revolution," *New Republic*, August 4, 1920, special supplement.

Officials of the American government with a few exceptions were no more realistic than the *New York Times* in their appraisal of Russian reality. In his war message to Congress on April 2, 1917, President Woodrow Wilson hailed the Russia of the Provisional Government as a "fit partner for a league of honor." He insisted that despite her czarist rule, Russia was "always in fact democratic at heart, in all the vital habits of her thought, in all the intimate relationships of her people that spoke their natural instinct, their habitual attitude towards life." George Kennan, the leading American "expert" on Russia, saw in the February Revolution "the complete triumph of democracy." In the spring of 1917 Wilson sent a commission headed by Elihu Root to Russia, to "reassure the Provisional Government of American friendship and to inspire Russia back into the war." According to the historian Peter Filene, the commission saw what they wanted to see and failed to assess the looming power of the Bolsheviks. Root presented Secretary of State Lansing with an optimistic picture of a free, democratic Russia that would effectively fight Germany. See Peter G. Filene, *Americans and the Soviet Experiment, 1917–1933* (Cambridge, Mass.: Harvard University Press, 1967), pp. 13–19.

42. George F. Nolte, *Case Histories of Loans, 1929–1953* (New York: First National City Bank, 1960). Meserve's letters to Vanderlip from Russia during 1915–1917 are deposited in the General State Historical Archives in Leningrad. See V. V. Lebedev, *Russian-American Economic Relations, 1900–1917* (Moscow, 1964, in Russian). Meserve's chief interests, apart from establishing a branch of National City Bank in Russia, were the promotion of railroads and the exploitation of natural resources.

43. October 8, 1917, Vanderlip MSS.

44. Cf. Nolte, *Case Histories.* Ultimately, the courts determined that the bank's liability to depositors was payable in rubles in Russia. Some claims were settled by negotiation; in these cases the bank paid dollars in New York. In addition, the bank lost $5 million on its holdings of Russian government bonds.

45. Interview, Howard C. Sheperd, August 1976.

46. Arthur Pond and Samuel T. Moore, eds., *They Told Barron: Conversations and Revelations of an American Pepys in Wall Street* (New York: Harper, 1930), p. 36.

47. Vanderlip, *Farm Boy*, p. 272.

48. *New York Times*, May 27, 1919. Vanderlip presented his views at greater length in a book entitled *What Happened to Europe?* (New York: Macmillan, 1919), which he dictated during his return voyage.

49. *Monthly Economic Letter*, May 1919, p. 5. At the time of the armistice National City had warned of the dangers of imposing overly harsh peace terms on Germany and stressed the need to revive the German economy, if only for the purpose of enabling Germany to pay reparations (ibid., November 1918, p. 5). John Maynard Keynes later emphasized the danger to the future economic prosperity of Europe of exacting too great an indemnity from Germany. See *The Economic Consequences of the Peace* (New York: Harcourt, Brace, and Howe, 1920).

50. Harold G. Moulton and Leo Pasvolsky, *War Debts and World Prosperity* (Washington, D.C.: The Brookings Institution, 1932), pp. 58–60; Robert K. Murray, *The Politics of Normalcy: Governmental Theory and Practice in the Harding-Coolidge Era* (New York: W. W. Norton, 1973), pp. 1–15.

51. Vanderlip, *Farm Boy*, p. 302.

52. Joseph H. Durrell, "History of Foreign Branches of American Banks and Overseas Division, N. C. B." (New York, unpublished memoir, 1940), p. 77.

53. John K. Winkler, *The First Billion: The Stillmans and the National City Bank* (New York: Vanguard, 1934), p. 13.

54. Ralph A. Young and Charles H. Schmidt, *The Effect of War on Business Financing: Manufacturing and Trade, World War I* (New York: National Bureau of Economic Research, 1943), pp. 8–10.

55. Milton Friedman and Anna J. Schwartz, *A Monetary History of the United States, 1867–1960* (Princeton: Princeton University Press, 1963), pp. 223–224.

56. National City Bank, Call Report, December 31, 1919. At this date the interest rate on new loans ranged as high as 25 percent for call money.

57. Elmus R. Wicker, *Federal Reserve Monetary Policy, 1917–1933* (New York: Random House, 1966), pp. 37–45; Friedman and Schwartz, *Monetary History*, pp. 222–231.

58. National City Bank, Executive Managers, Minutes, June 1, 1920. The executive managers noted that "as loans on Government securities have a preferential rate," the bank should "endeavor to secure as many Government bonds from our borrowing customers . . . as possible."

Evidently customers were willing to oblige, since shortly afterward it was reported that the bank was obtaining two-thirds of its borrowings from the Federal Reserve at preferential rates. National City Bank, Executive Managers, Minutes, June 7, 1920. On the bank's total borrowings of $93 million it paid the following rates: 5.0 percent on $17.9 million; 5.5 percent on $36.3 million; 6.0 percent on $7.7 million; and 7.0 percent on $31.1 million.

Even at 7 percent it was profitable in some cases to borrow from the Federal Reserve in order to book new loans. For example, on July 12, 1920, the bank purchased a promissory note of the U.S. Rubber Company that yielded 8 percent. National City Bank, Executive Managers, Minutes, July 12, 1920.

59. Comptroller of the Currency, Stenographic Transcript of Conference with the Active Officers of National City Bank, National City Bank, February 22, 1921.

60. National City Bank, Condensed Statement of Condition, April 28, 1921. The loan data are from National City Bank, Executive Managers, Minutes, April 28, 1921.

61. Henry C. Wallich, *Monetary Problems of an Export Economy: The Cuban Experience, 1914–1947* (Cambridge, Mass.: Harvard University Press, 1950), pp. 57, 68.

62. Durrell, "Foreign Branches," pp. 42–46.

63. National City Bank, *Annual Report, 1922* (New York: National City Bank, 1923).

64. New York Clearing House, Clearing House Committee, Minute Book, March 28, 1922 (Confidential meeting); Charles E. Mitchell to Clearing House Committee (Letter), April 3, 1922; Seward Prosser, acting chairman, Clearing House Committee, to Mitchell (Letter), April 10, 1922.

65. Cited in Nolte, *Case Histories*, p. IV-4. The following discussion is largely based on Nolte and National City Bank, Executive Committee, Minutes, February 15, 1927. See also Isaac F. Marcosson, *Colonel Deeds: Industrial Builder* (New York: Dodd, Mead, 1948), pp. 307–316; *Number Eight*, January 1922, p. 3. On the development of the sugar industry in the 1920s see League of Nations, Economic Committee, *The World Sugar Situation* (Geneva: League of Nations, 1929).

66. General Sugar operated 6 percent of the active mills in Cuba and produced over 5 percent of the crop in the 1922–23 season. Other American-owned sugar producers in that season together operated 37 percent of the mills and produced nearly 60 percent of the crop. These included a number of National City customers. See R. W. Dunn, *American Foreign Investments* (New York: B. W. Huebsch and Viking Press, 1926), p. 122.

67. Mitchell could not bring himself to sell the sugar properties outright in 1927. He continued to expect that "the cycle in the sugar industry will come around like it does in every agricultural commodity." National City Bank, *Annual Report, 1927* (New York: National City Bank, 1928).

68. As of June 15, 1923, sixty-seven large stockholders held 215,000 shares of a total of 400,000. The Taylor and Stillman families held 41,548 and 20,470 shares, respectively. In contrast, Mitchell held only 4,725 shares. Comptroller of the Currency, Examination Report, National City Bank, June 15, 1923.

69. Frank W. Taussig and W. S. Barker, "American Corporations and Their Executives: A Statistical Inquiry," *Quarterly Journal of Economics*, 40 (1925–1926): 1–50.

70. National City Bank, *Annual Report, 1923* (New York: National City Bank, 1924).

71. The management fund was a contract between the owners and management of the firm. National City Bank, Executive Committee, Minutes, May 1, 1923. Under its terms the bank's annual net operating earnings were to be divided among additions to retained earnings, dividends to shareholders, and payments to executives participating in the plan. As a first priority, an amount equal to 8 percent of shareholders' equity was allocated to the bank's surplus (undivided profits) account. Second, shareholders were paid a dividend of 16 percent on the par value of their stock. (At the time the fund was set up, this annual dividend obligation amounted to $6.4 million.) Third, a sum equal to 20 percent of the net operating earnings less the amount allocated to surplus was put into the management fund for distribution to participants. If earnings were not sufficient to meet both the allocation-to-surplus and the dividend obligations, there would be no allocation to the fund. Any shortfall of earnings in any year from the amount required to satisfy the dividend obligation would be carried forward as a debit against the fund, to be met out of future earnings before any monies were allocated to the fund for distribution. The plan worked in a manner similar to the *tantieme* scheme that had been successfully used for some time by the major German banks and industrial corporations.

Before implementing the agreement the owners and managers agreed to adjust the published estimate of stockholders' equity to account for investments and losses made before Mitchell took over the management of the bank. For the purpose of the management-fund accounting, the owners added to the equity base the difference between the market and book value of the International Banking Corporation ($7 million). From the equity base the owners then deducted the difference between the market and book value of the bad loans made before Mitchell became president of the bank and remaining on the bank's books ($26.3 million). These and subsequent adjustments later became the object of a suit against the directors by minority shareholders of the bank (cf. chapter 10).

The management fund is relevant to recent developments in the theory of the firm that have described the firm as a set of contracts among factors of production, each acting in its own self-interest. See Eugene Fama, "Agency Problems and the Theory of the Firm," *Journal of Political Economy*, 88 (1980): 289. The management fund was just such a contract. Through the management fund the owners and management agreed to tie the latter's compensation to the firm's profitability by sharing the risk and reward. In terms of this theory, the bank at this stage represents a transition stage between the entrepreneur/partial owner analyzed by Michael C. Jensen and William H. Meckling ("Theory of the Firm: Managerial Behavior, Agency Costs, and Ownership Structure," *Journal of Financial Economics*, 3 [1976]: 305–360) and the fully modern corporation analyzed by Fama in which managers own no stock.

72. *Number Eight*, November 1922, p. 2.

7. The Financial Department Store (I), 1921–1929

1. For a discussion of the economic history of the 1920s see Derek H. Aldcroft, *From Versailles to Wall Street, 1919–1929* (Berkeley: University of California Press, 1977); Milton Friedman and Anna J. Schwartz, *A Monetary History of the United States, 1867–1960* (Princeton: Princeton University Press, 1963), pp. 240–298. These two works counter the assumption underlying the New Deal banking legislation that the prosperity of the 1920s inevitably led to, indeed caused, the depression of the 1930s. They also counter the work of historians and economists who have frequently inferred from the stock market boom and the depths of the depression that the 1920s must have been unstable. For example, see George Soule, *Prosperity Decade* (New York: Holt, Rinehart, 1947), and Robert A. Gordon, *Economic Instability and Growth: The American Record* (New York: Harper and Row, 1974), pp. 17–45, 70–75.

2. In 1919 the Treasury began to dismantle the War Finance Corporation, an agency that had extended credit to business while the United States was at war. The Treasury also refrained from lending to foreign governments, calling instead on Allied governments to repay the credits that the United States had extended to them during the war. The Treasury itself reduced its borrowings and began to retire the debt built up during the war. Cf. Paul Studenski and Herman E. Krooss, *Financial History of the United States*, 2nd ed. (New York: McGraw-Hill, 1963), pp. 302–343, and Esther R. Taus, *Central Banking Functions of the United States Treasury, 1789–1941* (New York: Columbia University Press, 1943), pp. 171–183.

3. Even after the return of sterling to gold in 1925, the dollar remained an important international currency. During the 1920s the Federal Reserve System held at least one-third of the world's monetary gold stock, far more than any other country. This fact alone made the dollar a key international currency, and Federal Reserve officials consciously used the system's gold reserves as a basis for increasing the dollar's international role. Cf. Frank C. Costigliola, "Anglo-American Financial Rivalry in the 1920s," *Journal of Economic History*, 37 (1977): 911–934. In fact, by the end of the 1920s, even British bankers were speaking of a dollar standard. Cf. Reginald McKenna, "The Dollar Standard: America and the World Price Level," *Acceptance Bulletin*, February 1928, pp. 2–9.

4. On the rise of New York as a world financial center see W. A. Brown, *The International Gold Standard Reinterpreted, 1914–1934* (New York: National Bureau of Economic Research, 1940), pp. 535–538, and Paul Einzig, *The Fight for Financial Supremacy* (London: Macmillan, 1931), pp. 49–57. London's position as the world's financial market diminished considerably as a result of the liquidation of a large portion of British overseas investment during World War I, the inconvertibility of sterling into gold until 1925, and the controls placed on the U.K. capital market by the Bank of England.

5. John Henry Patterson, head of National Cash Register from 1884 to 1922, pioneered American sales methods: direct mail circulars, annual sales quotas and contests, formal sales training manuals and schools. His methods were adopted by Richard Grant, a vice president of General Motors in the 1920s, and by many others. On the General Motors methods of selling see "General Motors III: How to Sell Automobiles," *Fortune*, February 1939, pp. 71–78, 105–110. Reprinted in A. D. Chandler, Jr., ed., *Giant Enterprise: Ford, General Motors, and the Automobile Industry* (New York: Harcourt, Brace and World, 1964), pp. 157–170.

6. U.S. Bureau of the Census, *Fifteenth Census of the U.S. Manufactures, 1929*, 3 vols. (Washington, D.C.: GPO, 1933); Benjamin Chinitz, *Freight and the Metropolis: The Impact of America's Transport Revolutions on the New York Region* (Cambridge, Mass.: Harvard University Press, 1960), p. 21.

7. *New York Times*, May 9, 1921.

8. Ibid.

9. Although branching was not mentioned specifically in the National Bank Act, successive comptrollers of the currency based their interpretation that the act prohibited branching on two provisions. Section 6 stated that persons forming a national bank association had to specify "the *place* where its operations of discount and deposit are to be carried on, designating the state, territory or district and also the particular county or city, town or village" (emphasis added). Even greater emphasis was given to a provision found in section 8 that read in part: "and its usual business shall be transacted in the *place* specified in its organization certificate" (emphasis added).

National banks were thus left at a competitive disadvantage in a growing number of states where state-chartered banks were permitted to branch. Concern for this inequity was increasingly expressed by the national banks themselves and by the regulators of national banks, who feared an erosion of their authority. The Federal Reserve in its *Annual Reports* from 1916 to 1920 also recommended that national banks be allowed to establish branches within certain limits, but Congress did not act on these recommendations. Cf. Gerald C. Fischer, *American Banking Structure* (New York: Columbia University Press, 1968), pp. 19–20.

10. Fischer, *American Banking Structure*, pp. 19–20; Shirley D. Southworth, *Branch Banking in the United States* (New York: McGraw-Hill, 1928), pp. 12–13.

11. *New York Times*, May 9, 1921. The Commercial Exchange Bank was organized in 1872 under a state charter as the German Exchange Bank. Anti-German sentiment during World War I prompted it to change its name to the Commercial Exchange Bank of the City of New York. New York State, Superintendent of Banks, *Annual Report, 1918* (Albany: New York State Superintendent of Banks, 1919), p. 26. For most of its existence the Commercial Exchange operated out of an

office at the Bowery and Bond Street. It was granted permission to open its first branch office in 1914 on Broadway and Twenty-ninth Street. In 1919 this branch was discontinued in favor of an office on Broadway and Twenty-sixth Street. The other two offices Commercial Exchange brought to the merger—one at 321 Broadway and one at the Hotel Biltmore (Vanderbilt Avenue and Forty-third Street)—had been established just prior to the announcement of the merger with National City.

Under the financial terms of the May 10, 1921 consolidation agreement, the capital stock of the National City Bank was to remain at $40 million, divided into 400,000 shares of $100 each. Of these the shareholders of National City were allotted 393,000 shares, or 393/400ths share for each one already held. The remaining 7,000 shares were allotted to the shareholders of the Commercial Exchange, which amounted to a one-for-one share swap. Any Commercial shareholder not wishing to accept a share in the consolidated institution in exchange for his share of Commercial Exchange stock would receive $318 in cash. National City Bank, Executive Committee, Minutes, May 9, 1921.

12. *New York Times*, November 23, 1921. National City acquired the Second National under the terms of the 1918 National Bank Consolidation Act. At the time of the merger the Second National had total assets of $26 million; its stockholders' equity amounted to approximately $5.9 million. National City paid $680 per share for the Second National (National City Bank, Executive Committee, Minutes, November 21, 1921), a premium of approximately 45 percent over the market price prevailing immediately prior to the merger agreement.

13. In October 1923 Attorney General Daugherty rendered an opinion that such limited-service offices were legal. In 1924 the Supreme Court confirmed this (*First National Bank of St. Louis v. Missouri*). It ruled that nationally chartered banks were allowed only one full-service office. More positively, this ruling was interpreted as not precluding limited-service offices, such as teller's windows. Cf. Fischer, *American Banking Structure*, pp. 42–47.

14. From 1923 to 1926 National City received permits for five teller's windows, one in 1923, one in 1924, two in 1925, and one in 1926 (which did not open until after the McFadden Act became effective). For all national banks, the comptroller's office approved applications for 208 such offices from 1922 to 1926. Cf. John M. Chapman and Ray B. Westerfield, *Branch Banking* (New York: Harper, 1943), p. 98.

15. *New York Times*, March 5 and 10, 1926. By the early 1920s Brooklyn had surpassed Manhattan as New York's most populous borough (ibid., May 15, 1929).

In 1926 Mitchell pointed out Brooklyn's potential as a market for the bank: "This borough has shown tremendous development lately. It is the third greatest American city in point of population and the fourth industrially. Of the exports of New York, forty-five percent go from Brooklyn docks. Brooklyn controls one quarter of the country's foreign trade." *Number Eight*, June 1926, p. 3.

Some of the bank's competition already had offices in this rapidly growing area. Three retail-oriented, state-chartered banks, the Corn Exchange, Manufacturers' Trust, and the Bank of the Manhattan Company, had made full use of the liberal New York State regulations on branching. Each already had an extensive network of branches at key points in Brooklyn. Among National City's nationally chartered competitors Chase had acquired an office in Brooklyn through its merger with the Metropolitan Bank in 1921.

In June 1926 National City followed its competition into Brooklyn by acquiring the People's Trust Company under the terms of the National Bank Consolidation Act. Since its founding in 1889, People's Trust had grown through mergers and *de novo* expansion into one of the largest banking institutions in the borough, with eleven branch offices throughout Brooklyn and total resources of nearly $74 million, about 7 percent of National City's total. Most of that growth occurred under the administration of Charles A. Broody, who served as president of People's from 1907 until his death on February 1, 1926. See *Number Eight*, March 1926, pp. 13–20, and June 1926, p. 3.

Broody's death left People's without effective management, and its directors soon entered into negotiations with National City about a possible merger. An agreement in principle was quickly reached (National City Bank, Board of Directors, Minutes, March 3, 1926) and on May 2, 1926, People's converted to a national charter with trust powers prior to completion of the merger on June 25. National City paid approximately $16.9 million to acquire People's Trust. National City Bank, Executive Committee, Minutes, May 25, 1926.

After the merger, the People's Trust staff continued to administer the Brooklyn branches as a separate unit within the bank's Domestic Branch Division. The bank made an effort to keep the offices and staff of People's because of their extensive knowledge of Brooklyn conditions. By and large it was successful in doing so. Thus the merger catapulted the bank into a leading position in Brooklyn.

Finally, the acquisition of People's Trust also added a new dimension to the bank's own trust business—another of the diversified activities recently entered into by large commercial banks (see chapter 8).

16. Southworth, *Branch Banking*, pp. 163–184, and Fischer, *American Banking Structure*, pp. 47–49. The McFadden Act broke with the tradition that nationally chartered banks should be unit banks. Until 1923 the prohibition against branching had been based on rulings by the comptroller of the currency, rather than on specific legislation. But in 1924 the Supreme Court ruled that national banks had no legal power to establish branches.

This prohibition against branching by national banks suited advocates of unit banking, especially small banks in rapidly growing areas. It also suited state-chartered banks in those states with liberal branching laws. These banks made extensive use of their freedom to branch, winning business at the expense of their nationally chartered competitors. The Bank of Italy (later the Bank of America) grew through branching into the largest bank in the country outside New York. By 1927 it had 276 branches throughout California. Southworth, *Branch Banking*, p. 162.

Two factors led to a liberalization of the branching laws affecting national banks. The first was the failure of thousands of unit banks in the rural areas of the West and South. Branch banks were judged to be safer, since they had more diversified portfolios and a larger capital base. The second factor was the increasing number of national banks that were converting to state charters in order to obtain the power to branch. Once it had obtained a state charter, the bank also had the option of leaving the Federal Reserve System. Many did so, thus reducing its control over the banking system. As Congressman McFadden himself pointed out: "The primary object of the McFadden National Banking Bill is to amend the National Bank Act so that the national banks will be able to meet the needs of modern industry and commerce and also to establish competitive equality among all members of the Federal Reserve System. We must do this because otherwise national banks will seek the greater advantages offered by state banking laws and in that event the Federal Reserve System without the compulsory membership of national banks would be only a theory, not a reality. This is evidenced by the fact that out of 16,000 eligible state commercial banks and trust companies only about 10 percent have elected to become voluntary members of the system. National banks have been knocking at the doors of Congress for many years asking for the relief in the proposed legislation. If Congress denies that relief or defers action for any length of time it will strike a serious blow at the Federal Reserve System because the disintegration of the national system will continue and ultimately we will have to depend for a large amount of the resources of the Federal Reserve System upon the voluntary membership of state banks which can come in and go out of the system at will." Cited in National City Bank, *Monthly Economic Letter*, March 1927, pp. 50–51.

The McFadden Act itself was a compromise between those concerned about the safety and stability of the banking system and those opposed to branching. By allowing national banks to branch within the city of their headquarters (providing state banks were permitted to do so), the act put nationally chartered banks more on a par with state-chartered banks. Through the act, National City did gain parity with state-chartered banks, since New York State law limited their branches to New York City.

In addition to its branching provisions, the McFadden Act granted perpetual charters to the twelve Federal Reserve banks and to national banks (this facilitated their trust operations). It gave nationally chartered banks the right to buy and sell investment securities and it confirmed the legality of securities affiliates. It also extended the power of nationally chartered banks to make loans secured by real estate.

17. At the end of 1929 National City's domestic branch deposits were $305.3 million; those of the Corn Exchange, $243.6 million (excludes interbank and government deposits). Cf. New York State, Superintendent of Banks, *Annual Report, 1929* (Albany: New York State Superintendent of Banks, 1930).

18. U.S. Congress, House Committee on Banking and Currency, *Branch, Chain, and Group Banking: Hearings on H. Res. 141*, 71st Cong., 2nd sess., 1930, p. 1956.

19. National City Bank, *Annual Report, 1928* (New York: National City Bank, 1929).

20. "Pioneer Days of Uptown Service Pass," *Number Eight*, June 1921, p. 12.

21. National City Bank, *Annual Report, 1921* (New York: National City Bank, 1922).

22. N. C. Lenfestey (Cashier), "National City Absorbs Commercial Exchange Bank to Give Uptown Service," *Number Eight*, June 1921, p. 6. In a special marketing touch, the bank announced that certain officers at the Forty-second Street

branch had been designated "to provide every facility to women customers in the proper financial procedure in carrying out their business transactions." Apparently, management was well aware that women controlled much of the household wealth this new office was supposed to attract.

23. *New York Times*, December 27, 1921.

24. Phillip Cagan, *Determinants and Effects of Changes in the Stock of Money, 1875–1960* (New York: Columbia University Press, 1965), p. 319.

25. See National City Bank, Call Reports, June 1922 through June 1929, for number of accounts, total and average balances, and interest paid on accounts.

26. David H. Rogers, *Consumer Banking in New York* (New York: Columbia University Press, 1974), pp. 1–14.

27. New York State law set the usury ceiling at 6 percent but made no mention of discount or methods of repayment. National City followed the industrial banks in requiring periodic installments to be paid into a deposit account. At National City, this account earned interest. In 1933 a state court declared that the terms National City set on its consumer loans did not violate the state usury ceilings. Rogers, *Consumer Banking*, pp. 9, 14, 28–29.

28. *Number Eight*, April–May 1928, p. 25.

29. National City Bank, *Annual Report, 1929* (New York: National City Bank, 1930), and *Number Eight*, May 1930, p. 8.

30. Joseph H. Durrell, "History of Foreign Branches of American Banks and Overseas Division, N.C.B." (New York, unpublished memoir, 1940), pp. 117–120.

31. Clyde William Phelps, *The Foreign Expansion of American Banks: American Branch Banking Abroad* (New York: Ronald Press, 1927), pp. 161–166; *Federal Reserve Bulletin*, 7 (1921): 1267.

32. Mira Wilkins, *The Maturing of Multinational Enterprise: American Business Abroad from 1914 to 1970* (Cambridge, Mass.: Harvard University Press, 1974), p. 138, sums up the practices of American firms investing abroad in the 1920s as follows: "U.S. companies were (1) going to more countries, (2) building more plants in a particular foreign country, (3) manufacturing or mining more end-products in a particular foreign land, (4) investing in a single alien nation in a greater degree of integration, and (5) diversifying on a worldwide basis."

By the end of 1929 U.S. investments abroad totaled $7.5 billion, or nearly double the amount in 1919. Although Canada and Latin America accounted for nearly three-quarters of the total, U.S. corporations made investments in practically every region of the world. The subsidiaries that U.S. manufacturing firms set up overseas to crack additional markets and to vault tariff barriers were generally located in Western Europe, but the Far East also got a fair share. Latin America was the site of mining and crude oil production as well as assembly plants rather than manufacturing establishments. The public utilities tended to be more widespread but favored Latin America.

National City's customers were leaders in those industries that expanded most rapidly and accounted for the largest share of U.S. investment abroad—public utilities, petroleum, mining, and manufacturing. To old customers like Anaconda, W. R. Grace, International Harvester, and the oil companies, all of which had gone abroad well before World War I, were added the newly formed giant utilities, American and Foreign Power and ITT. Others like Firestone and General Motors made their first moves abroad in the 1920s.

An additional reason why National City chose to keep its branches open may have been the Harding administration's concern that closure of all U.S. foreign bank branches might harm U.S. trade. On the concern of the Commerce Department see the letter from G. Edwards (secretary, Public Relations Commission, American Bankers Association) to Julius Klein (director, U.S. Department of Commerce), July 28, 1922; Klein to Herter (Memorandum), August 1, 1922, National Archives, Record Group 151, Decimal File 612: Latin America.

33. Other U.S. banks with foreign branches in the 1920s included Guaranty Trust with eight, First National Bank of Boston with four, and Chase National Bank with three. By the end of the 1920s the banks that had joined together to form foreign banking corporations to operate foreign branches had abandoned these efforts. See Cleona Lewis, *America's Stake in International Investments* (Menasha, Wis.: George Banta Publishing, 1938), p. 197.

34. For a description of the prewar system of international finance in the United Kingdom see A. S. J. Baster, *The Imperial Banks* (London: P. S. King and Son, 1929; rpt. New York: Arno Press, 1977); A. S. J. Baster, *The International Banks* (London: P. S. King and Son, 1925); and Leland Rex Robinson, "British Banking: Foreign Policies of the 'Big Five' Banks," *Acceptance Bulletin*, October 1923, pp. 4–10.

35. Joseph Sykes, *The Amalgamation Movement in British Banking, 1825–1924* (London: P.S. King and Son, 1926).

36. Robinson, "British Banking," pp. 4–10.

37. Benjamin H. Beckhart, *The New York Money Market*, ed. Benjamin H. Beckhart, vol. 3, *Uses of Funds* (New York: Columbia University Press, 1932), pp. 321–323. See also "Rulings of the Federal Reserve Board," *Federal Reserve Bulletin*, 10 (1924): 638, and 13 (1927): 860. These rulings particularly affected cotton shipments to Germany. In *Uses of Funds*, Beckhart also discusses the substitution of acceptance credits for the drop in capital exports to Germany in 1928 and 1929 (pp. 324–325). Beckhart also reviews the growth of the U.S. acceptance market in the 1920s (pp. 310–329).

38. American Acceptance Council, *Facts and Figures relating to the American Money Market* (New York: American Acceptance Council, 1931), p. 86. The *Acceptance Bulletin* ranked National City first among banks in the United States as issuers of outstanding acceptances at the end of the years 1927 and 1928. In 1928 National City had $98.8 million in acceptances outstanding, or 7.7 percent of the total volume of $1,284 million given by the *Acceptance Bulletin*.

39. Beckhart, *Uses of Funds*, pp. 370–371.

40. Joseph H. Durrell, who headed the bank's Cuban branches during the 1920s and later the whole overseas operation, commented in a memoir in 1940: "The indirect asset that accrues to the Bank by reason of its ability to negotiate the bills of its clients and those of its competitors at reasonable rates at all times is more than considerable. This is only made possible by the carrying of positions.

"I am wondering if the Board [of directors of the bank] is aware that foreign exchange profits have always been the principal source of the income of the branches, and of the important part they have played in the Head Office P&L over the years." "Foreign Branches," p. 222.

41. Ibid., p. 224.

42. Ibid., pp. 117–120.

43. Comptroller of the Currency, *Annual Report, 1921* and *Annual Report, 1929* (Washington, D.C.: GPO, 1922 and 1930).

44. National City Bank, *Annual Report, 1928*.

45. As a correspondent, National City retained much of its prewar appeal: It was a large, strongly capitalized bank, so that its deposits seemed to be safer compared to those of other banks. Moreover, through its securities affiliate, National City could offer correspondents a complete investment service as well (cf. chapter 5).

After the 1921 recession a change in Federal Reserve policy helped promote National City's domestic correspondent bank business. During the 1920s the Federal Reserve System developed the doctrine that "continuous indebtedness at the reserve banks, except under unusual circumstances, is an abuse of reserve bank facilities." Federal Reserve Board, *Annual Report, 1928* (Washington, D.C.: GPO, 1929), p. 8. To borrow from a Federal Reserve bank became, not a right of membership, but a privilege that the Reserve bank could cancel without notice. In fact, borrowing from the Federal Reserve bank came to be regarded as a sign of weakness, something a bank should avoid, if possible. As a result, banks throughout the country continued to maintain a large proportion of their portfolio in liquid assets that could be used as secondary reserves. For the smaller banks, these included balances at other banks and marketable securities. On the adjustment of bank portfolios and the increased role of securities see Pearson Hunt, *Portfolio Policies of Commercial Banks in the United States, 1920–1939* (Boston: Harvard University, Graduate School of Business Administration, Bureau of Business Research, 1940).

During the 1920s the use of securities as secondary reserves prompted the development of the "shiftability" theory of bank liquidity, in which each individual bank could remain liquid through investments in securities, since these could be quickly and easily sold in the market with relatively small transactions costs to raise needed funds. Thus, securities holdings would provide liquidity to the individual bank, although not liquidity to the entire banking system. Cf. Waldo F. Mitchell, *The Uses of Bank Funds* (Chicago: University of Chicago Press, 1925), p. 3.

46. On corporate financial policy in the 1920s see Neil H. Jacoby and Raymond J. Saulnier, *Business Finance and Banking* (New York: National Bureau of Economic Research, 1947), pp. 71–166; Albert R. Koch, *The Financing of Large Corporations* (New York: National Bureau of Economic Research, 1943); Lauchlin J. Currie, "The Decline of the Commercial Loan," *Quarterly Journal of Economics*, 45 (1930–1931): 698–709.

47. National City Bank, Executive Managers, Minutes, September 23, 1920, February 14, 1921.

48. National City Bank, Comptroller's Report, 1928.

49. "The Servant of Business," *Number Eight*, February 1922, facing p. 1.

50. Donaldson Brown (vice president, General Motors) to M. L. Prensky (treasurer, General Motors), January 17, 1922, Stettinius MSS, University of Virginia, Charlottesville. See also Alfred P. Sloan, Jr., *My Years with General Motors* (Garden City, N.Y.: Doubleday, 1964), pp. 121–124.

51. National City Bank, *Twenty-fifth Anniversary of Transcontinental Banking Service* (New York: National City Bank, 1953).

52. On the call money market in the 1920s see Bartow Griffiss, *The New York Call Money Market* (New York: Ronald Press, 1925); Beckhart, *Uses of Funds*, pp. 1–211. During the 1920s call loans remained the nearest approximation to a liquid, risk-free, interest-bearing asset available in the marketplace. Although Treasury securities were free from default risk, they were chiefly long-term bonds, subject to interest-rate risk and not as liquid as call loans. The short-term Treasury bill was not introduced until 1929.

The bankers' acceptance, which the Federal Reserve had hoped to develop into a replacement for the call loan, never developed into a market where the bank or its customers could invest temporarily idle balances. The major reason for this was the Federal Reserve's discount policy. With discount rates set below market rates for much of the 1920s, there was little incentive for commercial banks to invest in acceptances. Consequently, an active market in acceptances never developed. Cf. Beckhart, *Uses of Funds*, pp. 409–462. In addition, the London discount market recovered much of its prewar vitality. After 1918 rates in London dipped below those in New York, so that while New York gained ground, the volume of acceptances in the London market was more than double the volume outstanding in New York. See Paul P. Abrahams, *The Foreign Expansion of American Finance and Its Relationship to the Foreign Economic Policies of the United States, 1907–1921* (New York: Arno Press, 1976), p. 90.

A third alternative to call loans, the Federal funds market, was in its infancy. Cf. Parker B. Willis, *The Federal Funds Market: Its Origin and Development* (Boston: Federal Reserve Bank of Boston, 1970), pp. 1–21.

53. In January 1929 Mitchell commented to National City's shareholders that "the danger to every period of prosperity lies in the development of overconfidence and a consequent tendency to unwise use of credit." National City Bank, *Annual Report, 1928*. A month later the bank referred in its economic bulletin to a special responsibility of the New York banks for the stability of the money market. "New York bankers . . . know from experience that they cannot be indifferent to conditions in the call loan market, even if their own commitments there are comparatively small. Every banker finds it important to take account of his contingent liabilities—that is, of all conditions which may create demands upon him—and the New York bankers know the vicissitudes of the call money market. They know that in an emergency that market and the entire stock exchange entourage will be on their door step begging for help and they cannot view with indifference the growth of dangerous possibilities with which they feel they might be unable to deal." *Monthly Economic Letter*, February 1929, p. 22.

54. Letter to Seward Prosser (chairman, Clearing House Committee), July 18, 1928, Archives, New York Clearing House, New York City. Mitchell proposed, and the Clearing House approved, a substantial increase in the minimum service

charge on loans placed for the account of others in the hope that it would lessen "the zeal of lenders who have no business in the market." The service charge proved an insufficient deterrent to the practice of placing loans for the account of others when in early 1929 interest rates in the call money market rose far above the interest-rate ceilings established by the members of the Clearing House. The Clearing House banks still refused to raise the rates paid on deposits. Rather than abandon their cartel-like behavior in an increasingly competitive environment, they merely bemoaned the 'irresponsibility' of other lenders.

55. Friedman and Schwartz, *Monetary History*, pp. 254–266, and Elmus R. Wicker, *Federal Reserve Monetary Policy, 1917–1933* (New York: Random House, 1966), pp. 129–143. As the stock market continued to rise in late 1928 and early 1929 criticism mounted in Congress and the country at large that "speculation" was diverting credit away from the "legitimate" needs of commerce. The plight of the farmer was attributed, not to the depressed price of his goods relative to manufactures, but to his inability to obtain credit. That Wall Street itself was financing new investment through a record volume of new bond and equity issues counted for nought in the debate. Neither did the thought that record earnings might be the reason for record stock prices.

56. Benjamin Strong to Owen D. Young (vice chairman, Federal Reserve Bank of New York), August 18, 1928, Archives, Federal Reserve Bank of New York, New York City. In light of the subsequent controversy, Strong's reasons for choosing Mitchell are of interest. The choice for Class A Director, Strong wrote, "probably narrows down to Mitchell of the City or Wiggin of the Chase. As to the latter, I am opposed to his election. The reasons for it I shall not recount, but they are ample and convincing and conclusive to me.

"As to Mitchell, I have a high regard for him. He is truly one of the ablest of our bankers. You probably know his characteristics as well as I do. For a long time he was a very bitter critic of what we were doing. The influence of some of my friends outside of the bank has been quietly exerted to educate him a bit as to our policy and philosophy . . . For the last year Mitchell has been much more reasonable . . .

"On the whole, I think he is my choice . . . The real point of this letter is to express my conviction that if Mitchell should be elected it would be best at the outset to have a very frank understanding with him on two points. One is that so long as he is a member of the board of directors he should be willing to accept the decision of the directors in all matters and not indulge in outside criticism but be loyal to the majority of his associates. I am convinced that a nice talk with him on this subject would insure that such would be the case, and it is not so much the need for having an understanding in advance as it is to avoid any possibility of misunderstanding in advance, and the distinction in Mitchell's case is important. The other point is as to the inevitable influence which his knowledge of what we are doing may exert upon his policy in running the City Bank. This is one of the oldest problems in central banking. How can a director who is interested in the other side of all banking problems be disinterested and impartial in his attitude in the Reserve bank as well as in his own bank, not take an unfair advantage of his confidential knowledge, and steer a clear course in a very delicate situation. Charlie Mitchell is one of these fellows who faces the facts honestly, and I think it can be discussed with him frankly and no possibility of misunderstanding rises."

57. Cited in Friedman and Schwartz, *Monetary History*, p. 260. According to the *New York Times*, March 29, 1929, Mitchell's bank would loan this sum "rather than permit a complete demoralization of the money market." John Kenneth Galbraith, *The Great Crash* (Boston: Houghton Mifflin, 1979, 50th anniversary edition), pp. 37–39, notes that by the end of trading on March 26, "money rates had eased and the market had rallied. The Federal Reserve remained silent, but now its silence was reassuring. It meant that it conceded Mitchell's mastery."

This statement reverses the actual situation. Mitchell acted with the foreknowledge and approval of George L. Harrison, governor of the Federal Reserve Bank of New York. When interest rates began to climb, Harrison telephoned Mitchell, stating that "in circumstances . . . bordering on the 'panicky' the Federal Reserve did not want and could not be in the position of arbitrarily refusing loans on eligible paper to member banks." Harrison told Mitchell, "the call money market was now the problem of the New York money market, that is the member banks and the private bankers." Memorandum of March 29, 1929, Conversations, vol. I, regarding events of March 26, 1929, Harrison MSS, Columbia University, New York (hereafter cited as Harrison MSS).

58. Friedman and Schwartz, *Monetary History*, pp. 260–261. Charles S. Hamlin, a member of the Federal Reserve Board, recorded in his diary (March 29, 1929) that "none of the Board criticized what Mitchell did—it was merely what he said." Hamlin MSS, Library of Congress, Washington, D.C.

59. *New York Times*, March 29, 1929, and March 30, 1929. Mitchell did not reply to Glass.

60. Senators George W. Norris and Duncan U. Fletcher joined Carter Glass's denunciation of Mitchell. *New York Times*, March 30, 1929. The coauthor of the Federal Reserve Act, ex-Senator Robert L. Owen, defended Mitchell for his aid to the market. *New York Times*, March 31, 1929. See also Cedric B. Cowing, *Populists, Plungers, and Progressives* (Princeton: Princeton University Press, 1965), pp. 187–188.

61. March 30, 1929, p. 1968.

62. "Crisis and Calm," March 30, 1929.

63. *Number Eight*, October 1925, p. 4.

64. *Time*, April 8, 1929.

65. *Number Eight*, March 1928, p. 1.

8. The Financial Department Store (II), 1921–1929

1. United States, Internal Revenue Service, *Statistics of Income, 1922–1929* (Washington, D.C.: GPO, 1923–1930).

Taxes also increased the importance of the smaller individual investor. A federal income tax had been instituted in 1916. Since Liberty bonds were at least partially exempt from income tax, they tended to gravitate into the portfolios of wealthier individuals and corporations, who found the tax-exempt feature attractive. As a consequence, corporate borrowers looked increasingly to the small investor for capital, rather than to the wealthy, to whom they would have had to pay higher rates in order to compete on an after-tax basis with government bonds. In 1919, Paul Warburg, a partner in the investment-banking house of Kuhn, Loeb, summed up the consequences for the securities distribution business: "Where heretofore investment banking addressed itself primarily to the comparatively few possessed of large incomes, taxation today strikes so heavily at the revenues and inheritances of the so-called well-to-do classes, and interferes so drastically with the accumulation of investment funds on their part, that successful distribution of large volumes of new securities can only be carried on by following wealth into the millions of small rivulets and channels into which it now flows, and where it is less subjected to the exactions of the tax-collector." Cited in Vincent P. Carosso, *Investment Banking in America: A History* (Cambridge, Mass.: Harvard University Press, 1970), p. 238.

2. National City Bank, "Lectures to Banking III Class, Lecture by C. E. Mitchell, March 18, 1919.

3. Ibid.

4. Ibid. Regarding the influence of the Liberty Loan campaigns on the development of investment banking see Carosso, *Investment Banking*, p. 226. It should be stressed that the National City Company's market was far narrower than that for Liberty bonds. What the City Company learned from the Liberty bond campaigns was the technique of mass marketing. The Guaranty Trust Company also attributed much of its success in the underwriting field to the Liberty bond campaigns. W. Nelson Peach, *The Security Affiliates of National Banks* (Baltimore, Md.: Johns Hopkins University Press, 1941), p. 33.

5. National City Company, *What You Should Know about Investment* (New York: National City Company, 1920).

6. Ibid.

7. National City Company, *Putting Your Dollars to Work*, 2nd ed. (New York: National City Company, 1928).

8. Charles E. Mitchell, "Investing for Independence," *Women's Home Companion*, November 1919, p. 150.

9. National City Company, *Putting Your Dollars to Work*.

10. Ibid.

11. National City Company, *Putting Your Dollars to Work*, 1st ed. (New York: National City Company, 1926).

12. National City Company, *Over a Century of Railroading* (New York: National City Company, 1929). Regulatory considerations also influenced this change. The McFadden Act of 1927 codified the investment-banking powers of national banks, formally recognized their security affiliates, and authorized the comptroller of the currency to determine what securities affiliates might underwrite. Although the comptroller ruled that banks themselves could underwrite only debt issues, he granted affiliates the power to underwrite equity issues as well. Cf. Edwin J. Perkins, "The Divorce of Commercial and Investment Banking: A History," *Banking Law Journal*, 88 (1971): 494n.

13. Benjamin Graham and David L. Dodd, *Security Analysis: Principles and Technique*, 2nd ed. (New York: Whittlesey House, 1940), pp. 17–30, describes the intrinsic value approach.

14. National City Bank, "Lectures to Banking III Class," Lecture by C. E. Mitchell, March 18, 1919.

15. Based on issues of U.S. corporate and foreign bonds, the leading originators of securities in the 1920s were J. P. Morgan and Company ($4.8 billion), Kuhn, Loeb ($2.8 billion), Harris, Forbes ($2.2 billion), the National City Company ($2.2 billion), and Dillon, Read ($2.2 billion). Cf. Terris Moore, "Security Affiliates versus Private Investment Banker—A Study in Security Origination," *Harvard Business Review*, 34 (1934): 480–481. For a history of investment banking in the 1920s see Carosso, *Investment Banking*, pp. 240–299; Arthur Galston, *Security Syndicate Operations: Organization, Management, and Accounting* (New York: Ronald Press, 1928). The City Company's strategy resembles the backward integration strategy later employed by retail-oriented firms in the 1960s and 1970s. Cf. Samuel L. Hayes III, "The Transformation of Investment Banking," *Harvard Business Review*, 79 (1979): 154–155.

16. George Whitney (partner, J. P. Morgan and Company), Testimony, U.S. Temporary National Economic Committee, *Investigation of Concentration of Economic Power*, pt. 23 (Washington, D.C.: GPO, 1940), pp. 11872–85, 11893–903, 12210–14. Until 1924, participants in the originating group received a one percent commission on sales to the syndicate. Thereafter, J. P. Morgan and Kidder, Peabody together took one-eighth of one percent as a managers' commission fee, leaving seven-eighths of one percent to be divided among the others in the originating group. Ibid., p. 12215.

17. On the bankers' agreement of 1914 see Thomas W. Lamont, "Discussion of Financial Administration, Budget, and Tax Rate," in *The Government of the City of New York* (New York: New York State Constitutional Convention Commission, 1915), pp. 160–164. In the interim between 1914 and 1918, the city agreed to finance non-revenue-producing improvements through a combination of fifteen-year bonds and one-year notes to be repaid from the following year's tax revenues. Cf. also *Municipal Year Book of the City of New York, 1916* (New York: Municipal Reference Library, 1917), pp. 53–54.

New York's net debt rose from $237.4 million in 1898 (the year of the consolidation of Manhattan and the outer boroughs into Greater New York) to $942.2 million at the end of 1914. Cf. Herbert H. Lehman, ed., *The Finances and Financial Administration of New York City* (New York: Columbia University Press, 1928), pp. 337–338.

18. On the development of international lending in the 1920s see Derek H. Aldcroft, *From Versailles to Wall Street, 1919–1929* (Berkeley: University of California Press, 1977), pp. 239–267; Douglass C. North, "International Capital Movements in Historical Perspective," in *U.S. Private and Government Investment Abroad*, ed. R. F. Mikesell (Eugene: University of Oregon Books, 1962); Cleona Lewis, *America's Stake in International Investments* (Washington, D.C.: The Brookings Institution, 1938), pp. 367–397.

19. Peacetime restrictions on capital movements were first imposed in 1919–1920 and were most severe from the middle of 1924 to the end of 1925. Later a duty on bearer bonds, relatively high interest rates, and the higher cost of floating issues in London combined to make the New York market extremely attractive to

foreign borrowers. D. E. Moggeridge, "British Controls on Long-term Capital Movements, 1924–1931," in *Essays on a Mature Economy: Britain after 1840*, ed. Donald N. McCloskey (Princeton: Princeton University Press, 1971), pp. 113–125; John M. Atkin, *British Overseas Investment, 1918–1931* (New York: Arno Press, 1977), pp. 28–75, 154–155.

20. Until 1927 France imported rather than exported capital. The government retained the right to pass on all foreign bond issues and exercised it quite vigorously in defense of the franc and the interests of French manufacturers and bondholders, and in order to promote French foreign policy. In addition, the heavy losses sustained by French investors on Imperial Russian bonds made them wary of new foreign issues. As a consequence of these economic and political factors, few new issues were floated on the Paris market for non-French borrowers during the 1920s. Cf. Paul Einzig, *The Fight for Financial Supremacy* (London: Macmillan, 1931), pp. 59–65.

21. Cited in Herbert Feis, *The Diplomacy of the Dollar: First Era, 1919–1932* (Baltimore, Md.: Johns Hopkins University Press, 1950), p. 6.

22. For a discussion of U.S. policy with respect to inter-Allied debt see Harold G. Moulton and Leo Pasvolsky, *War Debts and World Prosperity* (Washington, D.C.: The Brookings Institution, 1932), pp. 71–108. Prior to the entry of the United States into World War I, private lending to the Allies amounted to over $2.5 billion. The federal government then took over this function, lending $7.1 billion from April 1917 to November 1918 and another $3.3 billion after the war. U.S. Congress, Senate Special Committee Investigating the Munitions Industry, *Munitions Investigation: Supplemental Report on the Adequacy of Existing Legislation*, 74th Cong., 2nd sess., 1936, S. Rep. 944, pt. 6, pp. 2, 6, 123.

23. Cf. Feis, *Diplomacy of the Dollar*; George W. Edwards, "Government Control of Foreign Investments," *American Economic Review*, 18 (1928): 684–701; Jacob Viner, "Political Aspects of International Finance," *Journal of Business*, 1 (1928): 141–173, 324–363; John Foster Dulles, "Our Foreign Loan Policy," *Foreign Affairs*, 5 (1926–1927): 33–48.

24. Cited in Feis, *Diplomacy of the Dollar*, p. 11. The policy originated in response to a bond issue for the French government to be floated in the spring of 1921. The newly elected Harding administration did not look with favor on Europe's securing credit to aid its own industries at a time when American firms were suffering through a severe recession and when European governments, France foremost among them, had not made arrangements to repay their wartime debts to the United States. If credits to foreign governments were to be granted at all, the administration thought that the loans should be tied to the purchase of U.S. goods.

President Harding, therefore, invited a group of bankers to meet with him and the secretaries of state (Hughes), the treasury (Mellon), and commerce (Hoover) in order to discuss the proper role of credit to foreign nations. Among the bankers in attendance were Charles E. Mitchell, J. P. Morgan, Jr., Paul Warburg (Kuhn, Loeb), and Benjamin Strong (Federal Reserve Bank of New York). *Commercial and Financial Chronicle*, May 28, 1921, pp. 2247–48.

The cabinet members suggested policies that reflected the interests of their respective departments. Hoover wished the bankers to submit foreign loans to his department for a review of their quality as financial investments and their impact on American business. Mellon suggested that bankers refrain from making loans to nations that had not funded their intergovernmental debts. Hughes took a positive attitude toward bankers' loans to foreign governments, particularly since he thought they might paper over the complex tangle of reparations and Allied debts. But Hughes also wished to reserve to the State Department the right to advise against loans that it felt not to be in the national interest. Cf. Betty Glad, *Charles Evans Hughes and the Illusion of Innocence* (Urbana: University of Illinois Press, 1966), pp. 304–306; Feis, *Diplomacy of the Dollar*, pp. 7–9. On Hoover's position see Herbert Hoover, *The Memoirs of Herbert Hoover* (New York: Macmillan, 1951–1952), II, 85.

The bankers took the practical standpoint that the promotion of U.S. exports depended on Europe's ability to pay, and that in turn depended on Europe's access to the credit needed to reconstruct its industries. *Commercial and Financial Chronicle*, May 28, 1921, p. 2248. Thus each of the parties to the negotiation, bankers and cabinet members alike, took a position consistent with his own self-interest and each alleged his position to be not only consistent with the national interest but positively conducive to it.

Ultimately, the bankers and the administration reached a compromise along the lines suggested by Secretary Hughes. The bankers agreed to inform the State Department about contemplated public offerings of bonds in the United States so that the department might indicate whether it objected to a particular issue. But the State Department did not set the criteria on which it would judge a new issue, and these ultimately came to reflect the wishes of other departments.

In 1925 the Treasury Department gained formal acceptance of its view that "it was contrary to the best interests of the United States to permit foreign governments which refused to adjust or to make a reasonable effort to adjust their debts to the United States to finance any portion of their requirements" in the United States. The ban included national governments, political subdivisions, and private enterprises. U.S. Treasury, *Annual Report, 1925* (Washington, D.C.: GPO, 1926), p. 54.

25. Dulles, "Foreign Loan Policy," p. 33. Dulles also notes that the government had no statutory authority for the bond review policy. Viner, "Political Aspects," p. 169, makes this point as well.

26. In March 1922 all issuers of foreign loans to be sold to the public were told to ascertain the attitude of the State Department in writing before concluding the transaction. The comments of the State Department took one of three forms on the loan applications: (1) "the Department, in the light of the information at hand, offers no objection to the proposed transaction"; (2) "the Department is not in a position, therefore, to say that there is no objection to the proposed transaction"; or (3) "the Department is unable to view the proposed financing with favor at this time." Feis, *Diplomacy of the Dollar*, pp. 11–12.

At first, the State Department took extreme care to avoid giving the impression that its failure to object to an issue implied in any way a positive assessment of its merits as an investment. The State Department announced it would not "pass upon the merits of foreign loans as business propositions nor assume any responsibility whatever in connection with loan transactions." Ibid., p. 11. In sum, the

U.S. government thought that capital invested abroad "should conduct its own diplomacy, select its own assignments and make its own terms." Ibid., p. 6.

Nevertheless, it is doubtful that the government was entirely successful in this regard, for during the course of the 1920s economic as well as political considerations came to play a role in determining the attitude of the United States government toward a foreign issue. For example, it refused to allow issues financing foreign monopolies of raw materials and other commodities such as coffee. Inevitably, once such economic considerations came to play a role, passing the government's review process seemed to imply that the loan had the government's stamp of approval as an investment. Dulles, "Foreign Loan Policy," p. 44. In 1932 during hearings before the Senate Finance Committee, Francis White, assistant secretary of state, agreed with a statement of Senator Edward P. Costigan that "the practice of the State Department in passing upon certain foreign transactions has led the general public to assume that the security is ample and the investment is a good one." U.S. Congress, Senate Committee on Finance, *Sale of Foreign Bonds or Securities in the United States: Hearings Pursuant to S. Res. 19,* pt. 3, 72nd Cong., 1st sess., 1932, p. 1911.

In at least one instance government officials themselves adopted the notion that the government "approved" foreign bonds for issues in the United States. Cf. U.S. Department of State, *Papers relating to the Foreign Relations of the United States, 1925* (Washington, D.C.: GPO, 1940), I, 533-534.

27. For a survey of German economic history during the 1920s see Karl Hardach, *The Political Economy of Germany in the Twentieth Century* (Berkeley: University of California Press, 1980), pp. 16-52. For a broader perspective on the problem of postwar reconstruction see Aldcroft, *Versailles to Wall Street,* pp. 78-155; Charles S. Maier, *Recasting Bourgeois Europe: Stabilization in France, Germany, and Italy in the Decade after World War I* (Princeton: Princeton University Press, 1975); Stephen A. Schuker, *The End of French Predominance in Europe: The Financial Crisis of 1924 and the Adoption of the Dawes Plan* (Chapel Hill: University of North Carolina Press, 1976).

28. "Europe as Seen through the Eyes of Our Chief," *Number Eight,* December 1922, pp. 1-3.

29. In July 1922 the German government asked for a moratorium on reparations payments under the Treaty of Versailles until the end of 1924. Charles G. Dawes, who was later awarded a Nobel Peace Prize for his efforts, served on a committee charged with remedying Germany's financial distress. The Dawes Plan became operative September 1, 1924. See Moulton and Pasvolsky, *War Debts,* pp. 161-186.

30. Charles Evans Hughes (secretary of state) to Dwight Morrow (partner, J. P. Morgan and Company), n.d., Hughes MSS, Library of Congress, Washington, D.C.

31. National City Bank, *Monthly Economic Letter,* August 1924, p. 117.

32. The Dawes Plan provided that one billion gold marks were to be paid in 1925, with gradual increases up to 2.5 billion gold marks after five years. The Dawes committee had concluded that once the economic situation in Germany had stabilized, the German government would be able to meet a standard annuity of 2.5 billion marks. Moulton and Pasvolsky, *War Debts,* pp. 162-163, list the

four sources of revenue assigned to service the debt: (1) interest and amortization charges on German railway bonds; (2) interest and amortization charges on German industrial debentures; (3) the transport tax; and (4) the budget profit, out of which the receipts from customs duties, the alcohol monopoly, and the taxes on tobacco, beer, and sugar were specifically designated.

33. U.S. Congress, *Sale of Foreign Bonds*, pt. 1, after p. 162.

34. See U.S. Congress, *Sale of Foreign Bonds*, pt. 1, after p. 162, for data on National City Company originations on behalf of German borrowers.

35. Both Japan and China wished access to American capital in order to develop the Chinese mainland. The United States government wished development to occur under Chinese rather than Japanese auspices, but was unwilling to provide intergovernmental loans itself. Instead, it had consistently encouraged American banks to do so of their own accord and for their own account. With branches in both China and Japan, National City sought to negotiate a course between the conflicting aims of these two countries that would not antagonize the government of the United States.

In the revolutionary chaos following the overthrow of the Manchu dynasty in China (1911), Japan largely succeeded in its aim of subjecting China to its supervision. From the beginning of World War I Japan aggressively sought to extend its influence in China, most notably through the ultimatum of 1915 known as the Twenty-one Demands, in which Japan laid claim to broad economic and political powers in Manchuria and Shantung, the former German sphere of influence in China. In addition, Japan extended its colonization efforts from Korea to Manchuria.

Japanese actions in China directly contravened the United States policy of the Open Door first enunciated by Secretary of State John Hay in 1899. This policy advocated a free and independent China, strong enough to withstand the foreign powers who were trying to carve up China into separate spheres of influence. World War I effectively removed the European powers from the Far East, and Japan sought to exploit the resulting power vacuum to its own advantage. Japan's China policy inflamed the anti-Japanese sentiment present in California and other western states and strengthened American sympathy for China. In fact, part of the opposition in the United States to the Versailles Treaty resulted from its award of the Chinese province of Shantung to Japan. Cf. Richard Storry, *A History of Modern Japan* (Hammondsworth, England: Penguin, 1970), pp. 151–156; James E. Sheridan, *China in Disintegration: The Republican Era in Chinese History, 1912–1949* (New York: Free Press, 1975), p. 51; W. W. Willoughby, *Foreign Rights and Interests in China*, new ed. (Baltimore, Md.: Johns Hopkins University Press, 1927), I, 67–106.

36. *The Consortium* (Washington, D.C.: Carnegie Endowment for International Peace, 1921); Dulles, "Foreign Loan Policy," p. 40.

37. Feis, *Diplomacy of the Dollar*, p. 34.

38. Ibid.

39. Ibid., pp. 35–36; U.S. Department of State, *Papers relating to the Foreign Relations of the United States, 1923* (Washington, D.C.: GPO, 1938), II, 507–509.

40. James W. Angell, *Financial Foreign Policy of the United States* (New York, 1933; rpt. New York: Russell and Russell, 1965), pp. 63–84.

41. Peach, *Security Affiliates*, p. 88.

42. Ibid., p. 20.

43. Charles E. Mitchell, Testimony, U.S. Congress, Senate Subcommittee of the Committee on Banking and Currency, *Operation of the National and Federal Reserve Banking Systems*, 71st Cong., 3rd sess., 1931, p. 302.

44. From November 30, 1925, to September 30, 1929, the National City Company's profits are estimated to have been $25.3 million. This figure equals the change in the City Company's stockholders' equity (capital, surplus, undivided profits, and reserves) plus dividends paid minus increases in capitalization from new stock issues. Comptroller of the Currency, Examination Report, National City Bank, November 1925 and September 1929.

45. On the development of the trust business during the first three decades of the twentieth century see James Gerald Smith, *The Development of Trust Companies in the United States* (New York: H. Holt, 1928), pp. 340–390.

46. The Federal Reserve Act authorized national banks to perform trust functions if this did not contravene state or local law. Some trust companies contended that this provision of the Federal Reserve Act was unconstitutional, an argument that was later rejected by the Supreme Court. In September 1918 Congress amended the Federal Reserve Act to confirm the right of national banks to exercise fiduciary powers. This law was also challenged, but it too was upheld by the Supreme Court, in 1924. Cf. Edwin McInnis, *Trust Functions and Services*, 2nd ed. (Washington, D.C.: American Institute of Banking, 1978), pp. 16–17.

47. Smith, *Development of Trust Companies*, p. 357, cites $50,000 as the minimum profitable trust size.

48. National City Bank, "Trust News," March 30, 1929, cites estimates of Joseph F. McCoy, actuary of the U.S. government, based on the federal estate tax laws of 1927. Estates of over $50,000 amounted to $3.5 billion, or about 70 percent of the total.

49. *Number Eight*, May 1929, pp. 11–12.

50. Smith, *Development of Trust Companies*, pp. 365–370, relates that lawyers and trust companies viewed each other as competitors in the field of personal trust administration. Only after 1920 did cooperation between the two groups develop, after a meeting between the New York State Bar Association and the Trust Company Division of the American Bankers Association. The trust companies drew up forms by which a client could analyze his financial position and from which an attorney could draw a will suited to the client's needs. National City provided a similar service through its "estate survey." The practice of referring all legal work in the administration of an estate to the client's personal attorney became quite common and did much to eliminate the friction between the two groups.

51. National City Bank, "Trust News," April 13, 1929.

52. Smith, *Development of Trust Companies*, p. 376, notes that the insurance trust was first developed in 1877 but came to be widely used only in the mid-1920s. Title to the proceeds of the insurance became vested in the trust company upon the death of the creator of the trust and the funds were thus immediately available to meet the expenses of administering the total estate. In addition, there were certain tax advantages associated with the insurance trust.

In the funded insurance trust the client created a living trust into which he deposited some of his securities portfolio. The interest and dividend income of this portfolio was used to pay the premiums of a life insurance policy. Thus, the client's estate would consist of the value of the securities originally deposited plus the proceeds of the insurance policy. Cf. Smith, *Development of Trust Companies*, pp. 70–71; City Bank Farmers Trust Company, "Trust News," July 2, 1929.

53. Comptroller of the Currency, *Annual Report, 1928* (Washington, D.C.: GPO, 1929), lists the assets of individual trusts under management by national banks as of October 3, 1928, at $3.3 billion.

54. National City Bank, Comptroller's Report, 1928.

55. Gilbert T. Stephenson, *Reflections of a Trustman* (New York: n.p., 1960), p. 265. The original plan is described in a booklet by Edgar L. Smith, *Investment Trust Funds* (New York, 1927). See also James H. Perkins, "The Uniform Trust," *Number Eight*, February 1930, pp. 3–6.

56. *Number Eight*, March–April 1929, pp. 1–5, 22.

57. National City Bank, *Annual Report, 1929* (New York: National City Bank, 1930).

58. "Troubles of Mitchell," *Time*, November 18, 1929, p. 45.

59. *Time*, April 8, 1929.

60. Mitchell, Testimony, U.S. Congress, *Operation of the National and Federal Reserve Banking Systems*, p . 318.

9. Into the Abyss, 1930–1933

1. Milton Friedman and Anna J. Schwartz, *A Monetary History of the United States, 1867–1960* (Princeton: Princeton University Press, 1963), pp. 712–713. Figure in text is for M1, the narrowly defined money supply (currency in circulation plus demand deposits at commercial banks). Broader measures of the money supply fell by similar percentages. M2 (M1 plus time deposits at commercial banks) fell by 38 percent between October 1929 and March 1933. All figures are seasonally adjusted. For a survey of alternative theories of the causes of the Great Depression see Derek H. Aldcroft, *From Versailles to Wall Street, 1919–1929* (Berkeley: University of California Press, 1977), pp. 268–284. For a discussion of the depression's global aspects see Charles P. Kindleberger, *The World in Depression, 1929–1939* (Berkeley: University of California Press, 1973). Throughout this chapter the word *depression* will refer to the years 1929–1933.

2. Lester V. Chandler, *America's Greatest Depression, 1929–1941* (New York: Harper and Row, 1970), p. 27; Solomon Fabricant, *Profits, Losses, and Business Assets, 1929–1934* (New York: National Bureau of Economic Research, 1935), p. 2.

3. U.S. Bureau of the Census, *Historical Statistics of the United States: Colonial Times to 1970* (Washington, D.C.: GPO, 1975), ser. X510–515.

4. During the depression the City Company functioned primarily as a broker and dealer for securities in the secondary market. Although it managed to earn a small operating profit from these activities, it suffered tremendous capital losses on its holdings of securities. These losses were extraordinarily large, for at the end of the 1920s the City Company had embarked on a policy of acquiring "from time to time for short or long term investment account, bonds, stocks or equity inter-

ests, the holding of which will facilitate the development of its regular business or generally inure to the benefit of the Bank and the Company." *Number Eight*, March 1928, p. 1. In the context of the depression, this policy proved disastrous.

The first investment made by the City Company under this new policy had been the acquisition in 1927 of the General Sugar Corporation, the holding company for the Cuban sugar properties that the bank had taken over in 1921 (see chapter 6). As they had in 1922, Mitchell and Rentschler believed in 1927 that the Cuban sugar industry was fundamentally sound, and that an economic recovery would restore General Sugar to a prosperous condition. Thus, it seemed to make sense to await the recovery before selling it. As Rentschler commented in November 1929, "We are not content to liquidate it [General Sugar] until such time as we can get its fair worth, and as uncertainty continues in the sugar industry, that cannot be done." U.S. Congress, Senate Subcommittee of the Judiciary Committee, *Lobby Investigation*, 71st Cong., 1st sess., 1929, p. 1338. This was still the policy at the beginning of 1931. To the shareholders Mitchell stated that "we are prepared to support this investment until, with the inevitable turn of the agricultural cycle, a normal degree of prosperity asserts itself, and [it] can be disposed of to advantage." National City Bank, *Annual Report, 1930* (New York: National City Bank, 1931).

The market for Cuban sugar did not revive. To protect their own producers, the United States and other consuming countries raised tariffs on sugar imports. Prices on the world market dropped further, hitting Cuba's producers particularly hard. Although producing nations attempted to restore some order to the world sugar market, they could not reverse the slide in income suffered by General Sugar and other Cuban sugar mills. At the end of 1931 Mitchell and his directors recognized the loss involved, and wrote down the City Company's investment in General Sugar from $25 million to $1. National City Bank, *Annual Report, 1931* (New York: National City Bank, 1932).

With its other long-term investments, the City Company fared almost as badly. In the late 1920s it had made equity investments in a number of industrial and railroad enterprises for its own account. These long-term investments probably strengthened National City's relationships with corporations for which it was underwriting bonds, and the investments also pushed the overall National City organization a step further toward becoming a universal bank, along the lines of the great German banks.

Mitchell professed to be unconcerned by the drop in the prices of these stocks that accompanied the depression. At the beginning of 1931, he thought that their "intrinsic value" had changed little and that "in the light of the inactive and more permanent character of this portfolio, the day-to-day market quotations are not of controlling importance." National City Bank, *Annual Report, 1930*. Nonetheless, Mitchell abandoned the City Company's policy of making long-term investments for its own account. At the beginning of 1931 he stated that the company would henceforth limit its operations "principally to the purchase and prompt distribution of investment securities." Ibid. Mitchell expected that business to be profitable, since "a large amount of new and refunding financing of the highest character awaits the return of public confidence." National City Bank, *Annual Report, 1931*.

5. Howard Brubaker, "Of All Things," *New Yorker*, March 11, 1933.

6. On the behavior of the currency to deposit ratio during the depression see Friedman and Schwartz, *Monetary History*, pp. 332–350; James M. Boughton and Elmus R. Wicker, "The Behavior of the Currency-Deposit Ratio during the Great Depression," *Journal of Money, Credit, and Banking*, 11 (1979): 405–418.

7. Mellon is quoted in "How Is Business?" by Isaac Marcosson, *Saturday Evening Post*, April 14, 1928, pp. 6–7.

8. John Kenneth Galbraith, *The Great Crash 1929* (Boston: Houghton Mifflin, 1955), p. 119.

9. Ibid., p. 125. In a letter to the governors of the other Federal Reserve banks dated November 27, 1929, Harrison described the New York Reserve Bank's policy. "The very sudden and drastic liquidation in the stock market, accompanied by the calling of loans for out-of-town banks and others, naturally resulted in a tremendous shift in loans to our own member banks just at a time when the stock market itself was weakest and the mechanical apparatus of the exchange was taxed to its utmost. Our particular problem was to endeavor to maintain an easy money position throughout the whole period lest any evidence of a shortage of funds or an increase in money rates might lead to some sort of a money panic. If we should have added to the panicky state of mind relating to security values any fear of a money shortage, we might indeed have faced the most serious calamity. With this in mind, we kept our discount window wide open and let it be known that member banks might borrow freely to establish the reserves required against the large increase in deposits resulting from the taking over of loans called by others. In addition to this we went into the market, as you know, and bought large blocks of government securities, partly for psychological reasons but largely because we felt it so important that there should be no tightening of money during the period of such large transfers of loans to our own member banks. As we look back now, it is not at all unlikely that had we not bought governments so freely, thus supplementing the reserves built up by large additional discounts, the stock exchange might have had to yield to the tremendous pressure brought to bear upon it to close on some one of these very bad days the last part of October." Correspondence, Harrison MSS.

10. Friedman and Schwartz, *Monetary History*, p. 339. During the crash National City was one of the banks most active in supplying credit to the call money market. It took over from its customers the loans that it had placed for their account and credited the customer's demand deposit account. The resulting increase in deposits raised required reserves and led National City to borrow from the Federal Reserve. This activity reached a peak on October 29 and 30.

In the week ending October 30, 1929, National City increased its demand loans to brokers and dealers by $121 million, or 12 percent of the increase at all New York City weekly reporting member banks. Net nonbank demand deposits and interbank deposits rose more that $320 million, or 15 percent of the rise at other New York City banks. National City Bank, Daily Statement Book; Board of Governors, Federal Reserve System, *Banking and Monetary Statistics, 1914–1941* (Washington, D.C.: GPO, 1943), pp. 174, 498.

11. *New York Times*, September 19, 1929. In May 1929 the Corn Exchange Bank had converted itself from a state-chartered bank to a state-chartered trust

company. Concerning Vanderlip's plans to merge National City with the Corn Exchange see chapter 5, note 1.

12. *New York Times.*

13. New York State, Superintendent of Banks, *Annual Reports, 1922–1928* (Albany: New York State Banking Department, 1923–1929).

14. *Number Eight*, September-October 1929, p. 1. The cash option was required by a provision of the McFadden Act concerning the rights of shareholders of a state-chartered bank participating in a merger with a national bank.

15. Stock quotations are from the *New York Times.*

16. U.S. Congress, Senate Committee on Banking and Currency, *Stock Exchange Practices: Hearings on S. Res. 84 and S. Res. 239*, 72nd Cong., 1st and 2nd sess., 1933, p. 1811. During the crash other executives also bought stock in their own companies to stabilize its price. For example, A. P. Giannini attempted to support the price of Transamerica stock during the October 1929 crash, using corporate rather than personal funds for the purpose. See Marquis James and Bessie R. James, *Biography of a Bank: The Story of the Bank of America N.T. and S.A.* (New York: Harper and Bros., 1954), p. 302.

Some executives sold their company's stock short, profiting personally from the crash. A prominent example was Albert H. Wiggin, president of Chase National Bank. Between September 19 and December 11, 1929, Wiggin made over $4 million by selling Chase stock short. U.S. Congress, *Stock Exchange Practices*, Report (1934), pp. 188ff. Ferdinand Pecora, the counsel for the Senate Banking Committee, later wrote that Mitchell was "a heroic and laudable figure," who "at least went down with his ship in the hour of crisis," while Wiggin put "business . . . before sentiment" and "loyalty to [his] institution." *Wall Street under Oath* (New York: Simon and Schuster, 1939), p. 154.

17. National City observed in its *Monthly Economic Letter* of December 1929, "New conditions which had developed since the two bodies had formulated the plan had made the plan inequitable, inconsistent with the real purpose upon which the directors were agreed, impracticable of consummation and against the public interest at the time."

18. Diary, November 12, 1929, Hamlin MSS, Library of Congress, Washington, D.C.

19. Ibid., November 11 and 12, 1929.

20. Ibid., November 12 and 14, 1929. The directors of the bank strongly supported Mitchell. In a press release they stated, "In no sense or degree can the action of the National City shareholders be considered as an absence of confidence in or criticism of the official management or direction of the Bank. There is abundant assurance that the shareholders approved of the plan under the conditions which existed when the negotiations between the Boards were completed and the plan was prepared for submission. Proxies favorable to the plan were received from the holders of two-thirds of the shares, but after the new conditions had developed so many of these were withdrawn that less than two-thirds of the outstanding shares were represented at the meeting. No dissension has existed between the official management and the directors, or between the official management and directors on the one hand and the shareholders on the other. There has been no shadow of basis for any reports to that effect." *Number Eight*, December 1929, p. 16.

21. The total resources of National City Bank on December 31, 1929, were $2.21 billion (National City Bank, Statement of Condition, December 31, 1929), slightly ahead of those of the Midland Bank (£445.8 million, or $2.17 billion at the rate of exchange for that date). See *Bankers' Almanac and Yearbook, 1930–1931* (London: Thomas Skinner, 1930), p. 2429.

22. National City Bank, Comptroller's Report, 1929.

23. National City Bank, *Annual Report, 1929* (New York: National City Bank, 1930).

24. *New York Times*, March 19, 1930, announced the merger of Chase National Bank with Equitable Trust Company and the Interstate Trust Company, making the combined institution the world's largest bank. For the background to this merger, see Arthur M. Johnson, *Winthrop W. Aldrich: Lawyer, Banker, Diplomat* (Boston: Division of Research, Graduate School of Business Administration, Harvard University, 1968), pp. 99–106.

25. Friedman and Schwartz, *Monetary History*, pp. 340–341, note that high-powered money (bank reserves plus currency in circulation) declined despite an increase in the Federal Reserve's gold stock and its holdings of government securities. Discount policy was the reason. Although the Federal Reserve Bank of New York reduced its discount rate in six steps from 6 percent to 2.5 percent from November 1929 to June 1930, the difference between the discount rate and the market rate (renewal rate on call loans) actually narrowed. This reduced the profitability of borrowing at the discount window and led to a sharp decline in the volume of member bank borrowing during the first half of 1930.

26. National City Bank, Comptroller's Report, 1930.

27. National City Bank, *Annual Report, 1930*.

28. Friedman and Schwartz, *Monetary History*, pp. 309–311, ascribe "especial importance" to the failure of the Bank of United States. It "was the largest commercial bank, as measured by volume of deposits, ever to have failed up to that time in U.S. history. Moreover, though an ordinary commercial bank, its name had led many at home and abroad to regard it somehow as an official bank, hence its failure constituted more of a blow to confidence than would have been administered by the fall of a bank with a less distinctive name. In addition, it was a member of the Federal Reserve System. The withdrawal of support by the Clearing House banks from the concerted measures of the Federal Reserve Bank of New York to save the bank—measures of a kind the banking community had taken in the past—was a serious blow to the System's prestige."

29. Manufacturers Trust, Public National Bank and Trust, and International Trust were scheduled to merge with the Bank of United States on November 23, 1930, with J. Herbert Case of the Federal Reserve Bank of New York as chairman. The merger scheme collapsed according to Jackson E. Reynolds, president of the First National Bank and of the New York Clearing House Association (Oral History, Columbia University, p. 146), because of the "theory of relativity among three groups of stockholders who each wanted a larger piece of the melon than the other two were willing to accord, with the result that if you had put all their extreme views together you would have about 150 percent of a melon instead of one melon."

30. At a meeting of the board of directors of the Federal Reserve Bank of New York on December 18, 1930, Governor George L. Harrison stated that "the Re-

serve Bank had been working for a year or more to improve conditions in the Bank of United States . . . Perhaps we did not go far enough, but we did go as far as we felt we could legally go." Earlier in the same meeting, Harrison had pointed out that the Federal Reserve's powers were limited: "banks whose management is not considered satisfactory cannot be disciplined by the Reserve Bank, unless there are proven violations of the banking laws, and if any suggestions are made to the management by the officers of the Reserve Bank, without proof of such violations, a bank of that type is likely to decline to submit to the suggestions. The law would have to be changed before we could exercise regulation of member banks at all comparable to that exercised by the Clearing House Association." Minutes, December 18, 1930, Harrison MSS. The Bank of United States was not a member of the Clearing House Association.

31. Reynolds, Oral History, p. 148, recalled that the Clearing House would "arrange to pay every depositor 50 percent of his deposit upon the assignment of his claim against the bank with the proviso that to whatever extent realization of assets exceeded . . . 50 percent, we would turn such excess over to the depositor but we would not make any demand for any deficiencies of the 50 percent. This limited our liability, but at the same time, helped relieve the anxiety of the thousands of depositors."

32. Friedman and Schwartz, *Monetary History*, p. 311, state that the Bank of United States ultimately paid off 83.5 percent of its adjusted liabilities. But these repayments stretched out over fourteen years. Moreover, repayments did not exclusively result from the liquidation of the failed bank's assets. Under the double liability clause of the state banking law, stockholders of the Bank of United States were required to pay to the receiver the par value of their stock in order to help defray the depositors' claims.

Despite this record, there were differences of opinion regarding the solvency of the Bank of United States at the time of its failure. The New York State banking superintendent, who had primary responsibility for examining and supervising it, considered it solvent. Ibid., p. 310n. Bankers asked to buy stock in or support the Bank of United States took a more skeptical view. They were concerned about its large portfolio of real estate loans, especially those to the bank's real estate affiliate. For example, Jackson Reynolds adamantly opposed the suggestion that the New York Clearing House banks take over the Bank of United States. M. R. Werner, *Little Napoleons and Dummy Directors, Being the Narrative of the Bank of United States* (New York: Harper, 1933), recounts the history of the Bank of United States and examines its real estate operations in some detail. He comes to the conclusion that the bank's loans to affiliates and real estate subsidiaries were "so great that any institution that took over these loans would be compelled to guarantee transactions of doubtful profit to the extent of many millions of dollars" (p. 213). Later, the executives of the Bank of United States were tried and convicted on charges that they had violated various banking laws. This record weakens the inference made by Milton Friedman and Rose Friedman, *Free to Choose* (New York: Avon, 1981), p. 73, that anti-Semitism may have prompted New York Clearing House bankers to let the Bank of United States fail. But it in no way weakens the major point made by Friedman independently and together with Anna Schwartz, namely, that the failure of the Bank of United States contributed greatly to the severity of the banking panic of 1930 and severely weakened the prestige of the Federal Reserve System.

33. Cited in Friedman and Schwartz, *Monetary History,* p. 310n.

34. After the failure of the Bank of United States, the directors of the Federal Reserve Bank of New York acknowledged its adverse impact on public confidence in banks and in the willingness and ability of the Federal Reserve to stop bank failures. In a meeting of the board on December 18, 1930, Mitchell commented that "permission to use the phrase, 'Member of the Federal Reserve System', in the advertising of a bank, was almost as misleading to the public as was the name, 'Bank of United States', as the use of this phrase in advertising seems to imply a guarantee of safety." Another director said that he believed "the general public had been under the impression that a member bank could not fail; that the System was designed to prevent bank failures."

In a subsequent meeting (January 5, 1930) Owen D. Young, chairman of General Electric and vice chairman of the Federal Reserve Bank of New York, noted that there was considerable doubt concerning the Federal Reserve's legal authority to extend credit to a failing bank, and that this limited the Reserve Bank's ability to act. But the public knew little of these legal constraints. According to Young, "a large body of public opinion believed the Federal Reserve System to have great authority which it had not used to the full to correct an unsound banking situation." Minutes, December 18, 1930, and January 5, 1931, Harrison MSS.

35. Friedman and Schwartz, *Monetary History,* pp. 308–313. Elmus Wicker, "A Reconsideration of the Causes of the Banking Panic of 1930," *Journal of Economic History,* 40 (1980): 571–584, questions the Friedman-Schwartz hypothesis that the Bank of United States failure was the key event in the 1930 banking panic. Wicker ascribes the central role to the earlier (November 1930) failure of Caldwell and Company, a holding company with interests in commercial and investment banking and insurance. Wicker demonstrates that a large proportion of the 1930 failures were related to the failure of Caldwell and Company. Wicker ascribes only local significance to the failure of the Bank of United States, an opinion in accord with that of Jackson Reynolds (Oral History, p. 150). Eugene N. White, "A Reinterpretation of the Banking Crisis of 1930," *Journal of Economic History,* 44 (1984): 119–138, also contends that the failure of the Bank of United States was not especially significant.

Regardless of whether the Bank of United States or Caldwell was the precipitating event, the banking panic of late 1930 changed "the monetary character of the contraction." Friedman and Schwartz, *Monetary History,* p. 308. Starting in November 1930 the ratio of deposits to currency began to decline.

36. Friedman and Schwartz, *Monetary History,* pp. 311, 316–317.

37. Quoted in "To Keep Banks from Failing," *Literary Digest,* February 21, 1931, pp. 5–6.

38. On the Smoot-Hawley Tariff Act see Allan H. Meltzer, "Monetary and Other Explanations of the Start of the Great Depression," *Journal of Monetary Economics,* 2 (1976): 459–461. At the time National City Bank was primarily concerned about the tariff's adverse impact on U.S. exports. But it did not believe that significant harm would result. *Monthly Economic Letter,* July 1930, pp. 111–112. On the perverse effect of the standstill agreements see Stephen V. O. Clarke, *Cen-*

tral Bank Cooperation, 1924–1931 (New York: Federal Reserve Bank of New York, 1967), p. 186.

39. Immediately after the plight of the Credit-Anstalt became known, the Austrian National Bank injected $14 million in additional capital into the institution and issued a guarantee of its deposits, in order to calm fears regarding the Austrian currency. Foreign banks, including National City, agreed to renew their short-term claims on the Credit-Anstalt at maturity. But to make this play for financial stability, the Austrian National Bank itself required access to credit from abroad. According to one plan, a consortium of private commercial banks in the United States, the United Kingdom, and France would have provided substantial lines of credit to the Austrian National Bank and the Austrian government. National City indicated its willingness to take a 14 percent participation ($1 million) in the American share of the loan. National City Bank, Executive Committee, Minutes, June 16, 1931, June 23, 1931. When France set political conditions on its participation, the Bank of England extended the entire credit itself, rather than let the crisis assume greater dimensions. See Clarke, *Central Bank Cooperation*, pp. 186–189.

As of October 9, 1931, credits to Austrian borrowers at National City totaled over $2 million. This included only Head Office claims, all of which were short-term. Comptroller of the Currency, Examination Report, National City Bank, October 9, 1931.

40. For an in-depth study of the German crisis, see E. W. Bennett, *Germany and the Diplomacy of the Financial Crisis, 1931* (Cambridge, Mass.: Harvard University Press, 1962). See also Clarke, *Central Bank Cooperation*, pp. 189–201.

41. The BIS was a product of the negotiations that resulted in the Young Plan, which scaled down the German reparations payments as scheduled under the terms of the Dawes loan of 1924. The BIS was established to assume the administrative functions pertaining to Germany's reparations payments. Under the Dawes Plan the receipt and distribution of reparations was the responsibility of the transfer committee of the agent general of reparations payments. The committee absorbed the exchange risk. Under the Young Plan, Germany was to accept this risk, and the BIS was to facilitate the transfer process. In effect the BIS was to serve as a clearinghouse for the central banks of recipient countries so that the transfer payments could be effected with a minimum disturbance to the exchange markets. The BIS was also charged with the responsibility of arranging the public funding of the reparations debt and handling the administration of German requests for postponement of its annual payments.

It was also anticipated that the BIS would promote international financial cooperation. But its own resources were too small to cope with major problems, as the international financial crises of the early 1930s demonstrated. Moreover, the Federal Reserve Board did not join other central banks in forming the BIS. The administration feared that membership in the BIS would conflict with U.S. insistence on the separation of Germany's reparations obligations from the obligations of the Allies to repay their war debts to the United States. Clarke, *Central Bank Cooperation*, pp. 20, 47, 147, and National City Bank, *Monthly Economic Letter*, July 1929, pp. 101–103, and February 1930, p. 26.

42. Bennett, *Financial Crisis*, p. 222; Minutes, July 13, 1931, Harrison MSS. The standstill agreement was formalized on September 17, 1931.

43. Comptroller of the Currency, Examination Report, National City Bank, October 9, 1931. The $57 million figure mentioned in the text comprised $52.6 million in short-term claims and $4.7 million in securities. These figures refer only to Head Office credits to German borrowers and Head Office holdings of German securities. The figures exclude claims of the branches and the claims of the Bank of America (New York), which National City acquired as part of the merger. After the merger with Bank of America, National City's total claims on German borrowers may have exceeded $80 million, or about 15 percent of the total German debt held by New York City banks. Bennett, *Financial Crisis*, p. 137.

44. *New York Times*, July 17, 1931, and August 21, 1931; National City Bank, Comptroller's Report, 1931.

45. Friedman and Schwartz, *Monetary History*, pp. 316–319, 345–347.

46. The founders of the Bank of America, like those of City Bank, also hoped to fill the void left by the demise of the First Bank of the United States (cf. chapter 1). For the first half century of its existence the Bank of America was one of New York's leading banks. It was one of the original three "pet" banks designated by President Jackson and one of the original members of the New York Clearing House Association. After 1860 its prominence in the New York financial community began to wane. It remained a state bank, but it did not immediately take advantage of the opportunity to branch when New York State liberalized the banking law in 1898. By 1914 the Bank of America had become a "solid yet stuffy" institution. See Donald L. Kemmerer, *Life of John E. Rovensky* (Champaign, Ill.: Stipes Publishing, 1977), pp. 138–139.

In 1920 it sought a new lease on life by merging with the Franklin Trust Company of Brooklyn. Its young president, Edward C. Delafield, became the head of the combined institution, which had a total of six offices in Manhattan and Brooklyn, offering complete commercial banking and trust services. Although the Bank of America experienced severe losses in 1921 in connection with loans on Cuban sugar and other commodities, it not only paid dividends in excess of earnings but also continued its merger program. Kemmerer, *Rovensky*, p. 139. In 1922 it acquired the Atlantic National Bank, and in 1923 the Battery Park Bank. During the mid-1920s the eight-branch Bank of America caught the eye of Ralph Jonas, the hard-driving head of the Manufacturers' Trust Company. Rather than merge with Jonas, Delafield looked for a white knight through the offices of J. P. Morgan and Company. After Delafield and Morgan succeeded in blocking Jonas's right to vote his stock in the Bank of America, Jonas sold his interest, which was a controlling one, to A. P. Giannini's Bancitaly Corporation (February 1928). Giannini voted the shares, took control of the Bank of America, but retained Delafield as president. As one of his first acts Giannini converted the Bank of America into a national bank (March 1928). Then Giannini merged two other Bancitaly interests, the Bowery and East River National Bank and the Commercial Exchange Bank, into the Bank of America (April 1928). This more than doubled the New York–based Bank of America's total resources to $407 million.

At the end of 1928 Bancitaly Corporation became Transamerica, a name in keeping with Giannini's plans for a nationwide banking system. On the West Coast, Giannini was following the same procedure with the Los Angeles–based Bank of America and the Bank of Italy, the institution he had founded in 1904. In

September 1930 the Bank of Italy was merged into the California–based Bank of America, making it the third largest bank in the country. In 1929 Transamerica started to branch out into other financial services, imitating the trend toward department store finance initiated by National City and others. The New York–based Bank of America merged with Blair and Company, an investment house. The head of Blair, Elisha Walker, became head of Bancamerica–Blair Corporation, the security affiliate of the Bank of America (N.Y.). At the start of 1930, Giannini stepped down as chairman of Transamerica and handed control over to Walker. Walker began to move away from banking, and Transamerica acquired Occidental Life Insurance Company (March 1930) and General Foods (April 1930). Cf. James and James, *Biography of a Bank*, pp. 270–316.

47. New York Clearing House Association, *Condition of National Banks in the City of New York* (New York, 1931); Board of Governors, Federal Reserve System, *Banking and Monetary Statistics, 1914–1941*, pp. 73, 75.

48. *New York Times*, October 20, 1931.

49. James and James, *Biography of a Bank*, pp. 330–331.

50. Donald P. Jacobs, *The Impact of Examination Policies on Commercial Bank Lending Policies* (Washington, D.C.: GPO, 1964), suggests that examiners may have forced weak banks into insolvency by applying overly strict standards. In 1931 the comptroller of the currency ruled that national banks would not have to depreciate bonds fully except in the case of defaulted issues, and not at all if the bonds fell into the four highest-quality classifications for examination purposes. But if the full depreciation of all bonds plus losses on other assets exceeded capital, then the bank had to mark all its bonds to market. State examiners generally followed suit. Cf. Friedman and Schwartz, *Monetary History*, pp. 319n, 330n. For a general discussion of examination practices in the depression, see George J. Benston, *Bank Examination* (New York: New York University Graduate School of Business Administration, 1973), pp. 32–36.

Two effects of this bond valuation policy are worth mentioning. The first was an attempt in mid-1932 to raise the price of bonds by forming pools. This was intended to improve the balance sheets of banks and savings banks that had invested heavily in bonds. At the suggestion of the Federal Reserve Bank of New York, twenty leading New York banks formed the American Securities Investing Corporation in June 1932 "to make a profit out of the purchase of bonds for the 'long pull.' " Thomas W. Lamont of J. P. Morgan was president of the company, and Mitchell served as one of its directors. *New York Times*, June 4, 1932. Like the National Credit Corporation, on which it was modeled, the American Securities Investing Corporation had little effect in the long run. A similar corporation, the Commodities Credit Corporation, was established in August 1932 at the suggestion of Eugene Meyer, governor of the Federal Reserve Board, to help support the price of raw materials. National City also participated in this corporation. National City Bank, Executive Committee, Minutes, August 23, 1932.

The second and more serious effect was the erroneous belief that banks' investment in bonds had caused widespread bank failures. A Federal Reserve study (Federal Reserve Committee on Branch, Group, and Chain Banking, *225 Bank Suspensions: Case Histories from Examiners' Reports* [Washington, D.C.: GPO, 1932]) concluded that investment in low-grade bonds had contributed significantly to the failure of banks in the depression. This conclusion was widely shared, and helped lay the foundation for the Banking Act of 1933, which separated commercial and investment banking (see chapter 10).

This conclusion is not correct. The depression, not banks' investment in bonds, caused bank failures. The depression reduced the value of both loans and investments, reducing banks' net worth. It was merely easier to measure the depreciation in banks' bond accounts than in their loans, since bonds generally traded on a secondary market and could therefore be readily priced. Depreciation in other assets, such as loans, may have been equal to or greater than that in the bond account, but it was more difficult to measure, and unnecessary to measure if the bond depreciation was sufficient to exhaust net worth. Thus, in an accounting sense, there may have been many causes for the widespread bank failures.

51. Minutes, September 28, 1931, Harrison MSS.

52. James S. Olson, *Herbert Hoover and the Reconstruction Finance Corporation, 1931–1933* (Ames: University of Iowa Press, 1977), pp. 24–32. See also Albert V. Romasco, *The Poverty of Abundance: Hoover, The Nation, the Depression* (New York: Oxford University Press, 1965), pp. 87–96; Gerald D. Nash, "Herbert Hoover and the Origins of the Reconstruction Finance Corporation," *Mississippi Valley Historical Review,* 46 (1959–1960): 455–468.

53. Minutes, September 28, 1931, Harrison MSS. In part, the reluctance of the banks to lend and invest may have been attributable to their perception that the Federal Reserve would not be able to come to their aid, even if it promised to do so. The Federal Reserve's own resources were becoming strained. The run on the dollar was depleting its stock of "free gold" and this might have impaired its ability to discount.

The Glass-Steagall Act of 1932 addressed this concern. It made government securities purchased by Reserve banks eligible as collateral for Federal Reserve notes, increasing the amount of free gold and the ability of the Federal Reserve to conduct open market operations. Unfortunately, the Federal Reserve made only limited use of this power. The Glass-Steagall Act also broadened the collateral eligible for rediscount at the Federal Reserve to include government securities, making it easier for banks to discount. See Friedman and Schwartz, *Monetary History,* pp. 400–406.

54. Minutes, October 5, 1931, Harrison MSS.

55. Ibid.

56. National City Bank, Executive Committee, Minutes, November 4, 1931. Mitchell feared that once the plan had been publicized, it would "boomerang" if it failed to raise the necessary capital. Minutes, October 15, 1931, Harrison MSS. In early November 1931 National City and the other New York Clearing House banks subscribed the suggested 2 percent of their net demand and time deposits to the notes of the National Credit Corporation. Mitchell even suggested that the New York banks might find it necessary to double their subscription to the new corporation, although in his opinion the plan "should not be permitted to raise any doubts as to the position of the New York banks." Minutes, October 5, 1931, Harrison MSS. The New York banks also agreed to increase their direct loans to correspondent banks as a supplement to the work of the National Credit Corporation. Minutes, October 13, 1931, Harrison MSS.

57. For an evaluation of the work of the National Credit Corporation see Olson, *Hoover and the RFC*, p. 30. One of the few loans made by the National Credit Corporation was to the California–based Bank of America. James and James, *Biography of a Bank*, pp. 337–338. The National Credit Corporation addressed the symptoms of the depression, not its causes. It attempted to shift credit, not to create money. Although the announcement of the plan coincided with and possibly contributed to the decline in bank failures starting in mid-October 1931, the plan had virtually no impact on the fundamental cause of the depression, the failure of the Federal Reserve to expand reserve bank credit. Unlike the Aldrich-Vreeland associations, the National Credit Corporation did not directly lead to the creation of high-powered money. Nor did it liberate existing reserves, as did the Clearing House certificates employed in pre-1914 panics.

58. Comptroller of the Currency, Examination Report, National City Bank, October 9, 1931; National City Bank, *Annual Report, 1931*.

59. March 6, 1933, p. 48.

60. National City Bank, *Annual Report, 1932* (New York: National City Bank, 1933). Mitchell made these remarks on January 10, 1933.

61. At the time of the resolution, Garner was vice president–elect as well as Speaker of the House of Representatives. During the run on the banks in Michigan in February 1933, Garner stated, "I have contended consistently that there has been too much secrecy about what has been going on in the last twelve months. If the truth scares people, let it come. Let the people know all about everything the government does." See Jesse H. Jones with Edward Angly, *Fifty Billion Dollars: My Thirteen Years with the RFC, 1932–1945* (New York: Macmillan, 1951), pp. 82–83.

62. Joseph A Broderick (superintendent of banks, New York State) to Herbert H. Lehman (governor, New York State, Letter, December 14, 1935, Lehman MSS, Columbia University, New York. In a memorandum accompanying the letter Broderick wrote: "The last stage of the prolonged banking crisis which culminated in the nation-wide moratorium on March 4, 1933, may be said to have dated from January 26, 1933 with the publication by the House of Representatives of the list of financial institutions, to which loans had been made by the Reconstruction Finance Corporation, together with the amount of advances (and commitments) to each of such institutions. The proposed publication had been protested by banking organizations and supervisory authorities. We had telegraphed our objections to Speaker Garner and to the New York Representatives. We felt the publication would undermine confidence in a large number of institutions that had availed themselves of the loaning privileges of the Corporation, and it would bring a feeling of uncertainty and unsettlement in the communities which such institutions served. In fact, we stated in our opinion that the effect would prove disastrous. The effect of the widespread publicity was even worse than had been expected as subsequent developments showed."

63. "When All the Banks Closed," *Harvard Business Review,* 48 (1948): 129.

64. *The First New Deal* (New York: Harcourt, Brace and World, 1966), p. 134.

65. National City Bank, Daily Statement Book, February 1, 1933, February 23, 1933.

66. National City Bank, *Monthly Economic Letter*, April 18, 1929 (Special Edition), p. 64A. Mitchell later testified that he had written much of this particular issue himself. See U.S. Congress, *Stock Exchange Practices*, p. 1817.

67. Before 1931, *Saturday Evening Post* featured numerous laudatory articles about banks and bankers. See, for example, "The Freelance Allies of Wall Street," December 29, 1928, p. 20.

68. Lloyd W. Mints, *A History of Banking Theory in Great Britain and the United States* (Chicago: University of Chicago Press, 1945), p. 5, states that the real bills doctrine is "unsound in all its aspects," and is "utterly subversive of any rational attack on the problem of monetary policy." In 1803 Henry Thornton demonstrated the falsity of the real bills doctrine. In *An Enquiry into the Nature and Effects of the Paper Credit of Great Britain* (rpt. New York: Augustus Kelley, 1965), Thornton showed that at each stage of its production and distribution a commodity could be sold, creating a real bill. Thus, a single commodity could generate several "real bills." Regulating the quality of bank credit by restricting bank lending to real bills would not therefore guarantee economic stability, for it could not regulate the quantity of money in circulation.

69. U.S. Congress, Senate Subcommittee of the Committee on Manufactures, *Hearings on the Establishment of a National Economic Council*, 71st Cong., 1st sess., 1931, pp. 525–526.

70. Ibid., p. 526.

71. Ibid.

72. Ibid., pp. 528–529.

73. *Congressional Record*, 75, pt. 6 (March 15, 1932), p. 6052. The hearings on which Johnson based his remarks are available in U.S. Congress, Senate Committee on Finance, *Sale of Foreign Bonds or Securities in the United States: Hearings Pursuant to S. Res. 19*, 72nd Cong., 1st sess., 1932.

According to Johnson, the State Department was also to blame for the debacle. Its foreign bond review process (see chapter 8) lulled investors into a false sense of security. As Johnson put it, "the ordinary American, laboring still under the delusion that he participated by virtue of his citizenship in the Republic and that his Government would protect his interests as well as those of international bankers, fondly believed that if the State Department had no objection to his purchase of foreign securities his rights had been safeguarded. How his credulity was imposed upon, and how illusory was his belief concerning the protecting arm of his Government, his present plight demonstrates." *Congressional Record*, 75, pt. 6 (March 15, 1932), p. 6053.

This prompted a response from presidential candidate Franklin D. Roosevelt, who promised that if he were elected, it would no longer "be possible for international bankers or others to sell foreign securities to the investing public of America on the implied understanding that these securities have been passed on or approved by the State Department or any other agency of the Federal Government." Cited in Herbert Feis, *The Diplomacy of the Dollar* (Baltimore, Md.: Johns Hopkins University Press, 1950), p. 14.

74. See for example Peter T. Kilborn, "From Binge to Bust: The Legacy of the Crash," *New York Times*, September 23, 1979; Joel Seligman, *The Transformation*

of Wall Street: A History of the Securities and Exchange Commission and Modern Corporate Finance (Boston: Houghton Mifflin, 1982), pp. 23–37.

A scholarly study of the issue is Ilse Mintz, *Deterioration in the Quality of Foreign Bonds Issued in the United States, 1920–1930* (New York: National Bureau of Economic Research, 1951). Mintz examined the bonds originated by eleven banking houses for foreign governments (excluding Canada) during the years 1920 to 1930. Their bonds accounted for well over half of all (non-Canadian) foreign issues offered in the United States during those years. Mintz only considered the originations of each house, on the theory that the originating house undertakes the research and negotiates the terms and is therefore responsible for the issue.

Mintz clearly demonstrated that a higher proportion of the bonds issued during the years 1925 to 1930 ultimately went into default than bonds issued in the years 1920 to 1924. From this finding Mintz concluded that the quality of foreign bonds deteriorated during the 1920s. In addition, Mintz noted that the spread between yields on foreign bonds and domestic corporate Aaa bonds declined. From this she inferred that investors were not aware of the decline in the quality of foreign bonds. Finally, she implied that investment bankers were either unwilling or unable to make their customers aware of this decline. This allegedly promoted the acquisition of unsound assets by individuals and banks and contributed to the severity of the depression in the United States.

A study by Lawrence Fisher, "Determinants of Risk Premiums on Corporate Bonds," *Journal of Political Economy*, 67 (1959): 217–237, suggests a different and, we believe, more plausible hypothesis regarding the decline in the risk premium on foreign bonds than that provided by Mintz. The steady economic growth of the 1920s increased the stability of countries' income and export earnings, and lengthened the period of solvency. As more foreign bonds were underwritten, their marketability increased. These factors reduced the risk premium. In fact, each foreign bond probably improved in quality, in the sense that the factors determining risk diminished. Investors were aware of these factors and were offered prospective compensation for the risks they assumed.

Fisher's study shows that the risk premium on corporate bonds is inversely proportional to the stability of a firm's earnings, the length of its solvency record, its equity-to-debt ratio, and the marketability of its bonds (as measured by their outstanding value). Differences in the elasticity of the risk premium with respect to these factors were not statistically significant for cross-sectional regressions run for the years 1927, 1932, 1937, 1949, and 1953. This finding is not consistent with the hypothesis that investors in the 1920s had become less risk averse. If the market for foreign bonds in the 1920s operated similarly to that for domestic corporate bonds, then the decline in the risk premium on foreign bonds observed by Mintz may be explained by the improvement in foreign countries' economic conditions, rather than by reduced risk aversion on the part of investors.

Another possible cause of the decline in the risk premium was the U.S. government's preflotation review procedure (see chapter 8). Although the State Department asserted that this was a purely political process, its failure to object to the issue of a bond came to be interpreted as a sign of its approval of the bonds as investments. (See above, note 73, and chapter 8, note 26.) If held by investors, this would have lowered the risk, as perceived by investors, of foreign bonds floated in the United States.

75. *Moody's Foreign and American Government Securities, 1928* (New York: Moody's Investors Service, 1928), pp. ix, 715. This was written in late 1927. Professor Edwin Kemmerer, a Princeton University economist who acted as a consultant on monetary and fiscal issues for numerous countries during the 1920s, stated that Moody's manual was "used widely by investors in reaching decisions in regard to the purchase of bonds." U.S. Congress, *Sale of Foreign Bonds*, p. 1716.

76. *Moody's Foreign and American Government Securities, 1930* (New York: Moody's Investors Service, 1930), p. 905. This was written in November 1929. For an economic history of Peru during this period see Rosemary Thorp and I. G. Bertram, *Peru, 1890–1977* (London: 1978), pp. 112–115, 338–341.

77. U.S. Congress, *Sale of Foreign Bonds*, p. 1715. The report stated, "While this [Peru's internal and external funded debt] represents a heavy burden for a country in the position of Peru, it is less than that of many other countries similarly situated, and, when viewed in the light of actual and potential resources of the nation over a period of years, with normal world economic conditions and with political and social stability at home, it does not appear to be beyond the capacity of Peru to handle."

More generally, the Senate and later commentators also ignored the adverse impact on foreign bond prices of the Hoover administration's reversal of "dollar diplomacy," under which the United States had intervened militarily in Latin America to protect the interests of American holders of Latin American bonds. Cf. Alexander de Conde, *Herbert Hoover's Latin American Policy* (Stanford, Calif.: Stanford University Press, 1951), pp. 64–65.

78. Cf. Benjamin Klein and Keith B. Leffler, "The Role of Market Forces in Assuring Contractual Performance," *Journal of Political Economy*, 89 (1981): 615–641.

79. National City Company, *Foreign Dollar Bonds* (New York: National City Company, 1927), p. 6.

80. National City Company, *Sound Bonds of Foreign Governments* (Montreal: National City Company of Canada, 1925), p. 3. Victor Schoepperle (vice president, National City Company during the 1920s; after 1933, vice president, National City Bank), "Future of International Investment: Private versus Public Foreign Lending," *American Economic Review*, 33 (1943) Supplement: 337, makes a similar point.

81. *New York Times*, December 6 and 7, 1928.

82. C. W. Calvin (National City Company representative in Lima) to Ronald M. Byrnes (vice president, National City Company) (Memorandum on Peruvian government financing), December 3, 1925. Reported in U.S. Congress, *Stock Exchange Practices*, pp. 2103. This memorandum was inserted into the record of the Pecora hearings at the request of Victor Schoepperle, a vice president of the National City Company.

Calvin's support for Peruvian financing was not unqualified. He noted, "I do not and would not suggest the consideration at this time of making loans to Peru upon the unsecured obligations of the Government, but with designated revenues specifically set aside to guarantee the service of loans effected and provisions whereby such revenues would be paid direct to the Lima branch of our institution by the collecting agencies." U.S. Congress, *Stock Exchange Practices*, p. 2104. Such safeguards were in fact included in the 1927 issue underwritten by Seligman with the participation of the National City Company.

83. U.S. Congress, *Stock Exchange Practices*, p. 2102; *Moody's Foreign and American Government Securities, 1930*, pp. 901–906; National City Company, *Foreign Dollar Loans* (London: National City Company, 1928), pp. 84–85; William H. Wynne, *State Insolvency and Foreign Bondholders: Selected Case Histories of Governmental Foreign Bond Defaults and Debt Readjustments* (New Haven, Conn.: Yale University Press, 1951), pp. 186–187; U.S. Congress, *Sale of Foreign Bonds*, pp. 1706, 1742–45.

84. Other countries whose bonds had terms comparable to those of Peru and also rated A by Moody's were Italy, Finland, Chile, Colombia, and Uruguay. Bond prices used to calculate yields to maturity are from *Commercial and Financial Chronicle*, December 17, 1927.

85. *Moody's Foreign and American Government Securities, 1933* (New York: Moody's Investors Service, 1933), p. a–15.

86. Wynne, *State Insolvency and Foreign Bondholders*, p. 191.

87. A market is said to be efficient when prices fully reflect all available information. Thus it is fair to both buyers and sellers. Cf. Eugene F. Fama, "Efficient Capital Markets: A Review of Theory and Empirical Work," *Journal of Finance*, 25 (1970): 383–417.

88. See Henry C. Wallich, "The Future of Latin American Dollar Bonds," *American Economic Review*, 33 (1943) Supplement: 321–322.

89. U.S. Congress, *Stock Exchange Practices*, p. 785. Mitchell's reply refers specifically to the decline in Anaconda stock and was in response to a question from counsel for the committee.

90. "An Old Fashioned Banker," July 2, 1932, pp. 3–4.

91. "A Brief for the Bankers," September 1932, p. 20.

92. Pecora, *Wall Street under Oath*, p. 71.

93. January 2, 1933, p. 27.

94. *New York Times*, February 23, 1933. Senator Wheeler spoke on national radio on February 25, 1933, repeating what he said on the Senate floor three days earlier. Mitchell was by no means unique among Wall Street bankers. Thomas S. Lamont, a Morgan partner, sold stock to his wife at a loss on December 30, 1930, lending her the money to buy it. On April 8, 1931, Lamont repurchased the stock from his wife and his wife repaid the loan. Pecora, *Wall Street under Oath*, pp. 196–197. Lamont was never prosecuted for tax evasion; Mitchell was (see chapter 10).

95. U.S. Congress, *Stock Exchange Practices*, p. 1779. *Time*, February 27, 1933, pp. 37–38.

96. U.S. Congress, *Stock Exchange Practices*, p. 1818.

97. Ibid., p. 1835.

98. Ibid., p. 1818.

99. Ibid., p. 1807; Pecora, *Wall Street under Oath*, pp. 73–74. *Literary Digest*, March 11, 1933, p. 11, observed, "The biggest bankers may make mistakes when a nation-wide mania for stock speculation sweeps the most conservative financiers off their feet." Under a photo of Mitchell, the caption read, " 'We are human'— C. E. Mitchell's explanation of past errors."

100. Pecora, *Wall Street under Oath*, p. 71.

101. Harvey O'Connor, *Mellon's Millions* (New York: Blue Ribbon, 1933), p. 357. At parallel hearings in the Senate Finance Committee, witnesses stated that the national crisis required that the incoming Roosevelt administration be vested with dictatorial powers. *New York Times*, February 22, 1933. Some observers predicted riots unless the banking crisis came to an end. See Susan E. Kennedy, *Banking Crisis of 1933* (Lexington: University Press of Kentucky, 1973), p. 100.

102. February 28, 1933.

103. February 25, 1933, in the Heywood Broun column.

104. Diary, February 25, 1933, Hamlin MSS. At a meeting of the Federal Reserve Board, Meyer spoke of the injury to the Federal Reserve system resulting from Mitchell's testimony. Meyer also related that he had, without the knowledge or authorization of the board, attempted at the start of the hearings on stock exchange practices in June 1932 to have Mitchell removed from his office as chairman of National City Bank. This was six months after the expiration of Mitchell's term as a director of the Federal Reserve Bank of New York on December 31, 1931.

105. *New York Times*, February 28, 1933. President-elect Roosevelt later complained to his aide Raymond Moley that not a single editorial had ever attacked Mitchell and that the press lacked "moral indignation." Moley, *First New Deal*, p. 337. In fact, few editorials even mentioned Mitchell, although his resignation was front-page news. A notable exception was the *New York Herald Tribune*, which noted, February 28, 1933: "Such errors of judgment as Mr. Mitchell revealed are undoubtedly the defects of his qualities."

106. National City Bank, *Monthly Economic Letter*, March 1933, p. 33.

107. "Damnation of Mitchell," March 6, 1933, pp. 47–48.

10. Rehabilitation and Recovery, 1933–1939

1. Oswald Garrison Villard, "Issues and Men," *The Nation*, March 15, 1933, p. 279.

2. *New York Herald Tribune*, July 14, 1940.

3. Perkins served as an unofficial link between the president and the New York banking community. Roosevelt and Perkins exchanged a number of "Dear Frank" and "Dear Jim" letters during the former's first term in office. For example, in a "Dear Jim" letter dated September 28, 1934, Roosevelt urged Perkins to keep up his good work and "tell the boys to quit grousing and to start backing their own country." Roosevelt Library, Hyde Park, New York.

4. March 2, 1933, Archives, Bank of America, San Francisco, California.

5. National City Bank, Daily Statement Book.

6. Ibid.

7. Milton Friedman and Anna J. Schwartz, *A Monetary History of the United States, 1967–1960* (Princeton: Princeton University Press, 1963), pp. 326–327.

8. By the time the Clearing House bankers met, fifteen states had already declared banking holidays, and nine others had restricted withdrawals. For a record of the events of March 3 and 4, see Joseph A. Broderick (superintendent of banks, New York State) to Lehman, December 14, 1935, Lehman MSS, Columbia University, New York. For a general description of the events leading to the national banking holiday see Frank Freidel, *Franklin D. Roosevelt: Launching the New Deal* (Boston: Little, Brown, 1973), pp. 175–236.

9. *New York Times*, March 4, 1933.

10. Ibid., March 5, 1933. See also the *Chicago Tribune* of the same date on the crescendo of applause and cheers that "rose up in a wave that rolled forward and engulfed the high platform" when Roosevelt declared, "there must be an end to speculating with other people's money."

The development of Roosevelt's speech is described in Freidel, *Launching the New Deal*, pp. 196–212, and Raymond Moley with E. A. Rosen, *The First New Deal* (New York: Harcourt, Brace and World, 1966), pp. 96ff.

11. *New York Times*, March 7, 1933. See also Arthur A. Ballantine, "When All the Banks Closed," *Harvard Business Review*, 48 (1948): 129–143. Ballantine was under secretary of the treasury, "from the last years of the Hoover Administration through the first months of Roosevelt's and . . . could observe from the inside much that was going on at that time" (p. 129).

Some public figures thought that the Bank Holiday was unconstitutional. For example, Senator Carter Glass wrote in a private letter, "I think the President of the United States had no more valid authority to close or open a bank in the United States than had my stable boy." Glass to Russell Leffingwell (partner, J. P. Morgan and Company), July 12, 1933, Glass MSS, University of Virginia, Charlottesville. Moley, *First New Deal*, p. 156, also cites the Bank Holiday as an "extraordinary . . . extension of Executive power."

12. Perkins also wrote to Roosevelt on March 6, 1933, concerning the board's resolution to divorce the bank from the City Company. In addition Perkins noted, "I also cut the dividend of the Bank yesterday because of the feeling that while things were in this upset condition it was wise and conservative to reduce the outgo." Perkins concluded that he was not sure whether "I am going to be considered a great fellow or be hung." Roosevelt Library, Hyde Park, New York.

13. Ballantine, "When All the Banks Closed," pp. 140–141. For the provisions of the Emergency Banking Act of 1933 see Friedman and Schwartz, *Monetary History*, pp. 421–422.

14. Quoted in C. C. Colt and N. S. Keith, *Twenty-eight Days: A History of the Banking Crisis* (New York: Greenberg, 1933), p. 71. For a discussion of the licensing procedure see Cyril B. Upham and Edwin Lamke, *Closed and Distressed Banks* (Washington, D.C.: The Brookings Institution, 1934), pp. 45–48.

15. In contrast, the California–based Bank of America experienced considerable difficulty in obtaining a license to reopen. Roosevelt eventually decided that it should reopen; confidence would be undermined if the third largest bank in the country with its official sounding name were allowed to fail. Roosevelt had no desire to repeat the mistake made in the case of the Bank of United States. Relative to this consideration Giannini's Democratic credentials probably played a small part in Roosevelt's decision. On the difficulties of the Bank of America see Freidel,

Launching the New Deal, pp. 232–234; Moley, *First New Deal*, p. 192; Marquis James and Bessie R. James, *Biography of a Bank: The Story of the Bank of America N. T. and S.A.* (New York: Harper and Bros., 1954), pp. 371–374.

16. National City Bank, *Annual Report, 1933* (New York: National City Bank, 1934).

17. National City Bank, Comptroller's Report, 1933.

18. James H. Perkins, chairman, to the shareholders, December 5, 1933, Citibank Library, New York. Unlike many other banks, National City would have remained solvent without the infusion of additional capital, and this was well known. Therefore, its sale of stock to the RFC removed the stigma attached to receiving aid from the RFC (see chapter 9), allowing banks in weaker condition to receive required capital assistance without provoking runs. Cf. Friedman and Schwartz, *Monetary History,* p. 427n; Jesse H. Jones with Edward Angly, *Fifty Billion Dollars: My Years with the RFC, 1932–1945* (New York: Macmillan, 1951), pp. 26–53.

19. National City Bank, Comptroller's Report, January 13, 1934.

20. National City Bank, *Annual Report, 1933.*

21. *Celia Gallin and Others v. National City Bank of New York and Others,* 273 N.Y. Supp. 87 (Sup. Ct. N.Y. Cnty., 1934), 281 N.Y. Supp. 795 (Sup. Ct. N.Y. Cnty., 1935).

In an action of this kind, shareholders sue directors, alleging misconduct damaging to the corporation and therefore to its owners. If the plaintiffs win, damages are awarded and payable to the corporation, not to the plaintiffs. The court may and normally does require the defendant directors to pay both the damages and the plaintiffs' reasonable legal expenses, on the theory that the plaintiffs have rendered a service to all shareholders in bringing the directors to justice.

The case was complex, involving more than a dozen separate charges against the directors. If all or most of the plaintiffs' claims had been upheld, the damages would have meant financial ruin for the defendants; there was no directors' liability insurance at the time. As the Shearman and Sterling law firm's official history says, "It was a 'big' case in every way, calling for the resources of many lawyers working together. Countless transactions by the Bank and the Company during the previous twenty-two years were the subjects. There were myriads of documents to be examined and made ready for use." See *Shearman and Sterling* (New York: Shearman and Sterling, 1973), p. 274.

The main charges against the defendants were negligence or misconduct: in making and working out sugar loans in Cuba in the early 1920s; in making loans of $2.4 million to officers of the bank and City Company to help them carry bank stock they had purchased at high prices before the 1929 crash; and in authorizing the purchase by the City Company of seventy-one thousand shares of bank stock. The purchase took place on October 28, 1929, at the time the intended merger between the bank and the Corn Exchange Bank and Trust Company had been agreed upon but had not yet been ratified by shareholders. The purchase was made in an effort to support the price of bank shares in order to make the merger acceptable to National City shareholders. These shares were subsequently purchased from the City Company by Charles Mitchell for his personal account at the price the company had paid for them, so that Mitchell, not the City Company, bore the loss of the subsequent fall in price (see chapter 9).

The court disallowed these and several other, lesser charges but found that the directors had violated their legal duty to shareholders by failing to look at the underlying accounting that determined the size of the management fund. The court found a number of irregularities in the accounting; the most damaging was that management had failed to account properly for the City Company's large losses on its interest in the General Sugar Corporation. This had the effect of increasing allotments from the fund by $1.7 million. The court accordingly held the directors personally liable for this amount, on the theory that they should not have left the accounting entirely in the hands of officers who had a financial interest in the way it was done. As the court said, the directors were held "answerable to the stockholders for their failure properly to supervise the computation for the management fund" (281 N.Y. Supp. at 807). The total damages assessed to the directors of $1.8 million included about $100,000 because of another, minor irregularity in administering the management fund. An allowance for plaintiffs' legal expenses brought the directors' liability to $4 million.

22. George S. Moore, "History of First National City Bank during the Years 1927 to 1970" (New York: unpublished memoir, 1970), p. 36. See *New York Times*, June 16, 1934, for State Supreme Court Justice Edward S. Dore's opinion. The judge commented, "This is not a case such as many of those cited in the plaintiffs' briefs in which a board of directors by breach of duty has brought a bank into insolvency." *Time*, June 25, 1934, noted, "Many a U.S. banker big and little heaved a mighty sigh of relief last week, knowing that the National City decision would discourage similar stockholder suits."

Despite its victory in the *Gallin* case, National City chose not to contest a case brought by the comptroller of the currency and receiver for Harriman National Bank and Trust Company against National City Bank and the other members of the New York Clearing House Committee for 1932–1933 regarding their role in the failure of the Harriman National Bank. Perkins recommended that the bank settle the case out of court, for "in his judgment, the Bank stood to lose much more from the trial of the suit than the cost of settling it." In requesting the Executive Committee to approve this course of action, Perkins emphasized "the importance of avoiding damage to the good name and reputation of the Bank and conflict with public authorities which would interfere with the refunding in due season of the preferred stock of the Bank now held by the Government through the Reconstruction Finance Corporation." National City Bank, Executive Committee, Minutes, April 17, 1936. This recommendation was approved and National City paid $725,000 to settle the case.

23. Interview, Hon. Leonard P. Moore (assistant to Mitchell's personal counsel, Max Steuer), September 1979; interview with Charles Mitchell's daughter, Mrs. Allerton Cushman, March 1980.

24. The indictment alleged that Charles Mitchell had knowingly and fraudulently evaded federal income taxes for the year 1929 with respect to three transactions: first, the sale of 18,300 shares of National City Bank stock to his wife at the end of 1929 to establish a loss to offset income and capital gains that Mitchell had received earlier in the year, and second, the treatment of a mid-1929 payment from the management fund to Mitchell as a loan rather than as income. Under the terms of the management fund, distributions were based on the profits of the cal-

endar year. A midyear distribution was made in 1929 on the basis of the profits that the bank and its security affiliate earned during the first half-year and a forecast of profits anticipated during the second half-year. Profits for the second half-year did not correspond to the forecast; in fact, there were significant losses, so that the money advanced to management-fund participants at midyear substantially exceeded the payments due them for the year as a whole. Mitchell had declared the excess amount of the midyear payment to the U.S. Treasury as a loan and not as taxable income. The third transaction was a technical matter involving shares of the Anaconda Copper Company. In the first and second matters, Mitchell had acted on advice of counsel. Counsel's opinion concerning the management-fund matter was in writing and was on exhibit at the trial.

Roosevelt's secretary, Marvin H. McIntire, kept the president informed on the progress of Mitchell's indictment and arraignment. M. H. McIntire to Roosevelt, March 24, 1933, Roosevelt Library, Hyde Park, New York. Roosevelt later wrote to one of the prosecuting attorneys, commending him for "challenging the practices to which Mitchell resorted."

Mitchell's defense was carefully prepared and brilliantly conducted by Max Steuer, a famous courtroom lawyer of the day. Confident of his own integrity and of the justice of his case, Mitchell was a convincing witness. The jury found him not guilty on all counts.

After his resignation from National City, Mitchell remained in investment banking, becoming president of Blyth and Company in 1936. He built this regional firm into a major investment-banking house by competing for business with older, more established houses. He died in 1955, again a multimillionaire and again a respected figure on Wall Street.

25. Moore, "History," p. 38.

26. For a summary of the New Deal banking legislation see Friedman and Schwartz, *Monetary History*, pp. 434–449. The following is based on Thomas F. Huertas, "The Regulation of Financial Institutions: A Historical Perspective on Current Issues," in *Financial Services: The Changing Institutions and Government Policy*, ed. George J. Benston (Englewood Cliffs, N.J.: Prentice Hall, 1983), pp. 18–22.

27. Investment banks came under the regulation of a new agency, the Securities and Exchange Commission. In the Securities Act of 1933 and the Securities Exchange Act of 1934, Congress revamped the entire process of underwriting, distributing, and trading securities. The emphasis of the new regime was on disclosure. Together the acts required full and prompt dissemination of information considered by the Securities and Exchange Commission (SEC) to be relevant to a company's prospects. Strict controls were imposed on the use of inside information; the formation of pools to manipulate stock prices was prohibited. The legal liability of accountants, corporate officers, brokers, and others who participated in security transactions was defined and extended. It was presumed that investors in the securities markets were sophisticated enough to make and live with their own decisions. Ostensibly, the government's role was simply to ensure that relevant information be accurate and available. Therefore, the actual operation of the exchanges, and the structure of the investment-banking industry, continued to be characterized by self-regulation. In practice, this meant fixed brokerage com-

missions, a cartel device that limited the operational efficiency of the securities markets and resulted in higher prices to investors until removed in 1975.

28. Although interstate branching remained prohibited, the Banking Act of 1933 did extend the branching powers of national banks. Under the McFadden Act (1927), a national bank could branch to the same extent that state-chartered banks were permitted to do so but only within its headquarters city.

29. Cf. National City Bank, *Monthly Economic Letter*, July 1933, pp. 101–102. Subsequent studies of banks that failed in the Great Depression show no relationship between the payment of interest on demand deposits and the likelihood that a bank would collapse. See George J. Benston, "Interest Payment on Demand Deposits and Bank Investment Behavior," *Journal of Political Economy*, 72 (1964): 431–439, and Albert H. Cox, Jr., "Regulation of Interest on Bank Deposits," *Michigan Business Studies*, 17 (1966). Subsequent studies have also shown that the prohibition of interest payments on demand deposits was ineffective. See Benjamin Klein, "Competitive Interest Payments on Bank Deposits and the Long-run Demand for Money," *American Economic Review*, 64 (1974): 931–949. Banks substituted services for direct interest payments, and depositors invested directly in money market instruments, bypassing banks entirely (cf. chapter 13). Even in 1933 National City clearly recognized that such disintermediation would occur. Cf. *Monthly Economic Letter*, July 1933, p. 102.

30. Cf. Carter Golembe, "The Deposit Insurance Legislation of 1933," *Political Science Quarterly*, 75 (1960): 181–200. National City opposed the introduction of deposit insurance, for it lowered the value of the reputation for safety that National City had built up over the years. In its July 1933 *Monthly Economic Letter* (p. 101), the bank commented: "The fundamental objection to the plan is that it makes good bankers responsible for the losses of the poor ones, and naturally this is more likely to eliminate the former than the latter. It makes all banks equally safe for depositors and hence relieves the public of responsibility in the choice of banks. Thus it puts the burden of maintaining sound banking upon regulation by the Government, and takes it off the public, which should bear part of it.

"The element of character in the choice of a bank is eliminated, and the competitive appeal is shifted to other and lower standards, such as liberality in making loans. The natural result is that standards of management are lowered, bankers may take greater risks for the sake of larger profits, and the economic loss which accompanies bad bank management increases."

Subsequent studies have suggested that National City's early skepticism was justified. Cf. Sam Peltzman, "Capital Investment in Commercial Banking and Its Relationship to Portfolio Regulation," *Journal of Political Economy*, 78 (1970): 1–26.

31. For a broader discussion of the New Deal's reliance on cartels as a means of ensuring economic stability see Ellis Hawley, *The New Deal and the Problem of Monopoly* (Princeton: Princeton University Press, 1966).

32. James H. Perkins (chairman) to the shareholders, April 1, 1933, Citibank Library, New York.

33. To John Neylan (director, National City Bank), March 15, 1934, Neylan MSS, University of California, Berkeley (hereafter cited as Neylan MSS).

34. Perkins saw various difficulties in this plan. As he wrote Giannini, "The men in the organization have some idea of trying to raise money to start out on their own, in which case we should have to make a deal with them to enable them to look after the old issues that are in default and need reorganization, because they and nobody else knows about them. I hesitate very much to suggest that we take any of our shareholders' money and allow it to be used in a security business which we haven't control of; and it is clear to me that I can't take any part of the operation of such a company." J. H. Perkins to A. P. Giannini, March 13, 1934, Archives, Bank of America.

35. June 4, 1934, Citibank Library, New York. When National City Company was dissolved, a new company, the City Company of New York, Inc., was formed as a subsidiary of National City Bank. The assets of the National City Company were transferred to the subsidiary. The subsidiary was carried on the bank's books at a value of $1 until 1940, when it went out of business. Upon liquidation the subsidiary paid the bank a dividend of $10 million. See National City Bank, *Annual Report, 1940* (New York: National City Bank, 1941).

36. National City Bank, *Annual Report, 1933.*

37. James H. Perkins (chairman) to the shareholders, April 1, 1933.

38. Ibid.

39. On the economics of the recovery from the depression see Friedman and Schwartz, *Monetary History,* pp. 493–545; Kenneth D. Roose, *The Economics of Recession and Revival* (New Haven, Conn.: Yale University Press, 1954).

40. Charles P. Kindleberger, *The World in Depression, 1929–1939* (Berkeley: University of California Press, 1973), pp. 232–261.

41. To the shareholders, December 5, 1933, Citibank Library, New York. Relatively little could be done to cut expenses without undermining the long-term strategy to which National City was committed. Wages of the domestic staff were cut 10 percent in 1933 and new hiring was slowed. The total domestic staff was reduced from 5,500 at the end of 1932 to 4,800 at the end of 1934. Operating expenses were reduced by $1.5 million in 1933 and by another $1.8 million in 1934. But this was the limit. As Perkins remarked in January 1935, "As regards the number of our people and their rate of compensation we probably are at as low a point as we can reach without endangering the efficiency of our service." National City Bank, *Annual Report, 1934* (New York: National City Bank, 1935).

42. For a study of banks' excess reserve policy during the 1930s and previous panics see George R. Morrison, *Liquidity Preferences of Commercial Banks* (Chicago: University of Chicago Press, 1966). Morrison demonstrates that banks' excess reserve ratio varied positively with respect to expected deposit withdrawals and the risk premium on corporate bonds and inversely with respect to the interest rate on short-term Treasury securities. For a discussion of the impact of banks' excess reserve policy on the economy, see Friedman and Schwartz, *Monetary History,* pp. 449–462. See also notes 47, 48, and 49.

43. Banks across the country uniformly reduced the maturity structure of their U.S. government security portfolios. This was more true of banks in New York City, and at National City Bank it was even more pronounced. Outside New York City, banks substituted notes for bonds, and after 1931 these banks reduced their

holdings of short-term Treasury bills and certificates. At New York City banks, holdings of short-term investments increased almost uninterruptedly after 1929 until the middle of 1936. At the latter date, member banks held 73 percent of all Treasury bills outside the Federal Reserve banks; 85 percent of these represented the investments of New York City banks. National City's holdings, by themselves, accounted for nearly 25 percent of this total, or 15 percent of the total of Treasury bills outside the Federal Reserve banks. See National City Bank, Call Reports, 1929–1936; Board of Governors, Federal Reserve System, *Banking and Monetary Statistics, 1914–1941* (Washington, D.C.: GPO, 1943), p. 84, and *Banking and Monetary Statistics, 1941–1970* (Washington, D.C.: GPO, 1976), p. 80; and Friedman and Schwartz, *Monetary History,* p. 451.

The concentration of Treasury bills at banks in New York City and at National City Bank can be explained by the uncertainty of the times, since deposits that flowed into these banks after 1933 were likely to be more volatile than deposits at other banks. Consequently, National City Bank and other New York City banks would have had a greater preference for assets that could be readily sold with no loss.

At National City, Perkins's firm belief that interest rates would rise played a decisive role in the accumulation of short-term Treasury securities. A comparison of the bank's portfolio of government securities with those of other banks suggests the degree to which Perkins's expectations differed from those of the bank's closest competitors. National City Bank had generally favored a government securities portfolio with a somewhat shorter maturity structure than those of other banks in New York City. During the 1930s, this difference became more pronounced. By the middle of 1936, Treasury bills amounted to over half of the bank's portfolio of U.S. government securities; at other New York City banks, Treasury bills accounted for less than 25 percent of government securities. This disparity persisted until the middle of 1938 when Perkins finally realized that interest rates would not soon rise. Even then he opted for the shorter end of the spectrum, investing less than 40 percent of the portfolio in long-term bonds though the bank's closest competitors had invested more than 60 percent of the portfolio in such assets. See National City Bank, Call Reports, 1929–1941; Board of Governors, Federal Reserve System, *Banking and Monetary Statistics, 1914–1941,* p. 84, and *Banking and Monetary Statistics, 1941–1970,* p. 80. See Friedman and Schwartz, *Monetary History,* pp. 453–456, and see pp. 455–456n for a discussion of the role of liquidity preference and expectations in the determination of the structure of interest rates in the 1930s.

It remains a puzzle why Perkins bothered to invest such large sums in assets commonly thought to have yielded less than the transaction costs involved. If there were limits below which Perkins could not cut staff or expenses if the bank were to survive intact and follow its traditional strategy, it may be that for much of the time in the 1930s the staff was underemployed. If so, even the very low return on Treasury bills could have been worthwhile.

It should be noted that inferences drawn from the data presented here can only be tentative because the data on bank holdings of U.S. government securities reflect original maturity, not time remaining until maturity. The heavy concentration of Treasury bills at New York City banks nevertheless does suggest that the maturity of the government securities protfolio at these banks was much shorter than at banks outside New York City and that this tendency was even more pronounced at National City Bank than at other New York City banks.

44. Perkins to Giannini, July 25, 1935, Archives, Bank of America.

45. National City Bank, Daily Statement Book; Board of Governors, Federal Reserve System, *Banking and Monetary Statistics, 1914–1941*, p. 389. End-of-month data show a similar pattern and again demonstrate that National City accounted for a significant proportion of the total change in excess reserves held by member banks during the height of the excess reserve controversy (see below, note 48). From June to November 1935 member bank excess reserves rose $686 million, peaking at $3.1 billion at the end of November. National City accounted for one-third of this increase. From November 1935 to June 1936 excess reserves at member banks fell by $383 million. At National City they declined by $164 million, or 43 percent of the total for all member banks.

46. February 8, 1938, Neylan MSS.

47. June 15, 1938, Archives, Bank of America.

48. National City Bank, Comptroller's Report, 1933–1939.

49. Within the administration, Jesse Jones, chairman of the RFC, was a particularly vocal critic of the banks. He thought them too timid. He contended that banks were turning even credit-worthy borrowers away, so that they might pile up cash and government securities. In a speech to the New York State Bankers Association in 1934, Jones commented, "I appreciate that our bankers have been through a terrific ordeal and have felt their responsibility to depositors, but if we continue waiting on the sidelines for complete recovery and assured values, readily marketable, naturally there can be no recovery."

He continued, "I would be the last man in the world to advise loose credits or unsound banking, but am of the opinion that too little credit and too severe terms at this time would be worse than too much credit . . . With deposit insurance in effect, there is no longer any occasion for extreme bank liquidity." Jones concluded with the admonition, "the Banker must be the leader, the morale builder and the one who really decides most of our business problems." *New York Times*, February 6, 1934.

A study by Charles O. Hardy and Jacob Viner, *Report on the Availability of Bank Credit in the Seventh Federal Reserve District* (Washington, D.C.: GPO, 1935), concluded that banks were denying credit to borrowers who could repay simply to protect their liquidity. A later study by the Federal Reserve Bank of New York came to the opposite conclusion. This study was completed in 1938, when banks were again building up their excess reserves. The New York study found that "very few legitimate cases of unsatisfied demands for credit or working capital, which can be extended on a reasonably sound basis, exist in this district." Federal Reserve Bank of New York, *Annual Report, 1938* (New York, 1939), p. 21.

50. By late 1935, official concern had shifted from the banks' apparent refusal to lend to what might happen if they did. The Federal Reserve became alarmed at the rapid rise in excess reserves, much of which was accounted for by National City Bank. Officials at the Federal Reserve Bank of New York became convinced that "excess reserves of the present magnitude must sooner or later set in motion inflationary forces which, if not dealt with before they get strongly under way,

may prove impossible to control." Hence, they concluded, "It seems very probable that with excess reserves of such extraordinary dimensions there comes a point when further increases have no constructive effects." Memorandum, Federal Reserve Bank of New York, prepared for Federal Open Market Committee, December 13, 1935. Cited in Friedman and Schwartz, *Monetary History*, pp. 523, 518.

In responding to the charges of the administration and the Federal Reserve, Perkins and National City found themselves doubly disadvantaged. Banks in general and National City in particular still retained some of the "bankster" reputation acquired at the height of the 1933 panic through the Pecora hearings. More importantly, Perkins, like Mitchell, was a firm believer in the credit view of the economy employed by the Federal Reserve. Cf. Perkins's testimony regarding the Banking Act of 1935 in U.S. Congress, Senate Subcommittee of Committee on Banking and Currency, *Hearings on S. 1715 (Banking Act of 1935)*, 74th Cong., 1st sess., 1935, p. 547.

Therefore, National City made no effective response to those, such as the Federal Reserve, who regarded banks' excess reserves as potentially inflationary. National City portrayed banks' accumulation of excess reserves as a reflection of the low "needs of trade." It was unreasonable, the bank's monthly bulletin argued in 1935, to assume that banks would willingly carry huge volumes of idle funds, or invest in government securities at nominal rates, if other safe employment of this money could be found. See National City Bank, *Monthly Economic Letter*, April 1935, p. 54.

Perkins feared that banks might be driven by earnings pressure "to a lowering of credit standards, thus leading to a deterioration in the quality of banking assets." Ibid., November 1935, p. 168. According to the credit view, this had been one of the chief causes of the depression. Perkins had no wish to see undone the progress made in restoring the bank's image. Thus National City subscribed to the view that "these great 'excess' reserves, if not controlled at the proper time, may constitute a serious menace for the future." Ibid., December 1935, p. 181.

Perkins accordingly recommended that the Federal Reserve increase reserve requirements for member banks. This extraordinary request was seconded by Winthrop Aldrich, chairman of the Chase National Bank, and by various bankers' associations. See Arthur M. Johnson, *Winthrop W. Aldrich: Lawyer, Banker, Diplomat* (Boston: Division of Research, Graduate School of Business Administration, Harvard University, 1968), pp. 211, 222–223.

The Federal Advisory Council made a formal recommendation to that effect in November 1935. *Federal Reserve Bulletin*, 22 (1936): 6. The Federal Reserve was happy to follow a suggestion that matched its own thinking. From August 1936 to May 1937 it doubled reserve requirements on demand and time deposits.

The results were not what the Federal Reserve and the bankers had expected. Some of what appeared to be unnecessary reserves were in fact desired by the banks as protection against a possible loss of deposits. Accordingly the banks tried to rebuild their excess reserve position. As a result, the money supply fell and the recovery halted abruptly. Mindful of 1929–1933, banks' desire for liquidity increased further. Loans fell off sharply from the peak reached in late 1937. A rash of bank failures and a deep recession followed.

51. Neil H. Jacoby and Raymond J. Saulnier, *Business Finance and Banking* (New York: National Bureau of Economic Research, 1947), pp. 81–100; Friedrich H. Lutz, *Corporate Cash Balances, 1914–1943: Manufacturing and Trade* (New York: National Bureau of Economic Research, 1950), pp. 9–16, 37–59; Helen M. Hunter, "The Role of Business Liquidity during the Great Depression and Afterwards: Differences between Large and Small Firms," *Journal of Economic History,* 42 (1982): 883–902. See also Roose, *The Economics of Recession and Revival,* p. 186. A sample of eighty-four large manufacturing corporations constructed by the National Bureau of Economic Research showed that the ratio of cash to total assets rose from 6.3 percent in 1933 to 8.0 percent in 1935. After a decline in 1936 and 1937 the cash ratio rose dramatically in 1938 and 1939, reaching a peak of 9.7 percent in 1939. National Bureau of Economic Research, Financial Research Program, *Corporate Financial Data for Studies in Business Finance,* Section A (Large Corporations), Confidential and Preliminary Draft, May 1945.

52. Deposits from domestic correspondent banks rose even more rapidly, increasing 82 percent from 1933 to 1935, for reasons similar to those behind the rise in corporate balances. One additional factor leading to an increase in correspondent balances was the discount policy of the Federal Reserve System. All during the recovery the discount rate significantly exceeded the market rate of return, making borrowing from the Federal Reserve a relatively expensive way of meeting short-term liquidity needs and raising the incentive for banks to hold interbank balances. Friedman and Schwartz, *Monetary History,* p. 514.

53. Memoranda regarding United Parcel Service account, Rovensky MSS, in possession of Jane Rovensky Grace, Palm Beach, Florida.

54. To Neylan, March 15, 1934, Neylan MSS. Perkins wrote a similar letter to Giannini on March 13, 1934. Archives, Bank of America. National City made much the same argument in the aftermath of the 1937–1938 recession, when banks were again criticized for failing to lend: "As between carrying idle reserves and making loans and investments at excessive risk, soundly managed banks will unhesitatingly follow the first policy, as they have been doing. Since they are custodians of other people's money, they have no other choice.

"This limits the area of prudent credit expansion to loans of good quality and to high grade investments. The banks have increasingly tried to find good loans throughout the depression, but with small success, for demand from good borrowers for accommodation which banks can properly grant, is slow." National City Bank, *Monthly Economic Letter,* May 1938, p. 50.

National City freely acknowledged that this assessment was subjective, but contended that such judgments were the heart of the banking business. As it reminded the readers of its monthly letter, banking is the business of bearing risk. It necessarily requires the banker to act on his current assessment of future economic conditions, and that assessment will vary. In 1933 the bank argued that "the question as to what constitutes a good credit risk is to a certain extent a matter of individual judgment, which may vary between different persons, and also with the same person at different times. It is natural and proper that bankers should scrutinize loan applications more carefully under present conditions than in normal times." National City Bank, *Monthly Economic Letter,* October 1933, p. 151.

55. Neil H. Jacoby and Raymond J. Saulnier, *Term Lending to Business* (New York: National Bureau of Economic Research, 1942), p. 26. In addition, the comptroller of the currency limited bank purchases of securities to top-rated bonds issued by well-known firms. This reduced banks' ability to buy bonds. Jacoby and Saulnier, *Business Finance and Banking*, pp. 212–213.

56. Avery B. Cohan, *Cost of Flotation of Long-term Corporate Debt since 1935* (Chapel Hill, N.C.: University of North Carolina Press, 1961), pp. 68–69. See also Vincent P. Carosso, *Investment Banking in America: A History* (Cambridge, Mass.: Harvard University Press, 1970), pp. 357, 363–367.

57. Interview, J. Howard Laeri, February 1980.

58. National City Bank, Comptroller's Reports, 1938–1939.

59. Thomas R. Wilcox, a young bank employee, reflected these views in a 1940 thesis. He concluded that term loans were "the result of more recent changes in the securities markets. For these reasons, a large volume of the intermediate loans . . . will disappear with a reversal of the revenue and regulatory statutes." Thomas R. Wilcox, "Intermediate Loans for Commercial Banks" (Senior thesis submitted to Department of Economics and Social Institutions, Princeton University, 1940), p. 102. Wilcox, who started as a page in 1934, received a scholarship from the bank to attend Princeton. He later became head of the New York branches and vice chairman of the First National City Corporation (see chapters 14–16).

60. Wilcox, "Intermediate Loans," pp. 64–66.

61. Statement before the U.S. Congress, Senate Banking and Currency Committee, cited in National City Bank, *Monthly Economic Letter,* July 1939, p. 79.

62. National City Bank, *Annual Report, 1933.*

63. National City Bank, Executive Committee, Minutes, April 18, 1933.

64. Gordon S. Rentschler (president) to shareholders (Memorandum), December 1933, National City Bank.

65. Perkins to Giannini, September 18, 1934, Archives, Bank of America.

66. National City Bank, Comptroller's Supplemental Report, 1939.

67. National City Bank, *Annual Report, 1938* (New York: National City Bank, 1939).

68. Kindleberger, *World in Depression,* pp. 88, 172; Simon Kuznets, *Modern Economic Growth: Rate, Structure, and Spread* (New Haven, Conn.: Yale University Press, 1966), p. 308.

69. The description of the bank's activities in China are based on 1976 interviews with James MacKay (supervisor of Chinese branches in the 1930s), Henry M. Sperry, and Kenneth Rounds. In addition, Thomas C. Cochran, "The National City Bank and Warfare in the Far East," unpublished memorandum, July 28, 1943, National City Bank, provided valuable information. For a history of China during the 1930s see James E. Sheridan, *China in Disintegration: The Republican Era in Chinese History, 1912–1949* (New York: Free Press, 1975), pp. 183–244.

70. Joseph H. Durrell, "History of Foreign Branches of American Banks and Overseas Division, N.C.B." (New York, unpublished memoir, 1940), p. 228.

71. National City Bank, *Annual Report, 1933.*

72. Regulatory changes also helped pave the way to faster loan growth. Prior to 1933, there was considerable uncertainty about the legality of certain loan con-

tract provisions, such as repayment schedules. These were cleared up in a 1933 court decision upholding National City's method of interest calculation and by the Stephens Act (1934). Cf. David H. Rogers, *Consumer Banking in New York* (New York: Columbia University Press, 1974), pp. 27-31.

73. National City Bank, Comptroller's Report, 1939.

74. Ibid.; National City Bank, Executive Committee, Minutes, June 22, 1937, and May 23, 1939.

75. National City Bank, Comptroller's Report, 1939.

76. *Polk's Bankers' Encyclopedia*, 91st ed. (Detroit, Mich.: R. L. and Polk, 1940), p. vii, lists Chase National Bank as the largest bank in the country with assets of $3.1 billion as of December 31, 1939, followed by National City Bank with assets of $2.5 billion.

77. National City Bank, Comptroller's Report, 1933-1939.

78. July 25, 1935, Archives, Bank of America.

79. In a letter to Giannini, Perkins explained why he recruited Burgess. "I have been studying ways and means that will enable me to contribute all I have to contribute and relieve myself of a good deal in the way of dealing with the public. After a very careful canvas I have come to the conclusion that if the Board will elect Randolph Burgess as a Vice-Chairman of the Bank I can turn over to him a great many of the people I have to see, and he can keep me in touch with the essentials; he can watch our foreign exchange position from a long time point of view, and our bond account, and be useful to many of the officials of the Bank, as a consultant. I am sure you know him. I consider him the highest grade fellow in the Reserve System. He hasn't been trained as an executive, and I don't know that we should want to use him for that, unless as time went on he developed those qualities. He has kept free and clear of entanglements, is the man [Secretary of the Treasury] Morgenthau turns to more than anybody for the Government financing; he is comparatively young from your and my point of view; and has a fine character and personality.

"As a matter of fact, between you and me and the post, he is the only fellow I know of I should like to bring in at the moment. Of course, later on, it may be that the time will come when we want an executive and we might want to bring Curtis Calder [Chief Executive, American and Foreign Power, and a director of National City Bank] or somebody like him in here; but I don't think the time has arrived either for him or for us yet. Among other things, he is doing a swell job in working out a company that owes us a large sum of money, and I don't want him disturbed.

"In other words, the bringing of Burgess into the picture I don't consider as a final solution, although it may be that he will prove to have the qualities we want. Meanwhile, I believe it would do a lot to strengthen the name of the Bank and very greatly help me in its operation." July 5, 1938, Archives, Bank of America.

11. War and Peace, 1940-1949

1. National City Bank, *Annual Report, 1939* (New York: National City Bank, 1940).

2. Concerning monetary policy and the role of the banking system in World War II, see Milton Friedman and Anna J. Schwartz, *A Monetary History of the United States, 1867-1960* (Princeton: Princeton University Press, 1963),

pp. 546–574; Lester V. Chandler, *Inflation in the United States, 1940–48* (New York: Harper, 1951), pp. 190–91.

3. Reserve requirements for all banks had been raised in November 1941 to the levels prevailing prior to April 1938. Between November 1941 and October 1942 reserve requirements were lowered three times, but only for central-reserve-city member banks. These reductions were a response to the drop in excess reserves that banks in New York and Chicago suffered in mid-1941 partly as a result of the geographical patterns of Treasury expenditures. To offset this decline and thereby encourage these banks to continue to buy Treasury securities, their reserve requirements were reduced. "Bank Credit, War Finances, and Savings," *Federal Reserve Bulletin*, 28 (1942): 869–872.

The tax code was also changed to encourage banks to invest in government bonds. Beginning in 1942 banks were permitted to deduct losses on bonds from ordinary income but to treat profits as capital gains, which were subject to a lower tax rate. This provision was repealed in 1969. Cf. Robert C. Clark, "The Federal Income Taxation of Financial Intermediaries," *Yale Law Journal*, 84 (1975): 1631–32.

4. Cited in National City Bank, *Monthly Economic Letter*, December 1942, p. 136.

5. National City Bank, Call Reports, June 1941 and June 1945.

6. Ibid.

7. Delmont K. Pfeffer, "Victory Loan Closes Series of War Bond Campaigns," *Number Eight*, December 1945, p. 6; National City Bank, *Annual Report, 1945* (New York: National City Bank, 1946).

8. National City Bank, Comptroller's Report, 1945.

9. "W. R. Burgess Appointed to U.S. Treasury Post," *Number Eight*, January 1953, p. 4.

10. Neylan MSS, University of California, Berkeley (hereafter cited as Neylan MSS).

11. "Number of Women Employees Doubles in Two Years," *Number Eight*, March 1943, p. 34.

12. January 26, 1944, Neylan MSS.

13. Lewis B. Cuyler, "The Development of Personnel Administration, Citibank, 1928–1965," (New York: unpublished memoir, 1977), pp. 60–65.

14. National City Bank, *Annual Report, 1945*. Management's emphasis on recruitment and training of college graduates as future leaders of the bank created a serious morale problem among the operations supervisors who had kept things running during the war. Now these old hands were going back to less interesting jobs, while the college trainees would soon be passing them by and moving on to positions of responsibility. Yet the cooperation of the operations supervisors was vitally necessary in the training of the next generation. President William Brady took the offensive on this problem at the request of Cuyler and his boss, cashier Nathan Lenfestey. In a speech to approximately two hundred operations supervisors, Brady acknowledged that their timing had been wrong and that the young trainees would indeed pass them by. Nevertheless, their most important responsibility was to the bank, and therefore they should help train the future leaders. According to Cuyler, "This speech opened the way for executing training programs

that became more and more important in the years that followed." Cuyler, "Development of Personnel Administration," p. 92.

15. W. Randolph Burgess, "The Banker Looks Abroad," Address delivered before the American Bankers Association, September 1946, p. 14. Rentschler was puzzled by the postwar environment as well. In mid-1947 he wrote to Neylan: "Things are so confused that it seemed to me best to break a life long tradition of never stopping just to look around and see what it is all about. I have been at it for a full two weeks and can assure you that I have not even reached a first step towards a solution of the confusion." July 28, 1947, Neylan MSS.

16. National City Bank, Call Reports, June 1945 and June 1948.

17. National City Bank, *Annual Report, 1948* (New York: National City Bank, 1949).

18. David H. Rogers, *Consumer Banking in New York* (New York: Columbia University Press, 1974), pp. 41–43.

19. National City Bank, Call Reports, June 1945 and June 1948.

20. National City Bank, Call Report, June 1948.

21. National City Bank, *Annual Report, 1947* (New York: National City Bank, 1948).

22. "Leo Nelson Shaw: Forty-two Years of Service," n.d., Citibank, New York.

23. National City Bank, *Annual Report, 1947.*

24. National City Bank, *Annual Report, 1945.*

25. Ibid.

26. Interview, August 1976.

27. In addition to the political chaos, the civil war also produced economic chaos. To keep its armies fighting against the communists, the Nationalist government of China resorted to the printing press. A large part of the domestic tax base had been destroyed in the war with Japan, and U.S. and United Nations (UNRRA) aid covered only a small part of the government's huge deficit. Hyperinflation was not long in developing. At the beginning of 1946, the general price level in Shanghai stood at sixteen times its prewar (1937) level. During the next twelve months prices rose five times, and in 1947 prices rose a further seventeen times, or 27 percent a month. Prices rose another twenty times in the first half of 1948—more than 10 percent a day—as the tide of battle turned increasingly against Chiang Kai-shek's armies. Cf. K. N. Chang, *The Inflationary Spiral: The Experience in China, 1939–1950* (New York: MIT Press and John Wiley and Sons, 1958), pp. 372–373. On political conditions in postwar China see O. Edmund Clubb, *Twentieth-Century China,* 3rd ed. (New York: Columbia University Press, 1978), pp. 252ff.; James E. Sheridan, *China in Disintegration: The Republican Era in Chinese History, 1912–1949* (New York: Free Press, 1975), pp. 269–271.

As a consequence of the economic situation, activity at National City's branch in Shanghai was hectic. Everyone wanted to borrow money. No sooner did people receive their pay than they rushed to withdraw their funds to purchase anything of value. The branch's banking floor was a madhouse, with peddlers jamming the entryways and coolies unloading bank notes from the Bank of China's issue department. The bank had to wait until after closing to pay its own tellers, lest they leave their stations during the day to spend their salaries.

Branch profits in local currency were excellent, but exchange control made it impossible to convert most of them into dollars for remittance to New York. To the extent regulations allowed, the China branches advanced funds to New York. Against branch deposits equivalent to $3,980,000 in mid-1948, the branches had only $1,705,000 of Chinese currency assets, the difference representing advances to New York that Head Office had invested in dollar assets outside China. As the local currency was depreciating rapidly against the dollar, the branches' short position in Chinese currency and long position vis-à-vis Head Office in dollars yielded a gain on the bank's books. This discussion is based on interviews with Henry M. Sperry, Robert E. Grant, and Raymond A. Kathe in 1979, and on Kathe's article "Before the Curtain Dropped," *Citibank Magazine*, November 1976.

28. Jean Le Pelley, "A Contribution to the History of the European Division of the First National City Bank of New York," (New York: unpublished memoir, June 4, 1963).

29. George S. Moore, "History of First National City Bank during the Years 1927 to 1970" (New York: unpublished memoir, 1970), p. 44. By closing, National City lost its license in Spain and was not able to reopen a branch in that country until 1978. A representative office was opened in Madrid on May 5, 1973. Ironically, the bank had kept its branches open all through the Spanish Civil War. The manager of the Overseas Division, Joseph H. Durrell, stated, "In view of the Bank's sad Russian experience, we were determined that the branches be kept open and on an operating basis." Durrell to Perkins, August 5, 1939, Citibank, New York.

30. The Argentine election of 1946 brought to power a kind of regime hitherto unknown in that prosperous country. Juan Perón was a populist whose power base was the urban working population of Buenos Aires. His economic program was to raise real wages by encouraging the unions and to cope with the resulting unemployment by massive increases in public sector employment, financed by heavy taxes on agricultural exports and by the printing press. Inflation, stagnation of agricultural output and exports, and tight exchange and credit control followed. Banks could make loans only by rediscounting them at the central bank, which would only rediscount paper that accorded with its views about the proper allocation of credit. The central bank set interest rates on loans, deposits, and rediscounts. Exchange controls prevented National City's branches from remitting all but a small part of the profits they managed to make under this restrictive regime. Cf. Carlos F. Diaz Alejandro, *Essays on the Economic History of the Argentine Republic* (New Haven, Conn.: Yale University Press, 1970); Laura Randall, *An Economic History of Argentina in the Twentieth Century* (New York: Columbia University Press, 1978), pp. 71–80.

31. In Brazil, the fall of Getúlio Vargas at the end of World War II appeared to promise a period of expansion for National City's branches at Rio de Janeiro, Santos, São Paulo, and Recife. The country's principal exports, coffee in particular, were growing rapidly. In 1946, the Brazilian branches remitted record profits of nearly $1.3 million and the bank readied plans to reopen a branch at Pôrto Alegre that had been closed since 1921. But the next year remitted profits fell to $350,000. The Dutra government, which succeeded the wartime Vargas regime,

followed an inflationary policy, and exchange controls wiped out the free exchange market. For the next nine years, remittances remained at a low level, and the bank marked time in Brazil. For a discussion of the postwar Brazilian economy see Celso Furtado, *The Economic Growth of Brazil* (Berkeley: University of California Press, 1963), pp. 239–240; Thomas E. Skidmore, *Politics in Brazil, 1930–1964: An Experiment in Democracy* (New York: Oxford University Press, 1967), pp. 69–70. The above discussion is also based on interviews with De Koven Pulford and Ercole Carpentieri in 1979 and on William A. Prendergast, "Memorandum of Citibank Service, 1929–1965" (New York: unpublished memoir, 1966).

32. "Members of a Famous Team," March 15, 1948. Ownership appears to have been irrelevant in the choice of Sheperd. The Stillman and Taylor families' holdings in the bank had been significantly reduced during the 1920s as a proportion of the total. The largest shareholder, Transamerica Corporation, had also reduced its stockholdings. Although Giannini remained a director of National City, he rarely came to meetings, preferring to remain in California. There Transamerica built up its interests in banks in other western states and in insurance, much to the consternation of the Federal Reserve Board (see chapter 13, note 8).

33. Once again, the real bills doctrine inspired these restrictive measures. About a year before the 1948 elections, President Truman sent a message to Congress in which he pointed to the "alarming degree of inflation" and singled out "inflationary bank credit" as one of its primary causes. Cited in National City Bank, *Monthly Economic Letter*, December 1947, pp. 133–134. To allow the rapid rise in the cost of living to continue was, Truman contended, to invite catastrophe. To Truman, the postwar inflation was the first stage of a classic boom-and-bust cycle. In his view, expansion would inevitably give way to contraction unless some way could be found to moderate the demand pressure underlying the boom. Accordingly, Truman instructed the federal agencies responsible for bank supervision to develop policies "designed to confine extension of private bank credit to legitimate production requirements." *Economic Report of the President, 1948* (Washington, D.C.: GPO, 1948), p. 50.

34. National City Bank, *Annual Report, 1948*.

35. B. T. Stott (secretary of the Survey Committee), Minutes of Meeting with Howard C. Sheperd, April 6, 1949. The words quoted are Stott's paraphrase of Sheperd's remarks.

36. B. T. Stott (secretary of the Survey Committee), Confidential Memorandum, December 1, 1948.

37. George S. Moore, "History," p. 48.

38. George S. Moore to Howard C. Sheperd (president), Memorandum on Survey Committee, Final Report, July 5, 1950.

39. Stott and Sheperd, Minutes, April 6, 1949.

40. George S. Moore to Howard C. Sheperd (president), Survey Committee Memorandum, December 29, 1948, p. 1.

41. Moore to Sheperd, July 5, 1950. Formal divisional earning and expense statistics were prepared on a regular monthly basis beginning in May 1952 and submitted to top management. These statements divided the bank into independent profit centers. The three major centers were the Domestic Division, the Domestic Branch Division, and the Overseas Division. Each division was credited

with the income from loans it had booked and with any fees. It was debited with any interest paid to its depositors. Deposits in excess of loans were lent to the bank's general investment pool, with the division receiving credit for funds supplied at the average rate of return earned on the bond portfolio. Divisions with loans in excess of deposits could borrow from the pool at the same rate.

The allocation of noninterest expense was problematic. The wide variety of services performed for customers and the sheer number of transactions made accurate expense allocation almost impossible. Inevitably, a large portion of total outlays was buried in Head Office with little information on its precise contribution to overall profitability. These expenses were therefore allocated to the divisions on the basis of samples of operations.

Overall profitability was calculated relative to deposits. This tended to favor divisions with high loan-to-deposit ratios, such as Moore's own Domestic Division.

42. Although the bank welcomed the Federal Reserve's attempt to dampen postwar inflation, it was convinced that such "a prolonged and violent price rise will be succeeded, not by stabilization at the top, but by a drop of unknown proportions." National City Bank, *Monthly Economic Letter*, February 1948, p. 14. Thus, it decided to curtail credit, especially term loans, noting that "with tighter money and the threat of further moves by the authorities the banks are more cautious about term loans, and much more likely to reject the applications of marginal borrowers." National City Bank, *Monthly Economic Letter*, January 1948, p. 3.

43. Moore, "History," p. 48.

12. Back in the Business of Banking, 1950–1956

1. National City Bank, Call Reports, June 1948 and June 1950.

2. Cited in Landon Jones, *Great Expectations* (New York: Coward, McCann and Geoghegan, 1980), p. 45. The speaker was a Seattle banker; the date, 1955.

3. The value of plant and equipment increased at an average annual rate of 9 percent between 1945 and 1950 and 8.4 percent between 1950 and 1956 at a sample of the nation's largest firms. Moreover, the volume of annual expenditures on plant and equipment more than doubled in the 1950s over what it had been in the years right after World War II. Board of Governors, Federal Reserve System, "Financial Data for 300 Large Corporations" (Washington, D.C.: mimeo, October 19, 1953), and Board of Governors, Federal Reserve System, "Composite Balance Sheet and Income Statement, 1953–1956" (Washington, D.C.: mimeo, n.d.).

4. The gap between expenditures on plant and equipment and internal funding sources grew both absolutely and relatively in the 1950s. In the postwar boom corporations had cash and marketable securities in excess of their demands for liquidity. Board of Governors, Federal Reserve System, "Financial Data for 300 Large Corporations," and "Composite Balance Sheet and Income Statement, 1953–1956."

5. National City Bank, Call Reports, June 1950 and June 1957. These figures include the growth in loans resulting from the acquisition of the First National Bank in 1955.

6. National City Bank, Comptroller's Reports, 1950–1957; Appendix D.

7. Cf. George S. Moore, "Term Loans and Interim Financing," in *Business Loans of American Commercial Banks*, ed. Benjamin H. Beckhart (New York: Ronald Press, 1959), pp. 208–282.

8. Interview, Walter B. Wriston, May 1977.

9. The following discussion is largely based on interviews with C. Sterling Bunnell, July 30, 1980; Thomas Creamer, March 9, 1981; and P. Henry Mueller, July 31, 1978. See also George S. Moore, "History of First National City Bank during the Years 1927 to 1970" (New York: unpublished memoir, 1970), pp. 20, 25.

10. *Number Eight*, October 1952, p. 3. As a compliment to Forward, Sheperd restored the bank's tradition of naming a single senior vice president. William A. Simonson had held this position from 1922 until his death in 1937. On September 30, 1952, the board of directors amended the bank's bylaws to this effect and created a new title, executive vice president, which ranked below senior vice president. The new executive vice presidents were James Stillman Rockefeller (Domestic and Domestic Branch divisions), Leo N. Shaw (Overseas Division), and Nathan C. Lenfestey (cashier).

11. The above discussion relies largely on *Number Eight*, January 1953, pp. 1–4, and January 1954, p. 2. In addition interviews with James Stillman Rockefeller, March 26, 1980, and George S. Moore, May 15, 1978, provided useful information concerning the 1952 top management succession and the careers of the individuals involved.

It should be noted that Alan H. Temple, the head of the bank's Economics Department, was promoted to executive vice president along with Laeri and Moore. He took over many of Burgess's administrative duties, especially in public relations.

12. As Robert L. Hoguet said in an interview, "I think the idea [of industry specialization at National City] . . . probably came from George [Moore], who'd observed the success of the First National Bank of Chicago, who, because they were all under one roof, had come to that form of organization a long time ago." May 9, 1978.

13. Interview, Lawrence S. Heath, May 1980.

14. Chase had begun to organize along industry lines during the 1930s, when it formed the Public Utility Department to oversee the extensive public utility holdings acquired through foreclosure during the depression. Arthur M. Johnson, *Winthrop W. Aldrich: Lawyer, Banker, Diplomat* (Boston: Division of Research, Graduate School of Business Administration, Harvard University, 1968), pp. 127–128. Shortly thereafter it established the Petroleum Department. Ibid., p. 218.

15. Interview, Robert L. Hoguet, Jr., May 9, 1978.

16. First National City Bank, Comptroller's Reports, 1954–1957.

17. Interview, William I. Spencer, May 5, 1978, and William I. Spencer and James R. Rowen, *The ABC Transaction* (Englewood Cliffs, N.J.: Prentice-Hall, 1957). See also Charles R. Dodson, "Proposed Organization and Functions of a Petroleum Engineering Staff at the First National City Bank of New York" (Thesis for the Graduate School of Credit Research, Foundation of the National Association of Credit Men, Amos Tuck School of Business Administration, Dartmouth

College, 1957), and A. W. Austin, "Bank Credit in Oil Production" (Thesis, Graduate School of Banking, American Institute of Banking, 1941).

18. First National City Bank, Comptroller's Reports, 1954–1957.

19. For a discussion of Baker's career and Baker's bank see Sheridan A. Logan, *George F. Baker and His Bank, 1840–1955: A Double Biography* (New York: George F. Baker Trust, 1981). See also N. S. B. Gras and Henrietta M. Larson, *Casebook in American Business History* (New York: F. S. Crofts, 1939), pp. 512–527.

20. *New York Times*, March 3, 1955.

21. Interview, Edwin Thorne (then vice president, First National Bank), June 1981.

22. Ibid.

23. *Moody's Bank and Finance Manual, 1945* (New York: Moody's Investors Service, 1945), p. 19, and *Moody's Bank and Finance Manual, 1955* (New York: Moody's Investors Service, 1955), p. 58.

24. Interview, Edwin Thorne, June 1981.

25. Ibid.

26. Moore, "History," p. 49.

27. *New York Times*, October 15, 1954.

28. Ibid., February 24, 1955, and March 25, 1955.

29. Ibid., January 18, 1961.

30. Ibid., January 14, 1955, January 15, 1955, and March 29, 1955.

31. Ibid., February 9, 1959.

13. The Funding Squeeze, 1957–1961

1. First National City Bank, *Annual Report, 1956* (New York: First National City Bank, 1957).

2. First National City Bank, *Annual Report, 1959* (New York: First National City Bank, 1960).

3. On the "accord" see Milton Friedman and Anna J. Schwartz, *A Monetary History of the United States, 1867–1960* (Princeton: Princeton University Press, 1963), pp. 623–627. On the economics of cash management see William J. Baumol, "The Transactions Demand for Cash: An Inventory Theoretic Approach," *Quarterly Journal of Economics*, 66 (1952): 545–556; James Tobin, "The Interest Elasticity of Transactions Demand for Cash," *Review of Economics and Statistics*, 38 (1956): 241–247. As in the 1920s, the bank helped corporations economize on cash balances. Through its transcontinental banking service, founded in 1928, the bank concentrated a corporate customer's cash from accounts around the country into a single disbursement account. Cash in excess of immediate corporate needs was invested in Treasury securities.

4. First National City Bank, *Annual Report, 1956*. On the economics of credit rationing see Dwight M. Jaffee, *Credit Rationing and the Commercial Loan Market* (New York: John Wiley and Sons, 1971), pp. 31–57.

5. Richard A. Smith, "Big Banking's Troubled Giants," *Fortune*, April 1959, pp. 114ff.

6. First National City Bank, *Annual Report, 1961* (New York: First National City Bank, 1962).

7. Originally, the Stephens Act was a liberalization of New York's branch-banking restrictions. As in many other states, the disappearance of many banks during the depression had left a number of areas in New York State without banking facilities. Branching offered a way to alleviate the shortage of banking facilities in order to serve better the public interest. The Stephens Act divided the state into nine banking districts. Commercial banks could branch or merge in any part of its own district. But all cities except New York City were "home-office protected." That is, a commercial bank could not enter a community with a *de novo* branch if the community housed the headquarters of another bank. New York City was excluded from this protection. While the districts for banks outside New York City provided broad, multicounty areas, for the most part encompassing a major upstate city and its surrounding suburbs, New York City banks were still prevented from going outside the five boroughs. Again it was fear of the banking giants that motivated the confinement of the New York City banks. In a memorandum to the New York State legislature dated May 21, 1934, Governor Lehman, who signed the Stephens Act into law, stated that he was assured that the act contained "solid, strong safeguards" against upstate penetration by the Manhattan banks. Cited in Federal Reserve Bank of New York, *Monthly Review*, November 1971, p. 267.

It was not until the 1950s that the New York City banks felt confined by the Stephens Act. As the economy prospered their upstate counterparts began to use their branching authority to the fullest extent. The New York City banks pressed for a legislative redistricting of the state that would permit them to enter the expanding suburban market. Upstate bankers, invoking the fear that the big New York City banks would wield monopoly power and end healthy competition, resisted any change in the law. Actually, it was the upstate banks that were trying to avoid competition. As Senator Carter Glass, who as a member of the congressional banking and currency committees had played an important role in banking regulation from the turn of the century, said in 1932, "the appeal of the little bank . . . against the 'monopolistic' tendencies of branch banking, is misleading when we come to reason about it. The fact is that the little banker is the 'monopolist.' He wants to exclude credit facilities from any other source than his bank. He wants to monopolize the credit accommodations of his community. He doesn't want any other bank in his state to come there." Quoted in *Bank Stock Quarterly*, December 1969, p. 13.

8. On the Bank Holding Company Act of 1956 see Gerald C. Fischer, *American Banking Structure* (New York: Columbia University Press, 1968), pp. 143–149, and *Bank Holding Companies* (New York: Columbia University Press, 1961), pp. 69–75. The Holding Company Act is also discussed in chapter 16, below.

Multibank holding companies were by no means a new phenomenon in 1956. During the 1920s, a number of banks used the device to avoid restrictive state and national branch-banking laws. Within New York State, the Marine Midland Corporation had formed a statewide bank holding company in 1929.

The Transamerica Corporation was the most successful of all bank holding companies. As mentioned in chapter 8, A. P. Giannini used this holding company to build a chain of banks during the 1920s, first in the state of California and then across the nation. Its acquisition of the Bank of America (New York) and the subsequent merger of that bank with National City made Transamerica for many years National City's largest shareholder. During the 1930s and 1940s Transamerica continued to expand its bank holdings, buying the shares of small banks in five western states.

The growth of bank holding companies, particularly the Transamerica Corporation, had long concerned the Federal Reserve, which felt that such companies were engaged in banking and should therefore be regulated like banks. See Federal Reserve Board, *Annual Report, 1927* (Washington, D.C.: GPO, 1928), p. 32. The banking acts of 1933 and 1935 applied to bank holding companies, but such companies remained free to acquire banks within and across state lines and to acquire nonfinancial businesses. See Federal Reserve Board, *Annual Report, 1943* (Washington, D.C.: GPO, 1944), p. 37.

In 1948, the Federal Reserve Board initiated an investigation of the Transamerica Corporation, alleging that it had secured a monopoly in the loan and deposit markets in the states of California, Oregon, Nevada, Washington, and Arizona. In March 1952 the board found Transamerica in violation of the Clayton Act, but this finding was overturned by the U.S. court of appeals and the U.S. Supreme Court.

The implication of the Supreme Court's decision was clear: If the Federal Reserve was to control effectively the activities of bank holding companies, Congress would have to pass legislation covering them.

In 1956 the Congress acted. The bank merger movement of the time alarmed small banks throughout the country. They saw their existence as independent institutions threatened and they rallied to support the Federal Reserve's proposal to bring bank holding companies under control. The Bank Holding Company Act was the result. Under the new law a holding company was required to register with the board of governors of the Federal Reserve if it owned 25 percent or more of the voting stock of two or more banks. One-bank holding companies were exempted from regulation. The new law applied whether or not a bank was a member of the Federal Reserve. The board was given regulatory and examination authority over registered multibank holding companies.

Under the new law, no multibank holding company could be formed without prior approval of the Federal Reserve, nor could existing registered companies acquire more than 5 percent of any bank's voting stock without the board's approval. The act also prohibited a holding company from engaging in any business except banking, managing banks, furnishing services to affiliated banks, or a business determined by the Federal Reserve to be "closely related" to banking. The holding company could not acquire more than 5 percent of the voting shares of any nonbank business. Existing companies were given two years to divest themselves of nonbanking interests previously acquired. The 1956 law also limited certain intra-holding-company transactions. Upstream loans were prohibited and certain downstream loans were restricted.

In granting or denying a bank holding company's application to expand through acquisition, merger, or consolidation, the 1956 act required the board to consider five factors: "(1) the financial history and condition of the company or companies and the banks concerned; (2) their prospects; (3) the character of their management; (4) the convenience, needs and welfare of the communities and the area concerned; and (5) whether or not the effect of such acquisition or merger or consolidation would be to expand the size or extent of the bank holding company system involved beyond limits consistent with adequate and sound banking, the public interest, and the preservation of competition in the field of banking." These factors were substantially the same as those later included in the Bank Merger Act of 1960. See. J. L. Robertson, "Taking a Long View of the Bank Holding Company Act," *Commercial and Financial Chronicle*, November 1, 1956, p. 1855, quoted in Fischer, *Bank Holding Companies*, p. 71.

The Bank Holding Company Act of 1956 also restricted holding company mergers and acquisitions across state lines. The so-called Douglas amendment provided that an out-of-state bank holding company could not acquire shares or assets of any bank in a state that had not specifically authorized such an acquisition by statute. Since local banks could be expected to block such legislation, this provision amounted to prohibition of interstate holding company acquisitions.

After enactment of the 1956 law, Transamerica elected to divest its bank holdings, retaining its nonbank businesses. It had already disposed of its holdings in the Bank of America and in National City Bank. Its other remaining banks were spun off to form the Western Bancorporation, now the First Interstate Bank Corporation, a multibank holding company with banks in several western states. Western Bancorporation had been grandfathered under the Douglas amendment, along with five other interstate bank holding companies.

9. *Federal Reserve Bulletin*, 44 (1958): 921–922.

10. Ibid.

11. *New York Times*, January 13, 1957. See also M. A. Schapiro and Company, *The Triple Banking System: Impact and Significance of the Bank Holding Company Act of 1956* (New York: M. A. Schapiro, 1956), p. 1.

12. *New York Times*, January 13, 1957.

13. New York State, Superintendent of Banks, *Annual Report, 1957* (Albany: New York State Banking Department, 1958), p. 16. The freeze had no effect on existing bank holding companies. As the *New York Times* noted on March 20, 1960, Marine Midland "has been forbidden to add to its present chain of eleven regional banks. But there has been nothing to prevent the eleven from merging with or acquiring additional units." Marine Midland made six bank acquisitions in this period involving a purchase of assets for cash. The "freeze" did not prevent Marine Midland from offering shares in the affiliates in exchange for assets in the banks acquired, retiring the minority shares, and supplying the affiliates with additional capital to make possible acquisitions of assets for cash.

14. *Federal Reserve Bulletin*, 44 (1958): 902–903.

15. Ibid., p. 914.

16. *New York Times*, July 11, 1958.

17. *Federal Reserve Bulletin*, 44 (1958): 918.

18. The Omnibus Banking Act of 1960 dealt with three matters of bank structure: branch banking, merger standards, and the formation and expansion of bank holding companies. The law enlarged the branching powers of New York City banks by allowing them to enter Nassau and Westchester counties. Banks in these two counties could, in turn, branch in New York City. The 1960 act also contained the same standards for regulating bank mergers and bank holding companies within the state that were contained in the federal Bank Holding Company and

Bank Merger acts. As mentioned in the text, the enactment of the Omnibus Banking Act ended the freeze on the formation and expansion of bank holding companies in the state that had been precipitated by the plan to form the First New York Corporation in 1956.

Various studies had indicated that banking competition would be fostered by allowing New York City banks to offer their services in the city's suburban areas. The public interest would accordingly be served by price competition and the increased services provided. In a discussion of the developing banking structure in New York under the Omnibus Banking Act, the New York State superintendent of banks, G. Russell Clark, reviewed the public benefits of the bill:

"First, wider branch powers for the New York City commercial banks would serve to enhance competition in those suburban areas which are now dominated by one or two institutions. Various studies had been made, including one financed by a group of suburban institutions themselves, indicating that rates on loans for small business and for consumer credit were significantly lower at the New York City banks. The omnibus law will permit the benefits of these lower borrowing costs to be made conveniently available to the public in the suburban areas. Second, the essence of a competitive system, whether in banking or in industry, is to offer the public a choice among types of institutions in which it wishes to place its funds, a choice which was unduly restricted by the previously existing branch laws. By permitting wider branch powers, the public will be afforded a broader choice as between commercial banks and institutions, and among mutual institutions themselves." New York State, Superintendent of Banks, *Annual Report, 1960* (Albany: New York State Banking Department, 1961), pt. 1, pp. 30–31.

Nevertheless, the superintendent also noted that under the new law existing institutions would still be protected from "too much competition." Home office protection was retained. An outside institution was prohibited from opening a new branch in a locality containing the home office of an existing commercial bank, while New York City banks were not so protected. An outside bank could enter a protected locality only through a merger or a holding company affiliation with a bank already there.

19. *New York Times,* September 8, 1960.

20. *New York Times,* February 9, 1961, and February 10, 1961.

21. *Number Eight,* May 1961, p. 17. On the federal Bank Merger Act of 1960 see Fischer, *American Banking Structure,* pp. 149–162. The act required regulatory approval of bank mergers through asset acquisitions. In the case of a national bank, approval of the comptroller of the currency rather than the Federal Reserve Board was required. Such mergers had previously been exempt from regulatory review, and many of the major bank mergers of the mid-1950s, including National City's acquisition of First National, had been through asset acquisition.

22. First National City Bank and National Bank of Westchester, Memorandum on Proposed Merger Submitted to the Comptroller of the Currency on May 15, 1961.

23. Decision of Comptroller of the Currency James J. Saxon on the Application to Merge National Bank of Westchester of White Plains, New York, and the First

National City Bank of New York, New York, December 1, 1961. U.S. Comptroller of the Currency, *Annual Report, 1962* (Washington, D.C.: GPO, 1963), p. 147.

24. *New York Times*, April 14, 1961.

25. *New York Times*, May 1, 1962. See also *New York Times*, January 31, 1962, for Comptroller Saxon's letter to the Federal Reserve Board opposing both the Chemical and the Chase Manhattan mergers.

26. *New York Times*, May 5, 1962. The Federal Reserve Board voted unanimously to bar the formation of the Morgan New York State Corporation as "unduly cutting competition," employing the same reasoning that it had used in the First New York Corporation case in 1958, before New York State's liberalization of its branch-banking law: "The transaction would result in the creation of a holding company the size and extent of which would be inconsistent with preservation of competition in the field of banking." *Federal Reserve Bulletin*, 48 (1962): 581.

27. Smaller New York City banks were able to merge with suburban banks. In 1967, the Bank of New York and the County Trust Company announced a plan to form a statewide holding company system with other banks. *New York Times*, August 11, 1967. The New York State Banking Board approved the plan, which included four upstate banks. *New York Times*, November 7, 1968. New York Banking Superintendent Wille acknowledged that the merger would eliminate some potential competition but concluded that it would "serve the convenience of the public."

In 1970, the Federal Reserve Board blocked as anticompetitive the acquisition by the Long Island Trust Company of the Bank of Westbury Trust Company (*New York Times*, January 31, 1970) but the board later reversed itself (*New York Times*, September 23, 1970).

28. First National City Bank, *Annual Report, 1959*.

29. New York Clearing House Association, "Report of the Special Deposit Study Committee, September 25, 1959" (New York: mimeo, 1959), p. 9. Alan H. Temple, vice chairman of First National City Bank, served as chairman of the committee.

30. Parker B. Willis, *The Federal Funds Market: Its Origin and Development* (Boston: Federal Reserve Bank of Boston, 1970), pp. 1–21, gives the early history of the federal funds market. In the late 1950s several regulatory changes promoted the growth of the market for federal funds and repurchase agreements. In April 1958 the comptroller of the currency exempted loans collateralized by U.S. securities with maturities of eighteen months or less from the legal lending limit of 10 percent of capital and surplus. This enabled smaller banks to execute repurchase agreements with money center banks, since the securities serving as collateral were usually actually in the custody of the smaller bank's New York correspondent. In addition, the comptroller ruled that federal funds were sales and purchases of funds rather than lending or borrowing; thus, the sale of federal funds was exempt from the legal lending limit of 10 percent of capital and surplus. More importantly for First National City, the ruling also implied that the borrowing limit of a national bank of 100 percent of capital stock plus 50 percent of surplus no longer applied to federal funds transactions. In 1961 the Federal Reserve changed the calculation of reserve requirements, permitting vault cash to be counted as part of re-

quired reserves and introducing lagged reserve requirements. This induced a one-time jump in excess reserves and permitted more effective management of reserve positions. Cf. G. Walter Woodworth, *The Money Market and Monetary Management*, 2nd ed. (New York: Harper, 1965), pp. 46–58.

31. First National City Bank, Comptroller's Reports, 1954–1961.

32. First National City Bank, *Annual Report, 1959*.

33. On the origins and early development of Eurodollar banking, see Paul Einzig, *The Eurodollar System* (London: Macmillan, 1964); E. Wayne Clendenning, *The Eurodollar Market* (Oxford: Clarendon Press, 1970); Ramachandra Bhagavatula and Harold van B. Cleveland, *Global Financial Intermediation* (New York: Citibank, 1980); Gunter Dufey and Ian H. Giddy, *The International Money Market* (Englewood Cliffs, N.J.: Prentice-Hall, 1979), pp. 110–112; and Ronald I. McKinnon, *The Eurocurrency Market*, Essays in International Finance, no. 125 (Princeton: International Finance Section, 1977), pp. 1–10.

34. On Eurodollar borrowings as a substitute for the discount window at First National City, see Comptroller's Report, 1959. In an interview in July 1980, Sterling Bunnell recalled that Eurodollar borrowings were not to exceed $500 million because of fears over the future of the market. Bhagavatula and Cleveland, *Global Financial Intermediation*, pp. 33–49, point out that the concerns over the market are essentially groundless so long as central banks fulfill their function as lenders of last resort. This follows from the fact that the Eurocurrency markets are inextricably linked to national monetary policies. In the late 1950s and early 1960s, these linkages were not well understood.

35. It was roughly three years before the new vehicle, the negotiable CD, surpassed the Eurodollar market as a source of funds for the bank. Between 1962 and 1967, outstanding CDs increased five and a half fold to $1,379 million measured on a daily average basis. Eurodollar borrowings climbed from $162 million to $570 million over the same period. First National City Bank, Comptroller's Reports, 1959–1967.

The bank continued to rely on Eurodollar borrowings for several reasons. For one thing, the market helped the bank to diversify its access to funds. Moreover, Eurodollars were cheaper than domestic CDs because the market spread between the two sources was on average below the cost of reserve requirements and FDIC assessments on domestic CDs. At that time, borrowings from a bank's own overseas branches were not subject to reserve requirements. The volume of Head Office borrowing from the foreign branches, however, also depended on the dollar funding requirements of the branch network overseas.

As time went on, the bank began to realize the benefits of closer integration of its funding activities in the Eurocurrency market and domestic money markets. Late in 1965, the bank took steps to improve communications between London and New York to this end and began to analyze more carefully the cost of Eurodollars and the need for Eurodollars as an adjunct to domestic funds. See First National City Bank, Comptroller's Report, 1965, pp. 12–13.

36. Howard D. Crosse, "Bank Liquidity and Time Deposits," *Proceedings of the Thirteenth National Credit Conference* (New York: American Bankers Association, 1961), pp. 110, 114.

37. *New York Times*, February 21, 1961.

38. A. Gilbert Heebner, "Negotiable Certificates of Deposit: The Development of a Money Market Instrument," *Bulletin*, No. 53–54 (New York: New York University, Graduate School of Business Administration, Institute of Finance, 1969): 6–7; Statement of J. L. Robertson (vice chairman, Federal Reserve Board) before the Committee on Banking and Currency of the House of Representatives, *Federal Reserve Bulletin*, 52 (1966): 791.

39. Interview, Lawrence S. Heath, May 1980. The quotation is Heath's paraphrase of the Union Bank official's remarks.

40. Interview, Walter B. Wriston, May 1977.

41. Ibid. On the advent of liability management see Jack Beebe, "A Perspective on Liability Management and Bank Risk," Federal Reserve Bank of San Francisco, *Economic Review*, Winter 1977, pp. 12–24.

14. A New Era, 1961–1967

1. Measurement of the bank's commercial and industrial (C & I) loans in this period is complicated by series breaks in the bank's internal reports and in reports to the authorities. Until June 1959, C & I loans included loans to financial institutions other than banks. Loans in this category were reported by some banks in the catchall category "other loans." To arrive at a consistent series for this bank and other banks, for purposes of comparison, a series was constructed as follows. After June 1959, C & I loans are defined as C & I loans plus loans to financial institutions other than banks plus other loans. Before that date, C & I loans are defined as C & I loans plus all other loans. For First National City the series for end-of-June dates in millions of dollars is: 1955, $1,471; 1956, $2,091; 1957, $2,488; 1958, $2,509; 1959, $2,486; 1960, $2,797; 1961, $2,611; and 1962, $2,817. (Earlier data are not comparable because of the merger with First National Bank in 1955.) C & I loans increased by 69 percent between 1955 and 1957, and by 13 percent between 1957 and 1962. First National City Bank, Call Reports, 1955–1962.

The bank's internal Comptroller's Reports, based on yearly averages, show that CDs and Eurodollar borrowings added over $250 million to resources between 1960 and 1962. Business loans increased by $56 million in those years and total loans increased by $157 million. Most of the bank's added resources at this time were invested in securities. Investments in U.S. federal, state, and municipal securities rose by over $450 million.

2. On the basis of C & I loans as measured in note 1, the bank's C & I loans grew by 13 percent, compared with 19 percent for other New York City banks. First National City and its major competitors lost market share over ten years, with the bank's share declining slightly more than that of other New York City banks. First National City Bank, Call Reports, 1957–1962; Board of Governors, Federal Reserve System, *Banking and Monetary Statistics, 1941–1970* (Washington, D.C.: GPO, 1976), pp. 79–80, 136.

3. George S. Moore, "International Banking Tomorrow," Address to the Bankers Association for Foreign Trade, Hot Springs, Va., May 17, 1978.

4. First National City Bank, *Annual Report, 1961*, (New York: First National City Bank, 1962).

5. Walter B. Wriston, Address to Overseas Division Dinner, New York 1963. Herbert G. Grubel, "A Theory of Multinational Banking," *Quarterly Review*

(Banca Nazionale del Lavoro), December 1977, p. 353, offers a theoretical explanation for this strategy. According to Grubel the ability to draw on the information and personal contacts between the bank's and manufacturing firm's parents in the United States at very low marginal cost represents the main comparative advantage of the bank's foreign branch in dealing with the firm's subsidiary abroad in competition with the local banks. Failure to use this comparative advantage leads to the development of information capital and personal relationships between foreign-owned manufacturing subsidiaries and local banks that can eventually be used to take away business from the U.S. bank in dealing with the manufacturing firm in the United States and its subsidiaries in other countries. Because of this risk, the move abroad is "defensive."

6. Interview, George S. Moore, October 3, 1980.

7. In 1955, the Chase Manhattan Bank had nineteen overseas branches, the First National Bank of Boston had fourteen, and the Bank of America, nine. Cf. Comptroller of the Currency, *Annual Report, 1955* (Washington, D.C.: GPO, 1956), and *Polk's Banking Directory*, September 1955.

8. Interview, Robert W. Feagles, May 12, 1978: "Moore saw that many doors of opportunity . . . open for Citibank around the world would be closed unless we got in place, but that consideration was in terms of decades, whereas Moore's personal ambition, which was the force driving him, gave a much shorter deadline."

9. George S. Moore, "History of First National City Bank during the Years 1927 to 1970" (New York: unpublished memoir, 1970), p. 54.

10. Ibid.

11. Interview, Robert W. Feagles, May 12, 1978.

12. Interview, Walter B. Wriston, May 1977.

13. Interview, John Rudy, May 5, 1978.

14. Moore, in "International Banking Tomorrow," stated that "banking, like insurance, is a risk-taking business. The name of the game is to select good risks, and to diversify total exposure, by geographical areas, by industries, by maturities . . . But, risk and profit go together. The successful banker, hopefully by superior knowledge, assembling available facts, can accept risks others are not positioned to take. One example is Citibank's decision, in 1958, to open branches in Paraguay and in South Africa. Citibank superiors questioned the Paraguay opening, preferred the relative stability of South Africa. I pointed out that Paraguay needed us and the opportunity was great, the competition nil, and that there were 3,000 banks in South Africa. We opened in both. In Paraguay we had 30% of the country's deposits in a year and earned a high return on our capital each year. It took us several years to break even in South Africa. We had men who were capable of reducing the risks of banking in Paraguay to acceptable limits."

15. Wriston, Address, 1963.

16. In 1960 a Dutch bank, the Rotterdamsche Bank, had acquired the Mercantile Bank, the smallest of the Canadian clearing banks, by virtue of its acquisition of the National Handelsbank, another Dutch bank. The Handelsbank had organized the Mercantile Bank in 1953 under a charter granted by the Canadian Parliament. It was understood but not stipulated in the charter that the Mercantile Bank would specialize in financing foreign trade and would not compete for domestic business. As a result, the Mercantile had less than one percent of all Canadian

bank deposits. The Mercantile did not fit the Rotterdamsche Bank's plans, and late in 1962 one of its officers told Wriston that he would be interested in a sale. Wriston responded positively and negotiations were completed in June 1963. After receiving Federal Reserve Board approval, First National City bought a controlling interest of 50 percent in the Mercantile on October 1, 1962, for $3.85 million.

17. T. A. Wise, "The Bank with the Boarding House Reach," *Fortune*, September 1965, pp. 278, 280; John Fayerweather, *The Mercantile Bank Affair* (New York: New York University Press, 1974), tells the story in full detail.

18. First National City Bank made two other major investments in foreign banks in the 1960s. One was in the Banque Internationale pour l'Afrique Occidentale (BIAO), a French-owned colonial bank with fifty-five offices in Central and West Africa and six offices in France, including a headquarters in Paris. At this time, First National City had been unable to get permission to open branches anywhere in the former French colonies in Africa. When the opportunity to buy 40 percent of the BIAO was presented, Wriston and Moore decided the opportunity to get into a large, new territory was too good to pass up, despite the minority position. The sale was consummated on April 1, 1965, for $3.3 million. The acquisition was not a success. The bank's directors on the BIAO board were not able to influence the French bank's policy sufficiently to exploit the potential of its large branch network. First National City ultimately sold its BIAO shares in 1977 to a Brazilian and Swiss bank.

In 1968, the bank had an unexpected opportunity to buy into National and Grindlays Bank, an old British overseas bank with 293 offices in the Middle East, South Asia, Africa, and the United Kingdom. Lord Aldington, chairman of the British bank, visited George Moore in New York and told him that National and Grindlays was looking for capital and that he was on his way to see David Rockefeller, chairman of Chase Manhattan, about the possibility of Chase making a large investment in Aldington's bank. As Moore recalled the conversation in an interview, October 10, 1980, "Aldington said, 'I'm on my way to Chase. I want a godfather. Lloyds Bank won't give me any capital and I need more capital. I've got $1.5 billion in assets and $50 million in capital, and if I make a $50 million mistake . . . so I'm going to see David Rockefeller.' I said, 'Stay right here!' He said, 'You compete with us.' I said, 'No, we really don't. You're in India with 25 percent of the rupee deposits of the country. We've been there since 1901 and we've got one percent. Your customers in India are Shell, Dunlop, Imperial Chemical. Ours are Exxon, Firestone, Du Pont, and your customers want dollars while ours want rupees. We've got different customers and different businesses. Stay right here.' And we bought it at lunch that day, with Wriston. He, Aldington, canceled his date with the Chase." The deal was consummated on April 1, 1969, for 40 percent of National and Grindlays's shares at a price of $37.8 million. First National City Bank, *Annual Report, 1968* (New York: First National City Bank, 1969).

19. The bank's branch in Cairo had been opened in 1958, shortly before Gamal Nasser came to power in Egypt. A socialist and the leading Arab nationalist, Nasser was hostile to the United States and to Western business and determined to nationalize all banks in Egypt, foreign banks included. John Goodridge, manager of the bank's Cairo branch, had seen nationalization coming when Nasser had sent British and French banks packing after the Suez crisis. Goodridge had arranged a

sale of his branch's net worth to the Egyptian central bank for more than $1 million, payable in dollars. When the nationalization decree was promulgated, the Egyptian authorities at first insisted the sale was off. Goodridge succeeded in getting the money on the ground that the agreement to sell predated the decree. He may have been helped, according to George Moore, by the presence of the World Bank in Egypt in connection with financing of the Aswan Dam. The World Bank's president, Eugene Black, had been a New York investment banker and was close to the Eisenhower administration. Interview, John Goodridge, n.d.

20. Before Fidel Castro's successful revolution in 1958, the bank's eleven Cuban branches had been highly profitable, placing Cuba regularly among the first three or four countries in profits remitted during the 1940s and 1950s. Fortunately, the branches were not nationalized immediately, and the bank had time to minimize the impact. In charge of the branches was Juan D. Sanchez, who had been a branch manager in Colombia during the 1948 revolution and knew what to do. Sanchez never doubted that Castro's victory meant the end for First National City in Cuba. He began immediately to prepare for the worst. When nationalization was decreed in 1960, there was not much left to take. The Cuban government got the bank's building in Havana, but on the bank's books it had been entirely written down. Interview, Juan D. Sanchez, September 1976.

Loans totaling $40 million made by Head Office to firms and individuals in Cuba went into default when the Cuban authorities clamped down exchange controls and nationalized many firms. Several large loans were to subsidiaries of U.S. firms without the parent corporation's guarantee, so that the parent could not assume the debt without risking a stockholders' suit. Up to $25 million in Head Office loans were eventually written off. The bank's long and checkered history in Cuba had come at least temporarily to an end.

21. Interview, Robert W. Feagles, May 12, 1978. The quote is Feagles's paraphrase of Moore's remarks.

22. First National City Bank, *Annual Report, 1967* (New York: First National City Bank, 1968).

23. A list of all First National City Bank and First National Corporation subsidiaries, bank and nonbank, foreign and domestic, as of the end of 1969 may be found in the bank's annual report for 1970.

24. Mira Wilkins, *The Maturing of Multinational Enterprise: American Business Abroad from 1914 to 1970* (Cambridge, Mass.: Harvard University Press, 1974), p. 330. These figures exclude Canada and refer to the book value of U.S. firms' direct foreign investment expressed in current dollars.

25. Sidney M. Robbins and Robert B. Stobaugh, *Money in the Multinational Enterprise: A Study in Financial Policy* (New York: Basic Books, 1973), p. 11.

26. On average in the mid-1960s, each of these 165 firms maintained balances of slightly over $3 million. Their total demand deposits were approximately $519 million, about 10 percent of the bank's total demand deposits. First National City Bank, Internal Records.

27. John M. Stopford and Louis T. Wells, Jr., *Managing the Multinational Enterprise* (New York: Basic Books, 1972), p. 25.

28. Interview, Heinz Riehl, July 17, 1981. An analytical and operational description of the international treasury function in a bank may be found in Heinz

Riehl and Rita M. Rodriguez, *Foreign Exchange and Money Markets* (New York: McGraw-Hill, 1983).

29. Federal Reserve Board, *The International Operations of U.S. Banks* (Washington, D.C.: Board of Governors, Federal Reserve System, 1968), p. III-9. A monograph published by First National City Bank in July 1964 noted that European banks were playing a similar role: "Because local European money markets are characteristically too small and inelastic, many banks on the Continent entrust the task of running their money positions to foreign exchange departments. These departments have access to the developed money markets of New York and London. What the Eurocurrency market has done is to give the Continent a money market of its own, using internationally minded London as its central depot and the internationally minded dollar as its currency." Norris O. Johnson, *Eurodollars in the New International Money Market* (New York: First National City Bank, 1964), p. 12.

30. First National City Bank, *Annual Report, 1964* (New York: First National City Bank, 1965). Concerns about a worsening U.S. balance-of-payments situation initially led the Kennedy administration to impose the interest equalization tax (IET) in 1963 to discourage the purchase of foreign securities by U.S. residents. But the measure only succeeded in substituting bank loans for securities as a source of credit for foreigners. In 1965, the U.S. government responded not only by extending the IET to long-term bank loans but also by authorizing the Federal Reserve to inaugurate the Voluntary Foreign Credit Restraint Program (VFCR). Voluntary in name more than in reality, the VFCR put quantitative ceilings on lending by Federal Reserve member banks to foreign borrowers when loans were made from U.S. locations. At the same time, a number of large corporations were requested to finance overseas investments outside the United States. Despite these drastic measures, the gold parity of the dollar came under increasing pressure in the latter half of 1967. To stem the tide, President Johnson further extended the web of controls on New Year's Day 1968 and made mandatory the voluntary restraints on the financing of U.S. corporate investment overseas. The effect of the U.S. balance-of-payments controls was to force U.S. banks, if they wished to maintain relationships with their foreign customers, to book dollar loans in their London branches and to fund them with offshore or Eurodollar deposits in London. The controls gave strong encouragement to U.S. banks to plunge wholeheartedly into dollar banking in London, where their competitive position vis-à-vis British banks was strong. The London branches of large U.S. banks had an advantage over their British competitors in funding offshore dollar loans because, as dollar-based banks, they could attract dollar deposits at slightly lower rates than British banks. Cf. Board of Governors, Federal Reserve System, "Interest Equalization Tax," *Federal Reserve Bulletin*, 42 (1965): 242–243, 256–257; Board of Governors, Federal Reserve System, "Balance of Payments Program: Guidelines for Banks and Nonbank Financial Institutions," *Federal Reserve Bulletin*, 42 (1965): 369–376; *Economic Report of the President* (Washington, D.C.: GPO, 1968); Walter Lederer and Evelyn M. Parrish, "The U.S. Balance of Payments: Second Quarter of 1969," *Survey of Current Business*, September 1969, p. 35; and Sanford Rose, "Capital Is Something That Doesn't Love a Wall," *Fortune*, February 1971, pp. 101ff.

31. In the mid-1960s, First National City began to syndicate some of the floating-rate Eurodollar loans it was making to major corporations. An early example was a large loan to the Shell Oil Company to finance an acquisition in Italy. As recalled by Donald S. Howard, who oversaw the bank's United Kingdom operations from New York at the time, "they [Shell] called us on Thursday, and they had to have the money on Monday, and they needed $100 million dollars, which in those days was a lot of money. And they said they wanted Manufacturers Hanover and Irving to be included. So Bob Breyfogle, the manager of the London branch, called Walt Wriston, Walt Wriston called me [and] George Scott, who was in charge of credit for the Overseas Division. Walt said we want to do this, go home over the weekend and figure out how we're going to do it and come back Monday and we'll put our heads together and decide what to do. Well, out of that, we syndicated the deal, we took $55 million, we gave Manufacturers $30 million and we gave Irving $15 million and we decided that we would have to float the rate. And we decided that the rate that we would quote would be ¼ percent over our average cost of dollars taken for the previous 90 days." Interview, August 14, 1981.

32. Interview, Lawrence A. Heath, May 1980. In 1966, the bank organized what may have been the first syndicated Eurocurrency loan involving a front-end fee for arranging and administering the credit. The credit was to the IBM World Trade Corporation and was booked at the bank's Brussels branch. In the event, the line was not drawn on.

33. Ramachandra Bhagavatula and Harold van B. Cleveland, *Global Financial Intermediation* (New York: Citibank, 1980), p. 8.

34. Federal Reserve Board, *The International Operations of U.S. Banks*, p. III-30.

35. First National City Bank, *Annual Report, 1961* (New York: First National City Bank, 1962).

36. Richard A. Smith, "Big Banking's Troubled Giants," *Fortune*, April 1959, pp. 114ff.

37. First National City Bank, Call Reports, June 1959 and June 1962; Board of Governors, Federal Reserve System, *Banking and Monetary Statistics, 1941–1970* (Washington, D.C.: GPO, 1976), p. 79. This comparison is based solely on reported C & I loans and not on C & I loans as adjusted in notes 1 and 2, which show loans adjusted rising between 1959 and 1962 for First National City Bank.

38. First National City Bank, *Annual Report, 1963* (New York: First National City Bank, 1964). A change in the Federal Reserve Board's Regulation Y in 1964 confirmed the bank's right to own and lease property as a means of extending secured credit.

39. First National City Bank, Comptroller's Report, 1967, p. 25, and Supplement to 1967 Comptroller's Report, p. x-7.

40. First National City Bank, *Annual Report, 1965* (New York: First National City Bank, 1966).

41. Interview, Thomas R. Wilcox, May 22, 1980.

42. First National City Bank, Comptroller's Report, 1967, p. 25.

43. First National City Bank, Call Reports, June 1961 and June 1967.

44. First National City Bank, Call Reports, June 1961 and June 1967.

45. First National City Bank, *Annual Report, 1963*. Interview, Robert L. Hoguet, May 9, 1978.

46. First National City Bank, *Annual Report, 1965*. The data on pension funds are from Daniel M. Holland, *Private Pension Funds: Projected Growth* (New York: National Bureau of Economic Research, 1966), pp. 2–3.

47. First National City Bank, *Annual Report, 1966* (New York: First National City Bank, 1967).

48. First National City Bank, *Annual Report, 1967*.

49. Penetration is defined as percentage of the business of a sample of six hundred of the twelve hundred largest U.S. companies reporting important banking connections with each of the three banks. See the Opinion Research Corporation Survey (1967) reprinted in "Ensuring Preeminence in a Dynamically Changing Market Environment: The Challenge for Citibank in Wholesale Banking," a draft report by the McKinsey Study Team, June 1968, Exhibit IV.

50. First National City Bank, *Annual Report, 1960* (New York: First National City Bank, 1961).

51. First National City Bank, Call Reports, June 1960 through June 1967; Board of Governors, Federal Reserve System, *Banking and Monetary Statistics, 1941–1970*, pp. 79–80.

52. First National City Bank, *Annual Report, 1961*.

53. Federal Reserve Board, *Bank Credit Cards and Check Credit Systems* (Washington, D.C.: GPO, 1968), p. 7; F. M. Struble, "Bank Credit Card Plans in the Nation and the District," *Federal Reserve Bank of Kansas City Monthly Review*, July–August 1969, p. 5.

54. "Bank Credit Cards: An Appraisal," *American Banker*, May 18–24, 1971.

55. First National City Bank, *Annual Report, 1965*. Interview, Thomas R. Wilcox, May 22, 1980.

56. According to W. M. Cockrell, president of Carte Blanche, the joint venture with First National City had great international potential. Cockrell was quoted in the *New York Times*, August 25, 1965: "We want to take Carte Blanche around the world. That takes people and organization. First National City has at least 115 branches abroad. It looks like a logical combination."

57. *New York Times*, December 31, 1965.

58. Interview, Thomas R. Wilcox, May 22, 1980.

59. First National City Bank, *Annual Report, 1967*. Carte Blanche was reacquired by Citicorp in 1978.

60. First National City Bank, *Annual Report, 1969* (New York: First National City Bank, 1970).

61. Interview, James A. Farley, June 19, 1978.

62. First National City Bank, Comptroller's Reports, 1961–1967. According to *Polk's Banking Directory* (New York: R. L. Polk, 1967), the three largest banks in terms of assets were Bank of America ($21.5 billion), Chase Manhattan ($18.0 billion), and First National City ($17.5 billion).

63. First National City Bank, Comptroller's Reports, 1961–1967.

64. Ibid.

65. Ibid.

15. The Global Financial Services Corporation, 1968–1970

1. Since 1929, the bank's chairman had been the chief executive officer, as the bank's bylaws provided. But Rockefeller believed that Moore was inclined at times to make important decisions without sufficient reflection and consultation. He therefore recommended to the board that Moore be appointed chairman, but that the definition of the president's and chairman's roles be changed, making the chairman the second man. In June 1967, at the directors' meeting at which Moore and Wriston were elected, the bylaws were amended to provide that the "President . . . shall be responsible for formulation and execution of policy for the Association," and "the Chairman shall have general executive powers." The directors also passed a resolution providing that the president rather than the chairman "shall preside at meetings of the Policy Committee." The bank's news release about the elections did not mention the bylaw changes, noting only that the chairman would exercise "general executive authority" and that the new president would assume the "maximum possible responsibilities." *Wall Street Journal*, June 7, 1967.

2. First National City Bank, Call Reports, 1950 and 1965; Board of Governors, Federal Reserve System, *Flow of Funds Accounts, 1946–1975* (Washington, D.C.: Board of Governors, Federal Reserve System, 1976). Cf. also George Kaufman, Larry Mote, and Harvey Rosenblum, "Implications of Deregulation for Product Lines and Geographical Markets of Financial Institutions," *Journal of Bank Research*, 14 (1983): 14–15.

3. Walter B. Wriston, "Presentation to the Officers on the First National City Bank Reorganization Plan," New York, November 1968.

4. Interview, Walter B. Wriston, August 1, 1978.

5. McKinsey and Company, Inc., "Summary of Key Organizational Issues Facing First National City Bank: Progress Report on Phase I Findings," New York, December 1967, p. 1.

6. P. Henry Mueller, "The Account Domicile Conflict in Commercial Banking," unpublished lecture, May 9, 1958.

7. Ibid.

8. First National Bank, Comptroller's Report, 1961.

9. Wriston, "Presentation."

10. Mueller, "Account Domicile Conflict."

11. Wriston outlined the reason for a separate group devoted to the medium-sized company as follows: "Our existing organizational structure has been successful against the *Fortune* 500 group and no doubt would continue to maintain that position; however, it is not the best organizational approach to the medium-sized company . . . We believe the growth of our corporate business, both services and loans, will require increasingly greater professional knowledge and insight into the customer's industry. This market needs bankers with professional qualifications, who have a sufficient understanding of their customer's business to originate creative new services and make the unusual loan." Wriston, "Presentation."

12. Report of the Worldwide Account Management Task Force, and Discussion Draft, New York, June 1969.

13. "Seventh Senior Overseas Policy Conference," *Overseas Citibanker*, June 1969, p. 6.

14. Interview, Walter B. Wriston, August 1, 1978.

15. James Stillman Rockefeller, "The View from the Fifteenth Floor," Address to the First National City Bank Correspondent Bank Forum, February 6, 1965. Cf. also Lewis B. Cuyler, "The Development of Personnel Administration: Citibank, 1928–1965" (New York: unpublished memoir, 1977).

16. Interview, Donald S. Howard, August 14, 1981.

17. Robert W. Feagles, "Tomorrow's Management Crop—Reap or Weep," Address delivered to First National City Bank Insurance Forum, New York, November 2, 1967.

18. Robert W. Feagles, "Personnel Management," Address delivered to First National City Bank Correspondent Bank Forum, New York, February 7, 1970.

19. McKinsey and Company, Inc., "Ensuring Preeminence in a Changing Wholesale Market Environment," Study prepared for First National City Bank, September 1968, pp. 2–6.

20. Interview, Richard Neuschel, May 26, 1978.

21. Edward L. Palmer, "Asset and Liability Management," Address to First National City Bank Correspondent Bank Forum, New York, February 6, 1971.

22. First National City Bank, Comptroller's Report, 1966, pp. 53–54. Cf. also Robert V. Owen (budget director, First National City Bank), "Management Information at FNCB," Address to the First National City Bank Correspondent Bank Forum, New York, February 3, 1968. Charles W. Kelly, "The Construction and Use of Organizational Profit and Loss Statements in Commercial Banks" (New York: First National City Bank, n.d.), describes the early management profitability report.

Traditionally, budgets in the bank had been simple, merely projecting salaries and other operating expenses. Under Rockefeller and Moore the budget became a planning tool, "the dollar expression of an integrated plan of operation." "Citibank Does It Differently," *Citibank Magazine*, July 1965, p. 12. In addition to expense projections, budgets contained forecasts of loan and deposit volumes. The end result was a department-by-department projection of revenues, expenses, and earnings. The aim was to put a "profit and loss yardstick" on as many aspects of the bank's business as possible. But Rockefeller was reluctant to push the concept too hard. As he commented in 1965, "the P&L concept may have drawbacks if not controlled. With too rigid an application there is a tendency for a man responsible for a unit to think only of the unit and forget the overall interest of the bank. There is also a tendency, in the desire to do a good job and make a good showing, to ask for a great deal of allocation of expense in intra-bank accounting. If you don't look out, the accounting will eat up all the profit." Rockefeller, "The View from the Fifteenth Floor."

Although this danger remained, the management profitability report enabled the new regime to take budgeting one step further. It transformed budgets from a guide for planning into targets that line officers strove to achieve.

23. Palmer, "Asset and Liability Management." Cf. also Walter B. Wriston, chairman, Memorandum to All Officers on Asset and Liability Management Policy Committee, July 27, 1970.

24. E. Newton Cutler, Jr., "The Making of a President," Address to First National City Bank Correspondent Banking Forum, New York, February 5, 1966.

25. P. Henry Mueller, *Learning from Lending* (New York: Citibank, 1979), p. 134.

26. Ibid., p. 169.

27. Interview, Walter B. Wriston, May 1977; interview, Edwin A. Reichers, Jr., September 1976; interview, Heinz Riehl, July 17, 1981.

28. On check volume at First National City, see Carl Desch, "The Impact of Automation," Address to First National City Bank Correspondent Bank Forum, New York, February 2, 1964. Other banks generally were experiencing the same problems as First National City. According to the Federal Reserve Bank of New York, the number of checks used each year was about 3.5 billion before World War II. It grew to more than 8 billion in 1952, and hit over 12 billion in 1959. Federal Reserve Bank of New York, "Electronic Check Handling," *Monthly Review*, August 1960, p. 143. Since each check was handled approximately ten times by an average of two and one-half banks before being returned to its maker, the paper flow through banks took on truly awesome dimensions. Raymond C. Kolb, "The Paperwork in Banks," *The Banker's Handbook* (New York: Dow Jones-Irwin, 1966), p. 159. For a review of what banks were doing to cope with this paper flow see Federal Reserve Bank of Philadelphia, "How Banking Tames Its Paper Tiger," *Business Review*, May 1960, pp. 5–6.

Although paperwork mounted, the task of check processing was potentially profitable, for it helped attract interest-free demand balances to the bank. Thus if the bank could process checks at a cost lower than the sum of the fees collected and the interest (that is, the revenues it earned on net funds available for investment), check processing would add to the bottom line. Assuming that the funds available for investment earned the average federal funds rates paid by First National City, transaction revenue per check processed at the bank seesawed between 20 and over 35 cents a check between 1958 and 1961 and then rose to more than 45 cents a check in 1966. First National City Bank, *Annual Reports, 1958–1961, 1966* (New York: First National City Bank, 1959–1962, 1967); First National City Bank, Comptroller's Reports, 1958–1966. Data on which these numbers are based are not available for 1962–1965.

29. Interview, Carl Desch, n.d. The bank committed three serious mistakes in the ITT deal. First, it failed to conduct any type of cost-benefit analysis on what turned out to be a major capital investment. Second, it left the problem of how to automate check processing entirely in the hands of technicians who had insufficient appreciation of the purpose of the exercise: reducing the cost of check processing. The result was a cumbersome attempt "to do conventional banking as usual, only faster." In the terms of Professor Anthony Oettinger of Harvard, this initially made First National City a victim rather than a benefactor of the computer revolution. "The Coming Revolution in Banking," *Proceedings of the National Automation Conference* (New York: American Bankers Association, 1964), p. 37.

The third and most fundamental error was the bank's attempt to develop a check-clearing process on its own. Of necessity, each bank had to be able to process not only checks drawn on itself but also checks drawn on other banks that customers deposited to their accounts. This is the essence of the money transfer function. If all checks were to be machine handled, then all banks in the nation had to adopt a standardized system. Without this uniformity, automation at one bank made little sense. Thus, First National City could not solve its check-processing problem on its own. The cooperation of the industry was needed.

This led to the MICR system, developed by the American Bankers Association in cooperation with the Federal Reserve System. On the development and adoption of the MICR standard see "Automation at Commercial Banks," *Federal Reserve Bulletin*, 48 (1962): 1408–18; James A. O'Brien, *The Impact of Computers on Banking* (Boston: Bankers Publishing Co., 1968), pp. 1–14; Boris Yavitz, *Automation in Commercial Banking: Its Process and Impact* (New York: Free Press, 1967), pp. 21–27.

30. First National City Bank, *Annual Report, 1961.*

31. First National City Bank, *Annual Report, 1963* (New York: First National City Bank, 1964).

32. Interview, H. Lansing Clute, May 1977.

33. Cuyler, "Development of Personnel Administration," pp. 104–110.

34. The *New York Times* commented on March 18, 1970: "Mr. Spencer is under no illusions that all the problems have been solved, but through the highly imaginative use of sophisticated management techniques he believes that he has 'some handles on the greased pig.' "

35. *National Association of Securities Dealers v. S.E.C.; Investment Company Institute v. Camp*, 274 F.S. 624 (1967), rev'd 420 F. 2d 83 (1969), rev'd 91 S.Ct. 1091 (1971). First National City Bank was a party to both actions, which were consolidated. The court of appeals opinion supporting the bank's position includes an exegesis of the legislative intent of the Glass-Steagall Act as applied to the question at hand. The opinion points out that the securities in question ("units" in the Commingled Investment Account) were not the bank's own investments but were administered by the bank for the account of customers. In this respect, they did not differ from other securities held in a bank's trust department under regular trust or agency arrangements. Issuing or holding such securities did not run counter to the purpose of Glass-Steagall, which was to prevent banks from risking their depositors' funds by making speculative investments for the bank's own account. Justice Blackmun repeated this reasoning in his dissent from the majority's decision in the Supreme Court overruling the court of appeals.

36. First National City Bank, *Annual Report, 1968* (New York: First National City Bank, 1969).

37. "Current Banking Problems," Address before the First National City Bank Correspondent Bank Forum, New York, February 2, 1964.

38. On the 1966 credit crunch see Benjamin M. Friedman, "Regulation Q and the Commercial Loan Market in the 1960s," *Journal of Money, Credit, and Banking*, 7 (1975): 277–296. On the economics of Regulation Q see Milton Friedman, "Controls on Interest Rates Paid by Banks," *Journal of Money, Credit, and Banking*, 2 (1970): 15–32; James Tobin, "Deposit Interest Ceilings as a Monetary Control," *Journal of Money, Credit, and Banking*, 2 (1970): 1–14.

39. *Federal Reserve Bulletin*, 52 (1966): 1172.

40. New York Laws 1961, Chapter 146 (March 17, 1961); New York Banking Law, III-A, s. 142.

41. The memorandum, dated June 28, 1967, was written by Patrick J. Mulhern, a bank attorney.

42. *New York Times*, July 3, 1968.

43. Carter H. Golembe and Associates, *The Bank Holding Company Act Amendments of 1970* (Washington, D.C.: Financial Publications of Washington, 1971), p. 2.

44. First National City was not the first bank to form a one-bank holding company. According to the *New York Times* of July 3, 1968, that distinction belonged to the Union Bank of Los Angeles. In addition, the three major banks in North Carolina—Wachovia Bank and Trust, North Carolina National Bank, and First Union National Bank—had either announced or completed plans to form a one-bank holding company prior to July 2, 1968 when First National City announced that it would create a holding company to own the bank.

45. The procedure by which ownership of the bank was transferred to a holding company owned by the bank's former shareholders was more complex than this summary statement suggests. The desired result might have been accomplished by asking bank shareholders to accept, voluntarily, shares in the holding company in exchange for their bank shares. But this procedure would have been time-consuming, with the attendant possibility that some shareholders might have refused to make the exchange and the holding company would then not have been able to acquire 100 percent control of the bank, so that management might subsequently have had to contend with minority shareholders in the bank.

To avoid this possibility, an alternative procedure was followed: On July 18, 1968, an entirely new national bank was organized. All of the shares of this phantom bank, as it was called at the time, were initially owned by a few of the bank's directors, who then transferred them to a holding company that had been organized on December 4, 1967, as a Delaware corporation, under the name of First National City Corporation.

The next step was to merge First National City Bank into the phantom bank under an agreement of merger dated July 23, 1968. The agreement provided for the issue of one share of holding company stock to bank shareholders in place of each share of the bank's stock. The agreement of merger was ratified by the bank's stockholders at a meeting held on October 31, 1968. This procedure guaranteed the holding company 100 percent ownership of the merged bank, because the merger extinguished the old bank's corporate charter.

The phantom bank had been incorporated under the name of the City Bank of New York; under federal law, it could not be given the same name as an existing bank. But once the old bank ceased to exist, the phantom bank, now a flesh-and-blood institution, was renamed First National City Bank. Few people apart from senior management and legal counsel were aware of these esoteric transactions by which the bank spawned its own parent.

46. *New York Times*, August 13, 1968. The holding company made prompt use of its new powers. In quick succession agreements were reached to acquire the Chubb Corporation, a major insurance company; Advance Mortgage, the leading mortgage banker in the country; and Cresap, Paget and McCormick, a management consulting firm. In addition, the holding company announced its intention to establish a travel agency and the formation of a data-processing subsidiary. First National City Bank, *Annual Report, 1969 and 1970* (New York: First National City Bank, 1970 and 1971). The Chubb merger was dropped following objections from the Justice Department (*New York Times*, June 14, 1969), and the other acquisi-

tions were subsequently disallowed. Nevertheless, the holding company did retain the right to engage in data processing.

47. On the Bank Holding Company Act Amendments of 1970 see Golembe, *The Bank Holding Company Act*; Sidney M. Sussan, "An Evaluation of the Non-Banking Expansion of Bank Holding Companies under the 1970 Amendments to the Bank Holding Company Act of 1956, As Amended" (Thesis, Graduate School of Banking, Rutgers University, 1978), pp. 30–116.

16. The Dynamics of Success

1. See Alfred D. Chandler, Jr., *The Visible Hand: The Managerial Revolution in American Business* (Cambridge, Mass.: Harvard University Press, 1977).

2. See for example Kenneth R. Andrews, *The Concept of Corporate Strategy* (New York: Dow Jones–Irwin, 1971); Michael E. Porter, *Competitive Strategy: Techniques for Analyzing Industries and Competitors* (New York: Free Press, 1980); Richard E. Caves, "Industrial Organization, Corporate Strategy and Structure," *Journal of Economic Literature*, 18 (1980): 64–92.

3. James Stillman to Frank A. Vanderlip, February 12, 1907, Vanderlip MSS.

4. January 12, 1915, Vanderlip MSS.

5. James Stillman Rockefeller, "The View from the Fifteenth Floor," Address to the First National City Bank Correspondent Bank Forum, New York, February 6, 1965.

6. John Brooks, "The Money Machine," *New Yorker*, January 5, 1981, p. 53.

Index

HARVARD STUDIES IN BUSINESS HISTORY

(Some of these titles may be out of print. Write to Harvard University Press for information and ordering.)